Shakespeare's Theatre

The De Witt drawing of the Swan playhouse.
Source: ART Vol. d57, no. 45c, Folger Shakespeare Library.

Shakespeare's Theatre

A History

Richard Dutton

WILEY Blackwell

This edition first published 2018
© 2018 Richard Dutton

All rights reserved. No part of this publication may be reproduced, stored in a retrieval system, or transmitted, in any form or by any means, electronic, mechanical, photocopying, recording or otherwise, except as permitted by law. Advice on how to obtain permission to reuse material from this title is available at http://www.wiley.com/go/permissions.

The right of Richard Dutton to be identified as the author of this work has been asserted in accordance with law.

Registered Office
John Wiley & Sons, Inc., 111 River Street, Hoboken, NJ 07030, USA
John Wiley & Sons Ltd, The Atrium, Southern Gate, Chichester, West Sussex, PO19 8SQ, UK

Editorial Office
9600 Garsington Road, Oxford, OX4 2DQ, UK

For details of our global editorial offices, customer services, and more information about Wiley products visit us at www.wiley.com.

Wiley also publishes its books in a variety of electronic formats and by print-on-demand. Some content that appears in standard print versions of this book may not be available in other formats.

Limit of Liability/Disclaimer of Warranty
While the publisher and authors have used their best efforts in preparing this work, they make no representations or warranties with respect to the accuracy or completeness of the contents of this work and specifically disclaim all warranties, including without limitation any implied warranties of merchantability or fitness for a particular purpose. No warranty may be created or extended by sales representatives, written sales materials or promotional statements for this work. The fact that an organization, website, or product is referred to in this work as a citation and/or potential source of further information does not mean that the publisher and authors endorse the information or services the organization, website, or product may provide or recommendations it may make. This work is sold with the understanding that the publisher is not engaged in rendering professional services. The advice and strategies contained herein may not be suitable for your situation. You should consult with a specialist where appropriate. Further, readers should be aware that websites listed in this work may have changed or disappeared between when this work was written and when it is read. Neither the publisher nor authors shall be liable for any loss of profit or any other commercial damages, including but not limited to special, incidental, consequential, or other damages.

Library of Congress Cataloging-in-Publication Data

Names: Dutton, Richard, 1948– author.
Title: Shakespeare's theatre : a history / by Richard Dutton.
Description: Hoboken, NJ : Wiley, 2018. | Includes bibliographical references and index. |
Identifiers: LCCN 2017024307 (print) | LCCN 2017036417 (ebook) |
    ISBN 9781119101376 (paperback)

Subjects: LCSH: Shakespeare, William, 1564-1616–Dramatic production. | Shakespeare,
    William, 1564-1616–Stage history. | Theatre–England–History–16th century. |
    Theatre–England–History–17th century. | English drama–Early modern and Elizabethan,
    1500-1600–History and criticism. | English drama–17th century–History and criticism.
Classification: LCC PR3095 (ebook) | LCC PR3095 .D885 2018 (print) | DDC 822/.309–dc23
LC record available at https://lccn.loc.gov/2017024307

Cover Design: Wiley
Cover Images: (Theatre Swan De Witt) Chronicle/Alamy Stock Photo;
(Background) © ke77kz/Gettyimages

Set in 10/12pt Warnock by SPi Global, Pondicherry, India

10 9 8 7 6 5 4 3 2 1

For Hollea, who likes books

Contents

List of Illustrations *x*
List of Boxes *xi*
Preface *xii*

Introduction *1*
Palamon and Arcite was Performed with
the Queen Herself Present on the Stage *1*
The Upstart Crow *7*
Notes *17*

1 The Early Years *19*
Stratford and Staging Practices *19*
Princely Pleasures at Kenilworth *25*
Mystery Cycles and Trade Guilds *27*
Competing Authorities *28*
Straws in the Wind *29*
A System of Protection and Control *33*
Roads Not Taken *34*
Notes *36*

2 Possible Beginnings *38*
Shakespeare and the Queen's Men's Theory *39*
Tarlton *44*
Shakespeare and Alexander Hoghton's Will *50*
Strange's Men *60*
Notes *71*

**3 Shakespeare on the Record and the Stages of 1594:
Newington Butts, the Theatre, Greenwich Palace, and Gray's Inn** *75*
Plague *75*
Duopoly *77*

Shakespeare in the Records   *81*
Four Playing Places   *82*
The Theatre   *83*
Burbage   *102*
Kemp   *103*
Motley   *105*
The Cross Keys Inn   *114*
Greenwich Palace   *117*
Gray's Inn   *130*

Notes   *136*

4 The Chamberlain's / King's Men and their Organization   *140*
Sharers   *140*
Hired Men (and Women)   *156*
Hired Men as Actors   *157*
Gatherers   *159*
Tirewomen   *167*
Tiremen   *169*
Musicians   *174*
Book-keepers   *177*
Stage-keepers   *180*
Apprentices   *182*
Conclusions   *188*

Notes   *188*

5 A Stormy Passage, from the Theatre, via the Curtain, to the Globe   *193*
2 The Seven Deadly Sins   *205*
The Stories   *209*
Commentary   *213*
The Text   *213*
Authorship and Dating of the Play(s)   *213*
"Those Playhouses ... Shall be Plucked Down"   *221*

Notes   *227*

6 "The Great Globe Itself"   *230*
The Galleries   *232*
Lords' Rooms   *234*
Stage Directions   *242*
Playhouse of the Spoken Word   *257*
Robert Armin   *264*
The War of the Theatres   *271*

Notes   *274*

7   **A New Reign**   *277*
    A Royal Master   *279*
    Little Eyases and *The Malcontent*   *281*
    Notes   *288*

8   **The Blackfriars**   *290*
    "Your Master Worship's House, here, in the Friars"   *299*
    The New Repertoire   *303*
    Descent Machinery   *305*
    Jonson and Shakespeare in the New House   *309*
    Notes   *319*

    Appendix: Chamberlain's/King's Men's Plays 1594–1614, Other than by Shakespeare   *322*
    Extant Texts, with Dates of Performance and Publication, and Probable Playhouse of First Performance   *322*
    Anon   *323*
    Non-Extant or Unidentified Plays Associated with the Company   *324*

    Bibliography   *325*
    Primary Material from the Sixteenth and Seventeenth Centuries   *325*
    Secondary Material   *329*

    Index   *341*

List of Illustrations

Frontispiece   The De Witt drawing of the Swan playhouse. *Source*: ART Vol. d57, no. 45c, Folger Shakespeare Library.
Figure I.1   Portrait of Edward Alleyn. *Source*: akg-images   *11*
Figure 2.1   Image of Richard Tarlton (or Tarleton). *Source*: © British Library Board All Rights Reserved / Bridgeman Images   *45*
Figure 2.2   Interior of the Great Tudor Hall at Rufford Old Hall (showing the lower hall, with carved screen). *Source*: The National Trust Photolibrary / Alamy Stock photo   *56*
Figure 2.3   Interior of the Great Tudor Hall at Rufford Old Hall (showing the upper hall, with the high table in place and windowed alcove to the right). *Source*: The National Trust Photolibrary / Alamy Stock photo   *57*
Figure 3.1   Digital reproduction of a page in Philip Henslowe's *Diary*. *Source*: Dulwich College, MS VII f9r, © David Cooper.   *76*
Figure 3.2   A Map Showing the Theatres of Shakespeare's Day. *Source*: First published in *Shakespeare's Playhouses*, by John Quincy Adams (1917)   *79*
Figure 3.3   Image of Will Kemp and Companion on the title-page of *Kemp's Nine Days' Wonder*. *Source*: PN2598. k6, 1839, Folger Shakespeare Library   *104*
Figure 3.4   Diagram of Seating Arrangements in the Great Chamber at Whitehall. *Source*: College of Arms, MS Vincent 151, pp. 156–7   *120*
Figure 3.5   Portrait of Henry Carey, 1st Lord Hunsdon. *Source*: Berkeley Castle   *128*
Figure 6.1   Section of Hollar's Map Vista, *London from the Bankside*. *Source*: Map L85c, No. 29, Part 1, Folger Shakespeare Library   *237*
Figure 6.2   Portrait of Nathan Field. *Source*: Dulwich Picture Gallery, London, UK / Bridgeman Images   *262*
Figure 6.3   Portrait of Richard Burbage. *Source*: Dulwich Picture Gallery, London, UK / Bridgeman Archive   *262*
Figure 6.4   The Image of Robert Armin on the title-page of *The Two Maids of Moreclacke*. *Source*: STC 773 Copy 1, Folger Shakespeare Library   *265*

List of Boxes

Box I.1   Swan Drawing   *8*
Box I.2   Philip Henslowe   *12*
Box 1.1   James Burbage   *30*
Box 2.1   *Sir Thomas More*   *42*
Box 2.2   A Postscript to Strange's Men: Prescot   *66*
Box 3.1   Masters of the Revels   *84*
Box 3.2   A Day at the Theatre   *106*
Box 3.3   "Dramatic" or "Back-Stage" Plots   *113*
Box 3.4   Patronage and its Practices   *123*
Box 4.1   Martin Slater and the Children of the King's Revels   *144*
Box 4.2   The Contracts of William Shakespeare and John Heminge   *147*
Box 4.3   Augustine Phillips: Shakespeare's Fellow-Sharer   *152*
Box 4.4   Women in the Theatres   *161*
Box 5.1   The Falstaff Issue and the Use of the Blackfriars   *194*
Box 5.2   The Jig   *218*
Box 6.1   Contentions About The Globe: Size, Audience, Seating on the Stage   *236*
Box 7.1   *Court Masques*   *287*

Preface

Shakespeare's Theatre is a narrative history of the playing spaces that Shakespeare wrote for – not just the famous ones, like the Globe and the Blackfriars playhouses, but the country houses, inns, guild halls, Inns of Court and the royal palaces where he knew that his plays would also be performed. It is a history in that it follows a chronological arc, from about the time of his birth in 1564 until his retirement from the stage around 1613/14.

This is to underline the point that there was no single "Elizabethan stage." The theatrical profession underwent revolutionary change during Shakespeare's lifetime, developing from forms that were largely based in households of the aristocracy and gentry, academic institutions and royal palaces. Some troupes toured locally and then further afield, advertising the status of their patrons but also becoming increasingly professional. Theatrical venues specifically for them (and also for boy companies from some of the leading choir schools) were built in and around London from the 1570s. Around 1590 companies began to take up residence in these playhouses on a more-or-less permanent basis, as London developed a population capable of sustaining daily playing, setting the conditions for the career of a man like Shakespeare.

Acting thus passed from being a largely localized activity, much of it amateur, within a patronage culture; and it became a professionalized business, a proto-capitalist enterprise within which men (and boys, and even a few women) could build a living for themselves, and a very few become extremely wealthy. But the new never entirely threw off the old. The companies with which we can associate Shakespeare were called the Lord Chamberlain's Men and the King's Men – they had (and had to have) patrons of high, and ultimately the highest, status to succeed as they did. And aspects of this dual nature were visible in virtually every playing space.

Moreover these changes did not happen without resistance. The players had constantly to adapt to live within attempts to limit, control – or even try to eradicate – their activities. This history is largely the story of those adaptations. Like all histories it was never as straightfowarwardly linear as the writing process makes it seem: change happened erratically and at different speeds in different contexts. I shall, therefore, frequently cross-reference you to other parts of the book, especially to pick up where a minor development in one context became a larger phenomenon in another. Another distinctive feature of my story-telling is what I have called the Box features. Each of these recounts a story in itself, a significant anecdote within the larger tale – but one with which I did not want to interrupt the narrative flow. So, for example, you will find Box items on Philip Henslowe and on the Masters of the Revels. Henslowe and those Masters of the Revels who censored Shakespeare's plays (Edmund Tilney and Sir George Buc) figure repeatedly in the through-narrative and I trust their roles are comprehensible there: you do not *need* to read the Box items, certainly when you first encounter them. But I hope that your interest will be sufficiently picqued that you will want to read them, at your own time and pace. I think you will find the effort rewarding, giving depth and perspective to the wider tale.

No one writes a book of this nature alone. I have written in the company of many scholars who have scouted the territory before me, and to whom I owe an enormous debt of gratitude. These include giants of the past, like E. K. Chambers and G. E. Bentley, who compiled and analyzed vast compendia of information on early modern playing – *The Elizabethan Stage* and *The Jacobean and Caroline Stage* respectively – on which all subsequent scholarship has been built, even as some of those foundations have begun to show their age. But most of my companions have been people I have been privileged to know and work with in the field of Shakespearean-era scholarship over the last quarter of a century. Some I have been lucky enough to communicate with in person about this book; others have just inspired me with their writing. Let me mention John Astington, Peter Greenfield, Andrew Gurr, William Ingram, David Kathman, Roslyn Lander Knutson, Sally-Beth MacLean, Lawrence Manley, Alan Nelson, Tom Postlewait, Tiffany Stern, and William Streitberger. I also owe particular thanks to all other members of the theatre history seminar that miraculously reinvents itself annually at the meeting of the Shakespeare Association of America; I have attended more often than not since 1992 and profited enormously from it. Lastly I must acknowledge a different kind of debt to Emma Bennett, who first gave me the green light to work on this book, longer ago than I care to remember.

Quotations in the book from Shakespeare are normally taken from *The Complete Works of Shakespeare* edited by David Bevington, 6th edn (New York and London: Pearson Longman, 2009), though I have occasionally needed to draw in unmediated form on the quartos and the First Folio in which they were originally printed. You will find in the Bibliography details of all the editions on which I have drawn for the works of other authors of his era. A word of explanation: wherever a quotation comes from, if it is not already modernized, I have made it so. Most of us know Shakespeare in modernized texts. I do not want to obfuscate the wider picture of his times for the general reader by leaving his contemporaries four hundred years behind. Some terms associated with the playhouses, however, may well still be unfamiliar – "sharer," "book-keeper," "tireman," etc.; most of them are explained in Chapter 4, "The Chamberlain's/King's Men and their Organization."

The Bibliography is arranged by author and date, allowing you to find full details from a brief citation. Several texts, however, will be quoted so commonly that I have cited them parenthetically in quite distinctive forms. E. K. Chambers' *The Elizabethan Stage* is cited simply as *ES*; *English Professional Theatre, 1530–1660*, ed. Glynne Wickham, Herbert Berry and William Ingram as *EPF*; *Henslowe's Diary*, edited by R. A. Foakes (2nd edn, 2002) as *Henslowe*; and Sir Henry Herbert's office-book, from *The Control and Censorship of Caroline Drama*, ed. N. W. Bawcutt, as *Herbert*.

Richard Dutton
January 2017, Croston, Lancashire

Introduction

Palamon and Arcite was Performed with the Queen Herself Present on the Stage

The following passages all relate to theatrical events staged during Queen Elizabeth's visit to the university city of Oxford in September of 1566, when William Shakespeare was only two years old. They provide some of the most detailed accounts of any theatricals in the entire era. Although the experiences they record are very different from the Elizabethan theatre with which we are most familiar, as epitomized by the reconstructed "Shakespeare's Globe" on the south bank of the River Thames, they probably give us an indication of the kind of staging that Shakespeare would have encountered when his plays were performed at the royal court, and indeed (albeit on a less lavish scale) at other grand indoor venues, such as the Inns of Court, the great houses of the nobility and eventually the Blackfriars theatre.

And it will be my contention that some of the social and ideological assumptions that underlie this staging did in fact carry over into the public playhouses, even though the practicalities of outdoor playing made for very different conventions.

Several people left accounts of the royal visit to Oxford and I quote from three of them. The first passage comes from a full but rather solemn Latin commentary by John Bereblock, a Fellow of Exeter College, who first describes how the hall of Christ Church was set up on September 1 to accommodate the Queen and other worthies.[1] This was the site of all theatricals on the visit, and it tells us a good deal about the place of theatre in Elizabethan England (and not just at court or in the university colleges) that so much of her entertainment should have been planned in the form of stage shows. Elizabeth did not in fact attend the first play, a Roman history of *Marcus Geminus* in Latin, being so weary with the day's business. But, as entries for September 2 and 4 show, Elizabeth did attend Richard Edwardes's two-part play, *Palamon and Arcite*, based on Chaucer's *The Knight's Tale*. These come from a Latin manuscript "Of

Shakespeare's Theatre: A History, First Edition. Richard Dutton.
© 2018 Richard Dutton. Published 2018 by John Wiley & Sons Ltd.

the Acts Done at Oxford," compiled by Nicholas Robinson, Bishop of Bangor. Edwardes, the Master of the Children of the Chapel Royal, and author *Damon and Pythias*, which had pleased the Queen at court, staged the show with students of the university. Later passages are from a rather livelier, but less organized, set of recollections by one of those students, Miles Windsor, of Corpus Christi College.

> (1 September, Bereblock) As night was approaching the most elaborate shows were given, which for many, who being at leisure were anticipating them the whole day, were the pinnacle of reward in their distinction. And nothing indeed more precious or more magnificent could be devised than their provision and construction. First there was an elaborate approach (to the hall) by means of a doorway that was open in a large, solid wall and from it, a raised wooden platform placed on posts runs forward by a small [i.e. narrow] and skilful track across transverse steps toward the great hall of the college. It is equipped with a festive garland and an engraved and painted canopy so that by it, without the bustle and disturbance of the pressing crowd, the queen could make her way to the prepared shows with, as it were, an even step. There was the hall with a gilded panelled ceiling, a ceiling both painted and arched within, and you might say that it imitates the size of the ancient Roman palace in its grandeur and pride, and the image of antiquity in its magnificence. In its upper end, which faces west, a great and raised stage is built up, one also elevated by many steps. Along every wall raised steps and platforms have been constructed, benches were atop the same (raised steps and platforms) of many (different) heights, from which distinguished men and ladies might be admired, and the people all around were able to observe on all sides of the plays. Burning lamps, hanging lamps, and candles made a very bright light there. With so many lights arranged in branches and circles and so many torches (or chandeliers) providing flickering light here and there with unequal brightness, the place shone, so that like daylight, (the lights) seemed to sparkle and help the splendor of the shows with the greatest radiance. On either side of the stage, magnificent palaces and most sumptuous houses are constructed for the comedies and masques. A seat had been fixed on high, provided with pillows and tapestries and covered with a golden canopy: (this) place was appointed for the queen, but she, in fact, was not present on this night. [2]
>
> (2 September, Robinson) As on the previous night, on this one also this stage was decorated splendidly so that *The Knights Tale*, as Chaucer calls it, translated from Latin into English speech by Mr Edwardes and other students of the same college, was set forth to the public ... After her royal majesty had entered onto the stage and all the entrances were

closed, part of a wall by which one goes into the hall – by what chance or for what reason I do not know – fell down and crushed a scholar of St Mary's Hall and a townsman by the name of Penny. They died there and also another scholar's leg was broken. And both of a cook's legs were shattered and his face was cut up, as if by blows, by the fall of stones. Nevertheless, the show was not interrupted but continued to midnight.

(4 September, Robinson) On this night what had remained of the story or tale of Palamon and Arcite was performed with the queen herself present on the stage.[3]

Much could be said from Bereblock's account about the magnificence bestowed on Christ Church hall for these events; about the importance attached to them such that they were not suspended despite multiple deaths and injuries on September 2; about the elaborate arrangements to seat the spectators; about the blaze of lights which lasted until midnight, about the "magnificent palaces and most sumptuous houses" on either side of the stage. And I shall address them all in the course of the book. But what I particularly want to draw attention to here is the striking assertion that Edwardes's play "was performed with the queen herself present on the stage." Elizabeth was not only a spectator, she was also a performer. And, as Miles Windsor's account shows, she was not just a passive one.[4]

Bereblock and others commented on the realism and spectacle of several scenes in *Palamon and Arcite*, including sound effects to evoke Theseus hunting, when hounds were released in the courtyard outside the hall and students blew horns and hallooed.[5] According to Windsor Elizabeth cried out "O excellent ... those boys are ready to leap out of [the] window to the hounds." He also tells of John Dalaper, playing Lord Trevatio, "being out of his part and missing his cue, and offering his service to the ladies, swearing 'by the mass' or 'Got blutt, I am out.' And like to Master Secretary [William Cecil], whistling up a hornpipe in very good measure. 'Cod's pitty,' saith the Queen, 'what a knave it 'tis.' And likewise Master Secretary: 'Go thy ways, thou art wider out; thou mayst be 'llowed to play the knave in any ground in England.'"[6] The scene resembles nothing so much as the bantering with which Theseus and his courtiers respond to "Pyramus and Thisbe" in *A Midsummer Night's Dream*.

The original plan was that the two parts of *Palamon and Arcite* should be staged on successive nights. But, as on the first day of her visit, Elizabeth was so exhausted by the schedule the university had set for her that she could not face the second night; she graciously accepted, however, that it be deferred a further day. So she was present for some of the most spectacular scenes in the second part; the play climaxed with a subterranean fire by which Saturn struck down Arcite in his moment of triumph; and there was a magnificent pyre for his funeral. The latter was so realistic that a spectator tried to stop one of the actors from placing a cloak on it, crying "God's wounds ... what mean ye?

Will ye burn the *King Edward* cloak in the fire?" Edwardes had to intervene to allow the play to resume. But in all important respects the show was a great success.

Elizabeth complimented Edwardes and promised him reward ("she said it did surpass *Damon & Pythias*, than the which nothing could be better"). She also bantered with him about his principal actors, saying (according to Windsor) of Marbeck, who played Palamon, "I warrant him he dallyeth not in love when he was in love indeed"; and of Banes, playing Arcite, "he was a right martial knight, who had indeed a swarse & manly countenance."[7] She also singled out the boy playing Emilia: "The lady Emilia for gathering her flowers prettily in the garden & singing sweetly in the prime of May received 8 angels for a gracious reward by her Majesty's commandment." In similar vein "afterward her Majesty gave unto one John Rainolds, a scholar of Corpus College which was a player in the same play 8 old angels, in reward." With hindsight this moment can be seen as extremely ironic. That scholar of Corpus Christi would later be Dr John Rainolds, President of his college, one of the translators of the King James Bible – and author of *Th'Overthrow of Stage Plays* (1599). The book is one of the most famous of the Puritan attacks on the Elizabethan stage and the one that argues in greatest detail for the evils of cross-dressing boys as girls. Rainolds played Hippolyta in *Palamon and Arcite*, and we might not unreasonably conclude that the experience had scarred him for life (see p. 186).

I have dwelled at some length on one of the less familiar scenes of Elizabethan theatre. The universities were privileged, establishment institutions which had strong traditions of academic theatre, encouraged by the humanist conviction that dramatic performance was an ideal practice for honing rhetorical and musical skills. The first great generation of Elizabethan dramatists – Lyly, Marlowe, Greene, Nashe, Peele – were all "university wits," attending either Oxford or Cambridge. Robert Greene's infamous death-bed gibe at Shakespeare as "an upstart crow, beautified with our feathers," addressed to his "fellow scholars about this city," specifically scorns him as someone who did *not* have a gentleman's university education but in writing plays usurps the role that properly belongs to those who do.[8]

Shakespeare's skills as a dramatist, however, allowed him to transcend such distinctions. These doubtless derived in part from the classical and humanistic education he would have derived from the King Edward VI School in Stratford-upon-Avon, and in part from observing the example of his predecessors. And while he wrote initially for the public stages he came increasingly to cater also for privileged audiences, including the most privileged audiences of all, those at the courts of Elizabeth I and James I. Wherever his plays were performed, however, I suggest that the figure of the monarch *on the stage* was always figuratively present.

Those audiences at *Palamon and Arcite* saw her through the action of the play, something facilitated by the fact that the audience was situated virtually in the round (as they later would be at amphitheaters like the Theatre and the

Globe). Every member of the audience would, in effect, see other members of the audience through the action of the play; they were all participants in the same event. But for the great majority of those present what they saw was an elite and privileged audience, presided over by majesty itself (note Bereblock's "benches were atop the same ... from which distinguished men and ladies might be admired"). Although the Queen was clearly demarcated in a space of her own, she was not alone: leading members of her court, like her Principal Secretary of State, William Cecil, were clearly nearby and "the ladies" were evidently close enough to the stage for the embarrassed John Dalaper, "out" of his role, to bluster his apologies to them. So the upper echelons of the society were defined by their proximity to the stage, something most spectators absorbed even as they absorbed the play. As John H. Astington puts it, "Protocol demanded that the monarch be in a central position, a rival with the entertainers as a focus for the gaze of the assembly" (1999, 88–119, 90).

(See also the seating diagram for the Great Chamber at Whitehall in 1601, Figure 3.4, p. 120.)

Staging of precisely this nature was never used for plays staged in commercial playhouses during Shakespeare's lifetime. But Shakespeare's company performed their own works at court from 1594 onwards and provided the speaking roles for court masques – while the aristocrats in them danced and posed in outrageously expensive costumes, but did not "act." The players understood the literal and symbolic centrality of the monarch, wherever they performed. In a famous and influential essay on *A Midsummer Night's Dream* – a play dogged by the supposition that it was written for a wedding attended by the Queen – Louis Montrose argued that it was an unnecessary conjecture: "For whether or not Queen Elizabeth was physically present at the first performance of *A Midsummer Night's Dream*, her pervasive *cultural presence* was a condition of the play's imaginative possibility" (Montrose, 1983, 62). What I am suggesting is that this "pervasive *cultural presence*" was a condition of *all* the drama of the era.

I am not the first to point out that much Elizabethan theatre placed the Queen (or her representatives) literally on the stage. In *Shakespeare's Wooden O* Leslie Hotson presents a wealth of evidence that it was a *normal* feature of Elizabethan staging – both in England and on the Continent – for the most senior persons present at private theatricals (at court, colleges, the Inns of Court [the law schools in London] and elsewhere) to be seated in this way on the stage: to be objects of observation as much as the play. Unfortunately this led him into some unwise conjectures about the implications of such staging for public theatres like the Globe, which I discuss in the Box Item, "Contentions about the Globe: size, audience, seating on the stage" (p. 240). Probably as a result of this all that evidence has been largely ignored by scholars since, though theatre historians like Alan H. Nelson and John H. Astington have unearthed further evidence in the universities and at court (Nelson 1989, 1992, 1994,

1999, esp. pp. 59–60; Astington, 1999, 88–119). As we shall shortly reflect, there is an awful lot about Shakespeare's theatre that we simply do not know and can only guess at. And, ironically, a good deal of what we *do* know is commonly passed over, often because it seems not to square with what we expect or want of Shakespeare.

Reminders of the monarch's "cultural presence" in the theatre took many forms. One of the most immediate was the requirement throughout Shakespeare's professional career that all major acting companies be under the patronage of an aristocrat, a baron or an earl, next in rank to royalty itself. When James I came to the throne all the most successful companies were taken into direct royal patronage. A practical manifestation of the royal "presence" was the oversight of plays and players in this time by the Master of the Revels, an officer of the court who censored their plays and licensed their playhouses (and made a healthy income from doing so: see Box Item, "The Masters of the Revels," p. 84). Perhaps more surprising to modern sensibilities was the recitation of prayers at the end of plays, seeking blessings on the Queen and her ministers, and sometimes on the lord who patronized the acting company. These prayers appeared commonly in play texts early in Elizabeth's reign. *Apius and Virginia* (circa 1567–8), for example, contains an epilogue with a prayer for the queen, nobles and commons; *New Custom*, an interlude printed in 1573, ends with a prayer for Elizabeth.[9] *Horestes* (circa 1567) offers prayers for the Queen and the Lord Mayor of London, while *Cambyses* (circa 1570) ends with one for the Queen and her Privy Council.

E. K. Chambers suggests that "A practice of offering up a prayer for the lord's well-being at the end of a performance was probably of ancient *derivation*, although whether it survived in the public theatres may perhaps be doubted" (*ES*, 1: 311). Nevertheless, as late as 1596, the witty Sir John Harington could write: "I will neither end with sermon nor with prayer, lest some wags liken me to my L[ord —] players, who when they have ended a bawdy comedy, as though that were a preparative to devotion, kneel down solemnly, and pray all the company to pray for them with their good Lord and master" (Harington, 1960, 185). And Thomas Middleton evidently expected the practice still to be familiar in 1606 when he has a boy player at Paul's playhouse say "This shows like kneeling after the play; I praying for my Lord Owemuch and his good countess, our honourable lady and mistress" (*A Mad World, My Masters*, 5.2.208–10; 2007c).

The practice of praying for individual lord patrons may have phased out by James I's reign (started 1603). But prayers for the monarch remained a consistent element at the end of performances. *A Knack to Know a Knave* (pub. 1594), *A Looking Glass for London and England* (pub. 1594), and *Locrine* (pub. 1595) all appeared with prayers for Elizabeth. *Two Wise Men And All The Rest Fools* (pub. 1619) concludes thus: "It resteth that we render you very humble and hearty thanks, and that all our hearts pray for the king and his family's enduring happiness, and our country's perpetual welfare. *Si placet, plaudite*" (Chapman, 1874–5, 2: 427). And we know that William Shakespeare was familiar with the convention because he followed it in *2 Henry IV*, where the epilogue is spoken by a dancer: "My tongue is weary; when my legs are too, I will bid you good night; and so I kneel down before you, but, indeed, to pray for the Queen" (30–3).[10] Prologues and epilogues were often composed for particular performances, such as those at court, and not necessarily regarded as a permanent element of the text (Stern, 2009*a*, 81–119). This one may have been preserved because it contains Shakespeare's disingenuous denial that the character of Falstaff was based on the historical Sir John Oldcastle ("for Oldcastle died a martyr, and this is not the man," 29–30: see p. 194). But others that invoked prayers for Elizabeth and later James surely once existed.

So a performance of *2 Henry IV*, a play that ends with Henry V's cold-hearted renunciation of Falstaff ("I know thee not, old man," 5.5.47), actually concluded with a lively dance or jig – an entertainment we shall discuss later (see p. 218) – followed by prayers for the Queen. These are alien conventions to us, hard evidence that the past really was a foreign country and they did things differently there. But they were conventions that shaped William Shakespeare as a dramatist and the theatrical landscape within which he operated. As I shall argue, the authority of the Queen (and later the King) prescribed many of those conventions, determining the kinds of stage on which he would work.

The Upstart Crow

We do not know how William Shakespeare became involved with the world of the stage. Nor do we know how or when he moved from the small market town of Stratford-upon-Avon, in the south midlands of England, to London, by far the biggest city in the country. We can first trace him in the capital in 1592, when his success seems to have generated enthusiasm and resentment in equal measure from more established playwrights there. But by then he was already twenty-eight years old: more than half of the fifty-two years he was to live had passed. And we know virtually nothing about how he spent them.

We know that he obtained a licence to marry Anne Hathaway in late November 1582, though we do not know when the wedding took place; we do know that their first daughter, Susanna was christened on May 26, 1583 and their twins, Hamnet and Judith, were christened on February 2, 1585; in both cases baptisms took place in Holy Trinity Church, Stratford. Whether this means that Shakespeare was tied to Stratford until that last date, perhaps following in his father's trade as a glove-maker; or that he might have worked elsewhere – possibly as a traveling player – and only returned home for occasional visits, we have no way of knowing.

Nor do we know nearly as much about the profession in which he was to make his mark as we would like. We look back to his time as a golden age of theatre, in which not only his own plays but also those of Christopher Marlowe, Ben Jonson, Thomas Middleton, John Webster, John Marston, and many others were staged for the first time. Their contemporaries did not quite see it like that. We hear most often about what they did *not* like about the players and their playhouses (to use the terms most current at the time). They were noisy; they attracted pick-pockets, prostitutes, and other criminals; they lured people away from divine service; they were a breeding ground for the plague. Even though the London playhouses were some of the most original and striking buildings of their time, Londoners left little comment about them, except to complain about their inconveniences. It was left to foreigners, who were genuinely impressed, to record some really useful information – like the Swiss physician, Thomas Platter, who saw an early performance of *Julius Caesar* at the newly-opened Globe in 1599, one of very few eyewitness accounts of a Shakespeare play as it was originally performed.

Or like the Dutchman, Johannes De Witt, who left a sketch of the Swan theatre, the only visual impression we have of the interior of one of the great outdoor auditoria like the Theatre and the Globe (see Frontispiece). This in itself is an object lesson in the limits of our knowledge. Those primarily interested in Shakespeare would prefer the sketch to be of one of the theatres he is known to have used; and we would all prefer to have the original. But that is lost, and only a copy by his friend, Arendt van Buchell survives; we have no way of knowing what was omitted, added or distorted in van Buchell's copying.

> **Box I.1 Swan Drawing**
>
> Around 1596 a Dutchman named Johannes De Witt visited London and recorded his impressions, including those arising from going to the Swan playhouse on the Bankside, at that time the newest of the great outdoor auditoria. They also included a sketch of the interior of the theatre. Unfortunately what De Witt wrote and drew has not survived, but by great good luck his picture and some of his observations (such as an estimate that the playhouse could hold 3,000 people) were copied by his friend, Arendt van Buchell. That copy is the only visual impression we have of the interior of one of the great Elizabethan amphitheaters.
>
> We cannot know, however, how accurate De Witt's original drawing was, or how much van Buchell may have distorted it in making his copy. So we have to treat it with great caution. A particularly forceful critic of relying too heavily on the drawing for an understanding of Elizabethan theatre practice has been R. A. Foakes: "It seems to me … that we have little reason to be sanguine about the accuracy of the van Buchell/De Witt drawing, and should treat all of its features

with skepticism" (Foakes, 1993, 351; see also Foakes 2004; Postlewait 2009). To take one small example: a performance is evidently in progress, with three figures on stage (two, apparently female, one of whom is seated, while a man approaches them, staff in hand) and the playhouse's flag is flying, as we know it did during performances. But a trumpeter is in an upper turret, apparently blowing one of the three "soundings" which advertised as broadly as possible that a performance was *about* to begin (see p. 267). The picture obviously contains composite impressions and does not attempt to capture a single moment. Moreover it is apparent that De Witt had been struck by the likeness of features of the playhouse to those of ancient Rome (see p. 234), and this may have colored what he drew (and what van Buchell made of it).

Nevertheless, the drawing seems very clearly to show two large doorways at the rear of the stage platform (marked *proscenium*), in the wall of a structure marked *mimorum ædes* (the buildings of the actors), which most theatre historians designate as the tiring house. Above the doors is a row of six windows or openings, from each of which one or two persons look out; it could be a single gallery or possibly a row of boxes. This was evidently what was known as the Lords' room or rooms (see p. 95).[11]

The rear half of the stage is covered by a canopy (usually known as the "heavens" from the habit of decorating the underside of such covers with celestial images), and this is held up by two very substantial pillars. (Some have supposed that the Swan had a removable stage so that it could double as an arena for bear-baiting, as was the case with the later Hope. But those pillars seem to preclude that.) The stage itself is held up by stout legs, which seem to suggest that it was possible to see underneath, though this is contradicted by practice elsewhere. The area before the stage is labeled *"planetres sive arena"* ("level spaces [?] or arena" – the latter being what the Romans called the performance spaces in amphitheaters like the Colosseum), apparently what the Elizabethans knew as the pit, where the lowest-paying members of the audience stood, without protection from the elements.

To the left and right of the stage are what might be steps up to a higher level, one marked *"ingressus"* ("entrance"). This might well square with what we know about paying progressively to reach the better accommodations in the playhouses (see p. 160). Above this are what we might interpret as three levels of enclosed audience space. One is marked *"orchestra,"* apparently from the Roman *orchestra*, the seating in theatres reserved for the senatorial class (and so perhaps denoting what are elsewhere referred to as "gentlemen's rooms": see pp. 232–4). Above that *"sedilia"* – seating. And above that *"porticus"* – gallery. (In other contexts a gallery might suggest a place to walk, rather than sit. The levels apparently offered different comforts.) Top right is marked, *"tectum"* – roof, suggesting that all of these accommodations, as opposed to the "arena," were secured from the weather.

There is much the picture does *not* tell us. For example, we do not know how the items marked *ingressus* related to initial entry into the building, or indeed how many entry-ways there were. Perhaps most contentiously there is no sign of a discovery space between the two doors, which appear to be the only means of access to the playing area (see p. 96). Discovery spaces are deduced by scholars from stage directions such as that in *The Tempest*, where "*Prospero discovers Ferdinand and Miranda, playing at chess*" (5.1.172.1–2). Such actions *might* take place in one of the doorways, with the door folded back and the opening covered with a curtain. But for some scholars the cumulative evidence points to a third point of access to the stage, located between the two doors. Normally speaking, however, the discovery space would be covered with an arras or tapestry, so the fact that nothing is visible in the Swan drawing is far from conclusive (see p. 200). Indeed, that wall of the tiring house would normally have been covered with such tapestries, discovery space or no. The picture is no help in this regard.

Moreover, we must bear in mind that although the broad design of the Elizabethan amphitheaters remained settled from the time of the Theatre onwards, there were minor amendments and refinements throughout the period. The earliest playhouses apparently did not have "heavens"; and the comforts offered in the "gentlemen's rooms" seem to have improved in the later ones (becoming correspondingly more expensive). Discovery spaces may similarly have been an innovation part-way through the period or simply not a feature of all playhouses.

Only a single extant play is known to have been written specifically for the Swan, Thomas Middleton's *A Chaste Maid in Cheapside*, and it has two stage directions which *might* imply a discovery space: it opens with "*Enter Maudlin and Moll, a shop being discovered*" and 3.2 begins with "*A bed thrust out upon the stage, Allwit's wife in it.*" But the play was not staged until circa 1613 and not printed until 1630; the text we have may not reflect performance at the playhouse De Witt drew.

(Continued from p. 8)

Another example of information that gets us close to Shakespeare and his playhouses, but not as close as we would like, is Philip Henslowe's so-called *Diary*.[12] Henslowe was a multi-faceted businessman, with interests in (among other things) dyeing, pawn-broking, money-lending, trading in goat skins and renting out property, mainly in Southwark, a borough on the south shore of the Thames. There he purchased what became the Rose theatre, and his *Diary* records his business dealings with the companies who used it from 1592 to 1603. Only very briefly, in June 1594, was one of these a company with whom Shakespeare performed (and then it was at a more obscure playhouse at

Newington Butts, not the Rose: see pp. 76–7). Moreover there is much about the information which Henslowe recorded which is baffling or incomplete. It was once common to belittle him as illiterate and only concerned with profit (by supposed contrast with Shakespeare and his fellows), but today we recognize that he was a typical businessman of his day and quite shrewd about theatrical affairs; from 1592 his stepdaughter was married to the great actor, Edward Alleyn (see Figure I.1). His *Diary*, for all its shortcomings, is the single most revealing document we have about theatrical practices at the beginning of Shakespeare's London career, in the 1590s.

Figure I.1 Portrait of Edward Alleyn. *Source*: akg-images.

Box I.2 Philip Henslowe

Philip Henslowe's[13] career and practices tell us a good deal about the place of theatre in early modern London, in relation to the circulation of money, power, and prestige at that time. Born around 1555, he was the son of Edmond Henslowe of Lindfield, Sussex, a family with links to the court and the Sussex nobility. Edmond's son-in-law, Ralph Hogge, was an English iron-master and gun founder to the queen. Philip's older brother, another Edmond, was in the service of the Lord Chamberlain. Drawing on such connections, Philip was appointed a Groom of the Chamber in 1593, not a high post but one that crucially made him a member of the court circle, a position from which to promote his interests for the rest of his life. Prior to this he secured his standing in the City of London by gaining his freedom in the Dyers' Company; this was one of the livery companies, who were responsible for the regulation of their trades, controlling, for instance, wages and labor conditions. Freedom (i.e. membership) in such a company was an essential first step to becoming a freeman of the City, a necessary status for anyone wishing to conduct business there.

Henslowe had been an assistant to Henry Woodward in the Dyers, and when Woodward died Henslowe promptly married his widow, Agnes (February 14, 1580). They had no children of their own, but the marriage made him stepfather to two daughters, Joan and Elizabeth. From 1577 they lived in a house located between the Clink prison and the Bell inn, in the Liberty of Clink in Southwark, just south and west of London Bridge. This was a location of considerable importance in the history of Elizabethan theatre, the site eventually of the Rose and later the Globe playhouses (see pp. 197–8). Henslowe seems to have had an entrepreneurial spirit from the start, investing – almost indiscriminately, it seems – in property (in Buxted, Sussex, for instance, but mainly in Southwark), starch making and pawn-broking. Between 1576 and 1586 he negotiated the sale of wood in Ashdown Forest; in June 1584 he was involved in buying and dressing goatskins.

In March 1585 Henslowe acquired a property called "the little Rose" (because of its distinctive rose gardens). Plans for a playhouse on that property – also in the Liberty of Clink – were drawn up in 1587 by Henslowe, in partnership with one John Cholmley, a grocer. These specified a garden plot, 94 feet (28.7 metres) square, on the Bankside in the parish of St Saviour's, Southwark, and "a play house now in framing [was] shortly to be erected and set up upon the same" (*ES*, 2: 406). This was to be the Rose, the first successful theatre on the Bankside.[14] Employing a carpenter, John Griggs, Henslowe undertook to erect "the said playhouse with all furniture thereunto belonging … with as much expedition as may be" (ibid.). Chomley was to pay Henslowe £816 (his portion, apparently the lion's share, of the construction costs) in quarterly instalments, for which he was to receive half of all profits as "shall arise, grow to be collected, gathered, or become due for the said parcel of ground and playhouse when and after it shall be erected and set up by reason of any play or plays that shall be shown or played there or otherwise howsoever" (ibid.). The partners were jointly to appoint "players to use, exercise and play in the said playhouse" and collect payment from audiences (though their friends could be let in free). Chomley was also to have the exclusive right to sell food and drink in the playhouse, together with use of a small property nearby from which to run those operations. Then as now, playing was not the only way income could derive from a theatre; concession stands could be highly profitable with a captive audience. In 1614, when Henslowe built the Hope theatre, he did it in conjunction with Jacob Meade, a waterman; ferrying affluent members of the audience across the Thames to the Southwark playhouses was also a significant ancillary business.

Henslowe's *Diary*, written abstemiously on the reverse of some of Ralph Hogge's old ironworks accounts, records his dealings with the companies which used the Rose (and later the Fortune theatre) from 1592 to 1603. They are not always easy to follow and used to be mocked as semi-illiterate, but it is increasingly clear that Henslowe was a shrewd businessman; he was certainly most successful. Chomley had by then disappeared, and was perhaps dead – in which case Henslowe was taking a full share of the profits, but also carrying all the debt. I write elsewhere about Strange's Men and the Admiral's Men and the details of their repertoires recorded in the early parts of the *Diary*; these were the companies which used the Rose most extensively (see pp. 62ff; 170ff). Henslowe was their landlord and later financier, taking their rents but also lending them money to buy playbooks from the dramatists and properties (most notably costumes) for their performances, which would be stored in the tiring house section of the theatre. In the early years, business decisions about playing remained in the hands of the players – every loan was advanced on the word of one or more of the sharers, who were held strictly to its terms.

Over time, however, Henslowe's relations with the actors appear more in the light of a controlling business manager than a landlord. The fact that he owned one (and later more) of the few officially sanctioned playhouses around London, together with the capital to allow the actors who used them to indebt themselves to him, made him a commanding figure. And this was compounded by his relationship with the leading actor in Strange's and subsequently the Admiral's Men, Edward Alleyn, who married his stepdaughter Joan in October 1592. Henslowe and Alleyn seem to have been close personally and were certainly a very effective business partnership, controlling not only several theatres but also the bear-baiting arena in Paris Garden, yet another section of the Bankside.

In 1599 the building of the Globe by the Chamberlain's Men apparently created serious competition for the Rose, and Henslowe and Alleyn jointly decided to construct a new playhouse, the Fortune, north of London Wall in the parish of St Giles Cripplegate. They engaged Peter Street, the carpenter who had built the

Globe playhouse, in a contract dated January 8 1600; the contract makes it plain that they intended to imitate the Globe in many particulars, except that the outer walls were to be square rather than quasi-circular and the roof was to be tiled rather than thatched (see p. 230). The Fortune cost £520 in addition to the lease for the property on which the playhouse was constructed (*ES*, 2:436–9). It opened that autumn and the Admiral's Men immediately transferred there (*Henslowe*, 306–10). Whether Alleyn was still playing at this date is a moot point; he certainly retired around 1598 but seems to have come out of retirement on occasion between then and 1604. Possibly he felt that his proven popularity would help draw audiences to the new playhouse. Henslowe and Alleyn owned the Fortune jointly until Henslowe's death in 1616; Alleyn somehow acquired complete control and by 1618 was leasing it to the players (by then the Palsgrave's Men) for £200 a year (*ES*, 2: 442).

Several acting companies continued to rent the Rose for a time after it was vacated by the Admiral's Men; these included Worcester's Men. But Henslowe and Alleyn's interests on the Bankside now focused on bear-baiting. They particularly wanted the lucrative court office of Master of the Royal Game of Bears, Bulls and Mastiff Dogs. After several years of hoping to acquire it by patronage they decided to buy it in 1604. It proved profitable enough that by 1613 they planned, in conjunction with Jacob Meade, to build a dual-purpose playhouse/bear-baiting pit even further west on the Bankside, called the Hope. By October 1614 it was being used by Lady Elizabeth's Men who performed Ben Jonson's *Bartholomew Fair* there. According to the play's "Induction" the place was "as dirty as Smithfield, and as stinking every whit" (2012*b*, lines 119–20) – that is, it smelled every bit as bad as the site of the real Bartholomew Fair, near the great meat-market.

In addition to his business interests Henslowe was assiduous in his civic and church duties. He served as a collector for the lay subsidy taxes in the Clink liberty, paying himself substantial tax of £10 per collection. He similarly served as vestryman (1607), churchwarden (1608), and overseer of the poor of St Saviour's parish. He was a governor of the free grammar school there (1612) and one of five to purchase the rectory of St Saviour's in 1613 "for the general good of posterity as good cheap as they might" (Warner, 30–1, 139, 266). He died on January 6, 1616 and was buried in the chancel of St Saviour's Church (now Southwark Cathedral) "with an afternoon knell of the great bell." In touches of piety typical of the age his will required that forty poor men should receive mourning gowns to accompany his body to the burial, and a bequest was left to the poor of the parish. He could afford it. Henslowe left a sizeable estate, by one estimate including £1,700 in property alone (see p. 16 on the value of money).

His aged widow, Agnes, inherited his estate but died a year later, in 1617. Edward Alleyn retained his interests in the Fortune and the Mastership of the

> Royal Game. Rich and pious in his later years, in 1619 he founded the College of God's Gift (popularly known as Dulwich College) as a "hospital" for orphans and homeless pensioners. He endowed it with the manor of Dulwich in Surrey. The College is where many of Henslowe's and Alleyn's business and personal papers were left, and are primarily housed in its Wodehouse Library. Many of them can now be accessed online.[15]

Another area in which we see darkly is in the licensing and censorship of plays in the period. As mentioned above, we know that a court official, the Master of the Revels, was responsible for these matters. This was Edmund Tilney from 1579 until his death in 1610, when he was succeeded by Sir George Buc. But almost nothing has survived of the business records of these two men, which might have given us some sense of their daily dealings with the players. We occasionally hear of them when they are involved in policy matters dictated by the Privy Council – effectively the national government of the day – but otherwise we have to look to the office-book of the man who succeeded Buc, Sir Henry Herbert, who was in office from 1623 to the closing of the theatres in 1642 (*Herbert*). We have to take it on trust that his working methods and standards were similar to those of his predecessors.

Other frustratingly limited information derives from the records of the courts of Queen Elizabeth and King James, and from a great store of legal cases in which the actors were involved. The court records tell us which companies appeared there each season, how often, how much they were paid, and at which palace (even within which room) they performed. They sometimes tell us the precise date on which they played but rarely (never between 1585 and 1604) the name of the plays put on – much less anything about costumes, properties, numbers or names of actors. In respect of the law: it was a litigious age and the records are full of claims over contracts broken, money not paid and outbreaks of violence involving players.[16] Without these we would lack, for example, a record of the great actor Richard Burbage shooing off his father's creditors with a broom; or details of the Theatre being dismantled at Christmas 1598 and its main timbers being shipped over the Thames to form the skeleton of the Globe; or knowledge of John Heminge, the business-manager of Shakespeare's company being sued by his own daughter, Thomasine Ostler, over his seizure of her deceased husband's estate, including his shares in the Globe and Blackfriars theatres. We shall encounter all these anon and many others besides. But the last is typical in being frustratingly incomplete: we have contradictory depositions from various parties, but no final ruling. Similarly, after the Blackfriars boys company was wound up in 1608, opening the way for Shakespeare's company to take over their playhouse, no less than six lawsuits were filed by former members of its management, leaving us with a bewildering array of bills of complaint, answers, replications and rejoinders (Smith, 512–46).

Let me make one final point about the difficulty of putting together a history of the Shakespearean stage. The business of playing – the terms and conditions under which it was allowed – changed considerably in the course of Shakespeare's lifetime. None of those theatres I have already discussed, for example, existed when Shakespeare was born. People used to speak of *the* Elizabethan stage, as if theatre was essentially the same phenomenon from 1576 (the building of the Theatre) to 1642 (the closing of the theatres at the outbreak of the Civil War). We now see much more clearly that it was constantly evolving, as individuals and troupes sought to exploit new niche positions opened up by the rapid growth of London, the proliferation of royal households after the death of Elizabeth, the opening and closing of opportunities to perform within the City limits, and so on. Hence my title, *Shakespeare's Theatre: A History*; he wrote for multiple acting spaces, multiple (and sometimes very different) audiences, as his career unfolded.

* * *

I conclude here with some details of procedures I have followed, and some basic information about early modern England, which I hope will make it easier to read what follows. I have already mentioned, for example, that I have silently modernized all quotations, even from texts. The dates used in the book have similarly been brought into line with modern usage. Especially in legal and court circles, England clung to a start of the year on Lady Day (March 25), one of the four quarter days of the year, on which servants were hired and rents were due. So, for example, Elizabeth I technically died on the last day (March 24) of 1602, though we now call it 1603. For many purposes, however, January 1 was recognized as New Year's Day. Dates between January 1 and March 24 therefore fell ambiguously between the two years and Henslowe (for example) sometimes gets muddled himself or leaves the ambiguity unresolved. Wherever it is clear I use the modern version; wherever it is unclear I draw attention to the fact.

Finally, some basic information about one of the essential threads running though this narrative: money. Comparisons between values then and now are all but impossible. But some indications of wages and costs may help readers to appreciate the relative values in play; it is helpful to bear in mind that there was rampant inflation in the early Jacobean period and most wages did not keep up with costs. (Jacobus is Latin for James, king after Elizabeth's death, hence Jacobean: 1603–25). The unit of currency was the pound (£), which was divided into 20 shillings (expressed 20s.) and that in turn was divided into 12 pence (12d.) Pennies could be further divided into half-pence or quarters (farthings). One penny in Elizabethan England could buy you a 24oz loaf of wheat bread, a pound of beef or mutton, or 2–3 gallons of beer (depending on its quality – "small beer," with very low potency, was usually a healthier option than water, having been boiled). 1d. was also the cost of entry to the early open-air playhouses like the Theatre or Globe, entitling a person to standing room in the "pit"; an extra penny bought admission to the galleries; 3d. (later 6d.) paid for an upgrade to the seated "gentlemen's rooms," while it would cost a whole shilling to get into the exclusive lords' rooms, where they existed (see p. 95).

These costs need to be compared with salaries. Those for most regular tradesmen, members of guilds, were set by statute, varying by trade and skill-level within prescribed limits. According to William Ingram: "In a world of annual wages where the bottom range was £3 to £4, a worker earning £8 to £10 a year should have been able to live adequately, perhaps even comfortably. We might therefore use £10 a year as our benchmark annual wage" (Ingram, 1999, 314–15). That would give the recipient a little more than $6^1/_2$ pence per day to live on: a penny to stand in the pit, even 2d. for a gallery, would certainly have been affordable to such a relatively well-recompensed worker (though hardly to someone earning only £3 a year). Compare that with the schoolmaster in Stratford-upon-Avon, who received £20 a year plus board and lodging. At the top end of the scale those with money to invest could make a lot more. Philip Henslowe seems to have spent about £800 on building the Rose in 1587, and a further £100 or so to improve it in 1592 (Ingram, 1999, 323). The returns, however, were equally impressive: "For the 1594–5 playing season, for example, Henslowe recorded some 275 performances of plays. His share of the paid admissions came to an average of thirty-three shillings on each of these days, for an annual total of some £450. At that level of profit it would have taken only two years to recoup the whole cost of his playhouse" (Ingram, 325).

Ingram does also note, however, that not all years were as profitable; and plague or fire constantly threatened to suspend playing for long periods, if not forever. As G. E. Bentley reminds us: "In plague years of 1593, 1594, 1603, 1604, 1625, 1630, 1631, 1636–37 and 1640 there were no London gate receipts for significant periods" (1984, 53). 1608–10 was little better, delaying the opportunity of the King's Men to use the Blackfriars playhouse when they had finally acquired it. But the first Globe burned down in 1613 and the first Fortune suffered the same fate in 1622. Yet both were rebuilt, some measure of the faith people had that theatre was a worthwhile investment. London playhouses were always a high-risk investment, but one that offered substantial returns – if you were lucky. And Shakespeare was.

Notes

1 Readers may well be familiar with the normal state of the interior of the Great Hall of Christ Church, since Hogwarts Hall in the *Harry Potter* movies was closely based on it.
2 Bereblock's *Commentary* is taken from *REED Oxford* (2004), ed. J. R. Elliott, Alan H. Nelson *et al.*, 1: 136–41. Translation from Latin is by Patrick Gregory, 2: 979.

3 Robinson's "Of the Acts Done at Oxford" is from *REED Oxford*, 1: 135–6; translation from Latin is by Patrick Gregory, 2: 978.
4 For an account of *Palamon and Arcite* in broader context, see Edwards, 2001, 84–6.
5 On the realism and spectacle of mid-century court theatre, see Streitberger, 2016, 73–88.
6 Miles Windsor's *Narrative* appears in *REED Oxford*, 1: 126–35. The passages quoted: 129, 133.
7 *The Oxford English Dictionary (OED)* does not recognize "swarse." Possibly "swart" = "swarthy"?
8 Robert Greene, *A Groatsworth of Wit Bought with a Million of Repentance* (1592), cited in Schoenbaum, 1987, 151. Thomas Kyd was another exception to those who went to university, but he did receive a fine education (like Shakespeare) from his grammar school, in his case Merchant Taylors' School.
9 E. K. Chambers lists twelve such instances in *ES*, 3: 180, n. 1.
10 In the 1600 quarto of *2 Henry IV* the call for a prayer occurs, oddly, mid-way through the epilogue; in the 1623 folio text, cited here, it is at the end.
11 Early modern punctuation does not make clear whether the lords are singular or plural, while different references mention both "room" and "rooms." For consistency I shall stick with lords' rooms.
12 See *Henslowe*; also the Henslowe–Alleyn Digitization Project, which aims to put all the Henslowe–Alleyn papers, preserved at Dulwich College, online.
13 This section is particularly indebted to Cerasano 2004*b*, Warner 1881 and Foakes 2002.
14 Newington Butts, the first theatre south of the river, never seems to have been a success, possibly being situated too far from the city; Henslowe may eventually have owned it. The Globe would eventually be built only slightly south-east of the Rose and perhaps drive it out of business.
15 See the Henslowe–Alleyn Digitization Project; http://www.henslowe-alleyn.org.uk/index.html.
16 To get an impression of the extent to which our knowledge of theatrical affairs is built upon the litigation they generated, I suggest that readers glance through "Part Three: playhouses, 1560–1660" in *EPF*, 285–674.

1

The Early Years

Stratford and Staging Practices

Even in remote, provincial Stratford, Shakespeare would have been familiar with professional theatre, some of it of the highest quality. When he was born, in 1564, playing was an itinerant profession: actors more-or-less nominally in the service of an aristocrat or one of the lesser gentry toured the country. They would wear the livery of their patron as they traveled from town to town, advertising his prestige. We will examine the practical realities of such a way of life later on, but for now let us note that several of these companies visited Stratford at times when Shakespeare might well have been there. Thanks to the efforts of Alan Somerset in collecting evidence of drama in *Warwickshire* for the ongoing *Records of Early English Drama* series (an invaluable project, which has already transformed our knowledge) we now have a complete picture of this, from payments made by Stratford Borough Corporation.[1]

We learn that the Earl of Worcester's Men played there in 1576–7, 1580–1, 1581–2, and 1583–4.[2] (On this last visit they probably included Edward Alleyn, then at the beginning of his stellar acting career; we shall cross his path again in the course of the book: see Cerasano 2004*a*). The great Earl of Leicester's Men came in 1576–7 and 1587, his brother Earl of Warwick's Men in 1574–5; the Earl or Countess of Essex's Men visited in 1578–9, 1583–4 and 1587. The Earl of Derby's Men came in 1579–80, a year after a troupe patronized by the earl's son, Lord Strange (who were probably acrobats rather than actors). Lord Berkeley's Men (often written "Bartlett's") played in 1580–1 and 1582–3; and Lord Chandos's Men (from whom Shakespeare's company would one day recruit the great comic player, Robert Armin) played in 1582–3. The Earl of Oxford's Men performed in 1583–4 and Lord Stafford's Men in 1587. And the Queen's Men visited in 1587, 1593, and 1594 (Mulryne, 2006, 20). These included some of the finest troupes of the era: Leicester's, Warwick's and Derby's Men (as well as Strange's "tumblers") all played at court in this period, as well, of course, as the Queen's Men, the preeminent company of the 1580s.

Shakespeare's Theatre: A History, First Edition. Richard Dutton.
© 2018 Richard Dutton. Published 2018 by John Wiley & Sons Ltd.

A significant number of these patrons had principal residences either in Warwickshire (Leicester, Warwick, Berkeley) or in neighboring counties (Essex at Stafford in Staffordshire, Chandos in Gloucestershire), so asserting their local stature (Tiner, 2006, 88). Others – Derby, Oxford, and, of course, the Queen – were underlining their national standing. Stratford itself was probably never a prime target for the players, but it conveniently straddled routes – Leicester and Coventry to the north-east, Shrewsbury to the north-west, Bristol and Bath to the south-west, and Oxford to the south-east – which most certainly were places where they expected to do well. The great and wealthy wool center of Coventry, with its magnificent guildhall, was the single most popular venue for traveling players in the era.

In earlier years young William may have had privileged access to their performances, because his father – John Shakespeare – was a man of some standing. Over the years he held several responsible offices in the borough: constable, chamberlain (administering property and revenue) and in 1568, bailiff, a position equivalent to mayor. In 1571 he was elected Chief Alderman and deputy to his successor as bailiff. While he held such positions he and perhaps some of his family would have had priority seating when the players performed in Stratford's Guild Hall. The procedures for town visits by the players are described by R. Willis in *Mount Tabor or Private Exercises of a Penitent Sinner* (1639), written when he was seventy-five years old. In it he recalls "a stage-play which I saw when I was a child":

> In the city of Gloucester the manner is (as I think it is in other like corporations) that when players of interludes come to town, they first attend the Mayor to inform him what nobleman's servants they are, and so get license for their public playing ... and if the Mayor likes the actors or would show respect to their lord and master, he appoints them to play their first play before himself and the Aldermen and Common Council of the city; and that is called the Mayor's play, where everyone that will comes in without money, the Mayor giving the players a reward he thinks fit to show respect unto them. At such a play my father took me with him and made me stand between his legs as he sat upon one of the benches where we saw and heard very well.
>
> *(Bentley, 1984, 189–94)*

Did Shakespeare also stand between his father's legs and watch some of the leading players of the day in his own home town? We specifically know that the "Mayor's play" at Stratford would be staged in the Guild Hall for the back-to-front reason that in 1602 the town Corporation forbade such use. (As I have already flagged, much of our information comes to us obliquely, often because of legal disputes of one kind or another.) Whether this ban was as a result of growing puritanical resistance to theatre or because the Corporation wished to preserve the dignity and fabric of the building we do not know (Mulryne, 2006, 10–13).[3] Moreover, we are not actually sure in which room performances had been given: I pursue this issue to tease out a number of matters associated with late sixteenth-century playing.

The two-storey building, formerly the property of The Guild of the Holy Cross, passed into the control of the town Corporation in 1553. They allocated the upper floor to the newly-founded King Edward VI School, which William Shakespeare (as the son of an alderman) was entitled to attend; and they retained the lower floor for civic use. This leads some scholars to suppose that this lower room, on the ground floor, was where the actors performed. Alan Somerset, for example, describes this space: "with approximately eleven ft of headroom and a flat ceiling free of medial supports ... It measures approximately sixty-six ft long by twenty ft wide [20.1 m × 6.1 m]" (2006, 84). The few doors are not particularly convenient to a stage pitched at either end of the room, but the great length would give scope to curtain off one end, or set up canvas "houses," as tiring room space (where actors changed costumes and kept props), allowing entrances and exits around the sides. Somerset estimates that it could have accommodated "an audience of between two hundred and three hundred seated ... upon benches"; this seems quite realistic, not least since the Elizabethans were, on average, smaller than we are – one reason why the reconstructed Globe on the Bankside holds only half the audience of the original.[4] And Somerset concludes that "[w]e cannot be absolutely certain, but we are reasonably certain that this commodious lower room in the Stratford guildhall is the room in which Shakespeare first saw a professional production" (84–5).

One objection to this theory, however, is that the 11' headroom would hardly have allowed for the construction of a stage giving the audience a full view of the actors. A stage less than 4' off the ground would hardly give many in the audience a view of the action, while higher than that it might well inhibit a player like Edward Alleyn, who was "apparently a man of exceptional physical stature" (Cerasano, 2008). This is one reason that J. R. Mulryne thinks "[t]he upper Hall seems marginally more probable" as the site of performances; it has a high, vaulted, timber-beamed roof, like many Tudor halls. Another reason is that "any actor/producer/director, then or now, would prefer the commodious, bright and ample upper Hall" (2006, 15). He argues from archaeological evidence that by the time of the players' visits the upper Hall was divided into a room in its south end, used for the School (with an access passageway running down its east side), and a larger open space at the north end, available for Corporation use and so for performances. Mulryne estimates that the space at the north end measured approximately 38'4"by 21'8" (11.68 m × 6.60 m), making it remarkably similar in size and general shape to one of the buildings where Shakespeare himself has been supposed to have first practiced as an actor (17, n. 45: see pp. 55ff).

The positioning of a stage is not obvious, since once more the doors are not ideal. One possibility is that they used a raised dais at the north end of the room, a permanent fixture at the time; but it only measured 11' 8" by 5' (3.6 m × 1.5 m), a very confined performance space. Another is that the stage might have been placed at the south end, with ready access to the passageway running down the side of the schoolroom, which might itself have been used as a tiring room. As in our consideration of the lower Hall, however, these are modern instincts about what would work best for the actors and we need to consider the very real possibility that this was not the primary consideration of the Elizabethans. Think back to the Queen "on stage" in *Palamon and Arcite* (pp. 1–6). Any theatrical event of the era involving figures of authority was first a social event and decorum required that the social hierarchy should be acknowledged and appropriately visible. This would later be true – though in rather different ways – in the purpose-built commercial theatres. But in venues like this – colleges, guildhalls, private houses, and of course the court – it dictated that the hosts of the occasion (college masters and their fellows; mayors, aldermen, and members of the council; the lord and lady; the monarch) should be the real focus of attention, together with their honored guests. And the business of acting was secondary to this. We shall see this again clearly when we consider the first performances of Shakespeare's company at court, given in the Great Chamber at Greenwich, during the Revels season of 1594/5 (see pp. 118ff).

Alan Nelson has assembled considerable evidence, from records at the Oxford and Cambridge colleges, that stages there were normally constructed, not *on* the high-table dais, but just below it. The set-up might not have been as elaborate and spectacular as that for the Queen's visit to Oxford, described in the Introduction, but the principle would have been similar. The Master, senior fellows, and visiting dignitaries were seated on the dias, literally overlooking the performance. Others present sat on benches lower down the hall, and possibly even in a minstrel gallery if there was one (Nelson, 1992). Doors at either end of the hall would thus facilitate the entrance of the audience rather than of the actors, who may have had to make do with cloth-covered booths or ad hoc curtained-off spaces rigged near the stage for entrance and exit points, costume changes, and keeping properties. Where, however, scaffolding was used to erect seating for the audience (both before the stage and to both sides) it was possible to provide something more substantial. The inventory for such scaffolding used at Queens' College, Cambridge, mentions tiring houses on either side of the stage (Nelson, 1989, 691–2).

We may recall that in Bereblock's account of the Great Hall of Corpus Christi in 1566 he observed "On either side of the stage, magnificent palaces and most sumptuous houses are constructed for the comedies and masques." These were almost certainly the kind of structures (called "houses") which were used by the actors at court at this time, when they had no convenient way of entering or leaving the performance space. In the 1571/2 Revels season, for example, we find William Lyzard paid the equivalent of a very respectable year's salary just for the paints used for these: "for gold, silver and sundry other colours by him spent in painting the houses that served for the plays, & players at the court … [£13 15s 1d]" (Feuillerat, 1908, 141). No college or city corporation would go to that expense when royalty was not there to be impressed. But such structures could be very cheaply made and easily constructed, and possibly carried around by traveling actors.

The same principle is true of the college seating arrangements described by Alan Nelson: the less privileged members of the audience, sitting lower in the hall, would have seen the action against a backdrop of the Master and senior members of the college. And there is every reason to suppose that this would have been replicated at civic events such as the "Mayor's play" at Stratford Guild Hall, with the audience seeing the actors perform against a tableau of the bailiff, aldermen, and other dignitaries. In an unpublished paper of 2001, reflecting on the evidence accrued from the first eighteen volumes of the *Records of Early English Drama*, Sally-Beth MacLean offered this opinion about staging in guildhalls and the like:

> Here we can only speculate, as we seldom have evidence even of demountable stage construction. However I think it is important to bear in mind [Robert] Tittler's emphasis on the symbolic significance of the mayor in his official capacity in the seat of town government – the power and authority of the host which would have been emphasized in these touring play performances. (a) If the mayor and other members of council were accustomed to sit at the high end of the hall, on the dais, how likely is it that they would have given pride of place there to mere players? The same question can be asked of players' performances in the private halls of the nobility. Alan Nelson's research and happy discoveries of descriptive documents for comparable performances in Cambridge college halls suggest that demountable stages were placed near the upper end, but not on the dais. (b) Certainly not at the lower or screens end where the honoured guests would have had to squint to get a view from their otherwise privileged seats at the opposite end! So much for another popular assumption. I would like to suggest that official performances in urban spaces were mounted with a keen awareness of civic hierarchy and that plays were more likely staged "in the round" but towards the upper end so that the mayor and council would have had the best view. And if we look at the stage sketch that survives of the Swan theatre in London, we will note the lords' viewing room above the stage rather than below it.[5]

For these reasons I am inclined to think that the upper Hall, with its dais, is where performances took place in Stratford. I also think it likely that similar staging arrangements would have been the norm in the great halls of the nobility and gentry which the traveling players would also have graced as they moved around the country. I discuss the practices and protocols of the traveling players, which Shakespeare himself continued to experience even after he was normally settled in London, in the next chapters.

I must pause briefly to acknowledge that this argument about the staging flies in the face of one of the most popular theories about Elizabethan theatre, that advanced by Richard Southern in *The Staging of Plays before Shakespeare* (1973) and still often invoked. He was particularly struck by similarities between the hall screens at the bottom ends of many great halls of the era and what the De Witt/van Buchell drawing appeared to show of the interior of the Swan playhouse (see pp. 8ff). The wooden screens, often quite intricately carved, separated the hall itself from the kitchens and ancillary rooms beyond, or sometimes from the outside doors of the building; they usually had two substantial doors (classically "one-in, one-out" when food was being served) and many of them had so-called "minstrel galleries" above. The drawing very clearly shows two large doorways at the rear of the stage platform. Above them is a row of six windows or openings, from each of which one or two persons look out: a single gallery or possibly a row of boxes. The doors and the upper openings translate so readily into the serving doors and "minstrel gallery" of the hall screen that it is very easy to suppose that the latter inspired the former. The supposition is thus that performances in great halls were organized to focus on the hall screen, which acted as the rear of the acting area; the doors very conveniently allowed for entrances and exits, and the introduction of properties; the kitchens or adjacent rooms served as ad hoc tiring houses; the "minstrel gallery" allowed for action on the upper level, like the "balcony" scene [2.2.] in *Romeo and Juliet* or the entry of "Brabantio *above*" [1.1.83.1] in *Othello*. So felicitous was it, the argument runs, that this arrangement was later incorporated in the London amphitheaters.

There are, as we noted earlier, many caveats about the De Witt/van Buchell drawing. But the most compelling argument against this theory is that it flies in the face of all the evidence we have that social rank took precedence over all other considerations in the disposition of audiences at Elizabethan theatricals – certainly at court and in colleges but also, as I argue, virtually everywhere else as well. Social protocol and the very clear evidence of practice in the colleges and at court demand that the upper-end of the hall was used, with senior dignitaries sitting on the dais, the stage below them, and the rest of the audience arrayed on benches (or, in bigger venues, scaffolding), watching both the performance and their superiors. The rooms "above" in the Swan drawing are the lords' rooms, a symbolic embodiment of that order, not a mistrels' gallery (see p. 234).

Unless there were convenient alcoves adjacent to the stage, they would have required one or more canvas booths as tiring houses: the recessed windows in the diagram of the Great Chamber at Whitehall and adjacent to the high table at Rufford Old Hall, for example, might well have been used (see pp. 120 and 57). But it is unlikely that the players would have been allowed to use doors that led to private quarters – such as that to the Queen's Presence Chamber in the former venue or those to the Heskeths' private rooms at the latter. They would have been treated with the respect due them as emissaries of their patrons, but there were limits to familiarity.

***

William Shakespeare may not have joined his father on the dias, but he would have seen him there – splendid in his robes and insignia of office, presiding over the players – from a relatively privileged position on the lower benches. But this cannot have lasted. John's business evidently did not thrive; by the late 1570s he was in debt and stopped attending Corporation meetings. In 1586 he was replaced as alderman. The family would no longer have privileged access to Guild Hall performances, though William could have paid to attend the players' commercial shows in town. Notice in R. Willis's account that there is an implicit *quid pro quo* in the agreement between the mayor and the players. The "Mayor's play" was offered in the spirit of a gift offering from the players' patron to the worthies of the town (who did not personally pay to see it) and would be rewarded with a gratuity from the borough measured in proportion to the status of the patron. The audience in the limited space would be there by invitations only.

But the council would also permit a strictly limited number of commercial performances to take place in the town. So, for example, in 1580 the Gloucester Common Council authorized the Queen's Men to play three times over three days in the town; those patronized by barons or nobles of higher degree (viscount, earl, or marquis) were permitted two performances over two days; and anyone with patrons of lower status would be allowed one performance. This is where the players would really hope to make their profit. In Stratford these shows probably took place in one of the inns in Bridge Street, of which the two principal were the Bear and the Swan – though records of such performances have rarely survived. I discuss playing in such inns in Chapter 2.

Princely Pleasures at Kenilworth

The issue of family status has a bearing on another theatrical event that the young Shakespeare might have observed. Did he attend any of the festivities that accompanied the great Earl of Leicester's sumptuous entertainment of Queen Elizabeth at his Kenilworth estate for nineteen extravagant days in 1575? The whole affair is rumored to have cost Leicester a staggering £60,000 – a figure put in proportion by the relatively comfortable income of

£10 per year which we considered earlier (p. 17). Kenilworth is only fourteen miles from Stratford and if anyone from the borough was invited to attend it might well be the still-respected alderman and members of his family. (William's mother, Mary Arden, came from a notable Warwickshire family in her own right.)

What fuels interest in this possibility is the fact that, some twenty years later, Shakespeare included a passage in *A Midsummer Night's Dream* which might just glance at one of the spectacles on view at Kenilworth. Oberon asks Puck if:

> Thou rememb'rest
> Since once I sat upon a promontory,
> And heard a mermaid on a dolphin's back
> Uttering such dulcet and harmonious breath
> That the rude sea grew civil at her song,
> And certain stars shot madly from their spheres
> To hear the sea-maid's music?
> (2.1.148–54)

On August 18, 1575 there was a water-pageant on a large lake in Kenilworth's grounds, with a show of the Lady of the Lake, which the Queen watched from a bridge. This is described in a letter, ascribed to Robert Langham or Laneham:

> And the Lady by and by, with her two nymphs, floating upon her movable islands (Triton on his mermaid skimming by) approached toward her Highness on the bridge: as well to declare that her Majesty's presence both so graciously thus wrought her deliverance ... and ... to present her Majesty (as a token of her duty and good heart) for her Highness's recreation with his gift, which was Arion that excellent and famous musician, in tire and appointment strange well seeming to his person, riding aloft upon his old friend the dolphin (that from head to tail was a four and twenty foot long) and swimmed hard by these islands. Herewith Arion, for these great benefits – after a few well couched words unto her Majesty of thanksgiving, in supplement of the same – began a delectable ditty of a song, well apted to a melodious noise, compounded of six several instruments all covert, casting sound from the dolphin's belly within; Arion the seventh, sitting thus singing (as I say) without.[6]

Interestingly, a different image emerges from a second account of the event, by the poet and courtier, George Gascoigne:

> From thence her Majesty passing yet further on the bridge, Proteus appeared, sitting on a dolphin's back. And the dolphin was conveyed upon a boat, so that the oars seemed to be his fins. Within which dolphin a consort of music was secretly placed, the which sounded, and Proteus

clearing his voice, sang this song of congratulation, as well in behalf of the
Lady distressed, as also in behalf of all the nymphs and gods of the sea.
(Gascoigne, 1576)

So one observer thought he saw an actor playing Arion, the Greek poet and lyre-player, singing on a dolphin; another saw Proteus, the shape-changing sea-god, doing it. The only mermaid involved, in Langham's account, was being ridden by Triton, another sea-deity. Did Shakespeare's memory play tricks on him over the years, or did he embroider the event for his own artistic purposes? Or, more prosaically, did Shakespeare simply read about these famous events in one or both of these printed accounts, and adapt them to his needs? Apart from anything else, there is no evidence that a wider public was allowed to witness the events at Kenilworth: Langham had a position at court and Gascoigne was employed by Leicester in devising some of the entertainments. We know that Shakespeare read widely and with a retentive memory. In *Twelfth Night* he would describe Viola's brother as "like Arion on the dolphin's back" (1.2.15), but surely from his copious reading of classical mythology rather than memories of long ago.

Mystery Cycles and Trade Guilds

One other possible experience of theatre in his youth may have made its mark. In 1579, when he was fifteen, Shakespeare could have witnessed one of the last performances of the great cycle of mystery plays at Coventry, staged on moving pageant wagons by the craft guilds around the streets of the old city.[7] He seems to reference them in Hamlet's advice to the actors:

> Oh, it offends me to the soul to hear a robustious periwig-pated fellow tear a passion to tatters, to very rags, to split the ears of the groundlings, who for the most part are capable of nothing but inexplicable dumb-shows and noise. I would have such a fellow whipped for o'erdoing Termagant. It out-Herod's Herod. Pray you, avoid it. (3.2.8–14)

Herod's role in the *Massacre of the Innocents* pageant was one of ranting violence, associated with over-the-top acting, as apparently was that of Termagant, a supposed Moslem deity. The Elizabethan authorities waged a long campaign to suppress these mystery plays, which were closely associated with their Roman Catholic roots and the midsummer festival of Corpus Christi, which was not recognized by the Protestant Church of England. The local authorities in towns where they were traditionally staged – York, Chester and Wakefield, as well as Coventry – fought long and hard to keep them going, as much for the trade they attracted as for their religious associations.[8] But eventually the

Queen's ministers prevailed. This brought to an end what must have been a strong tradition of amateur theatricals, tied closely to the local community and to the occupations of those who sponsored or performed in them. It perhaps opened up opportunities for the traveling players. As we shall see, many of Shakespeare's actor colleagues retained links with the trade guilds to which they had been attached (either by indenture or by family ties) before they became players. Robert Armin, for example, was apprenticed as a goldsmith; and Ben Jonson – a player before he became a dramatist – had been with the bricklayers. The organization of the London acting companies had some affinities with that of trade guilds.

Competing Authorities

What Shakespeare did not witness at first hand he doubtless heard discussed at great length by those who had. All the theatrical events we have discussed were staged with the clear intention of promoting their patrons and sponsors, of making an impact. Whatever attracted Shakespeare to the world of the theatre – the power of its language, the mystery of mimesis, the potential to travel away from provincial Warwickshire – there were some features of it that must have been apparent from his earliest years. Most particularly, professional acting – especially at its most accomplished levels – was closely associated with royalty and the aristocracy. It reflected Leicester's magnificence that he could stage such shows for his Queen and her court, as well as patronize the most famous acting troupe of the 1570s (who presumably took some of the roles that required professionals at Kenilworth: see MacLean, 2002). In this association the actors straddled at least two worlds. On the one hand they were formally household retainers, lowly members of an intensely hierarchical unit, organized around the service of their lord – and his representatives whenever they toured in his livery. On the other hand they were entrepreneurs, seeking to make a living in a developing marketplace – though one contested by a number of different parties, notably the Crown (the Queen's government); Parliament; their own aristocratic patrons; and local authorities, often in the form of their mayors and councils. The piecemeal suppression of the mystery plays shows that these parties did not always see eye-to-eye or work harmoniously together.

Much of Shakespeare's early career was to be overshadowed by tensions between the Privy Council (the Queen's leading ministers) and the City of London authorities over the control of the players. There is a classic demonstration of this in an incident involving James Burbage, builder of the Theatre and father of Shakespeare's colleague, Richard. (It is described on p. 31.) The incident resolved itself into a confrontation between Burbage, standing on his dignity as a servant of Lord Hunsdon, a Privy Councilor, and William Fleetwood, the City's most senior judge. The clash demonstrates the importance the players set by their lords' patronage: Burbage thought he was untouchable as a member of a Privy Councilor's household, and was somewhat abashed when Hunsdon himself lent support to Fleetwood. To their chagrin, the City had no authority over the Theatre and its neighbor playhouse, the Curtain (see pp. 83–4). But Fleetwood felt that the disturbance which led to the confrontation sufficiently affected the City (or could be represented as doing so) that it was necessary to take a stand. Hunsdon at least affected to take Fleetwood's concern seriously enough to allow him to take Burbage to law. The Court and the City sparred endlessly, but always with at least a show of respect for each other's authority.

Straws in the Wind

Let us consider a few of the straws in the wind, blown at the actors by those power struggles, in the years when Shakespeare was growing up. In 1572 Parliament passed An Act for the Punishment of Vagabonds, which was meant to control the growing numbers of "masterless men," people with no fixed abode or regular means of support, uncomfortably outside the traditional structures of control: Edgar's disguise as "Poor Tom" in *King Lear* gives us a flavor of the problem. Among those included in these categories were "Common Players in interludes, & Minstrels, not belonging to any Baron of this Realm or towards any other honourable Personage of greater Degree" (*EPF*, 62; see Beier, 1985). This made it essential for any players who wished to make a living by touring beyond the county in which they resided to have the patronage of one of the aristocratic elite of the country. There were only about eighty noble families in England in Elizabeth's reign and by no means all of them wanted to be associated with professional players. The Act removed the former right of knights and gentry to offer such patronage, making it an exclusive privilege. Sir Ralph Lane of Northamptonshire, for example, patronized a company led by Laurence Dutton, which was proficient enough to be called to perform at court in the winter of 1571/2. But the following year they had had to find themselves a patron of greater standing: the Earl of Lincoln, the Lord Admiral (Gurr, 1996, 170–1).

Even the Earl of Leicester's players were disturbed enough to seek reassurance from their patron:

> we therefore, your humble servants and daily orators your players, for avoiding all inconvenience that may grow by reason of the said statute, are bold to trouble your lordship with this our suit, humbly desiring your honour that (as you have been always our good lord and master) you will now vouchsafe to retain us at this present as your household servants and daily waiters, not that we mean to crave any further stipend or

benefit at your lordship's hands but our liveries as we have had, and also your honour's licence to travel amongst our friends as we do usually once a year, and as other noblemen's players do and have done in time past, whereby we may enjoy our faculty in your lordship's name as we have done heretofore. (*EPF*, 205)

They persist in the polite fiction that their touring amounts to "travel amongst our friends as we do usually once a year," as once it might have been. But it was by now a fully professional operation, albeit conducted within the courtesies of Elizabethan social constraint. The first signatory to this letter was the leader of Leicester's Men, the aforementioned James Burbage. No individual was more influential in shaping the theatrical world that Shakespeare knew. He probably visited Stratford with Leicester's Men in 1573/4 and possibly 1576/7, though by the latter date he had other business on his mind: the building of the Theatre, the first successful purpose-built playhouse in London since Roman times.[9]

Box 1.1 James Burbage[10]

James Burbage (circa 1531–1597) was a joiner (woodworker), actor, and theatrical entrepreneur. His family appear to derive from Bromley in Kent, some ten miles south-east of London. He was apprenticed in London as a joiner, but by 1572 was established as a player with Leicester's Men. Indeed by then he was their leader, so it is likely that he had been playing for some time. This troupe was founded in 1564 and, under the patronage of the Queen's favorite, had become a leading company. Burbage was the lead signatory on a letter to the earl, begging him to certify them as members of his household, in order to avoid legislation that would render them vagabonds and masterless men (p. 29). In May 1574 the first royal patent to players was issued to Leicester's Men, licensing them to play in London and elsewhere under the authority of the court.

On April 23 1559 Burbage had married Ellen, the daughter of Thomas Brayne, a tailor and freeman of the Girdlers' Company. Two of their children have significant roles in our narrative: Cuthbert Burbage, baptised on June 15, 1565, who was never a player but was closely associated with the theatrical business all his life; and Richard Burbage, baptized on July 7, 1568, who was to play Richard III, Hamlet, Othello, and (we believe) most of the other leading tragic roles in Shakespeare's plays. Ellen Burbage's brother, John Brayne, was a member of the Grocer's Company (guild). In 1567 Brayne hired two carpenters to build a playhouse in the yard of the Red Lion, a farmhouse east of Aldgate, near Mile End in East London. It apparently consisted of little more than a stage (5 ft [1.52 m] high, 40 ft [12.19 m] "in length," north to south, 30 ft [9.14 m] "in breadth," east to west, with a portion to be left unboarded, for a trapdoor), a "turret" rising some

30 ft above the stage, with a floor some 7 ft [2.13 m] from the top (possibly for upper-level playing), and scaffolding to hold the audience. But it was the first purpose-fitted professional playhouse in England since Roman times. It was due to open with *The Story of Sampson* on July 8, 1567; it did not, however, flourish and little more is known about it (*EPF*, 290–4).

In 1576 Brayne went into partnership with Burbage to build a much more substantial playhouse named, on Roman precedent, the Theatre; doubtless, like Philip Henslowe's grocer partner in the later building of the Rose, he expected to make a profit from the food and drink sold on-site, as well as the playing. The details of their enterprise are related below (see pp. 83ff).

By 1584 Burbage had left Leicester's patronage (possibly after Leicester's Men lost many of their leading players to the newly-created Queen's Men) and sought instead that of the queen's cousin Henry, Lord Hunsdon, already a Privy Councilor and shortly to become Lord Chamberlain of the royal household. This was of some consequence in June of that year, when a series of disturbances in the region of the Theatre and the neighboring Curtain led the City of London authorities to seek their "suppressing and pulling down" (*ES*, 4: 298). William Fleetwood, the Recorder of London (the City's principal judge), reported to Lord Treasurer Burghley in a letter of June 18 that he had been advised:

> to send for the owner of the Theatre, who was a stubborn fellow, and to bind him. I did so; he sent me word that he was my lord of Hunsdon's man, and that he would not come at me, but he would in the morning ride to my lord; then I sent the under-sheriff for him and he brought him to me; and at his coming he stouted me out very hasty; and in the end I showed him my lord his master's hand [signature] and then he was more quiet; but to die for it he would not be bound.[11] And then I, minding to send him to prison, he made suit that he might be bound to appear at the [court of] oyer and determiner, the which is tomorrow[12]; where he said he was sure the court would not bind him, being a Councilor's man. And so I have granted his request, where he shall be sure to be bound or else like to do worse. (ibid.)

It is not clear how matters were resolved, but the playhouses remained safe.

Burbage's relations with John Brayne deteriorated, with money at the heart of the contention. Keeping track of profits, probably derived from a share of the takings when a company of players used the Theatre as a London base, must have been difficult – and readily disputable. Brayne died in 1586 without making a will, and his widow Margaret pursued his claim to a moiety (half) of the playhouse and its profits. She made Robert Miles, a freeman of the Goldsmiths' Company, her agent. The matter dragged on in the courts between 1590 and Margaret's own death in 1593. This included the notorious events of

November 16, 1590, recounted elsewhere, when Richard Burbage repelled Miles and Margaret Brayne with a broom (see p. 61). A further confrontation occurred in May 1591, with James Burbage still loudly refusing to accede to any court orders. And only days after that there was a falling out between Burbage and members of the Admiral's Men, over the division of the take, which led to the Admiral's and Strange's Men leaving the Theatre and transferring to the Rose. Burbage was indeed a "stubborn fellow," given to "stout[ing]" people out.

As early as 1585 Burbage attempted to extend his lease on the land on which the Theatre stood. But the landlord, Giles Allen, evaded the request and it eventually became clear that he would not extend it beyond April 1597 – by which time it was the permanent base of Shakespeare's Chamberlain's Men. In 1596 the Burbages moved from their house in Shoreditch, near the Theatre, to Blackfriars, a prosperous liberty on the north bank of the Thames, within the City's walls but outside its jurisdiction. Between 1576 and 1584 the Children of the Chapel Royal, under their Master William Hunnis and his deputy, Richard Farrant, had performed their plays for the public in a playhouse constructed in the hall of the great former friary complex of the Blackfriars. Burbage now paid £600 for a different part of this old stone complex and a further £400 to have it converted to a splendid new playhouse. Clearly some of this was done on credit. As Cuthbert deposed many years later: "our father purchased it at extreme rates & made it into a playhouse with great charge and trouble" (Gurr, 2004a: Appendix 3, 278). In November 1596, however, some of the more distinguished residents of the Blackfriars petitioned the Privy Council to make known "what inconveniencies were likely to fall upon them by a common playhouse which was then preparing to be erected there, whereupon their honours then forbade the use of the said house, for plays" (ES, 4: 320). Embarrassingly these petitioners had included the second Lord Hunsdon, who had inherited the patronage of the Chamberlain's Men from his deceased father (p. 130). Apparently the boy players who were formally attached to the court had been acceptable in the Blackfriars, but the adult players would make this a "common playhouse," which was not.

James Burbage did not live to see the resolution of the problems this posed for Shakespeare's company, denied the use of both their old and new playhouses. I pursue this elsewhere (see p. 198). He died in February 1597. He left only a modest £37, but he had already conveyed the lease of the Theatre and its residual value to Cuthbert, and the Blackfriars property to Richard. Fortunately they were to collaborate amicably about realizing the potential of both properties. James Burbage's gambles in building both the Theatre and the second Blackfriars playhouse were foundational to the whole history of professional playing in Elizabethan London, and in particular to that of Shakespeare's Chamberlain's Men.

A System of Protection and Control

Leicester and others at the court may have reflected on the consequences for themselves of Parliament's statute restricting the patronage of players. Certainly in 1574 his players stole a march on their rivals. They were granted a royal patent calculated to protect them from the attentions of lesser authorities. It "licensed and authorised" them "to use, exercise, and occupy the art and faculty of playing comedies, tragedies, interludes, stage plays, and such other like as they have already used and studied ... as well for the recreation of our loving subjects, as for our solace and pleasure when we shall think good to see them." This applied "as well within our City of London and liberties of the same, as also within the liberties and freedoms of any our cities, towns, boroughs &c. ... throughout our realm of England." They were to be allowed to play "without any your lets, hindrance or molestation," subject to some key conditions: "Provided that the said comedies [etc.] be by the Master of our Revels ... before seen and allowed, and that the same be not published or shown in the time of common prayer, or in the time of great and common plague in our said City of London" (*EPF*, 206).

There were constant concerns about the players drawing people away from the churches and also helping to spread the plague in London – a problem which only grew as the city did. The patent looked to answer those concerns, and also to address what amounted to the issue of censorship: who should decide what was acceptable to be performed? The court put itself forward as the true arbiter, in the form of the Master of the Revels, whose primary function was to oversee theatricals and entertainment for the Queen. Any play "seen and allowed" by him was deemed to be fit to be shown before her and should not therefore be challenged by others. This was soon to be extended to a system of censorship and licensing for the plays of all major companies but was resisted, notably, by City of London authorities, who really wanted to apply their own terms and conditions (Dutton 1991 and see pp. 84ff).

The patent specifically draws attention to "our solace and pleasure when we shall think good to see them" – the Queen's royal plural. At Christmas 1578 the Privy Council wrote to the Lord Mayor of London, requesting him:

> to suffer the Children of her Majesty's Chapel, the servants of the Lord Chamberlain [the Earl of Sussex], the Earl of Warwick, the Earl of Leicester, the Earl of Essex and the Children of Paul's, and no companies else, to exercise playing within the City, whom their Lordships have only allowed thereunto by reason that the companies aforenamed are appointed to play this time of Christmas before her Majesty.
>
> *(Gurr, 1996, 55)*

The battle was developing over rights to perform in and around London. The Privy Council's trump card was invariably that playing must be allowed because it amounted to rehearsing for performance at court, before the Queen. But, with some concession to the City authorities, such playing was henceforth to be limited to an elite circle of troupes who had a realistic chance of being asked to perform at court. What the Privy Council expected in return was that the adult players be allowed to perform in inner-city inns, which was always their preference in winter until the practice was phased out in the 1590s.[13] The favored companies would change over time, as patrons faded away or tastes changed, but they never numbered above six (as here) and usually rather less. This would be critical to Shakespeare's career.

One last straw in the wind: in 1575 the Laurence Dutton whom we last observed moving from Sir Robert Lane's company to that of Lord Admiral Clinton now moved (with his brother, John) to that of the Earl of Warwick, one of those companies listed in 1578 as "appointed to play this time of Christmas before her Majesty." For some reason the two brothers moved again in 1580, to a new company established by the Earl of Oxford. This elicited an anonymous satirical response: "The Duttons and their fellow-players, forsaking the Earl of Warwick their master, became followers of the Earl of Oxford, and wrote themselves his *comedians*, which certain gentlemen altered and made *chameleons*" (*ES*, 2: 98). (The Elizabethans commonly described players as "comedians." It does not imply that they only appeared in comic plays.) Wry verses followed. But this pointed to serious underlying issues: the quasi-feudal ties of servants to their masters were being preempted by other forces, which must have boiled down to money. The precise motivation here is actually rather opaque. The defection of the Duttons and some of their followers seems to have ensured that Warwick's Men never appeared at court again and the company may even have been wound up. But Oxford's Men were not invited to court until 1584, by which time (as we shall see) the Duttons had moved on again. They were evidently chancers, but the market was moving in their direction.

Roads Not Taken

We may pause to consider that there were various forms of theatre hypothetically available to Shakespeare for which, whether by choice or otherwise, he did *not* write. If he did see any of the *Princely Pleasures* at Kenilworth, he did not himself script any such occasional drama for royalty or aristocracy. These were often scripted by gentlemen amateurs like George Gascoigne, using their pens to seek other forms of advancement; but Shakespeare's friend and rival, Ben Jonson, a true literary professional, eventually built a career around writing such entertainments, especially the court masques which graced the court of King James and Queen Anne almost every year from 1605 to 1625. Shakespeare might offer a representation of such shows in *Love's Labor's Lost* or *The Tempest*, but never the real thing. Nor did he write shows for the artisans of the great London livery companies (trade guilds). Although the mystery plays had been suppressed in the provinces, the guilds were still involved in theatricals in London, most notably in the Lord Mayors' Shows which developed from the mid-sixteenth century. Every year on October 28 the new Lord Mayor was installed in the City; on the following day he went upriver to Westminster to take the oath to the king, and that day became an occasion for revelry both on water and on land, with pageants paid for by the livery company to which this Lord Mayor belonged. George Peele, Anthony Munday, Ben Jonson, Thomas Dekker, Thomas Middleton, John Webster, and Thomas Heywood all wrote "books" for these shows – but not William Shakespeare (Bergeron, 2003; Lancashire, 2009).

And one final omission: although Shakespeare wrote many memorable female roles for the boy actors who were recruited into his companies, he never wrote for any of the all-boy companies (see p. 270). The Children of the Queen's Chapel and the Children of Paul's (early favorites of Queen Elizabeth and both mentioned in the 1578 Privy Council letter) went out of business, the one in 1584, the other shortly after 1590, but both were revived around 1599/1600. As we shall see, the Children of the Chapel – the "little eyases" mentioned in the folio text of *Hamlet* (2.2.338–62) – have a role in Shakespeare's career, but he never wrote for them or their ilk: unlike John Marston, Ben Jonson, George Chapman, Thomas Middleton, John Day, Francis Beaumont, John Fletcher, and others (see Shapiro 1977, 2009; Bly 2000, 2009; Munro 2005). All of these omissions may have arisen from the contractual conditions Shakespeare negotiated with the companies for whom he did write, but they do make his career distinctively different from those of many of his contemporaries.

To the best of our knowledge, Shakespeare wrote exclusively for adult playing companies, normally performing in the purpose-built outdoor amphitheaters in the London suburbs. Over time we know that his plays were performed specifically at Newington Butts, the Theatre, the Curtain, and the Globe. They were also performed at inns within the city. And latterly they were performed at the indoor Blackfriars playhouse. But they were also performed at court, in a variety of royal palaces: Hampton Court, Greenwich, Richmond, and Whitehall. And at other great establishments, such as the Inns of Court (law schools), as in the 1594 fiasco when they performed *The Comedy of Errors* in impossible conditions at Gray's Inn (see p. 132); and at the London houses of grandees such as their patron, the younger Lord Hunsdon (e.g. March 6, 1600, when they performed *1 Henry IV* for the visiting Flemish Ambassador). But there were occasions, usually dictated by the plague, when they had to take to the roads, just as those companies which visited Stratford in his youth had done; the 1603 first quarto of *Hamlet* tells us that it had "been divers times acted … in the City of London: as also in the two Universities of Cambridge and Oxford, and elsewhere" (title page). The university authorities, particularly at

Cambridge, often tried to prevent professional players from performing near the colleges (though there was an active tradition of *amateur* playing and play-writing within them). But the players found venues just outside university jurisdiction, to which students and scholars flocked (White 2009; *EPT*, 113–16).

And these would just have been two of the stops in tours which took in numerous guildhalls, inns and great houses (such as that of Sir John Harington of Exton at Burley on the Hill in Rutland, where it was probably Shakespeare's company who performed *Titus Andronicus* on New Year's Day 1596).[14] Elizabethan plays had to be portable in this sense, which meant that they had to be adaptable – few venues outside of the professional playhouses, for example, would have had upper stages or trapdoors; but it does not follow that they were all written to the same blue-print. *Shakespeare's Theatre* aims to trace such differences and the circumstances which generated them.

Notes

1 Somerset's volume awaits publication, but scholars such as Elza Tiner (2006) and J. R. Mulryne (2007) have been allowed access to his findings. Details of the REED project can be found at its web site, http://www.reed.utoronto.ca/. Of particular value is their *Patrons and Performances Web Site* (http://link.library.utoronto.ca/reed/).
2 Many records relate to a fiscal year spanning two calendar years and cannot be dated more precisely. A payment to Worcester's "players" in 1568–9 is much lower than others and may refer to musicians rather than to actors. Several other payments are similarly open to interpretation.
3 As early as 1571–2 Liverpool denied use of their town hall to all but the most prestigious companies, and even they had to pay 5s. in advance against the cost of subsequent repairs (George, 1991, 39).
4 The seating plan for "Shakespeare's Globe" allows for 857 bodies, plus 700 standing "groundlings." The original was said to hold 3,000. Fire regulations partly explain the reduction, but body size seems to be the main contributing factor.
5 MacLean, 2001, 8–9, kindly shared with me by the author. Her internal references are (a) "Tittler, 1991, 105–18"; and (b) "see Nelson, 1994, 16-60 for full discussion and diagrams of the Queens' and Trinity College hall stages in particular. For a popular (but I think erroneous) view of lower end hall staging, see J. Leeds Barroll *et al.*, 1975, 128–30." In private correspondence, Professor MacLean adds: "Evidence accumulated since that time has not changed my view, by the way."

6 Quoted from Langham, 1575. Langham is only identified from some clues within the letter. The *Letter* might be a joke at his expense, possibly by William Patten, another courtier who was certainly at the Kenilworth entertainments.
7 "Mystery" here is an old term for a trade or craft and refers to the performers, not to the subject-matter of the plays.
8 The correspondence about the suppression of the mystery plays in Coventry is not very revealing. But see *EPT*, 64–9, for that relating to York, Chester, and Wakefield.
9 Strictly speaking the Red Lion, built in Mile End in 1567, was the first purpose-built Elizabethan theatre but it seems not to have thrived beyond its first season. see p. 30; Ingram, 1992, 92–113.
10 This section is particularly indebted to Wallace, 1913; Ingram, 1992; and Edmond, 2004.
11 This presumably refers to being bound over to keep the peace, or held responsible for keeping order, rather than physically restrained. The issue was one of authority over someone in the service of a senior minister of the Queen.
12 A commission of Oyer and Terminer (Anglo-French, literally meaning "to hear and determine") was one under which a judge of assize sat. He was charged with enquiring into all treasons, felonies and misdemeanours committed in its jurisdiction and resolving it by law. Burbage doubtless assumed that such a court would respect his status as Hunsdon's man more than Fleetwood did.
13 The boy companies did not need this permission. The Blackfriars playhouse was outside the City's jurisdiction (see p. 197), while Paul's playhouse was in the cathedral precinct, on church property.
14 The element of doubt is when the Lord Chamberlain's Men acquired ownership of *Titus*, which was written before Shakespeare joined them. The 1594 quarto tells us that it had been "been played by the Right Honourable the Earl of Pembroke, the Earl of Derby, and the Earl of Sussex their servants" – probably successively, as companies broke up and reorganized during the prolonged plague. The 1600 quarto adds "and the Lord Chamberlain" to the list.

2

Possible Beginnings

Most people today associate Shakespeare with the Globe, the playhouse on the Bankside in Southwark which became iconic because of its associations with him, though it was not actually built until his a career was half over (1599). When he himself imagines a performance in his plays it is not in a public playhouse but in the private space of a royal palace or a lord's house. Traveling players come to Elsinore in *Hamlet* and to the house of the Lord in *The Taming of the Shrew*; Ariel and his spirits perform for Duke Prospero in *The Tempest*; enthusiastic but inept artisans offer their service to Theseus and Hippolyta in *A Midsummer Night's Dream*. Ben Jonson, by contrast, often builds references to the London theatres into his plays, as when Fitzdottrel in *The Devil is an Ass* (1616) announces "Today, I go to the Blackfriars playhouse" – topping the joke by telling us that he is going to see … *The Devil is an Ass* (2012*d*, 1.6.31: see also 1.4.21). Jonson was always preeminently a Londoner, an urban dramatist (though he was a traveling player for a time in his early years). But Shakespeare always retained something of a pre-urban sensibility, in which playing was closely attached to the service of a lord and to great private houses.

Despite the most assiduous research, we still do not know how Shakespeare's move from Stratford to London took place. And we know nothing for certain of his employment or the patrons he might have cultivated prior to his arrival in London. Terence G. Schoone-Jongen is the latest scholar to look for answers, but eventually he concludes: "Ultimately, it seems Shakespeare's pre-1594 company affiliations present the biographer with a jigsaw puzzle. Yet because the puzzle is missing key pieces, it cannot be fully assembled. Or, more to the point, it can be assembled in a number of different, plausible-yet-incomplete ways" (2008, 199). What I propose to do is to examine two of those "plausible-yet-incomplete ways" in which the puzzle can be assembled, to show between them the variety of theatrical situations Shakespeare may well have confronted – and with which he must certainly have been familiar – before the recorded part of his career began. The first is the Queen's Men theory; the second is Hoghton Will theory.

Shakespeare's Theatre: A History, First Edition. Richard Dutton.
© 2018 Richard Dutton. Published 2018 by John Wiley & Sons Ltd.

Shakespeare and the Queen's Men's Theory

This explanation of how Shakespeare may have entered the theatrical world centers on the first visit the Queen's Men paid to Stratford, in 1587 (p. 19). It assumes that he had probably stayed in his birthplace up to that date, perhaps working alongside his father. The speculation focuses on the fact that the company probably arrived a man short. A coroner's inquest reports that on June 13,1587, between 9 and 10 p.m., one of their leading players, William Knell entered a close called White Hound in Thame, Oxfordshire (not so far from Stratford) and assaulted his fellow actor, John Towne. Towne, fearing for his life, took to the high ground of a nearby "mound." As the official report put it, "William Knell continuing his attack as before, so maliciously and furiously, and Towne ... to save his life drew his sword of iron (price five shillings) and held it in his right hand and thrust it into the neck of William Knell and made a mortal wound three inches deep and one inch wide." Knell bled to death within the half-hour. The Queen pardoned Towne on August 15 after it was agreed he acted in self-defense (Eccles, 1961, 82–3, 157–8).

Violence among the players was, sadly, not uncommon, though the Queen's Men seem to have been unusually prone to it. In September 1598 Ben Jonson and Gabriel Spenser fought a duel in Hoxton fields. They had formerly been fellows together in the Earl of Pembroke's Men and shared imprisonment for a play that Jonson co-wrote, *The Isle of Dogs* (see p. 221). But both had a history of violence, Jonson killing an opponent in a personal duel when he fought in the Low Countries, Spenser killing one James Freake in an affray in 1596. Spenser apparently wounded Jonson in the arm, but Jonson managed to strike back, killing him. According to the inquest, he died from a six-inch deep stab wound in his right side. Duelling was illegal and Jonson only escaped hanging by pleading benefit of clergy and reading "neck verse," an old legal loophole for those who could prove they could read Latin (Donaldson, 2011, 95; 113–15; 132–7). Elizabethan theatre was not an arena for shrinking-violet aesthetes.

The Queen's Men were certainly no strangers to violence before 1587. An incident in Norwich on Saturday June 15, 1583, shortly after their formation, is testimony to this and also gives us some real information about playing on the road, as this company commonly did.[1] They had previously given their "Mayor's play" at the guildhall and were now performing for the public at the Red Lion inn. There was an affray. A man recorded only as "George" was killed and two of the players, John Bentley and John Singer, were imprisoned while the city authorities investigated. It all began when, as Edmund Brown, a Norwich draper, deposed:

> one Winsdon would have entered in at the gate, but would not have paid until he had been within; and thereupon, the gatekeeper and he striking, Tarlton [the clown] came out off the stage and would have thrust him

out at the gate; but in the mean-time one Bentley – he which played the Duke – came off the stage; and with his hilts of his sword struck Winsdon upon the head, and offered him another stripe, but Tarlton defended it; whereupon Winsdon fled out of the gate, and Bentley pursued him: and then he in the black doublet, which kept the gate [identified elsewhere as the player, John Singer, in costume and wearing a false beard] ran up into the stage and brought an arming sword: and as he was going out the gate, he drew the sword, and ran out at the gate.

Another "examinate," Henry Brown, deposed how he saw "one in a blue coat ['George'] cast stones at Bentley and broke his head, being one of Her Majesty's servants; whereupon this examinate said 'villain, wilt thou murder the Queen's man?' and the fellow called this examinate 'villain' again, and thereupon this examinate struck him with his sword and hit him on the leg." Various depositions establish that Singer and Bentley also stabbed "George," Singer in the shoulder (though he denied drawing blood) and Bentley "thrust at him twice with his naked rapier; the one thrust was about the knee, but he [Brown] knoweth not where the other thrust was." Since Bentley and Singer were released, they were apparently not held at fault; possibly Brown's blow was the one deemed responsible for "George's" death, but even he could claim that he was defending Bentley. One Thomas Holland heard Brown say "I have sped him" and Bentley reply "well done, boy, we will bear thee out in it." Brown's own version of what Bentley said is "be of good cheer, for if all this matter be laid on thee, thou shalt have what friendship we can procure thee."

Being the Queen's servants at the very least ensured that they would get a careful hearing, with powerful patronage in London should it be needed. The whole incident seems to have started as a result of Winsdon's ignorance of the conventions of payment for a performance at an inn. He was probably used to performances in the street, where the actors would erect a stage and solicit payment during the course of the play or at its end. This of course could be subject to any manner of abuse, some of the audience slipping away without paying, others offering less than full payment if they had not been happy with what they saw. One of the attractions of playing in the inns must have been that the actors could control a limited number of entrances and demand payment in advance, as would happen in the purpose-built London playhouses. For the Queen's Men collecting the take was so important that one of their own sharers (senior players), John Singer, was entrusted with the role of gatekeeper – and he did it in costume, ready to take his place in the performance on cue. Presumably one of his fellows would relieve him at this point. As we shall see, ensuring that gatekeepers were trustworthy was an important consideration in the London theatres; although there are no records of sharer-players doing it there, hired players – who would be needed on stage from time to time – were certainly sometimes employed (p. 166).

By comparison with the Norwich and Thame incidents the Stratford authorities may have been relieved in 1587 that they got away, after the "Mayor's play," with only having to pay sixteen pence "for mending of a form that was broken by the Queen's players." This sort of damage may well have been one reason that Stratford was among the first towns to stop players using their Guild Hall for performances, in 1602 (Mulryne 2006: 20; 19, 10–13). At all events, with the death of Knell the Queen's Men would have been a player short. Shakespeare could have been recommended to them as literate and articulate, not able of course to fill Knell's shoes but able to help out as the others adjusted.

If this happened, he stepped quickly into elite company. The company bearing the Queen's name and scarlet livery came into being by Privy Council *fiat*, following a meeting called by its Principal Secretary, Sir Francis Walsingham: "Edmund Tilney Esquire, Master of the [Revels] office being sent for to the court by letter from Master Secretary, dated the 10 of March 158[3]. To choose out a company of players for her Majesty" (*ES*, 2: 104). Elizabeth must certainly have given personal permission for this. Only two years earlier Tilney, a distant cousin of hers, had been given a Special Commission which conferred upon him virtually plenipotentiary powers over all actors and their playing-places; the underlying motive was to ensure that he could provide entertainment of adequate quality at court whenever it was needed (Dutton, 1991, 41–55; Streitberger, 2016, 169ff). The creation of the Queen's Men was clearly seen as a way of fulfilling that mandate: "there were twelve of the best [players] chosen, they were sworn as the Queen's servants and were allowed … liveries as grooms of the chamber … Among these twelve players were two rare men, viz. Thomas [i.e. Robert] Wilson, for a quick, delicate, refined extempore wit, and Richard Tarlton, for a wondrous plentiful pleasant, extemporal wit; he was the wonder of his time. He lieth buried in Shoreditch church. He was so beloved that men use his picture for their signs."[2]

The whole process, a clear demonstration that royal will trumped personal ambitions and profit in the business of playing, robbed all the existing leading companies of star players. Besides Wilson, Leicester's Men lost William Johnson and John Laneham; Oxford's Men lost John Dutton (who before 1588 would be joined by his brother, Laurence); John Adams, another clown, came with Tarlton from Sussex's Men. The total of twelve leading players made it a super-troupe of its era, easily capable of staging plays requiring casts of fifteen or more (including boys), without the need to recruit added hired men. It has been shown that their plays which have survived require about that number (Crockett, 2009, 234). Earlier in the century troupes had usually been significantly smaller. Mid-century plays originally written for private performance later passed into print and the public repertoire, and title pages made a virtue of how few players they needed. The interlude, *Lusty Juventus* (circa 1550), for example, was printed with the claim that "Four may play it easily, taking such parts as they think best." Thomas Preston's *Cambises* (1570) was printed with a doubling chart on the title page, showing that eight people could play it. And that would include boys.

Box 2.1 *Sir Thomas More*

A play with some slight Shakespearean connection offers a memory of sorts of playing in earlier days.[3] *Sir Thomas More*, a play which survives in manuscript, stages a play-within-a-play, as it might have been done in early Tudor times, by Cardinal Wolsey's players. They arrive unannounced at More's London house when he is just about to entertain the Lord Mayor and several aldermen. They have "four men and a boy" (4.1.54) and a repertory of seven interludes or morality plays: *The Cradle of Security, Hit Nayle o'the Head, Impatient Poverty, The Play of Four Pees, Dives and Lazarus, Lusty Juventus*, and *The Marriage of Wit and Wisdom* (41–4). More chooses the last of these. He observes that, with only one boy, "there's but few women in the play" (56). The lead player replies: "Three, my lord: Dame Science, Lady Vanity, and Wisdom, she herself" (57–8). More considers this a lot for the one boy: "By our lady, he's laden" (59).

In fact the boy only gets to play one of his roles, Lady Vanity, in what we see. When More asks if the players are ready, "*Enter* … Inclination, *the Vice, ready*" (i.e. in costume). He beseeches More: "We would desire your honour but to stay a little; one of my fellows is but run to Ogle's, for a long beard for young Wit, and he"ll be here presently" (124–5). More jokingly observes that Wit does not need a beard until he is married, so they should start the show, and stop if needs be when the missing player's part begins. "*The trumpet sounds. Enter the Prologue*" (147.1), followed by "*Wit ruffling* [swaggering]*, and Inclination the Vice.*" Inclination – who flourishes his traditional dagger at boys supposedly encroaching on the stage space – tempts Wit to take a wife; Wit casually assumes this will be Wisdom, but Inclination has arranged a liaison with Lady Vanity: "*Enter* Lady Vanity *singing, and beckoning with her hand*" (199.1). More calls out "This is Lady Vanity, I'll hold my life; / Beware, good Wit, you take not her to wife" (202–3). Wit pays no heed and flirts with her, but the performance comes to a halt when Inclination calls out "Is Luggins come yet with the beard?" / *Enter another player.* / "No, faith, he is not come: alas, what shall we do"? (229–30). Inclination explains to More that "we can go no further till our fellow Luggins come, for he plays Good Counsel, and now he should enter, to admonish Wit that this is Lady Vanity, and not Lady Wisdom" (231–3). More himself, however, supplies the role of Good Counsel *extemprically* (270), until "*Enter* Luggins *with the beard*" (253.1).

At that point More decides it best to suspend the performance until after a banquet and we never see the end of the morality play, though we see the players rewarded by More as he is called away on the king's business. Clearly the whole show has been included to emphasize Sir Thomas More's role as the wise and witty counselor.[4] It is evidently fictionalized, but seems authentic enough in its depiction of traveling players earlier in the century – a very small group by later standards; twelve to fifteen was not uncommon by Shakespeare's day. They were prepared to put on one of seven plays, most in a familiar interlude or morality-play mode, and probably all authentic: four have survived in print, and *The Cradle of Security* was the play R. Willis remembered so many years later (see p. 20).[5] It seems unlikely that traveling players actually ever turned up without ensuring beforehand that they would be welcome; apart from anything else, it would avoid wasted journeys. But they would be always limited by the resources they could carry with them (see Dekker's vignette of Jonson "ambling" by a cart: p. 273), so the possibility of mislaying a long beard – or any other prop or costume – must have been quite plausible; Ogle's may have been a familiar shop that dealt in wigs and other hair items.

Inclination lives up to the traditional model of the Vice, "shaking his wooden dagger" as Jonson recalls in *The Devil is an Ass* (2012d, 1.1.85) and carrying a bridle because, as he tells More, "I must be bridled anon" (134). The foolish Wit would presumably ride off on his back, a variant on the Vice himself riding off on the devil's back. The literal Vice had disappeared by Shakespeare's maturity, but in the figure of Falstaff he is barely below the surface: "that reverend Vice, that grey iniquity … that vanity in years" (2.4.448–9), carries a "leaden dagger" (377) in place of the more traditional one made of lath – but harmless in either case.

What we are not told is how the play and its audience of More and his guests are deployed onstage. In fact it makes sense for them to be seated at a high table and for the performance to take place immediately below them, so that the audience in the playhouse always sees More and the city fathers *through* the performance – as we know the general audience would at court and colleges, and presume it did in other great halls (see pp. 4–5). This would also make sense for other plays-within-plays, such as those in *A Midsummer Night's Dream* and *Hamlet* – where senior members of the court also preside over the performance, and interrupt at will, much more arrogantly than More.

Cardinal Wolsey, as the most powerful royal servant of his time, would doubtless in reality have employed the best players available – probably somewhat more accomplished and professional than those we see here. But the size of the troupe and its repertoire seems plausible, given the more limited opportunities for earning a living by playing earlier in the century. The vignette we see of them shows them more as recipients of the patronage of the wealthy, not as hardened veterans of public stages.

(Continued from p. 41)

When Leicester's Men wrote to their patron in 1572 for confirmation of their status as his servants (see p. 29) only six players signed it, presumably the sharing members of the company. It may well be that the attempts to limit the patronage of playing, to which that letter responded, reduced the number of touring companies but increased the size of those that remained, helping turn them into more substantial commercial enterprises. In the case of the Queen's Men, however, the figures may be somewhat deceptive, since it is apparent that they often split in two during their travels and perhaps only played as a unified company on special occasions, such as when summoned to court.[6]

We may compare this evidence with the Lord Chamberlain's Men and the Lord Admiral's Men as they came into being in 1594; the former had about eight sharers, the latter nine (Gurr, 2006, 303, 253). But those operations, being London based, could also draw on a reliable pool of hired men to fill the lesser roles. We do know that when the Earl of Derby's Men played at Chatsworth in 1611 there were fourteen in the party, which doubtless included hired men and boys as well as sharers; the following year, at the Earl of Cumberland's Londesborough, there were thirteen of them (Bentley, 1984, 185–6). So the Queen's Men, in their early years, were capable of matching other companies of the era without having to hire journeymen players, though they would certainly have needed perhaps three boys to play their female roles. Alternatively, of course, they could have mounted extremely lavish productions by hiring extras. The presence among them of both Wilson and Tarlton, both playwrights as well as comedians, gave them the potential to be highly self-reliant. Wilson was the probable author of three extant plays, *The Three Ladies of London*, *The Three Lords and Ladies of London*, and *The Cobbler's Prophecy*; Tarlton wrote the two-part *Seven Deadly Sins*, a "plot" of the second part of which I reproduce and discuss later (see pp. 205ff)

Tarlton

For all their talent, Tarlton was the undoubted leading light and we can still catch a flavor of what made him so special. We have a good idea what he looked like in performance, where his clown persona was built on the country rustic. Henry Chettle says he knew him in a dream "by his suit of russet, his buttoned cap, his tabor, his standing on the toe, and other tricks … to be either the body or resemblance of Tarlton, who living for his pleasant conceits was of all men liked, and dying, for mirth left not his like" (1592, B2v). *Tarlton's Jests*, an untrustworthy collection of jokes and anecdotes, nevertheless tells us that he had a squint and a flat nose, and these characteristics certainly appear in the woodcut on the title-page of the volume (see Figure 2.1). E. K. Chambers says that it "represents a short, broad-faced, cunning-looking man, with curly hair, an elaborate moustache and a starved beard, wearing a cap, and a bag or money-box slung at his side, and playing on a tabor and a pipe" (*ES*, 2, 344).

The *Jests* also gives us these plausible tales of the man in performance: "At the Bull in Bishopsgate Street [a London inn], where the Queen's men oftentimes played, Tarlton coming on the stage, one from the gallery threw a pippin at him … [there] was a play of Henry the Fifth [*The Famous Victories of Henry the Fifth*] wherein the judge was to take a box on the ear, and because he was absent that should take the blow, Tarlton himself (ever forward to please) took upon him to play the same judge, besides his own part of the clown" (quoted in *EPF*, 301).[7]

Figure 2.1 Image of Richard Tarlton (or Tarleton). *Source*: © British Library Board. All Rights Reserved / Bridgeman Images.

Ben Jonson has the stagekeeper in the Induction to *Bartholomew Fair* remember a routine with Adams: "I kept the stage in Master Tarlton's time, I thank my stars. Ho! An that man had lived to have played in *Barthol'mew Fair* you should ha' seen him ha' come in and ha' been cozened i'the cloth-quarter so finely! And Adams, the rogue, ha' leapt and capered upon him, and ha' dealt his vermin about as though they had cost him nothing" (2012*b*, lines 27–32).[8] Thomas Nashe also gives us a glimpse of Tarlton at work in this anecdote about a choleric country justice:

> that, having a play presented before him and his township, by Tarlton and the rest of his fellows, her Majesty's servants, and they were now

entering into their first merriment (as they call it) the people began exceedingly to laugh, when Tarlton first peeped out his head. Where at the justice, not a little moved and seeing with his becks and nods he could not make them cease, he went with his staff and beat them round about unmercifully on the bare pates, in that they being but farmers and poor country hinds would presume to laugh at the Queen's men, and make no more account of her cloth in his presence.

(Pierce Penniless, *1592, D1v*)

The anecdote cuts several ways, since Tarlton's clown persona was that of the rustic fellow, liable to be defrauded even of his verminous clothes – or, like the justice, to misunderstand that the audience was *supposed* to laugh, even at the Queen's own servants. But the priceless touch is of Tarlton peeping out his head from behind the scenes, playing his audience, an instantly funny man who was either already known to them or whose fame had gone before.

He had a talent for extempore doggerel, sometimes inviting topics from the audience; the Queen is said to have enjoyed his wit, though it is possible that on occasion he overstepped the mark (*ES*, 2, 342). He channeled this talent into jigs, often performed as endpiece entertainments after a performance; they involved music, often topical fare set to popular tunes; dancing; comic, sometimes bawdy routines, perhaps built around a folk tale (see Box item, p. 218). The form was preserved by Will Kemp, who was to act with Shakespeare in the Lord Chamberlain's Men. Not the least of Tarlton's many talents was as a swordsman; in 1587 he achieved the prestigious title of Master of Fence by the Society of the Masters of Defence, requiring a mastery over several forms of swords and knives. The Elizabethans had a taste for fighting competitions, many of which were staged at the Theatre, Curtain, and Rose, as well as city inns like the Bull. Shakespeare's plays – *Romeo and Juliet, Richard III, Hamlet, Macbeth*, and many others – feature prominent sword-fights, which clearly also cater for that taste. Richard Burbage, who certainly played Richard III and Hamlet, must himself have been an accomplished swordsman and there would have been others in the company able to offer him a plausible challenge.

There is no wonder that Tarlton's fame lingered, as the posthumous anecdotes and jest-books attest. When Burbage played Hamlet and remembered how Yorick, "the King's jester … hath bore me on his back a thousand times" (5.1.180–6) many in the audience must have identified Yorick with Tarlton. The Queen's Men certainly sometimes used the Theatre, when they played in London. And indeed Tarlton probably had his home near there, in Shoreditch; he was certainly buried there in 1588. So young Burbage, growing up in the environs of his father's Theatre, almost certainly knew the great clown from an early age. Shakespeare perhaps knew him at the end of his career, and more as a traveling player than as a London presence. One of the distinctive features of the Queen's Men is that, for all they would be expected to entertain the Queen and certainly took up residence in London from time to time (see pp. 48–9), they were clearly also expected to spend much of the year touring.

They came into being at a time when a Spanish invasion to unseat Elizabeth and her Protestant regime was a very real possibility, and indeed came perilously close to succeeding with the Armada of 1588. The Queen's Men, traveling in her scarlet livery, spread her presence throughout the country, and indeed beyond. Their repertoire, including some of the earliest chronicle history plays, such as *The Troublesome Reign of King John*, *The True Tragedy of Richard III*, and *The Famous Victories of Henry V*, contained distinct elements of national and religious propaganda. And there were few places of substance that they did not visit. They had circuits that took in Kent – Canterbury, Faversham, Lydd, Maidstone, Dover, New Romney, Rye; East Anglia – Norwich, Aldeburgh, Ipswich, Cambridge, Saffron Walden; the West Country – Bristol, Gloucester, Bath, Lyme Regis, Exeter, Bridgwater, Southampton; the Midlands – Coventry, Leicester, Nottingham, Oxford, Worcester, Shrewsbury, and of course Stratford; the North – York, Carlisle, Chester, and the three main properties of the Stanley Earls of Derby, New Place, Lathom, and Knowsley in Lancashire. In 1589 they even visited Dublin and in October of that year accepted an invitation (forwarded by the governor of Carlisle while they were at Knowsley) to perform at the wedding of James VI and Anne of Denmark in Edinburgh. Unfortunately winds delayed Anne in Oslo by a month and the company could not linger indefinitely. But the diplomatic correspondence shows that they did attend in good faith and were honorably treated by their hosts (McMillin and MacLean, 58).

Until quite recently touring has been seen as a second-best option for the actors, indeed usually as an option of last resort. G. E. Bentley is typical in this prejudice: "For the London companies, touring was nearly always an unpleasant and comparatively unprofitable expedient to compensate for London misfortunes, and as the metropolitan companies became more prosperous they resorted to the road less frequently than they had in the reign of Elizabeth and in the early years of James" (1984, 179). But this is very much from the perspective of what was achieved in London in the 1590s and beyond, which involved radical changes for a few elite companies that no one had yet contemplated. And there is no reason to suppose that players in the 1580s were so gloomy about touring, especially if they were the Queen's Men. For one thing, they invariably received a higher gratuity for the "Mayor's play" than any other company – performing it probably as described at Stratford in the local town or guildhall, though they sometimes even played in cathedrals at Norwich, Chester, and York. As Andrew Gurr has noted, at "Bristol, Gloucester, Cambridge, Dover and other parts of Kent, Nottingham, and Shrewsbury ... they were usually paid twice as much as the other companies. This may reflect their greater size. It certainly reflected their pre-eminent name and greater prestige" (1996, 201). This is what R. Willis was getting at when he wrote that the players received from the Mayor "a reward he thinks fit to show respect unto them." In Stratford in 1587, for example, they received 20 shillings, exactly twice as much as Leicester's Men, four times as much as Essex's Men and six times as much as Stafford's Men that same year.

The assumption of Bentley and others that touring was "comparatively unprofitable" is partly based on the assumption that such payments in the town and city accounts constitute a significant proportion of the take while on tour. It alone, even combined with money we know they would also have received from performances at the houses of the nobility and gentry along their route, would indeed hardly have covered their costs.[9] William Ingram has estimated that, around 1600, food and lodging on the road would cost around 1s. a day per person, while the hire of horses – either to ride or to pull a wagon with all the company's costumes and properties – would cost a similar amount. So a company as large as the Queen's Men (assuming the boys could double up on most items) might spend as much as 25s. a day just to get by. This puts Stratford's 20s. in proportion. But of course that 20s. was a prelude to performances at inns like the the Bear or the Swan in Bridge Street, or indeed the Red Lion in Norwich (where the depositions about the fray suggest quite a crowded house; see pp. 39–40). The nature of the staging would have been dictated by the space available, either indoor or outdoor. But they could have charged more for a smaller but well-appointed indoor venue, while inns yard were likely to have covered galleries on at least two sides (leading to rooms for rent), and they would have been able to charge extra to those willing to pay for the comfort. In the differences between the "Mayors' plays" and those in public inns we see the professional players of the late sixteenth century poised between a patronage economy which required them formally to be servants of grandees and a proto-capitalist one, where the profit motive was unmistakable.

Towns seem normally (as we saw at Gloucester, p. 20) to have limited such commercial performances to two or three, but that was quite enough to be profitable, especially if innkeepers were prepared to allow the players some slack in respect of food and lodging as a trade-off against profits from the business they would generate with large audiences. By the same token, when they visited great private houses the players might expect to be fed and put up (probably with the servants) in addition to any gratuity. They might also receive additional, unrecorded gratuities from any of the lord's guests. Alan Somerset quotes an itinerant singer who claimed that he could survive simply by moving "from gentilmans house to gentilmans house upon their benevolence" (Somerset, 1994, 1.280; see also Greenfield, 2009). All in all, a well-planned tour by a premier troupe like the Queen's Men might expect not merely to cover costs but to be quite profitable.

Nevertheless, London was always an important stop on their travels. As we have already noted, anecdotes about Tarlton place the Queen's Men at times in the large outdoor auditoria, the Theatre, or its near neighbor, the Curtain. But for their first winter, that of 1583/4, the Privy Council specifically negotiated with the city authorities that they be allowed to play "at the signs of the Bull in Bishopsgate Street, and the sign of the Bell in Gracechurch Street and nowhere else in this city." Andrew Gurr observes: "The Bull in Bishopsgate Street was an inn ... with a square of galleries open to the sky. The Bell in Gracechurch Street, by contrast, seems to have been an inn with a large indoor hall available for playing. Specifying the two allowed the company a large good-weather and a smaller bad-weather venue, both inside the city."[10] David Kathman is more cautious about the evidence for indoor playing at any of the inns, suggesting that their key virtue was probably the greater convenience they offered the audience, being at the heart of the city (Kathman, 2009*b*). The specification of two inns might also have catered for the company continuing in its split form.

As I shall discuss further in Chapter 3, several issues are in play here. First, during the 1580s no company seems to have played for really extended periods in any of the available London playhouses. They hired one for the duration of their visits and then passed on. Second, they seem to have been happy enough with the outdoor auditoria (the Theatre, Curtain, and, from 1587, the Rose) in the summer months, but in the winter their first preference was always to play in one of the inns within the city itself, rather than outside in the suburbs. With the shorter hours of daylight and the worse weather it must surely have been easier to attract audiences there, possibly charging higher prices, even if the inns could not accommodate as many people. Third, this was an issue that created constant friction between the City authorities and the Privy Council. The former only wanted players in the City on their own terms; the latter insisted (as in their 1578 letter to the Lord Mayor) that certain companies it nominated must be allowed to play, as a form of rehearsal for their appearances at court.

In this instance the Lord Chamberlain, Lord Howard of Effingham, had negotiated these rights *exclusively* for the Queen's Men.[11] And they were the only adult company to perform at court that 1583/4 season, making four appearances in all; their only competition was from boy companies, who had long been among the Queen's favorite entertainments. The following year the Queen's Men gave five performances and again the only competition was Oxford's Boys (based at a theatre in the Blackfriars liberty, which was controlled by the playwright, John Lyly). In subsequent years, until 1590/1, they remained the dominant company, though it was a dominance that was increasingly challenged. The death of Tarlton in 1588 (following that of Knell the previous year) must inevitably have weakened them and may have entrenched the practice of splitting the company into two troupes, both still calling themselves the Queen's Men, but one led by John Laneham and the other by the Dutton brothers. Presumably about half of the surviving sharers went with each and they made up numbers to be able to continue playing from their established repertoire with hired men. It may even have been a more profitable arrangement as far as the sharers were concerned. In 1589/90 the Chamber Accounts at court show that John Dutton and John Laneham were jointly paid "for themselves and their company" for two performances, suggesting that the two sections came together for these court appearances. But in 1591/2 there are clear demarcations: "Lawrence Dutton and John Dutton, Her Majesty's players & their company" were paid for four performances and "John Laneham and his company, Her Majesty's players" only one (*ES*, 4: 163).

As we shall shortly see, they were then eclipsed by Strange's Men (with whom, indeed, Shakespeare *may* have been associated by 1592: Manley and MacLean, 2014, 280ff). After 1594 they survived only as a single touring company, with none of their former star players, and never again appeared at court. Why exactly they were allowed to lose their preeminent position is not certain. One explanation is that their style of drama may have begun to seem old-fashioned by comparison with the work pioneered around this time by Christopher Marlowe, Thomas Kyd, and others, including Shakespeare. It was certainly within Edmund Tilney's power to reinforce them, if he felt it was in the court's interest that he should. The fact that he did not do so perhaps suggests that their time had come and gone. If Shakespeare did indeed join them in 1587, it would have been sufficient to allow him to see a great company in its pomp, but also its rapid decline. He would presumably only have been with them quite briefly, but long enough to get him to London, where another model of theatrical practice was being formulated.

There is, however, absolutely no documentary evidence that Shakespeare was ever with the Queen's Men. The strongest argument for his involvement with them is well advanced by McMillin and MacLean: "The plots of no fewer than six of Shakespeare's known plays are closely related to the plots of plays performed by the Queen's Men. *King John* resembles *The Troublesome Reign [of King John]* virtually scene for scene. *King Lear* and *Richard III* cover the same stories as *King Leir* and *The True Tragedy of Richard III*. The sequence of *1 Henry IV*, *2 Henry IV*, and *Henry V* is in part an elaborate version of the material covered in *The Famous Victories [of Henry V]*. The plays of the Queen's Men are the largest theatrical source of Shakespeare's plots" (1999, 161). But did Shakespeare need to be a member of the company to have known these plays? Hardly. He could have had many opportunities to see them performed, or to speak to men who had played in them. Several were in print before he wrote the plays that seem to draw on them.

Shakespeare and Alexander Hoghton's Will

An entirely different scenario for Shakespeare's "lost years" and how he might have entered the theatrical profession starts earlier than the Queen's Men hypothesis and finishes somewhat later. It covers rather different terrain in terms of the kinds of acting experience it could have involved him in.

On August 3, 1581 Alexander Hoghton of Lea Hall in Lancashire, dying without a male heir, wrote a will with bequests to his family and faithful servants. This is the passage that most directly concerns us, even if it is not (as some would claim) about William Shakespeare of Stratford:

> Item: it is my mind & will that the said Thomas Hoghton of Brynescoules, my brother, shall have all my instruments belonging to musics, & all manner of play clothes, if he be minded to keep & do keep players. And if he will not keep & maintain players, then it is my mind & will that Sir Thomas Hesketh, knight, shall have the same instruments & play clothes. And I most heartily require the said Sir Thomas to be friendly unto Fulke Gillom & William Shakeshafte now dwelling with me & either to take them unto his service or else to help them to some good master, as my trust is he will ...[12]

In the twentieth century several people argued that "shakshafte" is actually a variant of "shakespeare" (a name much given to punning) and that this refers to the seventeen-year old future playwright.[13] There are several supporting circumstances, though they collectively fall well short of absolute proof. "shakshafte" turns out to have be quite a common name in central Lancashire and this was more likely a local man; conversely that very fact might explain why Hoghton muddled the name (Bearman, 2002). The likeliest reason for Shakespeare being a hundred miles or so from his Stratford home would be that his family were recusant Roman Catholics, like the Hoghtons, and that the young Shakespeare had gone to find employment in a part of the country where Catholicism was still strong and to an extent shielded. The possible association of John Shakespeare with a Catholic "spiritual Testament" perhaps speaks to this, though here too there are doubters (Schoenbaum, 1987, 45–54). But one of the Stratford schoolmasters in 1579–81, John Cottam, was the brother of a Jesuit priest and he came from that same part of Lancashire, suggesting possible lines of communication. Might he have recommended a star pupil from the grammar school to Hoghton? The whole circumstance, moreover, might bear out John Aubrey's anecdote from the late seventeenth century, that Shakespeare "had been in his younger years a schoolmaster in the country."[14]

Yet even if Shakshafte was not Shakespeare it tells us interesting things about theatricals in the community when he was growing up. The will strikingly puts goods before persons. Alexander starts with a bequest to his half-brother, Thomas, of "all my instruments belonging to musics, and all manner of playclothes, if he be minded to keep and do keep players"; if not, "the same instruments and play-clothes" were to go to Alexander's relative by marriage, Sir Thomas Hesketh of Rufford, some ten miles away. Only then does he bring to mind two faithful retainers: "And I most heartily require the said Sir Thomas to be friendly unto Fulke Gillom & William Shakshafte now dwelling with me &

either to take them unto his service or else to help them to some good master." There is an immediate ambiguity about whether "players" here means musicians or actors (an ambiguity which dogs many early records of theatre); but musicians do not specifically need "play-clothes" so it is not unreasonable to suppose that it means actors. The passage obviously suggests a tradition of music and playing at Lea Hall – and likewise at Sir Thomas Hesketh's properties, Rufford Hall and Martholme. Alexander is less sure about his brother's establishment, though he thinks it not impossible – and that Thomas might take it up as a result of the bequest.

In Hesketh–Hoghton circles playing was a regular fact of life, especially around Christmas, as it doubtless was in the households of many of the substantial gentry (I am speaking here of those below the status of a baron), though it has left little trace in the written records. Their household papers have not survived nearly as well as those of the grander aristocracy or the official records of towns and cities. Where they *have* survived, however, they can be quite revealing. For example, the records of Dunkenhalgh Hall in Lancashire, home of a wealthy judge, Thomas Walmesley, record fifty-one visits by performers in the period 1612–36. These include some of the major companies, including the King's Men, Prince Charles's Men, and Princess Elizabeth's Men; but they also include visits by companies not recorded anywhere else, including one by Sir Cuthbert Halsall's Men in August 1616.[15] Halsall was a relatively close neighbor, his principal residence being near Ormskirk in Lancashire. The visit seems to have coincided with a Walmesley family wedding, so this was perhaps a friendly festive wedding present. Visits are also recorded between 1612 and 1618 by John Warren's Men and Sir Edward Warren's Men. The latter must be a mistake, since Sir Edward died in 1609 and was succeeded by his son, John, who was doubtless the true patron over all five visits recorded under the Warren name.[16] The Warren family home was in Poynton, Cheshire, the county south of Lancashire; but John also acquired some property in Woodplumpton, some twenty miles west of Dunkenhalgh (and very close, as it happens, to Lea Hall). These visits by his "players" were perhaps in the spirit of generating and sustaining neighborly relations.

We should notice, however, that only one other record of an event involving the Warren players has surfaced; this was in 1611 at Gawthorpe Hall (close to Dunkenhalgh), and they are expressly recorded as "musicians."[17] As I say, it is a frustratingly common ambiguity in the records. It seems unlikely that John Warren patronized troupes of both musicians and actors (that level of patronage is normally associated with the aristocracy), so it is possible that none of these recorded visits involved theatricals at all. But it is also possible that the persons concerned were equally adept at both types of "playing." We just do not know. There is a parallel example in the records of Smithills Hall, also in Lancashire (one of the properties of the wealthy Shuttleworth family who later occupied Gawthorpe Hall); in 1584 they were visited by Sir Peter Legh's musicians and in 1588 by Sir Peter's "players."[18] Sir Peter held property and offices in both Lancashire and Cheshire, but it is still unlikely that he maintained two different troupes.

At all events, such entries suggest that there was some tradition of welcoming traveling players of various kinds in the Halsall, Warren, and Legh households, but it has left only these small traces and that only because their players traveled on a neighborly basis and were given lodging and board and a small gratuity. Warren's Men earned one shilling or two on each of their visits; Legh's Men 1s. and 5s.; Halsall's Men received quite a handsome 10s., perhaps inflated by the fact that it was associated with a wedding. Unless the *Records of Early English Drama* project unearths further references, this is the sum total of what we know of each of them. The Halsall visit might have been a one-off; Warren's Men presumably called at other properties in the region, to justify journeys from Cheshire, but all records of this have been lost. Legh's men surely did not only perform twice, and in the same property.

The situation must have been replicated all over the country – localized troupes visiting the properties of friends, relatives, neighbors and allies, but leaving at best the scantiest of records. Such troupes did not have the prestige to present themselves to the mayors of towns they might pass through; at least, they are not recorded as receiving payment from them. This was playing on a much more modest and domestic scale, and those who took part could not possibly have earned a professional living by it. They presumably held other positions in their master's household and only entertained the family or the neighbors when occasion called for it.

As to Sir Thomas Hesketh, although Alexander Hoghton seemed confident that he kept players, they have left very little trace. In 1569 one of his minstrels (James) was left a bequest by Robert Nowell of Read Hall (near Dunkenhalgh), where perhaps he had once performed. The only other, much debated, record is an entry in the household book of the steward of the Stanley family, Earls of Derby, who were the great magnates of southern and central Lancashire. An entry for December 1587 reads "Sir Tho[mas] Hesketh players went away." There are in fact several records of Sir Thomas visiting Henry Stanley, the fourth earl, and his son, Ferdinando, Lord Strange. He was clearly on sociable terms with them, a fact of some consequence in our hypothetical account of Shakespeare's theatrical experience.

But for now, the question is whether the "players" mentioned in the household book were Sir Thomas's own; or whether these were the company patronized by Lord Strange himself, back with the family for the festive season, but happening to leave at the same time as Sir Thomas – the timing of whose visit might well have been arranged to see their performances. We simply do not know. The Stanleys were used to the highest quality of theatrical entertainment, having visits (besides those of their own very accomplished troupes) from the Queen's own players as well as those of the Earls of Leicester, Hertford, and Essex; but it is possible that they followed the pattern at Dunkenhalgh and also accepted visits from much lowlier, local companies in the spirit of Theseus in *A Midsummer Night's Dream*: "For never anything can be amiss / When simpleness and duty tender it" (5.1.82–3). But there are no records of payment to them.

We have little evidence of what precise "playing" may have gone on in households of Hesketh's scale. At the beginning of the sixteenth century, a great house such as that of the fifth Earl of Northumberland, maintained four salaried players; it was made clear, however, that they would be in attendance for important religious and family events, but would otherwise tour to spare his household the cost of maintaining them – which in essence was the derivation of all the patronized touring companies (Westfall, 1990, 124). They perhaps supported the members of his chapel who were required to play the "Play of Nativity upon Christmas Day in the morning," the "Play of Resurrection on Easter Day" and the "Play before his Lordship upon Shrove Tuesday at night yearly" (Westfall, 2009, 276). Such performances were part and parcel of an intense celebration of the Twelve Days of Christmas, with feasts, masques, concerts, and processions, and then beyond to Shrovetide, before the great drawing-in of Lent. This festive season – known at the royal court as the Revels – was central to the business of playing in early modern England, though by Shakespeare's day theatricals were clearly distinguished from Christian (and most particularly Catholic) liturgy and tradition.

At Hesketh's Rufford Hall we might perhaps expect a scaled-down, more domesticated version of this pattern, with those who acted as players during festive periods of the year earning their keep in other ways for the rest of the time rather than touring extensively. It is highly unlikely that any were salaried for playing as such, or were full-time professionals. In 1542 the Earl of Rutland allowed one Anthony Hall board in the household for four weeks, because he was "learning a play to play in Christmas," though later he was paid for "scouring away the earth and stones in the tennis play" (Westfall, 1990, 127). If John Aubrey's evidence carries any weight, such a position for Shakespeare might have been as a "tutor" to household children. Baptista in *The Taming of the Shrew* talks of such appointments:

> And for I know she [Bianca] takes most delight
> In music, instruments, and poetry,
> Schoolmasters will I keep within my house
> Fit to instruct her youth …
>   … to cunning men
> I will be very kind.
>
>   (1.1.92–8)

Holofernes in *Love's Labour's Lost* could be one such, though it seems more likely ("he teaches boys the hornbook": 5.1.46) that he is master over a whole school.

Either way, when the King instructs Don Armado that he wants "some delightful ostentation, or show, or pageant, or antic, or firework" for the Princess (107–9), it is to Holofernes and the curate, Nathaniel, that he turns, understanding that they "are good at such eruptions and sudden breaking out of mirth, as it were" (107–9, 110–11). Holofernes immediately proposes a show of the Nine Worthies and volunteers the three of them to perform in it. Might this offer us some shadow of how Shakespeare got into writing and performing drama?

If Hesketh was personally interested in drama, rather than just prepared to patronize it, he might have done as Sir Edward Dering (of Surrenden Dering in Kent) did, collecting printed playbooks on a prodigious scale – Dering is the earliest known person to purchase the Shakespeare First Folio – and adapting some for amateur theatricals in his own home. A manuscript survives of an abridgement of *1* and *2 Henry IV*, stripped around 1622 of its comic scenes to make a single play for private performance (Krivatsy and Yeandle, 1992; Williams and Evans, 1974). Perhaps even more intriguingly, a partial cast-list is attached to that manuscript, apparently for an amateur performance of Fletcher's *The Spanish Curate*, marked up with roles for Dering himself, family, and friends, their servants and one "Jack of the Buttery" (Gibson, 2002, 1383, note to p. 916). The evidence ties this to 1622–24, which is remarkable since the play was not licensed until 1622 and not printed before 1647; Dering would have had to approach Fletcher or the King's Men for a copy. In 1623 he also bought six copies of a comic university allegory, "Ruff and Cuff," in which articles of clothing argue with each other; six copies would probably have been enough to allow the cast to rehearse (Wiggins, 2005). And he recorded buying "heads of hair and beards" (Krivatsy and Yeandle, 139). Clearly, Dering took household performance seriously and personally, performing himself and expecting family and friends to do likewise, with help from the servants. He had grown up through the theatrical revolution to which Shakespeare himself was central, with its attendant explosion of plays in print. The same resources would only have been available to a Sir Thomas Hesketh back in the 1580s on a much more modest scale. But there is no reason to suppose that the same enthusiasm might not have been there, perhaps relying on more traditional fare. Christopher Sly, tricked in the induction to *The Taming of the Shrew* into thinking he is a lord, can only imagine that his players might offer "a comonty [comedy?] a Christmas gambold [gambol, lively merrymaking and leaping] or a tumbling trick" (133–4). The Page patiently explains that the "pleasant comedy" that has been announced will be "more pleasing stuff ... a kind of history" (126, 135, 137). The Slys of the world, rather like the "rude mechanicals" of *A Midsummer Night's Dream*, are not really conversant with fashionable, sophisticated theatre.

One significant resource available to Hesketh was a room big enough to stage theatrical events. Rufford Hall (see Figures 2.2 and 2.3), built in the early

Figure 2.2 Interior of the Tudor Great Hall at Rufford Old Hall. *Source*: The National Trust Photolibrary / Alamy Stock photo.

sixteenth century, boasts a Great Hall which survives to this day. It is very similar in size to the upper Hall in Stratford Guild Hall, some 39 ft long and 23 ft wide (14.2 m × 6.7 m), a typical ratio for such rooms. It boasts a splendid hammerbeam roof, the timbers of which sit on a low stone wall. The woodwork is heavily decorated (each hammerbeam has a carved angel at either end), with some conservative religious iconography. At the low end of the hall is a unique wooden, elaborately carved screen, creating a spere passage leading to the

Figure 2.3 Interior of the Tudor Great Hall at Rufford Old Hall. *Source*: The National Trust Photolibrary / Alamy Stock photo.

original kitchen and buttery (Fig. 2.2). At the high end, where the principal dining table would normally sit, there are two doors (Fig. 2.3). These originally gave access to living quarters in the west wing of the house, which is no longer there (so they lead out now into the grounds). Looking towards that high end, on the right wall there is a bay measuring 10' 7" [3.21 m] wide and a similar depth at its deepest point.

The bay and the screen are somewhat unusual, but in other respects this is quite a typical Tudor hall in size and shape. It does not, however, have a minstrel gallery or any other potential upper playing space, as many do. As in the discussion of Stratford Guild Hall it is readily possible to imagine performances at either the high end or the low end of the room; doors are conveniently located at both ends (though whether actors could have used those to the family's living quarters is another matter). The screen creates a somewhat unusual configuration but ultimately would not interfere. The evidence, however, that playing commonly took place in colleges and at court immediately *below* the high table weighs heavily, and that probably happened here too. Significantly, a padded bench runs along the wall for the use of those at high table; at its center is a more elaborate seat for the head of the household – a more modest version of Elizabeth's "state" (see p. 120). The bay, curtained off, might well have served as a tiring room. The Heskeths and their principal guests would have presided over all – unless, like Sir Edward Dering, they were minded to be involved in the entertainment themselves. Fulke Gillom and William Shakshafte might well be imagined to have suspended their other duties for the festive season to take an active role in staging it all.

With any arrangement, even in daylight hours and certainly at night (theatricals elsewhere are recorded both in afternoons after dinner, around 2 p.m., and after supper, around 9 p.m.), it would be necessary to increase the provision of lighting in the room for the performance to be visible to all. At court and the Blackfriars there was an elaborate provision of candles throughout the hall (not just on the stage), which needed to be trimmed and replaced several times during a performance, necessitating breaks in the action. Here it seems likely that extra torches or standing candelabra around the room would serve. Wherever the stage was set, it is easy to imagine a hundred people, possibly more, on benches in an audience; Hesketh could readily assemble family, friends, and servants for a cohesive festive occasion.

We may imagine all this in the spirit of convivial recreation, but that was evidently not always quite the case. In 1609 Sir John Yorke, of Gouthwaite (or Gowlthwaite) Hall in West Yorkshire, entertained some hundred of his friends and neighbors at Christmas, in an event which acquired some notoriety. Sir John at least notionally conformed to the Church of England, but his wife, Lady Juliana, was actively Roman Catholic. Entertainment was provided by Sir Richard Cholmely's players, based at Cholmely's estate in Whitby and led by Christopher and Robert Simpson. They offered the Yorkes a repertoire of four plays from which to choose: interestingly *King Lear*, *Pericles*, *The Travailes of Three English Brothers* (all King's Men plays, all published far away in London recently), and a traditional saint's play, *The Play of St Christopher*, with inevitable Catholic associations. They chose the saint's play. Whether the Yorkes knew about it in advance or not, the players included a raucous scene of a dispute between two characters, a Protestant minister and a Catholic priest, which ended with the Protestant being dragged to hell by the Devil and the Catholic going to heaven. Most of the audience (many of whom were later recorded as being recusant Catholics) enjoyed this immensely, but one Elizabeth Stubbs, a former servant at Gouthwaite, reported it to the Justice of the Peace (Boddy 1976; Jensen 2004).

There were serious consequences all round, some of which are informative about playing in general. In 1614 Sir John and Lady Juliana were tried in Star Chamber (mainly composed of the King's chief ministers) for allowing a seditious play to be performed. They were fined £1,000 each for allowing the extra scene to be acted, and were imprisoned in the Fleet Debtors' Prison for three years, being released in February 1617 when they paid part of the fine.

The Simpsons and their associates probably lost Sir Richard's patronage as a result of what happened at Gouthwaite Hall and acquired a substantial track-record between 1612 and 1619 of prosecutions for being "vagabond" players and recusants. From these we learn that the players were all, like the "mechanicals" in *A Midsummer Night's Dream*, qualified tradesmen. The Simpsons were both shoemakers; their associates included weavers, a tanner, and a mason. We do not know if they continued to work at their trades when not performing, though it is likely. But it is quite clear that they persisted in their playing despite all the harassment and that there were plenty of households prepared to welcome them, despite (or perhaps because of) their reputation, even though they risked being fined for doing so (*ES*, 1: 305, n.1).

An interesting deposition to emerge from the enquiries which followed the *St Christopher* performance contains the complaint of one Thomas Pant, who actually gave one of the most detailed accounts of the play. He was apprenticed to Christopher Simpson, doubtless in his capacity as a shoemaker, but complained that he had been "trained up for these three years to wandering in the country and playing of interludes" – that is, he was being used as a boy player, not learning the trade of shoemaker (ibid.). Whether Pant had ever really expected to become a shoemaker may be questionable, but he took this opportunity (perhaps feeling threatened by the attention of the authorities) to challenge the terms of his apprenticeship; he was released from his indenture as a result. There were, of course, no women on Elizabethan stages. Their roles were normally played by boy actors liked Pant, who would be apprenticed like this to adult players under the aegis of their trade guild affiliations. But it is unlikely that any of those Shakespeare worked with in London were under any illusions about what they were training for. I discuss the boy actors further in Chapter 4.

The whole history of the Simpsons and the kinds of records we have seen in Lancashire attest to robust traditions of playing in provincial England during Shakespeare's lifetime, ranging from semi-professional to neighborly to purely domestic, tied to some extent to local affiliations, traditions, and beliefs. And it all went on, as it were, under the radar, since under the terms of the 1572 Act for the Punishment of Vagabonds (and an even more draconican measure passed in 1598) all traveling players were supposed to be attached to a "baron of the realm or any other honourable person of greater degree" (*ES*, 4: 324). Custom and practice doubtless kept such local playing in being, with the tacit assumption that the local gentry would keep their own in order. But there were obviously exceptions. Remarkably, the Yorkes seem not to have learned their lesson. In 1628 a player named Christopher Malloy was prosecuted in the Court of Star Chamber for playing the devil in a performance at their house; in the course of the role he carried someone playing the late King James on his back to hell, and alleged that all Protestants were damned (*ES*, 1: 328, n. 3). In an age of such divided religious loyalties theatre always had the potential to be inflammatory, contentious, or subversive, even in remote provincial manor houses. Sir Thomas Hesketh was never involved in any such scandal and to all appearances was a stalwart of the Tudor regime, serving as High Sheriff of Lancashire in 1562. But his wife and at least one of his sons were actively Catholic, and Samuel Schoenbaum maintains that he was too (1987, 114).

Strange's Men

This doubleness also characterizes the Stanley Earls of Derby, who were the Heskeths' own patrons. The first earl won his title for supporting Richmond (Henry VII) at the Battle of Bosworth Field – events depicted by Shakespeare in the closing scenes of *Richard III*. Thereafter the family were staunch supporters of the Tudor regime, though successive earls were suspected of Catholic sympathies. This plays into the last link in the Hoghton Will theory of Shakespeare's move to London. Hesketh died in 1588. Then if not before it has been supposed that "William Shakshafte" passed into the service of the Stanleys, and specifically of the enigmatic Ferdinando, Lord Strange heir to the earldom.

They had long welcomed traveling players at their three great estates in south Lancashire, Lathom House, New Park, and Knowsley Hall. We can catch a glimpse of the splendor in which they lived from the description of an elaborately carved hall screen at Lathom House, done by one Parker and celebrated in a poem by Thomas Chaloner. It depicted landscape, together with the astronomical and astrological workings of the heavens, showing:

> how and when the moon in every month doth change,
> And how she doth her light augment; and how she fades again,
> And how she quarterly doth stand. Here may'st thou see full plain
> The course of all the planets brought arising at the east,
> By *prim' mobile*, being led to sit again at west:
> A deep design, it represents a practice good also,
> That with his pains on earth the manor of the heavens doth show,
> And how therewith the dozen signs are led and brought about,
> A needful thing in such a place and to effect no doubt,
> To show thee when the day is long and how it shortens night …[19]

It stood as both astrological chart and perpetual calendar, "amount[ing] to a *theatrum mundi* or depiction of the cosmos" (Manley and MacLean, 2014, 268). This was obviously by several orders of magnitude grander even than the fine hall screen at Rufford Old Hall, which gives some measure of the Stanleys, only one step below royalty (see p. 56). Lawrence Manley describes it as a possible "microcosmic backdrop" to playing at Lathom. I have argued earlier that it would be against necessary seating protocol for hall screens to act as "backdrops" to theatrical performances (p. 24). But it would certainly be a significant presence in a room doubtless also hung with fine tapestries, locating plays and players within their widest social and political contexts.

The Stanleys also had a long tradition of patronizing players, not just locally but in troupes which traveled the country extensively (MacLean, 2004). As mentioned when we considered Stratford, both the fourth earl and his son had troupes that were received at court in the early 1580s, though Strange's troupe at that time seem to have been primarily acrobats; their court visits in late 1581 and early 1583, for example, are recorded as "activities" rather than play-performances. But by the Revels season of 1591/2 we find them putting on no less than six *plays* there, an unprecedented number by a single company in a season; even the Queen's Men (who that year only appeared once) had never performed more than five times.

Quite how the company managed this transformation into the highest league remains uncertain, though Lawrence Manley and Sally-Beth MacLean's *Lord Strange's Men and their Plays* (2014) puts everything in much clearer perspective than it has been before. The following details, however, seem pertinent. The Earl of Leicester's Men, already fractured in 1586 when Leicester took a troupe with him on his expedition to fight Spain in the Low Countries, was finally dissolved when he died in 1588. Some of his former players became Strange's Men, including the great clown, Will Kemp. By November 1589 the company can be traced playing in London. The Lord Mayor attempted to close the playhouses and summoned the two troupes he could trace, the Lord Admiral's and Strange's. As he reported to Lord Burghley and the Privy Council: "The Lord Admiral's players very dutifully obeyed, but the others in very contemptuous manner departing from me, went to the Cross Keys [an inn] and played that afternoon, to the great offence of the better sort that knew they were prohibited by order from your Lordship" (*ES*, 4: 305). Like James Burbage on an earlier occasion (see p. 31), players in the service of a great aristocrat stood on that dignity to resist "lesser" authorities. In this instance Lord Mayor Harte, who was acting on Privy Council instructions, imprisoned some of them for their contempt.

By this time the company seems to have lost the services of John Symons, their leader when their forte was acrobatics. In 1590 they apparently formed an association of sorts with the Admiral's Men, then working with James Burbage at the Theatre; they put on a joint play and activities at court that December.[20] But even by November 1590 there were tensions between Burbage and the Admiral's Men, some of whom became involved in a dispute between him and Margaret Brayne, the widow of his former partner, who was claiming a moiety (share) in the profits of the Theatre. John Alleyn (Edward's elder brother, also a player) later deposed that he "found there ... Richard Burbage, the youngest son of the said James Burbage there, with a broom staff in his hand, of whom when this deponent asked what stir there was, he answered in laughing phrase how they came for a moiety. But quod he (holding up the said broom's staff) I have, I think, delivered him a moiety with this and sent them packing" (*ES*, 2: 307). The man with the broom staff was shortly to become one of Shakespeare's closest colleagues and one of the great actors of the era. When Alleyn threatened to "complain to their lord and master, the Lord Admiral [Howard]" about their behavior, the irascible James Burbage "in a rage" declared "by a great oath that he cared not for the three of the best lords of them all."[21]

By February 1592, and probably somewhat earlier, Edward Alleyn had joined Strange's Men (while anomalously remaining in the service of the Lord Admiral), possibly bringing a few of his fellow Admiral's Men with him. And they had transferred to Henslowe's Rose, on the Bankside (p. 32). Apparently in anticipation of this Henslowe spent over £100 rebuilding the Rose's stage and tiring house, built only five years earlier, installing for example a permanent roof over the stage for the first time – which would not only keep the stage and the actors dry but might allow for relatively sophisticated "descent" scenes (J. Greenfield, 2007; Bowsher 2007). In October 1592 Alleyn married Henslowe's stepdaughter, Joan.

It seems indisputable that what finally transformed Strange's Men into the leading company of its day in 1591/2 was Alleyn's star power. In *Pierce Penniless, His Supplication to the Devil* (1592) Thomas Nashe praised him extravagantly: "Not Roscius nor Aesop, those admired tragedians that have lived ever since before Christ was born, could ever perform more in action than famous Ned Allen" (F4v). But something else about this company was distinctive. Wherever exactly they played immediately after the falling out with Burbage they must have done so long enough and with a sufficiently varied repertoire to convince Edmund Tilney, Master of the Revels, that they warranted six slots on the Revels calendar of 1591/92 and a further three (again the highest number) the following year. What we can say incontrovertibly is that between February 19 and June 22, 1592 they performed the first fully recorded London *season*, playing continuously at the Rose; we know this – with the names of all the plays they performed, and Henslowe's share of the takings – because of Henslowe's so-called *Diary* (see pp. 13ff).

Prior to this, to the best of our knowledge, no company had attempted to set up more-or-less permanent residence in London. Companies had visited London as part of their touring circuit, hiring amphitheaters like the Theatre and the Rose, or (in winter) inns within the city for a time, probably exhausting their limited repertoire; but then moving on. There must have been some calculation on the part of Alleyn and Henslowe, in conjunction with the senior sharers in Strange's Men that the time was ripe – the population of London was now around 200,000 – for a settled operation there. Attempts to identify the personnel of the company, and to estimate its size, are bedeviled by the contested status of two "plots" of plays that may have belonged to them, those of *2 The Seven Deadly Sins*, and *The Dead Men's Fortune*, which name quite a few players (see pp. 205–6 and Kathman, 2004*a*). But we can be certain of the core personnel as of May 6, 1593, since the Privy Council gave them a special licence to tour during the time of plague, naming "Edward Alleyn, servant to the right honourable the Lord High Admiral, William Kemp, Thomas Pope, John Heminges, Augustine Phillips and George Bryan, being one company, servants to our very good the lord the Lord Strange" (*ES*, 2: 123). Leaving aside Alleyn, all the others named were to be founder-members with Shakespeare of the Lord Chamberlain's Men in 1594/5.

All this strictly tells us is that Shakespeare was not one of the sharers of the company, the senior personnel who normally put capital into the enterprise and shared in the profits (see p. 140). He might have been a hired man, acting as required for a weekly wage. And/or he may simply have been employed to write for them. Among the plays which Henslowe lists in that first season is "harey the vi," which was probably *1 Henry VI*.[22] Even as Nashe was praising Alleyn he was also deeply struck by this play: "How would it have joyed brave Talbot (the terror of the French) to think that after two hundred year in the tomb, he should triumph again on the stage, and have his bones new embalmed by the tears of ten thousand spectators at least (at several times), who, in the tragedian that represents his person, imagine they behold him fresh bleeding" (*Pierce Penniless*, F3r). This was one of twenty-seven plays that Strange's Men staged in the 105 days of that first recorded season, a portent of one of the most striking differences between London playing and what had been the practice of traveling companies. As we saw, the Simpsons had precisely four plays that they were ready to perform (though three of them were surprisingly new). But even the grander companies would hardly have needed twenty-seven plays in repertoire as they toured to be able to offer their customers variety. They could probably have made do with half as many, and there would be relatively little pressure to renew them. But in London there was a constant need for novelty to keep a limited pool of customers coming back for more. That was an essential precondition of the kind of career Shakespeare was to have from now on.

"Harey the vi" was certainly one of the hits of that early 1592 season. It is first recorded on March 3, marked a "ne," one of Henslowe's enigmatic annotations which usually seems to mean that it was a new play that day or at least a revised and relicensed one; companies charged novelty-seeking audiences more, usually double, for such first performances. Henslowe also recorded takings of 76s. 8d. (£3 16s. 8d.).[23] This was not the full income for the day but reflected Henslowe's own proportion of the take, his income for allowing the actors to use his theatre (*Henslowe*, xxxii). We are not certain about his arrangement with Strange's Men, but it would be typical if his share derived from takings in the galleries, the tiered, covered sections around the inner wall of the Rose, where customers paid more for the luxury of shelter and seating (see p. 93). Whatever precisely was the case, this was a healthy return for the new play.

It was staged again on March 7 (60s.); March 11 (47s. 6d.); March 16 (31s. 6d.); March 28 (68s.); April 5 (41s.); Apri l 13 (26s.); April 21 (33s.); May 4 (56s.); May 7 (22s.); May 14 (50s.); May 19 (30s.); May 25 (24s.); June 12 (32s,); June 19 (31s.). Marlowe's *The Jew of Malta* – not, apparently, new but a famous role for Alleyn – actually did better in the run overall, but *I Henry VI* generated the second best returns. There were three other "ne" plays in this season, *Titus and Vespacia* (or *Vespasian*), *The Tanner of Denmark*, and *A Knack to Know a Knave*[24]. All three started with takings over 60s. but, though the other two settled into the repertory well enough, *The Tanner of Denmark* never recurs again in Henslowe's accounts. Our best guess for an explanation would have to be very negative audience response to the first performance. In a business where the margins were probably always tight and interruption by the plague was a constant threat, failure had to mean failure.[25]

Plague was certainly part of the undoing of Strange's Men, but the loss of their patron was the final blow. The Privy Council ordered all London playing to stop on June 23, 1592 because of the level of plague deaths. The company took to the road by July 13 and were still traveling on December 19. They were back at the Rose for a very brief season, from December 29 to the end of January 1593. But that is their final appearance in Henslowe's *Diary* (19–20). The plague set in again with a vengeance and scarcely remitted until the middle of 1594. They seem to have hung on as long as they could in London, until need drove them back on the road, under the special Privy Council licence quoted above. Among various letters that have survived from this period, between members of the Henslowe/Alleyn family, one from Edward Alleyn to his wife, Joan, gives some sense both of the terror of the plague and of the privations of touring:

Emmanuel
My good sweet mouse, I commend me heartily to you, and to my father, my mother and my sister Bess, hoping in God though the sickness be round about you yet by his mercy it may escape your house. Which by the grace of God it shall therefore use this course: keep your house fair and clean, which I know you will, and every evening throw water before your door and in your backside, and have in your windows good store of rue and herb of grace, and withall the grace of God which must be obtained by prayers. And so doing no doubt but the lord will mercifully defend you.

Now, good mouse, I have no news to send you but this that we have all our health, for which the Lord be praised. I received your letter at Bristol by Richard Cowley [an actor], for which I thank you. I have sent you this bearer, Thomas Pope's kinsman, my white waistcoat, because it is a trouble to me to carry it; receive it with this letter. And lay it up for me till I come. If you send any more letters, send to me by the carriers of

Shrewsbury or to Westchester or to York to be kept till my Lord Strange's players come. And this sweet heart with my hearty commendations to all our friends I cease.

From Bristol this Wednesday after St James his day, being ready to begin the play of *Harry of Cornwall*. Mouse, do my hearty commendations to Master Griggs [the carpenter who built the Rose and refurbished it in 1592], his wife and all his household, and to my sister Phillips.

Your loving husband, E. Alleyn

Mouse, you send me no news of any things you should send of your domestical matters, such things as happens at home, as how your distilled water proves, or this or that or anything what you will.

[*vertically in margin*] And Jug, I pray you let my orange tawny stockings of woolen be dyed a very good black, against I come home to wear in the winter. You sent me not word of my garden, but next time you will. But remember this in any case: that all that bed which was parsley, in the month of September you sow it with spinach, for then is the time. I would do it myself but will not come home till Allholland tide [All Saints' Day, November 1]. And so sweet mouse farewell, and brook our long journey with patience.

[*addressed*] This to be delivered to Mr Henslowe, one of the grooms of Her Majesty's Chamber, dwelling on the Bankside, right over against the Clink [a prison].

(Henslowe, 276–7)

It tells us something that this Bristol performance appears in no official city record. Those records, as we have seen, only record payment for the "Mayor's play" but no such record for Strange's Men appears in this period. Possibly that formality was sometimes overlooked, yet some commercial performances allowed. It would indeed have been a long journey, from Bristol, up the Welsh marches and on to York. But the record shows that they in fact turned to Bath before heading all the way to Norwich on the east coast, and then the usually lucrative east Midland centers of Coventy and Leicester. Possibly the change of plan was linked with a change in status of their patron: on September 25 Lord Strange succeeded his father as Earl of Derby, and henceforth his players were Derby's Men. But this only lasted until April 16, 1594, when the new earl in turn died, amid rumors of poison (Kathman, 2004c). A troupe of the same name toured under the patronage of his brother, the sixth earl, but by then they had lost all their key personnel and their access to court.

Strange's Men have the unique distinction of being the first known truly London-based company and the presence of what at least seems to be *1 Henry VI* in their repertoire associates Shakespeare with them. The title page of *Titus Andronicus*, as we have seen, also suggests a link with them (see p. 37, Note 14). But nothing else strictly does, though Shakespeare's depiction of the Stanleys in his history plays and the use of Lord Strange's unusual name, Ferdinand, for the King of Navarre in *Love's Labour's Lost* fuel speculation (Manley and MacLean, 2014, 280–320). Shakespeare's name appears in none of the "plots" possibly associated with the company, nor in the Alleyn–Henslowe correspondence, nor in their special traveling licence. So possibly he was just a hired man, or simply a playwright who wrote for a fee. Nevertheless, as Terence G. Schoone-Jongen observes, "The belief that Shakespeare performed with Strange's [Men] is probably the most popular" of all the theories about Shakespeare's early career (2008, 103). But none of this requires that he should have been part of Strange's Men *before* they settled in London.

Box 2.2 A Postscript to Strange's Men: Prescot

Given the circumstantial evidence that Shakespeare was associated with Strange's Men in the early 1590s, whether as a performer, playwright, or both, we should at least consider the possibility that he accompanied them to the little-known but remarkable Prescot playhouse in what was then Lancashire (now Merseyside). The bare facts of this shadowy enterprise are as follows: It is first mentioned around 1603 by the vicar of Prescot, Thomas Meade, who noted that 2s. 6d. was owing to Prescot Grammar School for "the play house builded upon the wast by Mr Richard Harrington" (George, 1991, 77). This sum was evidently a ground rent. Several subsequent documents refer to this same building as a "play house," confirming its existences and apparent usage. The "wast" on which it stood was probably common ground ("In legal use … a piece of such land not in any man's occupation, but lying for common": *OED* "waste," *n*. 2). David George has argued that it was specifically on the Town Moss, though that would have implied a bog or swamp, which would hardly have been appropriate for such a building (2004, 230). Elspeth Graham and Rosemary Tyler locate it on the north side of Newgate Street, the modern Eccleston Street, close to the town's Flat Iron Building (2011, 114.) In a document of 1615 we learn the dimensions of the plot on which the playhouse stood: 57 feet (17 m) long on its north and south sides, 29 feet (8.8 m) on the east and 15 feet (4.6 m) on the west, giving it the shape of a tapering trapezoid. This would give the property a floor space approximately half of that of the Globe or Fortune playhouses in London. Unfortunately we have no idea how the stage or the accommodations for the audience were disposed.

We do not know, moreover, when Harrington had built "the play house." There is a survey of Prescot from 1592, which makes no reference to such a distinctive feature, so it presumably did not exist at that date. It may or may not be suggestive that in 1595 Harrington had acquired a cottage and garden which was only 150 yards from the playhouse site and which might have been useful in its management. David George concludes from this that we "can put the construction date confidently between 1593 and 1595" (2004, 234). He himself pushes the argument for 1593, at the height of the prolonged plague in London, when Strange's Men took to the road and may have felt the need of a playing base well outside the capital (see p. 63). More recently Elspeth Graham and Rosemary Tyler, supposing the involvement of the *sixth* Earl of Derby in the enterprise – rather than Shakespeare's putative early patron, the fifth earl, formerly Lord Strange – have argued for a start date of 1597/8 (Graham and Tyler, 115).

By then Shakespeare was securely a member of the Lord Chamberlain's Men, who are never known to have toured in Lancashire. So the argument for Shakespeare's personal involvement with the Prescot playhouse hangs rather precariously on the earliest, 1593, dating – for which there is no documentary evidence. The appearance of *Venus and Adonis* that year, dedicated to the Earl of Southampton, rather suggests that he was pursuing another patronage strategy, though of course there was nothing to prevent him from backing two horses at the same time. But it also seems telling that he is not named alongside the six senior players in the special licence granted to Strange's Men by the Privy Council on 4 May 1593 – the permission they needed to travel out of London and the earliest date they could have taken up residence in Prescot; there is evidence, however, that at least two hired men – Thomas Downton and Richard Cowley – accompanied the named sharers on their travels, so Shakespeare could conceivably have done the same (Gurr, 1996, 264–5). But, all in all, Shakespeare's personal involvement with Prescot hangs by the thinnest shred of supposition.

Nevertheless the mere existence of a playhouse there (on the face of it such an improbable occurrence) tells us something of the theatrical world within which Shakespeare operated and the forces which shaped it. Prescot was in many ways the antithesis of London, a place of no more than 400 inhabitants and in an area which, as Graham and Tyler note, was described at the time as "so unbridled & badde an handfull of England." The main local industries were the making of clay pots and mining coal, and in 1586 Thomas Mead, reporting to his masters at King's College, Cambridge, the landlords of the whole area, gave a bleak picture of conditions there: "There is in this poor town of Prescot one hundred and five several families, among which there be scarce 20 that be able to help themselves without begging" (George, 2003, 227). It is clear that there was no resident community with the wealth to support a professional playhouse in the way that Londoners supported the Theatre or the Globe. If we ask why Harrington should have built it where he did the answer must somehow be tied in with the interests of the Stanleys, the Earls of Derby, and their family. He was himself the younger brother of Percival Harrington, deputy steward of Prescot for the Stanleys; Percival presided over the local assizes, the court leet, on their behalf. One of the principal Stanley estates, Knowsley, was only three or four miles from the town; the family had a long association with actors and acting, and regularly welcomed traveling companies to Knowsley, as well as to their other major Lancashire estates, Lathom and New Hall (MacLean, 2004). The fourth, fifth and sixth earls all patronized their own companies and any one of them might have sanctioned the building of the playhouse in a part of the country where they wielded royal or quasi-royal authority. Henry, the fourth earl, died in September 1593, Ferdinando, the fifth, died the following April, and William, the sixth, lived on until 1642, so which might first have supported Harrington's project depends entirely upon its unknown date.

But Harrington was not going to make a profit by staging daily performances to the local populace, with prices starting at 1d. a head, on the business plan of the Theatre or the Globe. The nearest town of any substance was Liverpool, but even there the population was less than a thousand, and that was some nine miles away – an impractical distance to travel on foot just to see a show. So what might he have had in mind? Graham and Tyler have argued that too strong an emphasis on the poverty of the town ignores important social, cultural, and economic features of the wider community of south Lancashire, describing Prescot as a "surprisingly complex small town that contained quite anomalously high levels of entertainment provision and activity" (2011, 124). The town sustained a weekly market on Tuesdays, where the rich and varied agricultural produce of neighboring regions was traded, alongside goods from much further afield. And in summer it held a fair on the Thursday and Saturday of Corpus Christi, which involved livestock sales and was known of as far away as London. The town apparently adapted to cater for these regular influxes of traders and their customers, having a surprising number of hostelries: "Prescot indeed had a disproportionately large number of alehouses: nineteen in 1592 and an astonishing forty-three by 1626" (121). The town also boasted a cock-fighting den at a time when there were only five in the whole of Lancashire, and it was apparently a magnet for the gentry of much of the county. In a journal entry of June 2, 1618 Nicholas Assheton of Downham Hall near Clitheroe, in the far east of the county, recorded: "We all to Prescod to a cocking. Sir Ric. Cooz Assheton to Leaver. Sir Jo. Talbot of Bashall, Cooz Bradyll, and very pleasant. Tabled all night" (quoted, p. 123). This outing involved a round trip of ninety miles. The pleasure of the cockfighting was magnified many times by the gambling associated with it, and clearly some of those alehouses catered for those who wanted to play backgammon into the early hours.

Looked at in this light Prescot was quite a dynamic community, adept at relieving those who came to visit of their money. And Harrington's playhouse may have been a calculated attempt to cash in further. Even with all these visitors to the town, however, there could hardly have been audiences sufficient to fill even a smallish playhouse on a daily basis in the manner reflected in Henslowe's *Diary*. His marketing strategy must, moreover, have been driven by the availability of performers. It is pretty much unthinkable that he could have employed a permanent local troupe: it was only in the early 1590s that any troupe tried to settle quasi-permanently even in London. It was still overwhelmingly the norm for acting companies to tour, looking for a welcome variously in great houses, guildhalls and town inns (pp. 47–8). South Lancashire, however, posed problems in this regard. Although there were certainly the great houses of the Stanleys in the region and a few lesser gentry who might have welcomed them, there were few towns of any substance and so (one supposes) few inns capable of accommodating substantial audiences in the manner of the inn at Norwich where the Queen's Men had their unfortunate affray (pp. 39–40).

This may help to explain why records of visiting players in the region are so sparse. We do know that the most prestigious groups, including the Queen's Men and Leicester's Men, visited the Stanley properties in the 1580s, but otherwise the record is extremely thin. David George found records of only four notable companies – the Earl of Essex's Men (1594), Lord Vaux's Men (1602–3), the Earl of Hertford's Men (1606) and James Lord Strange's Men (1609) – in the region throughout the entire period of 1593–1609 when he supposes the Prescot playhouse was in operation (2003, 237). He found a few more recorded in Cheshire to the south and Cumberland and Westmoreland in the north and supposes that they may have also visited Lancashire. But there is nothing to substantiate the notion of flourishing professional theatrical touring in the region at this time. This may well in part be the consequence of so few records having survived. Even with the Stanleys, only a single household book, spanning 1587–90, is extant; a few more of those might have painted a very different picture. Yet the geography of the region may also have played its part. The River Mersey to the south and the Pennine hills to the east were significant barriers, neither insurmountable but both deterrents to players who had easier or more lucrative routes to pursue.

Nevertheless, the situation cannot have been so grim that Harrington did not see ways of capitalizing on its opportunities. And one stray piece of information may point to some success. In June 1618 the Prescot Court Leet records give details of an altercation in the town; its constables "present[ed] James Ditchfield for making a tussle upon one of the Queen's Servants, a player, and the said player with others of his fellows for the like upon James Ditchfield. Pledge for them all Henry Stanley Esquire" (Gurr, 1996, 334). As Graham and Tyler show, Ditchfield was an interesting character, the owner of the cockpit and various other properties, operator of an alehouse, and someone repeatedly in trouble for brawling and defying ordinances against gaming. We have no idea why he made "a tussle" with one of Queen Anne's Men. The real question is why members of Queen Anne's Men would have been in Prescot at all at this time. They might, admittedly, have been en route to or from Knowsley. We do know, however, that they had visited Gawthorpe Hall, some thirty miles east, on March 10 of that year, which suggests that they had circulated in the region for at least three months. One possibility is that the Prescot playhouse had been revived by this date (as we shall see, it was certainly out of action in 1609) and that they were in residence for some of that time, as traveling companies continued to do at playhouses like the Curtain and the Swan which never seem to have had permanently resident tenants.

Yet how could this work, given the low level of population? I suggest that it might have worked in precisely the way that the cockpit worked, not by drawing in very large crowds, but by enticing significant numbers of high-end customers like Nicholas Assheton and his cousins to pay a visit on an occasional but regular basis. The real model for the Prescot playhouse may not, then, have been the Theatre but the indoor "private" playhouses favored by the boy companies. Two of these were revived in 1599/1600 – one playing at Paul's playhouse and the other at James Burbage's Blackfriars playhouse (see p. 270). Interestingly, William Stanley, the sixth Earl of Derby, helped finance the revival of the Children of Paul's and worked himself with its playwrights, including John Marston; in the summer of 1599 we was said to have "busied" himself "only in penning comedies for the common players" (Berry, 1986, 34). He would well have understood the business model I am suggesting: offering a select experience for the moneyed class, who would pay higher than ordinary fees; on such a basis, like the reopened boy companies, it might only be necessary to perform as little as once a week to be profitable. Instead of the likes of Queen Anne's Men having to visit multiple gentry houses, the gentry would come to them. With the added attraction of the cockpit and the gaming tables, Prescot's playhouse might have offered an attractive temporary base for traveling companies passing through.

There is, to be sure, not a scrap of evidence that this is how the playhouse was actually operated. But there is one detail in the records of the place which suggests that it might have been an enclosed building rather than an open auditorium, "private" rather than "public" in the London distinctions. Harrington died in 1603, the year the playhouse is first documented, and it passed to his widow, Elizabeth. By 1609 there were problems. The Court Leet presented a Thomas Malbon for converting the playhouse into "a howse for habitacion" and letting it to an undesirable tenant named Whiteside. It seems likely that this Malbon had married the widow Harrington and so taken control of her property. He ignored the Court Leet's findings and did nothing to remove Whiteside, but the following year the Court Leet decided that the tenant was so undesirable that it ordered him to be driven from the town. There is no record of any further tenants and in 1614 Malbon lost control of the property when Elizabeth died. It came under the control of Henry Stanley, the steward of the manor.[26] It seems possible therefore, as I have supposed, that the playhouse was returned to its intended purpose some time after 1610.

So the most persuasive evidence that the playhouse may have been an indoor one lies in the fact that it had, at least for a time, been converted into "a house for habitation." It is difficult to imagine anything built along the lines of the Theatre or the Globe being converted for domestic use. Only the tiring house and any galleries would be covered, and they would constitute an odd domestic dwelling. An indoor theatre, however, would have been roofed from the start and, while its inner space would have been oddly distributed, would have been much more readily adaptable as a habitation. Such conditions might also help to explain how the building survived as late as 1668, still apparently generating "rent, revenue, and profit" for its tenants (George, 2003, 229). A building which was mostly open to the elements would surely have required substantial maintenance to last productively – either as habitation or playhouse – for so long.[27]

Of course the Prescot playhouse was a monopoly. It did not, like the revived boy companies, have to fight to establish niche positions in a competitive market. It was clearly in its interest to try to attract higher-paying gentry on the model I have suggested. But this need not preclude the possibility of catering to more popular audiences, say on market day. Adaptability would have been an important virtue.

The Prescot theatre remains an enigma. It was, for a time, the only purpose-built professional playhouse in the British Isles outside of London. Others would follow, but in substantial cities like York or Bristol. Samuel Daniel's brother, John, set up the Children of Bristol. Their 1615 patent allowed them to play "in and about our ... city of Bristol in such usual houses as themselves shall provide" (*ES*, 2:68). A burgeoning city like Bristol seems, on the face of it, a much more likely prospect for a resident playhouse than Prescot, but we hear little more about the company except for a couple of records of it on tour. In 1635 James Ogilby built a playhouse in St Werburgh Street in Dublin, which would be run for several years by the dramatist, James Shirley; as I have surmised about Prescot, it was an indoor, "private" theatre, catering for a monied audience from among the residents of the Irish pale (Dutton, 2006). But it never exactly flourished, if the tone of the prologues that Shirley wrote are to be trusted, and it was killed off by the Civil War. On the face of it, Prescot faced even greater challenges from the start. London remained stubbornly the home basis of English theatre for many years to come, and Shakespeare's presence there from 1595 onwards played no small part in making that so.

Notes

1 Full documents from the investigation that followed are in Galloway, 1984, 66–76. Quotations here are from *EPF*, 246–50. See also Roberts-Smith, 2006.
2 Edmund Howes in his expansion of John Stowe's *Annals* (1615), 697; as quoted in *ES*, 2: 104–5. Shoreditch, beyond the City walls to the north-east, was the site of the Theatre and the Curtain.

3 This is no place to debate the authorship of *Sir Thomas More* and the additions made to the original manuscript (apparently) after being severely censored by Edmund Tilney. For a thorough recent survey of these issues, see Bate and Rasmussen, 2013, 683–97 (written by Will Sharpe); quotations are from the play in that volume, pp. 349–420. The various parts of the surviving manuscript have, at different times, been dated between 1593 and 1604; one section of the text, dubbed Hand D, is widely believed to be in Shakespeare's handwriting. Neither dating nor authorship is relevant to the discussion here. This part of the play (4.1) is mostly from the original text, in the hand of Anthony Munday and generally thought to be by Munday himself, perhaps with help from Henry Chettle. The last fifty lines or so (after line 275) are from one of the additions, possibly in Thomas Heywood's hand. See also McMillin, 1987.

4 For a fuller discussion of the interlude, and the significance of hair in it, see John Jowett, 2005.

5 *Impatient Poverty*, *Four PP*, *Lusty Juventus*, and *The Marriage of Wit and Wisdom* have all survived, though the text of *The Marriage* is very different from the fragment we see in *Sir Thomas More*.

6 McMillin and MacLean, 1998, 44. This section owes a good deal to their pioneering study.

7 The earliest extant edition of *Tarlton's Jests* dates from 1611, but it seems to have first been printed somewhat earlier.

8 The cloth-quarter was originally a line of booths leading to the site of Bartholomew Fair, which started out as a cloth fair. The joke is that Tarlton, playing a rustic, is cheated of his clothes by Adams, who then distributes the vermin in them – lice, fleas etc. – as if they were precious. Jonson, born in 1572, could have seen this routine.

9 For details of payments made by Henry, Lord Berkeley, one aristocrat fond of entertainment, see Greenfield 1983; also Greenfield 1988.

10 Gurr, 1996, 201, quoting from a licence of the Court of Aldermen, November 28, 1583. The number of their performances was restricted; the licence ran from November 28, 1583 to March 3, 1584 – Shrovetide, the end of the Revels season at court.

11 Charles Howard is better remembered as the Lord Admiral who oversaw the defeat of the Spanish Armada and who was patron of the chief rivals to Shakespeare's Lord Chamberlain's Men in the last decade of Elizabeth's reign. But he was Lord Chamberlain 1583–85 and always seems to have had a particular interest in theatrical matters. He was probably the single most influential figure at court in these matters in the last twenty years of the reign. Edmund Tilney, the Master of the Revels, owed his appointment to him. See Gurr, 2002; Dutton, 1991, 43–5.

12 Cited from Bearman, 2002, 93. Relevant portions of the will are reproduced, pp. 93–4.

13 The case was first fully made in Baker, 1937, and significantly reinforced by E. A. J. Honigmann, 1985. See also Wilson, 2004. The case has met with much resistance (see e.g. Winstanley, 2017). But I only explore it as a *possible* and *plausible* route for Shakespeare into his profession.
14 Quoted in Schoenbaum, 1987, 110. Aubrey had this from William Beeston, son of Christopher Beeston, a leading theatrical manager of the 1630s who was a member of the Chamberlain's Men with Shakespeare in the 1590s. Jonson tells us they performed together in his *Every Man In His Humour* (1598): see p. 140.
15 Details of all patrons and venues discussed here are primarily from the Records of Early English Drama's *Patrons and Performances* website (https://reed.library.utoronto.ca).
16 Such visits had probably been going on since Sir Edward's time, but surviving records only start at the time of his death. The steward who made these entries could not be expected to keep track of all such changes.
17 Details of Sir Cuthbert Halsall's players at Dunkenhalgh Hall are at https://reed.library.utoronto.ca/node/288632. Those for the Warrens' players are at https://reed.library.utoronto.ca/node/288630, 288617, 288644, and 288633.
18 For details of Sir Peter Legh's players, see https://reed.library.utoronto.ca/node/288595 and 288601.
19 Lines 46–55. From a transcript of the poem (BL MS Harley 1927, ff.10v–12), by Lawrence Manley, for which I am most grateful.
20 Andrew Gurr (1993) argues cogently that this was *not* a grand amalgamation of the two companies, as earlier scholars had suggested.
21 The dates and details of these disputes are not easy to follow, though they centered on the sharing of profits from the Theatre. The legal records were printed in C. W. Wallace (1913), from which quotations here derive (pp. 100, 127). But for differences in interpreting them see (e.g.), *ES*, 2: 392–3; and Manley and MacLean, 47–8.
22 There is a fairly general consensus these days that *1 Henry VI* is not solely by Shakespeare, though it was published in the First Folio of his plays. See Taylor, 1995; Vickers, 2007; Chernaik, 2014. But this is not relevant here. *1 Henry VI* remains the earliest text in which Shakespeare had a hand that we can identify in the performance record. It is widely thought that early versions of what we know as *2* and *3 Henry VI* were actually written and performed earlier, but we do not know where or by whom.
23 See p. 16, for an account of the value of money.
24 *A Knack to Know a Knave* is the only one of these to survive in print; on its title page it is uniquely and tellingly described as "played by Ed. Alleyn and his company." Other surviving plays from that season include *Friar Bacon and Friar Bungay*, *Orlando*, and "Jeronymo", which is very probably Kyd's *The Spanish Tragedy*. The attrition rate in terms of non-survivals is typical.

25 Several plays are known to have been notable failures in their first performances, including Ben Jonson's *Sejanus* (1603), *Catiline* (1611), and *The New Inn* (1629), all hissed from the stage – though by the end of the century *Catiline* was the most admired tragedy of its era. Francis Beaumont's *The Knight of the Burning Pestle* (1607) also failed; Walter Burre, its publisher, put it down to "the wide world ... not understanding the privy mark of irony."

26 Henry Stanley was the illegitimate half-brother of the fifth and sixth Earls of Derby; he presided over the Court Leet in the 1618 prosecution of James Ditchfield.

27 The tenants of the playhouse in 1668 were still descendants of Richard Harrington, through his daughter, Jane, who married one Edward Stockley. There is no evidence of when playing might have ceased, if indeed it had recommenced by 1618.

3

Shakespeare on the Record and the Stages of 1594

Newington Butts, the Theatre, Greenwich Palace, and Gray's Inn

Plague

The plague of 1593/4 brought turmoil to the theatre industry. It closed off many venues for playing, and not only in London. All the major companies either went out of business or were reduced to shadows of their former selves, clearly not fit to perform at court. We have already marked the fates of the Queen's Men and Strange's/Derby's Men (pp. 49–50; 65). The fates of others seem to be traced in *Titus Andronicus*'s 1594 claim that "it was played by the Right Honourable the Earl of Derby, Earl of Pembroke and Earl of Sussex their servants." There has been debate over whether this means that the survivors of these three companies collaborated to present it or whether the play was passed from one to the next as they successively failed. But either scenario speaks of some desperation.

The Privy Council and the London authorities were generally in agreement about the danger of the plague and the need to close playhouses there when deaths rose above a certain number. In the 1590s the agreed figure seems to have been thirty deaths a week reported from the combined parishes of London. The draft of a licence for Queen Anne's Men, from around 1604, speaks of them being allowed to play only "when the infection of the plague shall decrease to the number of thirty weekly within our city of London and the liberties thereof" (*ES*, 2: 230). In later documents, such as the King's Men's patent of 1619, the figure is raised to forty. In years like 1593/4 (1603, 1610, and 1625 were similar) the numbers far exceeded that: in a single week in August 1625 3,659 deaths of the plague were registered (Bentley, 1984, 182).

The first hint of final remission of the plague in 1594 is to be found in Henslowe's *Diary*, in a section which begins "In the name of God, Amen. Beginning at Newington my Lord Admiral's Men & my Lord Chamberlain's Men. As followeth" (see Figure 3.1) He then records ten performances between June 3 and 13 (*Henslowe*, 21–2). It is uncertain whether the two companies combined for these performances, or whether they played alternately. But they certainly put on

Shakespeare's Theatre: A History, First Edition. Richard Dutton.
© 2018 Richard Dutton. Published 2018 by John Wiley & Sons Ltd.

Shakespeare's Theatre

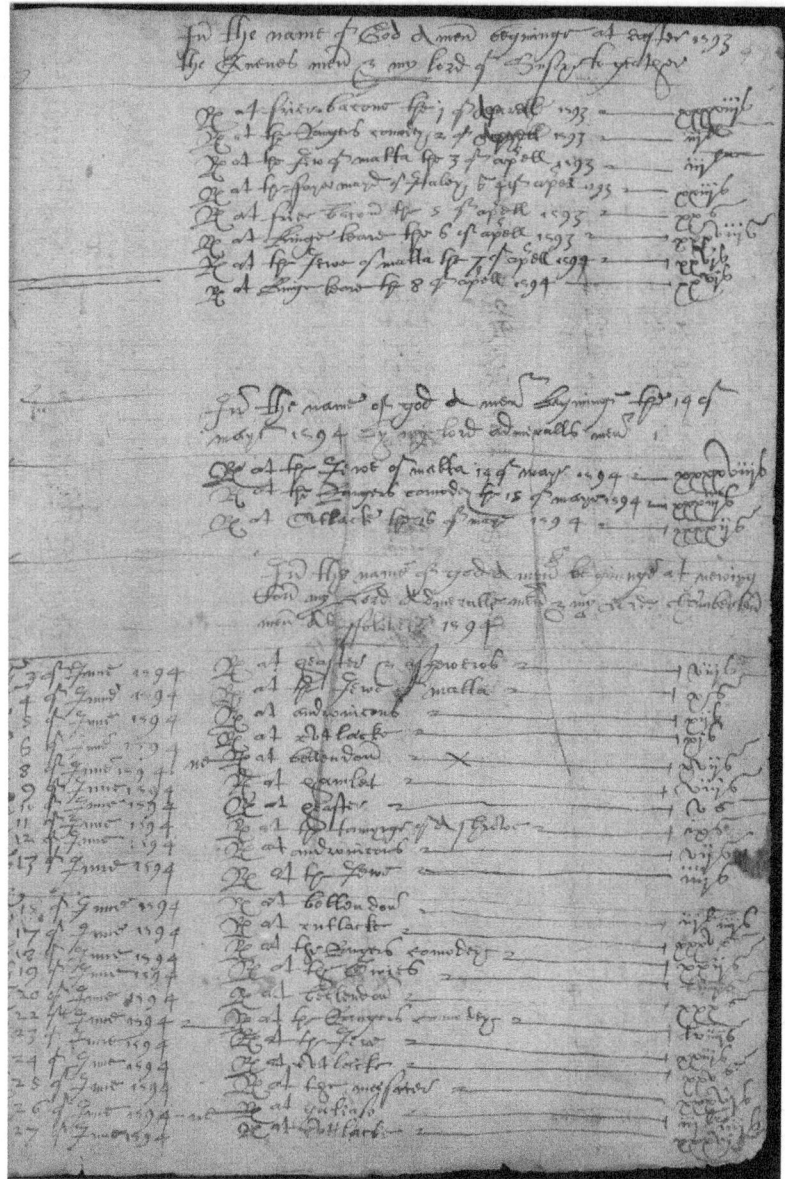

Figure 3.1 Digital reproduction of a page in Philip Henslowe's *Diary*. *Source*: Dulwich College, MS VII f9r, © David Cooper.

plays which would later be identified with the separate companies – Marlowe's *Jew of Malta* with the Admiral's Men and *Titus Andronicus* with the Chamberlain's. Two other titles – *Hamlet* and *The Taming of A Shrew* – are also intriguing, in view of plays subsequently associated with Shakespeare.

Newington Butts is one of the more obscure playhouses of the era. It was first built by Jerome Savage, a leading player with the Earl of Warwick's Men, about the same time that James Burbage was building the Theatre (Ingram, 1992, 163–81). As Burbage was, at least in part, providing a London base to Leicester's Men, Savage was presumably aiming to do the same for Warwick's. But they failed to flourish after the defection of the Dutton brothers (see p. 34); and the playhouse similarly did poor trade "by reason of the tediousness of the way," it was said in 1591/2, "and that of long time plays have not there been used on working days" (*ES*, 2: 405).

The village of Newington was indeed one mile south of London Bridge, which was itself a similar distance from the main residential areas of the city. And it could hardly have been very profitable if it normally only opened on holidays. The work-week was six days, but playing was (after 1579) at least notionally forbidden on Sundays – the one day when most working people would otherwise have been free to go.[1] Festival holidays included the Twelve Days of Christmas, Plough Monday, Candlemas, Shrove Tuesday, the four quarter days, May Day, and Halloween –about three a month in the Anglican Church calendar, averaged over the year. Henslowe's records make it quite plain that the Rose (and doubtless all the other successful theatres) operated on most days of the working week, doubtless attracting those who did not have to work, such as students at the Inns of Court, but also some workers and apprentices on afternoons when they really should have been at their trade.[2] The likeliest reason for the choice of Newington Butts as the first venue for what were in fact two new companies is that it was the furthest playhouse from the city – a prudent first step as the plague at long last receded.

Duopoly

But it lasted only briefly and by the middle of June the Admiral's Men moved to the Rose and the Chamberlain's Men to the Theatre. This was the beginning of what has come to be called the duopoly of these two companies in London playing. How exactly it came about is a matter for some debate. Andrew Gurr has argued most vigorously that it was engineered by the Privy Council – most specifically Lord Chamberlain Hunsdon and his son-in-law, Lord Admiral Howard – to continue the policy first evident in the creation of the Queen's Men:

> In effect, the Lord Admiral and the Lord Chamberlain worked together to set up a pair of new companies to replace the now divided Queen's Men.

> Setting up two companies was a better guarantee for the supply of the Queen's plays each Christmas than one had been. They drew the player membership from some of the major companies which had recently lost their patrons. They based the new groupings on the two chief impresarios who owned playhouses in the suburbs, James Burbage and Philip Henslowe, and their heirs, Richard Burbage and Edward Alleyn. They resolved the chronic problem of relations with the city by banning all playing from city inns, and instead specified as the only authorized playing places Henslowe's Rose and Burbage's Theatre. Henceforth the companies were denied any access to playing within the Lord Mayor's bailiwick.
>
> *(Gurr 2002, 236–7; see also Gurr, 1996, chapter 4)*

But we do not have the documentation for such Privy Council action as we do for the creation of the Queen's Men, and there have been several objections to the scenario Gurr outlines. Roslyn Knutson, for example, has argued that the two companies emerged this way by a process of friendly commercial rivalry rather than political fiat (2001, 8–9). And Holger Schott Syme has objected that Gurr builds inferences (such as that popularity at court equates with popularity in the public playhouses, or that it was specific policy to restrict the number of settled London companies to two) for which there is simply no evidence (2010). Gurr in effect argues from outcomes. It is certainly the case that these were the only two companies invited to perform at court in the seasons from 1594/5 to 1598/9 and they remained by some margin the dominant figures there until the end of the reign. It is less certain that the Rose and the Theatre were explicitly the only playing places to be allowed; the Curtain remained available and in 1595 Francis Langley, a goldsmith, built the Swan some distance downriver from the Rose and with others converted the Boar's Head Inn in Whitechapel into a true theatre in 1598/9 (see Figure 3.2). He presumably would not have done this if there was no question of their use by actors. On the other hand, the Swan project went seriously awry in 1597 and the Boar's Head was only successful for a short time. Other companies clearly did play in London from time to time, but it took serious patronage to allow them to settle there for prolonged periods or to gain access to court. On the question of playing in the city inns (the Boar's Head was outside the city): if there was an agreement with the city authorities to end this in 1594 Hunsdon himself broke it as early as that October with a request for his Lord Chamberlain's Men to be allowed to use the Cross Keys that winter (p. 114). Most scholars agree that the practice had indeed ceased by 1596, but even that has been disputed (Menzer, 2006*b*).

I will add this one observation to the controversy, which I have not seen voiced elsewhere. At some point in the 1590s, it became normal for plays in public playhouses to start at 2 p.m. Thomas Platter confirms this

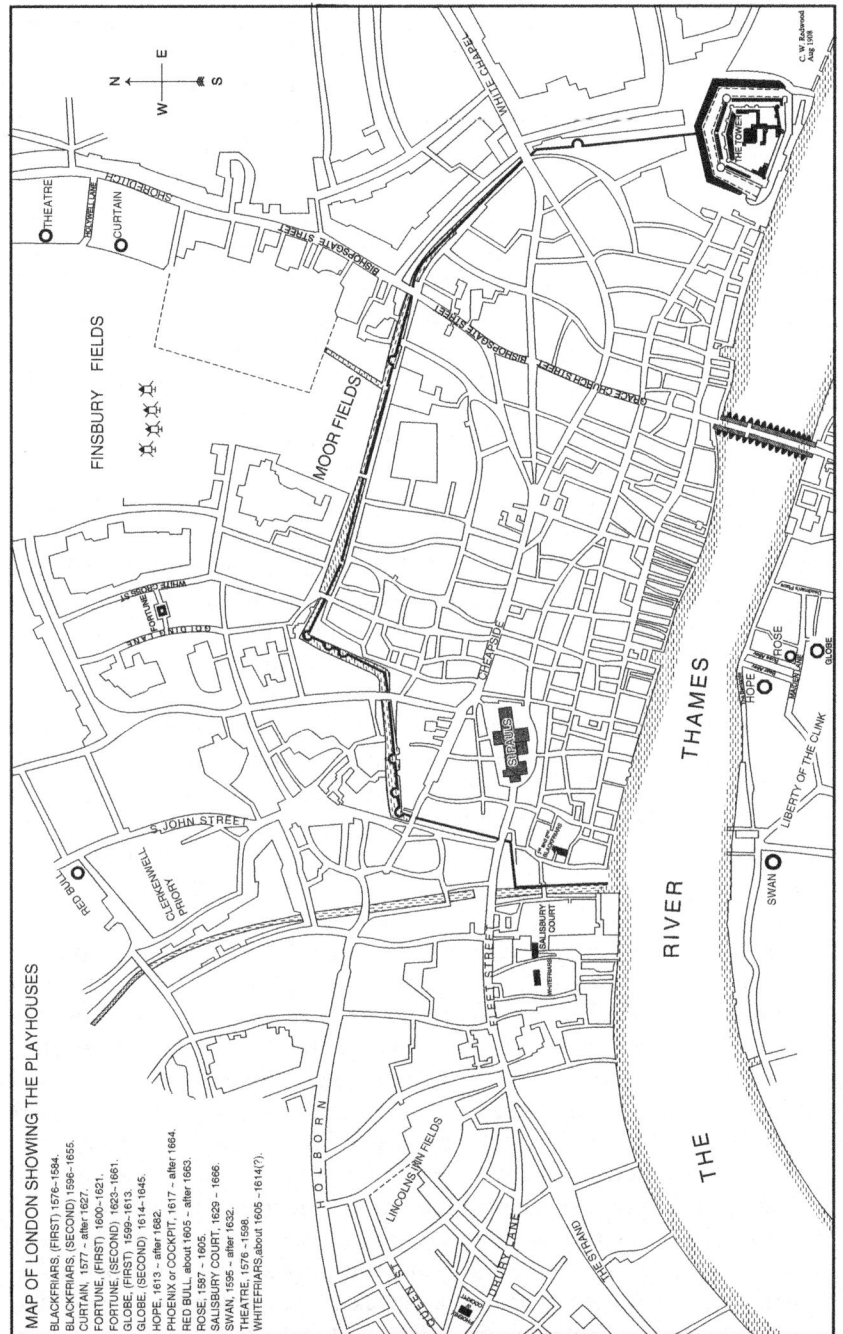

Figure 3.2 A map showing the London theatres of Shakespeare's day. *Source:* First published in *Shakespeare's Playhouses*, J. Q. Adams (1917).

in 1599: "And thus every day at two o'clock in the afternoon in ... London two and sometimes three comedies are performed at separate places wherewith folk make merry together" (*EPF*, 413). It is not clear if this included those festival holy-days which we noticed in respect of Newington Butts.[3] They had for years been a source of friction in negotiations between the Privy Council and the City of London authorities. On these days (and perhaps others) evensong was observed, between 2 p.m. and perhaps 4 p.m., and the Privy Council had respected a condition that playing should not clash with it. In the 1574 royal patent that Leicester's Men received, for example, it was an express condition that they should not play "in the time of common prayer" (*ES*, 2: 88).

In 1582 the Privy Council tried to argue with the Lord Mayor that playing should be allowed "*after* evening prayer, as long as the season of the year may permit" (*ES*, 4: 288; my emphasis). The Lord Mayor, however, replied that this could "very hardly be done. For though they begin not their plays till after evening prayer, yet all the time of the afternoon before they take in hearers and fill the place with such as be thereby absent from serving God at Church ... if for remedy hereof I should also restrain the letting in of the people till after service in the Church, it would drive the action of their plays into very inconvenient time of night ..." (ibid.). In 1584 the Queen's Men petitioned the Common Council of London for greater freedom to perform in the City, citing in turn the inconvenience of playing into the night. This drew sarcasm when the Council explained their response to the Privy Council:

> If in winter the dark do carry inconvenience, and the short time of day after evening prayer do leave them no leisure, and foulness of season do hinder the passage into the fields to plays, the remedy is ill-conceived to bring them into London, but the true remedy is to leave of that unnecessary expense of time, whereunto God himself giveth so many impediments. (*ES*, 4: 301)

We hear no more of this quarrel in the 1590s. And the first we hear of 2 p.m. as a regular start time for playing is that 1594 letter, mentioned above, in which Lord Chamberlain Hunsdon asked permission for his new company of players to perform at the Cross Keys, which stipulated that "where heretofore they began not their plays till towards four o'clock, they will now begin at two and have done between four and five" (*ES*, 4: 316). It is not clear if the previous start time of 4 p.m. applied *only* to holy-days, in order to avoid evensong, but Hunsdon makes no discrimination at all – as if the 2 p.m. start will apply in all cases, in which case performances would be in direct conflict with evensong. But they would end in time to avoid what all parties recognized as a major inconvenience, for players, audiences, and authorities alike – performances that ran on into darkness. Might this speak to some kind of negotiated settlement between the Privy Council and the City fathers?[4]

Shakespeare in the Records

On March 15, 1595 William Shakespeare finally entered the written record as the member of an acting company, the Lord Chamberlain's Men. The Treasurer of the Chamber's Accounts record: "To William Kemp, William Shakespeare and Richard Burbage, servants to the Lord Chamberlain, upon the Council's warrant ... for two several comedies or interludes showed by them before her Majesty in Christmas time last past, viz. upon St. Stephen's Day [26 December] and Innocents" Day [28 December] £13 6s. 8d. and by way of her Majesty's reward £6 13s. and 4d." (*ES*, 4: 164–5). Other than the inclusion of Shakespeare's name this is a very typical entry. It was normal that a senior member or members of the company, trusted by their colleagues, would be paid for performances at court. In later years the most regular payee was John Heminge, who emerged over time as a kind of company manager. But in this first year they sent Kemp, the most famous living clown; Burbage was not yet the great tragedian he was to become, but was presumably there because he represented the company's association with its now-normal London home, the Theatre; and Shakespeare's presence suggests that he had acquired some stature in his earlier company associations, even though we cannot trace them in the records.

The amounts they received add up to £10 per performance, normal totals when the monarch was present. The division of the sums into a fee and the Queen's "reward" was a formality, but a reminder that performance at court was not simply a commercial activity. The players were "servants" of a leading aristocrat (and indeed Elizabeth's first cousin) and they came to court – very much as they would come to another great house or a city guildhall – in the spirit of a gift-offering from their patron to their sovereign. So the Queen not only paid them for their pains, but awarded them a gratuity – a gift-offering of her own – in addition. In many ways this sums up the midway status of Elizabethan players between being lowly figures in a traditional, deferential, hierarchical class system (and "vagabonds" if they strayed outside it) and commercial entrepreneurs, a lucky few of whom made very substantial wealth by skill and shrewd investment.

It was clearly the case that those lucky enough to be allowed to play regularly in London made most of their money out of playing in their theatres; the court payments could never have been more than a fraction of their total income (Dutton, 2016, 13–14). On the other hand, they were well aware that regular London playing was a privilege only made possible by the court's authority. They needed each other. Besides, court performances took place at night, after supper, starting usually around 9 p.m.; in most cases the company would have given one of their usual performances at the Theatre in the afternoon and then made their way to court (another virtue of being "done between four and five"). This was an opportunity to make *extra* money that would not otherwise be available.

These Chamber Accounts tell us the dates of performances but not what was played. Between 1594 and the Queen's death in 1603 the only plays we know with certainty that Shakespeare's company put on at court (because title pages of early editions tell us) are *Love's Labour's Lost* and *The Merry Wives of Windsor*. But even there we do not know on which dates. We can make shrewd guesses about other titles and particular dates, but this is another of those glasses in which we see darkly. In the 1595 record we may not even be able to trust the Chamber accounts about one of the dates. On the evening of December 28, 1594, as we shall see, the Chamberlain's Men gave a performance of *The Comedy of Errors* at Gray's Inn, one of the Inns of Court or law schools in London; it is unlikely that they played twice in the same evening in venues so far apart (the court was then resident in Greenwich, some five miles south of the city). Besides, the Admiral's Men are also credited in the accounts with appearing at court on that date, and while it was not unknown for two companies to appear on the same evening it was not common. So the Chamberlain's Men probably appeared on the 27th. The St. Stephen's Day date, however, is almost certainly correct. In the latter half of Elizabeth's reign that was invariably the first day of the Revels season (which extended intermittently through Candlemas to Shrove Tuesday, the day before Ash Wednesday), and from 1595 the Chamberlain's Men occupied that opening slot until the end of her reign. That first year the Admiral's Men received payment for three appearances (one of their payees was Edward Alleyn), the Chamberlain's only two. But the proportions of court performances thereafter almost always favored Shakespeare's company.

Four Playing Places

After finding no trace of Shakespeare in earlier records we suddenly can place him with some precision in five distinct playing-places in 1594, assuming that he was part of the Chamberlain's Men from the company's inception: Newington Butts; the Theatre; the Cross Keys inn; the court at Greenwich; and Gray's Inn. I have already covered all that we usefully know about Newington Butts (p. 77) and will turn to the other four in order.

But first, a word of caution. I want to remind you that my Introduction devoted many words telling you how much we do *not* know about Elizabethan playing spaces. This is where that rubber touches the road. We think of a typical playhouse as having, like "Shakespeare's Globe" in Southwark, a "heavens" and supporting pillars, a "hell" beneath the stage, trapdoors, a discovery space, lords' rooms, descent machinery, and other familiar furniture. But we can only know whether any particular playhouse had any or all of these features – or had them from when it was first built – if evidence fortuitously survives: in building contracts, in records left by visitors (usually foreigners), in the texts of plays performed there (remembering always that if a play was printed long after its earliest performances, it might reflect staging in another place).

In the search for the historical truth about such matters we are in fact often forced to fall back on "best-guesses," hoping that something we can identify in one playhouse was common to them all or that something true in 1594 was still true in 1609. As I make my way through the public playhouses which Shakespeare is known to have used (after his presumed early experience at the Rose) – the Theatre, the Curtain and the Globe – and the one private playhouse for which he wrote, the Blackfriars, I shall address all of these issues as and when the evidence accumulates to a credible pitch, relying as much as I can on the plays likely to have been played in those venues. I can, however, immediately address the distinction between "public" and "private" playhouses, lest these terms give rise to misconceptions.

They were all in fact "public," in the sense that anyone who had the money could pay to see a play there. But the "private" playhouses charged considerably more for entrance – the minimum for the Blackfriars was 6d., against 1d. for the Globe – so some of the key distinctions were social and economic. But there were also very distinct differences in the designs of their theatrical spaces. The "public" playhouses were what we commonly think of as *the* Elizabethan theatres, amphitheaters largely open to the elements, whose design seems to have owed something both to animal-baiting houses and galleried inn-yards, such as that in Norwich where we observed the Queen's Men. The "private" playhouses were enclosed auditoria, perhaps more appropriately known as hall theatres, "built in large rooms on the model of the banqueting halls in royal palaces and great houses where plays were provided for banqueting guests" – the kinds of great houses Shakespeare would have visited with any major troupe touring the country in the 1580s (Gurr, 2004*b*, 14). The Blackfriars theatre in Staunton, Virginia, and the Sam Wanamaker Playhouse erected close to "Shakespeare's Globe" both approximate such a theatre, while the Prescot theatre planned by Shakespeare North on Merseyside is to be based on one, specifically the design by Inigo Jones for the Cockpit-in-Court theatre in Whitehall palace (1629). It was around the time the boy companies were revived in 1599/1600 – Paul's boys and the Children of the Chapel – that a kind of snobbish antagonism grew up in the use of "public" and "private" designations. The adult companies exclusively used "public" playhouses at this time, while the boys always performed in their "private" halls. But that distinction disappeared within a decade. The boy companies virtually went out of business, and Shakespeare's company found itself using both a public and a private playhouse. But their first resident base in London was the Theatre.

The Theatre

Why did Burbage and Brayne choose to locate the Theatre where they did in 1576? They built it in part of the dissolved priory of Holywell in Shoreditch, five hundred yards beyond the north-east wall of the City, across Finsbury

Fields – largely open land at that time.[5] We have already seen that when Philip Henslowe first built a playhouse, some eleven years later, he did so in the Liberty of Clink on the Bankside – diametrically the opposite side of London (p. 12). The key common feature of the two locations – and those of every new playhouse down to the Civil War of the 1640s – is that they fell outside the jurisdiction of the City of London authorities: the Lord Mayor, the Court of Aldermen, and the Common Council.

It seems very likely that what settled the minds of Burbage, Brayne, Henslowe, and all other builders of playhouses against sites within the City was an Act of the Common Council of December 6, 1574; this in turn was clearly a response to the royal patent issued to Leicester's Men earlier that year. That patent gave certain players royal authority to perform "as well within our City of London and liberties of the same, as also within the liberties and freedoms of any our cities, towns, boroughs etc. ... without any your lets, hindrance or molestation" (*EPF*, 206). It also required that their plays should be "seen and allowed" by the Master of the Revels. (Continued on p. 91).

Box 3.1 Masters of the Revels

The Masters of the Revels were the most important officials with whom the actors of Shakespeare's day had to conduct business on a regular basis. They had two functions: one was to ensure that entertainment of suitable quality was available to the royal court, especially during the midwinter Revels season that ran from Christmas (or, under James I, often as early as November 1, All Saints) until Shrove Tuesday, the day before Ash Wednesday and Lent; his other function was to censor and licence all plays that were to be performed in public.

There had been Masters of the Revels under all the Tudor monarchs, who were mainly concerned with helping the court to entertain itself, aided by an office staff which provided costumes and stage shows, supplying any necessary scenery, properties and lighting (Streitberger, 2016). The emphasis changed somewhat in 1579 when Edmund Tilney was appointed to the position. Expenses in the Revels Office had been running out of control and it was key to his remit that they be reined in. His main strategy for achieving this was to rely far less on expensive masques and shows staged by the courtiers themselves and to hire in the most successful professional players on a much more regular basis than hitherto. This was doubtless aided by the fact that leading troupes like the Earl of Leicester's and Earl of Warwick's Men now had London bases (the Theatre, Newington Butts), where they could build up their own stock of costumes and properties, relieving the Revels Office of the need to supply them.

In 1581 Tilney was given a Special Commission which empowered him to compel workmen to help with court theatricals at fixed wages and to require any players he saw fit to come and rehearse their repertory before him. So in his annual claim for attendance fees at court (this is for 1587/88) Tilney would claim for "attending, making choice, perusing, reforming & altering of such plays, comedies, masques and inventions as were prepared, set forth & presented before her Majesty" (Feuillerat, 1908, 379). And in his *Apology for Actors*, Thomas Heywood recalled how the players used to visit the old Palace of St John in Clerkenwell where Tilney lodged and kept "the office of the Revels, where our court plays have been in late days yearly rehearsed, perfected, and corrected before they come to the public view of the prince and the nobility" (E1v; 1607/8; printed 1612).[6]

By 1594 Tilney had been in office for fifteen years and knew more about London theatre than anyone else alive. He had been the one who enacted the Privy Council's order for the creation of the Queen's Men in 1583 and he had overseen a whole generation of playwrights – notably John Lyly, George Peele, Thomas Lodge, Robert Greene, Christopher Marlowe, and Thomas Kyd – who were either dead or had given up playwrighting by this date. He may well have had a hand in the formation of the Lord Chamberlain's Men, as he had the Queen's Men, but no record of this survives. He was certainly responsible, however, for ensuring that they performed at court every year for the remainder of Elizabeth's reign, never less than twice and once (1596/7) as often six times. We see that *Love's Labour's Lost* was published in 1598, proclaiming itself on the title-page to be "*A pleasant conceited comedy ... As it was presented before her Highness this last Christmas. Newly corrected and augmented by W. Shakespere*." Since no earlier version of the play exists we cannot know what was "*corrected and augmented*," but there is a good chance that the work was done in preparation for the mentioned performance at court and under Tilney's active supervision. *King Lear* was published in 1608 "*As it was played before the King's Majesty at Whitehall upon S. Stephen's night in Christmas Holidays. By his Majesty's servants playing usually at the Globe on the Bankside*." As Andrew Gurr argues, that play clearly glances at James I's wish to unite his two kingdoms: "It is difficult not to assume from this that the Master of the Revels could only have approved *King Lear* for a performance at court because he had thought the play supported the king's position over the question of uniting the kingdoms" (1996, 33). The wording on the title-page also opens up the possible inference that the version offered at court was not that audiences might see when the company was "*playing usually at the Globe*" (Dutton, 2016).

In such contexts we must see Tilney as an active collaborator with Shakespeare and others whose plays were being prepared for court performance. Contrary to the impression given by the film, *Shakespeare in Love* (1999; dir. John Madden), he was a man of some sophistication.[7] A distant cousin of the Queen, he had dedicated to her *A brief and pleasant discourse of the duties in Marriage, called the Flower of Friendship* (1568; Tilney, 1992), a dialogue in the manner of Baldasare Castiglione's influential *Book of the Courtier*: it went through at least five editions in his lifetime. He also prepared a substantial document called *Topographical Descriptions, Regiments, and Policies*; focusing on eight key European countries, it demonstrates his wide knowledge of international history, customs, diplomacy, and genealogy. Tilney intended to present it (handsomely decorated with the coats of arms of many of Europe's leading families) to the Queen, but she died before he completed it; he started work on a version dedicated to King James, but again never presented the manuscript to him (Streitberger, 1986*a*).

So Tilney might have been a congenial and knowledgeable colleague in preparing plays for the court. But he could also be a strict overseer when it came to censoring and licensing plays for public performance. In 1589, at the height of the Martin Marprelate scandal (a series of puritan satirical pamphlets, attacking the Church of England) order was given "for the stay of all plays within the City, in that Mr. Tilney did utterly mislike the same," apparently because "the players take upon themselves to handle in their plays certain matters of divinity and of state unfit to be suffered."[8] The wording of this suggests that Tilney was not disturbed that the players might support "Martin" but that he felt they should not involve themselves in matters of state at all, presumably defying his authority in presenting plays that he had refused to licence. We also have the evidence of one play manuscript which has survived, bearing the evidence of his censorship. This is *Sir Thomas More*, the main body of which is in the hand of the playwright Anthony Munday (see p. 42). At the head of the document Tilney has written: "Leave out the insurrection wholly and the cause thereof, & begin with Sir Thomas More at the Mayor's sessions [i.e. scene 2], with a report afterwards of his service done being Sheriff of London upon a mutiny against the Lombards. Only by a short report & not otherwise. At your own perils. E. Tilney" (Dutton 1991, Plate 7).

This refers to the play's graphic depiction of the notorious "Ill May Day" riots of 1517, which More was instrumental in suppressing. Those riots had been aimed at foreign workers in London, resented for edging out English jobs. There were similar disturbances in the early 1590s, particularly directed at Dutch, Flemish, and French Huguenot immigrants. It seems reasonable to infer that these were Tilney's principal concerns in respect of the play; he did not want it to further inflame public disorder. He does not want any live-action rioting on stage; he wants the report of the riots to specify the Lombards from Italy as targets (a less prominent group); and he wants the report *short*. Just as interesting as this peremptory intervention, however, is the relative lack of marking by Tilney elsewhere. This is striking in a play about a man who was executed for refusing to accept Henry VIII's Act of Supremacy, which made him something of a Roman Catholic martyr. We might have expected that this alone would have made it unacceptable. The play itself is careful about the most sensitive issues: Henry himself (the Queen's father) does not appear, while the text is studiously unspecific about the "Articles" to which More refuses to subscribe. There is to be sure one passage where More and the Bishop of Rochester refuse to subscribe while the Earls of Surrey and Shrewsbury do so all too avidly, to which Tilney evidently objected (his comment is now illegible). But this still demonstrates significant restraint in the face of what might be seen as serious provocation. Tilney did not reject the play out of hand and indeed seems to have wanted to work with the players and their author(s) to make it performable. Several passages not in Munday's hand have survived alongside the main manuscript, and these are perhaps evidence that there was indeed an attempt to rewrite the play in acceptable form, though there are debates about when exactly this might have happened (see p. 72 and note 3). One of the new passages is commonly thought to be in Shakespeare's handwriting (it is traditionally dubbed "Hand D"). None of the new passages shows Tilney's attentions and it is not known if the play was ever actually staged.

Another instance of a Master of the Revels doing his best to make a play acceptable is found in the manuscript of *Sir John Van Olden Barnavelt*, written by John Fletcher and Philip Massinger in 1619. The Bishop of London initially ordered that the play be "stayed" until it was shown to be acceptable. This play was also on a sensitive subject, since the executed Barnavelt had been an influential statesman in the Protestant Netherlands, which had for many years been England's closest ally. He had fallen out with Prince Maurice of Nassau (latterly Prince of Orange), who carried a degree of inherited status in what was otherwise a republic. Among their differences was religion, since Barnavelt had sided with the Arminians, a Christian sect at odds with the state's dominant Calvinists. This would resonate in England, where there were similar divisions and this is probably why, even after Sir George Buc, Tilney's successor, had licensed the play and the King's Men had spent money acquiring properties, the Bishop of London briefly prohibited its performance (Dutton, 1991, 207).

When we review the manuscript we can see the care Buc had taken. As T. H. Howard-Hill describes it:

> Buc read the manuscript pencil in hand, marking passages for scrutiny at another time in a variety of ways. Once the drift of the play was clear in his mind he went back to the manuscript again, paying particular attention to the passages he had previously marked in pencil. Some pencil markings he did not pursue; others elicited more emphatic ink crosses, marginal deletions, crossing out, and interlineations and … [a] well-known marginal note … *I like not this*. The second reading need not have been achieved at a single sitting, nor need Buc's markings have been inserted without consultation with the scribe, acting for the authors.
>
> (Fletcher and Massinger, 1980, ix–x)

All of this shows Buc's careful attention to numerous issues, including references to persons of note in both England and the Netherlands during

Barnavelt's career (including both Queen Elizabeth and King James), to religious affairs, and various other matters. A good example is a passage during Barnavelt's trial (lines 2343–55 in Howard-Hill's cited edition) in which he draws analogies between what was happening in the Netherlands and Augustus Caesar's transformation of the Roman republic into a monarchy, warning (with a blunt "you can apply this") against a time "when too late you see this government / Chained to a monarchy" (2349, 2353–4). It is a clear reference to Prince Maurice's supposed ambitions. Buc tried to make it acceptable. He crossed out the provocative "you can apply this" and "monarchy," but made several suggestions of his own. Only latterly did he mark the whole passage for deletion, apparently having decided that it could not be redeemed, something that rarely happens in the text. But he had worked hard to save it and evidently satisfied even the Bishop of London, since the play was shortly allowed to be performed.

The "well-known marginal note" to which Howard-Hill refers relates to the play's marked antipathy to Prince Maurice, which Buc monitored closely, finally snapping at lines 385–403, where he wrote in the margin "I like not this: neither do I think that the prince was thus disgracefully used. Besides, he is too much presented" (Dutton, 1991, Plate 9). This shows sensitivity to the status of a man who was virtually ruler of a friendly foreign state, something Masters of the Revels evidently kept their eyes on – they were not supposed to allow depictions of "living Christian monarchs" at all. But it also reflects Buc's personal knowledge of the people and circumstances of the play, since in 1601 he had been sent on a diplomatic mission to the Netherlands, carrying personal instructions from Queen Elizabeth and Sir Robert Cecil to Prince Maurice and other principals who appear in the play. Like Tilney, he was no faceless bureaucrat. Like Tilney too he owed his appointment as Master of the Revels (against strong competition from the dramatist John Lyly) to the patronage of Lord Admiral Howard (see p. 129). And he was a historian of some note. His account of the 1596 Cadiz expedition under Howard appeared in John Stow's *Annals* (1601). The first work under his own name was *Daphnis Polystephanos: an Eclog Treating of Crowns, and of Garlands*, a poem honoring James I's coronation and celebrating the king's ancestors. Later published work included his "Third University of England," printed as an appendix to the 1615 continuation of the *Annals*, and surveying the subjects – the arts, sciences, and professions (law, divinity, medicine) – which can be studied in London, even though the city boasted no university.

Buc's most important works, however, were not published in his lifetime and some have not survived at all. Most important of these is a revisionist *History of King Richard the Third*, a much more sympathetic account than the one we know from Sir Thomas More and Shakespeare (Buck, 1982). *The Baron* was a massive historical review of English titles and offices, but only some notes towards it have survived. We also know he wrote an "art of revels," but none of that survives. It suggests, however, that he saw his position as Master of the Revels as something that involved far more than simply importing the best commercial fare available.

Tilney continued in office until he died in 1610 and so would have licensed the great majority of Shakespeare's plays; Buc probably only licensed *The Tempest*, *Henry VIII*, *The Two Noble Kinsmen*, and the lost *Cardenio*. Tilney probably therefore had some involvement in what is usually regarded as the clearest case of censorship among Shakespeare's own works. When his *Richard II* was published in 1597 it did not include what is usually called the Parliament Scene, some 163 lines of Act 4 Sc.1 (from Northumberland's "May it please you, lords, to grant the Commons' suit to Richard's "Conveyors are you all, / That rise thus nimbly by a true king's fall," including the sequence where the fallen king examines his face in a mirror, which he then breaks). This passage did not appear until the fourth printing of the play, in 1608, when some copies carried a title-page which announced "With new additions of the Parliament Scene, and the deposing of King Richard."

Why the passage did not appear earlier is less clear than often assumed. It may have been part of Shakespeare's original manuscript but censored by Tilney. It may have been cut at the time of the 1597 printing. It did not go to one of the clerical censors who usually licensed printed books at this date – plays were often treated as ephemera like ballads, and the Master and Wardens of the Stationers' Company vouched for them without a formal licence. So it may have been they who called for the cut, or the players might prudentially have cut it themselves. Conversely, the passage may not have existed at all in 1597 and been written around the time of the 1608 printing ("With new additions").

One striking feature is that the "cut" is virtually invisible if you didn't know it existed. In 1597 the text jumps from the arrest of the Bishop of Carlisle for high treason to Bolingbroke announcing the date of his coronation and the Abbot of Westminster lamenting "A woeful pageant have we here beheld" – the "pageant" logically being Carlisle's arrest and Bolingbroke's assumption of royal power. The 1608 text inserts a long display of Richard's narcissistic self-pity in which he sidesteps admitting to any crimes, but ceremonially abdicates and ponders on the new identity – or lack of identity – this confers on him. In a play where Richard is clearly deposed, and later murdered, why should this apparently innocuous passage have been singled out for censorship? By far the most convincing explanation is one advanced by Cyndia Susan Clegg, who notes that the "new additions" are indeed clearly a "Parliament Scene," led off by Northumberland's introduction of a "the Commons' suit" – a motion from the House of Commons to the House of Lords – which seeks to confer legitimacy on the transfer of power (1997). In 1597, with Elizabeth's long reign drawing to an inevitable end, there was neither an acknowledged successor nor an agreed mechanism for finding one. The suggestion that Parliament alone might have the authority of do this was one that Elizabeth was unlikely to find welcome. By 1608, when James I had three healthy children and the succession was secure, the issue was far less loaded and someone may have felt it was safe to reinsert the passage. Conversely, however, there is also the possibility that the play was old and needed an injection of new material, which would take the form of a virtuoso passage for the lead role, presumably played by Richard Burbage. Tilney would certainly have had to be consulted (and paid) either way – to allow censored material to be restored or new material added for the revival.

Although it is difficult to discern exactly what happened here, it is a salutary reminder that the Master of the Revels was a constant presence in the working lives of the players and their authors. A later Master, Sir Henry Herbert, certainly had a reserved box in each playhouse and it is likely that Tilney and Buc had them before him (*Herbert*, 214). And, in the way of early modern monopolies, they made a handsome profit from their royal authority. In the 1590s they charged 7 shillings (about a third of a pound) to licence a play for performance; by the 1620s this had become one pound. They also charged the owners of the playhouses for a licence to stage their shows – 5 shillings a week in the early 1590s rising steeply to three pounds a month by 1600 (*Henslowe*, 32–7 ["mr pd"]; 162. *Herbert*, *passim*). These were heavy taxes to carry, but they were the cost of doing business. The Masters of the Revels, and the royal authority which they represented, were what allowed the leading companies, like Shakespeare's, to operate and flourish in the growing London market.

It was a symbiotic relationship, from which they both profited. As far as we can tell Shakespeare and his fellows recognized this fact and respected it. This impression may simply be down to the fact that the office-books of Tilney and Buc have not survived, as that of Sir Henry Herbert has, at least in part (E. Collins, 2013). Had they survived, the situation might have looked very different. Herbert, for example, records the King's Men performing an unlicensed play, *The Spanish Viceroy* in 1624 and resenting his peremptory order not to revive Fletcher's *The Tamer Tamed*, a play that had acquired topical overtones by the 1630s (*Herbert*, 183, 182–3). But there is no record of any such behavior in Shakespeare's time. They occasionally staged plays which caused some controversy, but in instances where Tilney's own judgment seems to have been at fault. Jonson's *Sejanus*, for example, incurred the wrath of the Earl of Northampton, and a lost play of *Gowrie* – about a well-known plot against James when he was King of Scotland – displeased some members of the Privy Council:

> the tragedy of Gowrie with all the action and actors hath been twice represented by the King's players, with exceeding concourse of all sorts of people. But whether the matter or manner be not well handled, or that it be thought unfit that princes should be played on the stage in their life

> time, I hear that some great councilors are much displeased with it: and so is thought shall be forbidden.
> (Chamberlain, 1939, 1.199)
>
> But in neither case is there any suggestion that the plays did not carry Tilney's licence, an offense which might have had serious repercussions, as indeed unlicensed performance of *Eastward Ho!* by the Children of the Queen's Revels (Hamlet's "little eyases") had for Jonson and Chapman in 1605. That company had its own separate licencer (see p. 281). All of these instances probably reflect the tensions in the early years of James's reign, where there was jockeying for power under the new regime, some of it by the Scots he had brought down with him. The licensing system operated by Tilney seems normally to have been effective in minimizing the overflow of these tensions on to the stage. In 1601 his regime had probably helped the Chamberlain's Men to represent their performance of a play of Richard II (very possibly Shakespeare's) on the eve of the Essex rebellion as a normal commercial transaction rather than an act of subversion (see p. 135).

(Continued from p. 84)

The Master of the Revels challenged the authority of the City to police playing, either in relation to playing places or in respect of censoring and licensing what was played. The 1574 Act of the Common Council robustly reasserted that authority (*EPF*, 73–7). It fulminated against "sundry great disorders and inconveniences [that] have been found to ensue to this City by the inordinate hauntings of great multitudes of people, specially youths, to plays, interludes and shows," "talking of frays," "evil practices of incontinency," "inveighing and alluring of maids" and more; it speaks as if playhouses were the only sites for the transmission of the plague, if not indeed its cause. It then imposes the City's own controls over what can be played and in what buildings, applying stiff fines for transgressions. And latterly it raises the issue of taxation: "every person so to be licensed or permitted shall ... pay or cause to be paid to the use of the poor in hospitals of the City, or of the poor of the City visited with sickness, by the discretion of the said Lord Mayor and Aldermen, such sums and payments and in such form as ... shall be agreed."

Rather than submit himself to such constraints, Burbage probably felt he had no real option but to build outside the City. It was not that Shoreditch was lawless; like the rest of the Middlesex it was subject to the authority of the county's Lord Lieutenant and Justices of the Peace. Since these were all crown appointments, however, they tended to view the regulation of theatre very much as the royal court saw it rather than as the City did. Nor would Burbage entirely avoid taxation by retreating to the suburbs; contributions to the upkeep or the poor (and sometimes the upkeep of local amenities, like roads) were a necessary cost of running a business like this. But it is likely that the rates of taxation could be negotiated lower in the suburbs, where the pressures of poor relief were much less, than they would have been in the City proper. Henslowe doubtless made similar calculations when building the Rose in the Liberty of Clink, which was also outside of the City's jusrisdiction. By asserting itself so aggressively the City may well have denied itself a source of real revenue. The Act also imposed stringent conditions, bonds, and potential financial penalties on the innkeepers who already operated within the City. Strikingly, this does not seem to have affected their business as much as we might have anticipated. As we have already noted, they remained in business for more than twenty years after this date (see p. 117).

Though John Brayne's first theatrical project, the Red Lion, antedated the Theatre by almost ten years (see p. 30), it has left very little trace, and the claim of the Theatre to be the first *successful*, purpose-built commercial playhouse in England since Roman times can hardly be doubted. It stayed in business for over twenty years, despite crippling financial difficulties on the parts of Burbage and Brayne, who went into the scheme expecting to pay about £200 and finished up spending £700, most of it coming out of Brayne's pocket. They went to law with each other (and on at least one occasion violence) over the money.[9] Brayne died bankrupt in 1586 but his wife Margaret continued the fight (see p. 31–2). There was a separate running battle with the ground landlord of the playhouse site, Giles Allen (see pp. 193, 223), both about the maintenance of other properties on the site and about extending the original twenty-one year lease. There were also several riots and affrays associated with the Theatre over the years, in connection with which the City was not slow to try to exert some authority (*EPF*, 341, 342, 345–6; see p. 31). There was even an earthquake in 1580, though no damage seems to have been done.

Yet the Theatre survived. On April 13, 1576 Burbage signed the fateful lease with Allen. It seems likely that he employed his younger brother or half-brother Robert, who was a fully-qualified carpenter – trained for large building projects – to erect the playhouse. He himself, as a trained joiner (a less skilled woodworker), might well have been involved with the fixtures and fittings, though doubtless his theatrical experience (and that of Brayne, such as it was) must have informed the grand design. We have already seen something of the long modern debate about what inspired that design, which was to be, with variations, the template for all the public playhouses of the era (Orrell, 1988, 7–29). Some have argued that it was based on the courtyard structures of the inns which the players had long used, both in the City and on their travels. We saw one in use in the Queen's Men's affray in Norwich: an open yard where a makeshift stage could be erected, overlooked by galleries (possibly two tiers of them) on two or three sides, which gave access to the inn's accommodation. Another possible model was the quasi-circular buildings used for animal-baiting, which certainly looked like the theatres from the outside, though internal arrangements were very different.

Yet another argument, most vigorously propounded by John Orrell, is that the main structures of the theatres were inspired by classical models, familiar to the Elizabethans through Sebastiano Serlio's *Architettura*, published in various parts between 1537 and 1575 (Orrell 1983; and 1988, 150–63). Burbage and Brayne would not have been set on a minute imitation of such models, but might have worked in the general spirit of what Serlio described, as mediated through the carpentry techniques of their day. It is certainly the case that foreign visitors like Johannes De Witt compared the theatres they saw to Roman precedents: "it [the Swan playhouse] seems to represent the general notion of Roman work" (*EPF*, 441; see pp. 97–8). In all probability multiple inspirations guided Burbage and Brayne in their final design.

Limited archeological excavations between 2008 and 2011 have revealed some details that we could previously only guess at (Bowsher, 2012, 55–62). It was a timber-framed building that seemed round, but which actually had fourteen sides and seems to have been about about 72 feet across (21.95m). These figures are strikingly similar to those of the Rose, whose foundations have been more extensively excavated, which suggests that Henslowe may deliberately have attempted to copy the Burbage/Brayne model (see Bowsher, 2012, 68–80; and Bowsher and Miller, 2009, 32–67. All measurements here come from these two works). The yard at the Rose was about 48 feet (14.63m) across, leaving around 12 feet on all sides for galleries (3.66m), which members of the audience could pay extra to use; these shielded them from the elements and some had seating – unlike the "pit" or "yard" where the lowest-paying "groundlings" stood. The Theatre excavations have shown that its lowest galleries were actually 12 feet 6 inches deep (3.81m), and we know from other evidence that a total of three tiers of galleries surrounded the yard, one above the other, the top one being covered by a tile roof (see next paragraph). The stage itself, like the 1587 Rose, does not appear to have had a roof, leaving it as open to the elements as the pit and significantly limiting any possibility of spectacular "descent" scenes. But it also meant that there would be no pillars holding up a roof – and obstructing the sight-lines.

The main timbers of the playhouse were presumably oak, possibly set on foundations of brick; the walls would then be constructed of lath and plaster (made of sand and lime), which we know Burbage and Brayne spent money on. We know little for certain about the stage and its furnishings, but again the evidence from the Rose is suggestive. Its stage was something of an irregular trapezoid, about 26 feet wide (7.92m) at the front and some 38 feet (11.58m) at its widest.[10] We do not know how deep the stage was, but at the Fortune it projected to the middle of the yard, so similar proportions here would make it 24 feet deep (7.32m). If the stage of the Theatre was indeed of such dimensions, it would have left at least 5 feet (1.52m) on either side (and considerably more nearer the front) between it and the galleries, such that the "groundlings" of the pit crowded up to it on three sides. We owe confirmation of the three tiers galleries all around the pit to a German visitor in 1585, Samuel Kiechel, who commented on the "daily comedies" in the city, adding "There are some peculiar houses that are so made as to have about three galleries over one another so that a great number of people always come in to see such entertainments" (*EPF*, 410) We infer tiles on the roof from the fact that no thatching was paid for in the construction, as it was in the Globe.

The fact that the Red Lion apparently had a trapdoor makes it reasonable to suppose that the Theatre had at least one, though none of the surviving plays that we can safely assume were written for it actually calls for it. One play that has (presumably) not survived, but may well have called for a trap, was the version of *Hamlet* which Thomas Lodge mentioned in 1596, featuring a pale-vizarded "ghost which cried so miserably at the Theatre, like an oyster-wife, *Hamlet, revenge*" (Lodge, 56).[11] All three versions of Shakespeare's *Hamlet* require the Ghost to call from "*under the stage*" (Scene 1.5 in modern editions) and it is widely assumed that it enters and exits via a trap. Similarly, *Titus Andronicus* would require a trap for the pit in which Bassianus's body is thrown and into which Martius and Quintus fall (2.3). That play almost certainly antedates the Chamberlain's Men's residence at the Theatre but, given its long popularity, would likely have joined the repertoire there.

All the surviving plays identifiable with the Theatre are by Shakespeare.[12] Their first performances are taken to have fallen between 1594 and April 1597, when his company vacated the playhouse. It seems likely that the following plays – at least in their original forms – had been staged elsewhere by other companies, before the Chamberlain's Men occupied the Shoreditch playhouse: *The Two Gentlemen of Verona*, *The Taming of the Shrew*, the *Henry VI* plays, *Richard III*, and *Titus Andronicus*. So their new repertory at the Theatre perhaps comprised *The Comedy of Errors* (though see below, under *Gray's Inn*), *A Midsummer Night's Dream*, *Richard II*, *Romeo and Juliet*, *King John*, *The Merchant of Venice*, *1* and *2 Henry IV*, and just possibly *Much Ado About Nothing*. *Love's Labour's Lost* might also first have been performed there, though many date it earlier; and the 1598 text explicitly tells us that the version we have has been revised from the original.

None of these calls for more than two entrances or exits (cf. the two doors on the Swan drawing: Frontispiece) or anything resembling descent machinery. One apparent requirement is for an upper acting space. I discuss the most famous instance, that in *Romeo and Juliet*, elsewhere (see pp. 111, 235), but assuming the company had taken over the *Henry VI* plays, they too needed such a facility.[13] In *Richard II* (3.3 folio text) a stage direction reads "*Parley without, and answer within: then a flourish. Enter on the walls* Richard, Carlisle, Aumerle, Scroop, Salisbury." The trumpeters earn their keep with a summons to negotiate, an answer, then a combined flourish to announce the king, who is on the walls, aloft. Later he descends, with exaggerated self-pity: "Down, down I come, like glistering Phaeton" (178). But he disappears for four lines of dialogue before Bolingbroke kneels, saying "My gracious lord" (189). This has presumably been enough for Richard to take a staircase down, linking the upper playing space to the main stage. Similarly in 3.5 *Romeo and Juliet*, Juliet "*goeth down from the window*" [Q1], not by the rope-ladder (fashioned from the nurse's "*cords*") which Romeo had athletically used, but by the staircase.

The upper stage was most likely part of a gallery of sorts in an upper level of the tiring house at the rear of the stage, fit to serve as a window, balcony or castle walls. The "attiring-house, or place where the players make them ready" was the hub of the stage, from which all action on it flowed (*EPF*, 362). It was almost invariably the place from which the actors entered, whether through doors on the main stage or "above," and where they stored costumes, properties and playbooks – though we have very little information about its internal arrangements. As the *Richard II* example shows, as many as five players could fit on the upper stage, but dialogue never involves more than two of them at once, so there was probably little space in which to move around and stay visible from ground level while doing so. If the Theatre contained a lords' room or rooms, their use might have limited space on the upper stage, but we have no evidence that it did (see p. 234).

William Lambarde attests that a version of the penny-by-penny entrance system was in operation here, with each section of the playhouse handled separately, thus ensuring (by Shakespeare's day) that James Burbage's distinct portion of the take as sole proprietor was accounted for. In the second edition of his *Perambulation of Kent* (1596) Lambarde explains how pilgrims were not able to avoid paying to see a shrine, "no more than such as go to Paris Garden, the Bell Savage, or Theatre, to behold bear baiting, interludes or fence play, can account of any pleasant spectacle unless they first pay one penny at the gate, another at the entry of the scaffold [i.e. stage] and the third for a quiet standing" (*ES*, 2: 359). This differs slightly from the system Thomas Platter described in 1599, but the principle is very similar (see p. 159). The most striking difference lies in the phrase "quiet standing," for which a third penny would be paid. Platter is quite explicit that there was seating in the galleries in the playhouses he described (including the Swan), of progressively higher comfort. Lambarde seems to suggest that what you were paying extra for at the Theatre (and at a city inn like the Bell Savage) was private standing space, rather than a seat; a gallery is, after all "A covered space for walking in" (*OED*, *n*. 1), rather than for sitting. Probably this is something that changed over time. The amount of seating available seems to have been a measure of the upmarket development of the playhouses. At the early Theatre, seating seems to have been distinctly the exception.

No description of the Theatre speaks of a "heavens" or canopy covering the stage, and modern excavations seem to confirm that it did not have one. Such features were certainly built into the Globe and the Fortune, and apparently added to the Rose when it was refitted before its use by Strange's Men (p. 62).

Their primary function was to keep the playing area dry from rain during performances, though there was nothing to protect the audiences in the yard. But they had an important secondary function in allowing ascent / descent machinery to be installed, making it possible for deities miraculously to appear and bodies to be winched up and down. Such effects can be found in many Jacobean plays, but none has been identified with a Theatre play.

Q1 *Romeo and Juliet* seemingly provides evidence of a discovery space at the Theatre though it appears to have been used quite sparingly there. The Elizabethans did not use this term, but their stage directions make clear that some such option was sometimes available to them. By a discovery space I mean a curtained-off opening in the tiring house wall, probably mid-way between the doors at either end of that wall, which were themselves towards the edges of the stage. Behind the opening was quite a shallow recess, probably itself hung with curtains or wall-hangings; it could be accessed from within the tiring house and so possibly used as an alternative door, or as a route through which substantial properties, such as beds, could be taken on to the main stage. As I shall show in all of Shakespeare's stages where it is relevant, the discovery space was only used occasionally and little action took place within it. It was mainly a "show" space, in which a tableau could be posed or a character shown in an enclosed space.[14]

When, in Q1 *Romeo and Juliet*, Juliet first drinks the Friar's "distillèd liquor," "*She falls upon her bed within the curtains*" (end of 4.3). This suggests that the bed was positioned at the front of the space, so that she could fall directly on it, letting the curtains fall shut to conclude the scene; she is found there two scenes later, when the Nurse opens the curtains. All that is required is that Juliet be seen there; there is no suggestion that other characters enter the space. We may infer – though the text is far less clear – that the discovery space also represents "the tomb" (i.e. vault) in which Juliet is laid to rest. First, "*Paris strews the tomb with flowers*" but this must be done *outside* the tomb, since he has neither the "*mattock and a crow of iron*" (Q1) nor the "*crow and spade*" (Q2) which Romeo and Friar Laurence respectively bring to open it. Indeed, Q1 makes it explicit that "*Romeo opens the tomb*," presumably with a show of difficulty. Paris confronts Romeo before he can enter the tomb and is killed in the fight that follows. His last wish is "lay me with Juliet" (5.3.73), to which Romeo agrees.

The precise deployments here are difficult to determine. Juliet is presumably lying on a dias or sarcophagus; Paris must lie on something similar, and both must be visible. Romeo dies kissing Juliet: "*Falls.*" Friar Laurence finds Romeo first and Paris second, then "*Juliet rises.*" She then "*stabs herself and falls.*" If this does indeed happen within a discovery space (which has been doubted, though alternative stagings pose at least as many problems), it is as much action as Shakespeare ever scripted for one. The Prince commands "seal up the mouth of outrage for awhile" (Q2, 5.3.216) and this is often read as a cue to draw the curtains, effectively removing the bodies from the stage – assuming they have all fallen backwards of that line. Q1, however, casts some doubt on that; here the Prince says "Come, seal your mouths of outrage for a while," asking people to cease their laments while they establish exactly what has happened. It is not impossible that both senses are operative: the curtains are drawn *and* people allow the Prince to examine the witnesses. Even by Shakespeare's standard, this would be a busy double meaning. But it is the best explanation we have.

One thing commentators did leave an unambiguous record of – even its puritan critics – is that the Theatre was an impressive building. The very choice of its name, as we have observed, was intended to evoke the classical Roman playing spaces of that name, and its appearance also did so. The Dutch visitor, Johannes De Witt, accurately described the four playhouses he saw around 1596 as "amphi-theaters" or double-theaters; as George Puttenham noted this was the classical usage for playhouses fully in the round: "Their theaters ... sumptuously built with marble & square stone in form all round ...were called Amphitheaters" (2007, 1.17.29). De Witt was particularly impressed by the newest he saw, the Swan and remarked on its "wooden columns which, on account of the colour of marble painted on them, can deceive even the most acute, whose form, at least ... seems to represent the general notion of Roman work" (*EPF*, 441). A foreign nobleman quoted by E. K. Chambers made the same Roman connection with what was evidently the Globe: "Monday 3 July 1600. We heard an English play. The theatre was built in the manner of the ancient Romans, out of wood, and so formed that from every side the spectators could see the details most suitably" (*ES*, 2: 366; my translation).

We can readily tell what an educated man of the period might know of Roman theaters, from a section of Thomas Heywood's *Apology for Actors*, where he wants to demonstrate the ancient dignity of his profession:

> The first public theater was by Dionysius built in Athens; it was fashioned in the manner of a semi-circle, or half-moon, whose galleries and degrees were reared from the ground, their stairs high, in the midst of which did arise the stage, beside, such a convenient distance from the earth, that the audience assembled might easily behold the whole project without impediment. From this the Romans had their first pattern, which at the first not being roofed, but lying open to all weathers, Quintus Catulus was the first that caused the outside to be covered with linen cloth, and the inside to be hung round with curtains of silk. But when Marcus Scaurus was *aedilis* he repaired it and supported it round with pillars of marble.
>
> Caius Curio, at the solemn obsequies of his father, erected a famous Theatre of Timber, in so strange a form, that on two several stages, two sundry plays might be acted at once, and yet the one be no hindrance or impediment to the other; and when he so pleased the whole frame was artificially composed to meet in the midst, which made an amphi-theater.

> Pompey the great ... saw in the city Mitylene a theatre of another form, and after his ... return to Rome, he raised one after the same pattern, of free stone, of that vastness and receipt [capacity], that within his spaciousness it was able at once to receive fourscore thousand people, everyone to sit, see and hear ... Julius Caesar ... exceeded him in his famous architecture. He raised an amphi-theater, Campo Martio, in the field of Mars, which as far excelled Pompey's as Pompey's did exceed Caius Curio's ... for the bases, columns, pillars, and pyramids were all of hewed marble, the coverings of the stage, which we call the heavens (where upon any occasion their gods descended) were geometrically supported by a giant-like Atlas, whom the poets for his astrology feign to bear heaven on his shoulders, in which an artificial sun and moon of extraordinary aspect and brightness had their diurnal and nocturnal motions; so had the stars their true and celestial course; so had the spheres, which in their continual motion made a most sweet and ravishing harmony. Here were the elements and planets in their degrees, the sky of the moon, the sky of Mercury, Venus, Sol, Mars, Jupiter and Saturn; the stars, both fixed and wandering: and above all these, the first mover, or *primum mobile*, there were the 12 signs; the lines equinoctial and zodiacal, the meridian circle, or zenith, the horizon circle or hemisphere, the zones torrid and frozen, the poles arctic and antarctic, with all other tropics, orbs, lines, circles, the *solstitium* and all other motions of the stars, signs, and planets. In brief, in that little compass were comprehended the perfect model of the firmament, the whole frame of the heavens, with all grounds of astronomical conjecture. From the roof grew a louvre, or turret, of an exceeding altitude, from which an ensign of silk waved continually: *Pendebant vela Theatro* [sails hung from the theater] ... In the principal galleries were special remote, selected & chosen seats for the emperor, *patres conscripti* [senators], dictators, consuls, praetors, tribunes, triumviri, decemviri, aediles, curules, and other noble officers among the senators; all other rooms were free for the plebe, or multitude.
>
> (Apology for Actors, *D2r–D3v*)

Of course the London playhouses did not seat eighty thousand (3,000 is several times given as the capacity of the Globe), nor were they built in marble; and Heywood omits to mention that Caesar's "theater" was built as much for sports and games as for acting. But there *were* correspondences. The English outdoor playhouses all adopted the amphitheater model, the evolution of which Heywood is careful to trace; they thus ensured that "everyone [could] ... see and hear" (if not sit), which was not the case with all theatre designs. Some Roman seats were reserved for the aristocracy, while all other rooms were free for the plebe, or multitude – effectively the same division as created by the lords' rooms and penny-by-penny payment. They may not have been built of marble, but parts of them at least were expertly painted to look like it.[15] And, where there was a "heavens," it was painted with astronomical and astrological signs, doubtless less comprehensive that that in the Field of Mars, but still tending to the same effect; when we remember that the space under the stage was popularly known as "hell" (see p. 137, Note 12), it is evident that the playhouses were meant to comprehend the three principal locations of the Christian universe. And Elizabethan playhouses also hung out signs or flags from a turret above the tiring house, when performances were in progress; the Swan drawing shows a flag, with a picture of a swan, flying from the highest place on the building (Frontispiece). All in all, it is hardly surprising that De Witt and others saw similarities with Roman theatres and it seems likely that, within their limited resources, Burbage and his successors deliberately tried to emulate them.

It is sometimes said that the English prefer to imagine their Elizabethan theatres austerely plain, like their medieval cathedrals. But we know that the cathedrals were once painted with vibrant color, which they only lost after the Reformation. This was almost certainly also the case with the playhouses. There is no specific evidence that the Theatre had such marbling paint twenty years earlier than De Witt, but even the puritan preachers saw it as "sumptuous" and "gorgeous" (though these terms were probably meant as reproaches); and it suggests something that a painter is on record as having regularly been paid in the playhouse.

It was presumably a tribute of sorts to the Theatre that within months it was joined by a neighbor, the Curtain, built barely two hundred yards to its southeast. It is difficult to believe that the demand warranted a second playhouse, especially in such close proximity. We do not even know who built it, only that the site was owned by one Henry Lanman or Laneman; he may or may not have been the builder, but in 1585 he came to an arrangement with Burbage and Brayne whereby the profits of the two properties would be shared 50–50 (*EPF*, 348–9; Ingram, 1992, 227–36). This presumably made for a *modus vivendi* and, as we shall see, eventually provided Shakespeare's company with an essential lifeline at a critical point in its history.

From the start, however, the two playhouses were commented on together. Their puritan detractors decried the uses to which they were put, even as they acknowledged that they were splendid buildings. One T. W. (Thomas White?) preached a sermon at Paul's Cross in November 1577, crying "Behold the sumptuous Theatre houses ..." while the following month John Northbrooke denounced them as "A spectacle and school for all wickedness to be learned in ... those places ... which are made up and builded for such plays and interludes, as the Theatre and Curtain is" (*Treatise wherein Dicing, Dancing, Vain Plays ... are reproved by the Authority of the Word of God*, quoted in *EPF*, 337). The following year John Stockwood preached against "The gorgeous playing place erected in [Finsbury] Fields ... as they have pleased to have called it, a Theatre" (339).

Little is known of the Theatre's use in early years, except the financial problems of and litigation between the various parties. But as early as August 1577 we hear that it had been in business some time. It is likely, though Leicester's Men continued to tour, that they used the Theatre as a London base, especially in summertime; but they did not have exclusive use of it. In 1578 we hear of a sword-fighting prize contest being staged there; such events were very popular and a theatrical arena was a logical place to hold them. But until 1594 there would be no permanent occupation of the Theatre. Traveling companies would book to use it as it suited their schedules, so it made sense to book alternative fare like the fencing when it was available. At the time of the 1584 brawl at the door of the playhouse which led to a confrontation between Burbage and William Fleetwood (p. 31), it appears that the Queen's Men were playing at the Theatre, while a somewhat lesser company, the Earl of Arundel's Men were playing next door at the Curtain. The whole incident was nearly disastrous, since Fleetwood got a majority of the Privy Council to agree to "the suppressing and pulling down of the Theatre and the Curtain. All the lords agreed thereunto, saving my Lord Chamberlain [Lord Howard of Effingham] and Mr Vice-Chamberlain [Sir Christopher Hatton]" (*EPF*, 345–6). Presumably Howard and Hatton – the officers who would be most sensitive to the theatrical needs of the Queen – eventually prevailed, since we hear no more of the matter. As we shall see, there would be other moments when playhouses seemed in danger of being suppressed and pulled down, but it did not happen until the Civil War. The link between the players and the court – and specifically those at the court who understood the practicalities of providing entertainment for the Queen – was always their key lifeline.

It must, then, have seemed an ideal arrangement for all parties when, in 1594, the Chamberlain's Men settled into the Theatre. For James Burbage it gave him secure tenants, who would normally play in his house rather than tour. Moreover, the company included his son, Richard, which would hopefully take the edge off any business frictions between the landlord and his tenants. And it was one of only two companies with court privileges – along with the Admiral's Men, who were likewise normally resident at the Rose. This did not cut off all competition from traveling companies making occasional visits to London, as before; the Curtain and, from 1596, the Swan were available to such "incomers." But, for the Chamberlain's Men, being as it were *in possession* gave them an advantage over the competition. They had the opportunity to make the higher profits on a more regular basis which we may assume came with London playing at this date; this in turn probably made them a desirable company to join, either for an established player as a sharer, as a hired man, or as an apprentice – issues discussed in the next chapter. Having the Theatre as a permanent base also gave them room in the tiring house to keep costumes, properties, and playbooks, allowing them to build deep resources in ways that companies constantly on the road could hardly ever have done. A potential downside is that they would *need* those resources, because they would have to stage a steady turnover of plays, old and new, as we saw with Strange's Men.

So Shakespeare was critical to this new business strategy. He was expected to keep turning out the box-office successes – the kind of plays that could be recycled time after time – for which he already had a track record. Naturally, he stuck to an extent to tried formulas. He had scored a lasting hit with his early revenge tragedy, *Titus Andronicus*, and this seems to have been one of the plays that the Chamberlain's Men acquired. We have already noted the existence of a *Hamlet* in the company's repertoire; if this was not indeed Shakespeare's own work, he was to make the story his own within a few years. The sequence of history plays we now know as the First Tetralogy and which we usually follow the First Folio in calling *Henry VI* Parts 1, 2, and 3, and *Richard III* – about the disintegration of English power in France after the death of Henry V, England's collapse into civil war in the Wars of the Roses, and its final delivery from chaos by the triumph of Henry VII at the Battle of Bosworth Field – had proved extremely popular and here again Shakespeare seems to have carried their performing rights with him into the new company.

The Epilogue to *Henry V* speaks of how:

> Henry the Sixth, in infant bonds crowned King
> Of France and England, did this king succeed;
> Whose state so many had the managing
> That they lost France and made his England bleed,
> Which oft our stage hath shown.
> (9–13)

In 1594/5 Shakespeare promptly set about writing a prequel to that earlier sequence, of which *Henry V* was to be the culmination. That Second Tetralogy, however – like the First – was probably never as neatly preplanned as the First Folio sequence of English history plays suggests.

Richard II (circa 1595) was perhaps the first serious drama he wrote for the company's new base, homing in on the deposition and murder of a king which destabilized the course of English medieval history. This is, in effect, the starting point for all of Shakespeare's English histories, barring only *King John* and *Henry VIII*. But any plan to pursue that history soon seems to have been blown off-course by Shakespeare's engagement with a long poem by Arthur Brooke, based on Italian novellas, *Romeus and Juliet* (1562); this engagement seems to have resulted in the writing of the tragedy, *Romeo and Juliet*, back-to-back with the comedy, *A Midsummer Night's Dream*. Both borrow so much from Brooke's poem that, as Brian Gibbons puts it "one might see them as a kind of diptych, portraying the attraction and repulsion of opposites – love and hate, light and darkness, wit and folly, action and dream – in opposed modes of tragedy and comedy, written close together about 1595" (Shakespeare, 1980, 31). Only then (circa 1596/7) did he return to the narrative of the man who deposed Richard II, Henry IV, though his real focus falls on Henry's son, Prince Hal, the future Henry V. It is not clear if he always planned to spread that story over two plays, or whether the possibility only came to him when he was part way through what became *1 Henry IV*. In either case he was probably again blown sideways by the enormous popularity that immediately attached to the chief comic character in that play, Sir John Oldcastle – and equally by the scandal which required him to change that character's name to Falstaff (p. 194). *The Merchant of Venice*, a different mix of the serious and the comic, was written about the same time.

Burbage

In all of this Shakespeare must have been adjusting to the novel experience of writing for the same theatre and the same group of players over a period of time.[16] We know distressingly little about the specific skills of Shakespeare's fellow sharers, or for the most part which roles they played. But we can say something about Shakespeare's two fellow payees for the company's first court performances, Richard Burbage and Will Kemp. We shall have occasion to revisit both of them again in due course, but it is appropriate to spell out the basics here (see pp. 257ff; 224ff). Burbage was thirty-five in 1594 and had been playing for about ten years, according to testimony by his brother, Cuthbert (Gurr, 2004*a*, 222). The earliest Shakespearean role with which he was identified in his own day was that of Richard III, though we cannot be sure whether he created the role or only took it up when the play became part of the Chamberlain's Men's repertoire at the Theatre.[17] He would later almost certainly perform the roles of Hamlet, Othello and Lear (see p. 164 and Van Es, 2013, 232–48). It would be surprising on that basis if he did not create the roles of Macbeth, Antony, and Coriolanus as well. We know that he played Malevole (a variation on the melancholic revenger) in Marston's *The Malcontent* (1604) and Ferdinand, the Duchess's melancholic twin brother, in Webster's *The Duchess of Malfi* (see pp. 281; 183, 187).

Such a track record, however, does not always help us to locate him in other plays, especially comedies. It must be likely that he created the role of Richard II and that Shakespeare invested that play with such a rich poetic texture in part because he already appreciated his colleague's capacity with blank verse. In *A Midsummer Night's Dream* he must surely have played Theseus. Did he also originate the common practice of doubling that role with Oberon? Doubling of roles was a common feature of Elizabethan theatre, an economic way of handling more speaking roles than the company could otherwise carry – and perhaps at times (like this) a way of drawing attention to parallels between two characters. But it was more common with lesser characters than with the leads. In *Romeo and Juliet* the obvious question is whether a man in his mid-thirties was ideal for a teenager (or at most early twenties) like Romeo; but when we consider that he must have been nearly forty when he probably first handled Shakespeare's "young Hamlet," and again consider the richly ornate poetry which this role is asked to deliver, the odds must be in his favor. What, however, of *The Merchant of Venice*? Bassanio? Antonio? Or Shylock? None of the roles seems an automatic fit. And when we come to *1 Henry IV* would he have taken the ageing dignity of the king's role or the vitality of the prince's? A possible deciding factor might be swordplay. The man who played Hamlet had to be more than proficient (though so too did the man who played Laertes). That also weighs in the role of Romeo – and the climax of *1 Henry IV* is the contest between Prince Hal and Hotspur at Shrewsbury. Indeed, it seems that many of Burbage's roles in histories and tragedies ended in swordplay – which must have asked a lot of him, on top of the already daunting speaking parts beforehand. Consider also the sheer number of those he had to keep at almost instant readiness at any one time, perhaps thirty over a two-month period, if what Henslowe shows to have been the Admiral's Men's practice also applied to the Chamberlain's Men (see pp. 63, 106). It called for supreme fitness.

Kemp

The role of the leading comedian was no less demanding. Will Kemp (see Figure 3.3) had a reputation well before he came to the Chamberlain's Men, having worked with Leicester's and Strange's Men; he had toured on the continent, including the Low Countries and Denmark (Wiles, 1987; Van Es, 2013, 40–1, 85–90). In the dedication to *An Almond for a Parrot* (1590, probably by Thomas Nashe) he is hailed as "that most comical and conceited cavalieri [knight], Monsieur du Kemp, jester-monger and vice-gerent general to the ghost of Dick Tarlton." There is an example of his "merriment" in Scene 12 of *A Knack to Know a Knave* (a Strange's Men's play). We know specifically that at the Theatre Kemp played Peter, the Nurse's "man" in *Romeo and Juliet* and (just possibly within the company's time there) Dogberry in *Much Ado About Nothing*. This is because early texts sometimes call for him by name, rather than by his role. In the 1599 second quarto of *Romeo*, a stage-direction for Peter reads "Enter Will Kemp" (4.5); and in 4.2. of the 1600 *Much Ado* the directions for Dogberry read at one point "Andrew" (= "Merry-Andrew," one who publicly plays the clown) and for the most part "Kemp." These show us very clearly – since both texts seem to derive from manuscripts either in Shakespeare's own hand, or very close to it – that he was writing with the specific performer in mind. Indeed, they suggest that Kemp's overall stage persona, "the clown," was primary, and the specific roles to which he was allocated somewhat secondary. In the 1597 first quarto of *Romeo* his role is designated "clown" before he is

Kemps nine daies vvonder.
Performed in a daunce from
London to Norwich.

Containing the pleasure, paines and kinde entertainment
of *William Kemp* betweene *London* and that Citty
in his late Morrice.

Wherein is somewhat set downe worth note; to reproove
the slaunders spred of him: many things merry,
nothing hurtfull.

Written by himselfe to satisfie his friends.

LONDON
Printed by *E. A.* for *Nicholas Ling,* and are to be
solde at his shop at the west doore of Saint
Paules Church 1600.

Figure 3.3 Image of Will Kemp and companion on the title-page of *Kemp's nine daies wonder*.
Source: PN2598.k6, 1839, Folger Shakespeare Library.

identified as Peter, and even earlier than that it is likely that he played the undistinguished, illiterate "serving-man" who has to ask Romeo to read the names of the guests to the feast on the list old Capulet has given him.

Inadequacies with language are part of his stock-in-trade, whether it be an inability to read at all, or a constant predisposition to malapropisms in the case of Dogberry. Like Dogberry himself, he is determined it be known "that I am an ass" (5.1.251). The mode of his clowning is very much that of the country fellow, out of his depth in the sophisticated society of the city or the court, despite a high opinion of himself.[18] He must surely have created the roles of Bottom and Lancelot Gobbo in *The Merchant of Venice*. Kemp's role in *Romeo* is particularly revealing, since his designation as the Nurse's "man" is anomalous; the Nurse is a servant herself and is unlikely, therefore, to have her own "man" – only possibly a fellow servant who was directed by their masters to help in some particular task. But this designation is an excuse to put two comic roles side-by-side and in the end allows Kemp to introduce his distinctive comedy into many corners of the play, including a set-piece with the musicians at the end of 4.5, a counterpoint to the rising tide of tragedy in the narrative.

Kemp was also noted for bawdy, irreverent, and energetic entertainments called jigs, which were often staged after the performance of a play. We shall have occasion to examine them elsewhere (see p. 218).

Motley

Something should be said about "motley," the clothing so often associated with Elizabethan comedians. Shakespeare actually seems to reserve it for the roles played by Kemp's successor in the company, Robert Armin, who specialized in "fool" roles, which were rather different from the clown roles pioneered by Tarlton and Kemp (see pp. 264ff). Jaques in *As You Like It* (circa 1599) particularly identifies motley with Touchstone, which seems to have been Shakespeare's first major role for Armin: "Oh, that I were a fool! / I am ambitious for a motley coat" he says, having met the character variously described as "the clownsish fool" and "the roynish [scurvy] clown" (2.7. 2.7.42–3; 1.3.128 and 2.2.8). Unfortunately we still do not know what it meant in terms of what a stage comedian actually wore. Leslie Hotson wrote a whole book on *Shakespeare's Motley* (1952), arguing that it was a long coat of fairly coarse woolen cloth, made with variegated colors, of which green or yellow was usually predominant: the clothing given to mentally-challenged people in real life, often called "naturals" or "fools." But his argument was systematically dismantled by David Wiles (1987, 182–97), who among other things showed the shifting sense of the term. What I think *is* clear is that Kemp did not regularly wear "motley" or carry the traditional accompaniments of the fool/jester employed in some noble households, a cockscomb and a bauble (cf. Lear's Fool). It is still likely, however, that he did wear a distinctive dress which singled him out as "the clown," which would give a kind of continuity to his various servant roles in *Romeo and Juliet*, keeping him somewhat separate from his fellow servants.

Kemp was not the only comedian in the company. Augustine Phillips is credited with writing a lost jig, *Phillips His Slipper*, entered in the Stationers'

Register in 1595, which might suggest his own comic facility; his stepbrother, Thomas Pope, is once described as a clown.[19] Richard Cowley played Verges to Kemp's own Dogberry. There may have been something of a comic star-cluster in the company, which particularly raises the question of who played the most famous comic role of them all, Falstaff, another role first created at the Theatre. The fact is that we do not know. David Wiles has argued cogently that it was Kemp (1987, 116–35). Others, however, have objected that the kind of comedy generated by Falstaff – a knowing, wordsmart, blasphemous rogue – is very different in temper from anything else he is known to have played. Whatever the competition, however, it is clear that Kemp was the preeminent comedian and star draw of the Chamberlain's Men's days at the Theatre. But those days were numbered.

Box 3.2 A Day at the Theatre

Let us try to reconstruct a typical performance day for the company at the Theatre. Of necessity, many of the details derive from Henslowe and the practice of the Admiral's Men, but there is every reason to suppose that the Chamberlain's Men operated in broadly the same way. The schedule, in fact, would have begun a couple of days earlier, when some of the hired men would have gone into the City and the suburbs, posting bills advertising this particular performance (however much this may have irritated the City authorities). On the morning of the performance the message would be reinforced by the company's trumpeters and drummers (see p. 174). In this instance it is to be the first performance of *Romeo and Juliet*. The earliest text of that play was printed in 1597 and most scholars date it two or three years earlier, at around the same time as *A Midsummer Night's Dream*. So there is a strong presumption that the 1597 text reflects its staging in the Theatre.

The morning of the performance was almost certainly taken up with something else, very probably associated with future performance(s). In the mid-late 1590s Henslowe shows the Admiral's Men introducing a new play about every three weeks, a phenomenal challenge not only in terms of learning the lines but also of making all the other necessary preparations – and most of these the players had to do for themselves (see pp. 64, 76). Even working out how long to keep new plays in the schedule and which plays to revive, in what sequence (and then ensuring that costumes and properties were still to hand and in good order), would have been a taxing business. On our hypothetical day, the sharers (core company members) might listen to a proposal for a new play from one of the many playwrights they commission, other than Shakespeare.[20] Henslowe, for example, lent Jonson an advance on a proposed new play that the Admiral's approved of: "Lent unto Benjamin Jonson the 3 of December 1597 upon a book which he was to write for us before Christmas next after the date hereof, which he showed the plot unto the company: 20s" (*Henslowe*, 73).²¹ Jonson was doubtless already sufficiently a man of the theatre to have produced an outline that provided for characters in numbers the company could handle, and with roles appropriate for their principal players. We assume that John Heminge handled the Chamberlain's Men's money – in later years it seems to have become his principal responsibility – and, like Henslowe, would have to keep track of such commitments, loans and outright payments.

The play would very probably be delivered piece by piece. Henslowe's records usually show payment to the dramatists in stages. This is often taken to show just how hand-to-mouth some of them lived: we hear, for example, of both Henry Chettle and Thomas Dekker being arrested for debt at various times. But it also shows them being paid by results, as they delivered portions of the play. So, for example, on July 24, 1599 Henslowe "lent" Dekker 10s. "at the request of Samuel Rowley and Thomas Downton [two of the sharers] in earnest of a book called *Stepmothers' Tragedy*." This apparently means that the company had accepted his "plot" scenario, which was perhaps the limit of his involvement with the play; all further references are to Henry Chettle, such as a month later, when Chettle was "lent" £1 "in earnest of his play called *The Stepmothers' Tragedy*," possibly having produced some early scenes or at least convinced members of the company that they were imminent. Only two days later (August 25) Henslowe lent three of the sharers – William Bird, Edward Juby, and Downton – a further £1 "to pay Harry Chettle for his book called *The Stepmothers' Tragedy*": payment now (to the playwright), rather than lending. Finally on October 14 Robert Shaa, yet another sharer, entered an affidavit into Henslowe's *Diary*, attesting that he had received £4 "to pay H. Chettle in full payment of a book called *The Stepmothers' Tragedy* for the use of the company" (*Henslowe*, 123, 125). So, over about two months, Chettle produced the play, receiving loans until he delivered something tangible and then payments; overall he received £6 (and Dekker 10s.) for this work.²² The fact that as many as six of the sharers were involved in authorizing these payments at different times may just have been an accident, but it might also suggest that they were being particularly careful about advancing company money when they were not entirely confident that either Dekker or Chettle was going to deliver. The company still, of course, had to repay Henslowe for all the money he had advanced. Such negotiations with the playwrights and with Henslowe (or Heminge, in the case of the Chamberlain's Men) must have been a constant and sometimes unpredictable process for the sharers and often occupied them on mornings before a performance.

Once the play was delivered in full, the sharers would hear it read together, presumably before making the final payment. This might be something of a social occasion. Henslowe records lending 5s "for to spend at the reading of [*The Famous Wars of Henry the First and the Prince of Wales*] at the Sun in New Fish Street" and similarly 2s "lent out for the company when they read the play of

Jephtha for wine at the tavern" (88, 201). This latter was the middle of May 1602; earlier that month they had paid Anthony Munday and Dekker £5 in earnest of the play. Subsequent payments suggest that they were happy with what they received, and that would have set off a flurry of business. First the Master of the Revels needed to "peruse" the book – either the version delivered by the dramatists or a fair copy, reproduced either by them or by a scrivener – for licensing, which he apparently did in late June, though Henslowe received a gentle reminder on August 4 that he had not yet been paid for it (296). This "allowed copy" became valuable company property, under the watchful care of the book-keeper.

Then the company would need to cast all the parts which had not been settled upon when they accepted the "plot." They would use their collective professional judgment (probably steered by Jonson, who would have written with it some individuals in mind) about any roles that could be doubled by a single actor, since that would save money. Once the sharers' own roles were settled there would need to be calculations about hired men who would be required for any remaining parts – weighing in the balance the possibility of using money-gatherers and stage-hands for crowd scenes. There would also have to be decisions about any music required. The sennets, flourishes and alarums of ceremonial entries and battlefield maneuvres would pose no problems (see p. 175). But new songs, especially those which did not rely on familiar ballad tunes, might need commissioning.

Parts

Then, for the speaking roles, a scrivener would have to be hired to draw up their "parts." This entailed copying out just the words to be spoken by each individual actor, with the very briefest of cues from the previous speaker to alert him to when he was to start speaking (Palfrey and Stern, 2007; Menzer 2008). This would be written out on conventional folios of papers, and then cut in strips, as Tiffany Stern describes in the "role" of Orlando, from Robert Greene's play, *Orlando Furioso*: "it was clearly originally kept as a roll … Each sheet was once joined to the other, top to tail, making a strip that was 18 or so feet in length; this appears to have been anchored at the very top and bottom with rods. The part will then have been wound around its two sticks, creating a text that could be 'scrolled,' probably with one hand" (Stern 2009*b*, 503).[23] This constituted the actor's roll [i.e."role"], from which he would learn his lines. The lion's share of preparing for a new production would entail each member of the cast "conning" his roll individually. Although they might be aided in this by an "instructor" it remained largely a solitary process and, as Stern puts it "plays will never have been as familiar to actors in their entirety as they were in parts" (511).

Costumes and Properties

At the same time attention would have to be paid to any new costumes or properties that would be required for the new play. There was a flurry of payments associated with this late in June: 30s. "unto the tailor for making of suit for *Jephtha*," 25s. "to pay unto him which made their properties for *Jephtha*" and 22s. "to pay the cutter for the play of *Jephtha*" (203).[24] Thomas Downton was the sharer who authorized all of the recorded payments for costumes and properties in connection with *Jephtha*, so this was presumably a delegated responsibility for him; the *Diary* suggests that it was something he did regularly. It was a serious obligation, because the company evidently spent a small fortune on costumes, probably their largest single commitment (pp. 170ff). Presumably all the other senior members of the company took responsibility for particular aspects of the complex business of bringing a new play to the stage.

There does not seem to have been much time for rehearsals (a "general rehearsal") as we would understand them, and when they did occur it seems that "verbal content of a play [was] not the emphasis of collective rehearsal; that a general rehearsal [was] largely intended to determine action that affect[ed] the group" (Stern 2009*b*, 509). It would in effect have been a walk-through, with the actors expected already to be familiar with their cues and written parts, while the readthrough should already have given them a general scene-by-scene sense of the business of the play, with a record presumably kept of properties that would be needed, and some possibly newly acquired. These would all have to be assembled at convenient places in the tiring house on the morning of a performance. But all kinds of issues might need to be resolved in a general rehearsal: which doors to use for particular entrances and exits; who would handle larger properties like beds and cauldrons, or remove dead bodies; at least a basic scenario for any fighting and its outcome (any deaths or woundings requiring suitably concealed bladders of animal blood for realistic effect).

Food and Drink

There was presumably a break for dinner, the main meal of the day, around noon. Inns and ordinaries are commonly associated with the playhouses, doubtless springing up to service players and audiences alike. But there may have been no need to leave the playhouse. We recall that James Burbage's original partner in the Theatre, John Brayne – like Henslowe's partner in the Rose, John Chomley – was a grocer; and Chomley's contract certainly gave him exclusive rights to sell food and drink at the Rose, with the use of a small house nearby "to keep victualing in." The concessions must always have been a profitable element in the whole enterprise, though we do not know who controlled them at the Theatre after Brayne died. We do know that John Heminge, the actor, always apparently shrewd with money, secured the position of tapster at the Globe, cornering the doubtless lucrative drinks market. Thomas Platter tells us that "in the pauses of the comedy food and drink are carried round amongst the people, and one can thus refresh himself at his own cost" (*ES*, 2: 365). As with modern sports auditoria, which in many respects the public playhouses resembled, it is likely that such refreshment was available an hour or so before the show began.

Performance

A general rehearsal for *Romeo and Juliet* had perhaps taken place the day before, leaving a final morning to ensure that everything was in perfect readiness. I shall basically follow the 1597 Q1 version that we may assume was used at the Theatre, though glancing at the much longer Q2, which perhaps shows how it was revised ("newly corrected, augmented, and amended" as the title-page says) for the court or the Curtain.[25] I discuss elsewhere the play's distinctive use of both an upper stage and a discovery space (especially at the end), so I shall not go into detail here (see pp. 111, 235). After three soundings of the trumpet high in the turret above the tiring house, the book-keeper would be seated in the prompt-corner, following the "allowed copy" both as prompter and as overseer of preparations backstage (see p. 201 on soundings). He would be adjacent to the wall-mounted "plot," available to himself and anyone who needed to check the essentials of the running order (see p. 267). His job was both to act as a prompter if necessary and to keep the action flowing smoothly offstage, sending boy assistants to alert cast and crew to upcoming cues.

The Prologue would commence the play at 2 p.m. Scene1.1 involves two unnamed servingmen of the Capulets (Samson and Gregory in Q2, which also tells us that they have "*swords and bucklers* [shields]"), who confront two similarly anonymous servingmen of the Montagues (one named Abraham in Q2). They would be differentiated by distinctive liveries. There is a fight, which would have needed some basic choreographing, before "other citizens" ("three or four … with clubs or partisans" [a type of spear] in Q2) assault both sides and then all are divided by senior members of the Capulets and Montagues – wordlessly in Q1, with dialogue in Q2. The stage already holds at least thirteen players before the Prince enters ("*with his train,*" Q2) – and this is before Romeo, Juliet, and Kemp in his various roles have appeared (see p. 113), figures who could not be doubled. Shakespeare wanted a show of the company's extensive personnel early on. It may be an effect of quoting more specific numbers, but the Q2 text does seem to call for a larger ancillary cast of servingmen and attendants – possibly a mark of the company prospering in the years between the two versions.

Kemp first appears in 1.2, designated as "*Clown*" on entry, a Capulet servant within the plot; he reappears briefly at the end of 1.3, a scene which otherwise involves three female roles – Lady Capulet, the Nurse, and Juliet, all presumably played by "boys" though we might expect the two older roles to be performed by young men near the ends of their apprenticeships (see p. 183).1.4. shows Romeo, Mercutio, and Benvolio ("*with five or six other maskers, torchbearers*," Q2), masked and approaching the Capulet's house. Torches throughout (see also 5.3) flag that it is night-time, just as the direction in 5.1 that Balthazar enters "*booted*" flags that he has traveled a long way (see p. 246). 1.5. shows a difference in staging between the two versions: Q1 defies the usual conventions of continuous staging; Romeo and his colleagues, who were only approaching in 1.4 are somehow (like a filmic lap-dissolve) within the Capulet's house when the new scene begins – it is very unusual for characters on stage at the end of one scene to be immediately present at the beginning of the next; in Q2 they merge into the action by mingling with some busy servingmen, who are preparing for a banquet. Q2 explicitly directs that "*Music play and they dance*" (it is implicit in Q1 too) – a crowded stage-full of at least eight Montagues and as many Capulets, including Juliet.

At the beginning of 2.1 Romeo enters "*alone*" but is quickly followed by Benvolio and Mercutio, whom he is able to overhear unseen. If there was indeed no "heavens" at the Theatre, and so no supporting posts, we might suppose he hides behind an arras on the tiring house wall. When he reemerges in 2.2 Juliet has appeared; the dialogue makes clear that she is "above," on the upper stage, as she will be again later. The company would have had to make accommodations in respects of admissions to the lords' rooms, and the gatherers at the tiring house door informed, given the amount of activity on the upper stage (see pp. 235–6). In 2.3 Friar Laurence appears ("*with a basket*," Q2), carrying herbs and flowers, possibly freshly acquired for the show. 2.4 again showcases Kemp as "*Peter, [the Nurse's] man*."

3.1 tilts the whole play towards tragedy as Mercutio and Tybalt duel with rapiers. Q1 is explicit about the key choreography: "*Tybalt under Romeo's arm thrusts Mercutio in, and flies* [i.e. runs away]." The contest between Romeo and Tybalt is less fully recorded: "*Fight. Tybalt falls.*" Presumably in a performance where swordplay was so prominent, and where audiences would have been knowledgeable because of the prize contests in the art, some effort would have been made to provide different action for each new fight. In 3.2 a direction reads "*Enter Nurse, wringing her hands, with the ladder of cords in her lap*" – a careful preparation for a prop which will not actually be needed until 3.5, when Romeo "*goeth down*" from Juliet's bedroom, which in that scene (but perhaps not always) is "*aloft*" (Q2). The only significant new prop in 3.3 is Romeo's dagger ("*He offers to stab himself, and Nurse snatches the dagger away*"), but he presumably wore that throughout. The following scenes raise few staging issues, apart from Romeo's climb down from Juliet's bedroom in 3.5, using the Nurse's "*ladder of cords.*" In 4.4 the Nurse brings "*herbs*" to make the house fresh for County Paris, and a servingman brings logs and coals to make it warm. (In Q2 the preparations are grander: Lady Capulet calls to "fetch more spices" (4.4.1) rather than herbs, a much more expensive option, and there are now *"three or four"* servingmen, who between them carry *"spits and logs, and baskets"* containing "[t]hings for the cook"). As Paris approaches *"Play music,"* the first call on the musicians since the ball; this would have been stringed instruments and perhaps woodwind, rather than the trumpets – music for a bridegroom.

As noted elsewhere, at the end of 4.3 Juliet *"falls upon her bed within the curtains,"* as clear a direction for a curtained discovery space at the rear of the stage as one could imagine (see p. 250). In 4.5 she is discovered, apparently dead; eventually *"They all but the Nurse go forth, casting rosemary on her and shutting the curtains."* Rosemary, of course, is "for remembrance" (*Hamlet*, 4.5.179) – so many features of Elizabethan life had symbolic value (different herbs, gems, metals, colors, for instance) and the players often went out of their way to invoke them. The curtains shield off the body and there follows a sequence which some have found in dubious taste, where Will Kemp jokes with the three musicians, at a loose end since "this is no time to play." (It is here in Q2 that Kemp is identified by name, rather than by the role he plays: 4.5.99.1: see p. 103). I have assumed that Shakespeare was responsible for this, though the book-keeper – who most particularly had to keep track of the actors during performance – may have influenced the usage. I discuss elsewhere the complex final scene at Juliet's tomb, which involves the most extensive use of a discovery space in any Shakespeare play (see p. 201).

We should expect the play to be over by 4.30 pm or 5.00 pm at the latest, which for most of the year would allow audience and players alike to get home in daylight, or at least twilight, if they did not stop at an ordinary or other eating establishment for supper on the way. It was a long day for the players. And it went on like this, usually six days a week (not Sundays) for much of the year, except when plague or other disturbances intervened. They were generally not supposed to perform in the forty days of Lent, but Henslowe makes it clear that they found ways around this – very probably paying the Master of the Revels for a dispensation. Even when there was no playhouse business to be conducted, the players had always to be "conning" new roles or brushing up old ones as they were revived. Moreover, as members of the company moved on or died all their old roles would have to be redistributed: the conveyor belt never stopped. It was a deeply taxing repertory system, but it gave them great resources. When they went on tour they might have as many as the seven plays to hand for a host to choose from that Wolsey's Men are said to have in *Sir Thomas More*, or even more (p. 42). In October 1633, Sir Henry Herbert "sent a warrant by a messenger of the chamber to suppress *The Tamer Tamed* [an old play being revived] for that afternoon ... They acted *The Scornful Lady* instead of it" (*Herbert*, 182). So, at perhaps four hours' notice, they were able to stage a completely different play. Never less than entirely professional.

Shakespeare on the Record and the Stages of 1594 | 113

> **Box 3.3 "Dramatic" or "Back-Stage" Plots**
>
> When Henslowe recorded a loan to Ben Jonson as an advance against a play he would write, "which he showed the plot unto the company," he meant something like an outline, enough of a description of the planned work to convince the company sharers that Jonson could produce a satisfactory play (see p. 107). He was not referring to the surviving pasteboard items called "plots" or "plats," several of which survive among Alleyn's papers at Dulwich College and which evidently served some practical function within the playhouses (see p. 62). Those other "plots" or "plats" are what concern me here. Baffling if we look to them for information about the story of the play or its authorship, they reveal a good deal about the practical organization of performances.
>
> Tiffany Stern, who has given them the closest recent attention, calls them "back-stage plots" (2009a, 201–31). She observes that:
>
>> plots were, as everything about them broadcasts, made with heavy and repeated use in mind. All surviving plots are made of substantial pulp boards on to which folio-sized paper (roughly 12 by 16 inches [0.30-0.41m]) are affixed. The pulp remains perfectly preserved for the plots of *The Dead Man's Fortune* and *Frederick and Basilea* ... Written at the top of the folio sheet stuck onto the board is the nature of the document (the word "plat" or "plot") and the title of the play for which it is the map ... Under the title, and using most of the rest of the sheet in every plot ... are two vertical columns ruled in ink in a thin nib. The boxes into which these are subdivided are filled with writing that fits exactly into its space ... Lastly ... they are pierced through by an oblong hole inserted about a third of the way down the central margin ... hanging the documents on a square peg was the last in the act of making them, and the first in the act of publicly using them. (208–9)
>
> In summation, she argues: "Plots ... define box-by-box when the stage is empty and when it is full, but they are interested only in what is happening onstage, not off it; in particular, they carefully list who is to enter first and who is then to enter to them, but they are only sporadically taken with mid-scene exits" (214). She then develops a convincing argument that these were publicly-hung call-sheets, presupposing the situation of "a 'prompter' who spent his performance staring at his 'book,' and a call-boy who aided him during production" (219). But "they must have been available to more than one person ... such plots as have marginal annotations for property and music calls anticipate use by at least three sets of caller" (226). They constituted, as John Gillies puts it, "a bird's-eye view of the whole action – a grid of entrances, exits, and stage-effects" (1998, 27). They are another mark of the players' sheer professionalism, the first

> resource they would draw upon whenever a play was revived, an instant reminder of its workings and challenges. Of the seven surviving "plots" the one of most immediate interest is that for *2 The Seven Deadly Sins*, because it is my belief that it relates to performances of that play by Shakespeare's own company while at the Curtain. See "The 'plot' of *2 The Seven Deadly Sins*" (pp. 205ff).

The Cross Keys Inn[26]

The Chamberlain's Men were barely settled in the Theatre before their patron, Lord Hunsdon, the Lord Chamberlain, wrote to the Lord Mayor of London, 8 October 1594:[83]

> Where my now company of players have been accustomed for the better exercise of their quality, and for the service of Her Majesty if need so require, to play this winter time within the City at the Cross Keys in Gracious Street: these are to require and pray your lordship (the time being such as, thanks be to God, there is now no danger of the sickness) to permit and suffer them so to do. The which I pray you the rather to do for that they have undertaken to me that, where heretofore they began not their plays till towards four o'clock, they will now begin at two and have done between four and five and will not use any drums or trumpets at all for the calling of people together and shall be contributors to the poor of the parish, according to their abilities. (*ES*, 4: 316)

This is among the clearest evidence we have that the players always really preferred playing in the City center, at least in the dark, cold, wet days of winter, when the appeal of the large, open-air suburban amphitheaters must have been considerably muted for actors and audiences alike. Hunsdon's letter, with an old soldier's concision, anticipates the full raft of all the City father's usual objections to the players: service of the Queen; no plague; start and end times to ensure they will be done before full dark, even in winter; no disruptive drums and trumpets; reasonable taxes for the poor. We have no actual proof that the Lord Mayor agreed to this, but the letter leaves little room for dissent (Gurr, 2005).

One curious feature of it is the way it talks of "my now company of players" as if they have regularly performed at the Cross Keys in this way in the past. Hunsdon had not patronized players since the late 1580s until the new company was created earlier in this year. Possibly there was a recognition that the Chamberlain's players were, in many respects, essentially the old Strange's Men (albeit stripped of Alleyn) and this had been their usual winter recourse. They had certainly played there in 1589, in defiance of the Lord Mayor's attempts to restrain them from playing at all (*EPF*, 213).

Professional playing in the City inns can be traced back at least as far as the 1540s, but it was around the time that the Theatre was being built in 1576 that four inns emerged as regular playing places and they would be used by the actors until at least 1596. This was despite the 1574 Act of the Common Council which, as we have noted, played its part in driving the purpose-built amphitheaters into the suburbs, but under whose conditions the inns' owners were apparently prepared to operate (see p. 117). The inns themselves may have been somewhat adapted for the purposes of playing, but not radically. Unlike, say, the Boar's Head in Whitechapel and the Red Bull in Clerkenwell, which were later converted into playhouses, the City inns – the Bell Savage on Ludgate Hill, the Bull in Bishopsgate Street, and the Cross Keys and Bell, both on Gracechurch Street – remained in business as inns, putting up travellers, handling cargoes, and purveying food and drink.

"Inn-playing in London was largely ... a winter phenomenon" (Kathman 2009*b*, 158). The Queen's Men had been granted permission to play in two of the inns in the winter of 1583/4, and Lord Hunsdon's letter explicitly ties his company's occupation of the Cross Keys to winter. Their preference for the City inns seems to have been driven by the realities of securing an audience. In 1584 the Corporation of London ruled "that no playing be in the dark, nor continue any such time but as any of the auditory may return to their dwellings in London before sun set, or at least before it be dark" (*ES*, 4: 302). One suspects that this was not only what the City authorities required but also what most respectable members of the audience would prefer. Negotiating the minimally policed city after dark, its roads always in a dubious state of repair and cleanliness, would always have been a daunting prospect. Performances in a nearby inn would always be preferable at that time of year to a playhouse in the suburbs.

Although some have rather hastily jumped to the conclusion that performances at inns were indoor, most of the accounts we have of their actual use speak of *outdoor* playing, such as we observed with the Queen's Men's affray in Norwich. Robert Greene describes the trickery of pickpockets at the Bull inn, in his *The Third and Last Part of Conny-Catching* (1592), in a context where it is clear that the audience is outside: a thief, having "nipped" a purse "stepped into the stable to take out the money" (D4^r). The story is probably fictional, but Greene certainly knew the Bull, where several of his own plays had been performed. He describes a stage and the audience being free to move about to get the best view. This is consistent with what we know of the Bull, which was a very large, L-shaped property with three courtyards – which meant that two could cater to the inn's regular trade while the third was being used for plays. As David Kathman puts it "The Bull's northernmost yard would seem to be ideal for [playing] ... The dimensions of the northern yard, roughly 45 ft by 35 ft [13.72 × 10.69 m], would have made it comparable in size to the original yard of the Rose playhouse" (2009*b*, 161). If we combine this with the characteristics

I have described before – galleries to accommodate higher-paying members of the audience, as well as accessible doors for stage and tiring house business – we have all the elements necessary for playing. (William Lambarde's account of penny-by-penny payment specifically mentions the Bell-Savage inn and the Theatre, but doubtless applied also to the Bull: see p. 95).

We know less about the Cross Keys inn than we do some of the others. But what we do know suggests that playing there may not have been outdoors. For one thing it only had one courtyard, so that playing there would seriously have interfered with the regular business of the inn. Another argument against it is that, unlike the Bull and the Bell Savage (especially the former), neither the Bell nor the Cross Keys is known to have hosted fencing prizes, which were probably better suited to outdoor presentation, in larger arenas. So we may cautiously hypothesize that the Cross Keys contained a room large enough for commercial playing, possibly not as big as the Stratford Guildhall, but surely no smaller than the country houses we reviewed earlier, capable of holding a hundred people. Even at that size, it would barely be economic – unless the players were able to charge a significant premium for indoor accommodation, some of it possibly seated. That was the formula pioneered by the management of the boy companies, though on a larger scale, and which the King's Men were to replicate, when they took over the Blackfriars. It is not impossible that the specific appeal of the Cross Keys over other potential venues among the inns was that it gave the company its first experience of this end of the market. But this is pure speculation.

Virtually everything we do know about the Cross Keys is contained in David Kathman's article, "Alice Layston and the Cross Keys" (2009c). Like so many of the theatrical properties, it was surrounded by vexatious, spiteful, and deceitful litigation over a number of years. Between 1571 and 1590 it was owned by Alice Layston, a legacy from her late (second) husband. Playing began there "probably by 1576 and certainly by 1579" (Kathman, 154), though renting the property to the actors was more likely a business decision of the leaseholder rather than the owner. From 1564 to 1584 the leaseholder was a Yorkshireman, Richard Ibbotson. By 1588 the lease passed to John Franklin, who "spent considerable money on wainscott, glass, settles (high-back wooden benches) and ironwork, among other things, to get the inn into presentable shape" (161). He was thus the leaseholder when Strange's Men defied the Lord Mayor and played there in 1589. Is it possible that Franklin's outlay on putting "the inn into presentable shape" was associated with a business plan to attract higher-paying customers?

Physically, we know that the Cross Keys was "located on the west side of Gracechurch Street ... immediately north of the parish church and immediately south of the Bell inn ... It was about 140 ft [42.67m] long extending west from the street, and was 80 ft [24.38m] wide at the back end but narrower on the Gracechurch Street end, with 32 ft [9.75m] of street frontage. There was a single yard in the middle, roughly 48 ft long (east-west) by 32 ft wide (north-south)" (147).²⁷ The proximity to the parish church doubtless explains why Hunsdon was so explicit about no drums and trumpets, and about the timing of shows. One of the striking features of his letter is that the proposed 2 p.m. start time would clash with evensong, whenever that service was being conducted (see p. 114). This might only have been on holy-days, and Hunsdon does not go into sufficient detail to explain if there would be special arrangements for such eventualities. But if there was tacit acceptance that shows and services would overlap it was certainly important that there be no drums and trumpets in the streets.

The dimensions show that the building was certainly large enough to contain a substantial interior playing space, especially if (as we may suppose) it rose more than one storey. But just as we do not know the size of this room we cannot know how the players adapted their shows to it. There was, presumably, no need to arrange the seating to include places of honor, but in other respects it might have been very like playing in a great house. Securing payment from an audience would have been very straightforward, with a limited number of doors, especially if there was no differentiated pricing.

On Alice Layston's death in 1590 the inn passed to her late husband's brother, William Layston, who went to law to dispossess John Franklin of his lease. He installed in his stead James Beare, who was somewhat improbably a sailor and privateer (some would say pirate). He was thus the leaseholder with whom Shakespeare's company presumably did business in 1594 and for as many years thereafter as they might have been allowed to play there. It is commonly assumed that playing in the City inns came to an end by 1596, when the petition by Blackfriars residents to stop the company using the new theatre which James Burbage had built there contained the passage "now all players being banished by the Lord Mayor from playing within the City ... they now think to plant themselves in liberties" (*EPF*, 508). It is also the case that none of the foreign visitors to London mentions the inns in their surveys of the theatres after this date. Paul Menzer, however, has recently argued that players continued to perform in the City inns almost up to the end of Elizabeth's reign (2006*b*). There is, however, no specific record of the Chamberlain's Men doing so (or even requesting to do so) after 1594/5, and my assumption is that they did not. Their experience of playing at the Cross Keys was brief, but if my speculation about the business model it involved is correct, it was far from unimportant.

Greenwich Palace

On December 26, 1594 the Chamberlain's Men performed at court for the first time. The Queen had elected that year to spend Christmas at Greenwich, one of the four royal palaces then in use. The previous year she had used Hampton

Court, the next year she would use Richmond, and the year after that Whitehall – which James was to make virtually his settled place of residence and entertainment. But Elizabeth followed the old tradition of moving regularly – carrying virtually her entire government and household with her – partly in order to allow these intensely-occupied buildings to air out after use.

Greenwich itself had been built by her father as a mark of particular royal magnificence. It stood on the site of what is now Sir Christopher Wren's Royal Naval Hospital, overlooking the River Thames, as did all the royal palaces. This was a practical as well as an aesthetic consideration. Access to water was critical, not least for dealing with sewage. And transport by river was much easier and faster than on land, horseback only excepted. One of the attractions of performing at the Cross Keys must have been that it made getting to Greenwich – on the south shore of the Thames, east of the City – much easier than it would have been from Shoreditch and the Theatre. They most likely took boats to the palace, carrying their costumes and properties; the land journey, having to cross over London Bridge, would have been much more arduous. Using the river also made it quite practical to perform at the inn that afternoon, concluding before five, and to be at the palace well before their performance was to begin, which would be after supper, around 9 p.m.

In each of the palaces dramatic performances were normally staged in one of two rooms, the Hall or the (usually smaller) Great Chamber. Whitehall additionally had structures known as Banqueting Houses. The decisions about which to use would be driven by considerations of the whole festive calendar, planned attendance, and the practicalities of mounting and demounting everything required. In 1594/5 the Great Chamber at Greenwich seems to have been used for all the plays performed by the Chamberlain's and Admiral's Men (see pp. 182–3). But the Hall was used after the Revels season, in March, when the Gentlemen of Gray's Inn presented the Queen with a masque, *Proteus and the Adamantine Rock*.

The Great Chamber at Greenwich, as in all the palaces, was the antechamber to the Queen's private quarters in the royal suite; it was constantly busy and always guarded (it was also known as the Guard Chamber). The fact that it could be set up at this time to use for plays was a mark that this was truly a holiday season. It would also have been decorated to impress, especially since this was the room where visitors were first brought. As John Astington explains: "The royal department of the Wardrobe looked after the preparation of rooms in this fashion [hanging the vertical surfaces with arras or woven cloth], and their responsibilities could easily have been extended to the stage facilities. The chamber was 'made ready' with hangings covering the walls, and following a particular event the yeomen and grooms busied themselves 'taking down stuff and laying it up' – returning the valuable fabrics to the rooms or cupboards where they were stored" (Astington, 1999, 151). Sometimes we have details of the designs. For the wedding of Prince Arthur and Catherine of Aragon in 1501 the Hall of Richmond Palace was splendidly decorated: "The walls of this pleasant hall are hanged with rich cloths of Arras, their works representing many noble battle and sieges, as of Jerusalem, Troy, Alba, and many other; that this whole apparement [equipment, outfit] was most glorious and joyful to consider and behold" (60–1, quoting Grose, 1808, 2: 315.) And after the execution of Charles I in 1649 many royal hangings were sold off: "Tapestries to hang in chambers came in matching themes ("Six pieces of *Vulcan and Venus*," "Five pieces of hangings of *King David*," etc.), but also in landscape designs and with other non-figurative motifs ("Flower pots and pillars"; "flower Deluces"; "beasts bearing the Arms of England")" (153, quoting W. G. Thomson, 1930, 314–29). Such hangings adjacent to the stage must always have been in a dialogue of sorts with the narrative of a performance.

John Astington describes what a court playing space would normally look like. The audience were:

> mostly seated, and no one would have occupied the space between the Queen's seat, set on a dias somewhere near the centre of the auditorium, and the actors' stage, a custom-built platform set across one end of the space, and possibly as large as their playhouse playing area. The court audience would have sat ... in sloping banks of seating set against the side walls and the rear wall behind the Queen's seat, creating more of the effect of a modern sports arena. The chief difference as one looked out from the stage, Shakespeare's point of view, would have been the effect of the glow and shimmer of numerous candles, suspended on decorated chandeliers hung from the roof, and burning in candleholders set against the wall and posts all around the room. The aura of this scintillating lighting would have been picked up in the jewels and spangled fabrics of the richly-dressed and high-born audience assembled to watch the play. Brilliance was the mark of court performance.
>
> *(Astington, 2009, 309)*

As was usual the Great Chamber at Greenwich was on the second storey, and seems to have been similar in size to that at Whitehall, about 60 ft (18.28m) by 30 ft (9.14m).[28] Somewhat less usual, the Hall was little bigger, some 68 ft (20.73m) by 30 ft, making it not much more than half the size of the equivalent room at Whitehall (approximately 90 ft [27.43m] by 40 ft [12.19m]) or Hampton Court (the only one of the four which still stands, 106 ft [32.31m] long overall and 40 ft wide). Those larger rooms must really have tested the vocal range of the actors, being almost twice as long as any distance they would have to carry over the yards of one of the amphitheaters, though indoors. As a general rule, therefore, the Halls were usually used for larger events, with an expanded attendance; the Great Chamber for somewhat more intimate occasions, though probably still involving up to 500 attendees.

There is a ground-plan for a banquet in the Great Chamber at Whitehall on Twelfth Night 1601, which we have noted was very similar in size to that at Greenwich. The plan is highly suggestive for the use of that room when theatricals were performed there, as they were later that night – including Shakespeare's company (see Figure 3.4).[29] We see that the Queen's Presence Chamber lay to the south of the Great Chamber; she would enter from there, requiring that her "state" or ceremonial seat would be at that end of the room. Indeed, it is apparent that there were special fittings to hold the "state" in place, so that protocol required that all the other seating would *always* be arrayed so as to make it the center of attention. In this ground plan we can see that all tables and cupboards have been pushed back to the walls and the seating is arranged in such away that the Queen and the space below her, where the actors would perform, were always the focus of attention. To a slightly lesser extent so to were her most notable quests, who on this occasion included Virginio Orsino, Duke of Bracciano, and ambassadors from Muscovy, seated close by her in positions of honor. For most spectators, they were all backdrops to the theatricals, very much as the hangings on the walls were (Astington, 1991, 6–11).

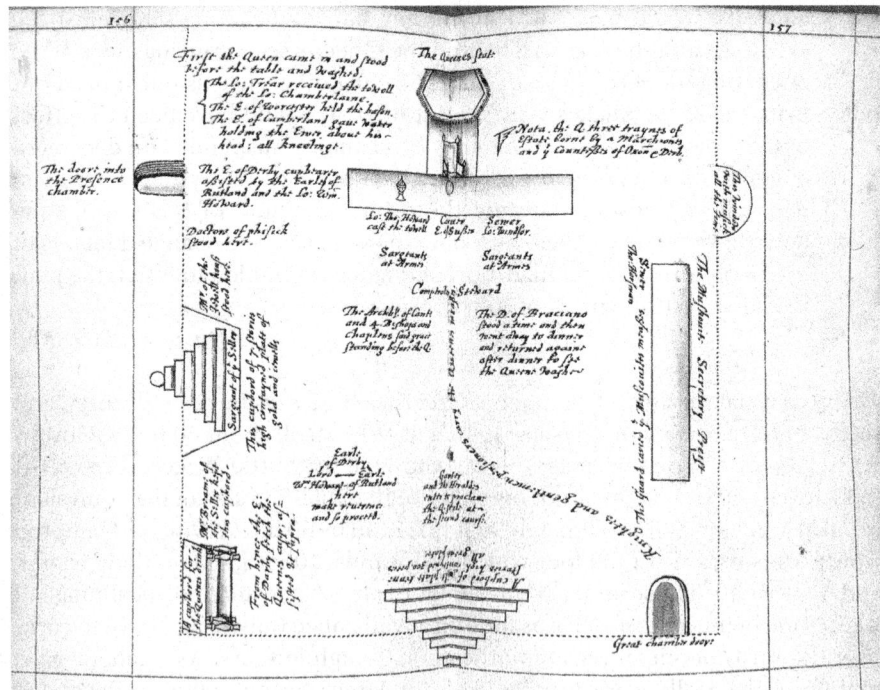

Figure 3.4 Diagram of seating arrangements in the Great Chamber at Whitehall.
Source: College of Arms, MS Vincent 151, pp. 156–7.

This arrangement afforded the actors no equivalent to their tiring houses in the theatres: no base for entrances and exits, no place to change costumes or conceal properties until they were needed. They were simply too far from the door at the north end of the room, via which they and most of the audience would have entered, and there are no alternative options. As they had been doing for decades, the players would have improvised. That is, a "house" or "houses" would have served as a tiring house. The Revels Accounts for the end of Elizabeth's reign are lost. But the early Jacobean Accounts bear out this supposition. Those for 1604/5 charge "For 12 ells of canvas for the Office of the Revels for the tiring house" (Streitberger, 1986b, 12). This might conceivably have been augmented by the use of smaller, similarly canvas-covered but richly painted "houses" or booths as localized points for action, and entry and exit, within the action of the play proper and defining its geography (see pp. 2, 21). The Revels Office had regularly provided these for court entertainments in earlier decades; their use seems to have been declining by the 1590s, but as late as 1614 Sir George Buc's Revels Accounts record expenditure on "canvas for the booths and other necessaries for a play called *Bartholomew Fair*" (70). (I discuss them further in relation to Gray's Inn, in the next section). Those same accounts also record "Music houses three at Whitehall," one requiring "taffeta for a curtain," presumably similar temporary constructions (ibid.).

We have a brief glimpse of Elizabeth seated on her "state" for the last-ever performance at court of the Queen's Men, early in 1594. Thomas Birch recorded that "Mr [Anthony] Standen was at the play and dancing on Twelfth Night, which lasted until one after midnight, more by constraint than by choice, the Earl of Essex having committed him to the placing and entertaining of certain Germans. The Queen appeared there in a high throne, richly adorned, and "as beautiful," says he, "to my old sight, as ever I saw her; and next to her chair the earl, with whom she often devised in sweet and favourable manner" (Birch, 1754, 1.146). The Queen and the last of her great favorites were of more interest than the Queen's Men, a salutary reminder of the place of theatricals in the great scheme of things.

As at Oxford in 1566, the focus on the Queen is all-important. She is as much the center of attention (indeed, more so) than the actors – it is crucial that the audience can see her as well as the stage. She is the courtly equivalent of the hosts in great houses, mayors in towns and cities, senior academics in colleges being placed in seats of honor, where they are as visible as the players (see pp. 57–8). This would have been enhanced by the lighting that was a distinctive feature of court shows, which were almost always staged in the dead of night. Shakespeare had encountered something of this in great houses where he played, but the court would be lit to a much higher level.

By this time it fell to the Office of Works to set up the stage and the seating, but the Revels Office still deployed its traditional skills in installing the candle lighting, using twisted copper wire. The 1608/9 Accounts are typical in charging for "Branches 16, viz. 8 at 40s the piece (£16) and 8 at 20s (£8) ... wire rods, 8 containing 140 foot the piece being twisted three great wires into one rod ... ropes to hang the branches, 8 ... pipes of plate to save the ropes from burning, 16 ... pulleys for branches, 8 ... staples to strain the wires, 4 dozen ... pendants ... candleplates, 4 dozen ... candlesticks, 4 dozen" (Streitberger, 1986*b*, 32–3). As in other venues, the whole room was lit, not just the stage, and there was presumably some scope to enhance lighting and coloring around the action for particular effects: the 1612–13 Accounts charge for "Looking glasses, 40 dozen to set upon the branches" and "bladders gilt to hang upon the branches, six dozen" (58). There were also the usual practical consequences of the candles, which here more than anywhere needed to be trimmed from time to time to stop wax dripping. The play had thus to be stopped, requiring (as we have noted before) what were in fact, if not in intention, act breaks (p. 58).

We see an instance of this in one of the rare accounts we have of a play by professionals being performed at court. The departure of the French Ambassador, La Trémoille, was marked by feasting and a play at Whitehall in May 1619, hosted by the King's cousin, the Duke of Lennox. The King's Men performed *Pericles* for the event:

> The Marquise Trenell on Thursday last took leave of the King: that night was feasted at White Hall, by the Duke of Lennox in the Queen's great chamber ... to the King's great Chamber they went to see the play of Pericles, Prince of Tyre, which lasted till 2 o'clock. After two acts, the players ceased till the French all refreshed them with sweetmeats brought on chiney voiders, & wine & ale in bottles, after the players began anew.[30]

This is the most precisely timed and detailed description of a court play (as distinct from masque) that we have. Assuming they had supper at the usual time, the performance began before 10 p.m. and certainly finished at 2 a.m., taking far longer than any modern performance of *Pericles* would – the text we have is quite short – even with intermissions. But it was interrupted for a relatively modest dessert after the second act, and we have no way of knowing how much time that took.[31] The fact that plays at court took breaks for refreshments, and had seating for the majority of those present, must have made the performance of ultra-long plays like *Hamlet* or *Bartholomew Fair* far more acceptable from an audience's point of view (Astington, 1999, 84, 117, 172–3). The rhythms of playing at court must have been very different, from the actors' point of view, from those in their regular theatres. Getting back to the Theatre in the dead of night on those winter nights – the Shakesperean era was a mini ice-age, when the Thames several times froze over – must also have been a daunting task.

We have no idea what plays the Chamberlain's Men staged at Greenwich late in December 1594, though we do know that they had *The Comedy of Errors* prepared for performance at Gray's Inn on the 28th and Edmund Tilney might well have thought it suitable fare for the court Revels season. Whatever the plays, the opulence must have been impressive. Not only would the Queen and her courtiers have been resplendent in their best dresses and doublets, while sergeants-at-arms and other guards would have been in full uniform, and the walls and stage would have been covered with hangings we have described. Like much of the clothing in the room, some would be shot through with gold and silver thread, further enhancing the glittering light from the candles. The tapestries' depictions of Biblical, classical, or mythological scenes placed the plays in ancient traditions of storytelling. The platform on which the players acted may literally have been pretty much bare, but the whole room in which they performed when at court was a richly embellished meta-stage in which their playing blended into a larger pageantry of royal majesty, visually very different from the common playhouses.

Box 3.4 Patronage and its Practices

"Patronage" is a broad term, which encompasses many of the characteristic practices of early modern England. "Patronage, broadly defined, was the central social system of the era. It dominated political life and permeated the structure of the church and universities. Its influence on the economy was enormous, and the assumptions behind it were reflected in religious thought, in cosmological speculation, and in the organization and daily detail of family life" (Evans, 1989, 23). Through it, offices, gifts, employment, rewards, authority, land tenancy, influence, opportunities all flowed from the highest in the land down to the lowest in society, in a rigidly hierarchical structure; it forged bonds of reciprocal beneficence and obligation, binding patron and patronized in quasi-familial ties.

A writer, like Shakespeare, might seek to exploit the benefits offered by the patronage system in one of various ways. At a very basic level he might seek permission to dedicate a work to someone of stature, ideally a wealthy aristocrat; this honored the patron and spread his fame, and might bring the author a reward of perhaps a few pounds. This is what Shakespeare was after when he dedicated both *Venus and Adonis* and *The Rape of Lucrece* to the young Earl of Southampton, though it is not impossible that he hoped for a higher level of patronage beyond that: perhaps employment in a role where his linguistic skills were of value, such as a tutor or a secretary. So, for example, the poet John Donne achieved a significant position as chief secretary to the Lord Keeper of the Great Seal, Lord Egerton (though he threw it away when he secretly married Egerton's niece); the poet and dramatist, Samuel Daniel, served as a tutor in the household of the great Countess of Pembroke, and later as tutor to Lady Anne Clifford, daughter of the Earl and Countess of Cumberland (see Robbins, 2003).

Patronage of an acting company was a rather different business. As we have seen, its origins lay in the fact that aristocrats and gentry employed household players and musicians, some of whom toured to neighboring establishments and earned gratuities, a practice which gradually extended and became professionalised. Some notable aristocrats seem to have encouraged their players to carry their livery widely around the country as a testament to their prestige, cementing relationships and alliances. So, for example, in 1559 Lord Robert Dudley (later the great Earl of Leicester) wrote to the Earl of Shrewsbury, in his role as Lord President of the North, seeking the latter's permission for his players to travel in Yorkshire, as they already traveled widely elsewhere: "Where my servants ... be such as are players of interludes, and for the same have the licence of divers of my lords here under their seals ... I have thought among the rest by my letters to beseech your good lordship's conformity to them likewise, that they may have your hand and seal to their licence for the like liberty in Yorkshire; being honest men, and such as shall play none other matters (I trust) but tolerable and convenient ... for whom I shall have good cause to thank your lordship and to remain your lordship's to the best that shall lie in my little power" (*EPF*, 205). So Dudley begs a favor of Shrewsbury, while promising to reciprocate (with "my little power") in the future; in this he financially benefits his players, but they in turn reflect his magnificence across the country, at essentially no cost to himself. Patronage oiled many wheels simultaneously.

We have already observed later provisions in the 1570s, prompted by both court and Parliament, which sought to limit such theatrical patronage to the narrow ranks of the aristocracy (excluding the gentry), so reducing the number of troupes and keeping them more securely within the proper limits of authority (see pp. 29–30). What we know very little about in all of this is the nature of the personal relationship between a lord and his players. To what extent were men like Leicester or Lord Strange, or Shakespeare's theatrical patrons, the Hunsdons, actually interested in theatre or in the plays they performed? To what extent did the players and their writers feel obliged to reflect their patrons' interests in their works? The evidence is very thin.

Writing for Patrons?

To return for a moment to the Revels season at Greenwich in the winter of 1594/5 (see p. 22): it is possible that the Chamberlain's Men made one further appearance in Great Chamber there, though there is no record of it. As John Stow's *Annals* record: "The 26 of January [1595], the Earl of Derby married the Earl of Oxford's daughter at the court then at Greenwich, which marriage feast was most royally kept" (Stow, 1605, 1279). The Queen then accompanied the couple to Burghley House (*ES* 4: 109, notes 10 and 11). This is one of the occasions on which it is often supposed that the Chamberlain's Men performed

A Midsummer Night's Dream – a wedding play with its polite obeisance to the "fair vestal thronèd by the west" (2.1.158), which is certainly an allusion to the Virgin Queen as a votaress of Diana and possibly one to the Earl of Hertford's entertainment of Elizabeth at Elvetham in 1591. The bridegroom was the younger brother of the late Lord Strange whom many of the company had served and the bride was the grand-daughter of William Cecil, Lord Burghley, so this was a marriage of consequence and one for which it would be fitting for Shakespeare's company to provide entertainment. The date is, moreover, close to when for other reasons scholars usually place the composition of the play.

If this supposed performance took place while the "marriage feast was most royally kept" at Greenwich, then it took place in the Great Chamber – the only room at that time set up for theatricals. The main problem with this hypothesis is that there is no record of any performance at court at that time; the Chamber Accounts detail costs of the feasting, but no payments for a play. It is not impossible, however, that those responsible for the wedding would have paid from their own pockets. (One Arthur Throgmorton desperately petitioned Sir Robert Cecil to be allowed to contrive a masque for the wedding, as a way to return to Elizabeth's favor. There is no evidence that he was successful [*ES*, 1: 168n].) Proponents of the *Dream* theory have alternatively suggested that there could have been a performance at Burghley House, though there is no record of a performance there either.

Others, however, have favored different weddings at which the play might have been performed.[32] One is the February 1596 wedding of Elizabeth Carey to Thomas, son of Henry, Lord Berkeley; it took place in Blackfriars, presumably at the residence of the bride's father, Sir George Carey. Elizabeth Carey was the grand-daughter of Henry, Lord Hunsdon, patron of Shakespeare's company. Yet again, however, there is no recorded performance. Neither of these suggestions is inherently implausible and the absence of records is more the norm than an invalidating objection in chronicling Elizabethan theatre. The more critical issue is whether – as many proponents of these notions suppose – the play was not just performed *at* such an event but written *for* one.

As we saw in relation to Strange's Men, Shakespeare's early history plays seem to show particular care in their treatment of the Stanley family, Lord Strange's ancestors. This is most notably the case in *Richard III* where Ernst Honigmann (one of the key proponents of the "Lancastrian Shakespeare" thesis) argued that "Shakespeare rearranged history so as to make Stanley's [i.e. Thomas Stanley, first Earl of Derby] services to the incoming Tudor dynasty seem more momentous than they really were."[33] He also points to the sympathetic treatment of Old and Young Clifford in *2* and *3 Henry VI*, noting that "Ferdinando, Lord Strange, was the son of Margaret Clifford and was therefore the direct descendant of the Cliffords represented in *Henry VI*" (154).

Lawrence Manley and Sally-Beth MacLean further develop these points in their chapter on "Shakespeare and Lord Strange's Men," arguing also that changes (softening?) to the depiction of the Duchess of Gloucester's witchcraft between the quarto version (*The First Part of the Contention ... of York and Lancaster*) and that in *2 Henry VI*, may have been in deference to striking parallels between what happened to her and to Strange's mother, Lady Margaret Stanley (Manley and MacLean, 2014, 280–320). Both Honigmann and Manley/MacLean also make much of the possible parallels between Ferdinando Stanley and Ferdinando, King of Navarre, in *Love's Labour's Lost*. All of these arguments assume a deeper and more extended connection between Shakespeare and Lord Strange's Men, or Stanley patronage more generally, than the historical record can vouch for. They also require some assumptions about the dating of plays, or of versions of plays, that may be open to question. The only version of *Love's Labour's Lost* that we have, for example, was published in 1598; but that text explicitly tells us that the play has been revised. We neither know when the original was written nor what it looked like. In short, there are a lot of intriguing possibilities here, but no smoking gun.

The same might be said of *The Merry Wives of Windsor*. Ever since Leslie Hotson suggested in 1931 that the play might have been written in connection with the elevation of the second Lord Hunsdon to the Order of the Garter in 1597, most editors of the play have treated this as established fact (Hotson, 1931). There is in fact no record of any theatrical performance connected with the Garter ceremony that year, or with the Garter feast some months later. And 1597 is earlier than other indications might suggest for the play.[34] Moreover, the play's detailed references to St George's Chapel at Windsor Castle, the chapel associated with the Garter Knights, only appear in the 1623 folio version of the play, not in its 1602 quarto. The folio version of the play is certainly associated with the Garter, the senior order of chivalry in England, but whether the play should really be linked with Shakespeare's patron's becoming a member of it has to be questionable (Dutton, 2016, 245–58).

In the Jacobean phase of his career, questions about the topicality of his plays hang most pointedly over *King Lear* and its associations with King James's known desire to unite the parliaments of his two countries, as he had united their crowns. As Andrew Gurr puts it: "Nobody there for the presentation of the play at court at the opening of the 1606 Christmas season could possibly have missed [the play's] applications as an inverted image of the still disunited kingdoms of England and Scotland ... the court's spectators might see the King's Men offering support to their patron through their play's obvious 'application'" (1996, 300; Marcus, 1988, 148–59). But in trying to assess the weight of such "applications" in relation to a court performance we must always bear in mind the regulating figure of the Master of the Revels, who insisted that all plays be "rehearsed, corrected and perfected" under his guidance before they were put on at court (see p. 85). The play was printed in 1608 "*As it was played before the King's Majesty at Whitehall upon St. Stephen's night in Christmas Holidays. By his Majesty's servants playing usually at the Globe on the Bankside.*" That leaves plenty of scope for assuming that the performance differed in some respects from what would have been staged in public. Any "application" that might have been drawn that St Stephen's Night was one sanctioned by Edmund Tilney and need not have squared with Shakespeare's original intentions – though of course Tilney would hardly have chosen the play in the first place, if it had not seemed to him to have proper potential.

These questions ask us to determine where Shakespeare and his fellows precisely were in a spectrum of royal service, company patronage, and commercial operation. There is no proven instance of a playwright for the public theatres being commissioned to write a play for an aristocratic event like a wedding or some mark of royal recognition. Of course one or two (Ben Jonson is the prime example) were commissioned to write masques for the court and entertainments for such as the London livery companies (see p. 12). But that is not the same thing as a play, which is a *company* undertaking, especially if it is written (as it would be by Shakespeare) by their "ordinary poet." To return to our original example, Francis Meres mentions *A Midsummer Night's Dream* in *Palladis Tamia* (1598), so it was certainly public knowledge by then; and it was published in 1600 "As it hath been sundry times publicly acted." There is no *evidence* that it was ever performed anywhere else until a play of "Robin Goodfellow" was staged at court on New Year's Night, 1604. A betting man would lay strong odds that it had been performed before Elizabeth on one of the thirty-two occasions when we know the Chamberlain's Men were at her court, but we do not know what they played (Dutton, 2016, 34–7; Streitberger, 2016, 281–92).

An intriguing example of a patron who clearly did take a real interest in his players and their work is the sixth Earl of Derby, brother of Lord Strange, who was described in 1599 as "busy penning comedies for the common players" – presumably his own Derby's Men, who that year briefly broke into the privileged ranks of chosen performers at court, though possibly the revived Paul's boys, in whom he invested (see p. 70). It may also tell us something that Thomas Heywood dedicated all his non-dramatic works to the Earl of Worcester or his son, long after Worcester ceded patronage of Heywood's acting company to Queen Anne in 1604; this continued until Worcester died in 1628, suggesting a genuine link between patron and client. But in the absence of evidence to the contrary, it is perhaps safest to conclude that Shakespeare and commercial playwrights like him were not specifically commissioned to write plays for their patrons and their particular occasions. Yet it is difficult to believe that *some* level of identification with their patrons did not make its mark on the plays written for them, in the manner of those plays apparently associated with Lord Strange.

While we might speculate that Shakespeare may have worked with the Queen's Men and/or Strange's Men there is no evidence that he was ever a permanent member of either company. The only companies in which he was a sharer were the Lord Chamberlain's Men (1594–1603) and its subsequent reincarnation, the King's Men (1603–circa 1613): see p. 277. So, leaving aside James I (see p. 277), the only theatrical patrons we can be sure Shakespeare served were the father and son, Henry and George Carey, first and second Lords Hunsdon, who both served as Lord Chamberlain – the man who oversaw the running of most aspects of the royal household, and so had particular influence over access to the Queen – for most of the time between 1594 and 1603.

Henry Carey (1526–96) (Figure 3.5) was first cousin to Queen Elizabeth on her mother (Anne Boleyn's) side. Largely because of this he received early honors when she came to the throne (1558), including being created Lord Hunsdon and made a Knight of the Garter. But he had to work hard in her service to achieve the influence and rewards he sought. Early in the reign this service focused mainly on the Scottish borders, a sensitive region at a time when Mary, Queen of Scots laid claim to the English crown and Scottish politics were in turmoil. In 1568 he was appointed governor of the key border town of Berwick and next year was involved in resistance to the revolt of the northern earls

Figure 3.5 Portrait of Henry Carey, 1st Lord Hunsdon. *Source*: Berkeley Castle.

against Elizabeth, making a name for himself in 1570 when he defeated the larger forces of the rebel, Leonard Dacre. He was promoted to warden of the east marches (i.e. the eastern section of the Scottish border).

In 1577 he achieved a central position in Elizabeth's administration when he was made a Privy Councilor, one of the body that effectively ruled England in the Queen's name. He got on well with the key figure, William Cecil, Lord Burghley, the Lord Treasurer, but also managed to stay on good terms with the Queen's great favorite, the Earl of Leicester. He gained a reputation as a blunt, plain-speaking man of affairs, with little of a courtier's proverbial guile. In 1585 he was appointed Lord Chamberlain of the Household, succeeding his son-in-law, Lord Howard of Effingham (husband of his eldest daughter), who in turn became Lord Admiral. As noted earlier, Lord Admiral Howard retained an interest in theatrical affairs, so that father- and son-in-law potentially represented an important axis within the Privy Council whenever theatrical issues came to their attention – a factor in Andrew Gurr's assumption that the situation in 1594 was engineered by the Council (pp. 72, Note 11; 77–8).

By the 1570s most Lord Chamberlains had assumed the responsibility of patronizing a leading troupe that might serve the Queen. The office required that he be at court with the Queen even over Christmas, so it made sense that they should perform there rather than at his own country estate. The Earl of Sussex, for example, who was Lord Chamberlain from 1572 until 1583 had one of the leading companies of the day and they performed at court most Christmases. Lord Hunsdon had patronized players intermittently since the 1560s, but by the time he came to office the formation of the Queen's Men in 1583 had effectively settled the choice of court playing for several years, until Strange's Men emerged (see pp. 41; 61). His players appear occasionally in provincial records, but he apparently patronized none at all between 1590 and the appearance of the Lord Chamberlain's Men in the record from 1594 onwards; they were clearly a new formation, built on what was left of Strange's Men, though critically without Edward Alleyn. He had left to lead Lord Admiral Howard's Men, the principal rivals to Hunsdon's own players for the next decade. Whether this was centrally planned or not, it effected a significant reorganization of London playing that set the pattern for the future. And Hunsdon, as Lord Chamberlain, played an important part.

Hunsdon was not an uncritical supporter of players. When in 1584 James Burbage defied the London authorities on the basis of his status as Hunsdon's "servant," he promptly backed the authorities (see p. 29). But, as I relate elsewhere, he was not opposed to James Burbage's building of a playhouse in the Blackfriars, where he was looking for new quarters himself, or to its use by his own players (see p. 196). Had he lived the scheme might have succeeded. But he died on July 22, 1596. Thomas Nashe's comments in a letter to William Cotton spell out the consequences: "now the players … are piteously persecuted by the Lord Mayor and the aldermen, and however in their old lord's time they thought their state settled, it is now so uncertain they cannot build upon it" (Nashe, 1904–10, 5: 194).

Ironically, his eldest son, George Carey, 2nd Lord Hunsdon (1547–1603), signed the petition of Blackfriars residents opposed to Burbage's plans, an unfortunate first involvement with the players he was to patronize (see p. 196). He dearly wanted to succeed his father in office, but Elizabeth as ever cannily spread her favors and appointed another long-serving retainer, William Brooke, tenth Lord Cobham. Cobham himself, however, died in March 1597, and the younger Hunsdon finally did succeed his father as Lord Chamberlain, a Privy Councilor and member of the Order of the Garter. The younger Hunsdon was not as prominent a figure as his father, but had a typical track-record of military, parliamentary, and judicial appointments before achieving real prominence. He assumed patronage of the players as soon as his father died; they were known simply as Lord Hunsdon's Men until he took on his father's old role. Towards the end of Elizabeth's reign he was a sick man and one of King James' first decisions in London was to relieve him of his duties as Lord Chamberlain (May 4, 1603). But this represented no threat to the players since only two weeks later they acquired the highest patron of them all, the king himself. The younger Hunsdon died on September 8 that year.

There is nothing in Shakespeare's works that connects them with the Hunsdons like those features of the early plays that may speak to his association with Lord Strange. If *A Midsummer Night's Dream* was written for a particular family wedding, there is no known trace of it in the text. The most teasing case is the figure of Falstaff, who appears in three plays – the two parts of *Henry IV* as well as *Merry Wives* – and was promised, in the epilogue to *2 Henry IV*, to appear in *Henry V*, though all we get there is an account of his death. It is just possible that all this was associated with Shakespeare's Hunsdon patrons. I pursue the case elsewhere (see pp. 194ff).

Gray's Inn

The last distinctively different staging with which we can associate the Lord Chamberlain's Men in 1594 relates to their performance of Shakespeare's *The Comedy of Errors* at Gray's Inn on the night of December 28 (Innocents' Day).[35] The occasion is recorded in the *Gesta Grayorum* ("A History of Gray's Men"), an account evidently written close to the date but not printed until 1688. It tells the story of a much longer charade, within which that performance was almost incidental. The students of the Inn, one of the four London law schools which virtually constituted a university in the capital city, had determined to hold protracted revels over the whole Christmas period (stretching from December to February). It was to be a release of festivity after the prolonged plague. These revels took the time-honored form in such institutions of electing a topsy-turvy lord-of-misrule, who "reigned" over the Inn during this period; he had a retinue which mirrored that of the Queen's own court, including a Lord Treasurer, Lord Chamberlain, Lord Chancellor, and many others. The student elected was Henry Helmes, dubbed the Prince of Purpoole after the manor of Portpoole in which the Inn stood. One thread running through these sophomoric revels was the intention to cement a bond of amity between Gray's and the students of their fellow inn, the Inner Temple. Accordingly an "ambassador" of the Inner Temple was among those invited on the night of the Chamberlain's Men's performance.

From the *Gesta Grayorum*:

> The next grand night was intended to be upon Innocents' Day at night; at which time there was a great presence of lords, ladies, and worshipful personages, that did expect some notable performance at that time; which, indeed, had been effected, if the multitude of beholders had not been so exceeding great, that thereby there was no convenient room for those that were actors; by reason whereof, very good inventions and conceits could not have opportunity to be applauded, which otherwise would have been great contentation to the beholders. Against which time, our friend, the Inner Temple, determined to send their Ambassador to our Prince of State, as sent from Frederick Templarius, their Emperor, who was then busied in his wars against the Turk. The Ambassador came very gallantly appointed, and attended by a great number of brave gentlemen, which arrived at our court about nine of the clock at night. Upon their coming thither, the King at Arms gave notice to the Prince, then sitting in his chair of State in the Hall, that there was come to his court an Ambassador from his ancient friend the State of Templaria which desired to have present access unto His Highness ... So he was brought in very solemnly, with sound of trumpets, the King at Arms and Lords of Purpoole making to his company, which marched before him in order. He was received very kindly of the Prince, and placed in a chair beside His Highness, to the end that he might be partaker of the sports intended. But first, he made a speech to the Prince ... Our Prince made him this answer, That he did acknowledge that the great kindness of his Lord, whereby he doth invite to further degrees in firm and loyal friendship, did deserve all honourable commendations, and effectual accomplishment, that by any means might be devised ... When the Ambassador was placed, as aforesaid, and that there was something to be performed for the delight of the beholders, there arose such a disordered tumult and crowd upon the stage, that there was no opportunity to effect that which was intended. There came so great a number of worshipful personages upon the stage, that might not be displaced; and gentlewomen, whose sex did privilege them from violence, that when the prince and his officers had in vain, a good while, expected and endeavoured a

reformation, at length there was no hope of redress for that present. The Lord Ambassador and his train thought that they were not so kindly entertained as was before expected, and thereupon would not stay any longer at that time, but, in a sort, discontented and displeased. After their departure the throngs and tumults did somewhat cease, although so much of them continued, as was able to disorder and confound any good inventions whatsoever. In regard whereof, as also for that the sports intended were especially for the gracing of the Templarians it was thought good not to offer anything of account, saving dancing and revelling with gentlewomen; and after such sports, a *Comedy of Errors* (like to Plautus his *Menechmus*) was played by the players. So that night was begun, and continued to the end, in nothing but confusion and errors; whereupon, it was ever afterwards called, The Night of Errors.[36]

I have quoted at such length to give an impression of the whole occasion and its social resonances for the participants. The following day, continuing the fantasy of misrule, the Prince's Privy Council launched an enquiry into the "great disorders and misdemeanours," which finally led to a charge against the "sorcerer or conjurer" deemed to be responsible "that he had foisted a company of base and common fellows, to make up our disorders with a play of errors and confusions; and that night had gained to us discredit, and itself a nickname of Errors" (32–3). This was of course in jest, but in such company there lingered the conviction that the Lord Chamberlain's Men were "a company of base and common fellows," however grand their lord might be.

Ironically, we learn that the real cause of the disorder was that too many of those in attendance that night felt that their status warranted them a place on the stage, with the Prince. The *Gesta* tells us that the collegiate form of staging was followed when it describes a "Running Banquet" and specifies "a table set in the midst of the stage, before the Prince's Seat" – imitating royal seating at court rather than (as long popularly supposed) using the lower end of the hall, with its convenient screen doors and mistrels' gallery, as the frame of the stage (see p. 24). As Ros King comments: "The stage must have been at the opposite end of the Hall from the screen" (2004, 34). In the chaotic conditions "there arose such a disordered tumult and crowd upon the stage, that there was no opportunity to effect that which was intended. There came so great a number of worshipful personages upon the stage, that might not be displaced ...." There is no way of knowing if these really were "worshipful personages" or only so in the fantasy of Purpool, but the Elizabethan convention of seating the dignitaries "upon the stage" proved in this company to be totally impractical – so much so that the most honored guest of the evening, the "Ambassador" from the Inner Temple, left in disdain.

This same section of the *Gesta* jokingly lays out how the "sorcerer" "had caused ... scaffolds to be reared to the top of the house, to increase expectation.

And how he had caused divers ladies and gentlewomen, and others of good condition, to be invited to our sports" (32). This speaks to two points discussed elsewhere. One is that if there was scaffolded seating reaching to the ceiling, there is a good chance that they made proper provision for substantial tiring houses lower down, adjacent to the stage, such as we know were built at Queens' College, Cambridge (see p. 22). The other is specific acknowledgment of the presence of ladies of quality in the audience. The Inns of Court, like the universities, were all-male establishments. But theatricals at both were festive occasions when ladies were invited in. Here, as elsewhere, they were a notable factor in the audience (see pp. 133, 162).

Only one text of *The Comedy of Errors* has survived, that in the First Folio, and it has some features that make it unusual by comparison with other Shakespeare works. It is particularly heavily indebted to its Latin source (as the author of the *Gesta Grayorum* noted, Plautus's *Menaechmi*, "The Brothers Menaechmus") but, more to the point its staging suggests features we do not associate with the public playhouses at this date. The action all takes place in Ephesus, and it repeatedly and pointedly circulates around the house of Antipholus of Ephesus, "the Phoenix," the house of the Courtesan, "the Porcupine," and the Priory where the Abbess is found.[37] The principal characters are either tied to these sites or in transit between them. They seem to be fixed and known points on the stage, rather than the very provisional designation of locations in most Elizabethan drama. If we compare it with *Twelfth Night*, for example, another Plautine play of twins and confused identities, we see there a very fluid shifting from Orsino's court to the seacoast ("This is Illyria, lady": 1.2.2) to Olivia's house, then alternating between the court and her house (or garden), or indeterminately to settings in the town or the country, as the action demands. This is what is sometimes called "successive staging," which takes for granted a change of scene whenever the actors clear the stage. This became the norm for Elizabethan public theatre.

A possible explanation for the relative rigidity of *The Comedy of Errors* might be that the text reflects a very specific, old-style staging of the play, possibly even that at Gray's Inn (for which some scholars think it might have been purposely written) or one at court: we know that it was performed at court on December 28, 1604, but it may well have been staged there earlier.[38] Academic institutions and the court are places where "houses" such as those we saw at Oxford in 1566 remained in use (see pp. 2, 21; Foakes, 1962, xxxiv–xxxix; Kernodle, 1944, 160–3). Where such "houses" were deployed, the effect was quite different from what we normally expect of the Elizabethan stage, as we see from McMillin and MacLean's discussion of the George Peele's Queen's Men's play, *The Old Wives Tale*:

> The action moves among four places: a cross, a well, Sacrapant's study, and a hill with a light hidden behind removable turf. The system of

> staging uses emblematic props or "houses" to indicate the locations, and because the scenic indicators remain in view throughout the action, this has sometimes been called "simultaneous staging." The emblematic nature of the scenic properties must be kept in mind. These are not so much acting places as indicators of location ... By keeping the locations visible and within easy reach of one another, simultaneous staging implies a containable and organized world. It was perhaps for this reason that simultaneous staging was customary at court and at other institutions of authority, where the monarch might attend and be given her special seat in an auditorium which was also carefully organized. The Queen's Men were masters of the court schedule in their early years and (help on the settings coming from the Revels office, where new canvas "houses" could be built and old ones pulled from storage) they must have performed many plays on the simultaneous system evident in *The Old Wives Tale*.
>   (McMillin and MacLean, 1999, 138–9)[39]

It is widely assumed that the use of "houses" and simultaneous staging declined at court as the acting conventions developed in the public amphitheaters became more prevalent. But change would not have happened overnight. As we noted, as late as the Revels accounts for 1614 we find a charge for "canvas for the booths" for *Bartholomew Fair*," suggesting that those old practices had not been entirely abandoned (p. 121). Jonson may even have been deliberately evoking the old staging, as he evokes so much about old theatre in that play.

The Gray's Inn *Comedy of Errors* and an account by John Manningham of a performance of *Twelfth Night* at the feast of Candlemas (February 2) in the Middle Temple are both well-established pieces of Shakespearean lore (Schoenbaum, 1987, 213). It is not yet so widely known – a discovery of Alan H. Nelson in tracing the theatrical history of the Inns of Court – that once they became established as the King's Men, Shakespeare's company took on yearly commissions to perform at the Inner Temple on the feast of All Saints (November 1) and at Candlemas.[40] They presumably saw this as a lucrative extension of their existing commitment to be available to perform for the court's Revels season; it was clearly a further inhibition against their touring at that time of the year. These commissions lasted until the Civil War.

As this review of known theatrical venues for Shakespeare and his company in 1594 shows, they were busy and they had to be adaptable. Their plays had to be portable enough to fit a variety of stages; nothing of theirs originating from this time called, for example, for descent machinery or even a trapdoor. In most venues they would play continuously, without interruption, a convention that meant they had (for example) to plan carefully for the removal of dead bodies. Sometimes it is fully scripted, as when Falstaff carries off the dead Hotspur in *1Henry IV* or Fortinbras orders "Let four captains / Bear Hamlet, like a soldier, to the stage" (5.2.397–8). The dialogue around Desdemona in *Othello* suggests that she lay where a curtain could be pulled to hide her body, either on the bed itself or at the mouth of the discovery space: "The object poisons sight; / Let it be hid" (5.2.375–6). That was easily arranged in the playhouse, of course, but would have called for special preparations on the road – as, for example, when *Othello* was performed at Oxford in the summer of 1610 – or in a private household. But in other instances their removal was evidently a charge for minor players, something assigned in rehearsal. In these same plays there is no indication of how Sir Walter Blunt, or Claudius or Laertes, or Roderigo, leaves the stage – but it seems not to have been acceptable to breach the suspension of disbelief by having the actors unaided discreetly withdraw, as often happens today. The players had themselves to be as adaptable as their plays, since these different venues all had different social conventions, histories, and expectations. One wonders what this "company of base and common fellows," who were now used to conducting a large, successful and profitable business at the Theatre, made of their reveling patrons at Gray's Inn on that Night of Errors.

The commissions to perform at the Inns of Court should also remind us that the actors did also at times perform plays from their regular repertoire for more private occasions in London. The most notorious example of such a private commission was that by the supporters of the Earl of Essex on the eve of his rebellion in February 1601. They prevailed upon the Chamberlain's Men to perform "the play of the deposing and killing of King Richard" (in all probability Shakespeare's *Richard II*) in their usual way at the Globe, despite the players' protests that it was old and would draw no audience. They were promised "40s more than their ordinary [regular share of the profits] to play it" (*ES*, 2: 205; see p. 153).

Most special commissions were far less dramatic and usually involved performances in private houses. Rowland White's regular reports to his master, Sir Robert Sidney, included the information that Sir Walter Ralegh, the Earl of Southampton and others feasted Sir Robert Cecil, with "plays," before a mission to France (January 30, 1598); that Sir Gelly Meyrick, the Earl of Essex's steward, laid on "a very great supper" for numerous lords and ladies: "They had 2 plays, which kept them up till 1 o'clock after midnight" (February 15, 1598); and that Lord Chamberlain Hunsdon entertained the Flemish Ambassador, Louis Verreyken, "and there in the afternoon his players acted, before Verreyken, *Sir John Oldcastle*, to his great contentment" (March 8, 1600: Collins, 1746, 2: 86; 2:90; 2: 175). At the end of December 1601 Hunsdon also called on his players to entertain the Queen at his Blackfriars house. We hear of the letter-writer, John Chamberlain, going to a play at the house of Sir Robert Cecil's close associate, Sir Walter Cope (Chamberlain, 1939, 1.457). Earlier in the reign Sir Walter went to great lengths on Cecil's behalf to find entertainment for Queen Anne, when James was out of town; the King's Men offered a revival of *Love's Labour's Lost*, but it was already "appointed to be played tomorrow night at my Lord of Southampton's." Southampton and Cecil apparently came to some kind of accord over the play; they both entertained the Queen, and her brother the Duke of Holstein, two nights apart in early January 1605, and one or other of them had *Love's Labour's Lost* performed (Kernan, 1995, 69). In 1613 Sir Robert Rich arranged a play for the ambassador from Savoy (*ES*, 1: 220, n. 3). Clearly only the wealthy could afford to pay for private performances by the players in this way, but it seems likely there was much more of this than we have record of.

Notes

1 There are repeated references at least until 1603 of the ban on Sunday playing not being enforced. See, for example, *ES*, 1: 314–15; 4: 3045, 307, 310, 335.
2 There is evidence that the boy companies only performed one day a week, Saturdays. The epilogue to *Eastward Ho!*, for example, performed at the Blackfriars in 1605, concludes with the wish: "May this [pageant] attract you, hither, once a week" (Jonson 2012e, line 8).
3 Henslowe's *Diary* contains several entries later than 1594 detailing performances on holy-days, including May Day in 1596, and Candlemas and Shrove Tuesday in 1597 (*Henslowe*, 36, 56). But there is no information about the time those performances began.
4 A note in the manuscript plays of the amateur playwright, William Percy, addressed to "the Master of the Children of Paul's", explains how they might be trimmed if needs be, "the children not to begin before four, after prayers, and the gates of Paul's shutting at six" (*ES*, 2: 21). It is not clear exactly when this was written, but if it was after that playhouse reopened in 1599 it would reflect special circumstances under which it operated. Evensong might well be celebrated *every* day at St Paul's and the boy's company, performing in its precinct, may have been required to respect it even if other companies no longer had to.
5 See Figure 3.2. You can also locate the sites of the Elizabethan theatres in modern London by consulting the Shakespearean London Theatres project site: http://shalt.dmu.ac.uk/locations.html.
6 Tilney was required to vacate the old priory/palace in 1607 and his office later settled in Blackfriars.
7 As played by Simon Callow, Tilney is pompous, self-important, narrow minded, and uses his position to obtain sexual favors. It makes for good comedy, but it is pure fantasy.
8 This runs together quotations from a letter of the Lord Mayor of London, Sir John Harte, and the minute of a Privy Council letter (*ES*, 4: 305, 306).
9 The key documents relating to the history of the Theatre are conveniently collected in *EPF*, 330–87; see also Egan, 2009.

10 In the 1592 alterations it was made rather more rectangular, and moved some 6 feet 6 inches further north.

11 It is usually assumed that this refers to an ur-*Hamlet* that preceded Shakespeare's play, though some scholars hold that the Q1 text of Shakespeare's *Hamlet* represents that early version. See, for example, Bourus, 2014.

12 *Dr Faustus* may be an exception. Middleton writes in *The Black Book*: "He had a head of hair like one of my devils in *Dr Faustus* when the old Theatre cracked and frighted the audience" (lines 156–7; 2007a). But the play was in the repertoire of the Admiral's Men at the Rose for nearly a decade before it was first printed in 1604 and probably reflects the staging there. In fact, although it calls for a wide range of properties and effects, including a "chafer of coals", deer's horns, fireworks, thunder and lightning, and a detachable leg, it makes minimal demands on a stage. A discovery space was presumably used for Faustus's study, but there is no call for an upper stage. The ending may or may not call for a trapdoor, depending on how it is played. When Faustus says "Ugly hell, gape not" (5.2.114) it is not clear if there is an actual representation of hell on stage, like an old-fashioned hell-mouth, or whether Faustus evokes these horrors for himself. (The 1616 text is much more explicit that "*Hell is discovered*" (5.2.114), though that is at an earlier point in the rewritten scene.) There is an aptness to making the discovery space the opening to hell, since Faustus's studies were his road to it. References to all Marlowe's plays are to Marlowe, 1995.

13 For example, in the witchcraft scene of *2 Henry VI* (1.4) "*Enter Eleanor aloft*", while 4.5 directs "*Enter Lord Scales upon the Tower*, and in 4.9 "*Enter King, Queen, and Somerset, on the terrace*"; there are entrances "*on the walls*" in both 5.1 and 5.6 of *3Henry VI*. See Hosley, 1957.

14 Scholars have long since abandoned the notion of an "inner stage" in Elizabethan theatres, used for indoor scenes. Large parts of the audience would not have been able to see into it at all, and the visibility even for those who could would have been very limited, in the absence of artificial lighting. The use of the discovery space was doubtless conditioned by the need to make what happened there visible to most of the audience.

15 The Fortune contract expressly stipulated that the builder, Peter Street, should *not* be responsible for any of the painting, presumably because specialist painters would be commissioned for that purpose.

16 Bart Van Es's *Shakespeare in Company* (2013) is in part an extended study of this situation.

17 For the mildly salacious tale in John Manningham's *Diary* (March 13, 1602) of Shakespeare supposedly getting the better of a sexual assignation Burbage had planned with a lady infatuated with him in the role of Richard III, see Schoenbaum, 1987, 204–5.

18 The best account of Kemp as a clown remains Wiles, *Shakespeare's Clown*, 1987.

19 In Samuel Rowlands's *The Letting of Humour's Blood in the Head-Vein*, satire 4, Pope is linked with John Singer, a clown in the Admiral's Men: "What means Singer, then, / And Pope, the clown, to speak so boorish, when / They counterfeit the clowns upon the stage?"
20 There were doubtless many, but the number of plays and playwrights we can associate with the early Chamberlain's/King's Men is painfully small: see Appendix.
21 This is clearly "plot" in a different sense from the pasted boards which offered a running schedule of the play as staged (see p. 113). Here it seems to mean something like "outline."
22 In the period when Chettle was writing *The Stepmother's Tragedy* Dekker also received payment for his involvement with plays called *Better Late Than Never* (August 1), *Page of Plymouth* (August 10 and September 2, co-authored with Jonson), and *Robert 2, King of Scots* (aka *The Scots Tragedy*; September 3, 15, 16, 27, co-authored with Jonson and Chettle). Their writing schedules and commitments must have been chaotic.
23 See the entry on the part at the *Henslowe–Alleyn Digitization Project* website: http://www.henslowe-alleyn.org.uk/essays/orlando.html.
24 This is Henslowe's only use of "cutter", which could relate to /one of several trades. Tailor is most likely, though it could refer to a carver or sculptor.
25 The differences between Q1 and Q2 can be accounted for in many ways. The dominant view used to be that Q1 is a clumsy, cut-down version of Q2. My own view is that Q2 is an *expansion* of the text behind the Q1, possibly created for performance at court. See Dutton, 2016, 211–25.
26 This section is particularly indebted to Kathman, 2009*b* and *c*; also *EPF*, 295-305.
27 The metric equivalents of these measurements are, respectively, 42.67m, 24.38m, 9.75m, and 14.63 × 9.75 m.
28 Astington, 1999, 38. This section is heavily indebted to John Astington's work.
29 The illustration shows pp. 156–7 from a volume known as *Vincents Presidents*, preserved by the College of Arms (*Vincent* 151). Reproduced by courtesy of the College of Arms. Leslie Hotson famously argued that Shakespeare's company performed *Twelfth Night* on January 6, 1601, largely because of the presence in the audience of Virginio Orsino, Duke of Bracciano, whose name echoes that of the duke in the play. But the records show that multiple companies were paid for performing that night: the Chamberlain's, Admiral's and Derby's Men, together with the Children of the Chapel, in some kind of "show" (*ES*, 4: 113; Streitberger, 2016, 188, 287). They either collaborated in something spectacular or each offered entertaining scenes rather than a whole play.
30 Sir Gerrard Herbert, writing to Sir Dudley Carleton, quoted in Chambers, 1930, 2.346. I am grateful to John Astington for drawing this account to my attention. Voiders were baskets or trays for serving or removing food; "chiney" presumably means these were of (expensive) china, perhaps platters.

31 f. *OED* "banquet", *n*. 3a. "A course of sweetmeats, fruit, and wine, served either as a separate entertainment, or as a continuation of the principal meal ... a dessert."
32 Other marriages suggested for *A Midsummer Night's Dream* include that of the Earl of Essex to Sir Philip Sidney's widow, Frances; and that of Sir Thomas Heneage, Treasurer of the Chamber, to Mary, Countess of Southampton and mother of the man to whom Shakespeare dedicated *Venus and Adonis* and *The Rape of Lucrece*. None can produce a certified performance.
33 Honigmann, 1985, 63–4. The whole chapter, "Shakespeare and Lord Strange's Men", 59–76, is relevant to this paragraph.
34 Barbara Freedman (1994) did everything necessary to kill off the 1597 hypothesis. Unfortunately, like so many Shakespearean myths, it refuses to die – especially with editors, the people with the greatest power to perpetuate it.
35 On the dating, see p. 82.
36 Based on *Gesta Grayorum*, 1968, 29–32.
37 The inn where Antipholus and Dromio of Syracuse are supposed to be staying, "the Centaur", appears to be offstage – no one is seen to enter or exit it.
38 See Andrews, 1987, 324, which reproduces the court record of "Shaxberd Errors" being performed that night.
39 Alan H. Nelson suggests an alternative staging model: "the localized setting of an academic theatre, in which the stage platform represents a street in the city of Ephesus, with the stage houses (not necessarily limited to three) ranged on either side" (1997, 66).
40 Nelson, 2009, 286. The Middle Temple also established a similar pattern of commissions, but with various companies over time.

4

The Chamberlain's / King's Men and their Organization

My intention here is to give a sense of the organization of Shakespeare's company and the personnel they would have employed at their various venues. As ever in the theatrical world it took many more people to stage a performance than just the actors, though the Chamberlain's Men were distinctive, both in their own day and by later standards, for the level of control exercised by the principal actors.

Sharers

The core of any major acting company were its sharers, the leading actors who would contract an agreement among themselves – with rules they were expected to follow in the business, and agreed penalties if they failed. We do not have a formal list of the sharers of the Lord Chamberlain's Men when the company was first formed. Clearly Kemp, Burbage, and Shakespeare were among them, as payees at court. There is strong evidence, moreover, that four other former members of Strange's Men (along with Kemp) were among them; John Heminge and George Bryan were the company's payees at court the following year; and Heminge was accompanied by Thomas Pope in each of the three succeeding years. Augustine Phillips too was almost certainly an early sharer, because when the company fell under suspicion for having staged a play about Richard II on the eve of the Essex Rebellion in 1601, he was the man the authorities interrogated – that would not have been entrusted to a junior member (see p. 153). In Ben Jonson's 1616 folio of his *Works* he lists the "principal comedians" in the company who performed his *Every Man In His Humour* in 1598; these include six of the seven I have already mentioned (Bryan is the one missing: see p. 157), plus Henry Condell, William Sly, Christopher Beeston, and John Duke.

These were not necessarily sharers at the outset, but Condell and Sly certainly acquired shares eventually. Beeston, who was later to be one of the most powerful theatrical impresarios, left the company not much later, as did Duke.

Shakespeare's Theatre: A History, First Edition. Richard Dutton.
© 2018 Richard Dutton. Published 2018 by John Wiley & Sons Ltd.

An intriguing absence in all this – and something of a cipher throughout – is Richard Cowley. He had been with Strange's Men when they toured in 1593, though not one of their sharers (see pp. 63, 67). The first we hear of him with the Chamberlain's Men is when he is identified with the role of Verges in *Much Ado About Nothing* in its 1600 quarto; the following year he was a payee at court and in 1603 was definitely a sharer in the King's Men. But he appears in *none* of the actor lists that Jonson left with his plays for the company – *Every Man In*, *Every Man Out*, *Sejanus*, *Volpone*, *The Alchemist*, and *Catiline*. Some assume that he was a sharer from 1594 but we cannot be sure; see below (p. 206).

The Chamberlain's Men, like most of the other major companies, were in essence a joint stock company. The sharers, or "fellows" as they were often known, each contributed an agreed sum to the capital of the company, to buy essential equipment (such as costumes and playbooks) and cover necessary expenses. The value of a share would vary with the fortunes of the company and the number of sharers, but it was recognized as owing to the sharer if he left the company or died. In 1613 Charles Massey, a long-time member of the Admiral's Men (Prince Henry's Men after 1603) had cause to remind Philip Henslowe: "for sir I know you understand that there is the composition between our company that if any one give over with consent of his fellows, he is to receive three score and ten pounds (Anthony Jeffes hath had so much); if any one die his widow or friends whom he appoints is to receive fifty pounds (Mrs. Pavy and Mrs. Towne hath had the like)" (Greg, 1907, 64).[1] In his 1635 will, John Shank, a leading sharer in what was by then the King's Men exhorted his fellows: "do not abridge my said wife and executrix in the receiving of what is due unto me and my estate amongst them, as namely fifty pounds for my share in the stocks, books [i.e. play scripts], apparel, and other things according to the old custom and agreement amongst us" (Honigmann and Brock, 1995, 188).

These are quite substantial sums, even allowing for inflation – between four and seven times the £10 that William Ingram designated as a comfortable annual income around 1600 (see p. 16). It presumably explains why some players only achieved a half or even a quarter share. We know, for example, that in June 1595 Henslowe lent his improvident nephew, Francis, £9 "in ready money to lay down for his half share with the company which he doth play with" (*Henslowe*, 9). For legal purposes, however, the sharers *were* the company. Whenever a company was issued with a new patent or licence, it is the sharers who are mentioned by name; other employees are usually designated as "associates." It is reasonable to suppose that the sharers of the Chamberlain's Men drew up mutually binding contracts, specifying what was expected of them and probably prescribing penalties for failure to comply.

We have evidence of such contracts in other companies, though since the precise situations of the different companies varied, the contracts must have varied similarly. Some, for example, were heavily dominated by a manager/impresario, like Christopher Beeston with Queen Anne's Men in the 1610s and

Queen Henrietta's Men in the 1630s; such men would have been in a position to impose something of their own will. This is obviously the case in respect of the one full player's contract that has survived, that for Robert Dawes, who in 1614 contracted to play for Philip Henslowe and Jacob Meade with Lady Elizabeth's Men at their new theatre/bear-baiting house, the Hope:

> 7 April 1614
>
> [Articles of Agreement,] made, concluded, and agreed upon, and which are to be kept and performed by Robert Dawes of London, gentleman, unto and with Philip Henslowe, esquire, and Jacob [Meade, waterman] in manner and form following, that is to say
>
> Imprimis. The said Robert Dawes ... doth covenant, promise, and grant to and with the said PH and JM ... that he ... shall and will play with such company as the said PH and JM shall appoint, for and during the space of three years from the date hereof and at the rate of one whole share, according to the custom of players; and that he ... shall and will at all times during the said time duly attend all such rehearsal, which shall the night before the rehearsal be given publicly out; and if that he ... shall at any time fail to come at the hour appointed, then he shall and will pay to the said PH and JM ... 12d; and if he come not before the said rehearsal is ended, then the said Robert Dawes is contented to pay 2s; and further that if the said Robert Dawes shall not every day, whereon any play is or ought to be played, be ready appareled and ... to begin the play at the hour of three of the clock in the afternoon, unless by six of the same company he shall be licensed to the contrary, that then he ... shall and will pay to the said Philip and Jacob or their assigns 3s; and if that he ... happen to be overcome with drink at the time when he [ought to] play, by the judgment of four of the said company, he shall and will pay 10s; and if he ... shall [fail to come] during any play, having no licence or just excuse of sickness, he is contented to pay 20s; and further [he] ... doth covenant and grant to and with the said PH and JM ... that it shall and may be lawful unto and for the said PH and JM ... during the term aforesaid, to receive and take back to their own proper use the part of him, the said Robert Dawes, of and in one moiety or half part of all such moneys as shall be received at the galleries and tiring house of such house or houses wherein he ... shall play, for and in consideration of the use of the same house and houses; and likewise shall and may take and receive his other moiety [of] the moneys received at the galleries and tiring house dues, towards the paying to them, the said PH and JM, of the sum of £124, being the value of the stock of apparel furnished [to*] the said company by the said PH and JM of the one part of him ... or any other sums [owed] to them for any apparel hereafter newly to be bought by the [said PH and JM, until the said PH and JM] shall thereby be fully satisfied, contended, and paid.

> And further the said Robert Dawes doth covenant, [promise and grant to and with the said PH and JM, that if he ...] shall at any time after the play is ended depart or go out of the [house] with any [of their] apparel on his body, of if the said Robert Dawes [shall carry away any property] belonging to the said company, or shall be consenting [or privy to any other of the said company going out of the house with any of the apparel on his or their bodies, he ...] ... shall and will forfeit and pay unto the said Philip and Jacob, or their administrators or assigns, the sum of £40 of lawful [money of England].[2]

The document clearly demonstrates the power that owners of authorized theatres had once the system that tentatively emerged in 1594 bedded in. Access to such a theatre became a prerequisite of London playing, and Henslowe over the years had clearly accumulated costumes, properties, and playbooks in his own name that he expected companies using his playhouses to lease from him. So Dawes's contract is with Henslowe and Meade much more than it is with the company. James Burbage had no such leverage in 1594. But Shakespeare and his fellows probably had a contract which made each of them accountable to *the company* for precisely the same kind of things: attending rehearsals and performances in a timely fashion, and not being drunk when they were due to perform. Henslowe and Meade further spelled out that they had the right to make two deductions from the sharers' take in the galleries and the tiring house (where the lords' rooms would be situated: see p. 234), before the sharers saw that money: one to repay the £124 value of the costumes which Henslowe and Meade had supplied for the company, the other the house-rent for use of the playhouse. James Burbage would similarly have expected a house-rent for the use of the Theatre, though we do not know if this would have been based (as it was for Henslowe at both the Rose and the Hope) on a fixed proportion of the take from the highest-paying customers, in the galleries and the lords' rooms (see p. 63).

Fines for the earlier infringements are fairly stiff – but become a swingeing £40 for leaving the theatre with any of the costumes kept there for company use. Possibly this was inflated because Henslowe and Meade wanted to protect their own investment. But it is not unlikely that a company like the Chamberlain's Men would have felt similarly protective about their costumes, which must have been their biggest single investment. (We shall see examples of what the Admiral's Men paid out: pp. 170ff.) A parallel example of contractual restrictions lies in the Articles of Agreement entered into by the sharers in a short-lived boy company, the Children of the King's Revels, circa 1608. The shareholders were those who bankrolled the operation, rather than the boy players, but here too it was stipulated that "no apparel, books, or other property of the company is to be removed without the consent of the sharers" (*ES*, 2: 65). And control of company clothing was one of many issues that caused friction between Martin Slater and his fellow sharers (see Box Item, "Martin Slater and the Children of the King's Revels").

Box 4.1 Martin Slater and the Children of the King's Revels

The most active member of the Children of the King's Revels operation was Martin Slater, a man whose track record gives an intriguing insight into the opportunities for illicit (or borderline illicit) money-making in the theatre of the day. We first hear of Slater (or Slaughter), a citizen and ironmonger of London, as a sharer in the Admiral's Men from 1594 to 1597. Henslowe noted his departure from the company on 18 July 1597 (*Henslowe*, 60). In December that year Slater claimed to have found a playbook which had been lost by his fellow sharer, Thomas Downton; Downton sued for its return in the court of the Queen's Bench and was awarded £11 11s. in damages and costs (Eccles, 1993, 165–76). Five months later (May 18, 1598), Henslowe lent the Admiral's Men £7 to buy five playbooks from Slater: the two parts of *Hercules*, *Pythagoras*, *Phocasse* (*Focas*), and *Alexander and Lodowick* (*Henslowe*, 89). Henslowe records paying another 20s. on July 18, 1598, when Slater finally delivered *Alexander and Lodowick* (93). This is highly suspicious. All of these plays had formerly been in the company's repertory; besides which, £8 is far too little to pay for five new plays (which might easily cost £6 each). The implication must surely be that Slater walked off with these playbooks when he left the company. Possibly he made some limited claim to rights of possession; possibly the company just felt it was worth paying the money to get the playbooks back.

Slater then went to Scotland, in company with Lawrence Fletcher, who was to be one of the founder members of the King's Men in 1603 (p. 279). Slater reappeared in England as payee for the Earl of Hertford's Men when they played at court on Twelfth Night 1603 – an inexplicable, random appearance by a purely provincial troupe. By 1606, however, he had joined Queen Anne's Men. By 1607 he was at odds with his fellows. Their leader, Thomas Greene, sued him in the court of Common Pleas to get him to stop posting playbills advertising plays by Queen Anne's Men when in fact few, if any, of the sharers (other than perhaps Slater himself) were involved. It seems that he had been touring with a company made up of hired men, under the guise of the Queen's Men, which of course might hurt the real company's reputation.

Eventually Greene and the other sharers paid Slater £12 to desist from the practice, a bribe. For this he agreed that: "Although he be sworn one of her Majesty's players yet in respect and consideration of the sum of £12 to him by them paid he, the said Martin Slater, shall forbear and be restrained from setting up bills for playing or playing as in the name of her Majesty's service" (Bentley, 1984, 148n). The document later repeats that neither Slater nor any appointee of his will "set up or publish any plays or playbills … in the name of her Majesty's players unless he the said Martin shall then have in his company to play with him five other of the said her Majesty's servants" (ibid..) That they should need to resort to a bribe to restrain him suggests that it was a legal gray area whether a single sharer in the company could represent himself as playing in the name of the whole. Indeed, a copy of a 1606 warrant purporting to come from Queen Anne herself has survived, sanctioning Slater's touring practices, though there is no way of determining its authenticity (ES, 2: 234–5). The terms of this agreement limited Slater to doing this only when a great majority of the other sharers were involved.

In 1608 Slater became manager of the Children of the King's Revels, while still a member of Queen Anne's Men. Again there was nothing to stop him doing this, though it would surely have kept him away from rehearsals and performances. The enterprise actually folded quickly, as a result of the plague. But Slater had it written in the Articles of Agreement that, if the boys had occasion to tour, "it shall be for more credit of the whole company that the said Martin shall travel with the children, and acquaint the magistrates with their business" (ES, 2: 65; Greenstreet, 1885). During any such travel his own allowance was to increase from a single share to a share and half. How this was to be compatible with being a sharer in Queen Anne's Men is far from clear.

The issue of "acquaint[ing] the magistrates with their business" was obviously something that became a speciality for Slater. Despite his agreement with Greene and the others he joined his fellow, Thomas Swinnerton, in leading bogus "Queen's Men" troupes on provincial tours. This doubtless lies behind yet another legal agreement Slater reached with the main company, recorded in a Chancery Bill of Complaint of February 9, 1609:

> It is ... agreed that all such apparel as is abroad shall be brought in ... it is further ... agreed ... that if at any time hereafter any apparel, books, or any other goods or commodities shall be conveyed or taken away by any of the said parties without the consent and allowance of the said residue of his fellow sharers and the same exceeding the value of two shillings, that then he or they so offending shall forfeit and lose all ... benefits ... besides the loss of their places and all other interests which they may claim amongst us.
>
> (Bentley, 1984, 51)

But this did not stop Slater and Swinnerton from leading their bogus tours, becoming quite notorious for it. In 1616 the Lord Chamberlain, the Earl of Pembroke, sent an emissary around the country, advising provincial officials to be on the lookout for players traveling under false warrants. And these men headed his list:

> Whereas Thomas Swinnerton and Martin Slaughter, being two of the Queen's Majesty's company of players, having separated themselves from their said company, have each of them taken forth a several exemplification or duplicate of his Majesty's letters patents granted to

> the whole company, and by virtue thereof they severally in two companies with vagabonds and such like idle persons, have and do use and exercise the quality of playing in divers places of this realm, to the great abuse and wrong of his Majesty's subjects in general and contrary to the true intent and meaning of his Majesty to the said company ... These are therefore to pray, and nevertheless in his Majesty's name to will and require you, upon notice given of any of the said persons ... that you call the said parties' offenders before you and thereupon take their said several exemplifications or duplicates or other warrants by which they use their said quality from them. And forthwith to send the same to me.
>
> (Gurr, 1996, 49–5)
>
> Swinnerton was actually caught under this by the Norwich authorities, but overall it was of limited effect and Pembroke reissued the notice in 1624. In the meantime Slater pursued his chosen course. He turned up for Queen Anne's funeral in due order in May 1619 and as a Groom of her Chamber was presented with black mourning-cloth (*ES*, 2: 236). Yet thereafter he can be traced traveling with a warrant in Queen Elizabeth's name (presumably the former Princess Elizabeth, now Queen of Bohemia), and in 1625 in the name of the King's Men (Gurr, 43).
>
> Slater's record shows well enough that everything was not sweetness and light in the theatrical profession. The Chamberlain's Men were very lucky, so far as we can tell, never to have contracted with anyone as indifferent to the company's wellbeing, so shameless in his dealings with his fellows, and so determined to seek his own advantage as he saw fit, as Slater was. It is worth noting, however, that Slater – a man of considerable theatrical experience – presumably reckoned that there was more profit to be made from touring than from taking his place alongside his fellows in the Red Bull theatre. That may be, of course, because he was able to set his own terms about the proportion of the take he would retain for himself – and he did not have to worry about interference from his supposed fellows.

(Continued from p. 143)

We do not know how the Chamberlain's Men initially acquired their stock of costumes. Possibly the former members of Strange's Men had been able to salvage some from that enterprise. Possibly they were able to acquire some from other companies that had folded during the plague. Or possibly James Burbage had built up a store of them at the Theatre, which the company might have leased or bought; or they simply had to buy them on the general market. Either way, the sharers would pay – upfront in purchasing their share, or over time in deductions from the household take.

Box 4.2 The Contracts of William Shakespeare and John Heminge

Robert Dawes was contracted simply as a player, as most sharers would be (see p. 140). But what of Shakespeare? It is clear that he was writing plays for the Chamberlain's Men from the off, generally two a year, one comedy and one more serious piece, history or tragedy. He was thus what was known as their "ordinary poet," continuing a tradition we noted with the Queen's Men, where both Wilson and Tarlton among the sharers at least occasionally wrote for the company. Not all companies had such personnel among them. The Admiral's Men, for example, had no "ordinary poet" in the 1590s and bought all their plays on commission from the stable of playwrights – including Dekker, Chettle, Haughton, Drayton, Chapman, Porter, Munday, Jonson, Hathaway, and Day – whose business relations with the company are chronicled by Henslowe.

Indeed, the only true parallels with Shakespeare are Thomas Heywood with Queen Anne's Men and Nathan Field, who as an adult was with Lady Elizabeth's Men and briefly, in Shakespeare's wake, the King's Men (see Figure 6.2). Both were actor-sharers who also wrote plays. The parallel with Field is actually not all that strong. He was indeed a star player, having trained up with the boy company at the Blackfriars, so cannot have had much time for writing plays; only two plays by him are extant, though attempts have been made to find his partial hand in others. But Heywood is a very close parallel. After writing plays for the Admiral's Men that can be traced in Henslowe's *Diary*, he joined what became Queen Anne's Men when they were still patronized by the Earl of Worcester and remained with them until the Queen's death in 1619, turning out a steady and often very popular stream of plays. In his Epistle to *The English Traveller* (1633) he talked of "two hundred and twenty [plays], in which I have had either an entire hand or at least a main finger" – much more productive than Shakespeare, though over a longer period. It works out at about six plays a year over thirty-seven years, compared with Shakespeare's thirty-eight over, at most, twenty-five years.

It is a question why a playing company would choose to include men like these as sharers, at the heart of their operations. In later years the King's Men would maintain an unbroken chain of "ordinary poets": John Fletcher (briefly in tandem with Field), Philip Massinger, and James Shirley. But this was on a different footing; they were on a retained contract to write exclusively for the company, and presumably a fixed number of plays were expected. But they were never either actors or, to our knowledge, sharers. It seems likely that retaining "ordinary poets" was related to the phenomenon we noticed with Strange's Men, when *The Tanner of Denmark* was played once and apparently never again (p. 64). Such failures were simply bad business. Those who achieved positions as "ordinary poets" already had track records of writing plays that could be revived again and again and draw audiences: money in the bank. One thing that may have made Shakespeare attractive to his fellow sharers is that he not only had a track record of successful writing (a commodity in short supply, given the recent deaths of Christopher Marlowe, Thomas Kyd, and Robert Greene) but he seems to have been able to bring the rights to some of his plays with him. The *Henry VI* plays and *Richard III* all apparently carried over into his new company's repertoire, as did *Titus Andronicus* (see p. 94).

Of course, neither Shakespeare nor any of the others wrote anything like all the plays their companies performed. Henslowe's *Diary* shows that, in their first (1594–95) season at the Rose with him, the revived Admiral's Men put on a total of thirty-eight plays, of which twenty-one were new; the next year they staged thirty-seven, including nineteen new ones, and in 1596–97, thirty-four, of which fourteen were new, which set the average for the next few years. Two or three new ones from an "ordinary poet" (had they had one) would only have been a small proportion of the total. But there was a better than average chance that these would be among their regular earners for years to come. Indeed, over the years, the King's Men acquired such a back-catalogue of popular works from Shakespeare and Fletcher in particular (and a few other irregulars, like Jonson) that they commissioned fewer and fewer new plays through the 1620s and 30s. Well-chosen "ordinary poets" certainly proved a good investment for that company.

What, however, might this have meant for Shakespeare's contract with the company? The short answer is that we do not know, though we may catch some of its flavor from the one contract of an "ordinary poet" of which we have detailed information, that between Richard Brome and Queen Henrietta's Men, playing at the Salisbury Court theatre in the late 1630s. As so often, we only know of this from legal wranglings which began when the company sued Brome for breach of contract:

> Richard Brome ... well knowing that it would be very beneficial for him ... to write and compose plays for the actors and owners of the said house, did by himself and others whom he employed therein make means unto ... the then owners and actors in the said house to entertain them in that business. And after many parleys and treaties therein, it was at the last by articles of agreement indented bearing date on or about the twentieth day of July ... 1635 agreed ... that he, the said Brome, should for the term of three years the next ensuing with his best art and industry write every year three plays and deliver them to the company of players there acting for the time being. And that the said Richard Brome should not nor would write any play or any part of a play to any other players or playhouse but apply all his study and endeavours therein for the benefit of the said company of the said playhouse. And that the said covenantees [i.e. the owners and players] should pay unto the said

Richard Brome the sum of 15s per week during the said term of three years and permit the said Brome to have the benefit of one day's profit of playing such new play as he should make … the ordinary charges of the house only deducted.[3]

It all ended in tears. Brome received his weekly wage, which (given the inflation of the early years of the century) was not luxurious, but doubtless more comfortable than payment by results. And he would have the bonus of profits from an early performance – perhaps the second or third, a usual arrangement with other dramatists. But Brome did not deliver the stipulated three plays a year. He claimed that "howsoever they had desired to have three plays yearly for three years … to be undertaken and promised by this defendant, yet upon trust and confidence and by the true and fair intent and plain meaning of all parties, the plaintiffs neither should nor would exact nor expect from this defendant the performance or composition of any more plays than … this defendant could or should be able well to do or perform" (661). More guidelines than stipulations, he claimed. The plague intervened and they came to an impasse. In 1638 the parties attempted to retrieve the situation with a new contract, this time for seven years. Brome was to get 20s. a week, still to write three plays a year, and moreover also to make up the arrears then (in the company's view) owing. In response Brome blustered a good deal, claiming that one of the plays he had delivered "styled and called *The Sparagus Garden*, was worth to them … the sum of £1000 and upwards," also that he had been ill. By this time, he argued "he is only behind with them [the Salisbury Court company] two plays, in lieu of which he hath made divers scenes in old, revived plays for them and many prologues and epilogues to such plays of theirs, songs and one introduction at their first playing of the plague" (664). Such duties were apparently not contractually specified and Brome claimed that they represented equal time and effort to the two plays he owed.

Little of this can have applied to Shakespeare as a sharer. It looks as though he was expected normally to produce two new plays a year rather than three. It is more likely that he received payment like other sharers directly from the performance profits, rather than a weekly wage – but some remission from duties that other sharers would be expected to carry. It is possible, though, that he did also receive the exclusive profits (after deduction of regular expenses) from an early performance of a new play. It is also entirely likely that he patched old plays, and wrote prologues and epilogues as needed – especially when plays were performed at court. They were regarded as ephemera and often not reproduced in printed texts (Stern, 2009a, 81–119).[4] It is easy also to invent other business he could have seen to. There was no such figure as a director in Elizabethan theatre and it is tempting to assume that, Peter Quince-like, he might have steered his fellow mechanicals through the basics of a first performance. And might he have had a hand in finding playwrights to commission to write plays other than his own that the company would need?

The problem is that there are, in fact, too many functions that we might *suppose* Shakespeare's contract specified, given that he had to find clear time to write his plays, and that he certainly did act. It might have been a piety that Shakespeare should have been at the head of the list of "Names of the Principal Actors in all these plays" included in the First Folio of his plays in 1623. But, as we have noted, his name also appears quite prominently in the lists of players which Ben Jonson attached to plays in his *Works* (1616). Shakespeare is credited with roles in *Every Man In His Humour* (1598) and *Sejanus* (1603), though not in other Jonson plays that his company first staged. This is sometimes read as evidence that Shakespeare did not act after 1603, but the evidence from Jonson is not as categorical as that. Note that *Every Man Out of His Humour* fell between two plays in which he *did* act. And the comparison with Robert Armin is instructive. He would probably only have been with the company for *Sejanus*, *Volpone*, *The Alchemist*, and *Catiline*, but we think of him as the comic mainstay of the company after Will Kemp left. Yet the only Jonson list in which Armin appears is *The Alchemist*. It seems probable that Jonson only listed those in major roles, and that Armin may often have spread his comic talent around several smaller ones. Shakespeare may similarly have taken smaller roles after *Sejanus* – a change when they became the King's Men. But surely even his initial contract must have allowed him *some* remission from acting and other duties involved in the staging of plays, to give him the time to write.

It does seem to have been the case (eventually if not in the first instance), that there could be sharers who did not act. There is, for example, no concrete evidence of John Heminge performing after he appeared in the cast list for Jonson's *Catiline* (1611). He is not credited with any role in John Webster's *The Duchess of Malfi*, published in 1623 with a list of actors in the first production, circa 1613/14 and another circa 1621/22 (see pp. 183, 187). Yet from 1601 onwards Heminge was normally entrusted on his own to receive payments from the court on behalf of his fellows, and he continued to appear in every official list of company sharers until 1629. As the company flourished in London, and its relationship with the playhouses in which it performed changed, the volume of its official business doubtless increased: relations with the court and local authorities, negotiations with the Master of the Revels, contracts, building maintenance, payment of wages and bills. Moreover, he took a leading role in bringing boy actors into the company, apprenticing far more than any of his fellows; these included Thomas Belte, Alexander Cook, George Birch, John Wilson, Richard Sharp, Thomas Holcomb, Robert Pallant (the younger), and William Trigg. Heminge presumably proved capable and trustworthy and his fellow sharers allowed him to take on the role of a business manager; contracts must have been sufficiently flexible to allow that. Around the time the King's Men acquired use of the Blackfriars (p. 286) he took on a deputy, John Jackson. He obtained for himself the position of tapster at the Globe, selling the beer on-site, and had outside interests, such as being one of the ten measurers of sea-coal for London (*ES*, 2: 370–3; Gurr, 2004*a*, 230).

For most other companies the theatre-owners apparently took on the role of business entrepreneurs, while the actors stuck to acting and the immediate business of staging plays. Philip Henslowe, for example, was only the company financier and landlord when the Admiral's Men first moved into the Rose in 1594; but around 1597/8 their relationship changed and he seems to have run more of their business affairs, in conjunction with his son-in-law, Alleyn.

Although the roles of sharers in the Chamberlain's Men might evolve for the good of the company, in ways I have suggested for Heminge and possibly Shakespeare, in the early days the shares themselves did not pass out of the company. If one of the sharers left, as Will Kemp left around 1599, the expectation was that he would be repaid for his share at the current rate; by the same token, if one died, it was expected that his executors would receive the money. New sharers could only be introduced if they all consented. This meant that the value of shares and the income they generated would fluctuate as numbers did. This was also inevitable, given the ups and downs of playing conditions; but to the extent that the body regulated itself, they were masters of their own fates.

That corporate interdependence began to break down after Shakespeare retired from the business, as some widows tried to hold on to shares and more of the players also became sharers in the playhouses ("householders") as well as the company. Indeed a legal tussle broke out as early as 1615, between John Heminge and his daughter, Thomasine, over the householder shares of her late husband, William Ostler (p. 164). We do not know the outcome of the suit, though it looks as though Heminge managed to hold on to the shares – by the time of his death in 1630 he owned a quarter of the shares in both the Globe and the Blackfriars, an extremely lucrative investment that he bequeathed to his son, William. It was resented by members of the company who were excluded from the householder shares (Gurr, 2004*a*, 271–80). In Shakespeare's own time, however, his company seem to have worked loyally together – especially by the standards of the day – and with remarkably little known friction.

> **Box 4.3 Augustine Phillips: Shakespeare's Fellow-Sharer**
>
> It will not be practicable, or probably profitable, to traces the lives and careers of all Shakespeare's fellows. Burbage as his principal tragedian, and Kemp and Armin as his two principal comedians, will certainly require further comment in due course. But it may offer some general insights to trace the life of one of them, if only to show that they were not all like Martin Slater. As it happens Augustine Phillips is better documented than most of them (*EPF*, 191–203).
>
> Nothing is known, however, of Phillips's early life and origins. The earliest secure reference to him is as one of the members of Strange's Men given a special Privy Council licence of May 1593 to travel during the plague (p. 67). The subsidy commissioners regarded Phillips as living in the Liberty of the Clink that year, part of the parish of St Saviour's in Southwark, on the south bank of the Thames and just to the west of London Bridge – Henslowe territory. This is confirmed by the parish's communion token book for the winter of 1593/4, which notes him as living at the end of Horseshoe Court, near Bullhead Alley in the Liberty. The commissioners assessed his wealth as £3 and levied a tax on him of 8 shillings; the token book establishes that he was regularly (at least once a month) taking Holy Communion at St Saviour's, as required by law; and also that there were three adults in the property, probably Phillips, his wife, Anne, and a servant. The Liberty of Clink, an area notorious for its brothels, was still notionally under the authority of the Bishop of Winchester (on liberties, see pp. 64; 197 and Note 4). But it was free from city control, which is why Henslowe built the Rose there in 1587, and Phillips would have found it convenient to live nearby while he was with Strange's Men.
>
> St Saviour's parish register tells us that Phillips's first daughter, Magdalen, was christened on September 29, 1594; his second, Rebecca, was christened there on July 11, 1596. In the first entry he is mentioned as "Austin, *histrionis* [player]" and the second as "Augustine, player of interludes."[5] For some reason his third daughter, Anne, was christened in 1599 at Stephen's Church in Coleman Street, near the city Guildhall. Besides these daughters, who all survived him, Augustine and Anne had a still-born daughter who was buried at the church of St Botolph's without Aldgate (in east London) on September 7, 1597. They paid 3s. for the service; the digging of the grave, ringing of the bell, and a coffin cost a further 18d. Anne Phillips was churched there, receiving the traditional blessing for recovery from childbirth a month later, on October 5. The Phillips's only son, "Austin," was christened on November 29, 1601, back in Southwark; his burial is recorded on July 1, 1604.
>
> As these records show, the family had been moving about. They were still resident in Horseshoe Court in 1595/6 but not by the following year. Southwark was as inconvenient for the Theatre – north-east of the city, where the Chamberlain's Men normally played – as it was convenient for the Rose. Living in

St Botolph's must have made life much easier. Once the company moved to the Globe, however it made sense to return to Southwark. They were certainly there for the birth of Austin and back specifically in Horseshoe Alley by 1602/3, when the number of adults in the house was listed as six. Evidence of Phillips's membership of the Chamberlain's Men accumulates. He is listed in the "plot" of *The Second Part of the Seven Deadly Sins* (circa 1597) as playing the role of Sardanapalus (see pp. 205–6). And he is in the acting lists for Jonson's first three plays with the company, *Every Man In His Humour*, *Every Man Out of His Humour*, and *Sejanus* – but he would be dead by *Volpone* (1606).

In late 1598 Phillips became one of the original shareholders in the Globe, replacing the Theatre (see p. 224). This was in effect a syndicate, initially comprising Shakespeare, Phillips, Pope, Heminge, Kemp, and the Burbage brothers, a kind of inner membership of the playing company. It took on the additional responsibility (and, of course, the profits) of financing the theatre they would use. The kind of role played elsewhere by Philip Henslowe, Edward Alleyn, and Christopher Beeston – playhouse owners who effectively dictated terms to the players who used them – in the Chamberlain's Men was played collectively by senior members of their own company.

Probably the most stressful event of Phillips's life was his examination after the special performance of a play of Richard II (probably Shakespeare's), on the eve of the Essex Rebellion, when the disgraced Earl staged an abortive coup, supposedly against the Queen's evil councilors (see p. 135). Exactly why he should have been singled out for this is not clear; there is no record that anyone else was. But he kept a very cool head about him when he was examined by Chief Justice Popham (a bully of a man) and Justice Fenner:

> The examination of Augustine Phillips, servant unto the Lord Chamberlain and one of his players, taken the 18th of February 1601, upon his oath.
>
> He saith that Friday last was sennight [i.e. Friday of the previous week] or Thursday Sir Charles Percy, Sir Jocelyn Percy, and the Lord Mounteagle, with some three more, spoke to some of the players in the presence of this examinate, to have the play of the deposing and killing of King Richard the Second to be played the Saturday next, promising to get them more than their ordinary to play it. Where this examinate and his fellows were determined to have played some other play, holding that the play of King Richard to be so old and so long out of use that they should have small or no company at it. But at their request, this examinate and his fellows were content to play it the Saturday and had their 40s more than their ordinary for it, and so played it accordingly.
>
> *Augustine Phillips* (EPT, 197)

No one seems to have thought that the performance was meant to incite an uprising there and then. Essex himself was not even there. Francis Bacon, who later prosecuted many of his followers, argued that Essex's steward, Gelly Meyrick, wanted the play "so earnest he was to satisfy his eyes with the sight of that tragedy which he thought soon after his lord should bring from the stage to the state" (Chambers, 1930, 2: 326). The motivation was more psychological than incendiary, to put people in the right mindset.

It looks as though the authorities were more interested in establishing the intentions of the plotters than in the involvement of the players, but Phillips may not have known that. His examination affirmed that some of Essex's supporters had approached members of the company on Friday 6 or Thursday 5 February, with the proposal to put on the play. The players had resisted the idea, claiming that it was an old play with little appeal (though its text had in fact gone through three editions in 1597/8, making it – only three years earlier – one of Shakespeare's most popular works, at least in print). They had only agreed to stage it when offered £2 over and above their regular take; they duly performed it on February 7, a Saturday, the day before the failed coup. As Phillips told it this was a rather grudging business arrangement for the players, not a flirting with treason. And the authorities apparently took them at his word. The company played at court on February 24, the night before Essex's execution.

On May 17, 1603, Phillips and his fellows received a patent from King James, making them now the King's Men. In March 1604 James made a ceremonial entrance into the City of London, and Phillips was one of the players authorized to receive four and a-half yards of red cloth for their livery at the event (see p. 281). On November 2, 1604 Phillips lent one John Baumfeld, of Hardington in Somerset, the sum of £100 for six months at the maximum legal annual interest rate of 10 percent; the following May Baumfeld would owe him £105. It is a measure of the success of the company (or more particularly, we might hazard a guess, of the housekeepers who controlled the playhouse) that Phillips had that much ready money that he could afford to loan out. He also had enough to purchase a property in Mortlake, Surrey, some way removed from the city but accessible by river. That winter of 1603/4 the plague still gripped the city and in December the court removed for a time to Wilton in Wiltshire, the country estate of the Earl of Pembroke. The King's Men were summoned to appear there, and the Chamber Accounts record that John Heminge was paid £30 "for the pains and expenses of himself and the rest of the company in coming from Mortlake in the county of Surrey" (*ES*, 4: 168). There is a good chance that they were quartered in or near Phillips's property.

By the late winter of 1604/5 the Phillips family had moved out of Horseshoe Court, possibly removing altogether to Mortlake. Augustine may already have been ailing, since he made his will on May 4, 1605 and his widow was confirmed as his executrix on May 13. The will itself reveals the depths of his associations with the theatre. (He was in fact the stepbrother of the former fellow-sharer,

Thomas Pope, who predeceased him.) He made a bequest of £10 "to my sister, Elizabeth Gough"; she was married to an actor with the King's Men (though probably not a sharer) Robert Gough, who was a witness to the will. He left similar bequests to two sons of another sister, Margery Borne, who had very possibly been married to William Bird or Borne, a player with the Admiral's Men. He left £5 to be distributed equally among all the hired men of the King's Men. Then more specific bequests of "a 30s piece in gold" each to early members of the company, Shakespeare, Henry Condell, and "my servant Christopher Beeston," which suggests that Beeston might once have been his apprentice. To more recent fellows in the company, Lawrence Fletcher, Robert Armin, Richard Cowley, Alexander Cooke, and Nicholas Tooley, he left each 20s. in gold. He left two apprentices 40s. each and some more personal items, including musical instruments (see p. 176).

A slightly unusual feature of the will is that Phillips makes no bequests as such to some of his oldest fellows, Heminge, Burbage, and William Sly. It does, however, name them as executors of the will, if "Anne my wife do at any time marry after my decease" and before the business of the will was concluded. (She was also to be excluded from any inheritance under the will.) In that case, "for their pains herein to be taken, a bowl of silver of the value of £5 apiece." Presumably Phillips knew something about "my loving wife" that he was not letting on, since Anne Phillips did hastily marry one John Witter; the will went back to probate in 1607 and Heminge was declared executor, to be assisted by Burbage and Sly. This was not quite the last to be heard of the affair. After Anne died in 1618, Witter made a rather feeble attempt to sue Heminge and Condell over her inheritance, which (though not specified in the will) he claimed had included Augustine's share in the Globe. The court found against him and awarded the veteran players costs.

In so many issues relating to Elizabethan players, we are at the mercy of what happens to survive. Legal documents tend to predominate, followed by financial ones; places of residence are recorded because they relate to taxation. In the case of Augustine Phillips we can trace his movements as as player, from one company and playhouse to another. We find evidence that he found the theatrical business profitable and also one in which he bonded closely with his fellows, including the apprentices he was training up. The Essex affair is the one great anomaly in the record, doubtless a moment of great drama and tension. The births and deaths of children tell one tale of marital relations, the will a rather sad finale. This is a long way from the whole tale of a life, but it is more than we can usually expect for a man of such status.

Hired Men (and Women)

Everyone else who worked in the theatre, other than the sharers, was a paid associate. The great majority of the income from performances was divided, one way or another, between the theatre owners and the sharers who rented the theatres from them. But it fell to the sharers (i.e. the actors rather than the housekeepers) to pay the associates from their profits. (On the term "housekeepers" for part-owners of certain playhouses, see p. 224.) When some of the sharers in the King's Men in the 1630s sued to be allowed to become housekeepers by acquiring shares in the Globe and the Blackfriars, they pointed out the inequity of their situation – since the shares of the housekeepers were evidently far more profitable than those of mere players: "their shares fall shorter and are a great deal less than the housekeepers," they complained. "And yet notwithstanding out of those lesser shares the said actors defray all charges of the house whatsoever (viz.) wages to hired men and boys, music, lights etc., amounting to 900 or £1000 per annum or thereabouts, being £3 a day, one day with another, besides the extraordinary charge the said actors are wholly at for apparel and poets etc" (Gurr, 2004, 274). These, of course, were 1630s prices. And during Shakespeare's time these tensions between sharers and housekeepers were far less marked. Nevertheless the costs associated with hired men were not inconsiderable, even then.

It was a very different operation from that of the adult companies, but the arrangement for the Children of the King's Revels gives us a better idea of where the hired men figured in the economics of the theatre and who they were. One sixth of each day's take was to be set aside to cover "charges of the house," which included "the gatherers, the wages, the children's board, music, book-keeper, tireman, tirewoman, lights, the Master of the Revels's duties [i.e. fees], and all other things needful and necessary" (*ES*, 2: 65). The main differences for an adult company would be that this obviously makes no provision for paying any actors at all, sharers or hired men. But it does include a provision for lighting, which would be a major cost for a boys company playing indoors, though not for adults in the Theatre or Rose who relied almost exclusively on sunlight.[6] And board for the much smaller number of boy apprentices whom the adult players employed would not be handled in this way (see pp. 182ff). Otherwise it seems a realistic checklist, and it is perhaps surprising that an old hand like Martin Slater felt it could all be done for one sixth of the weekly take (which was also to be his own share – with an extra half-share whenever the boys were taken on tour).

I examine below each of the categories of hired personnel identified in the King's Revels list, together with the category of hired (adult) actors which that list naturally omits. In Chapter 8, where I look at the Blackfriars playhouse, we have very detailed information about the (male) personnel employed by the King's Men in 1624 (pp. 301ff).[7] From that I deduce that the total number they employed circa 1608, before they took over the Blackfriars – exclusive of women and minors – would have been in the region of sixteen, all of whom needed paying from the daily take.

Hired Men as Actors

In an analysis of seven cast lists for the King's Men printed with plays between 1626 and 1632, G. E. Bentley conclude that "the numbers of hired men assigned roles are four, three, four or five, one, one, three and one" (1984, 69). Another way of putting this is to say that they might expect to cast about as many hired men with speaking roles (sometimes dubbed "journeymen players") as they did boy players, rarely more than three or four. In the first days of the Chamberlain's Men we can, as I have shown, fairly confidently identify seven sharers (see p. 140). Besides them, the following are also known to have played with the company early: Henry Condell, William Sly, Christopher Beeston, and John Duke. Of these Condell and Beeston had certainly been apprentices and perhaps became hired men when their indentures ended. Condell became a sharer quite quickly, possibly (following an advantageous marriage) buying the slot vacated by George Bryan, who apparently left circa 1597 to take up a position at court as an ordinary Groom of the Chamber. And Will Sly too became a sharer; Augustine Phillips's will (1605) treats him as a fellow, alongside Heminge and Burbage. Thomas Pope is not named in the 1603 personnel of the King's Men (he would die by early 1604), so that too may have opened up a slot.

The remuneration for being a hired man varied quite considerably from contract to contract, and there are numerous complaints about being paid late if at all: several depositions in the 1623 *Worth v. Baskervile* case attest to hired men getting less than they had been promised, when audiences were thin (see pp. 158, 165). John King, for example, claimed to have been "a hired servant" with the Red Bull company for "30 years past and upwards," which is notable in itself – these were by no means necessarily transitory positions. King claimed that "if at any time it should happen the getting of the said company to be but small and to decrease that then he should not have his whole wages agreed to be paid unto him but to have his part of the loss thereof as well as the said company and to have a part proportionally only to their gettings" (Bentley, 1984, 110). King was deferentially ignoring the reality that he could never earn *more* than his agreed wage, whereas the "company" (i.e. the sharers – or perhaps their manager) would always do well out of large attendances.

But on the face of it hired men could do quite well. Edward Alleyn, for example, signed a contract with William Kendall in 1597, committing "to give him for his said service every week of his playing in London 10 shillings and in the country 5 shillings; for the which he covenanteth for the space of ... 2 years to be ready at all times to play in the house of the said Philip [Henslowe] and in no other during the said term."[8] Ten shillings a week is a princely £26 a year, in a context where we are regarding £10 as a comfortable wage; this assumes payment did not cease in Lent when, for the most part, playing was supposed to be suspended. Even the half pay in the country is not draconian; the company probably handled room and board centrally while they were on tour. Other contracts for the Admiral's Men were somewhat less generous. That same year three of the sharers hired Thomas Hearne "for 2 years in the quality of playing for five shillings a week for one year and 6 shillings 8 pence for the other year." And in 1599 a blank contract in the name of the sharer, Thomas Downton, specified payment of "8 shillings a week as long as they play and after they lie still one fortnight then to give him half wages" (*Henslowe*, 238–9; 45). Presumably lying still would most often be the result of the plague, so that even half wages (when the company would not be earning) had its attractions. In each case there was a "covenant," formally making the hired man a servant of the person issuing the contract for two years, giving some security on both sides.

What we can see of the business affairs of the Chamberlain's Men suggests that people once hired tended to remain with the company, perhaps in the hope of becoming a sharer. That does seem, however, to have largely been a case of waiting for dead men's shoes. The existing sharers would have hesitated to expand the pool, since that would diminish their own returns. This may be why Beeston and Duke left, when opportunities opened up elsewhere; by 1602 they are with the newly-formed Earl of Worcester's Men, playing at the Boar's Head, and very probably sharers in it. But those who hung on generally seemed to achieve promotion to the inner circle eventually. John Lowin is one of the most impressive examples. He appears in Henslowe's *Diary* as a member – possibly a sharer – of Worcester's Men, playing at the Rose in 1602–3; he authorized a number of payments for them. But he evidently transferred to the newly-created King's Men shortly thereafter. He performed in *Sejanus* (1603) and *The Malcontent* (1604) but was not in official lists of the King's Men in either year, and so was presumably still a hired man with them; nevertheless, in the Induction to *The Malcontent*, in which three members of the King's Men played "themselves", Lowin was one of the three, status not necessarily correlating with audience familiarity. Thereafter Lowin seems quite prominently placed in the cast-lists for *Volpone*, *The Alchemist*, and *Catiline*, played Bosola in *The Duchess of Malfi*, and is clearly a sharer by the next official list in 1619, if not long before. In later years he is recorded as playing several prominent roles with success, including Falstaff, Volpone, and Epicure Mammon in *The Alchemist* (he was evidently on the portly side) and eventually succeeded Heminge in 1630 as a co-manager of the company.

Three others to whom Augustine Phillips made bequests very probably rose in the ranks. Richard Cowley, whose indeterminate early status we noted above (see p. 141). Alexander Cooke, who started as a boy apprentice, was with the company until his death in 1613, when his will declared that he owned £50, "which is in the hand of my fellows, as my share of the stock." Nicholas Tooley was not in the 1603 patent of the King's Men but was in that of 1619; he died while lodging with "my good friend Mr. Cuthbert Burbage" in 1623.

Gatherers

If any hired men were *exclusively* actors, they were very much a minority, probably no more than three or four at any one time. The King's Revels arrangements put gatherers – also known as box-holders – at the head of their list of necessary employees. As we saw with the Queen's Men's affray in Norfolk, it was thought important that reliable people be employed to gather in the take at the doors in the playhouses (see pp. 39–40). *The Actors' Remonstrance*, a satirical gibe of 1643 (by when Parliament had closed the playhouses) suggests that this did not always happen; the gatherers "cannot now ... seem to scratch their heads where they itch not, and drop shillings and half crown-pieces in at their collars" (*ES*, 1: 356n). Such dishonesty was obviously undesirable, and the sharers did their best to guard against it, requiring the gatherers to place money they collected in earthenware pots, with just a slot to take the coins: "One of the distinctive features of this form of money box is the fact that it is entirely sealed: there is no opening which would allow for the removal of the money stored within. In order to retrieve the contents, the jar has to be smashed" (Simpson, 2013). Shards of such pots have been found in the excavations of the Rose and the Theatre. But unscrupulous gatherers evidently got around this, and the issue was exacerbated in part because there were multiple entrances and payment points, and also because the income from different parts of the theatre went into different pockets.

The number of doors at which money was taken is indicated in the account of the Swiss visitor, Thomas Platter, who seems to be reflecting on his experience of playgoing at both the Curtain and the Globe in late 1599. He broadly confirms the penny-by-penny admission system described by Lambarde (see p. 95), which called for more gatherers than might otherwise have been necessary: "The playhouses are so constructed that they play on a raised platform, so that everyone has a good view. There are different galleries and places, however, where the seating is better and more comfortable and therefore more expensive. For whoever cares to stand below [in the pit] only pays one English penny, but if he wishes to sit he enters by another door, and pays another penny [the twopenny galleries], while if he desires to sit in the most comfortable seats which are cushioned, where he not only sees everything well, but can also be seen, then he pays yet another English penny at another door" (Platter, 1937, 166). The "most comfortable seats" are probably what are sometimes referred to as the "gentlemen's rooms," well-appointed sections of the galleries, very possibly those immediately adjacent to the left and right of the stage – so that the occupants not only had a very good view of the action but were also quite visible to much of the audience. Neither Lambarde nor Platter mentions a fourth option, the lords' rooms, which were most expensive of all. Their omission is presumably because the elite contingent of the audience which used them gained access by a special entrance through the actors' tiring house, which would not have been used by the general public. This in itself, however, required at least one extra gatherer. I discuss the lords' rooms in relation to the Globe (p. 234).

There would thus seem to have been – assuming two general entrances, and one doorway to each category of gallery – at least five gatherers in such a theatre, though it must be likely that several would have been employed at a main external door to handle the crush. (And there is some evidence that there were eventually more than were strictly necessary, because of the patronage system by which many were appointed.) The main reason for this elaborate penny-entrance tiering must have been the common practice of paying rent to the theatre owner(s) which was not a fixed sum but a proportion of the take from all or some of the galleries. In the *Sharers' Papers* of 1635, for example, we learn that the housekeepers of both the Globe and the Blackfriars (those who held shares in the physical structure of the playhouses, rather than in the acting company) were entitled to receive a full moiety (half), "without any defalcation or abatement at all," of all takings from the galleries and boxes in both houses and from the tiring house door of the Globe.

There were presumably similar divisions elsewhere, though the proportions may have varied. In Henslowe's *Diary*, for example, we find the entries: "Here I begin to … receive the whole galleries, from this day being the 29 of July 1598" and "Here I began to receive the galleries again which they received, beginning at Michaelmas week, being the 6 of October 1599," listing and totaling weekly items thereafter (*Henslowe* 94, 120). This suggests that the contractual arrangement for the payment of Henslowe's rent changed at this time; he was henceforth to receive "the *whole* galleries" (my emphasis). Quite what the change amounts to is obscure to us, but must have been clear to the parties concerned. (There were, of course, no housekeepers for Henslowe to share these takings with.) And in such arrangements it was critical to know what sums were collected at which doors and to keep them separate. Dishonest gatherers might thus be trying to feather their own nests or tilt the balance in the division of the take. (Continued on p. 166).

Box 4.4 Women in the Theatres

It is a notorious truism that there were no women on the professional stage in England prior to the Restoration of Charles II in 1660.[9] It is not, in fact, entirely true, though the exceptions are such as effectively to prove the rule. We know, for example, that when Middleton and Dekker wrote *The Roaring Girl* about the notorious cross-dressing, pipe-smoking pickpocket and fence, Moll Frith, Moll herself appeared on stage during the play's run at the Fortune, though not actually performing the role; she is reported to have sat "upon the stage … in man's apparel and played upon her lute and sang a song" (Mullholland, 1977, 31). Another exception was in troupes visiting from the Continent where, by Shakespeare's time, the resistance to women on stage had been overcome. A troupe of Italian players, for example, visited England in 1574 and entertained Elizabeth while she was on progress at both Windsor and Reading; that November Thomas Norton fulminated against "the unchaste, shameless and unnatural tumbling of the Italian women" (*ES*, 2: 262). A *commedia dell'arte* company was rewarded at court in August 1602, and since that was the form of theatre in which women had first appeared on the professional stage in Italy there is a good chance that there were women among the "comedians," though there is no actual record of this – or of them performing on public stages (Nicoll, 1976, 169).

We can also find numerous exceptions to the rule outside the *professional* theatre. As Phyllis Rackin has argued, "there were many women who performed in the guild plays, May games, and civic entertainments that were regular features of village life, and there were many women among the itinerant musicians, acrobats, and other performers who toured the English countryside" (Rackin, 2005, 25; Brown and Parolin, 2005). Aristocratic women also appeared on stage in Jacobean and Caroline court masques, though their "performing" was limited to dancing, not speaking or singing (Wynne-Davies, 1992; McManus, 2002). By the same token, highly educated aristocratic women wrote plays, though they never intended them for commercial performance; the most notable in Shakespeare's own time were Mary Herbert, Countess of Pembroke (sister of Sir Philip Sidney), who translated the French tragedy of Robert Garnier, *Antonie*, and wrote an entertainment for a visit of Queen Elizabeth, *Astraea* (or "A Dialogue Between Two Shepherds, Thenot and Piers"); and Elizabeth Cary, whose *Tragedy of Mariam* was the first English tragedy by a woman to be printed (1613). At a later date, semi-private theatrical activity involving women flourished in some aristocratic households, such as that of William Cavendish, first Duke of Newcastle, whose daughters Jane and Elizabeth both wrote plays and performed in them (Cerasano and Wynne-Davies, 1996; Findlay and Hodgson-Wright, 2000). Such exceptions only underscore the reality that female roles on the English professional stage did not exist. Kathleen McLuskie observed that the commercial theatres "had no women shareholders, actors, writers, or stage hands," and, as Dympna Callaghan categorically puts it, "there were no women on Shakespeare's stage" (McLuskie, 1985, 92; Callaghan, 2000, 7).

There *were*, however, women in Shakespeare's theatres. Among those paid as "hired men" two groups certainly included women: the gatherers, who collected the entrance fees, and the tirewomen, whom I discuss below (see pp. 159; 167). But at least two other categories of women made an impact on the theatre, although their impact is difficult to measure. One was those who helped compose the audience; the other was the wives and widows of some of the principal players and theatre-owners, who were more actively involved in the business than we might have supposed – and did indeed become householder sharers. The presence of women in the audiences is widely attested (Wynne-Davies, 2009). The poet, Edmund Spenser, for example, wrote of "a troublous noise, / That seemed some perilous tumult to design, / Confused with women's cries and shouts of boys, / Such as the troubled theatres oftimes annoys" (*The Faerie Queene*, 4.3.37; 1596). But far too much of the evidence is filtered through the besetting misogyny of the era, fuelled it would seem by deep male insecurities, which blends all too readily with pervasive anti-theatrical rhetoric.

So commentators claimed that women were easily corrupted by what they saw on stage. As early as 1580 an anonymous writer (possibly, ironically, the playwright Anthony Munday) categorically writes that "some citizens" wives … have even on their deathbeds with tears confessed that they have received at those spectacles such filthy infections as have turned their minds from chaste cogitations, and made them of honest women light huswives [i.e. hussies]" (*A Third Blast of Retreat From Plays and Theatres*, 1580, 125). By 1631 Richard Braithwait had tied the generalization to a concrete example: "a gentlewoman of our nation, who so fairly bestowed the expense of her best hours upon the stage, as being surprised by sickness, even unto death, she became so deaf to such as admonished her, she closed her *dying scene* with a vehement calling on Hieronimo [i.e. the protagonist of *The Spanish Tragedy*]" (1631, 53). William Prynne was so taken with the anecdote that he embroidered it, telling how she "cried out Hieronimo, Hieronimo; oh let me see Hieronimo acted (calling out for a play instead of crying unto God for mercy)" (1633, fol. 556). This was in his rabidly anti-theatrical *Histriomastix*, over 1,000 pages long, which contains an entry in the index: "women players: notorious whores."

All of which suggests that respectable gentlewomen *were* indeed going to the theatres, or such admonitions would have rung false; it does not, of course, establish that they received such "filthy infections" there, though even the fantasy of a woman calling upon Hieronimo on her deathbed speaks to the impact of the perennially popular *Spanish Tragedy*. Other writers make much of the fact that the Bankside playhouses were notoriously adjacent to brothels, some even owned by the Bishop of Winchester so that their prostitutes were known as

"Winchester geese." Some claim that the prostitutes attended the theatre ("harlots, utterly beyond shame, press to the forefront of the scaffolds, to the end to show their impudency, and to be as an object to all men's eyes": *A Third Blast*, 139) and others imply that respectable women who attended reduced themselves to the level of prostitutes. Nervous husbands doubtless concurred with Samuel Rowlands's view of "a good wife" in *The Bride* (1617): "At public plays she never will be seen / … She knows how wise men censure of such dames" (E1r–1v).

Evidently none of this stopped women of all social ranks attending the theatre. Francis Beaumont, for example, was not fantasizing when he made a thoroughly respectable citizen's wife part of the onstage "audience" for *The Knight of the Burning Pestle* (1607). By the 1620s and 1630s aristocratic ladies certainly went to the theatres, especially the indoor private theatres, where authors sometimes acknowledged their presence in prologues and epilogues. It has even been argued that their presence affected the repertoires of those theatres (Neill, 1978). Most famously, the Queen herself, Henrietta Maria attended the Blackfriars theatre four times in the 1630s, twice accompanied by foreign royalty (Gurr, 2004b, 234). But that would have been unthinkable during Shakespeare's lifetime, when the theatre invariably went to court, rather than vice versa. There is ample evidence, however, of less elevated women attending his playhouses.

In *Playgoing in Shakespeare's London* Andrew Gurr lists all those who can positively be identified (I confine myself to the period pre-1620): Sarah Archdall twice met the astrologer Simon Forman, who was wooing her, at the Curtain; Elizabeth Cary's daughter attests that her mother was a frequent playgoer in her youth; Lady Anne Clifford is recorded as seeing *The Mad Lover* in 1617; Elizabeth Wybarn took a party to the Globe in 1612, which included one of her nieces, possibly Margaret Franke; Elizabeth Hattrell, a serving-woman of about twenty, visited the Curtain in 1611; Mrs Overall, wife of John Overall, Dean of St Paul's, is reported as being much admired by the gallants at the playhouse; Elizabeth Reignoldes was escorted to plays by John Cotton; Mrs Watton was reprimanded in a 1610 London Consistory Court – which tried sexual misdemeanors – for attending a play without her husband; Elizabeth Williams, sister-in-law of Sir Dudley Carleton, is recorded as attending the rebuilt Globe in April 1614 (224, 226, 227, 231, 246, 239, 240, 244). It was clearly expected that respectable women would be accompanied by a male relative or other chaperone, but otherwise their presence was unremarkable. The number of men who can be similarly identified is, unsurprisingly, considerably greater, but the difference shrinks appreciably if we exclude those reported for affrays and other criminal activity. In the end I am inclined to agree with Gurr: "Evidence for a plentiful supply of women playgoers is there throughout the period, although few assertions, beyond the bare fact that women were present, can be trusted entirely" (Gurr, 2004b, 67).

Evidence of the influence of the wives of actors and theatre owners is more difficult to pin down, but is in some respects more telling. For one thing, intermarriage within the theatrical community was very pronounced. Less than a year after William Knell of the Queen's Men was killed, his widow, Rebecca, married Shakespeare's future fellow, John Heminge (see p. 31); Heminge's own daughter, Thomasine, married the King's Man, William Ostler in 1611 – a union with unfortunate consequences for father and daughter (Edmond, 2004). Edward Alleyn married Henslowe's stepdaughter. Augustine Phillips' sister, Mary, married his fellow, Robert Gough. When Richard Burbage died, his widow, Winifred, married Richard Robinson, a former boy actor but by 1619 a sharer in the King's Men (see p. 187). And so on.

This must in general have reinforced the cohesive ties within the theatrical community, personal attachments overlaying professional ones. In the case of wives of theatre-owners we can sometimes glimpse them at work alongside their husbands; Agnes Henslowe, for example, sometimes appears in Philip's *Diary*, handling moneylending items, with players, members of the family and other customers alike. She lent ten shillings, for instance, to Thomas Towne, the actor who killed William Knell; and five shillings to William Bird or Borne, both sharers in the Admiral's Men. She also dealt with an Isabel Keys, who had property dealings with Philip (*Henslowe*, 62, 76, 83). Christopher Beeston, who in later years owned the Cockpit theatre, appointed his wife, Elizabeth Hutchinson, "full and sole executrix" of his estate, "by reason I do owe many great debts and am engaged for great sums of money, which no one but my wife understands where or how to receive, pay or take in"; he also directs "that my said executrix shall ... provide and find for the said company [the King's and Queen's Young Company] a sufficient and good stock of apparel fitting for their use" (Honigmann and Brock, 1993, 192–3). As Natasha Korda notes, "It seems unlikely that Beeston would have entrusted his wife with this task if she had no prior experience in the procurement of costumes for the stage" (Korda, 2009, 469).

Finally, and less harmoniously, some of the theatre widows played the specter at the feast when their husbands' former partners tried to overlook continuing contractual obligations after their deaths. We have already observed Margaret Brayne, widow of John, unsuccessfully suing her brother-in-law, James Burbage, over continuing rights she claimed in the Theatre (see pp. 31–2). Thomasine Heminge sued her own father to try to hold on to her late husband's estate. She had married William Ostler, a sharer in the company, who died intestate in December 1614, leaving her as his administrator. His shares of the leases in the Globe and Blackfriars should by rights have gone to her, but somehow passed into her father's hands – leaving her no means of support. In September 1615 she entered a bill in Chancery to claim the value of the shares; by October 9, despite promises to make good her loss, he had still not done so, and she entered a common law suit for damages amounting to £600, her estimate of the shares' value of. Unfortunately the outcome is unknown (p. 151).

But the most tenacious of theatre widows, and a presence in theatrical affairs from 1592 to the closing of the theatres, was Susan Browne Greene Baskerville, a multiple wife, widow, and mother of actors, and fierce defender of their legacies. She first married in 1592 the actor, Robert Browne, who was with the Earl of Derby's Men in 1599 and manager for them of the Boar's Head playhouse. One of their sons was William Browne, who acted with Queen Anne's Men and Prince Charles's Men between 1616 and his death in 1634. The Boar's Head enterprise was bedeviled throughout Robert Browne's time by the bad faith of some involved in the enterprise (Berry, 1986). Derby's Men were replaced by Worcester's, and when Browne died in October 1603 he seemed to Joan Alleyn, wife of Edward, "very poor" (*Henslowe*, 297). She was not aware, apparently, that Browne had a part-ownership in the Boar's Head, which passed to his widow.

Susan's second husband was the famous clown Thomas Greene, a leading figure with Queen Anne's Men; he died in August 1612. Susan married her third husband, James Baskerville in June 1613. Thomas Greene's will, dated July 25, 1612, had left the value of his share in Queen Anne's Men, worth £80, to his wife. At the time of his death, the company owed Greene an additional £37 10.s, also due to Susan. In an attempt to retrieve this money she appealed to Viscount Lisle, Chamberlain of Queen Anne's Household, whose authority derived from the Queen's patronage of the company; he arbitrated that she should receive half the company's profits until the sum was met (*ES*, 2: 237). Hardly any of this was forthcoming. In 1615, after negotiations, the Baskervilles agreed to invest another £57 10s. in the company; they would receive in return a pension of 1s. 8d. every day the company played, for the rest of the Baskervilles' lives. The company predictably fell behind in its payments; in 1616, in return for further investment of £38, they raised the payment to 3s. 8d. The Queen's Men were now even less able to meet their payments to Susan Baskerville; they also failed to pay her son William, then a hired man with them. At this point, James Baskerville, apparently a bigamist, abandoned Susan and left for Ireland in 1617. Undeterred, Susan sued Ellis Worth and other members of the Queen's Men. She pressed her suit again in 1623, against the only three sharers still with the company who had agreed to her latest settlement. She was successful to the extent that the company, now known as the Players of the Revels or the Players of the Red Bull (since Queen Anne had died in 1619) broke up.

William Browne, by then a sharer in the company, died in November 1634, leaving his mother as his executor; Susan Baskerville thus acquired control of his share in the Red Bull company. Less than a year later she was embroiled in litigation with William's widow, Anne Browne. Susan Baskerville also bought a share in the second Fortune Theatre, which Edward Alleyn rebuilt after the original burned down in 1621, bringing together a syndicate of investors; yet another lawsuit, begun in 1637, shows that Baskerville owned one of the twenty-four shares. The issue was still active in 1648, the year before she died,

> when Baskerville filed a deposition in the matter. It is a remarkably persistent record of involvement in theatrical affairs. Wives and daughters in Shakespeare's day were legally and socially at a considerable disadvantage; but widows were another story.
>
> There may have been no women *on* Shakespeare's stage, but women were certainly employed in the theatrical operation; they contributed a highly visible part of the audience; the gatherers among them would be familiar front-of-house, while the tirewomen played an essential role in the tiring house; and a few of them pulled considerable strings behind the scenes.

(Continued from p. 160).

It may not have helped matters that some of the gatherers' positions were contractually in the gift of people with a significant stake in the enterprise. When Aaron Holland built the Red Bull playhouse, around 1606, he assigned one-seventh of the house to the player, Thomas Swinnerton, "with a gatherer's place thereto belonging" (Bentley, 1984, 98). Such arrangements had much potential for embarrassment, since it fell to the actor-sharers to pay those appointed. It was so in a case where William Bird (or Borne), a sharer with Prince Henry's Men, had to write to Edward Alleyn to complain about the dishonesty of one John Russell, "that by your appointment was made a gatherer with us," accusing him of being "often false." He explains that the company will no longer let him "take the box," but will pay his wages as "a necessary attendant on the stage" and if he likes also employ him as a tailor (Greg, 1907, 85). Was Russell stealing for himself or falsifying the take on Alleyn's behalf? It would always be in the interests of individual gatherers to maximize the take of whoever controlled the shares by which their positions were allocated. Given the authority Alleyn had with Prince Henry's Men this must have been a difficult negotiation. Although they believe Russell to be dishonest they will continue to find paid employment for him (as Alleyn has the right to insist), but not in this most delicate of positions.

That case probably casts light on another general feature of the position of gatherers. They were only required in that specific role for a couple of hours during the afternoons; it was responsible work, but hardly a full-time job. Possibly it was normally the only work in the theatre for those appointed by patronage. But for other hired men it was probably one function among many, including working as "necessary attendant[s] on the stage," tailors or some such, when they were not actually collecting entrance money. In the "plot" for *Frederick and Basilea* (first performed by the Admiral's Men in 1597) various unnamed "gatherers" and other attendants are assigned to perform minor roles in the play (Bentley, 1984, 213). It suggests that there were more gatherers than were strictly necessary, if some of them could be called away to perform on stage as needed.

We may hazard a guess – since no one mentions the issue – that none of the gatherers who played minor roles were women. But this is one theatrical job that we know women performed. We know of a Joan Hewes (Hughes) who was a gatherer for the twopenny galleries at the Red Bull in 1607 and was still employed there in 1618; Mary Phillips was also a gatherer at that playhouse in 1607. *The Actors' Remonstrance* (1643) satirically describes the straits of those employed in the theatres, since their closing: "Nay, our very doorkeepers, *men and women*, most grievously complain that by this cessation they are robbed of the privilege of stealing from us with licence" (*ES*, 1: 356n; my emphasis). On April 11, 1612, a Robert Browne wrote to Edward Alleyn on behalf of his fellow player, Mr Rose, who was already with the Prince's Men; Rose wanted Alleyn's help to get a gatherer's position for his wife: "he hath requested me to be solicitous for him to you (who he knows can strike a greater stroke amongst them than this) as to procure him but a gathering place for his wife, for he hath had many crosses and it will be some comfort and help to them both, and he makes no doubt but she shall so carry herself in that place as they shall think it well bestowed by reason of her upright dealing in that nature" (Greg 1907, 63).[10]

We do not know if Rose was successful in his petition. But we do know that Henry Condell, Shakespeare's veteran colleague, exercised his patronage as a housekeeper at both the Globe and the Blackfriars to the benefit of his old servant, Elizabeth Wheaton. In his 1627 will he left her a mourning gown, 40s. and "that place of privilege which she now exerciseth and enjoyeth in the houses of the Blackfriars, London, and the Globe on the Bankside [for life] if my estate shall so long continue in the premises." Condell's widow, also Elizabeth, renewed the bequest in her own will, leaving her £20 and "the gathering place at the Globe during my lease" (Bentley, 1984, 94).

Tirewomen

The King's Revels agreement also specified a *"tirewoman."* It may be questionable whether tirewomen were ever on the weekly payroll of any of the adult companies, but it is certain that they used their services from time to time. The term broadly denotes a dressmaker, but would extend to someone who helped ladies (and boys dressing as ladies) to dress, and also more specifically to someone skilled in the making and attaching of the elaborate head-tires which were fashionable for high-born women in Shakespeare's day. Ben Jonson glances at them in his masque, *Love Restored* (1612), when he has Robin Goodfellow say that this was one of the disguises he adopted to try to get into court: "Then I took another figure, of an old tirewoman, but tired under that too, for none of the masquers would take note of me" (Jonson 2012*l*, lines 73–5). Part of the joke may well be that in this small-scale and rather ad hoc entertainment by

Jonson there were no lady masquers who would require her services to get dressed, though such persons would certainly be needed in the normal run of things for such masques as those commissioned by Queen Anne for herself and her ladies.

We know with unusual certainty that Shakespeare himself was acquainted with a tirewoman, because in 1604 he lodged in Silver Street, Cripplegate, with a Huguenot family, the Mountjoys, and that was the trade of the lady of the house, Marie Mountjoy. This circumstance has been explored at some length by Charles Nicholl in his *The Lodger: Shakespeare on Silver Street*, to which I am indebted here. Marie and her husband, Christopher, seem to have been at the high end of this profession, creating elaborate head-tires – complex hair-pieces – for fashionable ladies, and plausibly for use on the stage also. Marie twice appears in the household accounts for Queen Anne in 1604, perhaps not coincidentally the year of her first court masque, *The Vision of the Twelve Goddesses*. For the 1606 wedding masque of *Hymenaei* the Countess of Rutland's accounts record her paying "To the tire woman for a coronet, £6" – and this was only one among many items which she acquired for this lavish entertainment (Nicholl, 158; we recall yet again that £10 was a comfortable annual income for the lower orders). Head-tires involved expensive commodities: gold and silver wire and thread, silver-coated wire to form the base of the structure, and human hair, very possibly from corpses. They could normally only be afforded by the moneyed classes, but when it came to clothing of all kinds those would include the leading acting companies, who spent prodigious amounts on impressive costumes and accessories. A 1598 inventory of the Admiral's Men lists "6 head-tires" and Henslowe twice mentions a Mrs Goosen in 1601; on each occasion she is paid 12 shillings "for a head tire" (318, 185, 198). On New Year's Day 1603 a Mrs Calle received 10 shillings "for two coronets for head tires for the court" – one of several instances where it is clear that the company would lay out money especially to shine at court, though doubtless the items eventually found their way onto the public stage. The boy actor, John Rice, wore what was evidently an elaborate head tire ("a coronet of pearl and cockle-shells on her head") for a public entertainment staged to honor Prince Henry's installation as Prince of Wales in 1610 (see p. 187).

Shakespeare several times brings tires into his dialogue. As early as *Two Gentlemen of Verona* (1590/92) Silvia laments "I think / If I had such a tire, this face of mine / Were full as lovely as this of hers" (4.4.183–5) and in *Much Ado* (circa 1598) the maidservant Margaret is critical of the new tire that Hero will wear for her wedding: "I like this new tire within excellently, if the hair were a thought browner" (3.4.12–13). Evidently the color of the tire does not exactly match that of Hero's natural hair – a foreshadowing of the misfortune which will befall the wedding. But it is in *Merry Wives* that tires figure most prominently, as Falstaff tries to woo Mrs Ford with flattery: "Thou hast the right arched beauty of the brow that becomes the ship-tire, the tire valiant, or any tire of Venetian admittance" (3.3.47–51). That is, her brow is arched in such a way that it will show to advantage a tire shaped like a ship, or one perhaps of daunting ("valiant") proportions, or indeed any tire that would pass for fashionable in Venice – a city of sophisticated tastes in headware as much as sexual behavior. Mrs Ford easily deflates him: "A plain kerchief, Sir John. My brows become nothing else, nor that well neither" (52–3). In the horribly confused text at the end of the folio version of the play Fenton tells us that Anne Page shall represent the Fairy Queen and "That quaint in green she shall be loose enrobed, / With ribbons pendent, flaring 'bout her head" (4.6.41–2). In the outcome it may be Mistress Quickly who plays the Fairy Queen – but the point is surely that whoever played it would be wearing a tire of sorts, befitting fairy royalty. There are no other specific clues about which characters wore these headpieces, but it makes sense that female deities might be so distinguished, such as "proud Titania" in *A Midsummer Night's Dream* and Diana in *Pericles*. We might well imagine Juno descending in *The Tempest*, wearing a head-tire – mimicking the appearance of an aristocratic lady masquer in one of Queen Anne's court masques – while Hecate in *Macbeth* may have worn some malevolent antimasque equivalent.

Tiremen

It is unlikely that the Chamberlain's Men included a tirewoman (in the sense of someone who made head tires) among their weekly salaried staff, but it is certainly not impossible that a woman was employed – as with the Children of the King's Revels – whose duties included dressing and equipping the transvestite boy actors. But a *tireman* – or more likely *tiremen* – most certainly would have been on the regular staff. The male title alluded, not to headware, but to care of the stock of clothing that the company built up, which was its most valuable single asset. When Francis Langley's attempt to set up the Earl of Pembroke's Men in his Swan theatre went awry in 1597 it was a major point in his suit for reparations against the players that he should be reimbursed for "the great costs and charges he hath disbursed and laid out at and by their direction for … furnishing himself with sundry sorts of rich attire and apparel for them to play withal, whereof the defendant hath ever sithence had little use" (*EPF*, 444). Thomas Platter noted that "The comedians are most expensively and elegantly apparelled since" – he was apparently informed – "it is customary in England, when distinguished gentlemen or knights die, for nearly the finest of their clothes to be made over and given to their servants, and as it is not proper for them to wear such clothes but only to imitate them, they give them to the comedians to purchase for a small sum" (*ES*, 2: 365).

This account of how the players acquired their finery is not corroborated in Henslowe or elsewhere and may be something of an urban myth, since the

Diary makes it very plain that they laid out great sums of money to acquire clothing for their productions – often significantly more than to acquire the script. In just eleven days (August 18–28, 1602) Henslowe advanced Worcester's Men the following sums for costumes: £2 "to buy rebatos and farthingales"; £9 "to buy taffeta and other stuff to make two women's gowns"; 5s "to buy buckram to make a pair of gyente [giant?] hose"; £12 "to buy a suit for 'Oldcastle' and a suit and a doublet of satin"; £4 for "a cloak of camlet [costly eastern fabric, or imitation of] lined with crimson taffeta, pinked," followed by 14s. to pay the mercer for lace for the cloak; £6 for a man's gown of branched [adorned with a figured pattern] velvet and a doublet; and 34s. "to pay unto the tailor for stuff and making of two women's gowns" (*Henslowe*, 214–15).

However it was acquired, such attire needed to be stored safely and in such order that items could regularly be found. It needed to be cleaned and mended as use demanded. It needed to be aired and kept dry as – in an era before artificial fabrics – a defense against both rot and moths. (At court, it was one of the responsibilities of the Revels Office – and specifically the Yeoman of the Revels – to protect the extensive collection of costumes used in court entertainments in this way.)[11] All of this was the tireman's first responsibility. The scale of it may be judged from the inventories which Edward Alleyn drew up in March 1598, presumably demarcating what the Admiral's Men owned as distinct from the property of Henslowe and Alleyn themselves, at a point when the business relationship between them was changing.[12]

One list, ominously – and despite the draconian penalties for absconding with company stock – is headed "*Gone and Lost*" and contains some obviously valuable items, including "1 orange tawny satin doublet, laid thick with gold lace," "1 pair of carnation satin Venetians [hose or breeches], laid with gold lace," "1 longshank's [= Edward 1] suit," "1 Spanish [?] doublet, pinked [= cut so as to reveal the lining]," "1 Harry the Fifth's velvet gown." Another is "*The Inventory of the Clowns' Suits and Hermits' Suits, with divers other*" which contains many standard, reusable items, even when they were apparently bought for a particular play: "1 senator's gown, 1 hood, and 5 senators' capes," "1 suit for Neptune; firedrake's [fiery dragon's] suits for Dobe [unidentified]," "4 janissaries' gowns, and 4 torchbearers' suits," "3 pair of red strasers [trousers]," "4 Hereward's coats, and 3 soldiers' coats, and 1 green gown for Marian," "6 green coats for Robin Hood, and 4 knaves' suits," "2 russet coats, and 1 black frese [coarse woolen] coat, and 3 priests' coats," "2 white shepherds' coats, and 2 Danes' suits, and one pair of Danes' hose," "4 friars' gowns and 4 hoods to them, and 1 fool's coat, cape, and bauble, and Branholt's bodice, and Merlin gown and cape," "2 black saye [fine textured cloth] gowns, and 2 cotton gowns, and 1 red saye gown," "5 pair of hose for the clown, and 5 jerkins for them," "1 yellow leather doublet for a clown," "Eve's bodice, and 3 dons' hats," "1 red suit of cloth for Pig [John Pig, boy actor], laid with white lace," "1 pair of yellow cotton sleeves, 1 ghost's suit, and 1 ghost's bodice," "5 shirts, and 1 serpelowes

[? = surplice], 3 farthingales," "6 head-tires, 1 fane [flag, banner], 3 rebatos [large, stiffened collars], 2 gyrketruses [unexplained]" and "18 copes and hats." Some entries include properties, as if perhaps they were expected to be used in the same show: "The Moor's limbs, and Hercules's limbs, and Will Summers's suit," "2 Orlates [unidentified] suits, hats and gorgets, and 7 antics' [grotesques', clowns'] coats," and "Cathemer [unidentified] suit, 1 pair of cloth white stockings, 3 Turks' heads," "1 hat for Robin Hood, 1 hobby-horse."

A brief inventory covers items "*Left above in the tire-house in the chest*," another (see p. 109) lists properties, and yet another seems to list the more precious clothes:

Item, 1 pair of white satin Venetians, cut with copper lace.
Item, 1 ash colour satin doublet, laid with gold lace.
Item, 1 peach colour satin doublet.
Item, 1 old white satin doublet.
Item, 1 blue taffeta suit.
Item, 1 Moor's coat.
Item, Pig's [boy actor's] damask gown.
Item, 1 black satin coat.
Item, 1 harcollar [? = hair-colour] taffeta suit of Pig's.
Item, Vartemar [Valteger? Vortigern?] suit.
Item, 1 great peach-colour doublet, with silver lace.
Item, 1 white satin doublet, pinked [split to show the lining].
Item, 1 old white satin doublet, pinked.
Item, 1 pair of satin Venetians, satin embroidered.
Item, 1 pair of French hose, cloth of gold.
Item, 1 pair of cloth of gold hose with silver pane [lining or trimming].
Item, 1 pair of cloth of silver hose, with satin and silver pane.
Item, Tamburlaine's coat with copper lace.
Item, 1 red cloak with white copper lace.
Item, 1 red cloak with red copper lace.
Item, 1 short cloak of tawny satin with sleeves.
Item, 1 short cloak of black satin with sleeves.
Item, Labesha's cloak, with gold buttons.
Item, 1 pair of red cloth hose of Venetians with silver lace of copper.
Item, Juno's coat.
Item, 1 hood for the witch.
Item, 1 red stamel [coarse woolen cloth] cloak with red copper lace.
Item, 1 cloth cloak of russet with copper lace, called Guido's cloak.
Item, 1 short cloak of black velvet, with sleeves faced with shag [rough matted hair or wool].
Item, 1 short cloak of black velvet, faced with white fur.
Item, 1 man's gown, faced with white fur.

Item, Dobe's [unidentified] coat of cloth of silver.
Item, 1 pair of peach-colour Venetians uncut, with red copper lace.
Item, 1 red scarlet cloak with silver buttons.
Item, 1 long black velvet cloak, laid with broad lace black.
Item, 1 black satin suit.
Item, 1 black velvet cloak, laid with twist lace black.
Item, Perowe's [unidentified] suit, which William Sly wore.
Item, 1 pair of peach-colour hose with silver corlled [?curled] panes.
Item, 1 pair of black cloth of silver hose, drawn out with tufted taffeta.
Item, Tamburlaine's breeches of crimson velvet.
Item, 1 pair of silk hose, with panes of silver curled [?] lace.
Item, 1 Phaeton suit.
Item, Robin Hood's suit.
Item, 1 pair of cloth of gold hose, with gold curl [?] panes.
Item, 1 pair of rowne [? = roan, sheep-skin] hose, buff with old lace.
Item, 1 pair of mouse-colour Venetians with R. [?] broad gold lace.
Item, 1 flame-coloured doublet, pinked.
Item, 1 black satin doublet, laid thick with black and gold lace.
Item, 1 carnation doublet-cut, laid with gold lace.
Item, 1 white satin doublet, faced with red taffeta.
Item, 1 green jerkin with silver lace.
Item, 1 black jerkin with silver lace.
Item, 1 red Spanish doublet, stiched.
Item, 1 peach-colour satin casse [? = cassock, long coat]
Item, Tasso's robe.
Item, 1 murey [purple-red] robe with sleeves.
Item, 1 blue robe with sleeves.
Item, 1 orange-tawny robe with sleeves.
Item, 1 peach-coloured half-robe.
Item, 1 lane [?] robe with spangles.
Item, 1 white & orange-tawny scarf, spangled.
Item, Dido's robe.
Item, 3 pair of basses [? = bases, skirts of women's outer-petticoats or robes].
Item, 1 white taffeta shirt with gold fringe.
Item, the friar's truss [bag, package] in Robin Hood.
Item, 1 little jacket for Pig.
Item, 1 woman's gown of cloth of gold.
Item, 1 orange-tawny velvet gown with silver lace, for women.
Item, 1 black velvet gown embroidered with gold lace.
Item, 1 yellow satin gown embroidered with silk and gold lace, for women.
Item, 1 greve armour [for the lower leg].
Item, Harry the 5 velvet gown.
Item, 1 pair of crimson satin Venetians, laid with gold lace.

Item, 1 taffeta suit, laid with silver lace.
Item, 1 Longshanks suit.
Item, 1 orange-colour satin doublet, laied with gold lace.
Item, Harry the 5 satin doublet, laid with gold lace.
Item, 1 Spanish casse [?] doublet of crimson, pinked.
Item, 1 Spanish jerkin, laid with silver lace.
Item, 1 watchet [light-blue] taffeta doublet for a boy.
Item, 2 pair of basses [? = bases, skirts of women's outer-petticoats or robes], 1 white, one blue, of sarcenet [fine silk].
Item, 1 friar's gown of grey.

These lists are far from complete and the sheer quantity of clothing is staggering – but obviously necessary with such a repertoire and every play containing twenty roles or more. And the range of materials is impressive: from various forms of coarse woolen material to more luxurious taffeta, satin, velvet, and sarcenet. And an array of colors, favoring peach-colored, black, white, orange-tawny, and occasional bright red, as (fittingly) in Tamburlaine's breeches. Trimming with copper (white or red, to imitate silver or gold) was common and cheaper than the precious metals – but there was plenty of real gold and silver on display as well, just as there were "pinked" items, pierced or slashed in some way to show off a splendid lining.

And the tireman's first responsibility was to keep all this investment in good order. The Chamberlain's Men doubtless had a wardrobe as impressive and expensive. In the case of the Admiral's Men we actually have the name of their tireman, Steven Maggett, and it is apparent in Henslowe's pages that he was a trusted part of the team. We first hear of him January 1595, when Henslowe sold him a doublet and a pair of Venetians (trousers) with two laces, for 16s., agreeing to take payment at the rate of 1s. per week. In December 1596 Henslowe recorded: "dd unto Steven the tireman for to deliver unto the company to buy a head-tire and rebato [stiffened collar or ruff support] & other things … £4 10s" – a significant investment, and also responsibility. In August 1601 we hear of Henslowe repaying him 14d. of his own money which he had used to buy tiffany [fine, transparent silk] for the play of *Cardinal Wolsey* (37, 50, 180).

Thereafter Steven presumably transferred with the Admiral's Men to the Fortune and a different tireman – Henslowe refers to him only as "our tireman," even in his tenancy accounts – worked for Worcester's Men, who took over the Rose. We hear of him in September 1602, being paid 8s. 8d. "for making of William Kemp's suit and the boy's." The next month he was lent 8s. to buy soutage, a coarse cloth, "to make devils" suits for the new play of the *2 Brothers' Tragedy* and a further 18s. "to buy saye … to make a witch's gown" for the same play. He was paid later in the month for doing the work. The next year he was entrusted with over £5 to buy eight and a half yards of black satin to make a suit for "The Second Part of *The Black Dog*" (*Henslowe*, 247, 218, 219, 224). This tireman clearly had tailors' skills and was employed to make up at least some of their clothes rather than buy them ready-made. This may show thrift on the part of a company which was by no means as well established as the Admiral's Men, and suffered from having to compete with the Chamberlain's Men at the Globe, a very short distance away.

The tireman's duties clearly extended to helping with make-up and other functions around the stage. In Marston's *Antonio's Revenge*, a boys' play for Paul's playhouse, a character comes on complaining "The tiring man hath not glued my beard half fast enough" (2.1.30–1); both Lyly's *Endymion* and Marston's *What You Will* have a stage direction: "Enter tireman with lights," while in the Induction to the *The Malcontent* as staged by the King's Men the opening stage-direction is "Enter W. Sly, a tireman following him with a stool" (1.1.0). In the Induction to Jonson's *The Staple of News* (performed at the Blackfriars in 1626) the Book-holder (i.e. book-keeper) commands "Mend your lights, gentlemen. Master Prologue, begin" and the stage direction follows: "*The* TIREMEN *enter to mend the lights*" (40–1); evidently, in the candle-lit indoor playhouses, it fell to the tiremen (note the plural) to trim the candles (2012*o*). It is confirmed elsewhere that, like the gatherers, the tireman could on occasion be called on to take on walk-on parts (Greg, 1907, 152). This is thus another case of hired men having a very specific responsibility within the company, but being expected to help out wherever necessary at performance time.

Musicians

The King's Revels list of charges of the house includes "music," while (as we shall see) in the 1624 list of "necessary attendants" to the King's Men *musicians* are the only category specifically named (pp. 301ff). The Blackfriars theatre had its famous consort of musicians and they are presumably what Sir Henry Herbert had primarily in mind when he drew up that list, making musicians so prominent. But music was an essential element of all professional drama in the period; and every leading troupe employed professional musicians (doubtless in smaller numbers than the Blackfriars) to provide it. They fell into at least two categories. On the one hand there were those who played the drums and trumpets; on the other there were those who would play chamber music or accompany songs, playing woodwind or stringed instruments. Such sets of instruments would not have been expected to perform together at this date.

Drums and trumpets had a very specific role *outside* the playhouse: in announcing the arrival of traveling players at a new venue and in making people aware that a show was about to begin at one of the London theatres. Hence they figure prominently in the anti-theatrical literature. For example John Stockwood, in a 1578 sermon preached at Paul's Cross, bewailed "Will not a filthy play, with the blast of a trumpet, sooner call thither a thousand, than an hour's tolling of a bell bring to the sermon a hundred?" (*ES*, 4: 199). It was a point often made. And when the Lord Mayor in 1580 wrote to the Earl of Warwick about his players appearing in venues near the city, he is careful to spell out that if their leader "obtain lawfully to play at the Theatre or any other open place out of the City, he hath and shall have my permission with his company, drums, and show to pass openly through the City, being not upon the Sunday" (291). The Lord Mayor remains respectful, but he stands his ground: they must get proper permission, they mustn't perform on Sundays. In such a context allowing the use of drums at all is a gracious concession. When James Burbage was building the second Blackfriars theatre, however, it was part of the (successful) objection of the local residents "that the same playhouse is so near the church that the noise of the drums and trumpets will greatly disturb and hinder both the ministers and parishioners in time of divine service and sermons" (320). And when Lord Hunsdon negotiated with the Lord Mayor to allow his new company to use the Cross Keys inn during the winter of 1594/5, he made the very specific concession that they "will not use any drums or trumpets at all for the calling of people together" (316).

Nevertheless, there would always be work for drummers and trumpeters within performances themselves, since between them they provided the musical soundtracks of warfare and royal ceremony. In Act 4 of *Richard III* a stage direction reads "*Enter King Richard and his train, marching with drums and trumpets*" (Q1 1597, 4.4.135.1) and shortly thereafter Richard commands: "A flourish, trumpets! Strike alarum, drums" (149). The *OED* describes such a flourish as "A fanfare (of horns, trumpets, etc.), *esp.* to announce the approach of a person of distinction" (*n*, 7a) and it preceded warlike royalty everywhere in Elizabethan plays, while the alarum or call to arms goes up on almost every battlefield, accompanied by drums and/or trumpets. In *3 Henry VI*, for example, 4.6, 4.7, 4.8, 5.3, 5.4, 5.5. and 5.7 all begin with flourishes, while 5.2 begins and 5.4 ends with an alarum: as *2 Henry VI* puts it, "When the angry trumpets sound alarum" (5.2.3). These probably corresponded to actual signals on the contemporary battlefield, but for less warlike settings it seems that the Elizabethan theatre devised its own convention for announcing royalty, the sennet, which the *OED* describes as "A set of notes on the trumpet or cornet, ordered in the stage-directions of Elizabethan plays, apparently as a signal for the ceremonial entrance or exit of a body of players." So in Thomas Dekker's *Satiromastix*, a stage direction reads "*Trumpets sound a flourish, and then a sennet*" (3.2.0 SD); in Shakespeare and Fletcher's *Henry VIII*, 2.4 opens with "*Trumpets, sennet, and cornetts*." Fletcher's own *Valentinian* 5. 8 calls for "*A sennet with trumpets*."

The only other instrument so specifically and regularly called for in play texts for the public theatres is the hautboy, a precursor of the modern oboe, though Lucy Munro points out that they "are extremely rare in adult company plays performed before 1608" (2009, 548, n. 22). We find it required, for example, at the beginnings of both 1.6 and 1.7 in *Macbeth*, ominously contrasting scenes in which King Duncan approaches Macbeth's castle ("The castle hath a pleasant seat") and Macbeth plots murder ("If it were done when 'tis done, then 'twere well / It were done quickly"). In the second quarto (1604) of *Hamlet* the dumb-show commences with "*The trumpets sound*," but in the folio version (1623) the direction is "*Hautboys play*." Early in *Timon of Athens* a feast begins with "*Hautboys playing loud music*" (1.2.0 SD). These are all texts first printed in 1623, we note, and may well not reflect their earliest staging.

But the theatres certainly had a much wider range of instruments at their disposal than this. In Alleyn's inventories of the Admiral's Men's property at the Rose, beside three trumpets and a drum, he listed "a treble viol, a bass viol, a bandore, a cittern."[13] These are all instruments that might be used to accompany singing. It cannot be accidental that Augustine Phillips bequeathed to his "late apprentice," Samuel Gilburne, his "bass viol" and to his current apprentice, James Sands, "a cittern, and a bandore, and a lute" (*EPF*, 198–9). There was a consistent relationship between music and the boy players, and not just those in the all-boy companies, which had their roots in the choir schools.

I discuss this further under *Apprentices* (p. 182). For now I wish simply to point out that, so long as the adult companies retained apprentices – and, moreover, recruited a growing number of their sharers both from among those apprentices and from the boy companies – they were never short of musicians trained in singing and in the use of stringed instruments. In the Chamberlain's / King's Men, for example, Alexander Cooke made the transition from apprentice to sharer, while William Ostler, John Underwood, and Nathan Field all derived, directly or indirectly, from the Blackfriars boys.[14] This ensured, for example, that when the famous opening of *Twelfth Night* appears to call for onstage musicians – "If music be the food of love, play on" – it would not have been difficult to provide them from within the sharer players, without recourse to hired men. When Viola asks Feste "Dost thou live by thy tabor" (3.1.1–2) it probably indicates that Robert Armin was playing the tabor [small drum] and pipe as Tarlton had done in earlier years (see Figure 2.1 and p. 44). When Amiens sings "Blow, blow, thou winter wind" in *As You Like It* (2.7.180–93), and other songs, probably to the accompaniment of one or more stringed instruments, it would hardly have taxed resources at all.

Musical costs in the theatre would also have included some commissioning of new songs. To some extent they would have got by on their own resources, with authors setting their own words to existing popular tunes. For example, when Edgar as Poor Tom bursts into "Come o'er the burn, Bessy, to me" (3.6.25) he is singing a ballad by William Birche, first published in 1558; when Desdemona sang "The Willow Song" (*Othello*, 4.3.43–59), which she calls "An old thing" (31), she was probably doing so to a lute tune first published in 1583. But the King's Men certainly employed people to write original songs and settings for them, perhaps more regularly after they took over use of the Blackfriars. All those so employed that we know of held positions as musicians at court. The most notable of these was Robert Johnson, a lutenist who was for a time in the employment of the younger Lord Hunsdon, patron of the company while it was the Chamberlain's Men. Johnson wrote surviving settings for songs in Shakespeare's *Cymbeline* (circa 1609), *The Winter's Tale* (circa 1611), and *The Tempest* (1611), Webster's *The Duchess of Malfi* (circa 1613), Middleton's *The Witch* (circa 1616), Jonson's masque, *The Gypsies Metamorphosed* (1621), and five plays in the Beaumont and Fletcher canon, *The Captain* (circa 1612), *Valentinian* (circa 1614), *The Mad Lover* (circa 1616), *The Chances* (circa 1617), and *The Lover's Progress* (1623).

Alphono Ferrabosco, a viol player, was another composer who we know worked for them on at least one play, Jonson's *Volpone*, performed at the Globe in 1606; his settings included one for its famous seduction song, "Come, my Celia, let us prove." Jonson had worked with Ferrabosco on *The Masque of Blackness* (1605) and *Hymenaei* (1606), elaborate and extravagant court masques, to which music was central. Since the King's Men supplied the speaking and singing roles for these events (while royalty and aristocrats posed and danced) a natural connection grew up between the actors and such musicians. Jonson praised Ferrabosco in the printed text of *Hymenaei*: "I do for honour's sake, and the pledge of our friendship, name Master Alphonso Ferrabosco, a man planted by himself in that divine sphere, and mastering all the spirits of music; to whose judicial care, and as absolute performance, were committed all those difficulties both of song and otherwise; wherein, what his merit made to the soul of our invention would ask to be expressed in tunes no less ravishing than his" (Jonson 2012*j*, lines 584–8).

Such men were never regular employees of the company, and would be paid strictly on a commission basis. Songs always enjoyed a somewhat semidetached relationship to the plays in which they appeared and are often not printed with them (Stern, 2009*a*, 120–73). Most of John Lyly's plays for boy companies in the 1580s, for example, first appeared without their songs; it was only in the collection of *Six Court Comedies* (1632) that their lyrics found their way into print. The stage directions in the quarto text of *Merry Wives* tell us that the "fairies" who torment Falstaff at the end of the play "s*ing a song about him*" (G2, G3), but the words do not appear; they only survive in the folio version (5.5.93–102).

Book-keepers

The King's Revels agreement, lastly, called for a *book-keeper* to be paid among the hired men, to which I add another position we know of among the adult companies, that of *stage-keeper*. The positions are famously paired in the

Induction to Jonson's *Bartholomew Fair*, where the stage-keeper regales the audience with tales of how much better it was "in Master Tarlton's time, I thank my stars" (2012b, line 28), and the book-keeper appears "not for want of a prologue but by way of a new one" (44–5) to introduce a Scrivener, who will read Articles of Agreement supposedly binding the audience and the author of the play. It is not impossible that the actual book-keeper and stage-keeper of Lady Elizabeth's Men at the Hope playhouse played themselves in this sequence. Evidently the jobs they performed were familiar to the audience.

The *book-keeper*'s (sometimes called *book-holder's*) role, minimally, seems to have been to act as prompter during a performance, helping actors who were "out"; to track entrances and exits; and to ensure that properties were where they should be when needed. Benvolio in *Romeo and Juliet* speaks of a "without-book prologue, faintly spoke / After the prompter" (1.4.7–8: Q1 only) – a nonce-prologue which is not part of "the book," being spoken softly to the running prompts of the book-keeper. In *Every Woman In Her Humour* we hear of someone who "would ... stamp and stare (God bless us), like a playhouse book-keeper when the actors miss their entrance" (1609, B3). In a joke at his own expense, Jonson has one of the children in the Praeludium to *Cynthia's Revels* deny that they have the author "in the tiring-house to prompt us aloud, stamp at the book-holder, swear for our properties, curse the poor tire-man, rail the music out of tune" (Jonson 2012c, lines 128–30). The book-holder thus merged aspects of the modern roles of prompter and stage manager.

The precise function of the surviving "plots" or "plats" among the Henslowe–Alleyn papers (and others which may have originated there) has been much debated but were probably, at least in part, a "map" to help the book-keeper in his duty of keeping a performance on the rails (see p. 113). It is a common but unsubstantiated assumption that it was also part of the book-holder's responsibility to tidy up the company's playbooks and mark them up for production purposes, in the way we might expect of a modern prompt-copy. As William B. Long has demonstrated, the surviving eighteen playbooks of the period, manuscripts demonstrably used within the theatres, simply do not bear this out (1985; 1999). The book-holder's interventions are fewer than we might expect, and mainly aimed (it would seem) at making details more readily noticeable on the page, rather than regularizing the playwrights' stage-directions or specifying numbers of attendants and other minor roles (as editors of plays have often supposed). Such functions are much more apparent in the surviving "plots," but we do not know who was responsible for those. G. E. Bentley makes the logical point that "The prompter would have been the obvious man to make, or at least to supervise the making of such Plots," though when a play came from a company's "ordinary poet" he could just as readily have done the job (1984, 85). The book-holder had an important role in the company, but it was as a servant to a team of professionals, not in any directorial capacity.

It is possible that the distinct position of book-holder developed over time, once regular playing in the London playhouses was established. The earliest book-holder to whom we can put a name is recalled by John Taylor, the Water-Poet: "I myself did know one Thomas Vincent that was a book-keeper or prompter at the Globe playhouse near the Bank-end in Maid Lane" (1638, 66). He was referring to a time pre-1612. But that is all we securely know of Vincent (see p. 209). By the time Edward Knight held the position with the King's Men it carried some responsibility. He was the first of those named in the Sir Henry Herbert's 1624 Protection List of the company's "servants" (*Herbert* 158; see p. 301). In the 1630s he was on the fringes of one theatrical awkwardness and at the heart of another. In October 1632 Sir Henry recorded "Received of Knight, for allowing of Ben Jonson's play called *Humours Reconciled*, or *The Magnetic Lady*, to be acted … £2" (176). He did not normally keep a record of who delivered his licensing fee, but in this case he mentions Knight by name. Was this prudential on his part? A year later this play had both Herbert and Jonson in trouble with the Court of High Commission over some lines delivered in performance which caused offence, probably relating to Archbishop Laud's reforms of the church (Butler, 1992; Dutton, 2000, 42–3). Herbert and Jonson insisted that the lines were not in the "allowed" text, the actors that they were. In the end the Court found against the players (184). No one would actually have been better placed to know if unlicensed additions had been made to a text than the book-keeper.

A year later Knight was centrally involved. On October 19, 1633 Herbert most unusually gave a last-minute order to the King's Men not to stage a revival of Fletcher's *The Tamer Tamed* (or, *The Woman's Prize*) "upon complaints of foul and offensive matters contained therein" (see pp. 90, 112). "On Saturday morning following the book was brought me and … I returned it to the players the Monday morning after, purged of oaths, profaneness, and ribaldry" (182). In 1606 Parliament had passed an Act of Abuses, aimed at restricting the use of profane oaths in the theatres; it was mainly focused on preventing the naming of God and the Trinity. In the intense church politics of the 1630s Herbert became particularly sensitive to this issue and insisted on reviewing plays formerly allowed by his predecessors but possibly not meeting the standards he now required.[15] From 1606 onwards the company's book-holder would have been particularly well-placed to ensure that the "allowed" copy of their plays met the legal requirements, overseeing necessary revisions when an earlier play was revived.[16]

That was now more important than ever, as Sir Henry's message to Edward Knight spelled out:

> Mr. Knight,
>   In many things you have saved me labour; yet where your judgment or pen failed you, I have made bold to use mine. Purge their parts, as I have

the book. And I hope every hearer and players will think I have done God good service, and the quality no wrong;[17] who hath no greater enemies than oaths, profaneness, and public ribaldry, which for the future I do absolutely forbid to be presented unto me in any playbook, as you will answer it at your peril. 21 October 1633.

This was subscribed to their play of *The Tamer Tamed*, and directed to Knight, their book-keeper

(Herbert, *183*).

Knight thus found himself in the delicate position of messenger to the players and their playwrights in this sensitive matter. He had to make sure that both the "allowed book" and the players' "parts" were in line with Herbert's directions (on "parts," see p. 108).

On a more relaxed note, however, his role became the butt of repeated metatheatrical in-jokes. In the Fletcher and Rowley comedy, *The Maid in the Mill* (performed 1623), as the plot gets more complicated, the clown Bustofa, played by William Rowley himself, reflects "they are out of their parts, sure. / It may be 'tis the book-holder's fault. I'll go see" (1647, p. 8). Similarly, in Richard Brome's *Antipodes*, when a voice "*within*" orders "Dismiss the court," Lord Leroy says "Dismiss the court: can you not hear the prompter?" (2010*a*, 3.8.628–30). It has been argued, from experience at "Shakespeare's Globe," that the role of prompter was unworkable on the Elizabethan stage. But there are enough references in the texts from *Romeo and Juliet* (Q1) onwards to prove that there was such a figure, and that he doubled up as the book-keeper in wider senses. He was clearly a pivotal figure during performances but also important in taking care of the company's precious manuscripts and liaising with the Master of the Revels.

Stage-keepers

We know rather less about stage-keepers. We have no grounds to suppose that the men who actually performed this duty were as garrulous, fixed in their (poor) judgments, or convinced that everything was so much better in Tarlton's time as the character in the Induction to *Bartholomew Fair*. Little in that role relates to his real work, except when he talks of his "judgment" and the book-keeper asks him "For what? Sweeping the stage, or gathering up broken apples for the bears within?" (2012*b*, 37–9). Collecting up discarded apple-cores for the bears would only apply to the Hope, where Jonson's play was staged; it doubled as a bear-baiting arena. But stages doubtless always needed sweeping, being fairly open to the elements. And they would have been strewn with fresh green rushes for each performance, a common recourse in houses with wooden floors; they helped freshen a room, protected the floors, absorbed or hid stains, and possibly softened the sounds of movement (see p. 268).

We know that rushes were also used for freshness in the gentlemen's rooms and may suppose that was the case in the lords' rooms (p. 234). It would make sense for the stage-keeper to attend to all these contexts. And there would always have been need to tidy up the playhouse after a large crowd. Yet again, however, this hardly seems like a full-time job. Possibly he was responsible for overseeing stage machinery, such as descent apparatus and trapdoors, but there is no record of this. He also might have had some responsibility for the security of the building, which housed so much of the company's property.

The playwright Robert Daborne does suggests another function the stage-keeper fulfilled, in a letter to Henslowe: "I pray you, sir, let the boy give order this night to the stage-keeper to set up bills against Monday for *Eastward Ho* and on Wednesday the new play [i.e. the one Daborne was writing]" (Greg, 1907, 71). Bills were an important – and still quite novel – way of advertising the companies and their offerings: such mass entertainment as they were able to offer from the 1570s onwards was a new phenomenon, and it would be essential to spread the word when a company came to town, especially if it was putting on a play in a suburban amphitheater, some way from where most people lived (see p. 106). Even with an established company, it would be essential to keep spreading the word about an ever-changing repertoire. From at least 1587 these bills were printed rather than handwritten – the right to print them became a lucrative monopoly for one printer at a time – and so could be posted in numbers (Stern, 2006).

Hence in the anti-theatrical literature bills are often coupled with the drums and trumpets which similarly announced the company's presence, both signs of the devil at work. This is the thrust of an anonymous rant to Sir Francis Walsingham, the Queen's Secretary of State, in 1587: "The daily abuse of the stage plays is such an offence to the godly, and so great a hindrance to the Gospel, as the papists so exceedingly rejoice at the blemish thereof, and not without cause; for every day in the week the players' bills are set up in sundry place of the city ... so that when the bells toll to the lecturer [preacher], the trumpets sound to the stages" (*ES*, 4: 303–4). In 1581 the Lord Mayor of London had given specific orders to his officials not to allow theatrical bills to be posted: "give straight charge and commandment to all the inhabitants within the same ward that they do not at any time hereafter suffer any person or persons whatsoever to set up or fix any briefs upon any posts, houses, or other places within your wards, for the show or setting out of any plays, interludes or prizes within this city ... and that if any such shall be set up, the same presently to be pulled down and defaced" (*ES*, 4: 283). This order had no lasting effect – as the letter to Walsingham attests.

Some "person or persons," then, had the chore "every day of the week" of posting these bills for the players "in sundry places" ("posts, houses") all over the city. This apparently included the doors of the theatres themselves. During the Commonwealth period Richard Flecknoe bemoaned: "From thence passing on to the Blackfriars, and seeing never a playbill on the gate, no coaches on the place, nor doorkeeper at the playhouse door" (1653, 141). It is unlikely that the stage-keeper would have handled the whole operation on his own, but he does seem to have been involved.

Apprentices

The boy actors, more than any other single feature, define the distance between early modern theatre and our own.[18] Why precisely women did not perform on the English professional stage before the Civil War has never been explained; they certainly did so in Italy, France, and Spain, even if this was often a change within living memory. Contrary to the movie *Shakespeare in Love* (1999) there was no legal prohibition against it and there is no record of the Master of the Revels trying to enforce a ban. It was a matter of custom and practice, to some extent deriving from the peripatetic lifestyle of the players in the days before settled city playing; less scandal would attend on the men being accompanied by boys than by women, and that was an important consideration when they were representing a noble patron.[19]

Taking on boys as apprentices would have seemed natural in a context where many of the players were freemen of trade or livery companies. They would be used to the custom of boys being bound by indentures, usually for a period of seven years, until they themselves became freemen. The expectation was that they should be trained for a profession, and given board and lodging, but usually no wage – they were getting freeman status in one of the livery companies like the Merchant Taylors, Mercers, Grocers, Goldsmiths, or Haberdashers at the end of it, and that was a tangible social benefit in the City of London (see p. 12). In an era before social security, the status also offered a financial support structure in old age, times of poverty or bereavement. It was by no means necessary, however, that the boys should be trained in the trade with which their masters were associated. The earliest known theatrical apprentices were indentured with Richard Tarlton, who had served his own apprenticeship with the Haberdashers, but later transferred to the Vintners, probably because he ran an inn as a secondary profession (Kathman, 2006). There was nothing improper about him taking on apprentices to train as players, even though there was no guild of players for them to belong to (Kathman, 2009d, 422–3). They would themselves be free of the Haberdashers or Vintners, just as John Heminge's many apprentices would be free of his own company, the Grocers.

The boys usually started their indentures around the age of thirteen, though anything up to sixteen was not unusual; and their term was commonly for seven years, though again anything up to twelve years was not out of the ordinary.[20] It thus seems that boy actors performed the roles of women (as well, of course, as of pages, children, apprentices and others appropriate to their size and voice) between about the ages of thirteen and twenty-two; puberty generally came two or three years later in less well-nourished times than it does in the industrial world today. Although, as we have seen, Augustine Phillips took on at least two apprentices while he was with Shakespeare's company, and Robert Armin, a Goldsmith, took on at least one (James Jones, bound July 15, 1608: Kathman, 2004*b*, 18), John Heminge, took on by far the most for the company, at least ten over his long career. And it so happens that we can identify quite a few of the roles they played (Kathman, 2009*d*, 419–20).

Heminge bound Thomas Belte on November 12, 1595, and he must be the "T. Belt" assigned to play a servant and the female role of Panthea in the "plot" of *The Second Part of the Seven Deadly Sins*, a play which David Kathman assigns to the Chamberlain's Men around 1597/8 (see 205–17). Heminge then bound Alexander Cooke on January 26, 1597; in the same "plot" someone named "saunder" played the substantial female roles of Queen Videna and Progne and that is quite likely to have been Cooke, who went on to be a shareholder with the company. We may note here that in the period 1597–1601 the company contained at least two boy players capable of taking on challenging female roles and it is probably not coincidental that it is the time when Shakespeare wrote his three most famous cross-dressing roles, Portia in *The Merchant of Venice*, Rosalind in *As You Like It*, and Viola in *Twelfth Night*, besides the major role of Beatrice in *Much Ado About Nothing*. There is no record of John Rice being formally bound to Heminge, but when he presented a speech as the Angel of Gladness before King James in the guildhall of the Merchant Taylors in 1607 ("a very proper child, well spoken ... with a taper of frankincense burning in his hand") Heminge received £5 for supplying and preparing him, Rice himself 5 shillings; Rice would eventually be a sharer and leading player in the company.[21] Heminge did bind George Birch or Burgh on July 4, 1610; by 1616 he is noted as playing Doll Common in a revival of Jonson's *The Alchemist* and Lady Would-Be in a revival of his *Volpone* – two substantial comic female roles.[22]

John Wilson, bound on February 18, 1611, is to be found in a stage direction in the First Folio text of *Much Ado About Nothing*, "Enter Prince, Leonato, Claudio and Jack Wilson"; this in part replaces the 1600 quarto stage direction "Enter Balthasar with music" (2.3.41.0). So Wilson had presumably played Balthasar, who goes on to sing "sigh no more, ladies, sigh no more," in a revival of the play at some time between 1611 and 1623; he became free of the Grocers (as the phrase was) on October 21, 1621, ending his apprenticeship and so probably also his days of playing female roles. Richard Sharpe, bound February 21 1616, played the challenging title role in *The Duchess of Malfi* around 1621/22, and became a sharer in the company around 1624/5.[23] Thomas Holcombe (April 22, 1619) played the Provost's wife in *Sir John Van Olden Barnavelt* that same year; Robert Pallant (February 9, 1620) played Cariola, a lesser role, alongside the more experienced Sharpe in the same revival of *The Duchess of Malfi*. William Trigge, the last of Heminge's apprentices, is recorded as having played numerous female roles between 1626 and 1632.

There is no doubt that there could be genuine affection between apprentices and their masters. There is a charming letter which purports to come from the boy actor, John Pig or Pyk (see pp. 170–2), to Edward Alleyn's wife, Joan: "Mistress, your honest ancient and loving servant Pig hath this humble commendation to you and to my good Master Henslowe & mistress, and to my mistress's sister, Bess; for all her hard dealing with me, I send her hearty commendation, hoping to be beholding to her again for the opening of the cupboard: and to my neighbour, Doll, for calling me up in a morning and to my wife Sara for making clean my shoes & to that old gentleman, Monsieur Pearle, that ever fought with me for the block in the chimney corner. And though you all look for the ready return of my proper person yet I swear to you by the faith of a fustian king never to return till fortune us bring with a joyful meeting with lovely London. I cease your petty, pretty, prattling, parleying Pig. By me, John Pyk." In the left-hand margin there is a note: "Mistress, I pay you keep this that my master may see it, for I got one to write it, Master Downton [the actor] and my master knows not of it." The joke is that the letter is not in Thomas Downton's hand at all; it is in that of Alleyn (a true "fustian king") who, while on tour (with Pig doubtless in the company), wants to keep in loving touch with his wife and does so by evoking little details of their household life, as seen from Pig's perspective. It would hardly be an effective joke if Pig were not genuinely a fond presence ("petty, pretty, prattling, parleying") in their household whenever they were in "lovely London."

Strictly speaking, Pig may not have been an apprentice. There are certainly instances in the Henslowe/Alleyn papers of boys being taken on formally as household servants, for a period of three years. Alleyn, for example, bound Richard Perkins, then aged seventeen, to a three-year contract in 1596; Perkins went on to a long career in the theatre, becoming a sharer and notable leading man with the King's Men. In many respects this would be similar to an apprenticeship, but it would not result in being made free of a livery company, with all the benefits attached to it. In both arrangements the usual assumption was that the boy would receive board and lodging, probably in the master's household like Pig; as a servant he might well also receive wages. Philip Henslowe's arrangements in respect of James Bristow give us some idea of the likely economics of such arrangements. Henslowe paid the player William Augustine £8 for the boy on December 18, 1597 (*Henslowe*, 241). Clearly there was a market of sorts in talented youngsters. And those who purchased their skills, whether from the boys' parents or a third party, would expect a return on that outlay. Henslowe then effectively rented Bristow out to the Admiral's Men at a rate of three shillings per week; notionally it was a wage for him, but it is likely that everything left after board and lodging finished up in Henslowe's own pocket (*Henslowe*, 118, 164, 167). Presumably there were similar understandings in respect of apprentices. John Shank claimed in the 1630s that he had laid out £40 to retain the services of John Thomson for the King's Men and "his part of

£200 for other boys since his coming to the company" (Gurr, 2004a, 277); he did not reveal how much he, or Heminge and the others, would have made out of this investment, but this would have been one of the charges that fell to the sharers of the company to pay from their portion of the daily or weekly profits.[24]

We have evidence of even shorter-term arrangements for some boy actors. In 1577, shortly after building the Theatre, James Burbage and John Brayne entered into an agreement with John Hind, a citizen and haberdasher (Mateer, 2006). They signed an indenture whereby Hind's two sons, John Jr and Augustine, would be available twice a week to perform as boy players for the six months between October 13 and April 6, 1578. Hind would receive twelve shillings a week for this while they remained in London, seven shillings a week whenever they were on tour. These rates of pay put the boys on a par with some highly skilled artisans; they must have been star performers to be worth so much (see p. 17). The boys in turn were required to be available, on reasonable notice, to perform in plays and other entertainments; also to learn their lines for stipulated plays, and to play the cithern and sing as required.

We might have expected that the Hind brothers would have been used exclusively at the Theatre, but this is not the case. In the litigation which followed the falling-out of the parties, Burbage and Brayne claimed that the boys had been given reasonable notice to appear one Sunday in a production at the Bell Inn in Gracechurch Street, but were not available as required (Mateer, 373).[25] Burbage and Brayne were clearly not just theatrical landlords, but show promoters, possibly because the costs of setting up the Theatre had so taxed their resources. It is a testimony to the boys' skills that they were "borrowed" by Lord Howard of Effingham to contribute to the 1578 New Year festivities at his estate in Reigate in Surrey – causing an absence which further stirred the litigation (374). This short-term contract clearly ended in tears, but it indicates how important the boy players could be in the theatrical economy.

There is no record of what training exactly was given to apprentices "pur apprendre larte d'une Stageplayer" ("to learn the art of a stageplayer").[26] John Astington very reasonably suggests that "Working partners are always latent instructors" and that like most trade apprentices the boys essentially learned on the job, in conjunction with the masters who bound them and the other older players (2010, 99; see also Tribble, 2009). He argues that between 1613 and 1635 John Shank "was the principal working actor with responsibility for supervising the boys on the stages of the Globe and the Blackfriars" (ibid.). But there is evidence that those on the management side of theatre sometimes took a lead in training apprentices. In the case of John Heminge he cannot have been such a direct role-model after circa 1611, since he withdrew from acting and concentrated on the business side of the company; but that may well still have involved some training of his apprentices. The epilogue to Richard Brome's *The Court Beggar* (1640) commends to the audience the man [William Beeston, son of Shakespeare's former colleague, Christopher] "by whose care and directions this stage is governed, who has for many years both in his father's days, and since, directed poets to write and players to speak till he trained up these youths here to what they are now — ay, some of' em from before they were able to say a grace of two lines long to have more parts in their pates than would fill so many dryfats" (Brome, 2010*b*).[27] This may have been more the case in boy companies (Martin Slater undertook such a role with the King's Revels boys: see p. 145) than with the adult companies.

One consistent thread runs through the records of the boy players, and that is musical accomplishment. From the Hind brothers in the 1570s who were expected to sing and play on the cittern, through Augustine Phillips's two apprentices, one of whom received his bass viol in his will, and the other a cittern, bandore, and lute, to John Wilson among Heminge's apprentices, they all either were or trained to be proficient musicians. The first quarto text of *Hamlet* tells us that the boy who played "Ofelia" entered *"playing on a lute, and her hair down singing"* when she went mad (Q1, G4v). John Wilson went on to be a notable musician and composer, employed extensively by the King's Men; settings by him survive for songs in Thomas Middleton's *The Witch*; Richard Brome's *The Northern Lass*; John Fletcher's *The Beggar's Bush*, *The Bloody Brother*, *The False One*, *Love's Cure*, *The Loyal Subject*, *The Mad Lover*, *The Pilgrim*, *The Queen of Corinth*, *Valentinian*, *The Wild Goose Chase*, and *Women Pleased*; and John Ford's *The Lovers' Melancholy*.

The one question we can probably never really answer is what people made at the time of the boys' playing of female roles (see Barker, 2009). How convincing was it or did they attempt to make it? And what does it say about early modern ideas of sexuality? There were certainly those at the time who saw the practice as deeply unnatural. The most famous exponent of this view was the Oxford Puritan theologian, Dr John Rainolds, whose *Th'Overthrow of Stage-Plays* (1599) pursues in detail the Biblical objections: "And so if any man do put on woman's raiment, he is dishonest and defiled, because he trangresseth the bounds of modesty and comeliness, and weareth that which God forbiddeth him to wear, which man's laws affirmeth he cannot wear without reproof ... plays are charged, not for making young men come forth in whores' attire, like the lewd woman in *Proverbs*, but for teaching them to counterfeit her actions, her wantonness, her impudent face, her wicked speech and enticements" (16–17). Freudians may wonder what to make of the fact that the young Rainolds had himself played Hippolyta in Richard Edwarde's *Palamon and Arcyte* during Queen Elizabeth's visit to Oxford 1566, described at the beginning of this book (see p. 4).

An Oxford scholar also left us one of the most affecting accounts of a boy's acting, having seen the King's Men perform *Othello* there in 1610: "But that Desdemona, murdered by her husband in our presence, although she always pled her case excellently, yet when killed moved us more, while stretched out on her bed she begged the spectators' pity with her very facial expression."[28] This was very probably John Rice, who earlier that summer had appeared with Richard Burbage in a water pageant to mark Prince Henry's formal creation as Prince of Wales. Described by an observer as "two absolute actors even the very best our instant time can yield," Burbage played "Amphion, the father of harmony or music," and Rice "a very fair and beautiful nymph, representing the genius of old Corineus's Queen of the province Cornwall, suited in her watery habit yet rich and costly with a coronet of pearl and cockle-shells on her head."[29]

Rice then left the company for a number of years and was replaced as the leading boy actor by Richard Robinson, who years later would marry Burbage's widow. Jonson includes a (possibly apocryphal) anecdote about "Dick" Robinson in *The Devil is An Ass* – a play in which Robinson himself appeared – telling how he was brought to a "gossip's feast ... Dressed like a lawyer's wife." One character says "They say he's an ingenious youth" and another replies "Oh, sir! And dresses himself the best! Beyond / Forty o'your very ladies" (2.8.69–70; 75–7; Jonson 2012d). If there is any truth in this, his cross-dressing was not restricted to the stage. But on it he probably created the role of the Duchess of Malfi and earned this praise (along with Webster) from Thomas Middleton:

> Thy epitaph only the title be –
> Write "Duchess," that will fetch a tear for thee,
> For who e'er saw this duchess live, and die,
> That could get off under a bleeding eye?
> *(Webster, 2009, 78)*

Michael Shapiro has drawn attention to two passages in Lady Mary Wroth's *The Countess of Montgomery's Urania* (part-published 1621) which draw on the cross-dressing of boy actors for metaphoric effect (1989, 187–93). In one overwrought scene a queen has taken a lover and persuaded him to kill her husband; she then falls in love with a stranger who comes to pay his respects to the dead king. Her lover secretly sees the new wooing: "there he [the first lover] saw her with all passionate ardency seek and sue for the stranger's love; yet he [the stranger], unmovable, was no further wrought than if he had seen a delicate play-boy act a loving woman's part and, knowing him a boy, liked only his actions." The second passage, written in the narrator's voice, is a kind of character-study of a vain, insincere and deceitful lady, "being for her over-acting fashion more like a play-boy dressed gaudily up to show a fond loving woman's part than a great lady; so busy, so full of talk, and in such a set formality, with so many framed looks, feigned smiles and nods, with a deceitful down-cast look, instead of purest modesty and bashfulness; too rich jewels for her rotten cabinet to contain ..." . In both passages the underlying implication is that an observer can perceive a distance between the actor and his role, and admire his technical skill without being seduced by the credibility of the impersonation. The boy-actor remained a boy, for all his skill in appearing womanly.

Of course, the puritans who fulminated against cross-dressing did not see it that way and the repertory of, in particular, the Children of the King's Revels does seem to have gone out of its way to exploit their sexual ambiguity (Bly, 2000). Does it make a difference here that Lady Mary was a woman? Would a man have seen things differently? It is probably an irresolvable debate. We have lost the convention and, despite frequent all-male performances of Shakespeare these days, cannot resurrect it in this very different culture.

Conclusions

This exhausts the categories of persons known to have been employed by the sharers of the acting companies. The ten or so sharers themselves were always the dominant presences, both artistically and commercially. They commissioned, assessed and purchased all plays; they authorized all payments and hiring of personnel. Philip Henslowe and Sir Henry Herbert are usually careful to accord the sharers they deal with the honorific "Mr." But they were assisted by a substantial body of "hired men" or associates, perhaps sixteen or so in the years before 1608 (excluding women and boys). They included a few strong actors in line to become sharers, and a few others with very clearly designated roles, such as the book-keeper, the stage-keeper, and the tiremen; but many were multi-talented, able to act a little, or play an instrument, or perform some tailoring (assisting the designated tireman), or serve as a gatherer. There would also have been perhaps four or five apprentices or contracted servants, primarily to act the female roles and to add musical variety, but also possibly to serve as the call-boys which the book-keeper required when they were not otherwise involved in a production. And there would have been a smaller number of women, notably acting as gatherers but also assisting with dressing the boys, especially with specialist items like head-tires. The regular personnel at the Theatre and the Globe must have added up to over thirty persons, all with roles to play in getting a performance on stage and the paying customers accommodated.

Notes

1 See p. 277 on the taking of the Chamberlain's, Admiral's, and Worcester's Men, and the Children of the Queen's Chapel, into royal patronage in 1603/4.
2 The document used to be in the Henslowe papers at Dulwich College, where it was transcribed. But the original has been lost. I take it here from *EPF*, 282–3, with these differences: to make it more readable I have usually condensed the

names of Henslowe and Meade to initials and omitted phrases like "the said Robert Dawes" when "he" is clear enough. The "[to*]" in the transcript reads "[by]", but the sense is clearly that the apparel has been furnished *to* the company *by* Henslowe and Meade. I have omitted the ending of the document, which mainly relates to Dawes conceding the rights of Henslowe and Meade to one playing day in four at the Hope for bear-baiting, the profits from which were to be entirely their own. This would inevitably reduce the players' profits.

3 *EPF*, 657–6; see Haaker, 1968. Eleanor Collins has questioned the typicality of Brome's contracts, suggesting that such arrangements were a product of specific circumstances rather than normal, long-term practices. She does not speculate about Shakespeare, but notes of Fletcher that his "dramatic production does not resemble *exclusive* contractual behavior until after Shakespeare's death, after which he may have taken a share in the company that would effectively ensure his loyalty" (2007, 121). It is an intriguing idea, but there is no evidence for it.

4 An example of an ephemeral epilogue is one which Juliet Dusinberre argues may have been written for a Shrovetide court performance of *As You Like It*, replacing Rosalind's more familiar one in the printed text of the play (Dusinberre, 2003, 371–405; and Shakespeare, 2006, Appendix 1, 349–54). Her claims for Shakespeare's authorship and its relationship to *As You Like It* have not been universally accepted (Hattaway, 2009; Hackett, 2012).

5 Official Elizabethan documents have a range of terms for what we would lump together as plays, presumably to limit wriggle-room. The Royal Patent granted to Leicester's Men in 1574 specifically allowed them to perform "comedies, tragedies, interludes, and stage plays." By the same token, performers were variously comedians, tragedians, stage or common players, or players of interludes, but only rarely actors.

6 Of course, the sun in England did not always cooperate. John Webster, in his epistle to the 1612 text of *The White Devil*, performed by Queen Anne's Men at the Red Bull, complained that "it was acted in so dull a time of winter, presented in so open and black a theatre, that it wanted … a full and understanding auditory."

7 It is not clear if this number includes the gatherers, those who took the entrance money, or is restricted to those specifically involved in performances. It muddies the waters somewhat that we know gatherers did occasionally take minor roles.

8 Bentley, 1984, 107. Note that this contract binds Kendall to *the theatre*, rather than to *the company*, at a time when Henslowe was acquiring more managerial control of the company, doubtless aided by Alleyn. They may have been hedging bets against the Admiral's Men looking to find a different base. There were probably no parallels with the Chamberlain's Men.

9 This section is particularly indebted to Natasha Korda, 2009: 456–73 and to Gurr 2004*b*.

10 This was evidently not the Robert Browne (d. 1603) who had been married to Susan Baskerville. Herbert Berry explains: "There were obviously at least two and could easily have been three or more Robert Brownes who had to do with the companies and playhouses of the time" (1986, 197).

11 The Yeoman's oversight of costumes evidently opened up opportunities to make a profit. In 1572 there was a complaint from Thomas Giles, a haberdasher, against the Yeoman of the Revels, John Arnold. He accused him of hiring out costumes from the office (presumably for his private profit) and was quite specific about the competition this represented to his own rental business. On Valentine's Day Arnold hired out gowns for an event in Fleet Street; the week before Shrove Sunday he hired out others for a wedding masque in Kent; and on Shrove Tuesday he hired out yet more for an event at Charterhouse Yard (Feuillerat, 1908, 409–10; see also Streitberger, 2016, 108). Will Fisher wonders whether Arnold's successor, Edward Kirkham, was engaged in a similar business when he became part of the management team for the Children of the Queen's Revels, early in James's reign (2006, 84). When William Hunt fell ill in 1635, Yeoman since 1611, Sir Henry Herbert asked the King not to fill his place without consulting him (*Herbert*, 198). In fact Hunt lived four more years, but his eventual successor proved to be Joseph Taylor (patent November 11,1639), one of the leading players with the King's Men (Bentley, 1941–68, 2: 590–8). Taylor may have been handling costumes for some time. On January 6, 1634 Herbert recorded: "Fletcher's pastoral called *The Faithful Shepherdess* [was presented at Denmark House] in the clothes the Queen had given Taylor the year before of her own pastoral [i.e. Montagu's *Shepherd's Paradise*]" (*Herbert*, 186). The Queen's gift was for Taylor's rehearsing of herself and her ladies in their pastoral, so it was specifically to him rather than to the King's Men. Presumably Taylor then sold or loaned the costumes to the company. There was clearly profit to be made from costumes that might derive one way or another from the court. Taylor's later service as Yeoman of the Revels may in effect have institutionalized it.

12 These inventories were originally with Henslowe's *Diary*, but have since been lost. They were, however, transcribed by Edmund Malone (1790, I: pt.2: 300–7). R. A. Foakes dates them to "between 8 and 13 March 1598", noting that "a statement of debt was acknowledged by the sharers" of the Lord Admiral's Men to Henslowe at that time" (*Henslowe*, 316; my transcription is from pp. 317–23).

13 *Henslowe*, 318. The cithern or cittern was a guitar-like instrument, though strung with wire and played with a plectrum; the bandalore was guitar- or lute-like, and played as bass to the cithern.

14 Phillips's apprentice, Samuel Gilburne, appears in the First Folio list of those who performed in Shakespeare's plays, but there is no record of him as an adult player.

15 This can only partly explain Herbert's peremptory behavior over *The Tamer Tamed*, which (its heroine, Maria, gains complete control over her husband) was probably suspected of having acquired a particular relevance in respect of Queen Henrietta Maria, her influence over the king, and her Catholicism (Dutton, 2000, 41–61).

16 The Act of Abuses applied only to performance, not to printed texts. So as late as 1622 *Othello* was printed in quarto with its oaths as originally written, circa 1602–3. The version in the 1623 Folio had been revised, presumably for a later performance. The 1607 quarto of Jonson's *Volpone* similarly contains oaths, but efforts have been made in the 1616 folio to bring it into line.

17 "The quality" was a common term for the profession or brotherhood of players (*OED* n. 6a; see pp. 180, 263).

18 This section is particularly indebted to the pioneering work of David Kathman, especially in 2004*b*, 2005 and 2009*d*.

19 It is not within my remit to say much about the all-boy companies of the era, since Shakespeare never wrote for them. But they operated on a very different basis from the adult companies. Most had their origins in choir schools attached to the court (the Children of the Chapel Royal), cathedrals like St Paul's, and various regular schools, like Westminster and Merchant Taylors. Drama was part of their curriculum, helping to enhance their students' skills in rhetoric and public speaking; singing was part of choral duties. A tradition grew up of presenting plays as gift-offerings to Queen Elizabeth at Christmas and for the first half of her reign they were her favorite performers. By the 1580s if not earlier they had become commercial operations, their "rehearsals" being in fact public performances. All boy companies went out of business during the 1590s, but Paul's Boys and the Children of the Chapel Royal were revived in 1599/1600 and created real competition for the adult companies, their indoor ("private") theatres and sophisticated repertoires designed to appeal to the wealthy, educated and politically savvy classes. In 1601 one Henry Clifton complained to the court of Star Chamber about the impressment of his son, Thomas, by the management of the Children of the Chapel Royal, arguing that it was for the purposes of commercial playing and not – as the impressment powers of the chapels was intended – to maintain the quality of the choir. He was vindicated and thereafter impressment for the boy companies ceased (*ES*, 2: 43–5). Paul's Boys survived until 1606; the Children of the Royal Chapel, later Children of the Queen's Revels or simply the Blackfriars Boys, survived until 1608. Indeed they notionally reformed as the Queen's Revels in 1610. But by then few if any of them were truly children.

20 In the boy companies they sometimes started as early as ten.

21 Baldwin, 1927, p. 227; see also Jonson, 2012*n*, 220.

22 This assumes he is the "R. Birch" assigned these roles in early handwritten notes in a copy of Jonson's 1616 *Works* (Riddell, 1969).

23 He was one who signed an abject apology to Sir Henry Herbert in December 1624 for having performed in an unauthorized play, *The Spanish Viceroy* (*Herbert*, 183): see p. 90.
24 For evidence of apprentices playing with provincial troupes, see the case of Thomas Pant, p. 59.
25 It was not until 1579 that the Privy Council issued an order to prevent Sunday playing in London and Middlesex (i.e. the site of the Theatre and the Curtain).
26 The phrase in legal Norman French was used in William Trigge's petition to be released from his indenture after Heminge's death (Kathman, 2009*d*, 423–4).
27 The "youths" would be members of the King's and Queen's Young Company, also known as Beeston's Boys, a late recreation of a boy company (Gurr, 1996, 423–4).
28 The Latin original was first printed by Geoffrey Tillotson (1933, 494). The translation is by Dana F. Sutton (2006).
29 Cited from *The Athenaeum*. May 19, 1888: 641.

5

A Stormy Passage, from the Theatre, via the Curtain, to the Globe

When the Chamberlain's Men first took up residence in the Theatre in 1594 their future must have looked as settled as that of any company of players could in the era. They had exclusive use of one of the few playhouses about the city, which was owned by the father of one of their leading players. They were one of only two companies invited to court for the Christmas Revels for each of the next five years. In Will Kemp they had the leading comedian of the day, a box-office draw to rival Edward Alleyn, now with the Admiral's Men at the Rose. In William Shakespeare they had one of the few *proven* playwrights of the day. The death or retirement from the stage of Christopher Marlowe, Thomas Kyd, Robert Greene, John Lyly, and George Peele had left a notable gap in the market, while the fact that Shakespeare seems to have been able to bring much of his earlier work with him gave the company a real opportunity to build a viable repertory.

The only real shadow on the horizon was that the lease of the land on which the Theatre stood would expire in April 1597 and the landlord, Giles Allen, had so far avoided granting the ten-year extension for which the original contract allowed. Possibly against the risk that he would never do so – but equally possibly as a speculative venture of his own – James Burbage came up with a new plan. On February 4, 1596 he purchased parts of the extensive Blackfriars precinct that was owned by Sir William More and set about building a new playhouse there. This was not in the same part of the complex as the earlier Blackfriars theatre, built by Richard Farrant for the Children of the Chapel. What Burbage purchased was "the Seven Great Upper Rooms, the rooms on the floor below, and the rooms to the west in the Duchy Chamber" (Smith, 155). As Irwin Smith has demonstrated, the "Seven Great Upper Rooms" included what had been used as the Parliament Chamber in the time of Henry VIII, a commodious structure, within which Burbage was to build a splendid new indoor playhouse, perhaps for the use of the Chamberlain's Men (164–74).

This is not the place to discuss the playhouse he built, something I defer until the point in the narrative when the King's Men (as by then the company had

Shakespeare's Theatre: A History, First Edition. Richard Dutton.
© 2018 Richard Dutton. Published 2018 by John Wiley & Sons Ltd.

become) were actually able to use it – as they were not in 1596/7 (see p. 290). But something needs to be said about the business plan behind this development, and why it failed. The short answer for its failure is that some influential neighbors of the theatre objected to it in November 1596 on a string of very familiar grounds, including claims that this:

> common playhouse ... will grow to be a very great annoyance and trouble, not only to all the noblemen and gentlemen thereabout inhabiting, but also a general inconvenience to all the inhabitants of the same precinct, both by reason of the great resort and gathering together of all manner of vagrant and lewd persons that ... will come thither and work all manner of mischief, and also to the great pestering and filling up of the same precinct, if it should please God to send any visitation of sickness ... for that the same precinct is already grown very populous; and besides that the same playhouse is so near the church that the noise of the drums and trumpets will greatly disturb and hinder both the ministers and parishioners in time of divine service and sermons. (480)

And the Privy Council apparently agreed with them, though there is no record of their actual response. Embarrassingly, one of the signatories to the complaint was the company's own patron, a role now taken by the second Lord Hunsdon, his father having died on July 23, 1596 (see p. 130). Timing here was almost certainly everything, since they temporarily lacked a powerful patron in the highest quarters. The only upside to the whole affair is that it may have played its part in creating the character we know as Falstaff, who took shape around 1596/7 (see p. 102).

(Continued on p. 197).

Box 5.1 The Falstaff Issue and Use of the Blackfriars

It is widely known that Shakespeare originally called the character we know as Falstaff, Oldcastle. This identifed him with the historical Sir John Oldcastle, who was burned at the stake for the heresy of his Lollard (proto-Protestant) views in the reign of Henry V. Although Shakespeare later disavowed that identification (see p. 7), the name was clearly Oldcastle in the version of *1 Henry IV* first staged. It was changed before the play got into print, but unmistakable vestiges of the identity remain, as when Prince Hal addresses him as "my old lad of the castle" (1.2.41). It is also now well established that the change was made because of objections raised by the Brooke family, who held the family title of Lord Cobham; Oldcastle had held that title in the right of his wife, and Shakespeare's depiction of Oldcastle as a drunken, debauched coward (he had in fact been a distinguished soldier) was presumably taken as a slur on the family (Gary Taylor, 1985; 1987).

The question is why Shakespeare should have caricatured Oldcastle in this way, especially since William Brooke, the tenth Lord Cobham, was Lord Chamberlain around the time *I Henry IV* was very probably written. He held the post from August 8, 1596 until his own death on March 6, 1597. Samuel Schoenbaum offers one common explanation, treating the whole affair very laconically: "It has been suggested that Shakespeare's choice of a name was deliberately provocative, an act of retaliation against a dynasty hostile to the stage; but there is no evidence of the Cobhams' puritanical leanings, and more likely the dramatist took the name, without a second thought, from his source play, *The Famous Victories of Henry the Fifth*. A second thought would have been advisable" (1987, 194).

Schoenbaum is right that neither William Brooke not his son, Henry, the eleventh Lord Cobham, who was also drawn into the business, has been shown to have any puritanical hostility to the stage. But the idea that it was a casual oversight – and one that no one else in the company, or indeed the Master of the Revels, picked up on – is equally implausible. I suggest another possibility, which I have not seen advanced before. It was in November 1596, while the elder Cobham was Lord Chamberlain (and a Privy Councillor), that neighbors of James Burbage's Blackfriars theatre petitioned the Lords of the Privy Council to prevent its being used as a "common playhouse." Most of the attention focused on this petition has been directed to the fact that it bears the signature of the younger Lord Hunsdon, by now patron of Shakespeare's company.

I suggest, however, that attention ought first to be focused on the name which is *not* on the petition: that of William, Lord Cobham, himself though the document makes very plain that it could have been.

> Humbly showing and beseeching your honours, the inhabitants of the precinct of the Blackfriars, London, that whereas one Burbage hath lately bought certain rooms in the same precinct *near adjoining unto the dwelling houses of the right honourable the Lord Chamberlain* and the Lord of Hunsdon, which rooms the said Burbage is now altering and meaneth very shortly to convert and turn the same into a common playhouse, which will grow to be a very great annoyance and trouble. (*ES* 4: 319–20; my emphasis)

Cobham's signature was not on the letter purely because it was addressed to himself as one of the Lords of the Council (which Hunsdon would not become until he succeeded Cobham as Lord Chamberlain). Cobham was a long-time tenant of Sir William More, the owner of the Blackfriars complex, occupying the south end of the upper floor of the Old Buttery as well as the Porter's Lodge (Smith, 158). The Old Buttery actually adjoined the Parliament Chamber which Burbage was converting into the playhouse.[1]

Cobham had been incommoded by Richard Farrant's *first* Blackfriars playhouse, so there can have been little doubt about his views on a second one (Smith, 149). And it seems that his fellow Lords of the Council had little difficulty sympathizing with him and granting the petition – thus blocking Shakespeare and his company from using the new Blackfriars theatre, if that is what they planned. This squares perfectly with Thomas Nashe's comments after the first Lord Hunsdon's death, quoted earlier: "in their old lord's time they thought their state settled, it is now so uncertain they cannot build upon it" (see p. 129). The reference is surely not to all players, but specifically to the Lord Chamberlain's Men. "Their old lord" Hunsdon had interceded with the Lord Mayor to get them permission to perform at the Cross Keys in over the winter of 1594/5; himself a former tenant of Blackfriars and wishing to become one again, he had corresponded with Sir William More, in a way that suggests that he knew of and was probably supportive of the planned theatre: "understanding that you have already parted with part of your home to some that means to make a playhouse in it" (Smith, 162).

His death was a catastrophe for Shakespeare's company. With their lease on the Theatre expiring, it blocked the possibility of a move to the Blackfriars.[2] Patronage in the highest places was required for success in the London theatrical world, and just when they needed it they didn't have it. The second Lord Hunsdon would acquire the same status as his father when he in turn became Lord Chamberlain, but in the meantime his influence was limited. He would not have had influence with the Lord Mayor to ensure them winter playing in a City inn. He may well have felt that he had no option but to support Cobham and his other neighbors when the petition was drawn up; indeed, without the influence to do anything, he may have felt free to voice his actual reservations about having a "common playhouse" in his own backyard.

It is hardly surprising that Shakespeare and his fellows should look for a way to get back at Cobham. Whether they did so while he was still in office, or after his death, is unclear, but there *is* evidence that no love was lost between the younger Lords Hunsdon and Cobham (White, 2002). The latter, Henry Brooke, eleventh Lord Cobham, may have been the one who required Oldcastle's name to be changed. He was certainly the one who became identified with Falstaff. In February 1598 the Earl of Essex wrote to Sir Robert Cecil, jestingly asking him to tell their friend Sir Alex Ratcliff that "his sister is married to Sr. Jo. Falstaff" – rumor was linking Margaret Ratcliff with Brooke (Hotson, 1950, 148). And the Oldcastle association with Falstaff lingered for many years after (Dutton, 2016, 245–58). In part this may have been because Shakespeare's company kept it alive. When *Merry Wives* was first printed, in 1602, the jealous Ford adopts the Cobham family name of Brook ("tell him my name is Brook – only for a jest": 2.1.1.200–1) and this prompts Falstaff to a pun: "Such Brooks are welcome to me, that o'erflows such liquor" (2.2.143–5). In the folio text of 1623 the name has been changed to

"Broome," making nonsense of the pun, and so paradoxically calling attention to it, but proving that the original had been found as offensive as the use of Oldcastle. Lord Cobham's disgrace and imprisonment for involvement in the Main Plot against King James in 1603 can only have perpetuated the Cobham/Falstaff identification, not least since it led to Cobham's being stripped of the Order of the Garter ("degraded"), as happened to Shakespeare's original Falstaff in *1 Henry VI*.

We might see all this as a darker side of the links between patronage and playing that we considered earlier (see p. 124). The Admiral's Men, the Chamberlain's Men's chief rivals, chose to capitalize on the scandal by staging their own two plays on *Sir John Oldcastle*, offering a much more respectful account of the Lollard martyr; this was, in part, how their repertories were formed, playing off each other's successes (Knutson, 1991). But of course, however innocently, it helped to perpetuate the scandal. The Admiral's Men may have demonstrated a more graceful allegiance to their own patron, Lord Howard of Effingham, who was created Earl of Nottingham, when they hired Anthony Munday to write two plays about Robin Hood, the legendary outlaw strongly associated with Nottingham (*The Downfall* and *The Death of Robert, Earl of Huntington*, both 1598). As ever, the functioning of the players and the conditions of their writers' creativity, were highly defined by the Elizabethan world of patronage politics.

The mode of all this changed somewhat under James I, when all the companies were under royal patronage. But many of Shakespeare's Jacobean plays seem tuned to matters associated with the royal family, whether or not (as with *King Lear*) they have been suspected of glancing directly at court politics (see p. 126). The issue has been well treated from different angles by David Bergeron (1985) and Alvin Kernan (1995). *Cymbeline*, for example, with its partially Welsh setting, has been plausibly associated with the formal creation of Prince Henry as Prince of Wales in 1610, while Prince Henry's own players seem to have presented *The Valiant Welshman* (by "R.A.") in the same context (Cull, 2014). Such plays may well have been read as supporting one courtly faction or another, but they doubtless also played on the audience's fascination with the privileged and closed world of the court, into which the actors offered teasingly oblique access.[3]

(Continued from p. 194).

The petitioners almost certainly did identify Burbage's intentions, doubtless formulated on the back of his extensive knowledge of the players' preferences: "all the players being banished by the Lord Mayor from playing within the City by reason of the great inconveniences and ill rule that followeth them, they now think to plant themselves in liberties" (Smith, 480). Liberties like the Blackfriars (and the Clink) were anomalous pockets of territory, mostly within the City walls but outside the control of the City of London authorities. In most cases their status derived from their former privileges as church property. The Blackfriars had been a Dominican priory until the dissolution of the monasteries under Henry VIII. Liberties thus had all the advantages of suburbs like Shoreditch, where the Theatre and Curtain stood, in being free of the Lord Mayor's oversight; but they were as close to the population, and indeed to the quarters of some of the wealthiest citizenry, as the City inns – which, moreover, the Lord Mayor was doing his best finally to close down, something the petitioners noted. There would, therefore be little or no direct competition to the Blackfriars.

This is not to say, however, that the liberties were lawless.[4] As Irwin Smith puts it: "In the course of time, as civil administration succeeded ecclesiastical, the inhabitants appointed their own justices to try petty offenders, their own porters and scavengers, and their own officers ... to serve as civil magistrates" (1964, 114). Blackfriars did retain the ancient church privilege of sanctuary, protecting people from arrest for lesser crimes, including debt, which made it a haven for petty criminals. Yet despite this it was on the whole a prosperous, respectable neighborhood, one where aristocrats, courtiers, and successful businessmen chose to live. It was an ideal location for an upmarket theatre. Or would have been, but for the Privy Council.

This faced Lord Hunsdon's Men (as they briefly were) with a real crisis. They could not use the Blackfriars; the Theatre lease was about to run out. They found a lifeline in the Curtain. Quite early in the life of the Theatre (1585) James Burbage had negotiated an agreement with the proprietor of the Curtain, Henry Lanman, to share the profits on their two properties on an equal basis (p. 99). They were only two hundred yards apart and serious rivalry between them could have been bad business for both. This agreement, though it ran out in 1592, probably established easy relations between the parties; if so, it paid off significantly at this critical time, because the Chamberlain's Men now secured for themselves a long-term lease at the Curtain.

Until very recently, with the exception of Newington Butts, we knew less about the Curtain than we do about any other Elizabethan playhouse, despite the fact that it was there virtually from the beginning and outlasted all the others. What has changed is that in 2011 parts of the foundations of the playhouse were unearthed by archaeologists, revealing most unexpectedly in 2016 that the external structure of the Curtain was rectangular, taking advantage of neighboring structures.[5] And the galleries on its internal walls were straight, not curving around polygonal shapes such as those of the Theatre or the Globe. In both these respects it seems to have mirrored the kinds of inns that the players encountered on the road and in London, though it was probably larger (see pp. 39; 115ff). Unfortunately the archaeology has not been able to tell us anything about the size or disposition of the stage or its relationship to the tiring house. One unusual artefact to emerge is a small pottery "bird whistle" which, when filled with water, could be used to create bird noises, possibly echoing frequent references to such sounds in plays like *Romeo and Juliet*. For example:

> her eyes in heaven
> Would through the airy region stream so bright
> That birds would sing and think it were not night.
> (2.2. 20–2)

Or again:

> *Juliet.* It was the nightingale, and not the lark,
> That pierced the fearful hollow of thine ear;
> Nightly she sings on yon pomegranate tree.
> Believe me, love, it was the nightingale.
> *Romeo.* It was the lark, the herald of the morn,
> No nightingale.
> (3.5. 2–7)[6]

The Curtain seems hitherto normally to have catered for companies looking for a temporary London venue as part of their traveling circuit.[7] Unlike the Rose and the Theatre it was never a base for players more-or-less permanently resident in London – until this crisis for the Chamberlain's Men. The London-resident players, by and large, are those whose plays have survived, giving us some clues as to the particular qualities of their home bases. So we have very little such evidence regarding the Curtain. Of course we must assume that the plays from the Chamberlain's Men's existing Theatre repertory could be played there without too much adaptation, or this new arrangement would hardly have been viable. The company's stay at the Curtain lasted from around October 1597 to late 1599. But only one play survives which we can be categorically certain was written with the specific expectation of being played at the Curtain. This is Ben Jonson's first play for the Chamberlain's Men, *Every Man In His Humour*, the 1616 folio text of which assures us that it was first performed there in 1598. In fact we can date its first performance even more precisely, since there is a record of a German ("Almain") dignitary who "lost 300 crowns at a new play called *Every Man's humour*" on September 20, 1598 (*Calendar of State Papers, Domestic, 1598–1601*, 97). The critics were not wrong when they said that theatres attracted pickpockets; they also attracted foreign nobility who carried irresponsible amounts of money with them.

Every Man In as then staged was as it appeared in the 1601 quarto text, with a setting in Florence, Italy, rather than in the London of the folio version, which is quite radically different. In fact the quarto text provides us with no surprises. Entrances and exits can all be effected with two stage doors; there are no calls for use of an upper stage or a trapdoor; there is no use of pyrotechnics or other spectacular stage effects; all of the props required would have been quite standard – a tankard, a letter, tobacco, swords, papers, a book – with the exception of a red herring (a pun on the name of the character, Cob) and a striking clock (doubtless the one that Brutus anachronistically heard in *Julius Caesar* the following year, by when they had moved it to the Globe: see p. 268).

The only stage direction which is at all out of the ordinary occurs in 1.3, following line 62, where Cob is marked to exit and then "Bobadilla discovers himself on a bench." This is odd for a couple of reasons.[8] Cob's exit momentarily leaves the stage empty – unless Bobadilla has been on stage, silent and unobserved, throughout the scene. But there is no indication of that in the text. An empty stage usually marks the beginning of a new scene in successive staging and that is how this sequence is presented in the folio version of the play. But Jonson goes for something slightly different in the quarto version. "Bobadilla discovers himself" almost certainly means that he draws back a curtain to reveal himself; if so the reference might be to a so-called discovery space, which is generally agreed existed in the rear wall of the stage in at least *some* theatres (see pp. 96, 249). It could be used as a third entrance, or a place from which substantial properties (like beds) could swiftly be conveyed out on to the main stage. Or it could be somewhere that characters could be "discovered," often seated or in bed, by the drawing back of the curtain, cloth or arras which covered the mouth of the space.

But in general there is much fuller evidence for the use of discovery spaces from the era of the Globe onwards than from earlier. It is clear, however, that from early times a curtain, often described as an arras, hung on the rear wall of the stage and afforded sufficient space for people to stand behind it – possibly even without the need for a recess within the wall itself or for an opening from the tiring house, such as a true discovery space requires. So in *King John* (circa 1594) Hubert orders the executioners "look thou stand / Within the arras" (4.1.1–2), and in the first quarto of *Hamlet* (1603) Corambis famously undertakes to "shroud myself behind the arras," where he will be stabbed by Hamlet.[9] Robert Greene's old Queen's Men's play, published in 1594, contains this overloaded stage direction: *Enter Friar Bacon drawing the curtains with a white stick, a book in his hand, and a lamp lighted by him, and the brazen head and Miles, with weapons by him* (Sc.xi.0). Does this mean that Bacon emerges from behind the "curtains" in such a way as to reveal the "brazen head," or does he simply "discover" the head? Either way there is no requirement for any depth of recess behind the curtains, which need to conceal from view – at most – one person, the head and a lamp, which could easily be on a small table. *Dr Faustus*, an equally early play, does seem to call for a discovery space, but this might derive from later staging practices than those for which Marlowe wrote (see p. 137 Note 12). No text that indisputably reflects pre-1594 staging requires a discovery space.

To return to *Every Man In His Humour*: it is quite conceivable that Bobadilla might discover himself on a bench at the Curtain, simply by drawing back the arras. If so – if, that is, there was no actual space in the tiring house wall, and so no conventional way to enter but by the stage doors – it means that the actor playing Bobadilla had sat there through two and a half scenes. That seems unlikely on the face of it. But it might actually be the point of this quite unusual staging. It gives Bobadilla – the loud star-turn of the play, a trumpeting *miles gloriosus* or braggart soldier – a sudden, unexpected and dramatic "entrance," bellowing "Hostess! Hostess!" (63). But all in all, this one striking instance does not establish that the Curtain had a true discovery space, as distinct simply from a hanging arras.

There *might*, however, be more evidence for a Curtain discovery space if we accept Tiffany Stern's contention that the *second* quarto version of *Romeo and Juliet* was staged there (2009c, 81ff). We have presumed that the first quarto version, (Q1) published in 1597, relates to the Theatre (see p. 96); but the substantially different second quarto, (Q2) published in 1599, might logically be a Curtain piece. There is some confirmation of this in John Marston's *Scourge of Villainy*, where Luscus – who is obsessed by theatre – is said to steal all his conversation from *Romeo and Juliet* in performances at the Curtain.

> *Luscus*: what's play'd to day? faith now I know.
> I set thy lips abroach [i.e. set them flowing], from whence doth flow
> Naught but pure *Iuliat* and *Romio*.
> Say, who acts best? *Drusus*, or *Roscio*?
> Now I have him, that ne'er of ought did speak
> But when of plays or players he did treat.
> H'ath made a common-place book out of plays,
> And speaks in print; at least whate'er he says
> Is warranted by Curtain *plaudeties* [applause].
> (Scourge of Villainy, *1598, H4*)

It is commonly assumed that significant parts of the last act of *Romeo and Juliet* might take place inside the discovery space, or around its entrance, leaving the bodies of Paris, Romeo, and Juliet within. And the Q2 text seems to sanction that when the Prince orders that they should "Seal up the mouth of outrage for a while" (5.3.216), while he establishes what has happened. This *seems* to be a direction to draw the curtain over the discovery space as a convenient way of removing the bodies from the stage, and is often quoted as such. But in Q1 the Prince says "Come, seal your mouths of outrage for a while" (K3), cutting off Old Montague, who has begun to lament the death of Romeo, in favor of finding out what has happened. The phrasing "your mouths" can hardly refer to an open discovery space. Indeed, the Q1 reading might also alert us to ambiguity in Q2: "Seal up the mouth of outrage" need not refer to a discovery space at all, but might similarly speak to ending expressions of distress. In short, the evidence for a discovery space at the Curtain is inconclusive at best. Discovery spaces may have been more a feature of the next generation of playhouses, which began with the Swan in 1596 (though the De Witt / van Buchell drawing shows nothing resembling one: see Frontispiece).

One feature of the Curtain which Tiffany Stern draws attention to is its close association with prize fencing matches, though the Theatre also had such associations. Students of fencing needed to demonstrate their art in public contests in order to progress in rank; these contests were very popular and the playhouses obviously made ideal arenas. Jonson seems to allude to this side of the Curtain's trade when he makes Bobadilla a loud-mouthed "expert" in swordsmanship. He tells tall tales of how "with this instrument … my poor rapier, [I] ran violently upon the Moors that guarded the ordnance and put them pell-mell to the sword" (2.3.111–13) or "[u]pon my first coming to the city they assaulted me, some three, four, five, six of them together … at my lodging, and at my ordinary, where I have driven them afore me the whole length of a street in open view of all our gallants, pitying to hurt them, believe me" (4.2.31–5). He proceeds to brag about his ability to train others to be almost as good as himself, running off fashionable Italian terms for the various thrusts: "And I would teach these nineteen the special tricks – as your *punto*, your *reverso*, your *staccato*, your *imbroccato*, your *passado*, your *montanto* – till they could all play very near or altogether as well as myself" (55–8). This expands into a fantasy of annihilating an army of forty-thousand strong by challenging them all to "single" combat, twenty at a time. The comedy shades into something more serious when Cob speaks of Bobadilla as "that fencing Burgullian" (Q, 3.5.12–13), an allusion to John Barrose, a Burgundian swordsman who had challenged all comers earlier that year and was hanged on July 10 for murdering a City official who tried to arrest him. And the subject turned deadly serious for Jonson himself only two days after the German nobleman lost his money. On September 22, 1598 he went out into Hoxton Fields, north of the City, and slew Gabriel Spenser in a duel (see p. 39).

One other play has a reasonable claim to have been staged by the Chamberlain's Men at the Curtain, and that is *Henry V*. But the claim is a contentious one and it is unwise to hang too much on it. A *version* of the play was almost certainly staged in 1599, but the issues are *which* version and *exactly when*. If it was the version published in quarto in 1600 – without the prologue and choruses, without "Once more unto the breach, dear friends, once more" and (historically correct) without the Dauphin fighting at the Battle of Agincourt – then indeed it might have been staged at any date in 1599; and that would have meant performances at the Curtain any time up until the Globe was opened, which cannot be dated more precisely than late summer/early autumn, though no later than September/October when Thomas Platter saw *Julius Caesar* (see p. 267).

This is critical if it was the folio version of the play which was staged, containing the prologue and choruses. Critical because the chorus to Act 5 contains a famous reference to "the General of our gracious Empress," imagining him returning home "Bringing rebellion broachèd on his sword" (30, 32). It is widely believed that this refers to the Earl of Essex, who had been sent to

Ireland to put down a serious rebellion.[10] Unfortunately his expedition went disastrously wrong almost from the beginning and it would have been impolitic or worse to talk about it publicly any time after midsummer at the latest.

In terms of the theatres what is principally at stake is: does the famous "wooden O" invoked in the prologue refer to the Curtain or to the Globe (or indeed to a venue at court)? Is it an apology for old and unimpressive facilities which the company would prefer not to have had to use at all? Or is it calculated mock-modesty about the company's splendid new house on the Bankside? We simply do not know, though it is difficult to see how the line about "the General of our gracious Empress" could have been voiced in public as late as September 1599, since Essex's campaign had failed disastrously and he returned to London against the Queen's express orders, arriving on the 28th of that month. Nevertheless, people have, with equal facility, been able to read the "wooden O" reference either way. Of course, the discovery that the Curtain was rectangular rather than polygonal might seem to tilt the odds in favor of "the wooden O" being the Globe; but rich metaphors can embrace many forms of reality.

In other respects neither version of *Henry V* poses any new challenges in terms of stagecraft which would incline us to suppose that it was written for one of these playhouses rather than the other. Editorial tradition, which universally cleaves to the folio version as the original text, assumes that the Governor of Harfleur appears on the walls to surrender in 3.3, so requiring an upper stage. In fact both versions have a bare "*Enter Governor*," which tells us nothing about the staging.

A Warning for Fair Women is a difficult play to date, but was published in 1599 as it "hath been lately diverse times acted by the right Honourable, the Lord Chamberlain his servants," and thus might be a Curtain play. It does, however, contain many early stylistic features, including dumb shows (though *Hamlet* is evidence enough that dumb shows were far from dead at this date). In particular, *A Warning* is framed by heavy metatheatrical – and indeed melodramatic – elements. The play opens: "*Enter at door* History *with a drum and ensign,* Tragedy *at another, in her one hand a whip, in the other hand a knife.*" Later they are joined by Comedy. The point of this preamble is to establish the proper genre for the action to follow, and it is Tragedy who prevails. As History notes: "The stage is hung with black: and I perceive / The auditors prepared for tragedy" (A3r); Tragedy later refers to "these sable curtains" (C2v). It is not clear if there were equally distinctive stage decorations for comedy, history or tragicomedy, but such black hangings for tragedy were standard in public playhouses and seem to have been a feature also of the indoor private playhouses, though it is less often commented upon (see pp. 300).[11] The plot of *A Warning* is based on a famous murder in 1573, of which Arthur Golding published a prose account. Tragedy claims that this is a new style of drama, shunning the old conventions of revenge tragedy and concentrating on domestic violence in a familiar English setting. The claim to novelty may be belied by *Arden of Feversham* (pub. 1592), but it is not impossible that *A Warning* does indeed antedate it. Yet plays based on true-life murders did latterly become a stock-in-trade for the Chamberlain's Men, as we see with *A Yorkshire Tragedy* (circa 1605) and *The Miseries of Enforced Marriage* (1607), both based on the same events in Yorkshire. *A Warning for Fair Women* could have been a straw in that wind, whether as a belated printing of an earlier play, with a recent playhouse revival, or as a new play in an old style.

The story of the play unfolds quite conventionally, except that the action is interrupted several times by dumb shows, introduced and commented on by Tragedy, in which the protagonists interact with abstract and mythological characters, like Furies, Lust, and Chastity – spelling out the moral misdirections and the inexorable process of divine retribution. Tragedy's looming presence – "*Tragedy expressing that now he goes to act the deed*" – piles on the melodrama, which is stoked by very simple props and effects: "*Enter* Tragedy *with a bowl of blood in her hand*"; "*Here some strange solemn music like bells is heard within.*" Gruesome and gory it may be, but it is all very elementary stage-craft, calling on no unusual resources. The bowl of blood is a useful reminder that the staging of violent deaths and wounds was often very realistic, using concealed bladders filled either with vinegar or possibly real (calves' or lambs') blood. Three characters in *The Battle of Alcazar* – an Admiral's Men's play – are disembowelled on stage, and the direction on the surviving "plot" of the play calls for "*3 vials of blood and sheep's gather* [liver, heart and lungs]." *The Fair Maid of Bristow* (a Chamberlain's / King's Men's play, printed 1605) calls for nothing so extreme, but in the course of the murder: "*Here he stabs his arm and bloodies Sentloe's face, and plucks out Vallinger's sword and bloodies it, and lays it by him.*" Presumably the arm was where this substantial bladder of blood was concealed.

The ending of *A Warning for Fair Women* is the only other place where the staging calls for some comment. The murderer, George Browne, is brought to trial. It was evidently decided that the event should be treated with suitable gravity, so that a considerable presence of stage furniture was called for: "*Enter some to prepare the judgment seat to the Lord Mayor, Lord Justice, and the four Lords, and one clerk, and a sheriff; who being set, command Browne to be brought forth.*" This makes explicit something we may only have presumed: that with continuous staging it would sometimes be necessary for back-stage personnel to move properties in open view of the audience.[12] In this instance it ensures that something like half the cast – all, except the clerk, wearing impressive finery – would be seated in (probably tiered), awe-inspiring judgment. Browne is found guilty and sentenced to death. At the end of the execution sequence the direction reads only "*He leaps off.*" We may infer that before Browne delivers a penitent's speech, he has mounted a ladder, used as a make-shift gallows. (There is talk of proper gallows being built for his three co-conspirators, but that was hardly practical on stage). The actor would have been wearing a concealed harness, familiar to this day, which would take the strain of the rope without the noose endangering him. But the simulation of sudden death would have been effective, and the horror of the whole plot is rubbed in when Browne is denied his last plea, which was to be spared having his body hung in chains, to rot and be pecked at by crows. This is not a style of drama we would normally associate with Shakespeare (the play is sometimes credited to Heywood) but neither is Barnabe Barnes's *The Devil's Charter*, as we shall see. The Chamberlain's Men were never tied to a single style. That point is further underscored if we consider what we know of a play called *The Second Part of The Seven Deadly Sins*.

2 The Seven Deadly Sins

David Kathman's meticulous demonstration that the "plot" of *2 The Seven Deadly Sins*[13] relates not, as was long thought, to a company containing Edward Alleyn in the early 1590s but to the Chamberlain's Men in 1597–8 is to my mind utterly convincing – certainly more convincing than any other that has been advanced.[14] (On "back-stage plots," see p. 113). As such it offers us a unique insight into the inner workings and personnel of the company while it was based at the Curtain and around the time that Shakespeare was writing the *Henry IV* plays, *The Merchant of Venice*, and *Much Ado About Nothing*. One thing stands out immediately: that while Shakespeare was making striking innovations in the forms of history plays and romantic comedies, the company was still staging traditional, even old-fashioned, plays like this, a morality play which portrays the consequences of three of the Seven Deadly Sins, Envy, Sloth, and Lechery. (The other four, Pride, Gluttony, Avarice, and Wrath, had presumably been the subject of the lost *1 Seven Deadly Sins*, to which this was a sequel.) Neither *A Warning for Fair Women* nor *An Alarum for London* may be quite the outliers in the company's repertory they have hitherto seemed (see p. 203).

I start by recapitulating Kathman's identification of the adult actors included in the "plot." Their names are first given as they appear, then fleshed out if needs be, followed by the roles they played in each of the three sections (Envy, Sloth, Lechery) or the framing Induction:

Mr. Brian (George Bryan): Damasus/ Lord / Councillor (Envy); Warwick (Induction).
Mr. Pope (Thomas Pope): Arbactus (Sloth).
Mr. Phillipps (Augustine Phillips): Sardanapalus (Sloth).
R. Burbadg (Richard Burbage): King Gorboduc (Envy); Tereus (Lechery).
W. Sly (William Sly): Porrex (Envy); Lord (Lechery).

R. Cowly (Richard Cowley): Lieutenant (Induction); Soldier and Lord (Envy); Giraldus / Captain (Sloth); Lord (Lechery).

John Duke: Pursuivant (Induction); Attendant and Soldier (Envy); Will Fool?? (Sloth); Lord (Lechery).

John Sincler: Keeper/Warder (Induction); Soldier (Envy); Captain / Musician (Sloth).

John Holland: Attendant and Soldier (Envy); Captain (Sloth); Warder (Induction).

Ro. Pallant (Robert Pallant): 1 Warder (Induction); Attendant, Soldier, and Dordan (Envy); Nicanor (Sloth); Julio (Lechery)

Tho. Goodale (Thomas Goodale): Lucius / Councillor (Envy); Phronesius and Messenger (Sloth); Lord (Lechery).

As Kathman summarizes: "The first eight players in the above list – Bryan, Pope, Phillips, Burbage, Sly, Cowley, Duke, and Sincler – are all known to have been active with the Chamberlain's Men in 1597–8, if we assume that Bryan remained with the company for at least a while after December 1596 [see p. 157]. The other three men on the list – Holland, Pallant, and Goodale – have links with the Chamberlain's Men and can be plausibly placed with that company in the late 1590s, and none is known to have been with any other company at the time" (25). I concur with this analysis in all respects, except for one small caveat. The role of Will Fool does seem to be allocated to John Duke in Sc.14. But the company contained the most famous fool/clown of his day, and his name was Will – Will Kemp. So, as Andrew Gurr suggests: "It makes obvious sense to see ... Will Kemp playing the script-free clown, whose presence was registered only as 'foole' in scenes 14 and 15" (2007, 79).[15] On balance I agree with this, though I recognize that it renders John Duke's name at this point an anomaly which I cannot explain unless Duke simply *accompanied* Will Fool.

The list is obviously deficient in the sense that it never openly names not only Kemp but also two of the other most senior members of the company, John Heminge and William Shakespeare; they were all sharers in the company and so entitled to the honorific "Master" which is carefully accorded Bryan, Pope, and Phillips. But this can be explained by the fact that, besides "Will Fool," there are two roles in the Induction with no indication of who played them. These are King Henry VI and the poet Lydgate. Since they apparently remained on stage throughout the performance they were obviously substantial roles. But they were of less interest to the book-keeper and others who would consult the "plot," since they had no entrances and exits to track. Kathman suggests that Shakespeare might have played the king (an epigram in John Davies' 1610 *Scourge of Folly* suggests that he had "played some kingly parts in sport"), while Heminge played the venerable poet, and Kemp played [Mercury] the trickster messenger of the gods, an ideal role from which to guy the other characters (2004*a*, 31).[16] This is entirely plausible, though I do wonder if there might not have been an exploitable in-joke in making Shakespeare the poet who presents the scenes of Envy, Sloth, and Lechery to the king. Kemp as Mercury does make perfect sense; if he also played Will Fool that gave him stage-time sufficient to his status and appeal.

Such speculation aside, however, this still only gives us six sharers in the company – Bryan, Pope, Phillips, Heminge, Shakespeare, and Kemp – which is on the low side for a major company at this date. All but Phillips had by this date received money from court on behalf of the company, an important responsibility that normally fell to sharers; so too had Richard Burbage, in 1595. It seems inconceivable that he was not in fact a sharer, despite the inconsistency in the "plot" in not dubbing him "Master" – he had important and substantial roles as King Gorboduc and Tereus. (Possibly his initial was used to distinguish him from his brother, Cuthbert, who, though not an actor, had inherited the Theatre from their father and was always close to the company). Richard Cowley also received court payment on behalf of the company in 1601, so might also already have been a sharer by 1597/8 (see p. 141). All those mentioned in this paragraph were identified as sharers in the King's Men in 1603, except Bryan and Kemp who left, and Pope who died. By then Will Sly had risen to be a sharer and so had Henry Condell, who – as Kathman argues with conviction – was on the point of transition from boy player to adult at the time of *2 The Seven Deadly Sins*.

Identifying the boy players is more problematic because often only their first names are given. But again Kathman's deductions ring true in a striking number of cases:

Harry (Henry Condell?): Ferrex (Envy); Lord (Lechery).
Kit (Christopher Beeston?): Attendant and Soldier (Envy); Captain (Sloth).
Vincent (Thomas Vincent?): Musician (Sloth).
T. Belt (Thomas Belt): Servant (Induction); Panthea (Lechery).
Saunder (Alexander Cooke): Queen Videna (Envy); Procne (Lechery).
Nick (Nicholas Tooley?): Lady (Envy); Pompeia (Sloth).
Ro. Go. (Robert Gough?): Aspatia (Sloth); Philomela (Lechery).
Ned (Edmund Shakespeare??): Rodope (Sloth).
Will (William Ostler? William Ecclestone?): Itis (Lechery).

The identification of "Harry" with Condell and "Kit" with Beeston makes perfect sense. Both are named in Jonson's list of the "principal comedians" in *Every Man In His Humour*, staged in 1598. As I have said, Condell would buy his way into a sharer's position before 1603, while Beeston (remembered by Augustine Phillips as his "servant" in his 1605 will) moved by 1602 to be a member of Worcester's Men and to a spectacular entrepreneurial career with that company when it became Queen Anne's Men (pp. 141, 164). Both, that is, were really too old to be called boys by 1597, being close to the end of their apprenticeships.[17] Thomas Belt and Alexander ("Saunder") Cooke were both apprenticed to John Heminge, in 1595 and 1597 respectively – an earlier discovery by Kathman himself (2004*b*). Cooke would go on to flourish with the company, appearing in Jonson's cast-lists for *Sejanus*, *Volpone*, *The Alchemist*, and *Catiline*, dying as a shareholder-member in 1614. Nicholas Tooley, like Cooke, received a legacy in Phillips' 1605 will as his "fellow," and was certainly a shareholder in the King's Men by 1619, making him a strong candidate for "Nick." Robert Gough is an equally likely candidate for "Ro. Go." He would be remembered in the 1603 will of Thomas Pope, would witness Phillips' will, and be a shareholder in the King's Men by 1619. The other identifications are more speculative, especially that of Edmund Shakespeare for "Ned." This would be William Shakespeare's brother (b. 1580), presumed to be the man of that name buried in St Saviour's Church, Southwark, in 1607, as a "player." Nothing else is known of him, though it would be logical that a player living in Southwark at that date might be with the King's Men at the Globe.

Such speculations are not, in fact, necessary to make Kathman's hypothesis any more secure. The overwhelming majority of identifications make perfect sense and draw the "plot" (to my mind) closer to 1597 than 1598, given that this is the last we ever hear of George Bryan as a player. He was a payee for the company at court in December 1596, but not in the list for *Every Man In His Humour*. One striking feature of the list is how many of the boy players had an adult career with the company: Condell, Cooke, Tooley, and Gough all flourished with them. That makes it all the more likely that the "Will" in the list, playing a small role as a child, might be one of the Williams – Ostler and Ecclestone – who were with the King's Men from around 1610, though that does not square very readily with what we think we know of their earlier lives.

The "plot" of *2 The Seven Deadly Sins* thus shows us a company with fourteen adult players (the ones named plus Kemp, Heminge, and Shakespeare), of whom seven or eight were sharers. The other six or seven would all have been hired men, but it seems certain that they were not just employed casually; all have multiple roles that may have helped to bulk up the presence on stage (attendants, captains) but also probably called for some professional accomplishment. One of them, John Sincler (or Sinklo) would appear in the Induction to Marston's *The Malcontent*, alongside sharers like Burbage and Sly, as familiar members of the company (see p. 283). In addition to the adult players there were a surprisingly large number of boys, nine in all. Of these Condell and Beeston stand out for having been given roles of real substance, Ferrex and a Lord in the case of the former, Attendant, Soldier, and Captain of the latter. Indeed, Condell looks very comparable in his roles to Sly, who played Porrex to his Ferrex, while Beeston looks identical to most of the hired men. It seems reasonable to assume that both were on the brink of adulthood.

Of the younger boys Saunder Cooke seems to have the pick of the female roles, playing Queen Videna and Procne, wife of Tereus (Burbage) and sister of the

Philomela (Robert Gough), whom her husband would rape. (This makes him the leading candidate to have created roles such as Beatrice in *Much Ado* and Rosalind in *As You Like It.*) Although it is impossible to be sure, without knowing the script, most of the other female roles seem to have been more decorative than demanding. "Will" has only the role of the small boy, Itis, and may have been the youngest of them all. "Vincent" is the most difficult of all to place, since no known actor of that name seems to fit the time frame. David Kathman does, however, recall the anecdote about Thomas Vincent who is mentioned as a "book keeper or prompter" at the Globe not long after this (27; see p. 179). Possibly he moved into that position after starting as a boy player. Here he only appears briefly as a musician. Many if not all boy actors had some facility with instruments; and we note that originally only two musicians were called for and this was increased to three, his only role. He would have been available as "call-boy" to the book-keeper for most of the play, as would "Ned" and "Will" (see p. 113).

The "plot" is marked by a determination to describe the action in a number (26) of self-contained sections or scenes, rather than to tell the story. It helps us make sense of this, however, if we know something of the three tales incorporated by the play.

The Stories

Induction. The framing Induction focuses on the figure of King Henry VI, apparently after his deposition in 1461 by Edward IV, when he was held in the Tower of London – a fitting audience for the three tales of the fall of kings which make up the play. It seems to end with his restoration to the throne in 1470 by "Warwick" (Sc. 24), Richard Neville, Earl of Warwick, known as the "Kingmaker." This was a brief reprieve however since Warwick was defeated and killed the following year, Henry was recaptured and murdered. It is not clear if the sequence ends with the temporary triumph or the ultimate fall; it is also not clear if the play treats Henry as a near saint and martyr, a widespread view after his death though one fading by the end of the sixteenth century. Shakespeare's audience was familiar with a fuller version of the history in *3 Henry VI*. John Lydgate was an appropriate author to present these tales to Henry, venerated at the time alongside Chaucer and Gower (cf. *Pericles*) as one of great poets of English antiquity; he had lived in Henry's time (though he died before the deposition) and was famous for his enormous poem, *Fall of Princes*.[18]

Envy tells the tale of Gorboduc, one of the mythical line of early British kings including Brute, Lear, and Cymbeline, which was familiar to the Elizabethans from Holinshed's *Chronicles* and from the famous old play by Thomas Sackville and Thomas Norton. Gorboduc made the fatal mistake of dividing his kingdom while he was still alive, leading to a disastrous civil war between his sons, Ferrex and Porrex (Scenes 5–9).

Sloth is the tale of Sardanapalus, a more-or-less mythical king of ancient Assyria, whose name became a byword for sloth and sybaritic living. He had many concubines of both sexes, though in the play they are all female. His general, Arbaces (here Arbactus) led a revolt against this decadent lifestyle (Sc.15), which Sardanapalus seemed initially to crush but which eventually overcame him at Nineveh. Rather than allow himself to be captured he and all his concubines died in a blazing funeral pyre, with all his wealth and royal trappings (hence "with as many jewels, robes and gold as he ca < n > carry," Sc.16).

Finally *Lechery* tells the famous tale from Ovid and elsewhere of Tereus, married to Procne, who lusted after and raped his wife's sister, Philomena, cutting out her tongue to prevent her from talking about it. Philomena, however, told her tale by weaving a tapestry (here "the sampler," Sc. 23). She and Procne planned revenge, killing Tereus and Procne's son, Itis. They baked his flesh in a pie, and fed it to Tereus, then showed him Itis' severed head, from which he deduced what had happened (Sc. 23). Tereus tried to kill the sisters, but the gods intervened ("Mercury comes and all vanish") and all three were turned into birds. In older versions of the tale Philomela was turned into a swallow, which has no song, while Procne became the nightingale, forever mourning her dead child. Since the most famous version of the myth, however, in Ovid's *Metamorphoses*, the assignation of the birds has usually been reversed, with Philomela the nightingale lamenting her ravishment. Shakespeare notably adapted part of the tale for *Titus Andronicus*.

As I started this section by saying, it was clearly not the purpose of the "plot" to recount these stories. It was to convey to professionals within the playhouse how they had been converted into dramatic form, in such a way that anyone consulting it could see the sequence of scenes, entrances, and exits: exactly who should be on stage at any moment in the sequence (and so should be prepared to go on ahead of time). The great majority of scenes start with an entry, often followed with indications that other characters subsequently join those who enter first, but there is rarely any indication of what actions take place and no indication at all of what the characters talk about – the players are supposed to know all that from learning their parts. The scenes that do not begin with an entry almost all relate to the Induction/framing device involving Henry VI, Lydgate and (latterly) Mercury; the first two are apparently on stage throughout, until Lydgate exits at the very end. Henry may remain in his tent to watch the action, possibly emerging when he is involved with the Lieutenant of the Tower, his warder and the pursuivant (which might here mean either a royal warrant officer or a personal attendant). It is possible that he was meant to exit with Warwick at the end of Sc. 25, but that is not indicated.

Here, then, is a transcription of the "plot" of the play.

The Plat (Plot) of *The Second Part of the Seven Deadly Sins*
1) A tent being placed on the stage for Henry the Sixth. He in it, asleep; to him the Lieutenant, a pursuivant, R(ichard) Cowley, John Duke, and [2] 1 warder [s], [John Holland], Robert Pallant. To them Pride, Gluttony, Wrath and Covetousness at one door, at another door Envy, Sloth and Lechery. The three put back the four. And so exeunt.
2) Henry awaking, enter a Keeper, John Sincler; to him a servant, Thomas Belt; to him Lydgate and the Keeper. Exit then enter again. Then Envy passeth over the stage. Lydgate speakes.
3) A sennet. Dumb show. Enter King Gorboduc with 2 Councillors; Richard Burbage, Master (George) Bryan, Thomas Goodale. The Queen with Ferrex and Porrex and some attendants follow; Saunder (Alexander Cooke), Will Sly, Harry (Condell), John Duke, Kit (Christopher Beeston), Robert Pallant, John Holland. After Gorboduc hath consulted with his Lords he brings his two sons to two several seats. They evaing one another, Ferrex offers to take Porrex his crown. He draws his weapon. The King, Queen and Lords step between them. They thrust them away and, menacing [ecc] each other, exit. The Queen < and Lords depart > heavily. Lydgate speaks.
4) Enter Ferrex crowned, with drum and colours and soldiers, one way; Harry (Condell), Kit (Beeston), R. Cowley, John Duke. To them, at another door, Porrex, drum and colours and soldiers; W Sly, R. Pallant, John Sincler, J. Holland.
5) Enter [Gorb] Queen, with 2 Councillors; Master Brian, Thomas Goodale. To them Ferrex and Porrex several ways with [his] drums and powers. Gorboduc, entering in the midst between. Henry speaks.
6) Alarum with excursions. After Lydgate speaks.
7) Enter Ferrex and Porrex severally, Goboduc still following them. Lucius and Damasus; Master Bryan, Thomas Goodale.
8) Enter Ferrex at one door, Porrex at another. They fight, Ferrex is slain. To them Videna, the Queen; to her Damasus; to him Lucius.
9) Enter Porrex sad with Dordan, his man; R(obert) P(allant), W Sly. To them the Queen and a Lady, Nick (Tooley?), Saunder. And Lords, R. Cowley, Master Bryan; to them Lucius running.
10) Henry and Lydgate speaks; Sloth passeth over.
11) Enter Giraldus, Phronesius, Aspatia, Pompeia, Rodope; Richard Cowley, Thomas Goodale, Robert Gough, Ned (Shakespeare?), Nick (Tooley?).

12) Enter Sardanapalus, Arbactus, Nicanor and captains, marching; Master Phillips, Master Pope, R(obert) Pallant, Kit (Beeston), John Sincler, John Holland.
13) <Enter> A captain with Aspatia and the ladies. Kit (Beeston).

* * *

Lydgate speak.
14) Enter Nicanor with other captains; R. Pallant, J. Sincler, Kit (Beeston), J. Holland R. Cowley. To them Arbactus; Master Pope. To him Will Fool; J. Duke. To him Rodope; Ned (Shakespeare?). To her Sardanapalus like a woman, with Aspatia, Rodope, Pompeia, Will Fool. To them Arbactus and [2] 3 musicians; Master Pope, J. Sincler, (Thomas?) Vincent, R(ichard) Cowley. To them Nicanor and others; R. Pallant, Kit (Beeston).
15) Enter Sardanapalus, with the ladies. To them a messenger; Thomas Goodale. To him Will Fool, running. Alarum.
16) Enter Arbactus, pursuing Sardanapalus, and the ladies fly. After enter Sardanapalus with as many jewels, robes and gold as he ca<n> carry. Alarum.
17) Enter Arbactus, Nicanor and the other captai<ns> in triumph; Master Pope, R. Pallant, Kit (Beeston), J. Holland, R. Cowley, J Sincler.
18) Henry speaks and Lydgate; Lechery passeth over the stage. Enter Te<reus>, Philomele, <Julio>; R Burbage, Ro<R Pall.>, J<Sink>.
19) Enter Procne, Itis and Lords; Saunder (Cooke), Will (Ostler? Eccleston?), J. Duke, W(ill) Sly, Harry (Condell).
20) Enter Philomele and Tereus; to them Julio
21) Enter Procne, Panthea, Itis and Lords; Saunder (Cooke), T(homas) Belte, Will (Ostler? Ecclestone?), W. Sly, Harry (Condell), Th(omas) Goodale. To them Tereus with Lords; R. Burbage, J. Duke, R. Cowley
22) A Dumb Show. Lydgate speaks.
23) Enter Procne with the sampler. To her Tereus from hunting with his Lords. To them Philomele with Itis' head in a dish. Mercury comes and all vanish. To him 3 Lords; Th(omas) Goodale, Harry(Condell), W(ill) Sly.
24) Henry speaks. To him Lieutenant, pursuivant and warder; R. Cowley, J. Duke, J. Holland, John Sincler. To them Warwick; Master Bryan.
25) Lydgate speaks to the audience and so exits.

FINIS

Commentary

The Text

The text of the "plot" is based, with permission, on the "diplomatic" version offered by David Kathman, which has old spelling and original punctuation (2004a, 35–8). I have modernized spelling and punctuation, but followed Kathman in respect of use of brackets: square brackets represent material crossed out – so, for instance, in Scene 1 the original plan was to have two warders, but this was later reduced to one; pointed brackets indicate best-guess attempts to reconstruct text which has been lost to wear or damage, all of which I have accepted.

Round brackets represent my own expansion of abbreviated forms, purely to help the reader. The numbers designating the scenes are also my own, but very clearly suggested by the way the "plot" divides the action into two columns, each section of which is ruled off after a self-contained sequence (i.e. a scene). The line of asterisks is not on the "plot" but marks where the left-hand column ends and transitions to the right-hand side. It seems that the items at the foot of the left column and the top of the right represent a single scene.

Authorship and Dating of the Play(s)

George Harvey attributed the "famous play of *The Seven Deadly Sins*" to the great comedian, Richard Tarlton, "which most deadly but most lively play I might have seen in London, and was very gently invited thereunto at Oxford by Tarlton himself" (*ES*, 3: 497; see p. 44). It was evidently a two-part play, the first part of which is lost; but there is no reason to suppose that Tarlton did not write both parts. If so, they must have been written and performed (presumably by the Queen's Men) before Tarlton's death in 1588. As a morality / fall of princes play the Second Part does seem to belong to an earlier era than Shakespeare. Yet the Chamberlain's Men somehow acquired a manuscript of it and saw fit to perform it as late as 1597/8; there is no record of its ever being printed. We do know, however, that the Queen's Men sold a significant number of their plays to printers in 1594/5, at the time they lost their footing at court and became exclusively a touring operation. It is not impossible that the Chamberlain's Men, looking to build up a repertoire of plays as quickly as possible, might have purchased one or both parts of the play then or later, with the licence to perform them.

Scene 1: The tent on the stage represents Henry's cell in the Tower of London and apparently remains throughout the play, a vantage point from which the action can be observed. (The use of the tent would seem to preclude any use of a discovery space and is perhaps further evidence that the Curtain did not have one.) The Lieutenant is a senior officer of the Tower and important prisoners, like Henry, would formally be in his charge. "Pursuivant" here could mean either a royal warrant officer or (perhaps more likely) a personal attendant. The changes represent a decision to reduce the warders from two to one, freeing up John Holland for other business. It is possible that the change had been forgotten by Sc. 24, where two players seem to be nominated for only one warder role. The secondary action of the scene represents the symbolic triumph of the three deadly sins who feature in this play over the other four, who presumably featured in the lost *First Part of the Seven Deadly Sins*. The familiar formula of entry "at one door, at another door" usually denotes two doors, one at either side of the tiring house wall. It was common for opposed forces to enter on opposite sides; see Ferrex and Porrex in Sc. 4.

Scene 2: It is unclear here whether "keeper" is being used in the same general sense as "warder" or whether it denotes another important official at the Tower of London, the Keeper or Master of the Jewel House, where the Crown jewels are kept. The way he seems to introduce Lydgate perhaps suggests the latter. It is not clear who exits and enters again – Lydgate, the Keeper, or both? – or why, but would have been known to the relevant players. The formula "passeth over the stage," as each of the three Deadly Sins does (see Scenes 10 and 18), indicates that a character enters at one door and exits at the other, displaying herself conspicuously in the process. This opens Envy's sequence in the play, as Lydgate presumably explains.

Scene 3: "Sennet": see p. 175. The dumb show allows the players to establish the characters and their relationships, especially those within the royal family of Gorboduc, his Queen, and their two sons, Ferrex and Porrex. The councillors are probably consulted (in mime) about the decision to divide the country between the twins and advise against it. But it goes ahead anyway; the "two several seats" represent two thrones (OED, seat *n*. 8a). Ferrex and Porrex are then described as "evaing one another," probably in the sense of "vie with, contend for mastery with" (OED envy, v^2). The Queen and Lord depart "heavily" – sadly, in sorrow.

Scene 4: Presumably *both* Ferrex and Porrex have been crowned as kings, following Gorboduc's decision. The drum and colors (flags with their royal emblems) indicate armies in the field.

Scene 5: Perhaps the original staging plan was to have Gorboduc center-stage, with Ferrex and Porrex entering to him from either side. This was changed to the Queen and her Councillors entering first and perhaps making emotional pleas. Goboduc's "entering in the midst" means that he ends up between the forces of his two sons.

Scene 6: "Alarum" = alarm: a call to arms, a warning of danger (examples elsewhere suggest it was made by drums and/or trumpets); "excursion": "An issuing forth against an enemy; a sally, sortie, raid" (OED *n*. 3).

Scene 7: Lucius and Damasus are presumably the two Councillors mentioned in Sc. 5. Their names have no traditional association with Gorboduc. The most notable historical Damasus was a fourth-century pope, so it is just possible that the character was a man of the church. The events of the play, however, supposedly occur in the pre-Christian era, so this is pure speculation.

Scenes 8 & 9: In the original myth and play Porrex does indeed kill Ferrex. But then the Queen (Judon in the early sources, but Videna in the old play) kills Porrex in revenge for the death of her beloved elder son. This results in a civil war in which both Gorboduc and his Queen die and there is a long and devastating struggle over the succession. (In the play Dordan is *Ferrex's* man.) It is far from clear how far 2 *The Seven Deadly Sins* carries the story. There is no record of deaths after Ferrex's, though it may be significant that there is no mention of Gorboduc in this last section. Was his death offstage reported? The entry of "Porrex sad" could suggest that all ended on a note of repentance.

Scene 10: Sloth's passing over marks the transition to the next section of the show.

Scene 11: The introduction here of "Giraldus" (Giraldus Cambrensis, Geoffrey of Monmouth) is puzzling. His *History of the Kings of Britain* was the ultimate source of the mythology that included the Gorboduc story. But it has nothing to do with Sardanapalus, the subject of the second section of the show. Possibly his function was to suggest some thematic link between the two stories. "Phronesis" is Greek for a type of wisdom, perhaps best translated as prudence. "Aspasia" was the lover and partner of the Athenian statesman, Pericles; she was apparently very influential, though very little is actually known about her. "Pompeia" was a name shared by numerous women in ancient Rome, including the daughter of Pompey the Great and the second wife of Julius Caesar; it is impossible to know which, if any, this character represented. "Rodope" was a queen in Greek mythology; her vain husband compared the two of them to Zeus and Hera, who were offended and turned them into ranges of mountains (cf. the Rhodope Mountains, which run through Bulgaria and Greece). The four between them perhaps represent pairs of good and evil female counsellors.

Scene 13: For Sardanapalus and Arbactus, see *The Stories*. No Nicanor figures in standard histories of Sardanapalus, though a Seleucid-Syrian general of that name figures in the Bible (1 and 2 Maccabees); he died in a crushing defeat by the Jews at the Battle Adasa in 161 BC and his body was mutilated. None of that, except perhaps his name as a general, seems relevant here. It seems evident from Sc. 17 that Nicanor sides with Arbactus against Sardanapalus.

Scene 16: Did they attempt to represent Sardanapalus' funeral pyre? Richard Edwardes' *Palamon and Arcite* included a highly realistic pyre, but that was in very different staging conditions (see pp. 3–4). Somewhat later than this the Fortune and Red Bull theatres acquired a reputation for their pyrotechnics, though perhaps more in the form of fireworks than open blazes. (See p. 255 on the Chamberlain's Men's own "blazing star".) A trap-door could certainly facilitate business with fire. In Greene's *Friar Bacon and Friar Bungay* (circa 1589), for example, a stage direction reads "*Here Bungay conjures and the tree appears with the dragon shooting fire*" (Sc. 9, 83.1–2).

Scenes 18–21: Lechery's passing over introduces the third and final section of the show. Of the named characters, it is unclear what roles are played by Julio and Panthea, whose names do not relate to the original myth. "Panthea" means "of all the gods" and someone of that name was said to be the most beautiful woman in Persia, beloved of Cyrus the Great. But that may not be relevant at all.

Scene 22: The dumb show may foreshadow the death of Itis.

Scene 23: Procne's appearance with the sampler makes it clear that she knows what has happened to Philomela. Presumably food has been prepared for Tereus on his return from hunting, including the flesh of Itis. Only when he has eaten would Itis' head be produced. The direction "Mercury comes and all vanish" suggests a spectacular piece of stage-work involving a trapdoor. It brings to mind the direction in *The Tempest*: "*Enter Ariel, like a harpy, claps his wings upon the table, and with a quaint device the banquet vanishes*" (3.3.52 SD). If Will Kemp did indeed play Mercury the scene was presumably not without comedy, something which the entrance of the three Lords may have allowed to continue.

Scene 24: As suggested in the outline of the Induction story, this scene seems to represent the freeing of King Henry VI and restoration to the throne in 1470 by Warwick the "Kingmaker."

Plays that strung multiple stories together were quite common. *Four Plays in One* was in the repertoire of Strange's Men at the Rose in 1592; some have supposed it to be *1 The Seven Deadly Sins* (see p. 213). *A Yorkshire Tragedy* declares itself to be "One of the four plays in one" performed togther under that title (p. 204). Overall, *2 The Seven Deadly Sins* tells familiar tales of the falls of four princes: Henry VI, Gorboduc, Sardanapalus, and Tereus, the latter three destroyed by Envy, Sloth, and Lechery, as Lydgate doubtless moralized. But the fact that the play ends on an apparently positive note, with the restoration of Henry VI to his throne (albeit, historically, only briefly) does raise questions about the overall tone of the piece. The entry of Porrex "sad" does leave open the possibility of remorse and reconciliation which is not part of the traditional tale. The tale of Sardanapalus is counterpointed by the comic presence of Will Fool and the final emphasis is not on his death but on the triumph of the generals who restore his kingdom's moral compass. The tragedy of Tereus, Procne, and Philomela is prevented from an even more tragic conclusion by the intervention of the gods – in the form, apparently, of Will Kemp. All in all it contrives to be a tragicomic piece, with lots of scope for flamboyant costumes, action (battles, chases), sentencious speeches, comic diversions, and perhaps two spectacular set-pieces: Sardanapulus's funeral pyre and the "vanishing" with which the Lechery sequence ends.

I have dwelt at such length on this play because I believe that I am the first person writing on the Chamberlain's Men and their theatres to pick up on David Kathman's cogent argument for locating its "plot" in 1597/8, rather than several years earlier. It gives us unique insights into the personnel, roles, and staging practices of the company quite early in its existence. It also demonstrates that they were still performing plays of an earlier era and theatrical fashion than the sophisticated histories and comedies that Shakespeare was writing for them while they were housed at the Curtain.

The folio text of Jonson's *Every Man In His Humour*, as we have already partially seen, gives us one last substantial piece of information about the company during their time at the Curtain (pp. 199ff). It lists the "principal comedians" who performed in the original, quarto version; and this reinforces what we have inferred from the "plot" of *2 The Seven Deadly Sins*. These appear in two columns: on the left, William Shakespeare, Augustine Phillips, Henry Condell, William Sly, and William Kemp; on the right, Richard Burbage, John Heminge, Thomas Pope, Christopher Beeston, and John Duke. The principles on which Jonson compiled these lists are far from clear and attempts to correlate actors with particular roles are usually pure speculation. As mentioned earlier, neither Beeston nor Duke was ever a sharer with the Chamberlain's Men, though they were successful – in Beeston's case spectacularly successful – with other companies. All the others were certainly sharers. One name missing from the original line-up is George Bryan, who had left for his position at court (see p. 157). Another missing name is that of Richard Cowley (see p. 141). His omission here may only prove that he did not take any major role, though he may have taken a number of smaller ones, the apparent practice with Armin in most of Jonson's plays for the company while Armin was with them (see p. 150). If we omit Beeston and Duke from Jonson's list and add Cowley I suspect we have a tally of all the sharers in 1598.

Although in general it is fruitless to speculate who played what role (especially Shakespeare) an exception can be made for Kemp, since it was always likely that he would take one of the more distinctive comic roles. There are two of these in *Every Man In His Humour*, Bobadilla and Cob. Bobadilla is, as we have seen, a braggart soldier, a type which does not align itself with any other role Kemp is suspected of playing. But Cob readily compares with Bottom or Dogberry and I concur with David Wiles in seeing it as Kemp's role in the play:

> The clown's part is manifestly that of Oliver Cob. The part owes nothing to the theory of humours, everything to the clown tradition … Kemp's clowning is rooted in festival. "Cob" identifies himself as a herring cob [head] – that is, an emblem of Lent. But Cob loathes fasting days, because herring then are eaten, so Cob becomes, paradoxically, the

embodiment of Carnival ... Cob's English name distances him from the Italian world of the play, and he is English enough to deal in shillings and pence. A virtuoso mime routine is given him when he performs a balancing feat with his tankard to the nonsense words: "Helter skelter, hang sorrow, care will kill a cat, up tails all, and a pox on the hangman."

The central feature of Cob's clowning is that the audience do not know whether they are laughing at or with him. On the face of it, he is set up as the fall guy to be cudgeled, scratched, knocked on the head by a door, and duped into thinking he must go to prison. Yet at the same time he remains in control of the humour of every scene in which he appears. (1987, 94–5)

Kemp was also at this time, while resident at the Curtain, at the height of his fame for his jigs. John Marston in his satirical *Scourge of Villainy* (1598) declares that "the orbs celestial will dance Kemp's jig" (Sat. 11, line 30), while Everard Guilpin's *Skialetheia* that same year says "Whores, beadles, bawds and sergeants filthily chaunt Kemp's jig, or the Burgonians' tragedy" (Sat. 5). Dancing, singing and bawdry – some of it impromptu – seem to have parts of his stock-in-trade, and such jigs often closed an afternoon's performance.

> **Box 5.2 The Jig**
>
> As we have seen, Shakespeare may have been familiar with the jigs of the original master of the form, Richard Tarlton. But he certainly knew those of Will Kemp, the principal comedian of the Chamberlain's Men between 1594 and 1599. They were one of the company's selling points, an attraction over and above the show of the day. But it is very difficult for us to recapture the full flavor of these items, since they obviously depended for their effect on boisterous activity, spontaneity, unscripted bawdy – on action and song over written text. Yet we need to try, if we are to have a real sense of the theatrical experience in 1590s London.
>
> It will help us to understand them if we recognize that they have their roots in forms of folk drama, such as those which survived (and to an extent still survive) in the morris dance. By the late sixteenth century these typically focused on the wooing by a fool of a man–woman figure known as "Maid Marian" – in which we may see something of the origins of the distinctively English tradition of the transvestite pantomime dame. Thomas Nashe describes such a morris:
>
>> the Maid Marian trimly dressed up in a cast gown and a kercher of Dame Lawson's, his face handsomely muffled with a diaper napkin to cover his beard, and a great nosegay in his hand ... [The fool] dances round him in a cotton coat, to court him with a leathern pudding and a wooden ladle.[19]

Four texts of jigs ascribed to Kemp have survived, two in English and two in German – the jig was enormously popular in Germany, where English actors had toured since the 1580s.[20] David Wiles offers this account of one of the English ones:

> The jig of *Singing Simpkin* appears in the Stationers' Register in 1595 as "a ballad called Kemp's new jig betwixt a soldier and a miser and Sim the clown" … Simpkin keeps up a running commentary to the audience, even when hidden inside a chest, and the final line is repeatedly his to exploit. A sample will illustrate the nature of the material. In the husband's absence, a soldier (Bluster) has interrupted the wife's seduction of the servant (Simkin). Simkin is now hidden inside the chest.
>
> | | |
> |---|---|
> | *Bluster* | Within this chest I"ll hide myself, |
> | | If it chance he should come. |
> | *Wife* | Oh no, my love, that cannot be – |
> | *Simkin* | I have bespoke the room. |
> | *Wife* | I have a place behind here, |
> | | Which yet is known to no man. |
> | *Simkin* | She has a place before, too, |
> | | But that is all too common. |
> | | *Old man within.* |
> | *Old Man* | Wife, wherefore is the door thus barred? |
> | | What mean you, pray, by this? |
> | *Wife* | Alas! It is my husband. |
> | *Simkin* | I laugh now till I piss. |
> | *Bluster* | Open the chest, I'll into it; |
> | | My life else it may cost. |
> | *Wife* | Alas, I cannot open it. |
> | *Simkin* | I believe the key is lost. |
>
> While remaining notionally unseen, the clown is as free to participate in the conversation as he is to jest with the audience. The behaviour of the other characters, by contrast, is governed by the logic of the plot. In accordance with a dramatic mode that is primarily physical and mimemtic, Simkin's passions are strictly physical, with no hint of sentiment.[21]

It is the stuff of farce and fabliaux, as are other jigs associated with Kemp, with a stock cast of characters: lustful wife, braggart (but cowardly) soldier, duped old husband (*senex*) – and a clown who can rise to every occasion.

In this respect the jig seems to offer a counterpoint to the roles which Shakespeare crafted for Kemp in his comedies (see pp. 103–5).[22] With the limited exception of Peter, none of these characters takes control of the situation in which he finds himself; they are swallowed up in the plot, figures of fun emitting malapropisms rather than demonstrating superiority over others (despite their pretensions). Only Bottom inadvertently finds himself in a romantic situation, though he proves the most supine of lovers and later has only the dimmest memory of his time with Titania. There is certainly much bawdy in the comedies – *The Merchant of Venice* even ends with a bawdy pun ("I'll fear no other thing / So sore as keeping safe Nerissa's ring") – but sex is subservient to a romantic ethos and focused on the sanctity of marriage as the foundation of family and society. And the clown is never party to such outcomes. But the jigs have no such sentimental illusions. Sex is simply a physical appetite, and one which the clown will use his superiority over all competitors to gratify. It is a complete reversal of his role in the romantic comedies and perhaps a deliberate change of pace and tone for dramatic effect, akin to the satyr-plays that were performed alongside ancient Greek tragedies. The jig is an important reminder that the live experience of Elizabethan theatre was a long way removed from the reading of the the play-texts it has left behind.

On October 1, 1612 the bench of nineteen Middlesex Justices – who had authority over the amphitheaters north of the river – made an Order for Suppressing Jigs at the End of Plays, explaining "by reason of certain lewd jigs, songs and dances used and accustomed at the playhouse called the Fortune in Golden Lane, divers cutpurses and other lewd and ill-disposed persons in great multitudes do resort thither at the end of every play, many times causing tumults and outrages whereby his majesty's peace is often broke and much mischief like to ensue thereby: it was hereupon expressly commanded and ordered … that all actors of every playhouse [under their jurisdiction] utterly abolish all jigs, rhymes and dances after their plays" (*ES*, 4: 340–1). This therefore only applied to the Fortune and the Red Bull, playhouses that kept the tradition of the jig alive after the death of Kemp (then with Worcester's Men) in 1603. The suggestion is that the jigs attracted all kinds of undesirables who "do resort thither at the end of every play" – as if, perhaps, entrance late in the show was at a reduced rate.

The jig was certainly a feature of Chamberlain's Men's shows at the Theatre and the Curtain; if it was to be abandoned at the Globe, it may explain why Kemp left Shakespeare's company and "danced out of the world" (see pp. 226–7).

(Continued from p. 218)

Cob, however, was to be one of Kemp's last new roles for the Chamberlain's Men. As I shall explain, he left them before they moved to the Globe. But before we consider that major transition we need to consider events of 1597 and 1598 which did not centrally involve the Chamberlain's Men but had a major impact on their future.

"Those Playhouses ... Shall be Plucked Down"

The cause and effect of the events of July and August 1597, when theatre in London seemed to be in danger of being obliterated altogether, are not easy to piece together. On July 28 the Privy Council wrote to the magistrates in Middlesex and Surrey, ordering that "those playhouses that are erected and built only for such purposes shall be plucked down" both in Shoreditch, where the Theatre and Curtain were, and in Southwark, where the Rose and the recently-built Swan stood (*EPF*, 100–1; see also Dutton, 1991: 102–16; Dutton, 2000: 16–40). They also suspended all playing. The orders were signed by, among others, the patrons of both the Chamberlain's and the Admiral's Men. On that very day the Court of Common Council of London had written to the Privy Council with what looks like a routine complaint, listing the familiar objections to the theatres – immorality, crime, absenteeism, spread of plague – and petitioning "for the present stay, and final suppressing, of the said stage plays" (*EPF*, 99). But there is nothing to suggest why the Privy Council should have reacted so dramatically on this occasion. There is, however, also no indication that anyone acted on the order to pluck the playhouses down.

It seems likely – though final evidence is lacking – that the Privy Council order was somehow linked with specific activity on the Bankside, focused on the new Swan theatre. It had been occupied by the Earl of Pembroke's Men, who now constituted clear rivals to the Admiral's Men, playing nearby at the Rose. Indeed they had been poaching some of their senior players, including Martin Slater (Gurr, 1996, 239). Over the next few months, however, Henslowe's *Diary* shows that defectors were tempted back to the Admiral's Men, and indeed some others of Pembroke's Men joined them (*Henslowe*, 239–40).

A critical factor in reversing the flow was almost certainly the Council's action against *The Isle of Dogs*, co-written for Pembroke's Men by Thomas Nashe and Ben Jonson; Jonson also performed in it. We do not know precisely when they took this action, but by August 15 they certainly had Jonson and other players in custody for their parts in the play, which supposedly "contain[ed] very seditious and slanderous matter" (*ES*, 4: 323). Moreover, they were employing the notorious inquisitor and licensed torturer, Richard Topcliffe, in pursuit of those responsible – the only time in the entire era that they demonstrated such naked aggression in their response to theatrical infractions. And it may well have been this play, rather than the petition from the Court of Common Council, which prompted the Privy Council's actions against the playhouses (*EPF*, 101).

One clear outcome of all this – which, reading backwards, we might suspect had been intended all along – was that Pembroke's Men went out of business and the Swan was largely unused for several years (Ingram 1978: 167–86, 313–14). Its owner, Francis Langley, unsuccessfully sued five of the players who had abandoned the Swan for the Rose (*EPF*, 437–46). Over the following months measures were put in place which gave public standing to the *de facto* pre-eminence of the Chamberlain's and Admiral's Men, notionally making it more difficult for rival companies to challenge it. Parliament passed an even harsher statute governing the Punishment of Rogues and Vagabonds (February 9, 1598), restricting travel by professional players to those who carried their aristocratic masters' sealed warrant and removing certain privileges of mayors and justices in that regard in the earlier legislation (see p. 29). Then on February 19 Privy Council letters went out simultaneously to the Middlesex and Surrey magistrates and to Edmund Tilney, Master of the Revels:

> Whereas licence hath been granted unto two companies of stage players retained unto us, the Lord Admiral and Lord Chamberlain, to use and practice stage plays, whereby they might be better enabled and prepared to show such plays before Her Majesty as they shall be required at times meet and accustomed, to which end they have been chiefly licensed and tolerated as aforesaid; and whereas there is also a third company who of late (as we are informed) have by way of intrusion used likewise to play, having neither prepared any play for Her Majesty nor are bound to you, the Master of the Revels, for performing such orders as have been enjoined to be observed by the other two companies before mentioned. We have therefore thought good to require you upon receipt hereof to take order that the aforesaid third company may be suppressed, and none suffered hereafter to play but those two formerly named belonging to us, the Lord Admiral and Lord Chamberlain, unless you shall receive other direction from us. (*EPF*, 104)

Nothing earlier is as explicit about the interrelationship of these two "licensed" and "tolerated" companies, the Master of the Revels and the provision of plays for the Queen. Nor had anything specified that the individual authorities of the Lord Chamberlain and the Lord Admiral, in respect of the companies they patronized, carried the collective authority of the Privy Council. But this is unequivocal. Whatever understandings may have surrounded the emergence of these companies in 1594, these were now publicly stated policies of the Privy Council as far as the authorities in and around London were concerned.

This – following the appointment of their new patron as Lord Chamberlain, after Lord Cobham's death – must have offered reassurance to his players and helped steer them to the actions which followed. Denied use of both the Theatre and the Blackfriars, and not content with the old Curtain, they needed a new playhouse. But James Burbage had died in February 1597, having invested all his capital in the Blackfriars. The briefly remaining lease on the Theatre had earlier been conveyed into the hands of Cuthbert, the elder son, while the freehold of the Blackfriars building now passed to Richard. It was, however, a fact of some importance to the stability of the Chamberlain's Men that the Burbage brothers seem to have acted cooperatively in all their theatrical affairs. Cuthbert, though never an actor or a sharer in any company, was engaged in theatrical finance all his life, currently owner of the Theatre, and must have taken a lead over the next few months.

By the end of the year they had identified a site for a new playhouse. Either seeking to emulate the success of Henslowe's Rose or determined to make a clean break with the Shoreditch district, where there was continuing litigation with their landlord at the Theatre, they chose a piece of garden ground "situate in Maiden Lane on the Bankside in the County of Surrey" (from a Privy Council order of 1604; *ES*, 2: 416). Their new lease was executed on February 21, 1599, but backdated to run from the Christmas just passed for thirty-one years. This relates to the reality that they had actually been occupying the site since then. Under cover of darkness on December 28, 1598, the Burbage brothers, Peter Street (a carpenter) and some dozen workmen

> did riotously assemble themselves together and then and there armed themselves with divers and many unlawful and offensive weapons, as namely swords, daggers, bills, axes, and such like, and so armed did then repair unto the said Theatre. And then and there, armed as aforesaid, in very riotous, outrageous, and forcible manner, and contrary to the laws of your Highness's realm, attempted to pull down the said Theatre, whereupon divers of your subjects, servants and farmers, then going about in peaceable manner to procure them to desist from that their unlawful enterprise, they, the said riotous persons aforesaid, notwithstanding procured then therein with great violence, not only then and there forcibly and riotously resisting your subjects, servants and farmers, but also then and there pulling, breaking and throwing down the said Theatre in very outrageous, violent and riotous sort, to the great disturbance and terrifying not only of your subjects, said servants and farmers, but of divers others of your Majesty's loving subjects there near inhabiting.
> (*Wallace, 1913, 278–9*)

Thus the indignant legalese of their former landlord, Giles Allen, some three years later, as he pursued Cuthbert Burbage through the courts. In fact Allen was legally correct; property standing on the site when the lease expired formally passed to him. But he was never able to get a court to rule in his favor. Meawhile the timbers of the Theatre were shipped across the Thames to the Bankside, where they were to be re-erected, by Peter Street the carpenter, as the Globe. That will be the subject of the next chapter.

We do not know all the details of how the Burbages were able to afford all this; they may have borrowed money. But one feature of their arrangements is known and was to prove yet another element in preserving the stability and cohesiveness of the Chamberlain's Men. The lease on the Globe site was assigned to seven persons: the Burbage brothers, William Shakespeare, Augustine Phillips, Thomas Pope, John Heminge, and Will Kemp. But the division was not equal. The Burbages had one moiety (half, or five tenths) of the lease between them, while Shakespeare and the other members of the company divided the other half (one tenth each), contributing £70 each towards the construction costs. The logical inference of all this is that these men had all invested their own money in building the Globe and so were naturally entitled to share in its profits. They thus became what were called "housekeepers" – in addition to remaining sharers in the company, the Chamberlain's Men. So they became their own landlords and took a double profit in the operations of the Globe.

The disposition and value of the housekeeper shares would vary as their holders died or as agreement was reached to allow others into their ranks. There were attempts legally to bind the housekeepers into a "joint-tenancy," whereby they would only convey shares among themselves (*ES*, 2: 417–18). But this was certainly not observed in the long run; shares passed to widows and other heirs over time. There was also potential for friction between the housekeepers and those sharers who had no stake in the playhouse, not least since it would appear that there was more money (perhaps three times as much) in being a housekeeper than in merely being a company sharer. A replication of these divisions when the company also acquired use of the Blackfriars playhouse only compounded the pressures (see pp. 292–3). These issues certainly boiled over in the 1630s, when some players became aggrieved at not being given the opportunity to obtain housekeeper shares as their predecessors had done. The Lord Chamberlain was called upon to arbitrate the matter and the *Sharers' Papers* were the depositions put before him by various parties in the dispute, including Cuthbert Burbage who by then had a longer memory of everything that had happened than anyone else (Gurr, 2004*a*, 271–80). To all appearances these matters were handled amicably during Shakespeare's working lifetime, though as early as 1615 they caused major discord within John Heminge's own family (see p. 164).

The one really jarring note in early company relations came in fact with Will Kemp's withdrawal from the consortium that had bought shares in the Globe; he withdrew from the agreement before it went into effect and his share was redistributed among Shakespeare, Phillips, Pope, and Heminge, leaving them with one and a-quarter shares each. This was evidently a prelude to his departure from the company itself. Precisely when he left is unclear. The latest play we can associate him with, as we have seen, is Jonson's *Every Man In His Humour*. He is not in the cast-list for *Every Man Out of His Humour*, staged at the Globe in the autumn of 1599 – one of the first plays performed there (Jonson, 2012*h*, 239–40). And it seems likely that he had left before the company in fact moved to its new playhouse.

Thomas Platter, the Swiss tourist who described the penny-by-penny payment system, recorded visits to two performances where he had encountered it. He was only in England from September 18 to October 20, 1599, so both were in the same time-frame. One, which I discuss later, was of *Julius Caesar* at the Globe (see p. 267). The other was of an unknown play "in Bishopgate," which at this date must mean the Curtain. He described there a routine in which a master and servant "both got drunk, and the servant threw his shoe at his master's head and they both fell asleep" (*ES*, 2: 365). In *Every Man Out of His Humour*, the tavern jester, Carlo Buffone remarks: "would I had one of Kemp's shoes to throw after you" (4.5.118). Kemp in this scenario must have joined the company that succeeded the Chamberlain's Men at the Curtain, and devised this comic routine for them. This is his old company's salute to him.

Why Kemp left is a matter for conjecture. But it is surely telling that the break happened as the company prepared to cross the River Thames and take up residence at the Globe on the Bankside, very close to Henslowe's Rose. Whether by accident or by design the move proved to be not only a geographical one, but one that changed the tone of the company's repertory – in good part because of Kemp's departure. It is likely that the sharers of the company discussed their professional objectives at this time, thinking about the types of audience they would hope to attract. They might feel it important to distinguish themselves from their rivals, the Admiral's Men, who would now be performing barely 200 yards away – probably not knowing until their own plans were well advanced that the Admiral's Men in turn would move to a new playhouse, the Fortune, which Henslowe built for them north of the City.

At the same time, however, they may have heard that moves were afoot to resuscitate the boy players who had been out of business for the best part of a decade. Indeed Paul's boys re-opened in their tiny indoor playhouse in the grounds of St Paul's before the end of 1599, only weeks after the Globe welcomed its first audiences. And there were plans to revive the Children of the Queen's Chapel by May of 1600, because Richard Burbage drew up a lease for them to use his father's Blackfriars playhouse at a rent of £40 a year: it was executed on September 2. Evidently the company's at least notional association with the royal chapel made it possible for them to play there when adult players could not.[23] This must have been bittersweet for Burbage and the Chamberlain's Men in general. It gave Burbage a financial return after all his family's outlay on both the Blackfriars and the Globe. But it also gave an advantage to serious competitors, the "little eyases" who (in the folio version of *Hamlet*) are said to be responsible for driving the adult players out on their travels.

Any or all of these factors may have weighed with the company as they contemplated their move to the Bankside. And it may be that his colleagues felt that Kemp and his jigging, so long a mainstay of the company in the northern suburbs, were not well suited for attracting the kinds of audiences they hoped to bring to their new venue. What is indisputable is that they made no attempt to continue the tradition of jigs after Kemp left. It became a hallmark of the new playhouses in the northern suburbs, the Fortune (from 1601) and the Red Bull (1606), though even there it became disreputable (see p. 220). The Globe – and the boys – would offer different fare.

The change clearly left its mark on Jonson's *Every Man In His Humour*, which was radically revised before it appeared in his 1616 *Works*. The quarto text, as performed at the Curtain in 1598, clearly shows preparations for the jig that was to follow (Wiles, 54). Fifteen of the sixteen named characters come together to celebrate with "Doctor" Clement, who invites them all to "enjoy the very spirit of mirth" (5.3.379–80; Jonson, 2012*g*). The missing character is Cob, Kemp's clown part (see p. 217 and Wiles, 94–8). His long-suffering wife, Tib, is present and briefly condoled, but does not speak. And three characters are dismissed – Bobadilla, Matheo, and Peto – before the end of the scene. In the 1616 version all sixteen of the named characters are on stage by the end of the play and included in "Justice" Clement's determination to dedicate the night "to friendship, love, and laughter" (5.5.71–2; Jonson, 2012*h*). Cob and Tib are there with the others and, as the Justice puts it, "married anew" (57–8) among the romantic festivities.

The quarto thus clearly makes provision for Kemp and three fellows to stage a jig when the comedy winds up and the other characters leave the stage. But the 1616 text makes no such provision. The business of the afternoon's playing is fully resolved within the terms and conditions of the printed text. It might be that the company felt that they could not follow Kemp in a form he had made so much his own, though Augustine Phillips is also credited with writing a lost jig, *Phillips His Slipper*. Or simply that the audience at the Globe had less stomach for the boisterous, bawdy, lawless jig. But the change certainly happened.

There are signs that the parting of the ways was not amicable. In February–March of 1600, by which time he had clearly left, Kemp morris-danced from London to Norwich – a distance of some hundred miles – in nine days, spread over several weeks; it was an impressive physical achievement, which says much for his stamina and athletic ability. He took wagers against his failure as a way to profit from the stunt. Later that year he commemorated the achievement in *Kemp's Nine Days' Wonder* (see Figure 3.3). In his dedication of his book he acknowledges that he has "danced himself out of the world" (punning on "globe") and proudly announces himself to be "one ... that hath spent his life in mad jigs and merry jests." Later on, however, he addresses "the impudent generation of ballad-makers and their coherents" – apparently the originators of "slanders" against him mentioned on the title page – as "my notable Shakerags." It is difficult not to see this as aimed personally at Shakespeare, while the "coherents" might be the rest of the company.

But Shakespeare may not have been above some pointed comments of his own. In *Julius Caesar* (which may well have been the first new play in the Globe) Brutus refers contemptuously to jigging fools (4.3.136). Might this be one of Kemp's supposed "slanders"? Another one appears in *Hamlet*. The version printed in the first quarto (1603) seems related to the moment when the boy companies reopened; the "Tragedians of the City" are said to be traveling "For the principal public audience that / Came to them are turned to private plays, / And to the humour of children" (E3). This would be late 1599 or 1600. This text of the play contains a less familiar version of Hamlet's famous rebuke to certain clowns:

> And do you hear? Let not your clown speak
> More than is set down. There be of them I can tell you
> That will laugh themselves, to set on some
> Quantity of barren spectators to laugh with them,
> Albeit there is some necessary point in the play
> Then to be observed. O, t'is vile, and shows
> A pitiful ambition in the fool that useth it. (Q1, sig.F2)

In this, as indeed in everything he says about acting, Hamlet is at least partly talking about himself: his "antic disposition" is a kind of clowning, which repeatedly defers "some necessary point" in his own plans for revenge. But it is difficult to believe that this would not also be taken as an extra-textual reference to Kemp and the way his extempore clowning sometimes cut across the artistry of Shakespeare's plays.

There may, therefore, have been a personal edge in this parting of the ways. But it seems to have been all of a piece with what we might call professional and artistic differences. Kemp went on the continent for a time, before he returned and in 1602 joined Worcester's Men, resuscitating his trademark jig. But he died the following year. That company, however – later Queen Anne's Men, playing at the Red Bull – was one of those noted for keeping jigs alive and other forms of populist theatre, such as pyrotechnics, when such fare was no longer fashionable at the Globe. The Chamberlain's Men, as we shall see, replaced Kemp with a very different style of comedian (see p. 264).

Notes

1 Lord Hunsdon occupied the old Infirmary, which was also not far from the proposed playhouse.
2 Holger Schott Syme (2010) is right to point out that there is no evidence that Burbage built the Blackfriars specifically as a playhouse for the Chamberlain's Men. Family attachments apart, he may simply have been looking for a new investment and hoping to lease it to another company. The Oldcastle controversy, however, lends some support to the assumption that the Chamberlain's Men were aggrieved with Lord Chamberlain Cobham about *something* and his role in blocking the use of the Blackfriars seems to me the best explanation we have.

3 See Paul Yachnin's notion of "populuxe art" in Dawson and Yachnin, 2001; Yachnin 2005.
4 I am implicitly here questioning the account of the liberties given in Steven Mullaney's influential *The Place of the Stage* (1988), esp. pp. vii–ix, 21–2, 44–60. It is true that *some* of the liberties had unsavoury associations; that of the Clink had the Rose – and subsequently the Globe – rubbing shoulders with extensive brothels. But the playhouses always remained under direct royal control, policed by the Masters of the Revels and subject to the authority of relevant county justices. Blackfriars never had such unsavoury associations.
5 See, for example, early announcements in *The Guardian* and *The Evening Standard*, with pictures: https://www.theguardian.com/culture/2012/jun/06/shakespeare-curtain-theatre-shoreditch-east-lonfon; http://www.standard.co.uk/news/london/curtain-lifts-on-open-air-stage-at-shakespeare-theatre-site-in-shoreditch-8464712.html. The square shape was discussed on US radio (NPR): http://www.npr.org/2016/05/21/478962867/.
6 See http://www.bbc.co.uk/news/uk-england-london-36304627.
7 Virtually everything we used to know about the Curtain prior to the discovery of its remains is included in Stern, 2009c. My section here is indebted to it; also Ingram, 1979.
8 It is partly odd because the phrasing "discovers himself" normally means "removes his disguise." But the context here makes that extremely unlikely. This is the first we see of Bobadilla, who has no motivation at this point to be in disguise.
9 Corambis is renamed Polonius in the second quarto (1604/5) and folio versions of the play, where there is no overt reference to an arras.
10 I am one of a small minority who believes that the reference is not to Essex, but to his successor in Ireland, Charles Blount, Lord Mountjoy, the man who actually did bring "rebellion broachèd on his sword." See Dutton, 2016, 173–99.
11 In *Antonio's Revenge*, for Paul's boys, Marston signals the the different genre of this play from the earlier *Antonio and Mellida* when he refers in the Prologue to "our black-visaged shows" (20). In *Northward Ho!* (also Paul's boys) Webster and Dekker talk of "the stage hung all with black velvet," though the reference is specifically to plays at court – where the cloth would naturally be more expensive (1607, E3).
12 In instances such as those in *Thomas, Lord Cromwell* ("*The music plays, they bring out a banquet*") or *Macbeth* ("*Banquet prepared*", 3.4.0 SD) an illusion of realism could be maintained by having the stage personnel dressed as servants.
13 The "plat" or "plot" of *2 The Seven Deadly Sins* is catalogued as MSS 19 in the Henslowe–Alleyn papers at Dulwich College and can be accessed online: http://www.henslowe-alleyn.org.uk/images/MSS-19/01r.html.The online commentary suggests that the "Ned" named in the "plot" is Edward Alleyn but

this is *highly* unlikely. Other senior and adult players are identified either by the honorific "Mr" (Master) or at least given a full surname. "Ned" has the single, minor and *transvestite* role of Rodope and would be played by a boy or young man, not by Master Alleyn.

14 See Kathman, 2004*a*. This was challenged by Andrew Gurr (2007), to which Kathman replied – in my view definitively – in (2011). The long-standing assumption that the "plot" must reflect a production involving Edward Alleyn *and* Richard Burbage would locate it circa 1591; that starts with the presumption that it involved Alleyn, even though he is not named in it, since it can be traced in the Henslowe–Alleyn papers in Dulwich College for centuries. One strength of Kathman's argument is that he offers a plausible explanation for how it might have found its way there after Alleyn's death. It is an anomalous item there, whatever else we make of it. The debate is best chronicled in the *Lost Plays Database* established by Roslyn Knutson. See http://www.lostplays.org/index.php/Second_Part_of_the_Seven_Deadly_Sins,_The.
15 Gurr, 2007, 79. Gurr is in fact arguing for the old association of the play with Strange's Men in the early 1590s, which I do not agree with. But the unique status of Kemp was the same in both companies.
16 *The Scourge of Folly* is cited from Schoenbaum, 1987, 200.
17 According to Mary Edmond (2004), Condell was probably born in 1576 and so would be around twenty-one at the time of the "plot", a good age for Ferrex. He was married in 1596 to the daughter of a gentleman of means and it has reasonably been speculated that he might have bought his share in the company – perhaps taking the place of Bryan – with the dowry she brought.
18 Lydgate's reputation has fallen considerably since. It has never really recovered from a withering eighteenth-century description of him as "a voluminous, prosaic and drivelling monk."
19 From *Martin and Marsorius* (1589), B3v. The "pudding" was the pig's bladder on the end of the fool's stick and the wooden ladle was to collect money from the audience.
20 Kemp is not known to have visited Germany, though he certainly visited Denmark. He and two other future fellows of Shakespeare, George Bryan and Thomas Pope, entertained Frederick II of Denmark at the castle we know as Elsinore.
21 Wiles, 1987, 51. This section is indebted to the chapter, "Kemp's Jigs", pp. 43–60. See also West, 2009 and Astington, 2014.
22 The conventions for the clowns' roles in tragedies were different and it seems less likely that they were followed by jigs – though Thomas Platter's account of *Julius Caesar* certainly suggests it concluded with dancing (see pp. 267–8).
23 The licensing of the boy companies was on a different basis from that of the adult companies, which is why they were both free to compete with the near-monopoly of the Chamberlain's and Admiral's Men.

6

"The Great Globe Itself"

Far and away the most revealing document about the physical characteristics of the Globe[1] is the contract which Henslowe and Alleyn drew up with Peter Street for the construction of their new Fortune playhouse, dated January 8, 1600. Street was the master carpenter who had erected the Globe for the Burbage consortium and it is clear that he had done a sufficiently impressive job that it was to be used in almost every respect as a model for the Fortune. Leaving aside some of the legal preamble, and some of the terms and conditions to which Street was required to submit, it reads:

> The frame of the said house [is] to be set square and to contain fourscore foot of lawful assize every way square without and fifty-five foot of like assize square every way within, with a good sure and strong foundation of piles, brick, lime and sand both without & within to be wrought one foot of assize at the least above the ground. And the said frame to contain three storeys in height. The first or lower storey to contain twelve foot of lawful assize in height. The second storey eleven foot of lawful assize in height. And the third or upper storey to contain nine foot of lawful assize in height, all which stories shall contain twelve foot and a half of lawful assize in breadth throughout, besides a jutty forwards in either of the said two upper storeys of ten inches of lawful assize, with four convenient divisions for gentlemen's rooms and other sufficient and convenient divisions for two penny rooms with necessary seats to be placed and sett as well in those rooms as throughout all the rest of the galleries of the said house and with suchlike stairs, conveyances & divisions without & within as are made & contrived in and to the late erected playhouse on the Bank in the said parish of Saint Saviour's called the Globe; with a stage and tiring house to be made, erected & set up within the said frame, with a shadow or cover over the said stage. ... And which stage shall contain in length forty and three foot of lawful assize and in breadth to extend to the middle of the yard of the said house. The same stage to be paled in below with good strong and sufficient new oaken boards.

Shakespeare's Theatre: A History, First Edition. Richard Dutton.
© 2018 Richard Dutton. Published 2018 by John Wiley & Sons Ltd.

And likewise the lower storey of the said frame withinside, and the same lower storey to be also laid over and fenced with strong iron pikes. And the said stage to be in all other proportions contrived and fashioned like unto the stage of the said playhouse called the Globe; with convenient windows and lights glazed to the said tiring house; and the said frame, stage and staircases to be covered with tile and to have a sufficient gutter of lead to carry & convey the water from the covering of the said stage to fall backwards; and also all the said frame and the staircases thereof to be sufficiently enclosed without with lath, lime & hair [i.e. plaster], and the gentlemen's rooms and two penny rooms to be sealed with lath, lime & hair, and all the floors of the said galleries, storeys and stage to be boarded with good & sufficient new deal boards, of the whole thickness where need shall be; and the said house and other things beforementioned to be made & done to be in all other contrivitions [contrivances?], conveyances, fashions, thing and things effected, finished and done according to the manner and fashion of the said house called the Globe, saving only that all the principal and main posts of the said frame and stage forward shall be square and wrought pilasterwise [in the manner of pilasters, square or rectangular wooden pillars projecting from a wall, usually with bases and capitals], with carved proportions called satyrs to be placed & set on the top of every of the same posts; and saving also that the said Peter Street shall not be charged with any manner of painting in or about the said frame house or stage, or any part thereof, nor rendering the walls within, nor sealing any more or other rooms than the gentlemen's rooms, two penny rooms and stage before remembered ... And saving that the said Peter Street shall ... also make all the said frame in every point for scantlings [builders' regulated measures] larger and bigger in assize than the scantlings of the timber of the said new erected house called the Globe. (*ES* 2: 436–9)[2]

Street was to be paid £440, and the work was to be completed by July 25, some twenty-eight weeks from the date of the contract. If the construction of the Globe followed the same schedule, and commenced when the lease was signed, it should have been finished by the first week of September.

The most obvious difference between the Globe and the Fortune is that the latter was to be square, outside and in (as now know, somewhat like the Curtain: p. 198), whereas the Globe was polygonal in structure, possibly finished off with plaster to appear circular. The recent excavations of the Globe, though much less extensive than those of the Rose, have shown that it was indeed larger than that playhouse, or indeed than the Theatre and the Curtain. Whereas they were all about 72 ft (21.95 m) in diameter, the Globe either had sixteen sides and was 84 ft 6 in (25.76 m) in diameter or eighteen sides and was 95 ft (28.96 m) in diameter (Bowsher and Miller, 2009, 89–102; Bowsher 2012, 89–96).[3]

The specifications for the Fortune might incline us towards the former: 80 ft (24.38 m) square on the outside and 55 ft (16.76 m) square on the inside, the latter figure being arrived at by allowing for galleries on all sides 12½ ft (3.81 m) deep.

On the face of it the Globe's layout would give better sightlines, especially to those in the three storeys of two penny rooms, but perhaps Street was meant to adjust the groundplan in places to allow for this. Alleyn, of all people, must have known what he was asking for. The foundation was to be of brick and piles, the framework of wood, which would be boarded within, the whole being coated with plaster. There were to be three galleries, rising to a height of 32 ft (9.75 m); their roof was to be tiled. (In what was probably a cost-cutting decision – which proved to be singularly unfortunate – the Globe was thatched with reeds.) Also to be tiled were a "shadow or cover" over the stage, the "heavens," and the staircases. Here modeling it on the Globe works to our disadvantage, since Henslowe and Alleyn could assume Street knew what was expected – including any special provision in "the heavens" to fit descent machinery, and indeed the number of staircases. There are indications elsewhere that there would be two of them. That is the number specified in the 1613 contract for the Hope theatre (*ES* 2: 466–8), in which the Swan is several times mentioned as a model – as it may well have been for the Globe. And when the Globe burned down that year, it was noted that there were only "two narrow doors" by which to escape (Gurr, 2009, 203–4).

The Galleries

The fact that the staircases needed to be tiled and enclosed with plaster confirms that they were on the outside of the building. How, precisely, they afforded access to the various parts of the playhouse is a matter for some conjecture. It was, presumably, possible to pay a penny and pass without climbing through to the pit, a place for open standing, with no shelter from the elements. It might equally be possible to gain access to the stairs and move up, paying either a total two pence for access to the "two penny rooms" or three pence for the even more comfortable "gentlemen's rooms." What is least clear is the status of and access to the lowest of the three storeys of galleries. The Fortune contract is quite explicit that only the "gentlemen's rooms" and the "two penny rooms" are to be sealed with "lath, lime and hair" – presumably leaving parts of the galleries, both there and by implication at the Globe, less comfortably furnished and possibly without seating.

Indeed, Dekker, in the epilogue to *Satiromastix* (performed at the Globe in 1601) is quite explicit that some of the galleries were used for standing rather than sitting, though he does not specify which they were. His Tucca calls on one section of the audience to "bear witness, all you gentle-folks (that walk i'the galleries)" and finally bids them "Good night, my two penny tenants. Good night" (Epilogus 5–6, 31–4). This seems to suggest that a second penny at the Globe at that date got you entry to covered space where you might walk, though it might not guarantee you seating. If so, it differed from the Fortune, the contract for which explicitly requires seating *throughout the galleries*: "with necessary seats to be placed and set as well in those rooms [i.e. the gentlemen's and two penny rooms] as throughout all the rest of the galleries of the said house." Dekker does, however, confirm in the same play that there was seating in *some* Globe galleries, since Horace is told that henceforth he "shall not sit in a gallery, when your comedies and interludes have entered their actions and there make vile and bad faces at every line" (5.2.298–300).

As recently as 1596, William Lambarde had suggested that the best accommodation at the Theatre only afforded "a quiet standing," with no mention at all of seating. The 1600 Fortune contract is the first document to specify seating in *all* the galleries, though it seems also implicit in Platter's account of payment penny-by-penny. Between the refurbishment of the Rose in 1592 (see p. 62), the building of the Swan in 1595, the Globe in 1599, and the Fortune in 1600, there seems to have been a competitive drive for each new building to be grander and better fitted than its predecessor – we see it explicitly in the Fortune contract's stipulation that it shall *mostly* be like the Globe, but with *tiled* roofs and "scantlings ... larger and bigger in assize than the scantlings of the timber of the said new erected house called the Globe." (And did the Globe have any equivalents of the satyrs adorning the main posts of the stage?)

Possibly the Globe was caught betwixt and between in respect of the accommodations on offer, retaining standing in some galleries but not others. If so, the likeliest candidates for covered standing room would include (if they were not indeed restricted to) the lowest level of them. The Van Buchell drawing of the Swan shows two sets of steps from the pit to the lowest gallery, one clearly-marked "*ingressus*" (see Frontispiece). The affinity of the pit with the lowest gallery might have made them extensions of one another, with the audience standing in both but perhaps being prepared at times to pay an extra penny for protection from the elements. This would, however, have created an oddity when first entering the playhouse: having to choose between paying two pennies for covered standing – or exactly the same amount for the seated comfort of a "two penny room." Why not take the comfort?

There are, however, other possibilities. One is that there was seating in all the galleries, but that some people *chose* to stand and walk about some of the time rather than to sit. In the Fortune, the galleries other than the gentlemen's and the two penny rooms were not partitioned, so that it would have been possible to walk around three-quarters of the inner circumference of the playhouse, seeing the stage – and the audience – from various perspectives. In that scenario the two options simply catered to different tastes – the one to gregarious types (on the whole, perhaps more likely to be young men) who welcomed the opportunity to walk about and socialize in the lower gallery. Tucca's salute to his "two-penny tenants" that "walk in the galleries" suggests that it was, to say the least, a distinctive section of the audience, one that perhaps kept the players on their toes. The other option catered to those (including, we might suppose, well-bred young ladies) who preferred both comfort and private space to themselves.

Each of these scenarios does rather suggest that the entrances to the Globe dictated what was essentially a two-tier system, lower and upper, each of which offered a basic facility and an enhanced one – on the one hand, pit and "standing gallery," or on the other two penny rooms and gentlemen's rooms. Andrew Gurr sees in all this a marked social stratification of the audience in a "vertical divide" throughout the theatre: "the lowest of the three tiers of gallery was associated by its *ingressi* with the lowly in the yard, whereas the upper levels welcomed the gentry and richer citizens with their cushions" (2009, 205). The lords' rooms offered another level of distinction altogether.

Lords' Rooms

The size and facilities of the tiring house are even more of an enigma than the disposition of the audience; all the Fortune contract tells us about it is that its windows were glazed. We do not know its depth, though it presumably extended back into the gallery space behind the stage, minimizing the amount of actual stage space it took up. Nor do we know how many windows there were, or how the rooms behind them were divided or what each was used for. But there is a strong presumption ("as seems almost certain," is how E. K. Chambers puts it: *ES*, 3:118–19) that they included a lords' room, or multiple lords' rooms, for the wealthiest members of the audience, overlooking the stage.

We first hear of such a room when Henslowe repaired the Rose in 1592, paying out 10s "for sealing the room over the tirehouse" and 13s "for sealing my lord's room" (*ES*, 2: 535). Henslowe's latter phrasing suggests that at least one of these rooms was meant for the lord who was patron of the company playing at the theatre, so this may have been an innovation when specific companies became identified with particular theatres, as Lord Strange's Men were then becoming identified with the Rose. But Thomas Dekker's reference to "the lords' room" in *The Gull's Hornbook* (1609) suggests that they were – at least by then – more generally available to gallants willing to pay the price, perhaps as much as sixpence, six times what people in the pit paid, if not a shilling (*ES*, 4: 366; see pp. 293). This squares with the evidence from Jonson's first Globe play, *Every Man Out of His Humour* (1599), which describes a character boasting of familiarity with aristocrats "as if he had … ta'en tobacco with them over the stage i'the lords' room" (2012*i*, 2.2.234–6).

This almost certainly means that those buying such seating must have entered through a privileged doorway at the rear of the tiring house.[4] Even more decisively than those who used the staircases, they would not have to mingle with the lower orders – but would rub shoulders with the actors themselves and the playhouse personnel, a familiarity between the social élite and stars of the stage which persists to this day. As Richard Hosley puts it:

> In addition to the pleasures of seeing and being seen, hob-nobbing with the players (what we should call "going back stage") may also have been an attraction of sitting in the Lords' room, for one must have reached it by a stairway within the tiring-house. (On "going back stage" compare Gossip Mirth, a "presenter" sitting upon the stage in Jonson's *Staple of News*, 1626: "I was i' the Tiring-house a while to see the Actors drest.") And still another attraction of sitting in the Lords' room may have been, as Lawrence suggests, that one entered the theatre by a door leading from the street directly into the tiring-house, thus escaping contact with the mob.
>
> *(1957, 25; citing Lawrence, 1912, 33)*

Earlier playhouses like the Theatre and the Curtain may not have had such a facility. But these rooms seem to be what are indicated in the De Witt / van Buchell drawing of the Swan, a gallery or row of boxes above door height in the face of the tiring house.[5] There indeed people "not only see everything well, but can be seen," as Thomas Platter put it (though he was talking about the gentlemen's rooms: see pp. 159–60). This arrangement thus preserved, after a fashion, the social decorum we observed at performances in colleges and country houses, where the seating of the élite took distinct precedence over the convenience of the players. The rest of the audience could hardly see the action of the play without also seeing those in these rooms – as well as those only marginally socially inferior, occupying the "gentlemen's rooms," which seem to have been situated at stage-level, to its right and left. This would have been especially the case for action on the upper stage, such as when *"They heave Antony aloft to Cleopatra"* (4.15.38SD) – *Antony and Cleopatra* (circa 1606–8) is certainly a Globe play.

This presumably means that some of the space either within or adjacent to the lords' rooms could be used for playing when a show called for it. In the 1597 first quarto of *Romeo and Juliet*, which presumably describes staging at the Theatre, a stage direction reads *"Enter Romeo and Juliet at the window"* (3.5.0) which may suggest that, there at least, the upper tier in the tiring house contained a number of discrete rooms with glazed windows, which could be opened for playing as necessary – rather than an open gallery. This would make it relatively easy to limit the number of rooms available for audience use when an upper space was required for playing. As Richard Hosley argued: "the gallery over the stage was also used as a box or boxes for audience" but after showing that barely half of all Globe plays called for such a use, he concluded that it "functioned primarily and constantly as a Lords' room, and only secondarily, occasionally, and then for relatively short periods as a raised production area; and that during such periods it exercised both functions simultaneously" (1957, 23, 31).

There could be no stronger testament to the difference beween Elizabethan and modern attitudes to the social location of theatre, and the placement within it of its audiences, than this statement that appears in the Glossary section of the "Shakespeare's Globe" web site: "Lords' Rooms: located on the upper stage gallery, to the left and right of the musicians' gallery; these were the most expensive seats in Shakespeare's playhouse. Today, no one sits in the Lords' Rooms, as they are used for stage action, but the name has remained." (http://www.shakespearesglobe.com/discovery-space/adopt-an-actor/glossary: accessed 28 November 2016).

Box 6.1 Contentions About the Globe: Size, Audience, Seating on the Stage

Because of its association with Shakespeare, issues relating to the Globe have attracted far more attention and controversy than those relating to any other early modern theatre. It would be tedious to take the reader through them all, blow-by-blow. But I should acknowledge that my account of the Globe involves at least two assumptions which modern scholarship has found contentious: the overall size of the building and the issue of privileged seating. The Fortune contract may *imply* but does not categorically state that the new playhouse should be the same size as the Globe. Shakespeare's Globe on the Bankside – the modern reconstruction – is actually about 100 ft in outer diameter (30.48 m), significantly bigger than the 80 ft square specified in the Fortune contract. This is because of the scholarship of John Orrell, most particularly that in his *The Quest for Shakespeare's Globe* (1983), on which the reconstruction was based. It is a remarkable piece of work, in which Orrell demonstrates that the groundwork for Wenceslas Hollar's famous *Long View of London* (1647) was done in the 1630s using a perspective or topographical glass, from the top of St Saviour's Church (now Southwark Cathedral), ensuring a methodically high level of accuracy. But the *Long View* itself is not as photographically accurate as it might be, because its elements have been subtly adjusted for artistic effect, and besides the engraving itself was not done on the spot but in Antwerp. (So, for example, it infamously reverses the labels of the Hope and Globe playhouses, the latter being wrongly marked "bear-baiting": see Figure 6.1.) However, some preparatory sketches for the *Long View* are remarkably accurate, including one entitled "West part of Southwark towards Westminster," which is reproduced in *The Quest* on pages 2 and 3. Trusting to that accuracy Orrell deduced mathematically that the Globe measured just over 100 ft in diameter, and that was accepted by the builders of Shakespeare's Globe.[6]

Figure 6.1 Section of Hollar's famous map vista, *London from the Bankside*. Source: Map L85c, no. 29, Part 1, Folger Shakespeare Library.

Aspects of Orrell's methodology were, however, challenged by Franklin Hildy, who argued that he had introduced certain distortions which might exaggerate the figures. In his view the diameter was not more than 90 ft (27.43 m) (Hildy, 1993). And the controversy was intensified in 1989 by the discovery of the remains, first of the Rose playhouse, and second of the Globe. The archaeology of both sites (but especially the Globe) has been limited by their locations, but one thing to emerge is that the Rose was no more than 72 ft (21.95 m) across. The very small portion of the Globe's foundations to be uncovered were sufficient to convince Orrell that his original calculations of its diameter, close to 100 ft, were accurate, but some (especially archaeologists) have argued that 90 ft is more realistic.

The issue will presumably remain unresolved until or unless it is ever possible to excavate the Globe remains further. If we accept Orrell's 100 foot diameter, however, and assume the galleries were the same width as those at the Fortune, we are left with a yard 75 ft (22.86 m) across, and a stage extending more than 37 ft (11.43 m) into the yard – a much more spacious operation, and pretty much what Shakespeare's Globe offers. In staying with the Fortune's figures I am not assuming necessarily that they are *right*, but acknowledging that the relationship of the overall size (inside and out), the depth of the galleries, and the width and depth of the stage *to each other* is one that consummate theatrical professionals in Shakespeare's day chose to adopt. However accurate Orrell's external dimensions might be, all the other figures in his model are guesswork.

On the issue of privileged or conspicuous seating in the lords' rooms and the gentlemen's rooms, we need to consider the issue in relation to wider debates about the nature of Shakespeare's audience. Alfred Harbage first articulated a view of that audience which has lodged in the general consciousness: "I believe that Shakespeare's audience was a large and receptive assemblage of men and women of all ages and all classes ... Unlike some other audiences existing in and near his time, Shakespeare's audience was literally popular, ascending through each gradation from potboy to prince" (1941, 158–9). The timing of that assertion – as the English-speaking world was fighting a war to protect democratic civilization – was significant. The main "other audiences" he was probably thinking of were those in the much more exclusive (because expensive) indoor or "private" theatres, for which Shakespeare would write at the end of his career. For Harbage, the Globe was the home of *authentic* Shakespeare. Some forty years later Ann Jennalie Cook challenged Harbage, arguing that "the more leisured classes" (whom she defines as the "privileged" minority of a very hierarchical society, the ones with the wealth to behave independently) formed the overwhelming majority of his audience (1981). There is plenty of evidence that skilled artisans, apprentices, unskilled workers, and even paupers attended the playhouses, but Cook's claim was that they were statistical outliers. Much more typical would be students at the Inns of Court, like the young John Donne (described by a contemporary as "a great visitor of ladies, a great frequenter of plays, a great writer of conceited verses"). Those with money and free time would always predominate.

Later again, Andrew Gurr challenged the generalized demographic methodologies of both Harbage and Cook, arguing that it was important to recognize the extent to which different playhouses catered to different clienteles and so attracted different social and economic mixes (2004b; 1987). Moreover, reputations and repertoires changed over time. The reemergence of the boy companies around 1600, and particularly of the Blackfriars boys using the Burbages' theatre, represented a particular challenge to Shakespeare's company, since they certainly targeted an élite, high-paying audience which the Chamberlain's Men might well have wanted to cultivate.[7] Their "railing" style of satirical plays, aimed at the court and courtiers, generated numerous scandals, which I discuss elsewhere (see p. 284). At the other extreme the two northern amphitheaters, the Fortune near the site of the old Theatre and the Red Bull in Clerkenwell, seem to have cultivated audiences of citizens and apprentices, with popular Protestant patriotic fare such as the Elect Nation plays based often on John

Foxe's *Book of Martyrs* -- plays like Thomas Heywood's *If You Know Not Me, You Know Nobody* (1604), Samuel Rowley's *When You See Me You Know Me* (1604), and Thomas Dekker's *The Whore of Babylon* (1606). The Fortune may have been modeled on the Globe, but its repertoire was distinctively different, with a more populist edge. Heywood also entertained the Red Bull audience with his five "Ages" plays (*The Golden, Silver, Brazen* and *Iron Ages*, the last in two parts, all circa 1610–13), popularizations of classical myths and tales, staged on a grand scale and with spectacular properties and effects. *The Silver Age*, for example, includes these stage directions: "*Enter Pluto with a club of fire, a burning crown ... and a guard of devils, all with burning weapons*"; "*Jupiter appears in his glory under a rainbow*"; "*Thunder, lightnings, Jupiter descends in his majesty, his thunderbolt burning*"; "*fireworks all over the house.*" The northern amphitheaters developed particular reputations for pyrotechnics.

Shakespeare's company seems on the whole to have steered a middle course between catering for coterie audiences and pandering to popular tastes. As Andrew Gurr puts it: "As always ... its offerings and playgoers stood midway between the familiar extremes of amphitheatre reputation and hall [i.e. indoor] playhouse snobbery, which first began to show themselves in the year the Globe was built" (1987 ed., 190). In the latest edition he puts it slightly differently, arguing that "Shakespeare's company avoided the 'public' or popular tag which clung to Henslowe's companies and also the risks of being outrageous which the Blackfriars boys ran to get their 'private' or 'select' playgoers into their seats" (2004*b*, 188).[8]

The issue of seating within the Globe, and most particularly the conspicuous position of the lords' room and the gentlemen's rooms, can thus been seen as related to commercial competition. The Globe did not cater solely for the most privileged of playgoers, the most extravagant of whom at the Blackfriars paid as much as 6d. or even 12d. (over and above the 6d. entry charge) to sit on the stage itself, as much the center of attention as the play – up to twelve times the cost of entry to the Globe's pit. But it did cater at somewhat lower cost for a number of such customers wishing to display themselves in the prestige rooms (and, at least for a time, on the stage itself) and demonstrate the kind of social superiority they doubtless enjoyed outside of the theatre. At the same time, almost anyone could – and did – brave the weather and stand in the Globe's pit.

I need to say more in this context about Leslie Hotson's *Shakespeare's Wooden O* (see p. 5). As I mentioned earlier, Hotson describes many other instances of the kind of hierarchically-conscious audience arrangements such as I described in Christ Church Hall for Elizabeth at Oxford in 1566. It is perfectly clear that these were the *norms* in such private theatricals as those at court, university colleges, and other privileged institutions, such as civic guildhalls and the great houses of the aristocracy and gentry – indeed most of the playing spaces we have imagined Shakespeare using before he can be identified on the London stage.

But Hotson gets carried away and tries to argue that the model was transposed very substantially into the Globe. He argues, in particular, that not only were there lords' rooms above the stage but also that substantial numbers of wealthy and well-dressed people habitually sat on the stage. This is surprising because it is popularly supposed that sitting on the stage was a distinctive feature of the indoor, "private" theatres.[9]

The Fortune contract confirms that the stage at the Globe was 43 ft (13.11 m) wide, leaving about 6 ft (nearly two metres) on either side between its edge and the galleries.[10] It extended to the middle of the yard, some 27½ ft (8.38 m), though some of that depth would have been taken up by the tiring house. It was certainly large enough to accommodate some spectators – far more so, as we shall see, than the Blackfriars (see p. 294). And E. K. Chambers perhaps surprisingly claims, of seating spectators on the stage, that "as it certainly originated in the *public* houses, so it maintained itself there in spite of the grumbles of the ordinary spectators" (*ES* 2: 536; my emphasis). He cites two pieces of evidence. One is the *Epigrams* of Sir John Davies, published (and banned) in 1599, but apparently written some years earlier; Epigram 3 has Rufus, "the courtier at the theater" who "Doth … to the stage transfer" and Epigram 28 speaks of "He that dares take tobacco on the stage." The second item from 1599 is Jonson's *Every Man Out of His Humour*, which (as noted earlier) is the first printed play to have been written for and performed at the Globe. In it Carlo Buffone offers the foolish Sogliardo a lot of advice about, in effect, how to be even more foolish: "and when it comes to plays, be humorous, look with a good starched face, and ruffle your brow like a new boot, laugh at nothing but your own jests, or else as the noblemen laugh, that's a special grace you must observe … Ay, and sit o'the stage and flout – provided you have a good suit" (2012*i*, 1.2.47–52). Paul's playhouse, the smallest of the indoor "private" theatres, reopened late in 1599 but there is no reason to suppose that either of these items refers to arrangements there: the references are to public theatres, the latter to the Globe itself.

Chambers advances one last piece of evidence. In Dekker's *The Gull's Hornbook* (1609) the gallant is offered this advice: "Whether therefore the gatherers of the *public* or private playhouses stand to receive the afternoon's rent, let our gallant (having paid it) presently advance himself up to the throne of the stage" (*ES*, 4: 366; my emphasis). Hotson too quotes this passage, but Bernard Beckerman peremptorily dismisses it, accusing Hotson of taking "seriously what is patently a satiric description of a fool intruding where he does not belong" (1962, 97). Patently? Leslie Thomson has recently brought together a wider collection of references to playgoers sitting on amphitheater stages (2010). These include Middleton's *Black Book* (1604), which refers to "Barnaby Burning-Glass, arch tobacco-taker of England, in ordinary, upon stages *both common and private*" (sig. F2r; my emphasis). She also adduces evidence from litigation that people sat on the stage of the Red Bull ("of all places") in the latter half of the Jacobean period.

And Henry Hutton's *Follie's Anatomy* (1619) contains this passage: "The Globe tomorrow acts a pleasant play ... / Go take a pipe of to[bacco]; the crowded stage / Must needs be graced with you and your page" (B2v).

As far as the Globe is concerned, the most compelling evidence *against* the proposition that members of the audience sat on the stage is, as Beckerman argues, the Induction to John Marston's *The Malcontent*. Marston had written the play for the Blackfriars boys but in 1604 the King's Men somehow acquired it, claiming it was in retaliation for a play of theirs stolen by the boys. John Webster wrote an Induction for it, a piece of metatheatrical joking, in which three of the company play "themselves" – Burbage, Henry Condell, and John Lowin – while William Sly appears as a young theatergoer, accompanied by his cousin, "Doomsday," played by John Sinklo. It begins:

> *Enter W. Sly, a tire-man following him with a stool.*
> Tire-man. Sir, the gentlemen will be angry if you sit here.
> Sly. Why, we may sit upon the stage at the private house. (1–2)

"Immediately it is apparent that, contrary to Hotson's fancy, sitting on the stage was not the custom and its introduction was not happily countenanced by the 'gentlemen'" (Beckerman, 1962, 96). The joke is thus the same as in *The Gull's Hornbook* (if that passage is read ironically), at the expense of the gallant who simply does not know the different conventions at the public and private theatres. But Leslie Thomson counters: "Although the extreme metatheatricality of the whole Induction necessarily undermines any exclusively literal interpretation, if one begins with the premise that playgoers did sometimes sit on the Globe stage, it is possible to understand the Sly-Tireman exchange as an attempt to *discourage* the practice" (6) – but thereby also as evidence that it existed.

The references in *Every Man Out of His Humour* and *Follie's Anatomy* establish fairly categorically that there was audience seating on the stage at the Globe as early as 1599 and as late as 1619. The evidence from the Induction to *The Malcontent* and *The Gull's Handbook* proves to be more ambiguous about the years in between. Those included the years (1600–1609) when the company was in direct competition with the boys at the Blackfriars, who certainly allowed this practice, and Andrew Gurr maintains that "[s]itting on stools on the stage was clearly taken to be a very distinct mark of the difference between the audiences for the adult plays in the amphitheatres and for boy plays in the hall playhouses through the decade 1600–1609 when they were competing for audiences" (2004b, 36–7). I am less sure.

Hotson was not wrong, therefore, about audience members sitting on the stage of the Globe, though it may not have happened in that key decade when Shakespeare was primarily writing for that stage; and he must surely have overestimated the numbers – he speaks of "a many-hued insolent phalanx of several dozen" (1960, 26). But he was certainly not wrong about the prevalence of

> hierarchically-sensitive seating in many other places where Elizabethan drama was performed. Indeed his mistake was in not recognizing that simply in the lords' rooms and the gentlemen's rooms Shakespeare's company (and those in other public theatres by this time) had sufficiently adapted the convention to suit the circumstances of a public amphitheater playhouse. The Queen might never have been there in person, but as the lower-paying members of the audience looked through the performance to see the lords and the gentry in their finery, whether in the most exclusive rooms or seated on the stage itself, they saw everything she represented. To this extent, the Globe reproduced in its own way the same kind of hierarchical stationing as we have observed in all the other playing spaces where we have imagined Shakespeare performing.[11]

(Continued from p. 236)

There remains, however, much that the Fortune contract does not tell us. Despite its careful detail about the main structure, it tells us remarkably little about the stage proper; it does not specify its height; the number or location of doors; whether or not there was a discovery space or trapdoors. Presumably Street would remember all of these from the Globe. It also says nothing about painting the building (though it specifies carved satyrs as decorations), because this was expressly not left to Street and his team but doubtless left to skilled professional painters. We recall Heywood's description of the "heavens" in Rome's Campus Martius (p. 98) and even in the much more limited space of the Globe, we must assume that they went for something in rich, glowing colors. The pillars holding up the heavens doubtless emulated the Swan in being painted to look like marble. Hamlet/Burbage presumably gestured to the heavens themselves, decorated with stars, planets and zodiacs, when he spoke of "this brave o'erhanging, this majestical roof fretted with golden fire" (2.2.291–2).

From other sources, we can put together the following: the only contemporary record that specifies the height of a stage is the litigation over Brayne's Red Lion, where the stage was 5 ft (1.52 m) from the floor. This seems high, but it would certainly ensure everyone in the pit a clear view (though they might acquire a crick in the neck). It would also prevent persons in the pit from getting up on to the stage, probably a necessary precaution. The invasion of the stage by the Citizen, his Wife and Rafe in Beaumont's *The Knight of the Burning Pestle* (a Blackfriars play) is not something a company would want to contemplate in reality.

Stage Directions

On many of the other issues we see darkly because a good proportion of the plays we presume to have premiered at the Globe – including those by Shakespeare from circa 1599 (*As You Like It, Julius Caesar*) to 1609 (*Pericles,*

Coriolanus), and three by Jonson (*Every Man Out of His Humour*, 1599; *Sejanus*, 1603; and *Volpone*, 1606) – are strikingly thin in their stage directions and rarely call upon particularly outlandish stage facilities. It is difficult even to state categorically how many doors there were on the stage: certainly two, but we cannot rule out more. The earlier (1608) text of *King Lear*, for example, gives us instances of "*Enter Edmund, the bastard, and Curran meeting*" (Scene 6.0 SD), which strongly suggests entrance by different doors; the next scene has "*Enter the Earl of Kent, disguised at one door, and Oswald the steward, at another door*" (7.0 SD); Scene 8 begins "*Storm. Enter the Duke [sic] of Kent disguised, and First Gentleman, at several doors*" (8.0 SD). "Another" door can be one of multiple, and "several" here clearly means "separate," without committing to how many other doors there might be – possibly only one. The folio version of the play is no more helpful; it has "severally" in all three of these examples. We do indeed finally find something that looks categorical in *Pericles*: "*Enter Pericles at one door with all his train; Cleon and Dionysus at the other*" (4.4.22 SD). But the text has already used the "*at one door … at another door*" formula twice (Act 2 Chorus, 16 SD) so it is difficult to be sure. Is it possible that the option of using the discovery space as an entrance on occasions led to the common use of this evasive phrasing (see p. 200)?

Rather than squeezing the details out painstakingly in this manner I shall go to the other extreme and examine the play from Shakespeare's Globe years with by far the most detailed stage directions. This is *The Devil's Charter* by Barnabe Barnes. Barnes was not a professional dramatist, but a poet, pamphleteer and hanger-on at court, who in 1598 was tried in the Star Chamber for trying to poison someone. We have no way of knowing how he came to write for the King's Men, much less how the play came to be performed at court, but it was, and in the same Revels season as *King Lear* (1606), as the title-page tells us: "THE DEVIL's CHARTER: A tragedy containing the Life and Death of Pope ALEXANDER the Sixth. / As it was played before the King's Majesty, upon Candlemas night [February 2] last by his Majesty's Servants." There is thus the possibility that some features were *only* performed at court. Moreover, the title-page continues: "But more exactly reviewed, corrected, and augmented since by the author, for the more pleasure and profit of the reader." So there is a risk it also contains items never staged at all (which is also true, notably, of Webster's *The Duchess of Malfi*).

Yet nothing Barnes includes is inherently impossible or even improbable at the Globe, judging by what we know went on in other playhouses. It is only extreme in its specificity of detail by the standards of Shakespeare and Jonson, and we might say that it represents what a dramatist thought imaginatively possible in this playhouse. It gives perhaps the most vivid sustained description of any early modern play in performance, and demands attention even if some of it was not actually staged. Alexander VI was the most notorious of the Borgia Popes, and father of Caesar and Lucretia Borgia, whose evil deeds had been inflated to legendary proportions. Barnes makes of their lives a cross between Marlowe's *Dr Faustus* – Alexander makes a "charter" with the devil, and there are repeated scenes of devils and magic – and Middleton's *The Revenger's Tragedy*: lust, ghoulish murder, mayhem. *The Revenger's Tragedy* was itself a Globe play and had probably premiered the year before.

> *The Devil's Charter* begins with the Prologue who
> with a silver rod moveth the air three times./ Enter, At one door betwixt two other Cardinals, Roderigo [the future Pope Alexander] in his purple habit close in conference with them, one of which he guideth to a tent, where a table is furnished with divers bags of money, which that Cardinal beareth away: and to another tent the other Cardinal, where he delivereth him a great quantity of rich plate, embraces, with joining of hands.
> Exeunt Cardinal. Manet Roderigo
> To whom from another place a monk with a magical book and rod, in private whispering with Roderick, whom the Monk draweth to a chair on midst of the stage which he circleth, and before it another circle, into which (after semblance of reading with exorcisms) appear exhalations of lightning and sulphurous smoke in midst whereof a Devil in most ugly shape from which Roderigo turneth his face. He being conjured down after more thunder and fire, ascends another devil like a sergeant with a mace under his girdle: Roderigo disliketh. He descendeth. After more thunder and fearful fire, ascend [another devil] in robes pontifical with a triple crown on his head, and cross keys in his hand: a devil him ensuing in black robes like a Pronotary, a cornered cap on his head, a box of lancets at his girdle, a little piece of fine parchment in his hand, who being brought unto Alexander, he willingly receiveth him; to whom he delivereth the writing; which seeming to read, presently the Pronotary strippeth up Alexander's sleeve and letteth his arm-blood in a saucer, and having taken a piece from the Pronotary subscribeth to the parchment; delivereth it. The remainder of the blood, the other devil seemeth to sup up; and from him disrobed is put [on Alexander]the rich cap and the tunicle, and the triple crown set upon Alexander's head, the crosskeys delivered into his hands; and withal a magical book. This done, with thunder and lightning the devils descend: Alexander advanceth himself, and departeth.[12]

So, in a sequence rich in both Catholic pageantry (the Cardinals' "purple" robes, the Pope's Triple Crown and keys of St Peter) and black magic (blood, the circles on the floor), the Globe's back-stage staff went to town with lightning (a squib, or firework – gunpowder crammed in a tube) and thunder (a cannonball, possibly stone, rolled along the ground backstage: see p. 305). In the prologue to the 1616 version of *Every Man in His Humour* Jonson scorns to use such devices: "Nor nimble squib is seen, to make afeard / The gentlewomen, nor rolled bullet heard / To say, it thunders, nor tempestuous drum / Rumbles, to tell you when the storm doth come" (2012*h*, 17–20). But Barnes had no such aesthetic qualms. He also called on "sulphurous smoke" (playing on the audience's sense of smell) and fire, and a simulation of running blood, drawn with lancets, a popular effect.

We do not know precisely what stage devils looked like, though Middleton in *The Black Book* says of "a villainous lieutenant" that "He had a head of hair like one of my devils in *Doctor Faustus* when the old Theatre cracked and frighted the audience" (2007*a*, lines 153, 156–7). There are several allusions to devils being satyr-like, with the lower limbs of goats, as when Othello sees Iago as a revealed villain: "I look down towards his feet; but that's a fable" (5.2.294). In *Othello* all the devils are far too human, with no cloven heels, but that may not have been the case for Barnes, who is drawing on older, medieval traditions. And we notice that his devils ascend and descend, making full use of one or more trapdoors. It is not clear if they used steps of some design or, as some (probably fancifully) have supposed, mechanisms with mechanical counter-weights. But evidently the effect was meant to be spooky. The space below the stage was commonly known as "hell," and one reason for having the stage 5 ft off the ground would be to allow movement down there without too much impediment (*ES*, 2: 528 n. 3). Sealing off the front of the stage – apparently unlike the Swan (see Frontispiece) – as the Fortune contract prescribed ("paled in below with good, strong and sufficient new oaken boards") of course kept such activity secret.

The opening is by no means the last we see of black magic in the play. In Act 4 Scene 1, for instance, Alexander conjures devils to discover who has committed recent murders, and finds that it is his own children:

> *After Bernardo had censed he bringeth in coals, and Alexander fashioneth out his circle then taketh his rod ... standing without the circle he waveth his rod to the East.*
>
> - *And calleth upon VIONATRABA.*
> - *To the West. SUSERATOS.*
> - *To the North. AQVIEL.*
> - *To the South. MACHASÄEL.*
>
> *Conjuro, et confirmo super vos in nomine. Eye, eye, eye; haste up & ascend per nomen ya, ya, ya; he, he, he; va; hy, hy; ha, ha, ha; va, va, va; an, an, an.*
> *Fiery exhalations, lightning, thunder. Ascend a [devil like a] King, with a red face, crowned imperial, riding upon a lion, or dragon: Alexander putteth on more perfume ...* (612)

It is the mix as before, with lightning and thunder and incantations; to which is added the scary spectacle of a king riding a lion or dragon (presumably an actor riding on the backs of two or more others, draped in a suitable costume). The use of strong smell is increased, with Alexander's servant burning incense in a censer, and Alexander seeking to protect himself from noxious fumes with perfume, which he tells us is "red sandal[wood]."[13]

At Alexander's command: "*The devil descendeth with thunder and lightning, and after more exhalations ascends another all in armour.*" One of the devils "*goeth to one door of the stage, from whence he bringeth the Ghost of Candy, ghastly haunted by Caesar pursuing and stabbing it; these vanish in at another door.*" So Alexander learns that Caesar has killed his own elder brother. Another devil "*bringeth from the same door the Ghost of Gismond Viselli, his wounds gaping, and after him Lucrece undressed, holding a dagger fixed in his bleeding bosom: they vanish*" (all 63). So he learns that Lucretia has murdered her own husband.

Lucretia's "*undressed*" belongs to the convention of people wearing nightclothes to betoken night-time; when the actual murder took place in Act 1 Scene 5 – as distinct from this ghostly recapitulation – the directions read "*Enter Lucretia alone in her nightgown, untired, bringing in a chair, which she planteth on the stage*" (22), while shortly afterwards, "*Enter Gismond di Viselli, untrussed, in his nightcap, tying his points*" (23). "*Untired*" may simply mean "in a state of undress," though it could also relate to having no hair-pieces attached (see pp. 167ff); "*untrussed*" means with his clothes unfastened, while "*points*" were laces or cords which held doublets to hose in the days before buttons were widely used.[14] The most famous – but in some ways least typical – example of this night-time convention is recorded in the first quarto version (only) of *Hamlet*, when the ghost of the old king comes to Hamlet in his mother's study: "*Enter the ghost in his night gown.*" We may note that Lucretia's "*bringing in a chair*" is in preparation for tying Gismond to it while she stabs him; she carefully "*conveyeth away the chair*" when the deed is done – small but important attentions to stage management.

Conventions relating to night-time were important because, performing in daytime, there was no way of altering the light to show the hour. Barnes enterprisingly uses two of these in the scene (Act 3 Scene 5) where Caesar Borgia murders his brother, Candy. One is the use of a clock – doubtless the same we have encountered before in *Every Man In His Humour* and *Julius Caesar*. Caesar's accomplice knows his hour is come when "*The clock strikes eleven*" (56) and the suspension of disbelief is carried forward by the use of a lit torch, indicating the outdoors: "*Enter a Page with a torch, Duke of Candy and Caesar Borgia disguised.*" (Note, among properties listed by Henslowe, "4 torchbearers" suits," p. 170.) After "*the boy putteth out the torch*," Candy verbally keeps up the illusion going: "'Tis very dark" (57).[15]

This sequence, incidentally, draws attention to what must have been a very common piece of stage business, though rarely recorded. Caesar's accomplice says "Here will I stand till the alarum call," to which a stage direction adds: "*He stands behind the post.*" This will have been one of the two posts that held up the "heavens" over the stage, as at the Swan (see Frontispiece). We assume that most of the playhouses after the refurbishment of the Rose in 1592 will have had both a "heavens" and its posts, though the Hope contract expressly requires that there should be no posts. It was to double as a bear-baiting arena, so it was essential that the stage be removable in its entirety; the joints and underpinnings of its "heavens" must have been significantly reinforced. Where, like the Globe, there *were* posts we must assume that they sometimes irritatingly obscured sightlines. But they must also have been very convenient for the actors in moments like this, where a character wanted to remain hidden. Although it is entirely possible that a property was brought on to serve as the "boxtree" behind which Sir Toby, Sir Andrew and Fabian hide to spy on Malvolio reading Maria's letter in *Twelfth Night* (2.5.15ff), one of the posts would certainly serve quite adequately. They may also very well have served as the trees to which Orlando attaches his poems about Rosalind in the Forest of Arden (*As You Like It*, 3.4). The Admiral's Men did have among their properties "1 bay tree," "1 tree of golden apples" and "1 Tantalus tree" but these seem to have been items for particular productions, as the tree of golden apples was for *Fortunatus* (*Henslowe*, 319–20). In most contexts the posts would have served.

After the prologue and its dumb show, the regular action of *The Devil's Charter* starts with the following direction: "*Enter marching after drums & trumpets at two several places, King Charles of France, Gilbert Mompanseir, Cardinal of Saint Peter ad Vincula: soldiers. Encountering them Lodowick Sforza* [and] *Charles Balbiano. The King of France and Lodowike embrace*" (7). Here again, two points of entry, but this does not preclude there being more. This is the first of twenty-two references to drums in the text and stage directions, and sixteen references to trumpets. The action was kept at a high aural level throughout. For example, towards the end of Act 2 there is a dumb-show in which the drums play continuously, while the trumpet gives way to a fife or high-pitched flute:

> *Drums and Trumpets. Charles and his company make a guard ... Alexander being set in state, Caesar Borgia, and Caraffa advance to fetch King Charles, who being presented unto the Pope, kisseth his foot, & then advancing two degrees higher, kisseth his cheek: then Charles bringeth* [Cardinal] *S. Peter ad Vincula, and Ascanio, which with all reverence kiss his feet, one of them humbly delivering up his cross-keys, which he receiveth, blessing them and the rest of Charles his company: The drum and fife still sounding.* (40)

Just as Barnes makes full use of the trapdoor(s), he also takes several opportunities to put the action on the upper stage. Much of Act 2 Scene 1, for example, takes place with Alexander on the battlements of Castell Angello, in diplomatic wrangling with the French king below. This begins:

> Sound drums, answer trumpet.
> [Enter] Alexander upon the walls in his pontificals, betwixt Caesar Borgia and Caraffa (Cardinals); before him the Duke of Candy, bearing a sword; after them Piccolomini [and] Gasper de Foix. (33)

And continues:

> Sound drums and trumpets.
> [Exit] Alexander with his company off the walls, ordnance going off. After a little skirmish within, he summons from the Castell with a trumpet; answer to it below. Enter Alexander upon the walls as before. (36)

Similarly in Act 4 Scene 4, in a military standoff between Caesar (with Barbarossa) and the Countess Katharine, a good deal of the action happens with her on the battlements and them down below:

> Sound drum, answer trumpet.
> Enter upon the walls Countess Katharine, Julio Sforza, Ensign, Soldiers.
> Drums, Trumpets. (76)

Later we get:

> A charge with a peal of ordnance: Caesar, after two retreats, entereth by scalado; her ensign-bearer slain, Katharine recovereth her ensign, & fighteth with it in her hand. Here she sheweth excellent magnanimity. Caesar the third time repulsed, at length entereth by scalado, surpriseth her, bringeth her down with some prisoners.
> Sound drums and trumpets. (81)

These directions call for up to six persons on the upper stage, which speaks to there more likely being an open balcony than rooms with separate windows. The level of action in the last direction speaks to the same point. Countess Katharine could hardly show "excellent magnanimity" [great courage] from the depth of a room; nor is it likely that Caesar Borgia could storm her battlement using scaling-ladders without having reasonably free access at the top. *Antony and Cleopatra* also bears this out. Act 4 Scene 15 begins "*Enter Cleopatra and her maids aloft, with Charmian and Iras*" and subsequently "*They heave Antony aloft to Cleopatra*" (38 SD). So there seem to be four or five boys *aloft*, even before they begin the inevitably clumsy business of heaving Antony up to join them. Such a space must inevitably have eaten into what was available for the lords' rooms (see p. 235). Possibly when a play involved activity on this scale on the upper stage the audience would not be able to use the lords' rooms, or at least be restricted to limited numbers of them.

These two sequences of *The Devil's Charter* also remind us that firearms were very much a feature of the show. Both involve peals of ordnance, loud discharges of cannon, which were loaded with powder and wadding, but not shot. (In *A Larum for London* a direction reads: "*The piece discharges. A great screeke heard within.*") These were doubtless the "chambers" (cannon) which, when fired during a performance of *Henry VIII* in 1613, set fire to the thatched roof and burned the house to the ground; the cannon, which would have been too cumbersome to maneuvre on stage, were kept high up above the stage roof or "heavens," adjacent to the platform from which trumpeters gave the three "soundings" (see p. 110). That's why the cannon wadding got into the thatch. Alexander at one point enters "*with a linstock in his hand*"(30), the forked stick which gunners carried from which they could draw fire for their guns. Shortly thereafter "*Piccolomini, Gasper de Foix [enter], with small shot*" (31), a generic term for gunners who used small arms, like arquebuses. They were presumably armed with their pieces. Most of the male gentry in the play, except the churchmen, would have worn swords – and the fighting cardinal, Caesar Borgia, would have broken that rule too; his sister, Lucretia, uses a knife to kill her husband ("*Three stabs together*" (25)). The tiring house must have carried a formidable armoury.

The Devil's Charter also (to my mind) settles any doubt about the presence of a discovery space at the Globe, and gives more detailed indications of how it was used than usual. Here it mainly represents Alexander's study; the only exception seems to be in Act 4 Scene 4 where Caesar, having defeated Katharine, "*discovereth his tent where her two sons were at cards*" (82). We first see it used as the study in Act 1 Scene 4, which opens with "*Alexander in his study with books, coffers, his triple crown upon a cushion before him*" (15). He is subsequently joined by his sons, Candy and Caesar, and talks at length with them; nothing indicates that he leaves his study at all, but subsequent examples make it likely. For example, Act 4 Scene 1 begins with "*Alexander in his study beholding a magical glass with other observations.*" After brief reflections, "*Alexander cometh upon the stage out of his study with a book in his hand*" (60). We then have the long black magic sequence we have already observed, and at the end of the scene "*Exit Alexander into the study*" (65). Similarly Act 4 Scene 5 opens with "*Enter Alexander out of his study*" (83). He confers with his trusted servant, Bernardo, about getting Astor and Philippo Manfredi drowsy with doped wine and then "*Exit Alexander into his study*" (84). Bernado "*Knocketh at the study*" (86) to confirm they are asleep, Alexander answering from within. Then "*[Enter] Alexander upon the stage in his cassock and nightcap with a box under each arm.*" The "upon the stage" suggests that this is once again *from the study*, a different status of entry from that through the all-purpose doors. He then places "*aspics*," poisonous asps, on both their breasts and they die. Finally he has a simple *exit*, but almost certainly back into the study (88).

There is one variation, when at the beginning of Act 3 Scene 2 the direction reads "*Alexander out of a casement*" (43), presumably one of the "convenient windows and lights glazed to the said tiring house" specified in the Fortune document. This is when he expresses his passion for Astor Manfredi, a delicate subject and probably safer staged with distance between the characters. But otherwise the study is consistently the center of Alexander's machinations, the heart of his web; but for action or interactions with other people he repeatedly emerges "*upon the stage*." This suggests that the discovery space was quite small and that sightlines into it were limited. It is a place where Countess Katharine's two sons can literally be "discovered" or where Alexander on his own can be seen, possibly seated, and surrounded by symbolically potent aids: "*books, coffers, his triple crown upon a cushion before him*" (15), "*a magical glass with other observations*" (60), and the boxes with the deadly snakes. No heavy action takes place there, or interactions between characters. It was presumably quite a shallow alcove, probably created by a wooden framework draped with sheets or arrases – more for brief visual effects than for conducting the business of the plot. We must assume that it could be accessed from within the tiring house, so that actors and properties could be positioned there while a performance was taking place. Though there is no evidence for this, it is not impossible that some limited form of lighting was used to enhance those effects. Given the geographical axis of the playhouse, with the rear of the stage facing due south at midsummer, the area under the "heavens" was always likely to be in shade.

The final scene opens with "*Alexander unbraced betwixt two cardinals in his study, looking upon a book, whilst a groom draweth the curtain*" (104) – the curtain or arras across the face of the back of the stage, concealing the discovery space. Alexander's loose clothing betokens his sorry state, in contrast to his earlier pontificals; he needs the cardinals to help move him around. Yet again he comes out of the study for the main business of the scene: "*They place him in a chair upon the stage; a groom setteth a table before him*" (105). In an ironical twist, the discovery space serves one last turn: "*Alexander draweth the curtain of his study, where he discovereth the devil sitting in his pontificals. Alexander crosseth himself, starting at the sight*" (106).

The music of the play is heavily dominated by the drums and trumpets, but there are calls for some other tones. As the Manfredi brothers are being put to sleep, they ask "good Barnardo" to "let it be thy labour ... / To call for music." Philippo says "Let's hear this music" (85) and later "More music there": "*After one strain of music they fall asleep*" (86). This was presumably from stringed or woodwind instruments. One wonders if Barnes had already seen *King Lear* when he scripted this: it essentially inverts 4.7 of Shakespeare's play (Scene 21 in the quarto version), where Cordelia and her allies play soft music while Lear awakes from his madness; "Louder the music there," the Gentleman calls, as he begins to stir (line 26). There are, as it happens, interesting differences in the two versions of the scene in *King Lear* that may speak to Shakespeare's modest use of discovery spaces. Not only is it a "Doctor" rather than a "Gentleman" who assists Cordelia in the 1608 quarto version, but there are changes in the staging. At the call for louder music, the quarto text reads "*King Lear is asleep*," which reads very much like a discovery direction, with the curtain being pulled back to reveal him. If so the long conversation between Cordelia and Lear which follows was scripted to take place in the mouth of the discovery space. The folio text, presumably scripted later, has a direction: "*Enter Lear in a chair carried by servants*" (21 SD). There is no indication that the discovery space is used at all. Possibly experience showed that the scene was more effective if Lear was semi-upright and clearly visible on the stage.

This is not to say that Shakespeare never used the discovery space at the Globe, but that he used it sparingly and always with consideration of the sight-lines, minimizing what went on behind the entrance. In *Troilus and Cressida*, for example, it likely serves as the tent in which Achilles famously sulks. A stage direction tells us "*Achilles and Patroclus stand in their tent*" (3.3.37 SD). There is no other indication of an entry for them, so it is likely that they draw back the curtain and emerge. Ulysses says "Achilles stands i'th'entrance of his tent" (38) – visibly *outside* the space itself. It is also likely that, at the end of the scene, they withdraw into the space again (there is no scripted exit for them at all, in either the quarto or the folio text).

To return briefly to what Barnes may have learned from Shakespeare's example. In both versions of *King Lear* music helps restore Lear to sanity; in *The Devil's Charter* it consigns the boys to death, an ironic twist on the usual associations of music and harmony. (One also wonders if Barnes had had the opportunity to see *Antony and Cleopatra* when he wrote, since the use of asps seems very pointed, and the text freely makes comparisons with Cleopatra's death.) There is also further evidence of sophisticated musical stagecraft: at the end of the penultimate scene, anticipating their final triumph over Alexander, the devils resolve "Then let us for his sake a hornpipe tread. *They dance an antic*" (104). The hornpipe was traditionally danced to woodwind music, such as might be produced by the hautboys, ancestors of the modern oboe, which feature commonly in texts of Shakespeare's later plays, or later versions of early ones. In the folio text of *Hamlet*, for example, the "*Hautboys play*" at the beginning of the dumb show (3.2.135).[16] In *Macbeth* hautboys and torches usher in two successive scenes, 1.6 and 1.7 – where Duncan arrives at Macbeth's castle, and where Lady Macbeth steels her husband's heart to murdering the king. Later, in the last appearance of the witches, as they prepare the "*show of eight kings*," the text calls for "*Hautboys*" (4.1.105 SD). Perhaps most poignant of all is the brief scene in *Antony and Cleopatra*, where for some anonymous Roman soldiers "*Music of hautboys is under the stage*" (4.3.12 SD). It may not be accidental that all of these instances are in fact ominous. The "hornpipe" of the devils in *The Devil's Charter* is no less so. The *"antic"* that they dance would be a grotesque, bizarre or ludicrous action, of a kind that Jonson often built into his court entertainments, such as the 1609 *Masque of Queens*, as an antithesis to true order. The King's Men performed the speaking and comic roles in such productions and may well have borrowed something suitable here from their court experience – as the *"dance of twelve satyrs"* in *The Winter's Tale* (4.4.342 SD) was certainly borrowed from Jonson's 1611 masque, *Oberon* (see p. 313).

The last, ironic musical twist in the play heralds Alexander's demise: *"sound a horn within. Enter a devil, like a post."* Such messengers often announce themselves with horns. But the message here is a summons to hell: *"The devil windeth his horn in his ear and there [three?] more devils enter, with a noise, encompassing him. Alexander starteth"* (112). The posthorn is thus the final instrument we hear in the play, if not quite the final noise: *"Thunder and lightning, with fearful noise. The devils thrust him down, and go, triumphing"* (113). There is, then, a good deal of music in the play, helping to maintain its fevered pitch. But it is in a limited range: drums, trumpets, fife, hautboys, horn, punctuated with the percussion of squibs and rolled cannonballs. There is little call for stringed instruments. That is not untypical in a play which is a history of sorts. Lutes and viols would be much more in evidence in comedies and romances (as, for example, in the music Orsino calls for at the beginning of *Twelfth Night*).

Barnes has thus used a very wide range of the playhouse's facilities: the upper stage (at one point repeatedly assailed by scaling-ladders), the traps, the discovery space, pyrotechnics, sound effects, one of the posts supporting the "heavens," potent smells, lavish costumes, grotesque figures. *The Devil's Charter* may not be great drama, but it has unmistakable energy. And – even if the text was not staged in its entirety – it is so consistent and repetitive that there is no reason to doubt that most of it reflects the Globe's actual resources.

We may pause to note two things Barnes does *not* call for. One is that he does not call for any descents from the "heavens." This is understandable, in that such entries were normally reserved for deities, and this is a play concerned with devils rather than gods. Yet, given Barnes's liberal use of just about everything else, it was surely not beyond him to call on such machinery – if it was available. This was another stage device that Jonson scorned – no "creaking throne comes down, the boys to please" (prologue to *Every Man In His Humour*, 16) – so its absence in *his* Globe plays is not significant. But even Shakespeare seems to avoid it there. Hymen in *As You Like It* might well have made a descent, but apparently entered on foot, alongside Rosalind and Celia (5.4.106 SD). Even in *Pericles* – a play which offers a foretaste of the kinds of romances which would often use descents at the Blackfriars – it is far from clear that Shakespeare made use of it. The one possible exception is in the vision of Diana that comes to Pericles, which is often staged these days on high. But the text says merely *"Diana,"* which might mean any number of things (5.1.242 SD). It is a serious question whether the Globe that Shakespeare used had descent machinery at all.[17]

Barnes's second apparent omission is in not specifying a "hell-mouth" for Alexander's final exit. Of course, *"thrust down"* makes it perfectly apparent where he is going, but there is no indication of that legacy of the medieval stage, a vivid representation of the ghoulish jaws of hell through which the sinner will pass. We know that the Admiral's Men possessed "1 hell mouth," from an inventory of their properties taken on March 10, 1598 (*Henslowe*, 319). Of all their extant plays the one that would seem most suited to its use is Marlowe's *Dr Faustus*, but interestingly the 1604 version of the play gives no indication of it, the final direction being merely "*They* [the devils] *exeunt with him* [Faustus]" (1995, 5.2.115 SD).

The 1616 version, which most scholars now regard as based on a 1602 revision of Marlowe's text – and so definitely a Fortune play, rather than a Rose one – is notably more explicit (see Marlowe 1995, xvi; *Henslowe*, 206). As the end approaches, the Good and Bad Angel pay one last visit, and we read "*Music while the throne descends*," bearing them (5.2.104 SD); the Good Angel abjures Faustus to "behold / In what resplendent glory thou hadst set / In yonder throne, like those bright shining saints, / And triumphed over hell" if he had followed God's way (109–12). And shortly thereafter "*Hell is discovered*" (114 SD). Was this the "hell-mouth"? It seems quite possible, though it is apparently placed, not over a trapdoor but in the discovery space, where it can suddenly be revealed. Presumably it had been enhanced with images of suffering sinners, to contrast with "those bright shining saints." Thus the final *exeunt* probably took Faustus and the devils, not down through a trapdoor, but back into the discovery space where we had first seen him "*in his study*" at the beginning of the play. So the 1616 *Dr Faustus* uses both a descent and a hell-mouth at its climax, whereas *The Devil's Charter* calls for neither. We can hardly call Barnes's play reserved or understated in its stagecraft, yet these differences may point to some differences of general artistic policy between the Fortune and the Globe – or to differences in their facilities. The plays of Shakespeare and Jonson at the latter, in particular, seem distinctly restrained, and more focused on the spoken word, than what we know of the Admiral's (later Prince Henry's) Men's repertory.

The small sampling of Globe plays we know of other than by Shakespeare and Jonson does tend to bear this out. *The Merry Devil of Edmonton*, for eample, does start as if it intends to emulate *The Devil's Charter*, or indeed *Dr Faustus*. The Prologue introduces us to Peter Fabel, the "merry devil," when he "*draw*[*s*] *the curtains*," revealing the discovery space:

> Behold him here, laid on his restless couch,
> His fatal chime prepared at his head,
> His chamber guarded with these sable slights [black arts],
> And by him stands that necromantic chair …

The space is evidently just deep enough for Fabel's couch and necromantic chair, and decorated with signs of black magic. There is also the clock we have traced from *Every Man In His Humour* onwards -- and the action of the play begins dramatically with its chimes (see p. 200). But having led us to expect a re-run of *The Devil's Charter* the play entirely abandons this mode, discovery space and all. It makes no further special calls on the theatre's resources.

Thomas, Lord Cromwell (pub. 1602) makes more consistent use of the discovery space, notably in two scenes apparently meant to mirror one another. In the first we find "Cromwell *in his study with bags of money before him, casting his account*." The scene opens out for him to talk at some length with a post and then Mistress Banister. While it is conceivable that all this happens in the space, it makes more stage sense that, like Pope Alexander, he would hold the conversations on the main stage. Later we find "Gardiner *in his study*." The Bishop, plotting against Cromwell, is shown in this equal position of power; he then talks to witnesses from the nobility, Suffolk, Norfolk, and Bedford, which again makes more sense if it happens on the main stage.

Between these two scenes there is a comic scene that speaks to both of them. The clown, Hodge, occupies Cromwell's study ("Hodge *sits in the study*"). He is disguised as the Earl of Bedford ("*in his cloak and his hat*"), in a plot to secrete the real earl out of the country. Cromwell negotiates with the authorities then slips away with the earl (disguised as the clown), and Hodge distracts them long enough for the scheme to work. At one point the Governor orders: "Go draw the curtains, let us see the earl. / Oh, he is writing, stand apart awhile." The point is that the discovery space represents power in the play: whoever possesses it is dominant. Cromwell holds it in the first half of the play, and Gardiner towards the end, as Cromwell falls. Hodge's brief, comic reign in there is a marker of the scales beginning to tip against Cromwell. It is effective stagecraft which, however, calls upon few resources. Again, there is no evidence of extensive action in the discovery space. It only has to accommodate a desk. Its symbolic role is what matters most, and to that end the company may have lined its interior with the most impressive hangings they had to signify the authority of whoever possessed it.

The play also introduces us to an important prop, which the company recycled from production to production: a severed head ("*Enter one with Cromwell's head*"), presumably dripping with blood. Seasoned members of the audience would perhaps remember it as the head of Cade in *2 Henry VI*, of the conveniently dead pirate, Ragozine (substituting for Claudio) in *Measure for Measure*, and of the youngest son of the Duchess in *The Revenger's Tragedy*, whose "yet bleeding head" is presented to his deluded brothers (3.6.33). They would see it again as Macbeth's head, and Cloten's in *Cymbeline*. Presumably the make-up team backstage (the tiremen or women?) fitted it with a wig and facial hair to suit each occasion.

Middleton's use of his staging opportunities elsewhere in *The Revenger's Tragedy* is characteristically adept.[18] There is one certain and one likely use of the discovery space. The former reads:

> *Enter the discontented* Lord Antonio, *whose wife the Duchess's youngest son ravished. He discovering the body of her dead to certain* Lords; *and* Hippolito.
>
> L. Antonio:
> Draw nearer, lords and be sad witnesses
> Of a fair comely building newly fallen,
> Being falsely undermined: violent rape
> Has played a glorious act. Behold, my lords,
> A sight that strikes man out of me.
> (2007e,1.4.0 SD-5)

The tableau of the raped and dead woman becomes an opportunity for sententious moralizing. The next likely use of the space is nicely ironic, if I am right: "*Enter in prison* Junior Brother." The formula "*Enter in*" some kind of confined space, like a study or a prison cell, seems generally to betoken a discovery. Junior Brother is "*the Duchess's youngest son*," who raped the woman we last saw in the discovery space, so this would be a very fitting twist – especially since, by yet another mordant twist in the plot, he will shortly be escorted out (by mistake) to execution. Neither scene uses much depth in the space: the first is still tableau; the second presumably keeps Junior at his cell bars while he talks to his gaolers.

Close to the end of the play Middleton stages a good deal of pageantry and a spectacular effect: "*In a dumb show, the possessing* [coronation] *of the young Duke, with all his* Nobles. *Then sounding music. A furnished table is brought forth. Then enters the* Duke *and his* Nobles *to the banquet. A blazing-star appeareth*" (5.3.0 SD). It is uncertain how the blazing star (usually an omen of régime change) was effected. It was either a very elaborate firework, or a painted banner that could be pulled quickly across the stage under the "heavens." This is the only surving example of a blazing star used at the Globe, though it was evidently in common use, since we find the same effect as early as *The Battle of Alcazar* (circa 1589) for the Admiral's Men and as late as 1622 in Rowley's *The Birth of Merlin* with Prince Charles's Men, then at the Curtain (*Herbert*, 136). Here the star precipitates the climax of the play which, like many revenge plays, ends with theatricals gone awry – a masque, in which the masked dancing offers every opportunity for plots to unfold and fold in again upon themselves.

The London Prodigal (1605), a citizen comedy, calls for no elaborate staging or effects whatsoever. There is no recorded use of upper stage, trap, or discovery space. The only demands on properties are for a torch and rapiers, and costumes had to cover one simple disguise: "*Enter ... Luce like a Dutch Frau.*" *The Miseries of Enforced Marriage* (1607) is an interesting case, since there is evidence that Shakespeare knew its author, George Wilkins – an innkeeper and pimp – outside the theatre; it seems reasonable to suppose that Shakespeare may have had some hand in involving Wilkins in writing plays and guiding him on what the players could handle (C. Nicholl, 2008, 208–11, 220–6). It is likely that he collaborated with him in *Pericles* (Jackson, 2003). *The Miseries* is another play that calls for very little in the way of special stagecraft, beyond a couple of instances of swordplay, throwing wine in a drawer's face, and some business with letters. It calls twice for brief business *above*, and draws particular attention to the upper stage. A character below heavy-handedly points it out: "We cannot mistake it, for here's the sign of the Wolf and the bay window."

Even the perennially popular romance, *Mucedorus*, calls for nothing more sophisticated than a bear suit (with a detachable head), a pot, a few swords, "a wild man" and a hermit disguise for Mucedorus himself. The revision of the play for a performance at court circa 1610 – sometimes ascribed to Shakespeare – might have offered the opportunity to open the old-fashioned fantasy of the play to the Globe's extensive resources; but the revised text adds nothing more challenging than a blast of trumpets (see Bate and Rasmussen 2013, 503–7). This differentiates it from the later generation of romances, where descents and discoveries are quite common, when the King's Men had use of the Blackfriars theatre.

Shakespeare only once scripted a live animal in one of his plays. The dog, Crab, accompanies the clown, Launce, in *The Two Gentlemen of Verona*.[19] We do not know if this was ever performed by the Chamberlain's/King's Men, but the fact that he did not repeat the experiment perhaps tells us how successful he felt it had been.[20] Other playwrights, however, did bring animals on to the Globe stage. In Jonson's *Every Man Out of His Humour* the "humorous" knight, Puntarvolo, is accompanied throughout by a greyhound, under the control of his servants; in the latter half of the play he also has a cat with him, to accompany him (because his wife refuses to go) on his planned journey to Constantinople. In his edition of the play, Randall Martin judges that while the dog is certainly a live greyhound, the cat (which is kept in a bag) "is not a live animal," though it doubtless affords many opportunities for unscripted comedy (2012*i*, 1: 252). *The Merry Devil of Edmonton* directs "*Enter Brian with his man and his hound*," not impossibly the same as Puntarvolo's greyhound, though this was eight or nine years later.[21]

In this survey of Globe plays and the theatrical resources they call upon I have deliberately focused more on works that are not by Shakespeare, partly because his plays for the Globe make surprisingly few demands on its resources but also in the expectation that readers will in many cases be able to draw their own comparisons. *The Devil's Charter* is truly exceptional in calling upon so many features of the stage, which it is helpful to know that the company could draw on if they wished (virtually everything we know of in the era, except for descent machinery). But most of the other plays are remarkably modest in the demands they make. Only a few of them use the discovery space, though they do so imaginatively. Even the upper stage is relatively rarely called upon, and often then only briefly, as when Brabantio is called from his bed in the first scene of *Othello* or Celia appears at her window to throw down her handkerchief to Volpone disguised as a mountebank (*Volpone*, 2012p, 2.2); either of these could be staged using only a small portion of the lords' rooms. And the trap is almost never used: *Hamlet's* gravedigger scene is the great exception, and possibly Timon's digging in the woods, where he finds gold (*Timon of Athens*, 4.3), though there is no clear direction to this effect. *The Devil's Charter* is certainly eccentric in that, as in the use of fireworks. We do have to bear in mind, of course, that many of the plays premiered at other playhouses we have considered would have been revived at the Globe – bodies in *Titus* would continue to fall into the pit, Richard II would have still have appeared on the battlements, Juliet would continue to appear at her window.[22]

One thing easily forgotten in reading the texts of these plays is just how much color would have been on stage at some point in all of these performances. As we have noted, the woodwork of the stage and the "heavens" was splendidly painted, while there were arrases on the tiring house wall. But, as we saw with Henslowe, the players also spent a fortune on acquiring fine costumes (see p. 170ff). This was an issue for Sir Henry Wotton, who memorably commented on the splendor of the costumes in his letter describing the burning down of the Globe in 1613, while *Henry VIII* was in progress: "the knights of the order with their Georges and Garter, the guards with their embroidered coats, and the like: sufficient in truth within a while to make greatness very familiar, if not ridiculous" (Schoenbaum, 1985, 276). He perhaps felt the fire was fitting retribution.

Playhouse of the Spoken Word

But, at its core, the Globe was a playhouse of the spoken word, catering first to hearing (audience) and secondly to eyes (spectators). The trio of Shakespeare, Burbage, and Armin virtually assured that. So what kind of acting did this iconic theatre, the Globe, produce or encourage? This has long been a very contentious issue. It is not that we have no evidence, but that the evidence is susceptible to various forms of construction. The argument is sometimes framed in distinctions between "presentational" and "representational" acting, otherwise expressed as between "formal" and "naturalistic" (Thompson, 1997, 329ff). What is fundamentally at issue is whether Elizabethan actors were trained in a rigid set of conventions and gestures whereby they formally "presented" emotional states and appropriate social behavior to their audiences, or whether they naturalistically inhabited the mindset and personal histories of individuals, to "represent" people in their living complexity. As Marvin Rosenberg provocatively framed the argument, were they men or marionettes (1968)?

In many respects it is easier to argue the case that they were marionettes. Most of the "characters" in Elizabethan drama were defined socially by the clothing they wore before they even spoke – servants, lords and ladies, soldiers, priests – which is why costumes were always so important to the players. And in a repertory system which demanded a different play virtually every afternoon, a completely new play approximately every three weeks, lines learned separately in individual "parts," and precious little time to rehearse together – it is tempting to suppose that this must have relied on "presentational," formalistic acting and typecasting: something mechanical and familiar that ran within predictable parameters.

And the case for this seems, on the face of it, to be reinforced by the metatheatricality of Elizabethan plays, with their prologues and choruses, their dumb shows, clowns who wander "out of character," plays-within-plays, references to "this wooden O" or "this brave o'erhanging firmament, this majestical roof fretted with golden fire," and actors who directly address the audience, denying the illusion of a dividing line between the staged event and the wider theatrical experience. Shakespeare's audiences were never allowed to forget that they were watching – or, more to the point *part of* – a fictive experience in which Burbage is always Burbage, "presenting" Hamlet, Othello or Lear, not incarnating them. Our examination of Lady Mary Wroth's depictions of boy actors tended towards this same conclusion (pp. 187–8).

A passage often cited in the debate is this by Buckingham in *Richard III*:

> Tut, I can counterfeit the deep tragedian,
> Speak and look back, and pry on every side,
> Tremble and start at wagging of a straw;
> Intending deep suspicion, ghastly looks
> Are at my service, like enforced smiles;
> And both are ready in their offices,
> At any time, to grace my stratagems.
> (3.5.5–11)[23]

Is the actor playing Buckingham slyly imitating Burbage here, who was playing Richard III – the person to whom the speech was delivered? Does this not suggest that there were a set of poses and mannerisms that in effect constituted "the deep tragedian," reducing his individual interpretation of a role to a set of pre-scripted gestures?

The most developed argument along these lines was that advanced by B. L. Joseph, an extreme formalist, in his *Elizabethan Acting* (1951).[24] He saw the acting of the period as an extension of rhetoric and oratory, key classroom skills in a humanist education, where command over language was an essential attribute of the ruling classes: "'That what is applied to acting in oratory also applied to acting on the stage is evident in the description of [the 'character of'] *An Excellent Actor* ... 'Whatsoever is commendable to the grave Orator, is exquisitely perfect in him'" (p. 1).[25] He also cites Richard Flecknoe's claim in the preface to *Love's Kingdom* that Burbage "had all the parts of an excellent orator" (102). He supports this thesis by reference to John Bulwer's *Chirologia* and *Chironomia*, published together in 1644 as a manual of rhetorical delivery. The full title of these works explains their main arguments, based on empirical study of body movement in communication: ***Chirologia****: or the natural language of the hand. Composed of the speaking motions, and discoursing gestures thereof. Whereunto is added* ***Chironomia****: or, the art of manual rhetoric. Consisting of the natural expressions, digested by art in the hand, as the chiefest instrument of eloquence.* They contain pictures showing how hand, arm, and fingers might consistently and effectively be used in speech. Acting is thus reduced to a stylized eloquence, a mechanical use of predictable gestures, such as those proposed in the preface to the anonymous Caroline play, *The Cyprian Conqueror*: "The other part of the action is in gesture, which must be various as required; in a sorrowful part, the head must hang down; in a proud, the head must be lofty; in an amorous, closed eyes, hanging down looks, and crossed arms; in a hasty, fumbling and scratching the head etc." (cited in Plett, 2004, 441).

Others, however, turn such arguments on their head and argue that paradoxically the self-referentiality of Elizabethan drama creates the perfect conditions for what Coleridge dubbed "the willing suspension of disbelief": the audience, literally all around the players, is taken so far with them through the looking glass as to experience their acting as an authentic "representation" of reality. When we hear "This is Illyria, lady" we are right there with Viola, and have already even forgotten – or rendered irrelevant – the fact that "she" is a boy. We meet the actors more than half way in their attempts to represent their characters' realities.

So Marvin Rosenberg enjoyed himself demolishing Joseph's argument, quoting further from Flecknoe, where he says "Burbage was a delightful *Proteus*, so wholly transforming himself in to his part, and putting off himself with his clothes, as he never (not so much as in the tiring-house) assumed himself again until the play was done" (103). This sounds something akin to the teaching of Stanislavski or even Method acting, which in the terms of this argument would be an extreme version of "representational" acting, identifying entirely with the thing itself.[26] The *Cyprian Conqueror* looks as though it was written by an amateur, who may not have understood professional acting. Indeed, if we look back to the Buckingham speech at the head of this train of argument, we may ask ourselves just how "presentational" it is. Given the levels of irony and duplicity involved in this conversation between King Richard and his supposed ally, may this not be a "representational" account of "presentational" acting, which "Buckingham" is far too sophisticated actually to engage in – a double bluff? Of course, in the long run, "Richard" proves the better actor of the two, so the point is moot.

Peter Thompson is surely right to advise us against "any assumption that there was a single, uniform acting style on the Elizabethan stage. On the contrary, the professional stage accommodated a range of styles. Like all popular entertainment, it was not purist but eclectic" (334). The very mixed styles of the plays we have reviewed surely bear this out. This would in part be because theatre was evolving, and at a great pace. Acting styles were in flux; indeed, one way of reading Buckingham's speech is to see it as a recitation of old-fashioned expectations about acting, which are contradicted by the presence of new-style acting in the person of Richard III. When Falstaff is to play King Henry he demands "Give me a cup of sack to make my eyes look red, that it may be thought I have wept; for I must speak in passion, and I will do it in King Cambyses" vein" (*1 Henry IV*, 2.4.380–3). He paradoxically intends to be more convincing by playing in a style from the 1560s – which, however, was evidently still familiar to everyone thirty years later. Its essence is perhaps best conveyed by a stage direction in the old play when King Cambyses is mortally wounded: "*Here let him quake and stir.*" When Hamlet warns the actors against over-acting, we all know that he is steering them away from an old, Cambyses-like style of acting: "a robustious periwig-pated fellow tear[ing] a passion to tatters ... It out-Herods Herod. Pray you, avoid it" (3.2. 8–14). Nevertheless they continue to use the dumb-show, with its dated and stylized conventions of enacting the "plot" of the play wordlessly prior to presenting the spoken version.

It is too simplistic to suppose that Elizabethan acting in general had renounced the old excesses and conventions in favor of Hamlet's own preferences: "suit the action to the word, the word to the action, with this special observance, that you o'erstep not the modesty of nature. For anything so o'erdone is from the purpose of playing, whose end, both at the first and now, was and is to hold, as 'twere the mirror up to nature, to show virtue her feature, scorn her own image, and the very age and body of the time his form and pressure" (17–24). This is suspect as a generalized statement of Shakespeare's ideal or intention precisely because it speaks so exactly to Hamlet's own condition, a man continually failing to suit his actions to his words. It may be a kind of wish fulfilment, likely to be achieved only sporadically at best while many players hung on to older or less challenging ways, and indeed when playwrights scripted them characters built on old foundations, as Falstaff is built upon the Vice as well as Cambyes (see p. 43).

Yet Peter Thompson spells out the potential in such construction:

> the blending of Vice and human protagonist is at its most vivid in Richard III. It is my contention that the reference was metatheatrically reinforced when *Richard III* was first performed. Only five years dead, Tarlton was not forgotten. Most of the audience would have seen him, hunchbacked and outstandingly ugly, easily imitated by a shape-shifting actor like, say, Burbage. This, surely, is the man who strides across the platform stage at the explosive opening of *Richard III* to declare himself a Vice [he quotes *Richard III*, 1.1.18–30, concluding "I am determined to prove a villain"]. It is a fraught moment in the playhouse. Burbage as Tarlton as future king as Vice/Clown: the new drama encasing the old. The player is addressing the audience directly, partly as Burbage, partly as Tarlton, and only partly as the Duke of Gloucester. (335)

It was indeed in the great tragedians of the day that commentators saw what modern scholars have interpreted as something different, something perhaps akin to "representational" acting, or naturalism. Jonson tried to pin what was so special about Alleyn in saying "others speak, but only thou dost act" (*Epigrams* 59, line 10), as if (perhaps) he transcended mere oratory and took on a three-dimensional reality. Others might, however, conclude that Jonson is saying Alleyn's skill lay in infusing his delivery with the *energeia* which Aristotle had insisted was essential for moving the emotions of listeners. The evidence is never clear cut.

Whatever exactly prompted the departure of Kemp from the Chamberlain's Men as they entered the Globe, the moment seems symbolically apt. Clowns like Kemp built on old routines to cultivate a persona which transcended any particular play. They were only actors by special definition – always more Kemp than Bottom or Dogberry. But the stage was passing to "new" actors, like Alleyn and Burbage. And in recruiting Armin to replace Kemp, the Chamberlain's/King's Men recruited a comedian whose style would complement that of Burbage, not be (as some might conclude) at odds with it: Hamlet and the gravedigger, Lear and his fool, and (as some of us believe) Othello and Iago (see, p. 276 Note 30). Eventually Alleyn and Burbage would be replaced by a new generation in the same tradition, like Nathan Field (Figure 6.2), and the King's Men's great trio of the 1630s, John Lowin, Joseph Taylor, and Eliart (or Eyllaerdt) Swanston. But the tradition essentially ended with them, since the proscenium stage of the Restoration called for a completely different set of acting conventions. We can do our best to rebuild the physical Globe, but we can never recreate the social, aesthetic, and material conditions that produced precisely that style of acting.

Jacalyn Royce has most fully argued the case for the Theatre/Globe being the true making of Burbage (Figure 6.3), their proportions, size of stage and intimate relationship with the audience being what allowed this new style of acting.[27] She focuses on a different sequence in the "character" of *An Excellent Actor*:

Figure 6.2 Portrait of Nathan Field. *Source*: Dulwich Picture Gallery, London, UK / Bridgeman Images.

Figure 6.3 Portrait of Richard Burbage. *Source*: Dulwich Picture Gallery, London, UK / Bridgeman Archives.

"what we see him personate, we think truly done before us" (N2r). There are good grounds for supposing that Webster was specifically thinking of Burbage here, since he speaks of the actor being "much affected to painting," and there are several contemporary references to his being a skilled "limner," including payments of 44s. by the Earl of Rutland to both Shakespeare "about my lord's impresa" and to Burbage "for painting and making it."[28] Only the year before, Webster had written the role of Duke Ferdinand in *The Duchess of Malfi* for Burbage, so he knew better than most what he was talking about.

Royce takes "personate" here to be the key term, a synonym for what we have been calling "representational" or naturalistic acting. She argues that the "stability provided by James Burbage's Theatre precipitated a change in working conditions that revolutionized theatrical methods, particularly the methods of the company that called the Theatre its home. Staying in London presented conditions that made the shift to naturalistic acting possible," adding that "Shakespeare's dialogue provides much evidence of plausible body language and gesture, capitalizing on the visibility of the actor's body in the Globe's performance space." She concludes: "The Globe theater enabled actors to achieve an unprecedented level of physical verisimilitude by providing a new possibility for 'truth' in the visibility – or visible body – of a character" (484, 490, 495).

We can add a tiny detail which bears out the cases of both Thompson and Royce. Richard III was the role that made Burbage a star. In *The Letting of Humour's Blood* Samuel Rowlands, almost certainly thinking of that performance, describes gallants who would "like Richard the usurper, swagger, / That had his hand continual on his dagger" (1600, A2). Shakespeare had built his character of Richard from the brilliant if biased account by Sir Thomas More, which is embedded in the *Chronicles* of both Edward Halle and Raphael Holinshed: "when he stood musing, he would bite and chew busily his nether lip; as who said, that his fierce nature in his cruel body always chafed, stirred, and was ever unquiet: beside that, the dagger that he wore he would, when he studied, with his hand pluck up and down in the sheath to the midst, never drawing it fully out" (Bullough, 1957–75, 3: 300). Rowlands' gallants were evidently imitating Burbage in the role. But nothing in the text of the play tells us that he did this with his dagger, even though the dagger is indeed mentioned (3.1.110). Shakespeare must have communicated the detail to Burbage in rehearsal, helping to turn this frame-breaking role into a memorable – indeed a star-making – piece of naturalistic acting.

It is perhaps sensible to put all this in perspective by heeding the final sentence of *An Excellent Actor*: "But to conclude, I value a worthy actor by the corruption of some few of the quality, as I would do gold in the ore; I should not mind the dross, but the purity of the metal" (see p. 180 on "the quality"). There was only one Burbage and it was Shakespeare's rare good fortune to work in harness with him for at least twenty years. It is difficult to believe that they did not inspire and reinforce each other's strengths. Shakespeare left gold rings in his will to Burbage, Heminge, and Condell – the last survivors of the old team. Burbage outlived him by only three years. His passing elicited much comment, notably the Earl of Pembroke's touching grief: the Lord Chamberlain and richest man in England declined to attend the performance of *Pericles* we mentioned earlier, "which I being tender-hearted could not endure to see so soon after the death of my old acquaintance Burbage" (*ES*, 2: 308; see p. 122).

A Funeral Elegy for Richard Burbage, March 1619 was sadly corrupted by forgery in the nineteenth century. Some versions are palpably false, crediting him with roles such as Frankford in *A Woman Killed With Kindness* (Heywood) and Brachiano in *The White Devil* (Webster), which were never in the King's Men's repertory. This must also cast doubts on suggestions that he played "young Romeo" and "the red-haired Jew," for which we have no further sanction. The version printed in *English Professional Theatre, 1530–1660*, however, appears to be authentic (its invocation to a limner – a painter – once more rings true) and it pays sufficient tribute:

> Some skillful limner help me; if not so,
> Some sad tragedian help t'express my woe.
> But O he's gone, that could both best; both limn
> And act my grief ...
> He's gone, and with him what a world are dead,
> Which he reviv'd, to be revived so.
> No more young Hamlet, old Hieronimo.
> Kind Lear, the grieved Moor, and more beside
> That lived in him, have now forever died.
> Oft have I seen him leap into the grave,
> Suiting the person, which he seem'd to have,
> Of a sad lover, with so true an eye
> That there I would have sworn he meant to die ...
> (1–4, 12–20)[29]

A more pithy epitaph said only "Exit Burbage."

Robert Armin

We may perhaps link something of Burbage's success with what seem to have been deliberate changes in artistic policy which accompanied the move to the new Globe. The first is the choice of Robert Armin to replace Will Kemp; the second is the change in Shakespeare's choice of material for his plays. Armin was already a well-established comedian, having served for some years with Lord Chandos's Men. Although he too claimed to be a "son" of Tarlton, he was

THE
History of the two Maids of More-clacke,

VVith the life and simple maner of IOHN
in the Hospitall.

Played by the Children of the Kings
Maiesties Reuels.

VVritten by ROBERT ARMIN, seruant to the Kings
most excellent Maiestie.

LONDON,
Printed by N.O. for *Thomas Archer*, and is to be sold at his
shop in Popes-head Pallace, 1 6 0 9.

Figure 6.4 The image of Robert Armin on the title-page of *The History of the Two Maids of Moreclacke*. *Source*: STC 773 Copy 1, Folger Shakespeare Library.

a very different style of comedian. He was a small man, probably never robust enough for dancing a jig, and he cultivated the role not of a rustic buffoon but of a droll and wily fool (see Figure 6.4).

David Wiles spells out the differences:

> Kemp, the "Lord of Misrule," was allowed to develop an alternative order, unromantic, libidinal and egalitarian – an alternative to the dominant order of the gentry. Armin, however, played the fool's part. Just as the fool stayed outside of the ordered formation of the morris ... so Armin's stage fools remained perpetual outsiders. Just as the morris fool beat the dancers and watchers with his bladder, so Armin railed at the fools of the world. Kemp's art lay in convincing the spectators that he was their

elected representative, chosen in order to play out their most mischievous fantasies, because he was one of their number. Armin's art lay in being different, so that through parodying normal men he could point up the follies of normal men. (1987, 163)

If Kemp was Bottom, Peter, Dogberry, Armin was (almost certainly) Touchstone, Feste, Lavatch, Hamlet's gravedigger, Thersites, Lear's Fool, Macbeth's devil-porter, Autolycus, Trinculo, and probably other outsiders like Cloten and even Iago.[30]

If Hamlet's rebuke to unruly clowns is partly aimed at Kemp, it is reasonable to suppose that Viola's praise of Feste in *Twelfth Night* might be applied to Armin:

> This fellow is wise enough to play the fool,
> And to do that well craves a kind of wit.
> He must observe their mood on whom he jests,
> The quality of persons, and the time,
> And like the haggard [*untrained hawk*], check at every feather
> That comes before his eye. This is a practice
> As full of labour as a wise man's art.
> (3.1.60–6)

Armin was also apparently an accomplished singer: his singing in *Twelfth Night* entertains Orsino ("Come away, come away, death") even as it mocks his self-absorption, and delights Sir Andrew ("What is love, 'tis not hereafter") even as it points out the folly of his wooing Olivia. And the song he sings at the end – "When that I was and a little tiny boy" – pours cold water over the whole romantic fantasy that the audience has sanctioned ("For the rain it raineth every day" – a refrain that echoes even more painfully again amid the storm in *King Lear*: 3.2.74–7).

Shakespeare had always contrived to keep Kemp's roles thematically linked to the rest of the play, but usually in setpiece moments where he could pursue his clowning without seriously disrupting the action. Armin's roles tend to be more structurally integrated with the wider play – an arrangement which his recurrent casting as a retained household "fool" greatly facilitates. It gives him the freedom to speak uncomfortable truths, becoming – as Goneril complains of Lear's companion – his "all-licensed fool" (1.4.198). It is difficult to believe that he did not collaborate with Shakespeare in planning such roles. He was himself the author of a comedy, *Two Maids of More-Clacke* (pr. 1609) and two witty collections, *Fool Upon Fool* (1600, reissued as *A Nest of Ninnies*) and *Quips upon Questions*. He took the art of fooling seriously and in a way that surely complemented Burbage's skills.

If the pivotal role of principal comedian changed at the Globe, so too did the direction in which Shakespeare, as the company's "ordinary poet," steered their repertory – or, at least, such of their repertory as we can discern (see Appendix). His early career had been firmly based on two staples: chronicle English histories and (broadly) festive comedies. With *Henry V* (probably at the Curtain) he wrote the last of the eight English history plays which, although not written in sequence, traced between them the narrative of England through a tempestuous century from the deposition of Richard II to the death of Richard III and the beginning of the Tudor dynasty.[31] But Shakespeare never wrote an English history for the Globe. Late in his career he wrote the stylistically very different *Henry VIII* (known, before the first folio tidied it into the histories, as *All Is True*), and a performance of that would burn the Globe to the ground. But there are good reasons for thinking that he wrote *Henry VIII* with the Blackfriars primarily in mind (see p. 304).

The earliest play we can locate at the Globe with reasonable certainty is *Julius Caesar*, and this flags what was to replace the English histories. Thomas Platter once more records:

> After dinner on the 21st of September [1599], at about two o'clock, I went with my companions over the water, and in the strewn roof-house saw the tragedy of the first Emperor Julius Caesar with at least fifteen persons very well acted. At the end of the comedy they danced according to their custom with extreme elegance. Two in men's clothes and two in women's gave this performance, in wonderful combination with each other. (*ES*, 2: 365)[32]

Platter took a boat over the Thames, as gentlemen commonly would, so this was clearly the Bankside. It could just be the Rose, but other evidence dates *Julius Caesar* around this time, so there are good grounds for assuming it is the Globe. As we have noted elsewhere, Platter goes on to generalize the point that plays started at 2 p.m. (see p. 267). Here he fixes that time for a specific performance at the Globe. This was around the autumnal equinox, so assuming a show running between two and three hours (including the dancing) everyone could still get back to the City comfortably before dark. It would have been difficult to start much earlier, however, because dinner was the main meal of the day and usually started around noon. The actors were trapped between the audience's eating schedule and the limits of daylight. As the audience made their way towards the playhouse they would have heard the trumpeter high up above the tiring house deliver three "soundings" which marked the beginning of the show (pp. 78–80). It was by now a familiar convention. Jonson, an inveterate experimenter with the conventions, started the Induction of *Every Man Out of His Humour* – at the Globe that same autumn – at the second sounding, while the third marked the Prologue. In the printed text of *Satiromastix*, Dekker also jokingly alludes to the convention, entreating the reader to check the errata before commencing on the play "Instead of the trumpets sounding thrice, before the play begins" (1: 306).

Platter also identifies "at least fifteen persons" on stage. *Julius Caesar* has well over forty speaking parts (some, admittedly, very brief) so this must have meant a lot of doubling – requiring a very well-oiled arrangement for costumes changes in the tiring house – for those who were not in the main roles. Assuming there were by now nine sharers, this perhaps implies three boys to play the women (and probably Brutus's servant, Lucius) plus three hired actors. It would not be surprising if this was a production that occasionally required other company personnel, like the gatherers, to make up numbers in the most crowded scenes, such as the opening where the tradesmen mill about on the feast of Lupercal, or the people listen to the funeral orations, or the battle of Philippi. Still, Platter was obviously impressed to see as many as fifteen persons involved in such entertainment. Sadly, he does not comment on other aspects of the play, such as the costumes. Other evidence suggests that there might be an eclectic mix of historically appropriate clothing with modern items, which would echo the play's famous anachronisms, such as the "sweaty nightcaps" ancient Roman plebeians are supposed to have worn (1.2.245–6) and a clock striking (2.1.192.1). These are often quoted as evidence of Shakespeare's indifference to such niceties, by contrast to Jonson's punctilious accuracy in his two Globe tragedies, *Sejanus* (1603) and *Catiline* (1611). But such anachronisms might have alerted an audience to parallels between historical times and their own, never more relevant than in a play about resonant régime-change at a time when the sands of the Tudor régime were inexorably running out.

We also wish Platter had been more forthcoming about "the strewn roof-house" from which he watched the performance. In his penny-by-penny account of entry he never mentions the lords' rooms, so this is presumably not those. It is most likely one of the well-appointed "gentlemen's rooms" – strewn, presumably, with new rushes to keep it fresh. And since he describes it as a "roof-house" we might infer that it was in the highest galleries, almost certainly above the side of the stage. The drawing of the Swan actually places the "orchestra" – seating for the wealthiest spectators – on the lowest level and immediately adjacent to the stage (see Frontispiece). But we have to be wary of treating the drawing as gospel, and besides the Globe was not bound to imitate the Swan in all particulars. The third tier galleries doubtless gave a commanding view, almost on a par with that from the lords' rooms. Finally, we note that, though the production had no time for "jigging fools," the performance – like the one he saw at the Curtain – still ended with a dance. Platter describes its "extreme elegance" and praises the "wonderful combination" of the dancers, rather than raucous or lewd clowning. It remains, however, a measure of the difference between then and now that a play like *Julius Caesar* should end with any kind of dance at all. But this was obviously the expectation for plays both comic and serious. *2 Henry IV* ends with an Epilogue spoken by a dancer: "My tongue is weary; when my legs are too, I will bid you good night" (30–2).

Shakespeare had written two early tragedies, *Titus Andronicus* and *Romeo and Juliet*, but *Julius Caesar* was a mark of intensified concentration on the genre. The first version of his *Hamlet*, as we have seen, was apparently written circa 1600, and then revised (I would argue) circa 1603/4, and again sometime later (probably circa 1606/8: see Knutson, 1995). *Othello* was written between 1602 and 1604; *King Lear* 1605–6; *Macbeth* 1606; *Antony and Cleopatra* 1606–7; and *Coriolanus* circa 1607 (with *Timon of Athens* variously assigned between 1604 and 1608). People have wondered about the emotional and imaginative pressure behind this output, but there must also have been a commercial agenda: tragedies *worked* for the audience at the Globe, and for Burbage and Armin, or Shakespeare would not have kept writing them. This seems to have been a calculation that the company made, even as they moved there.

At the same time, something happened to Shakespearean comedy at the Globe. This was less immediate. Armin must certainly have performed in *As You Like It* in 1599/1600, since Touchstone is a pun on his status as a time-served freeman of the Goldsmith's company: a touchstone is a smooth, fine-grained, dark variety of quartz or jasper, used for testing the quality of gold and silver alloys by the color of the mark left from rubbing them on it. By analogy the fool rubs up against the people in the Forest of Arden, testing their quality. The role of Feste in *Twelfth Night* could hardly have been written for anyone other than Armin; and John Manningham, a student at the Middle Temple, saw the play performed there in February 1602, so we deduce it was written a little earlier than that. But these are the last two of what are often called Shakespeare's "festive" comedies, following a formula of social unrest or inversion, disguise or cross-dressing (especially in these last two), and processes of self-discovery which finally results in marriages and social reintegration. That gives way in *All's Well that Ends Well* (circa1602) and *Measure for Measure* (1603/4) to a much more skeptical comedy, whose use of bed-tricks (among other things) to effect the outcomes makes for difficult or unsatisfactory resolutions – hence the modern label of "problem" comedies. *Troilus and Cressida*, a mordantly anti-heroic version of the Trojan wars, also belongs to this period.[33] Here again, it is unlikely that these changes were not significantly driven by the company's expectations of what would appeal to their audiences on the Bankside.

But the landscape of the company's competition changed dramatically in the space of a year. On the one hand, Henslowe and Alleyn apparently appreciated that the challenge which the Globe represented was too much for the Admiral's Men – the Globe was hard by the Rose, which was moreover sinking into the marsh land on which it had been built. They resolved as soon as possible to build anew themselves, calculating that the Fortune had better chances of success if it was built on the other side of London; they too may have had thoughts about reshaping their repertory. The Rose did not immediately close down; Worcester's Men are used it occasionally, but we hear of no plays there after 1603. With the Swan also apparently largely inactive, the Chamberlain's Men perhaps unexpectedly faced no further significant competition on the Bankside until the Hope was built in 1614.

But the reopening of the boy companies certainly gave them something to think about. Paul's boys were always much the smaller operation of the two boy companies; though they clearly offered novelty when they opened their doors, it is unlikely that they offered serious commercial competition to the Globe. John Marston was their driving force in the early years, and Shakespeare clearly paid serious attention to the kinds of plays he was producing – and Marston repaid the compliment. Marston's *Antonio and Mellida* (1599), for example, is a romantic comedy of the type Shakespeare had been master of for years; but Marston introduces elements of burlesque and parody which give it a very different tone. And its sequel, *Antonio's Revenge* (1600), unpredictably leaps genre barriers and becomes a revenge tragedy, whose precise relationship to *Hamlet* scholars have been debating for years, never entirely sure who is indebted to whom. Marston's *The Malcontent* (1603/4), first written for the Blackfriars, is also very clearly inspired by *Hamlet*, in such original ways that Shakespeare's company found a way to include it in their own repertoire, as we shall see (see pp. 281ff).

The Children of the Queen's Chapel, who gallingly had occupied the Burbages' Blackfriars property, were always significant competition for the Chamberlain's Men. At least in their early days they only performed once a week, and in a playhouse which perhaps held an audience of 600, one-fifth of the 3,000 which it was said the Globe could accommodate.[34] But those 600 were all willing to pay *at least* 6d. for a seat and the comfort of indoor accommodation, the cost of the exclusive lords' rooms at the Globe (at least in its early years). And both the boys' theatres were within the City walls, easily accessible by its wealthier inhabitants, especially during the worst of the winter weather. Such competition clearly threatened to starve the Globe of its highest-paying customers. Shakespeare's company obviously looked to develop a business plan to meet that threat.

As if this were not enough, the Privy Council privileges which had seemed so clear in 1598 became somewhat less so as time passed. On paper all seemed well. In June 1600 the Privy Council issued a very explicit order restricting the number of (adult) playhouses to two, one in Middlesex for the Admiral's Men (the Fortune, once it was complete) and one on the Bankside in Surrey for the Chamberlain's Men (the Globe). The Curtain, which the Admiral's Men had apparently been using, was to be torn down once the Fortune was in use. Playing at any "common inn" was forbidden, and the number of performances was restricted to two per company per week, and none on Sundays, in Lent or in time of plague.

But it is unclear if *any* of these provisions, other than the plague restriction, was ever enacted. As the Privy Council must well have known, there was already a new playhouse, the Boar's Head, a converted tavern, on the east side of the City and just beyond the City's jurisdiction, in Whitechapel (Berry, 1986). Since the previous summer it had been occupied by a company under the patronage of the sixth Earl of Derby, and Derby's influence as one of the great northern magnates had secured them a performance at court this past February – the first breach in the Chamberlain's and Admiral's Men's duopoly there since 1594. They returned again the following Revels season, but then left London. They were immediately replaced in both venues, however, by a troupe which was formally a merger of companies patronized by the Earls of Worcester and of Oxford, but went under the former's name. Worcester was now Master of the Horse to the Queen – a position as prestigious as those of the Lord Chamberlain and the Lord Admiral – and a member of the Privy Council. Oxford was the seventeenth earl of that title, which carried enormous prestige. With such combined influence, their company breached the duopoly permanently.

The War of the Theatres

The move to the Globe thus coincided with a whole new, and possibly unanticipated, London theatrical marketplace. A much-mythologized symptom of this, in the early years of the new century, was the so-called War of the Theatres, in which a number of dramatists – notably Jonson, Marston, Chapman, and Dekker – traded boasts and insults in their plays. Scholars used to expend a lot of ink tracking these insults and the supposed personal rancour behind them. It is now more common to see the whole thing as a commercial publicity exercise, though informed by a keen sensitivity to new styles and experimentation, in which the boy companies sought to establish niche places within this new theatrical economy (see, in particular, Knutson, 2001; Bednarz, 2001; Steggle, 1998). It succeeded as well as it did not least because Jonson invested his considerable ego in championing the Children of the Chapel at the Blackfriars, who staged his next two plays.

Whether Shakespeare joined him and the others in this is something of a moot point. In *The Second Part of the Return to Parnassus*, a student satirical play written for festivities at St John's College, Cambridge (circa 1601/2), "Dick Burbage" and "Will Kemp" purportedly appear as themselves, and the latter says "Why here's our fellow Shakespeare puts them all down, aye and Ben Jonson too. O that Ben Jonson is a pestilent fellow; he brought up Horace giving the poets a pill, but our fellow Shakespeare hath given him a purge that made him beray his credit" (Anon, 1949, 4.3.1769–73). How much students at Cambridge really knew about London theatre is not easy to determine. But the reference to "Horace giving the poets a pill" is apt enough, referring to a scene in Jonson's *Poetaster* (5.3), one of the central texts in the "War," in which the urbane Roman satirist administered pills to thinly disguised versions of

Marston and Dekker, to make them belch up their turgid language. What "purge," if any, Shakespeare may have administered to Jonson has been a matter of much unresolved debate.

But the sense of a celebrity culture reflected in the student play (where Burbage, Kemp, Shakespeare and Jonson are all familiar names – though the authors seem not to know that Kemp and Shakespeare have parted company) does make it the more likely that London audiences entered into the spirit of these authorial and company antagonisms, and this may have boosted attendances for all concerned. An illuminating sidelight on the whole affair is cast by Thomas Dekker's *Satiromastix, or, The Untrussing of the Humorous Poet*, which tells us on its title-page that "it hath been presented publicly by the Right Honourable, the Lord Chamberlain his Servants, and in private by the Children of Paul's." This was a unique collaboration / cross-over, which must have been very different in style and resonance as presented in the two houses. But it makes sense. The Blackfriars operation was a threat to both of these companies, who were not really a threat to each other. Dekker at this date usually wrote for the Admiral's Men. But he had been one of Jonson's clear targets in *Poetaster*, and to an extent the satire of that play is aimed at *both* of the duopoly companies.

Satiromastix, staged later in 1601, is a clear riposte – the poet whose "humour" is to be "untrussed" is "Horace," a thinly veiled Jonson. But in addition to the *ad hominem* (but actually quite humorous) attacks on Dekker and Marston, *Poetaster* contains much darker satire, aimed at various constituencies. One of these is the adult players, Histrio and Aesop, who are associated with "your Globes and your triumphs" (3.4.163) and so, inevitably, with the Chamberlain's Men. They act as informers for the asinine magistrate, Asinius Lupus, and for this Aesop is promised "a monopoly of playing confirmed to thee and thy covey under the emperor's broad seal" (5. 3.103–4). Even the ultra-cautious E. K. Chambers is led to wonder whether this can be an allusion to the part Augustine Phillips played in speaking to the authorities about the *Richard II* performance given on the eve of the Essex rebellion (*ES*, 1: 385n: see p. 153). Is the suggestion that the Chamberlain's Men have secured their privileged playing position by acting as informers to the government?

If so, Jonson must certainly also have had in mind his own experience in respect of *The Isle of Dogs* (see p. 221). He later told of how, when he was imprisoned for it, "his judges could get nothing of him to all his demands but 'ay' and 'no.' They placed two damned villains to catch advantage of him, with him, but he was advertised by his keeper" (Jonson 2012k, lines 194–6). One agenda in the *Isle of Dogs* affair was clearly to preserve the Privy Council's privileges for its chosen acting companies. Government informers and the preservation of the "duopoly" would naturally go together in Jonson's mind. The whole arrangement rankled deeply with him – and doubtless with others outside the charmed circle – whose opportunities to perform in London were seriously circumscribed. The timely reappearance of the boy companies must have seemed a godsend to Jonson.

Dekker turns all of Jonson's self-righteous indignation back on itself. He has Tucca remind Horace / Jonson of his humble beginnings as a player and what has made him the scornful poet he is today:

> I ha' seen thy shoulders lapped in a player's old cast cloak, like a sly knave as thou art: and when thou ranst mad for the death of Horatio, thou borrowedst a gown of Roscius the stager, (that honest Nicodemus) and sent'st it home lousy, didst not? (1.2.354–8)
>
> thou put'st up a supplication to be a poor journeyman player, and hadst been still so, but that thou couldst not set a good face upon't. Thou hast forgot how thou amblest (in leather pilch) by a play-wagon, in the highway, and took'st mad Jeronimo's part, to get service among the mimics. And when the stagerites banished thee into the Isle of Dogs, thou turn'dst ban-dog (villainous guy) and ever since bitest; therefore I ask if th'ast been at Paris-garden, because thou hast such a good mouth. Thou bait'st well; read, *lege*, save thy self and read. (4.1.128–36)

Dekker's review of Jonson's humble beginnings as an actor casts an interesting light on the profession. He had evidently been a player in an itinerant troupe, without a London base, and was remembered for playing Hieronimo in *The Spanish Tragedy*, though he was only a journeyman or hireling, not a sharer; he had worn a distinctive rough leather outer-garment ("pilch"), the mark of a laborer – perhaps sneering at his former trade as a bricklayer. If there is any truth in the tale of the borrowed cloak, returned infected with lice, "Roscius" would have to one of the very finest actors – perhaps Alleyn or Burbage.

Dekker traces Jonson's current pretensions as a satirist "ban-dog" (attack-dog, such as would be used for bear-baiting in Paris Garden) specifically to the *Isle of Dogs* business. He turns the knife savagely in the exhortation to "read, *lege*, save thy self and read" – the touch of Latin making it clear that he is recalling the reading of "neck-verse" by which Jonson escaped hanging for the death of Gabriel Spencer (p. 39). And he rubs salt in this wound again later, referring to his "white neck-verse" and pronouncing a death sentence on him: "that presently he be had from hence, to his place of execution, and there be stabbed, stabbed, stabbed. (*He stabs at him*)" (4.3.105-6, 27–9). A man who has killed a fellow-actor should perhaps think twice before criticizing others of "the quality." If the "War of the Theaters" was at heart a publicity exercise among rivals finding their feet in the new marketplace, it was nevertheless fueled by genuine anxieties and antagonisms.

Notes

1 See *The Tempest*, 4.1.153.
2 The original document can be seen at http://www.henslowe-alleyn.org.uk/images/Muniments-Series-1/Group-022/01r.html, courtesy of the Henslowe–Alleyn Digitization Project.
3 The modern day reconstruction known as Shakespeare's Globe, on the Bankside, was built on the assumption that the original was 20-sided and 100 feet in diameter. The other major differences from the original are that it is some 750 feet from the original site, is further from the Thames – which was much wider in Shakespeare's day – and can only hold an audience of about 1,500, compared with 3,000 in 1599 (see p. 276 Note 34).
4 Note the complaint in the 1635 *Sharers' Papers* about the profits which the housekeepers derived from the galleries "and of the tiring house door at the Globe" (Gurr 2004a: 273).
5 It is not beyond dispute that the lords' rooms were in this position. Gabriel Egan argues that "the Lords Room was in the lowest gallery at the side of the stage" (1997, 308). With respect, I think he takes over-literally a passage in Dekker's *The Gull's Horn-Book* which speaks of the practice of sitting on the stage as it were upstaging the lords' rooms, rendering them "but the stage's suburbs" (see p. 295). He reasons that "the Lords Room is not in the stage balcony because such a position could not be obscured" (306). But surely it is at least as likely that Dekker means metaphorically overshadowed as literally obscured.
6 Strictly speaking Hollar's pictures are of the *second* Globe, built after the original burned down. But we know that it was built on the foundations of the original and so must have been very similar in size.
7 Paul's Boys were a much smaller operation than the Blackfriars and never really seen as a threat. In the so-called "War of the Theaters" they collaborated with the Chamberlain's Men in both staging Dekker's *Satiromastix*, a reply to Jonson's self-aggrandizement in his Blackfriars plays.
8 By 1603 Prince Henry's Men (formerly the Admiral's) were using Henslowe's Fortune playhouse, and Queen Anne's Men (formerly Worcester's) the Rose. The latter left circa 1606 to take over the new Red Bull playhouse, which was not owned by Henslowe.
9 Hotson also argues, much more eccentrically, that this arrangement rendered a tiring house non-viable in the position which we normally take it to have occupied, and that it was consequently placed underground. Skeptics would say it is perhaps surprising that the Fortune contract makes no mention of anything like this.
10 The contract calls this measurement the "length", but it clearly refers to the width at the front edge of the stage.

11   We may have to enter an exception for the public inns which the players used, in part because we know so little about their staging. It is clear that some of them, at least, had galleries for which patrons doubtless paid higher prices. But whether any of those patrons became a focus of attention for the rest of the audience, as I argue was the case at the Globe and elsewhere, we simply do not know.

12   Barnes, 1999, 5–6. (There is no lineation.) Note that I have not adopted editorial amendments, made in square brackets, but kept to the original text.

13   The burning of incense was a charged issue during the Counter-Reformation, but it was relatively common in the theatres. Elizabeth Williamson notes: "In at least ten plays [performed between 1573 and 1642] incense is used onstage during performance" (2016, 20). She includes Jonson's *Sejanus*, a Globe play, and Shakespeare and Fletcher's *The Two Noble Kinsmen* and Fletcher's *Bonduca*, both of which were either Globe or Backfriars plays, or both.

14   Cf. *The Merry Devil of Edmonton* (pub. 1608): "*Enter Sir Ralph Clare and Sir Arthur Jeringham, trussing their points new up*"; "*Enter Blague trussing his points.*"

15   Cf. Q2 *Romeo and Juliet* calls for "*torchbearers*" (1.4.0 SD); *The London Prodigal* (pub. 1605): "*Enter a citizen's wife with a torch before her.*"

16   The first quarto of *Hamlet* does not call for music; the second quarto specifies trumpets. Lucy Munro makes the point that when the adult companies moved into indoor playhouses, like the Blackfriars, they began "to use quieter instruments such as recorders, cornets, and hautboys more extensively" (2009, 549). All of the Shakespearean instances cited here occur in texts first printed in the 1623 folio, so they *may* reflect usage in the Blackfriars rather than the Globe. This is not to say that hautboys may not have been used at the Globe, only that their use was probably rarer than it was to be in the indoor playhouse.

17   If the first Globe did not have descent machinery there is a good chance that the 1614 replacement would have had it, so that it could accommodate plays written for the Blackfriars, which clearly did have it.

18   *The Revenger's Tragedy* was published as by Cyril Tourneur, but modern scholarship generally favors Middleton as the author.

19   The bear in *The Winter's Tale* was a man in a bear suit: see p. 313.

20   The Queen in *2 Henry VI* does enter "with her hawk on her fist", as the early version tells us (*The First Part of the Contention*", C1v); this is at 2.1.0 in modern texts. But the hawk is never involved in the action – its purpose is to symbolize royal power – and it is a moot point whether it was a live bird.

21   In *A Larum for London* (pub. 1602), the villainous Duke D'Alva pretends to be dead and is "*carried upon a horse covered with black.*" But he is later clearly on a *hearse*, so it is possible that the earlier reading was a mistranscription.

22   All three plays were reprinted during Shakespeare's time at the Globe, in 1611, 1608, and 1609 respectively, a possible mark that they were revived at that time (Knutson, 1991, 12–13, 81). None would require more than a portion of the lords' rooms.

23 *Richard III* was one of the most reprinted of all Shakespeare's plays, suggesting that it remained firmly in the repertoire in playhouse after playhouse. It first appeared in 1597 and then again the next year. During Shakespeare's Globe years it was reprinted in 1602, 1605, and 1612.
24 Joseph is much less hardline about all this in the second edition of his book (1964).
25 "*An Excellent Actor*" was included in Sir John Overbury's *Characters* (1615), but it is generally agreed to have been written by the dramatist John Webster. "Characters" of the kind presented by Overbury and others were prose essays modeled on the work of the classical Greek writer, Theophrastus, offering brief sketches of human types who demonstrate particular faults, such as vanity, toadying, or churlishness. English examples did not restrict themselves to characters embodying faults, but they retained the emphasis on *typicality* – human nature is conceived of predominantly as a matter of conforming to type, not of expressing individual complexity and difference. See pp. 257ff.
26 I am aware that, in relation to modern acting, the Stanislavski approach is sometimes called "presentational", which is confusing. I am trying to be consistent to the terms used about *early* modern acting.
27 Royce, 2009. The Theatre, of course, only became "home" to the Chamberlain's Men some twenty years after it was built. Joyce's argument is that having a fixed venue of these proportions allowed the new style of Burbage and others to flourish, after the peripatetic lifestyle of being traveling players.
28 "These *imprese* were insignia, allegorical or mythical, with appropriate mottoes, the whole painted on paper shields" and carried in the Accession Day tilts at court (Schoenbaum, 1987, 272).
29 On the reference to Hieronimo (i.e. Jeronimo) – the central character in Kyd's *The Spanish Tragedy* – see pp. 281–4.
30 The possibility that he originated the role of Iago as a kind of "diabolical" fool is given some credence by an eighteenth-century report that the role was first played by a comedian. See Wills, 2011, 88–90.
31 A ninth, *King* John, is the one outlier in terms of historical sequence.
32 I have slightly amended Chambers's translation, especially replacing "characters" with "persons." The German is *personen*. Platter is surely commenting on the number of actors, not on their roles.
33 A publisher tried to register *Troilus and Cressida* for printing in February 1603, but was required to get further authority (*ES*, 3: 487).
34 The Epilogue to Jonson, Chapman and Marston's *Eastward Ho!* (1605) concludes "May this [play] attract you, hither, once a week" (Jonson 2012e, line 8). On estimates of seating at the Blackfriars, see p. 270. De Witt estimated the capacity of the Swan as 3,000 spectators. When *A Game at Chess* played at the second Globe in August 1624, the Spanish Ambassador reported that "during these last four days more than 12,000 persons have all heard the play" (quoted in Middleton, 1993, 197).

7

A New Reign

Some of the concerns that underlay the "War of the Theaters" were allayed by the theatrical settlement reached when James I came peacefully to the throne, following the death of Elizabeth in March 1603. Considering how many other issues must have weighed with him, the beginnings of that settlement emerged surprisingly quickly. On May 19 a royal patent was issued to Shakespeare's company, creating them the King's Men. Over the next year or so all the other leading London companies similarly passed into royal patronage: the Admiral's Men became Prince Henry's Men, Worcester's Men became the Queen's (i.e Queen Anne's) Men, and the Children of the Chapel, the Children of the Queen's Revels (also patronized by Queen Anne). Only the small Paul's Boys were not so graced, and that company went out of business by 1606.

This was a logical development from the *de facto* situation at the end of Elizabeth's reign. As the Virgin Queen she had only one royal household. James initially had three – his own, his Queen's, and his elder son's, Prince Henry's; eventually this would extend to include households for the younger son, Prince Charles, and his daughter, Princess Elizabeth. All of these patronized acting companies over time, and all of them brought the players in to court to entertain them during the Revels season. This led to an enormous increase in theatrical consumption there. In James's first Revels season, for example, the King's Men were called to court nine times – they had never been called more than six times during Elizabeth's reign, and usually less. Moreover the new Queen's Men also played twice and the Prince's men five times; each of the boys' companies was also called once. Companies did not only play for their own patron. The King's Men, for example, performed twice for Prince Henry, who also paid for the two performances by the Queen's Men.

And even when the king paid for it, it did not necessarily mean that he attended. The great extra demand for performances has sometimes led to the assumption that James was inordinately fond of theatre. He liked it well enough, but probably not as much as his wife and son (Barroll, 1988, 454ff; 1991, 22–69). He did, however, recognize – as Elizabeth had – that court entertainment befitted his princely

Shakespeare's Theatre: A History, First Edition. Richard Dutton.
© 2018 Richard Dutton. Published 2018 by John Wiley & Sons Ltd.

magnificence and indulged it in that spirit. It was, however, by no means inevitable that he would choose the Chamberlain's Men as his personal players. Their patron, the second Lord Hunsdon, had been ailing and his successor as Lord Chamberlain, Thomas Howard, soon to be Earl of Suffolk, had been deputizing. This may explain why they had only been called twice during Elizabeth's last Revels season, 1602/3, against three times by the Admiral's Men.

Someone else must have advocated for them. Edmund Tilney may have been consulted, as Master of the Revels, but decisions of this nature were probably made at a higher level, and it is unlikely that much serious business was done without reference to Sir Robert Cecil, the man who had engineered James's smooth transition to the throne. The young Earl of Pembroke, one candidate for the "fair youth" in Shakespeare's *Sonnets* has also been suggested. A factor that may have weighed heavily against the Admiral's Men is that the incomparable Alleyn was known to be close to retirement. He had in fact retired once, in the 1590s, but had returned, possibly to boost the Fortune; some said at the request of the Queen herself. But he seems finally to have retired early in the new reign, pursuing other business goals.[1]

Since Shakespeare came into the public record with the Chambelain's Men in 1595, there had been an ever closer correlation between his career and the links of his company with the royal court. Their appointment as the King's Men was the last step in that process. We need to be clear, however, about the nature of this relationship. Some scholars have downplayed its significance by comparison with their commercial activities. Bernard Beckerman, for example, weighed its impact on their income:

> From Elizabeth, and later from James, the Chamberlain-King's Men received £873 between 1599 and 1609, of which amount £70 was for relief of the company during plague time, and £30 for reimbursement for expenses incurred during unusually lengthy travel to and from the Court. Thus the annual average for playing was £77.6s., with the court payments in the later years substantially greater than in the early one. Grants from Elizabeth never totaled more than 5 per cent of the income the company earned at the Globe. Under James the percentage rose to a high of about fifteen by 1609. The increase in Court support, evident in these figures, ultimately led the Globe company to appeal increasingly to an aristocratic audience. But throughout the decade we are considering [1599–1609], the actors depend on the pence of a large, heterogeneous public more than upon the bounty of their prince. (1962, 22–3, citing ES, 4:166–75)

Beckerman concedes that "The players certainly tendered courtesy and respect to the Court, which after all was their main defense against puritanical suppression" (23), but the economics of the situation required them to cater first and foremost to "a large, heterogeneous public."

I suggest that the logic of this is almost exactly back-to-front. The Lord Chamberlain's Men were only able to make the very substantial sums we presume that they did at the Globe *because* the court protected them and gave them very significant privileges. Both Elizabeth and James made extensive use of monopolies to reward people in their service, an indirect form of payment which cost them nothing (though, as the House of Commons repeatedly complained, it cost the people a good deal). Elizabeth, for example, granted the Earl of Leicester a monopoly to tax imports of sweet wines, a monopoly which passed after his death to the Earl of Essex. The situation of the leading players was not identical, but it was analogous. Only a small number of companies ever had access to the profits that could be generated from sustained playing in London, and that access was only granted to those who served the court. They always knew which side their bread was buttered on.

A Royal Master

The appointment of Shakespeare's company as the King's Men was thus a major coup. Their new licence names William Shakespeare, Richard Burbage, Augustine Phillips, John Heminge, Henry Condell, William Sly, Robert Armin, and Richard Cowley. A familiar name missing is that of Thomas Pope, one of the originators of the company and one of the first housekeepers in the Globe. He had apparently retired through ill-health, making out his will on July 22, 1603; it was proved the following February. With his death the first shares in the Globe went outside the company, to his legatees, though this did not raise any problems in the first instance. But Pope is replaced among the sharers by a new name, in fact the first on the list, Lawrence Fletcher.

The addition of Fletcher to the company's sharers is sometimes dismissed as a polite concession to the king, since he appears in no other record of the company's activities. Yet he could have been a useful colleague, even if only as a consultant. Fletcher had been connected with the new king since at least 1594, when he was one of the "Inglis comedianis" recorded in Edinburgh, perhaps to take part in festivities for the baptism of Prince Henry Frederick on August 30 (Dibdin, 1888, 20). They received a generous gift of £333 6s. 8d. (Scots) from the king.[2] Fletcher's association with this group, apparently its leader, is vouched for in the gossip of the English agent in Edinburgh. In March 1595 George Nicholson wrote to Robert Bowes, the treasurer of Berwick: "The King heard that Fletcher, the player, was hanged, and told him [i.e. Nicholson] and Robert Ashton [a Scottish courtier] so, in merry words, not believing it, saying very pleasantly that if it were true he would hang them also" (cited in *ES*, 2: 266). James was clearly already familiar with Fletcher.

He became much more so in the years 1599–1601 when the return of Fletcher's company caused a direct confrontation between the king and the

Kirk of Edinburgh.³ They performed several times before James and were then allowed to purchase a warrant "to the bailiffs of Edinburgh, to get them an house within the town. Upon Monday, the 12th of November [1599], they gave warning by trumpets and drums through the streets of Edinburgh, to all that pleased, to come to the Black Friars' Wynd [a narrow lane] to see the acting of their comedies" (Calderwood, 1842–49, 5: 765). The four sessions of the Kirk were convened and passed an act "that none resort to these profane comedies, for eschewing offence of God, and of evil example to others" (ibid.). This angered the king, who told their representatives that the act contravened the warrant he had granted the actors, which was clearly intended to allow them to perform before the public. He ordered them to rescind it or face the consequences, and eventually the Kirk backed down. Whatever James's personal interest in plays and players, he was fully prepared to stand up on their behalf to the Calvinist Kirk when it attempted to cut across his royal prerogative. The actors received several gifts from the king, culminating in December 1599 with one matching that of 1594. By 1601 they were able to travel to Aberdeen, bearing a letter of recommendation from the king and styling themselves his majesty's servants; the burgh register specifically records the presence of "Laurence Fletcher, comedian to his Majesty" (*ES*, 2: 269). All of this was a useful preparation for James's time in England. When he entered his new kingdom he did so well prepared to face down any threats to his court's consumption of theatre, and comfortable with the idea that royal players should normally earn their living commercially, with only modest subventions from their patrons.

People from the theatrical world in England, like everyone else, looked to see what would come with the new reign when Elizabeth died. Only a week after her death, when the pronouncement of James as her successor was unopposed, the Corporation of London began preparations for his triumphal entry into the city, with a number of ornamental arches along the route. Thomas Dekker was appointed to write appropriate speeches. Jonson was commissioned to write an entertainment for Queen Anne and Prince Henry on their journey south, at Althorp, the Northamptonshire estate of Sir John Spenser (2012*f*, 2: 393–412). He was also brought belatedly into the writing for James's entry into the city, which the plague delayed until March 1604. In all these quarters, people were anxious to know the tastes of the new royal family. Nobody knew James's taste in theatre, or that of Queen Anne, better than Fletcher, and that might have made him a useful ally in the early days of the new reign and of the reconstituted company.

The most immediate issue to the company in mid-1603 was the very plague which caused James's royal entry to be postponed. It followed hard on a precautionary closing of the playhouses when Elizabeth was clearly dying. They then remained closed almost continuously until the following Spring, losing the players a whole year's income. The situation became so acute during the winter (with touring impractical and no sign of the plague relenting) the king presented Burbage with £30 "for the relief of himself and the rest of his company, being prohibited to present any plays publicly in or around London ... by way of his Majesty's free gift" (*ES*, 4: 168–9). The extra performances at court must also have been welcome in this regard though, as we have noted, the income from such commissions was less significant than the profits from public performances which continuing royal favor normally made possible (see p. 278).

The plague also inhibited royal business. Protocol demanded that the king's coronation should take place as soon as possible, and it did so in July 1603, but the public were banned and a ceremonial procession through the streets of London was deferred until the plague lifted, which turned out to be March 15, 1604. For that event each of those named in the new patent for the King's Men was entitled to receive four and a half yards of scarlet-red cloth for his livery, being now an unpaid Groom of the Chamber and so a member (albeit a lowly one) of the king's household (Law, 1910). There is no record of them actually marching in the procession, but this is a marker of their growing status and prestige. The following year, moreover, they wore the livery in earnest. A long and intermittent war with Spain was ended in 1604 by the Treaty of London, and in August the first Spanish ambassador for many years was welcomed in some style; he stayed in the Queen's palace, Somerset House, and was waited on for eighteen days by twelve members of the King's Men (some of them evidently not sharers). They were paid the princely sum of £21 12s., and the line between acting and reality must have seemed very blurred. Such developments led the satirical writer, J. Cocke to observe a decade later how times had changed, now "that players may not be called rogues: *For they be chief ornaments of his Majesty's Revels*" ("A Common Player," 1615; quoted in *ES* 4: 257).

Little Eyases and *The Malcontent*

One unusual consequence of the change of reigns is that the licensing and censorship of one of the companies – the Children of the Queen's Revels – was taken out of the hands of the Master of the Revels, Tilney, and given to the courtier poet and dramatist, Samuel Daniel. As we shall see, this was an unfortunate decision. But I suspect it helps to explain the curious circumstance whereby *The Malcontent*, a play written by John Marston (switching allegiance from Paul's boys) for the Children of the Queen's Revels at the Blackfriars came into the hands of the King's Men at the Globe. Versions of the play – as performed both by the boys and by the adults – have survived, and a comparison of the two shows us a good deal about both operations.

The King's Men made several decisions about how the play was to be adapted. They decided they needed an Induction to explain how and why they had taken over a play with which the audience might already be familiar in another venue.

They judged that they could not match the music which accompanied performances at the Blackfriars, both before the show and during intermissions (see p. 300). As it happens, they had recently experimented along these lines. Ben Jonson, returning to their fold, had written a tragedy, *Sejanus*, in severely classical mode; it is the last play in which we have a record of Shakespeare performing. One breach of classical decorum, however, is that Jonson dispensed with the conventional chorus, and called for a *Musicorum Chorus* – chorus of musicians – between the acts instead. Thus the action would not have flowed continuously, as it usually did on the public stages, but more in the manner Jonson had been used to at the Blackfriars, with act-breaks. For whatever reason, *Sejanus* was an unmitigated disaster. In dedicating it to a cousin of the king, Jonson wrote: "It is a poem that, if I well remember, in Your Lordship's sight suffered no less violence from our people here than the subject of it did from the rage of the people of Rome" (2012*m*). One of the commendatory poems in the 1605 quarto of the play also recalled the event:

> When in the Globe's fair ring, our world's best stage,
> 　I saw *Sejanus*, set with that rich foil,
> 　I looked the author should have borne the spoil
> Of conquest from the writers of the age;
> But when I viewed the people's beastly rage,
> 　Bent to confound thy grave and learned toil …
> 　　　　　　　　(p. 228, lines 1–6)

The sharers of the King's Men had no interest in seeing *The Malcontent* subject to "the people's beastly rage" and abandoned the inter-act music of its "private" theatre staging. They were fortunate that this did not pose continuity issues. Where the boys' plays had such breaks there was no problem about having actors on stage at the end of one act back on stage (but in a different locale) at the beginning of the next; but that was not possible with the continuous staging in the public theatres. The nearest example of such a problem in *The Malcontent* was between Acts 1 and 2; the protagonist, Malevole, is on stage in the last scene of the first and the first scene of the second. But he leaves the stage nearly thirty lines before the end of Act 1, which would be more than adequate for a turnaround, even if a change of costume had been called for.

The other consequence of losing the incidental music was that the running time of the show was now less than the Globe customers were used to. At some 1,908 lines it would play (at modern acting speeds) for a bare two hours – though some people believe that Elizabethan actors spoke quicker than we do today (Erne, 2003, 140–4). At all events, the decision was made to expand the text, in addition to the Induction (137 lines), by some 457 lines spread over eleven passages (Marston, 1975*b*, lii). That might give half an hour's extra playing time. The Induction was written by John Webster, and the additions to the text seem to have been shared between Marston and Webster. A substantial part of those additions involved creating a fool's part (Passarello) for Armin, since the boy companies had no tradition of clown roles (xlix).

As we have noted, the Induction uses the conceit of having members of the company come on to play "themselves" and discuss the production (see p. 158). The three who do so are Burbage (referred to familiarly as "Dick"), Condell and John Lowin. To them comes Will Sly, playing a gallant who "hath seen this play often [i.e. at the Blackfriars] and can give [the players] intelligence for their action: I have most of the jests here in my table-book" (lines 14–16). In a neat metatheatrical twist Sly asks "Where's Harry Condell, Dick Burbage and Will Sly?" (11–12), which all speaks to the celebrity culture now surrounding the Globe. The jest of Will Sly asking to speak to himself would hardly work if many of the audience had not recognized him.

As a gallant Sly had come prepared to sit on the stage, as they do at the Blackfriars ("We may sit upon the stage at the private house": 2). The tire-man who has accompanied him on stage is carrying a stool (presumably a stage property), and Sly assumes he can hire it: "I would have given you but sixpence for your stool" (7–8) – the going price of an onstage stool at the Blackfriars (see p. 295). Perhaps Sly is not quite the gallant-about-the-theatre he pretends to be. When the tire-man will not loan him the stool he assumes he is being protected from adverse audience reactions to his preening behavior – not simply because this was not the custom in public playhouses. Eventually Lowin convinces him that he has to go: "Good sir, will you leave the stage? I'll help you to a private room" (125) – presumably one of the "gentlemen's rooms" (see pp. 240ff on sitting on the stage).

While Sly remains on stage, however, he pumps the actors on how they come to be performing this play, "another company having interest in it" (75–6). The Master of the Revels's licence normally conferred a copyright of sorts on the company to which it was granted, at least in the London theatres. Companies could not just steal from each other, even when a play got into print. So unless the King's Men had come to a private arrangement with the Blackfriars management, they had no right to perform *The Malcontent*. That may have happened or – I think the likelier – the change in the licensing of the Blackfriars boys opened up a gray area over performing rights, which the King's Men exploited. Tilney, as Master of the Revels, would hardly object to their theft of a play for which he had not been responsible; in fact he would now get a fee for (re)licensing it. And Daniel had no immediate authority over the King's Men. All that Condell evasively admits is that the play was "lost." He also justifies it as a *quid-pro-quo*: "Why not Malevole in folio with us, as Jeronimo in decimo-sexto with them?" (77–8). The reference is to paper sizes, folio big, decimo-sexto small, like the respective actors.

Malevole is the chief protagonist of *The Macontent*. "Jeronimo" is something of a puzzle. The name is that of the central character in Thomas Kyd's *The Spanish Tragedy*, a play long in the repertory of the Admiral's Men, not that of the Chamberlain's Men.[4] There was another play, called *The First Part of Jeronimo* or *The Comedy of Jeronimo*, but it never had anything like the reputation implied here. So what precisely the boys' theft amounted to is difficult to assess. One thing is clear, however: both the Blackfriars boys and the King's Men were acquiring revenge plays wherever they could. Shakespeare's *Hamlet* seems to have rejuvenated this elderly genre, as we saw with Marston's earlier work for Paul's Boys (though they seem to have concentrated on city comedies in the new reign). Henry Chettle wrote a revenge play, *Hoffman* (circa 1602), for the Admiral's/Prince Henry's Men, though there is less evidence that they built any reputation with such plays, except for Kyd's play. Nor, apparently, did the Blackfriars boys. This was one area where they could not keep up with the King's Men, even if they did commission *The Malcontent* and steal "Jeronimo"; there is no wider evidence of them building on this part of the repertory. But the King's Men certainly did. They very probably wanted *The Malcontent* to play it alongside *Hamlet*, which in so many respects it shadows. If they really had also secured *The Spanish Tragedy*, the great-grand-daddy of the genre, that would further compound their range; it was certainly consolidated again when they acquired *The Revenger's Tragedy* (circa 1606) from Thomas Middleton. They were cornering the market in revenge plays, with the incomparable Burbage taking the lead in all of them. Sequels had long been a stock-in-trade of the theatrical repertory, a way of cashing in on success – *1* and *2 Tamburlaine*, *1* and *2 Henry IV* (with *The Merry Wives of Windsor* tacked on), *1* and *2 Sir John Oldcastle*, and so on. But it was perhaps new to build a repertory, not around a single character, but around similar plot motifs and character-types, showing off Burbage's skills to the very best advantage (Knutson, 1991).

At around this time the management of the Children of the Queen's Revels went down a very different commercial route. They began to focus on recent history and political satire. At a time when the Essex rebellion was still a very touchy subject (see pp. 153–4), and there were tensions between the English and the Scots whom King James had brought south with him, this was an incendiary mix, which repeatedly brought them to the notice of the authorities. A play by their own licenser, Samuel Daniel, set the pattern; his *Philotas* (1604) was expressly accused of shadowing Essex's downfall, and it is likely this – at least in part – which also got Chapman's two-part *Byron* plays (1608) into trouble. Chapman, Jonson and Marston's *Eastward Ho!* (1605) and John Day's *Isle of Gulls* (1606) both satirized the Scots and got their authors into trouble. The company lost the Queen as its patron. They were henceforth known variously as the Children of the Revels or Children of the Blackfriars. There are signs that other playing companies worried that this policy might have consequences for the profession in general. Thomas Heywood concluded his *Apology for Actors* (written circa 1607–8) with this:

Now to speak of some abuse lately crept into the quality, as an inveighing against the state, the court, the law, the city, and their governements, with the particularizing of private men's humours (yet alive), noblemen and others. I know it distastes many; neither do I any way approve it, nor dare I by any means excuse it. The liberty which some arrogate to themselves, committing their bitterness, and liberal invectives against all estates, to the mouths of children, supposing their juniority to be a privilege for any railing, be it never so violent: I could advise all such to curb and limit this presumed liberty within the bands of discretion and government. But wise and judicial censurers, before whom such complaints shall at any time hereafter come, will not (I hope) impute these abuses to any transgression in us, who have ever been careful and provident to shun the like. (G3v)

And I follow Roslyn Knutson in thinking that it was probably about the same time that Shakespeare added a famous passage to *Hamlet*, which only appears in the folio text:

HAMLET:	Do they [the visiting actors] hold the same estimation they did when I was in the City? Are they so followed?
ROSENCRANTZ:	No indeed, they are not.
HAMLET:	How comes it? Do they grow rusty?
ROSENCRANTZ:	Nay, their endeavour keeps in the wonted pace. But there is, sir, an aerie of children, little eyases [hawks], that cry out on the top of question; and are most tyrannically clapped for't. These are now the fashion, and so berratle the common stages (so they call them) that many wearing rapiers, are afraid of goose-quills, and dare scarce come thither.
HAMLET:	What, are they children? Who maintains'em? How are they escotted [maintained]? Will they pursue the quality no longer then they can sing? Will they not say afterwards, if they should grow themselves to common players (as it is most like, if their means are no better) their writers do them wrong to make them exclaim against their own succession.
ROSENCRANTZ:	Faith, there has been much to-do on both sides, and the nation holds it no sin to tar [incite] them to controversy. There was for a while no money bid for argument, unless the poet and the player went to cuffs in the question.
HAMLET:	Is't possible?

> GUILDENSTERN: Oh, there has been much throwing about of brains.
> HAMLET: Do the boys carry it away?
> ROSENCRANTZ: Ay, that they do, my lord – Hercules and his load too.
> (2.2. 334–62; see Knutson, 1995)

So the "ordinary poets" of two leading adult companies – Queen Anne's Men and the King's Men – went out of their way to condemn the practices of the Blackfriars management and the authors they employ. Shakespeare projects them as shortsighted, endangering the future livelihood of the boys who want to go on to be adult actors. He also suggests that they are keeping the gentry ("many wearing rapiers") away from the public theatres, since they are scared of being satirized by the Blackfriars writers. He suggests that the Globe in particular is suffering – "Hercules and his load too" apparently refers to the sign or flag of the Globe, depicting Hercules carrying the world on his shoulders (Dutton, 1988).

Eventually the King himself lost his temper. The French ambassador complained about the *Byron* plays for an insulting depiction of the Queen of France (compounding the offense of their allusions to Essex) and shortly thereafter the company staged a play about a Scottish mine, with uncomplimentary references to James's Scots favorites. On March 11, 1608 Sir Thomas Lake, the Secretary of State, wrote to the Earl of Salisbury as secretary of the Privy Council:

> His majesty was well pleased with that which your lordship advertiseth concerning the committing [imprisonment] of the players that have offended in the matter of France and commanded me to signify to your lordship that for the others who have offended in the matter of the mines and other lewd words, which is the Children of the Blackfriars, that though he had signified his mind to your lordship by my Lord of Montgomery, yet I should repeat it again: that his grace had vowed they should never play more, but should first beg their bread, and he would have his vow performed. And therefore my Lord Chamberlain by himself, or your lordships at the table [the Privy Council], should take order to dissolve them and punish the maker [playwright] besides.[6]

The company was indeed dissolved and its licence was revoked; its goods were divided among the remaining management in July. The lease of the playhouse property was surrendered in August, and twelve years after James Burbage built the second Blackfriars playhouse, it became available for the use of Richard Burbage's company, now the King's Men. Whatever reservations the people of Blackfriars may have had about adult actors performing in their neighborhood, the fact that they now enjoyed the king's own patronage must have overridden any objections.

Box 7.1 *Court Masques*

Elizabethan court masques had been truly amateur events, devised by courtiers or by institutions affiliated with the court. Under King James they became much more elaborate and extravagant affairs, scripted (often by Ben Jonson) and staged (usually by the architect and stage-designer, Inigo Jones) by professionals. Queen Anne was the early driving force behind many of these shows, like the *Masques of Blackness* (1605) and *of Queens* (1609) in which she appeared herself, together with a group of her ladies. They were occasions for royal and aristocratic self-display, with flamboyant costumes, Italianate stagecraft, elegant music, allegorical and mythological subject-matter, and most particularly extensive dancing. The climax of any masque was the *revels*, when the masquers invited members of the audience to dance.

The aristocrats, however, did not otherwise *perform*: they did not speak or sing. But these increasingly sophisticated events required professional singing, often supplied by the gentlemen and boys of the Chapel Royal, and spoken roles, which were taken by unnamed members of the King's Men. Jonson led the way with many of these developments. His first court masque, *The Masque of Blackness*, for example, had the Queen and her ladies appear in black make-up, 'negroes and the daughter of Niger' (lines 34–5), who make their way to 'Britania' (205) because they have heard that it is 'Ruled by a sun ... whose beams shine day and night, and are of force / To blanch an Ethiop and revive a corse' (207–9). Whoever the performers are, King James is always the centre of attention; the masque is a gift-offering which celebrates his rule.[5] This action requires three speaking roles, those of Oceanus, Niger and Ethiopia, to explain what was going on; these were taken by three of Shakespeare's colleagues.

They must have been as astonished as members of the court were when they first saw Jones's staging, based on technology he had seen in Italy: 'an artificial sea was seen to shoot forth as if it flowed to the land, raised with waves that seemed to move, and in some places the billow to break, as imitating that orderly disorder which is common in nature' (16–19). This was obviously a large and complex machine, occupying much of the stage – one observer called it an 'engine' – since it was capable of carrying the scallop shell on which the lady masquers appeared. There were also elaborate visuals: 'the moon was discovered in the upper part of the house, triumphant in a silver throne, made in a figure of a pyramis; her garments white and silver, the dressings of her head antique, and crowned with a luminary, or sphere of light, which, striking on the clouds, and heightened with silver, reflected as natural clouds do by the splendor of the moon' (171–4). Nothing like this had been seen on English stages before.

In the *Masque of Queens* Jonson credited Queen Anne with an important development: 'some dance or show that might proceed hers, and have the place of a foil or false masque ... I therefore now devised that twelve women in the habit of hags, or witches ... should fill that part, not as a masque, but a spectacle of strangeness, producing multiplicity of gesture, and not unaptly sorting with the current, and whole fall of the device' (7–14). And so what he called the 'antimasque' became a major component of this and most future masques. For *Queen's* the King's Men were required to produce twelve performers – probably mixed men and boys – to play the eleven 'hags' and their Dame, counterpointing the famous and virtuous women personated by the Queen's party. Jones meanwhile added the *scena ductilis* to the *machina versatilis* (turning machine) used in earlier masques; this was a system of sliding flats which made possible instantaneous changes of scene, as when the antimasque of witches disappears: 'the whole face of the scene altered, scarce suffering the memory of such a thing. But in the place of it appeared a glorious and magnificent building ...' (321–2).

The *scena ductilis* was used to even more striking effect in *Oberon* (1611), a masque to honor Prince Henry as Prince of Wales: 'the discovery of each successive scene took the eye into the perspectival setting, at the furthest reach of which the Prince was enthroned' (Lindley, *Oberon*, 717). 'Then the whole palace opened, and the nation of fays [*fairies*] were discovered ... and within, afar off in perspective, the knights masquers sitting in their several sieges [*separate seats*]; at the further end of all, OBERON, in a chariot, which to a loud triumphant music began to move forward, drawn by two white bears ...' (211–14; see p. 311). It was the first full demonstration of perspectival staging behind a proscenium arch in England, used to induce awe and wonder among spectators appropriate to a show of royalty; it gave a glimpse into the future of theatre. But nothing like this was seen on public stages in Shakespeare's lifetime, or indeed before the closing of the theatres in 1642. The King's Men turned out again in force for *Oberon*, being paid a total of £15, mainly for playing unruly satyrs, when the going rate was £1 per player (against the princely £40 Jonson was paid for devising it all; see *ES* 1:201, Note 1; 210). But their own playhouses were not suitable to stage such theatre, which was besides fabulously expensive; *Oberon* cost well over £1000. They perhaps borrowed the 'dance of satyrs' in the show for *The Winter's Tale* (see p. 311), but in other respects Shakespeare and is fellows could only produce pale – if suggestive – shadows of what they saw at Whitehall, as in the masque of Amazons in *Timon of Athens* (1.2.120–56), the masque of Juno, Iris and Ceres in *The Tempest* (4.1), and the morris prepared by the schoolmaster and the country folk in *The Two Noble Kinsmen* (3.5), taken from Francis Beaumont's *Masque of the Inner Temple and Gray's Inn* (1613: see p. 314).

Notes

1   He and Henslowe jointly acquired the post of Master of the King's Games of Bears, Bulls and Dogs – bear and bull-baiting. It was profitable work.

2 When James became King of England the currency was regularized on a scale of 12 Scots pounds to 1 English one. So this payment was worth approximately £30 English.
3 The players are identified as "Fletcher and Mertyn [Martin Slater] with their company" in a letter of November 12, 1599 by George Nicholson to Sir Robert Cecil (*ES*, 2: 269). It tells us something that the affairs of players in a foreign country was deemed worth reporting to Elizabeth's Principal Secretary.
4 There have been attempts to argue that Shakespeare was responsible for the additions to the 1602 version of *The Spanish Tragedy*. See Bate and Rasmussen 2013: 207–11, 671–80. Also http://www.nytimes.com/2013/08/13/arts/further-proof-of-shakespeares-hand-in-the-spanish-tragedy.html. This would imply that the Chamberlain's Men had somehow acquired the rights to it, since he is unlikely to have done work like that for another company. We recall that *The Funeral Elegy for Burbage* hailed him in the role of Hieronimo; but that poem contains forged elements. I remain skeptical.
5 All the masques cited here are edited by David Lindley in Jonson 2012: *Blackness*, 2:503–28; *Queen's*, 3:281–331; and *Oberon*, 3:711–43. Citations are by line numbers.
6 *EPT*, 515. Lake is under the impression that the infractions were by two separate companies, but all other evidence points to them being the same company, the Children of the Blackfriars. A residual company of "boys" (though some were now in their twenties) did emerge, with personnel from the Blackfriars and the short-lived Children of the King's Revels. They performed at the Whitefriars theatre and in 1610 got a new patent as Children of the Queen's Revels. They had a star player in Nathan Field, but never posed the same threat to the King's Men that the Blackfriars operation had.

8

The Blackfriars

So many seemingly disparate pieces fell together so neatly in the winding up of the Blackfriars boys and the return of their theatre to Richard Burbage's control that it would be easy to suppose some behind-the-scenes planning, conceivably involving the Master of the Revels. Only a month after Burbage retook possession, the Blackfriars precinct (along with several others) ceased to be a liberty and became formally part of the City of London, under the authority of the Lord Mayor and the Common Council (see pp. 84, 197–8). Its playhouse was thus apparently open to all the unwelcome supervision that James Burbage had sought to avoid when he first built the Theatre outside the City walls. In fact there is no evidence that the City authorities tried to impose themselves in that way. On the other hand this change may have helped to persuade the playhouse's neighbors that its activities would be properly regulated.

Within the King's Men, however, the reacquisition of the Blackfriars theatre posed as many questions as it offered opportunities. If they moved their operation to it, as they had apparently planned to do in 1596/7, what would happen to the Globe? This was a matter of no small consequence, since the housekeepers of the Globe – who by this date included the Burbage brothers, Shakespeare, Heminge, Condell, and Sly – had invested significant capital in it. The only other adult players currently permanently resident in London, Prince Henry's Men and Queen Anne's Men, had their own playhouses, the Fortune and the Red Bull, so there was little prospect of leasing it.

Moreover, there is good evidence that the Globe had proved to be a *very* profitable enterprise, as the events of 1613 were to confirm (see p. 315). One detail seems particularly telling. Since reopening an embassy in London in 1603 Venetian ambassadors had been in the habit of visiting the playhouses: "Giustinian [in post January 1606 to November 1608] went with the French ambassador and his wife to a play called *Pericles*, which cost Giustinian more than 20 crowns. He also took the Secretary of Florence" (Chambers, 1930, 2: 335). Ambassadors carried the dignity of the state they represented, so it was a mark of the growing respectability of the playhouses –and of the Globe in

Shakespeare's Theatre: A History, First Edition. Richard Dutton.
© 2018 Richard Dutton. Published 2018 by John Wiley & Sons Ltd.

particular, the first playhouse known to have had such a visitation – that three of them should have been at a performance together.[1] Twenty crowns, moreover, translated to something more than £5, making it highly likely that Giustinian had hired the Globe's entire lords' rooms as a personal suite. This would surely only be done at at a fashionable and successful playhouse.Why abandon such success for the Blackfriars, which was about to lose its protection as a liberty?

No sooner, however, had the King's Men finally secured the potential use of the Blackfriars than it was denied them by another sustained visitation of the plague. The playhouses did not reopen until December 1609 at the earliest, and they were closed again for the second half of 1610 (Barroll, 2005, 159). In January 1609 the king presented the company with £40 "for their private practice in the time of infection," and £30 again the following winter; those Revels seasons they performed twelve and thirteen times at court respectively (*ES*, 4: 175–6). This still represented far less than they would have made if the playhouses had been open, but it is a measure of how far ahead of their rivals the King's Men now stood. No other company received free gifts or performed more than five times in either season. Indeed, the Prince and Queen's Men and the Children of the Whitefriars between them did not perform as often as the King's Men.[2]

One possible benefit of this break in playing is that they were able to give detailed thought to how they would manage with two playhouses. It might hypothetically have been possible to expand and split the company, occupying both houses, in friendly competition with each other; that would have been most profitable to the householders, though it would have required a major investment in new costumes, properties, and plays. But it would also have required approval by the authorities, which might well not have been forthcoming.

In fact the company did resolve to continue with both houses, but playing a summer season at the Globe (April/May–September, on evidence relating to the 1630s) and the rest of the year at the Blackfriars.[3] Why they should have done this is far from clear. It was a phenomenal extravagance, of a kind which would not be seen again until the subsidized theatres of the twentieth century. It may be relevant that when the boys had performed there, they were only expected to do so "the full time six months in every year" – the winter months (Smith, 514). Could it be that the Blackfriars got hot and stuffy in the summer months, with packed bodies, candles, and the windows closed to keep out sounds of traffic and trade? This arrangement would certainly give the King's Men the opportunity to air it out during the summer months, and anyway it meant that they would always have somewhere to play if something should happen to one of the playhouses. The memory of losing the lease on the Theatre and having to fall back on the Curtain must have haunted them, and it was to prove wise policy when the Globe was destroyed by fire in 1613.

This solution involved a striking, if perhaps necessary, act of generosity on the part of Richard Burbage. He set up for the housekeepers of the Globe a similar consortium for the Blackfriars. But where earlier they had paid to join, here they were given free shares, only having to contribute to the upkeep of the building and to the annual rent on the lease of £40 – so that what they lost in profits at the Globe they would make up in profits at the Blackfriars, and vice versa. There were initially seven equal housekeeper shares in the Blackfriars consortium: one each for the Burbage brothers, and for Shakespeare, Heminge, Condell, and Sly; and one for someone named Thomas Evans. The suspicion is that this was a placeholder for Henry Evans, a figure involved in the management of the Blackfriars boys since their reemergence in 1600.[4] If so, the further suspicion has to be that his share was a prearranged reward for expeditiously wrapping up the boys company and surrendering their lease (which provoked litigation from other members of the management: *EPT*, 517–21).

One other convenience arose from the winding up of the Blackfriars boys. Some of the boys themselves became available to join the King's Men, whose sharer ranks were thinning. Of those named in the 1603 patent (see p. 279), Phillips had died some while back, and perhaps been replaced by Nicholas Tooley, named as his "fellow" in Phillips' 1605 will. But William Sly died only days after becoming a housekeeper in the Blackfriars and Lawrence Fletcher about a month later. These were replaced in the company by William Ostler and John Underwood from the Blackfriars boys – but almost certainly no longer in boy roles. Both had been performing since at least Jonson's *Poetaster* (1601). Tooley, Ostler and Underwood all appear in the cast-list for Jonson's *The Alchemist* (1610) with the King's Men.

We might presume that maintaining the two venues would pose the company problems in respect of which plays to perform where. As we have seen, transferring *The Malcontent* from the boys' repertory to the Globe involved significant changes, which took time and money. The King's Men certainly kept on the Blackfriars consort of musicians, who continued to play for up to an hour before performances and again during the intermissions to keep the lighting trimmed (see p. 300). So we might expect that plays written for the Globe would have to be cut at the Blackfriars, to give a manageable playing time. By the same token, we might have assumed that some plays were better suited, either by style or subject matter, for one house (or its audience) than the other. But actually the evidence on this is far less clear cut than we might have anticipated.

Pericles and *Troilus and Cressida* were the last two Shakespeare plays published in his lifetime; both were printed in 1609 and both title pages speak of performance at the Globe.[5] None of the plays written after that date was printed until the 1623 First Folio, which says nothing about where they were staged. *Othello*, certainly written by 1604 but not printed before 1622, tells us that it had been played at both the Globe and the Blackfriars, but not whether the text reflects adaptations from one to the other. Similarly the 1631 *Taming of the Shrew*, not printed until the First Folio, names both playhouses. *Love's Labour's Lost*, reprinted in 1631, also mentions both playhouses; it offers the version of the play first printed in the Folio, but that differs little from what appeared in a

1598 quarto – which obviously relates to staging before either playhouse was in operation. From 1608 onwards reprints of *Richard II* associated it with performance at the Globe, as do those of *Romeo and Juliet* from 1609, and those associations continue into the 1630s – with no mention of the Blackfriars.[6] But some of that may simply be inertia: printers always preferred to work, as far as possible, from an earlier printing. For example, all twelve editions of *Mucedorus* printed with title-pages between 1610 and 1656 pronounce it to be "as it was acted before the Kings Majesty at Whitehall, on Shrove Sunday night. By his Highness' servants usually playing at the Globe." The reference to the actual court performance (in either 1609 or 1610) would have been meaningless to most people within a few years, while "his Highness' servants" no longer existed by 1656, nor did the Globe – but the printers churned out the same old formula. Amid all this imperfect information, the fact remains that *The Two Noble Kinsmen* (printed 1634; coauthored with John Fletcher) is the only play by Shakespeare *exclusively* associated textually with the Blackfriars.

* * *

Before pursuing this further, let us consider the physical characteristics of the Blackfriars, in part to assess the challenges of moving from one stage to another. Scholars broadly agree that the hall James Burbage constructed out of the seven existing rooms he bought in the Blackfriars complex measured 66 ft long by 46 ft wide (just over 20 m × 14 m), less than half the total floorspace of the Globe. The size of the stage is far less certain. There were certainly boxes on either side of the stage (and possibly also behind it), "and somewhere there was a tiring house" adds Herbert Berry, a laconic reminder of how imperfect our information is (2002, 156). The entire audience was to be seated. The pit lay before the stage but was here supplied with benches for even the lowest-paying (six-penny) entrants, while there were tiered galleries all around the remaining three sides of the auditorium for those prepared to pay more. Whether there were two tiers or three (as at the Globe) is less certain. Marston's reference in *The Dutch Courtesan*, written for the Blackfriars boys circa 1604/5, to "my worshipful friends in the middle region" (5.3.160–1; Marston, 1975*a*) is sometimes thought to support the argument for three, but options would have been restricted by the need to retain the use of the high Tudor windows of both long sides of the room for lighting. Seated bodies take up more space than standing ones, and since everything started with dramatically reduced floorspace, the pressure to squeeze in as much seating as possible must have been intense. The size of the stage must have been a trade-off between that pressure and the need for sufficient space to mount impressive productions.

If the galleries were as wide as those at the Fortune (12' 6"; 3.81 m) there would barely be 21 ft (6.40 m) left for the width of the stage; by the same token, if the stage reached out halfway along the length of the hall (33 ft; 10.06 m), that might allow for a stage of 22 ft (6.71 m), with 11 ft (3.36 m) to contain the tiring house (but only 33 ft for the lowest-priced seating on the floor of the auditorium). Irwin Smith calculated that 22 ft was the absolute minimum depth necessary to stage the battles, masques, and other setpieces of plays like Beaumont and Fletcher's *The Maid's Tragedy* (circa 1610, pub. 1619) and Massinger's *The Roman Actor* (pub. 1629), both printed as Blackfriars plays (1964, 306–8). Smith, however, assumed that there were no boxes adjacent to the stage, so that there would be much greater width; records, however, of a contretemps in 1632 between a Captain Essex and the Irish peer, Lord Thurles, make it clear that there *were* boxes immediately adjacent to the stage.[7] But they were not necessarily 12'6" deep – reducing them to, say, 8' (2.44 m) would give an extra 5' (1.52 m) of usable stage, 26' across (nearly 8 m). Even this, however, does not allow for the one factor which distinguished the Blackfriars from the Globe, the more preponderant presence of spectators (like Lord Thurles) on the stage itself. I shall consider the wider implications of this shortly, but for now want simply to point out that spectators on stools (and others standing or reclining) on the stage must have reduced the usable space even further. Smith had assumed that, without galleries to the side, two rows of stools on each wing of the stage would have accommodated them. *With* the galleries, however, they have to be accounted for in other ways, and Ben Jonson's testimony (see below) suggests that they were *not* neatly tucked away in the wings. All in all, Ralph Alan Cohen's estimate of usable acting space as 25' by 25' (approx. 7.6 m square) seems like a reasonable best guess (2009, 214).[8]

The presence of the spectators on the stage is the feature of the Blackfriars which elicited most comment. As we have seen, there were almost certainly spectators on other stages too, even in public playhouses (see pp. 240ff). But given the narrow confines of this stage they were a particular issue. In the Prologue to *The Devil is An Ass*, staged in 1616, Jonson tartly comments:

> *The Devil is an Ass.* That is today
> The name of what you are met for: a new play.
> Yet, grandees, would you were not come to grace
> Our matter with allowing us no place.
> Though you presume Satan a subtle thing,
> And may have heard he's worn in a thumb-ring,
> Do not on these presumptions force us act
> In compass of a cheese-trencher. This tract
> Will ne'er admit our vice because of yours –
> Anon, who, worse than you, the fault endures
> That yourselves make? When you will thrust and spurn,
> And knock us o' the elbows; and bid, turn;
> As if, when we had spoke, we must be gone,
> Or, till we speak, must all run into one,
> Like the young adders, at the old one's mouth?
>   (*1–15; Jonson, 2012*d)

The litany of thoughtless behavior by the ironically-named "grandees" is painfully plausible. You come to grace the play, but allow the actors no room to perform, forcing us to act in confines as narrow as those of a wooden trencher used to serve cheese. Our Vice will not be able to get on, because of the vices you yourself commit – when you will push and kick, and jostle our elbows and, when someone calls you, you turn around. It's as if you expect us to get off as soon as we have spoken, and until then we are all forced to stand in one small space.

The behavior of onstage gallants is most famously satirized in Thomas Dekker's *The Gull's Horn-Book* (1609), Chapter 6, "How a Gallant should behave himself in a Playhouse." It is worth quoting at some length for some of the doubtless acute observation of actual playhouse activity. Do note that he describes the practice of sitting on stage (to which he devotes almost the whole chapter) as one common to both public and private playhouses. We noted earlier that the evidence as to whether members of the audience sat on the stage at the Globe (and if so, when) is ambiguous; and Dekker continues that ambiguity here – he may be entirely sincere or he may be mocking those "gulls," like Will Sly's character in the Induction to *The Malcontent*, who do not understand the different conventions of public and private theatres (see pp. 283–4). But there is no ambiguity about the Blackfriars, which became the playhouse most celebrated (or notorious) for the practice.

> Sithence [*since*] then the place is so free in entertainment, allowing a stool as well to the farmer's son as to your Templar [*inns of court lawyer*]; that your stinkard has the selfsame liberty to be there in his tobacco-fumes, which your sweet courtier hath; and that your car-man [*carter*] and tinker claim as strong a voice in their suffrage, and sit to give judgment on the play's life and death, as well as the proudest Momus [*Greek god of ridicule*] among the tribe of critic: it is fit that he, whom the most tailors' bills do make room for, when he comes, should not be basely, like a viol, cased up in a corner.
>
> Whether therefore the gatherers of the public or private playhouse stand to receive the afternoon's rent; let our gallant, having paid it, presently advance himself up to the throne of the stage; I mean not into the lords' room [see pp. 234ff], which is now but the stage's suburbs; no, those boxes, by the iniquity of custom, conspiracy of waiting-women and gentlemen-ushers that there sweat together, and the covetousness of sharers, are contemptibly thrust into the rear; and much new satin is there damned, by being smothered to death in darkness.
>
> But on the very rushes where the comedy is to dance, yea, and under the state of *Cambyses* himself [*Persian king, subject of an early bombastic play*], must our feathered ostrich, like a piece of ordnance [*artillery*], be planted valiantly, because impudently, beating down the mews and

hisses of the opposed rascality. For do but cast up a reckoning, what large comings-in are pursed up by sitting on the stage. First, a conspicuous eminence is gotten; by which means the best and most essential parts of a gallant, good clothes, a proportionable leg, white hand, the Persian lock, and a tolerable beard, are perfectly revealed.

By sitting on the stage, you have a signed patent to engross [*monopolize*] the whole commodity of censure; may lawfully presume to be a girder [*sneerer*], and stand at the helm to steer the passage of scenes; yet no man shall once offer to hinder you from obtaining the title of an insolent, over-weening coxcomb [*conceited simpleton*]...

By sitting on the stage, if you be a knight, you may happily get you a mistress; if a mere Fleet-street gentleman, a wife; but assure yourself, by continual residence, you are the first and principal man in election to begin the number of "We three" ... [i.e. *to show yourself a fool*].

By sitting on the stage, you may, with small cost, purchase the dear acquaintance of the boys; have a good stool for sixpence; at any time know what particular part any of the infants present; get your match lighted; examine the playsuits' lace, and perhaps win wagers upon laying 'tis copper [*i.e. cheap alternative to gold*], etc. And to conclude: whether you be a fool or a justice of peace; a cuckold or a captain; a Lord Mayor's son or a dawcock [*jackdaw, chattering fool*]; a knave or an under-sheriff; of what stamp soever you be; current or counterfeit; the stage, like time, will bring you to most perfect light and lay you open. Neither are you to be hunted from hence; though the scarecrows in the yard hoot at you, hiss at you, spit at you, yea, throw dirt even in your teeth: 'tis most gentlemanlike patience to endure all this and to laugh at the silly animals. But if the rabble, with a full throat, cry "Away with the fool!" you were worse than a madman to tarry by it; for the gentleman and the fool should never sit on the stage together.

Marry, let this observation go hand in hand with the rest ... Present not yourself on the stage, especially at a new play, until the quaking Prologue hath by rubbing got colour into his cheeks, and is ready to give the trumpets their cue that he's upon point to enter; for then it is time, as though you were one of the properties, or that you dropped out of the hangings, to creep from behind the arras [*hanging tapestry*], with your tripos or three-footed stool in one hand, and a teston [*coin*] mounted between a forefinger and a thumb in the other; for, if you should bestow your person upon the vulgar when the belly of the house is but half full, your apparel is quite eaten up, the fashion lost, and the proportion of your body in more danger to be devoured than if it were served up in the counter amongst the poultry. Avoid that as you would the baton [*cudgel*]. It shall crown you with rich commendation to laugh aloud in the midst of the most serious and saddest scene of the terriblest tragedy, and to let that clapper, your tongue, be tossed so high that all the house may ring of it ... for by talking and laughing, like a ploughman in a morris [*morris-dance*], you heap Pelion upon Ossa, glory upon glory; as first, all the eyes in the galleries will leave walking after the players, and only follow you ...

Before the play begins, fall to cards; you may win or lose, as fencers do in a prize, and beat one another by confederacy, yet share the money when you meet at supper: notwithstanding, to gull the ragamuffins that stand aloof gaping at you, throw the cards, having first torn four or five of them, round about the stage, just upon the third sound, as though you had lost ... Now, sir; if the writer be a fellow that hath either epigrammed [*satirized*] you, or hath had a flirt at your mistress, or hath brought either your feather or your red beard, or your little legs, etc. on the stage; you shall disgrace him worse than by tossing him in a blanket, or giving him the bastinado [*beating*] in a tavern, if, in the middle of his play, be it pastoral or comedy, moral or tragedy, you rise with a screwed and discontented face from your stool to be gone; no matter whether the scenes be good or no; the better they are, the worse do you distaste them. And, being on your feet, sneak not away like a coward; but salute all your gentle acquaintance, that are spread either on the rushes, or on stools about you; and draw what troop you can from the stage [*after*] you; the mimics [*actors*] are beholden to you for allowing them elbow-room ...

Marry, if either the company or indisposition of the weather bind you to sit it out, my counsel is then that you turn plain ape; take up a rush, and tickle the earnest ears of your fellow gallants to make other fools fall a laughing; mew at passionate speeches; blare at merry; find fault with the music; whew at the children's action; whistle at the songs ...

Dekker's basic point is that pride of place on the stage is open to anyone with money; class and intelligence are not requirements, and are indeed conspicuous by their absence. The typical gallant on stage will arrive just as the show is beginning, to make the strongest impression he can with his splendid clothing; he will face down ridicule from the rest of the audience; he will be a constant critic and fool; he will respond inappropriately and loudly in the course of the play; and if he takes offense at some supposed affront from the author he may leave as conspicuously as possible. Dekker also hints at inappropriate familiarity ("dear acquaintance") between these moneyed gallants and the boy actors (see p. 188).

There is no doubt that these gallants on stage – there were perhaps no more than ten of them at a performance – were indulged for the extra sixpence they paid to get a stool. Cokes in *Bartholomew Fair* wonders if the puppets have "none of your pretty, impudent boys now, to bring stools, fill tobacco, fetch ale, and beg money, as they have at other houses?" (5.3.49–51; 2012*b*). Such services probably did not exist at the Hope (and certainly not at puppet shows); at this date they were most widely associated with the Blackfriars, where the King's Men's may have continued the practice of the boy actors attending to these elite customers. Dekker blames "the covetousness of sharers" for allowing all this to happen – here doubtless meaning the housekeepers, to whom such income flowed.

In allowing this section of the audience on stage the indoor theatres recreated the effect which we have repeatedly seen in early modern staging, especially in colleges and at court, whereby the majority of the audience saw a privileged minority as it were through the action of the play. And that association may have been entirely deliberate. Dekker specifically notes that "the throne of the stage" is no longer "the lords' room" ("which is now but the stage's suburbs" – an insignificant backwater), nor those prime boxes, the "gentlemen's rooms" (which he suggests are now used for rather sordid assignations); it is "on the very rushes where the comedy is to dance, yea ... [that] our feathered ostrich, like a piece of ordnance, [must] be planted valiantly."[9]

The indoor auditoria became known as "private houses," though they were in reality no more "private" than the outdoor playhouses. But they simulated something of the atmosphere of performances in the homes of aristocrats and gentry such as we saw associated with the early parts of Shakespeare's career – and such as those nearby in the Blackfriars precinct itself (see pp. 135, 198). Such venues had never been entirely left behind; whenever the King's Men had to tour because of plague in London (as they did in 1610) or they played in the city houses of aristocrats they would have reencountered the old status-driven arrangement of the audiences. The critical difference here was that privileged status was conferred entirely on the basis of ability to pay, not social or institutional rank. So, in Dekker's listings, farmers' sons, stinkards, and tinkers were as likely as lawyers, knights, and courtiers. Yet again we see the early modern theatre strung between an older, hierarchical world of social obligation and deference and a modern one governed by markets and economic opportunism.

Also as in the houses of the nobility, lighting was a significant issue. Although there has been speculation that the King's Men may have performed in the evenings there is no evidence of this – and significant indication that, as at the Globe, they performed in the afternoons, at least in part to allow audiences to get home at a reasonable hour. When in December 1618 neighbors of the playhouse complained of the great crush of coaches it attracted and the disruption they caused, they specified: "These inconveniences falling out almost every day in the winter time (not forbearing the time of Lent) from one or two of the clock till six at night" (*EPF*, 523). Nevertheless, even though the chambers which James Burbage converted into the playing space doubtless had the kinds of classic Tudor high windows that we associate, say, with the Great Hall at Hampton Court Palace or with Middle Temple Hall, these would rarely have cast direct light on the stage, but at best allowed a diffuse light to filter down over the room in general (Graves, 2009, 538). And in the depths of winter even that was gone by four o'clock.

"Your Master Worship's House, here, in the Friars"

Candlelight was an essential precondition of playing at the Blackfriars. But we should not assume that this even began to approximate to the levels of lighting we are accustomed to today. Our best evidence comes from the indoor Salisbury Court playhouse in 1639, where a mix of wax and tallow candles was used at a cost of 5 shillings a day. Depending on the mix of (more expensive) wax and tallow, R. B. Graves calculates that this paid for between two and four dozen candles daily, of which he observes "—a fair quantity, one would think, but in actual brightness not equivalent even to the power of one 60-watt light bulb" (2009, 535). [10] And these candles were not even concentrated over the stage but spread throughout the room: there was no equivalent of modern spotlights and footlights. It has been hypothesized that stage lighting might have been intensified with reflective cloths, screens, or mirrors such as may well have been used in the elaborately staged – and fabulously expensive – masques at court. But there is no actual evidence of that level of intervention in the moment-by-moment lighting of plays in commercial playhouses. It is perhaps best to bear in mind that the human eye adapts quickly to even the lowest levels of light, so that the mix of filtered sunlight and candlelight – a mix which would modulate as time passed through performances – may well have offered an acceptable medium for performance. Given the record of the playhouse between 1610 and 1642, when it was indisputably the most successful theatre of the era, there seems little doubt of this.

Within that medium the actors continued to use the conventions they imported from the Globe to represent the lighting conditions within the fictions they staged. The quarto text of *Othello* (1622), for example, which tells us that it was played at both houses, goes out of its way to emphasize that the opening scenes occur at night: "Enter Brabantio in his night-gown, and servants with torches" (1.1.159.1); "Enter Othello, Iago, and attendants with torches" (1.2.0; the formula recurs later in the scene for "Cassio with officers"); "Enter Duke and Senators, set at a table with lights and attendants" (1.3.0). The torches and lights symbolized night; they did not enact it. Similarly, when Iachimo in *Cymbeline* emerges from the trunk to spy on the sleeping Imogen he tells us that the flame of a taper he carries "Bows towards her" (2.2.20). The motion of a flame is something an actor could hardly control – this is something he *tells* the audience to see. We believe that the play was performed at the Globe (where Simon Forman probably saw it: see p. 320, Note 15); but we might suppose that so recent a play was transferred to the Blackfriars. In the former playhouse many spectators would be too far away to see the flame at all; in the latter it would be one light among many. But the key in both moments is a suspension of disbelief, created here by the magic of the spoken word, in which light and dark are whatever the theatrical conventions say they are.

In his satirical plague pamphlet, *The Seven Deadly Sins of London*, Thomas Dekker describes nightfall in the City: "all the city looked like a private playhouse, when the windows are clapped down, as if some ... dismal tragedy were presently to be acted" (1606, sig. D2). The suggestion seems to be that it was a convention to play tragedies entirely by candlelight, without the addition of light from outside. This was perhaps on a par with the convention of hanging the stage with black cloth for tragedies; I can, however, find no clear instance of *that* convention mentioned at the Blackfriars, though it certainly comes up in plays for Paul's boys (see p. 203 and p. 228, Note 11). The critical issue here is that neither of these conventions involved changes to either decoration or lighting *during the course* of a performance: they were a fixed convention from the outset, not manipulated during intense moments to heighten the mood.

One clear consequence of the indoor lighting, however, was that performances had to be interrupted occasionally to allow the candelabra to be lowered and the wicks of the candles to be trimmed, to avoid hot wax falling dangerously. This meant that plays were staged with predictable intermissions for the first time in an adult commercial playhouse, thus imposing something resembling an act-by-act, rather than scene-by-scene, structure. We shall observe this shortly in the text of *The Tempest*, one of the few plays by Shakespeare to have come to us marked as it was probably staged at the Blackfriars.[11] A detail in the folio (1623) text of *A Midsummer Night's Dream*, however, seems to reflect the changed conditions. At the end of what it marks as Act 3 it gives the direction *"They sleep all the act."* This refers to Hermia, Lysander, Helena, and Demetrius, who are all asleep at this point. There is no stage direction in the comparable point in the quarto text, for the simple reason that one is not necessary – it is obvious that they do not leave the stage, since the fairies enter immediately, to be followed shortly by Theseus and Hippolyta. But in the folio version there is clearly meant to be a break between Act 3 and Act 4, and normally the stage would have been cleared at the end of the former. Instead, in a little metatheatrical gesture, the lovers are directed to remain on stage, asleep, until the next act starts.

As they did so, we may assume that music played. The consort of musicans assembled by the Blackfriars boys was retained by the King's Men (see p. 174). Their duties included offering a concert of music for up to an hour before the play began, and also playing much more briefly between the acts. When Frederic Gerschow, secretary/tutor to the Duke of Stettin-Pomerania, saw the boy actors at the Blackfriars in 1602 he noted: "For a whole hour before the play begins there is a delightful performance with musical instruments, organs, lutes, bandores [large bass string instruments, to be plucked], mandolins, violins and flutes" (Gurr, 2004a, 80, in his own translation from the German.) John Marston's Blackfriars play, *Sophonisba* (pub.1606), calls variously for "cornets, organ, and voices," "organs, viols and voices," "organ and recorders play to a single voice" (B. R. Smith, 1999, 221). Philip Rosseter, a musician who became part of the management of the Children of the Whitefriars in 1609, published *Lessons for Consorts* that same year, all arranged for a broken consort of bandora, cittern, lute, flute, and treble and bass viol – "broken" in this context meant mixing multiple families of instruments, such as woodwind and strings. This precisely matched the six instruments prescribed in Thomas Morley's *First Book of Consort Lessons* (1599) and we might hazard a guess that these were the instruments used by the core consort at the Blackfriars. But contemporary accounts of the music played while the boys were resident there all describe use of one or more organs, while some also mention cornet and hautboys, which cannot reliably be placed in the Globe before 1608. [12] There is no knowing how much doubling of instruments went on, but it is quite possible that the King's Men inherited as many as nine musicians in total with the new playhouse.

We can in fact be even more specific than this if we look to 1624 and Sir Henry Herbert's "Protection List" of that year, which gives us a rare insight into the body of adult males employed by the Kings Men at that time, including their musicians. That December Sir Henry, the Master of the Revels, listed twenty-two people who "are all employed by the King's Majesty's servants in their quality of playing as musicians and other necessary attendants." He separately added two others to the list, making twenty-four. This list was to prevent those named from being "arrested, or detained under arrest, imprisoned, pressed for soldiers or any other molestation" and was backed by the Lord Chamberlain (*Herbert*, 158). England was going war with Spain and there was a serious risk that those employed by the King's Men might be pressed into service. The sharers themselves, as "the King's Majesty's servants" – by then approximately twelve in number – were Grooms of the King's Chamber and so exempt from impressment. [13] But these twenty-four were separately distinguished as "musicians and other necessary attendants," hired men, who would have been vulnerable without this protection.

The list repays attention because we can identify, or at least make informed guesses about, a surprisingly large number of the twenty-four and their functions – only five of them escape even provisional identification. And with this information we can make some reasonable inferences about what similar lists in the 1590s or 1610 might have looked like. Only one of the nineteen more-or-less identifiable was not a performer, either a musician or an actor – Edward Knight, the company's book-keeper, who heads the list (see pp. 177ff). Perhaps the other four were employed in occupations that left less of a record, such as stage-keeper and tiremen (see pp. 180, 169).

The most useful analysis of the list is that made by John P. Cutts, a musicologist, who concludes:

> of the twenty-four people mentioned in the 1624 Protection List the following seven can definitely be identified as musicians: Ambrose Byland (violinist), Henry Wilson (violinist and lutenist), William Saunders (violinist and wind instruments), William Tawyer (trumpeter), Edward Shackerly (instrument unknown), Jeffery Collins (instrument unknown) and Nicholas Underhill (trumpeter); and there is a possibility that four more were musicians too: William Chambers (singer), George Rickner (trumpeter?), John Rhodes (instrument unknown) and Alexander Bullard (recorder player; trumpeter?). (1966, 104)

This, then, (with Knight) accounts for up to twelve of the twenty-four. Some of these names are familiar from elsewhere. In the 1623 folio text of *A Midsummer Night's Dream*, when the mechanicals enter in the final scene the direction reads "Tawyer with a trumpet before them" (5.1.125.0). Nicholas Underhill had been a boy player, apprenticed to the Ambrose Byland (or Beeland) who is the first on the list named by Cutts.[14] Cutts identifies Underhill as a trumpeter by association with other trumpeters in his family, but there is evidence that he was certainly a violinist. Both he and Byland performed as violinists in James Shirley's 1634 masque, *The Triumph of Peace* (Gurr, 2004a, 219, 245). But it is entirely possible that Underhill was proficient with both instruments, which would have been used in different contexts. He is probably the "Nick" who played Barnavelt's wife in the 1619 Fletcher/Massinger play, *Sir John van Olden Barnavelt*, as well as the role of Shackle in *The Soddered Citizen* (1630) and minor roles (officer, attendants) in *Believe as You List* (1631). Such an adaptable performer would have been very useful to the company. By the same token, George Rickner, identified by Cutts as a possible trumpeter is almost certainly the "Geo. Rick" marked out to play a servant in *The Honest Man's Fortune* (1625).

Of those Cutts does not mention, we can certainly identify the following: Richard Sharpe who, with Edward Shackerly, was one of the two not on the general list; he was a player on the point of becoming a sharer in the company, which he remained until 1632 (see pp. 183, 314–15). He presumably had not yet been sworn into the king's service and so needed protection. William Patrick is on record as acting as a senator in *The Roman Actor* (1626) and in various minor parts in *Believe As You List* (1631). William Mago similarly had small parts in Massinger's *Believe As You List*, as did William Gascoyne, while George Vernon, formerly a boy player apprenticed to John Lowin, is recorded as playing small roles in *The Roman Actor* and John Ford's *The Lover's Melancholy* (1628). Robert Pallant was another boy player, apprenticed to John Heminge in 1620, who may have played the role of Cariola in *The Duchess of Malfi* circa 1621/2 (Bentley, 1941–68, 2: 519). Finally, the quarto text of *The Two Noble*

Kinsmen identifies Thomas Tuckfield as an attendant in a revival of the play circa 1625 (Shakespeare and Fletcher, 1989, 5.3.0.2n). So at least seven on the list are on record as non-sharer actors (one still formally an apprentice), to add to Cutts' seven probable and four possible musicians (among whom Underhill and Rickner also acted). Thus, with Knight, perhaps as many as nineteen are identified.

The Blackfriars broken consort, as we have noted, used an eclectic mix of instruments from various families. But they would *not* have used trumpets, which were not employed at this time in musical ensembles. Their role was to announce ceremonial entrances and exits, to give signals on the battlefield – all of which might have been highly resonant in an indoor theatre. And there is no mention in the list of drummers, who were similarly traditionally called for in ceremonial and martial scenes. Unless their use proved overpowering indoors, there must have been at least two of them, as there would be trumpeters. They also had other, offstage functions, connected with publicising the company's performances (see pp. 174–5). It is very likely, in fact, that most of the people named under the Protection List, except perhaps the core consort of musicians, would have performed multiple functions around the playhouse. If that consort used the regular number of six instruments (to which we may add up to the three other instruments known to have been used at the Blackfriars but not earlier at the Globe – cornets, hautboys and organs), that would mean that Shakespeare's company perhaps employed sixteen or so hired men at the Theatre, the Curtain, and the Globe, in the days before they acquired use of the Blackfriars. They were used primarily as actors in lesser roles, or in a range of smaller-scale musical positions (they certainly needed lutenists, as well as trumpeters and drummers, even before they took on the consort), but also to be available for other functions offstage. These figures may not account, however, for those like tiremen and gatherers, who may not have been deemed "necessary attendants" in Herbert's view – though it would not have been easy to cope without someone who knew his way around all the costumes.

The New Repertoire

How did the acquisition of the Blackfriars affect the nature of the plays the King's Men would henceforth commission? It is commonplace to associate the indoor playhouse with the new vogue for romances or tragicomedies, plays which John Fletcher distinguished from tragedies and comedies in this way: "A tragi-comedy is not so called in respect of mirth and killing, but in respect it wants deaths, which is enough to make it no tragedy; yet brings some near it, which is enough to make it no comedy. Which must be a representation of familiar people, with such kind of trouble as no life be questioned; so that a god is as lawful in this as in a tragedy, and mean people as in a comedy" (To the

Reader, *The Faithful Shepherdess*). Fletcher and his early collaborator, Francis Beaumont, started by writing for the boy companies and quickly became associated with this genre – though The *Faithful Shepherdess* itself was a failure when it was staged at the Blackfriars in 1608. They wrote *Philaster* (circa 1610) and *A King and No King* (circa 1611) in this mode for the King's Men, with great success; but when those plays were published, in 1620 and 1619 respectively, their title-pages associate them both with the Globe, and not the Blackfriars.

Shakespeare also contributed to this new genre, though in his own distinctive mode. Indeed, his highly successful *Pericles* has some claim to be the earliest romance/tragicomedy (certainly the earliest one to be conspicuously successful), and that was a Globe play. Where Beaumont and Fletcher focused on issues of love and honor placed under extreme pressure (issues that were close to the heart of the gentry who perhaps formed the core of the Blackfriars audience, and resonated even more strongly in the 1630s), Shakespeare concentrated on families divided, children and wives lost, strange reconciliations under challenging circumstances. He followed *Pericles* with *Cymbeline, The Winter's Tale,* and *The Tempest. Henry VIII* (staged as *All is True*) and *The Two Noble Kinsmen*, the latter co-written with Fletcher, are not quite in the same mode but they have affinities.

But of these *The Winter's Tale* and *All is True* were certainly staged at the Globe. The doctor/astrologer Simon Forman saw *The Winter's Tale* at the Globe in May 1611 and probably saw *Cymbeline* there at some time the same year.[15] *All is True*, described as a new play, was what was playing when the Globe burned down in 1613. This seems all the odder because some of the key events of the play – the trial of Katherine of Aragon – took place in the Parliament chamber in Blackfriars, the very space now occupied by the playhouse. And the text draws attention to the fact. Henry VIII says:

> The most convenient place that I can think of
> For such receipt of learning is Blackfriars;
> There ye shall meet about this weighty business.
> (2.2.137–8)

It was surely *meant* to be performed at the Blackfriars. But the only concrete evidence we have places it in the Globe. In short, the evidence we have is that tragicomedy was a genre that played as well, and at least as commonly, in the Globe as it did in the Blackfriars. And the plays we have mentioned here probably migrated between the theatres as readily as they migrated to court when they were called for there. We know with unusual specificity that *The Tempest* and *The Winter's Tale* opened the Revels season of 1611/12 in November, while *A King and No King* followed the night after Christmas, another major date in the festive calendar; the following winter *A King and No King* and *The Tempest* appeared again, along with *Philaster* and *Cardenio*, a lost Shakespeare–Fletcher collaboration.

There is no doubt about there being a vogue for romances/tragicomedies, or that the company went out of its way to meet it. But it is doubtful if the acquisition of the Blackfriars playhouse was the key driver in this. As Leeds Barroll puts it "narratives that assume a straightforward linkage between the 'romances' and the 'new Blackfriars playing space' fail to do justice to the complexities of the historical record" (2005, 168). Both playhouses seem to have played their parts. One issue, however, may suggest a difference between them, and that is the use of descent machinery. As I have been at pains to show, the Globe either did not have descent machinery (at least, prior to 1608) or the writers of those of its plays which have survived made a deliberate decision not to use it. But from 1609 onwards, descents become a fairly regular feature of the company's plays.

Descent Machinery

So in *Cymbeline* there is the extended vision of Posthumous, which is given with detailed stage directions:

> *Solemn music. Enter, as in an apparition, Sicilius Leonatus, father to Posthumous, an old man, attired like a warrior; leading in his hand an ancient matron, his wife, and mother to Posthumous, with music, before them. Then, after other music, follows the two younger Leonati, brothers to Posthumous, with wounds as they died in the wars. They circle Posthumous round, as he lies sleeping.* (5.4.29 SD)

His family laments what has happened to Posthumous and call on Jupiter to relieve him:

> *Jupiter descends in thunder and lightning, sitting upon an eagle. He throws a thunderbolt. The ghosts fall on their knees.* (92 SD)[16]

Later Jupiter demands "Mount, eagle, to my palace crystalline" and *Ascends* (113 and SD). It is a theatrical tour de force, drawing on extended music, rolling of cannonballs offstage for thunder, fireworks or a banner quickly drawn across the stage for lightning, and what was very likely an impressive "squib" for the thunderbolt. Amid all this Jupiter descends upon an eagle, on which he later re-ascends.

This differs in two particulars from what we have observed earlier at the Globe: the length, variety and/or complexity of the music called for, and the descent machinery. As I shall suggest, these are characteristic of plays expressly written for the Blackfriars. Yet, at 3264 lines, *Cymbeline* is over 50 percent longer than the 1908 lines of *The Malcontent* as the boys staged it at the Blackfriars; it is even 30 percent longer than the 2531 lines with which *The Malcontent* was staged at the Globe. This seems odd if we assume that Blackfriars performances also included music. We may note that Simon Forman says nothing at all about Jupiter or a descent in his record of the play as he saw it. Is it likely that he would overlook such a spectacular scene? (see p. 320, Note 15). But he says nothing, either, about anyone being pursued by a bear, or Hermione's statue "coming to life," in *The Winter's Tale*. Who can say why he recorded – or omitted – precisely what he did? This does, however, leave open the possibility that *Cymbeline* was not staged at the Globe as the text we have prescribes. Spectacular as the descent might be, it is not strictly necessary. If Hymen could simply enter as he does in *As You Like It* (5.4), or Pericles have his vision of Diana without a scripted descent (5.1), Jupiter could certainly make an impressive entrance without pulleys.

There is yet another possibility, but before exploring that it is time to look at plays from this period that have survived in texts very probably intended for Blackfriars performance. Of Shakespeare's plays two in particular suggest themselves: they are within 100 lines of the length of the original *Malcontent* and they both call for descents. One of them quite explicitly calls for a wider range of music than we have encountered with any earlier play. These are *The Tempest* and, more surprisingly, *Macbeth*. Latterly I shall look at a play that somehow defies the length constraints; possibly the pre-show concert was not a feature of *every* performance. *The Two Noble Kinsmen* is some 2800 lines long, but undoubtedly a Blackfriars play.

The Tempest is 2015 lines long and contains some of the most detailed stage directions of any Shakespeare play, a great majority of them involving sound of one kind or another. It opens with "*A tempestuous noise of thunder and lightning heard*" (1.1.0 SD). In the second scene, "*Enter Ferdinand; and Ariel, invisible, playing and singing*" (1.2.377 SD);[17] when his song reaches the word "burden" [refrain], the direction is *Burden, dispersedly* (385 SD) – it is picked up by other supposed spirits, probably in the tiring-house. In Act 2, "*Enter Ariel playing solemn music*" (2.1.185 SD) and again "*Enter Ariel, with music and song*" (298 SD). In the next scene, "*Enter Caliban with a burden of wood. A noise of thunder heard*" (2.2.0 SD) and "*Enter Stephano, singing*" (41 SD). When Stephano and Trinculo try to sing together, Caliban recognizes "That's not the tune" and Ariel obliges: "*Ariel plays the tune on a tabor and pipe*" (125 SD). When Prospero turns his magic on the king and his party "*solemn and strange music; Prospero on the top, invisible*" and "*Enter several strange shapes, bringing in a banquet, and dance about it with gentle actions of salutations; and inviting the king etc. to eat, they depart*" (3.3.17 SD and 19 SD). But then "*Thunder and lightning. Enter Ariel, like a harpy, claps his wings upon the table, and with a quaint device the banquet vanishes*" (52 SD). The masque which Prospero's spirits stage in Act 4 starts with *"Soft music"* (4.1.59 SD) and shortly *"Juno descends"* (72 SD), apparently taking nearly thirty lines of dialogue before she alights; as the masque turns to dancing, *"Enter certain reapers, properly habited. They join with the nymphs in a graceful dance, towards the end whereof Prospero starts suddenly, and speaks; after which, to a strange, hollow, and confused noise, they heavily vanish"* (139 SD). In the next scene, Stephano, Trinculo and Caliban receive less courtly treatment: *"A noise of hunters heard. Enter divers spirits, in shape of dogs and hounds, hunting them about, Prospero and Ariel setting them on"* (256 SD). As Prospero pursues his course with Alonso and the others, *"Ariel sings and helps to attire him"* (5.1.87 SD), changing his *"magic robes"* (5.1.0 SD) for his finery as Duke of Milan. The last piece of theatrical magic is *"Here Prospero discovers Ferdinand and Miranda, playing at chess"* (172 SD).

As Gurr and Ichikawa observe: "Its off-stage music, its songs, its two spectacles (a banquet visited by a harpy and a masque), its lack of fights or fireworks, the large proportion of scenes that call for few players on stage, in later years all became standard features of the plays written for indoor venues" (2000, 38). Yet the play is almost on a par with *The Devil's Charter* in exploiting its playhouse's resources – the discovery space, saved till the end (as usual, little happens within it, Ferdinand and Miranda speak from its mouth); a trap – perhaps more sophisticated than the one at the Globe – allowing the banquet to vanish *"with a quaint device."* The trap may also explain how the nymphs, reapers and goddesses of the masque *"vanish heavily."* (Smoke would be a useful accessory here, and they certainly knew how to use it). There is no conventional use of an upper stage scripted, but Prospero appears at one point *"on the top,"* which seems to point to an even higher spot above the tiring house, possibly a lantern in the ceiling of the building, a genuinely commanding height. The musicians are called upon to provide *Solemn and strange music* and *soft music*, to accompany dancing, and possibly to provide the *strange, hollow, and confused noise*, while noise-effects men behind the scenes are kept busy with the *thunder* and the sounds of hunters, and lightning flashes either with fireworks or with banners. And of course there is the descent, splendid with Juno in her chariot pulled by her sacred peacocks ("Her peacocks fly amain": 4.1.74).

When we turn to *Macbeth* there are two features which point to the version as we have it being prepared for the Blackfriars. One is the remarkable brevity: at 2084 lines it is over a thousand lines shorter than *Othello, King Lear, Antony and Cleopatra, Coriolanus,* or *Hamlet*, the length that we associate with the indoor theatre. It is one of very few Shakespeare plays, and the only tragedy, that can comfortably be performed within the traditional "two hours" traffic of the stage even today. More tellingly, however, it is apparent that the play has been revised. The play originally dates from circa 1606, since it has allusions to the Gunpowder Plot of the year before; and Simon Forman records having seen it at the Globe on April 20, 1611, presumably in its original form (Rowse, 1974, 308).

But in 3.5 and again in 4.1 the text calls for songs for Hecate and the three witches, only the titles of which are given in the printed version, "Come away, come away" (3.5.36) and "Black spirits" (4.1.44). Those songs are given in full in Thomas Middleton's tragicomedy, *The Witch* (circa 1615–16). And it is reasonable to infer that someone – possibly Middleton himself – incorporated them into a revised version of Shakespeare's play, perhaps at about the same time, giving us the version of the text that we now have. When we look, in particular, at "Come away, come away" in its full original setting we see that it accompanies both a descent and an ascent: "A spirit like a cat descends" (3.5.47.0) and Hecate departs with that spirit:

> Now I go, now I fly,
> Malkin, my sweet spirit, and I.
> O, what a dainty pleasure 'tis
> To ride in the air
> When the moon shines fair.
>   (59–63)[18]

The truncated version we have in the Shakespeare text has Hecate saying "My little spirit, see,/Sits in a foggy cloud and stays for me" (34–5). There is no other explanation of the "little spirit," so it is reasonable to suppose that the whole sequence with Middleton's spirit cat was reproduced there, with descent and ascent. And this marks the play as we have it, like *The Witch*, as probably a Blackfriars one.

I did, however, mention yet another possibility, which further complicates all this guesswork. That is that the Globe might have been adapted (perhaps in the extensive plague breaks of 1608–10), the more readily to allow effects from Blackfriars-orientated plays to be achieved in the amphitheater. As the company contemplated how to make best use of two playhouses, it would certainly have made sense to ensure that as much of their repertoire as possible could be played in both venues. That is, descent machinery might have been installed and some provision made to house the musicians – answering the question of how the consort were employed during the summer months, when it would seem they exclusively used the Globe. In the Prologue to the folio version of *Every Man In His Humour* (1616) Jonson derides how the "creaking throne comes down the boys to please" in plays other than his own, making it seem like a traditional feature of popular theatre. But, as we have seen, the surviving record of the Globe's repertoire, and certainly of Shakespeare's plays, makes no demands on such a facility until after the company's acquisition of the Blackfriars. Such texts may therefore actually reflect solely Blackfriars, or they may indicate that the Globe installed equipment for descents around this time.[19]

Housing for the musicians is an issue in itself. So long as the King's Men used the Theatre, Curtain, or Globe there was no call to make special provision for them – trumpeters and drummers would perform on stage, or within the tiring house, as would those who played an occasional flute or lute. But once they had the Blackfriars and its consort separate provision would have to have been made. Indeed, we might assume that there was already such provision in the playhouse as they acquired it from the boys. But some new thinking might have been necessary at the Globe, if indeed the consort also served there in some capacity.

There are several references in the era to "music houses" or "music rooms," in both public and private playhouse, though none in a public playhouse earlier than circa 1610. *Antonio's Revenge* (circa 1600), for example, requires that "*While the measure is dancing, Andrugio's Ghost is placed betwixt the music houses*" (5.5.17.2–3 SD). This was at the Paul's playhouse where, as E. K. Chambers puts it, "there was at the back of the stage a 'musick tree,' which apparently rose out of a 'canopie' and bore a 'music house' on either side of it" (*ES*, 2: 557). Middleton's *A Chaste Maid in Cheapside* (? 1613), the only play specifically known to have been written for the Swan, contains the direction "*there is a sad song in the music-room*" – but see p. 10 (5.4.0 SD; 2007*b*). And Jasper Mayne specifically praised Jonson, after his death, that "Thou laidst no sieges to the music room" (*Jonsonus Virbius*, 1638).

This last strongly suggests that music rooms might be on the same level as upper stages which, in addition to permitting windows or balcony scenes, were sometimes used to represent the battlements of a besieged town or castle. So, for example, "*Richard appeareth on the walls*" (3.3.61.3–4) and talks to Northumberland in *Richard II*, and "*Enter Henry the Sixth and Richard, with the Lieutenant, on the walls*" in *Richard III* (5.6.0 SD). In *The Devil's Charter*, as we saw, the action could be much more athletic and involve the use of scaling ladders. Mayne's point is that Jonson did not write plays that called for such derring-do – and as a result did not disturb the musicians in the music room. But he may indirectly be telling us that when plays did call for such action they cleared the music room temporarily for those purposes. That would mean that they would not have to disturb the spectators in the lords' rooms, which were also apparently on the same level as the upper stage, who would however have an unusually good view of the action. In respect of the Blackfriars, however, it should be said that there is no evidence of lords' rooms being used after the King's Men took over: Dekker's joke that the fashion of the gentry for sitting on the stage had rendered them theatrical "suburbs" may have been only too apt (see pp. 295, 298). They may still have been there but ceased to have pride of place, making them less worthy of mention. This may also have made it easier to install a music room on that level.

Jonson and Shakespeare in the New House

Let us begin to conclude this narrative of Shakespeare's theatre with a reflection on the moment, probably in 1610, when the playwright first faced up to writing for an indoor playhouse, something he had never done in a career of twenty years or more. Of course, as we have observed, the Blackfriars in many respects tried to recreate the ambience of the great houses of the gentry and he had long experience of working in such places. Moreover, he was well used to performances by candlelight, which he would have found at the Inns of Court and at the court itself – though the latter put on a blaze of light that it seems the commercial playhouses could hardly afford to emulate. Nevertheless there are signs that he payed careful attention to writing for his new venue, taking his cue from someone with long experience of indoor playhouses.

Ben Jonson had written *Cynthia's Revels* and *Poetaster* for the Children of the Chapel at the Blackfriars shortly after that operation opened in 1600. And most recently he had written *Epicene, or The Silent Woman* for the Children of the Whitefriars, a company put together from remnants of the Blackfriars boys and the King's Revels troupe – notionally a boy company, though most of them by now were young men. The King's Men had commissioned Jonson to write one of their earliest new plays for the Blackfriars, if not in fact the very first of them. Jonson wrote them *The Alchemist*, a play specifically set in the Blackfriars precinct: all the action takes place in or just outside Lovewit's house, "here, in the Friars" (1.1.17; 2012*a*) and the play abounds in local details (Jonson lived nearby), such as a gibe at Face for being an "apocryphal captain,/Whom not a Puritan in Blackfriars will trust/So much as for a feather" (1.1.127–9). There was a notable Puritan community in the district and they were leaders in the trade in feathers for the fashion industry.

In its close adherence to this single location the *The Alchemist* conformed to the classical unity of place, a most unusual choice for a Jacobean dramatist, though one that Jonson increasingly followed. He also followed the unity of time with an exactness that even Aristotle could hardly have contemplated, marking off the progress of the action with great deliberation. As Peter Holland and William Sherman put it, "The Prologue's 'two short hours' for the performance come remarkably close to the play's fictional time-span" (Jonson 2012*a*, 545). And Jonson pins the date of the action just as precisely: November 1, 1610. Some have thought this was the day of its first performance at the Blackfriars, and it might have been. But this would have been difficult to predict, given the long-running plague (which is also an issue within the play). The one context in which Jonson could be certain that a performance would take place on that set date was at court, where under King James November 1 was the usual first day of the Revels season – and court Revels continued, plague or no plague. We have no record of what plays the King's Men put on in that court season of 1610/11 but there were fifteen of them, and I would not bet against *The Alchemist* having been the first.

The old Master of the Revels, Edmund Tilney, had died that August and been replaced by Sir George Buc. Jonson already knew him; they mixed in the circle of Sir Robert Cotton and both drew on his famous library (Sharpe, 1979, 195–221). Shakespeare also knew him, since Buc had approached him for information about an old play, of which he had acquired a copy (Nelson, 1998). Buc was doubtless anxious to make a good impression in his first season in charge of the court Revels and Jonson – well known at court for his masques, which he produced almost annually – would have been a strong choice to lead it off, as he was to do three years later, when *Bartholomew Fair* led off the 1614/15 Revels. All of this could only have given Shakespeare more of an incentive to learn what he could from Jonson.

Andrew Gurr argues that "Shakespeare's *Tempest* ... was almost certainly written while *The Alchemist* was in rehearsal" (1996, 80). And we know that Jonson's play was ready by late summer (August/September) 1610 since it was alongside *Othello* in the repertory of the King's Men at Oxford, on tour to escape the plague (Sutton, 2006). It is as if Shakespeare took his cue from these lines of Jonson: "I will teach you/How to beware to tempt a fury again/That carries tempest in hand and voice" (1.1.60–2). Where *The Alchemist* barely moves outside Lovewit's house, *The Tempest* is entirely confined to Prospero's island (in a marked break from the wide-ranging geographies of recent plays like *Cymbeline* and *The Winter's Tale*). Jonson's play is about con-trickery centering on the figure of a (fake) alchemist – a magician of sorts; Shakespeare's is about a magician with real powers, working his spells on a range of different characters (Levin, 1971). And *The Tempest* "seems to parody Jonson's timing by matching the time of the plot immaculately not just to the time of a day but to the time of the performance ... Both plays were written for afternoon performance at the Blackfriars" (Gurr, 80).

But there the similarities end. Jonson sticks by his commitment to a kind of realism in the sorts of characters he portrays and their speech, offering "deeds and language such as men do use/And persons such as comedy would choose" (Prologue to *Every Man In His Humour*, folio text, 9–10; 2012h. See pp, 244; 308). The plot may operate with the finest artistry, but its raw materials are characters drawn straight from the streets of London. By contrast, Shakespeare presents us with airy spirits and a "servant monster" apparently spawned by a witch (3.2.3, 4 & 8); and they are located on a remote island, apparently in the Mediterranean but bearing touches of the Americas. *The Alchemist* calls for no music at all and the only scripted sound effect is "*A great crack and noise within*" as the alchemist's supposed "works/Are blown *in fumo*" (4.5.54.1, 57–8), whereas:

> The isle is full of noises,
> Sounds, and sweet airs, that give delight and hurt not.
> Sometimes a thousand twangling instruments
> Will hum about mine ears.
> (3.2.1369)

Caliban's wonder surely echoes the effect of this play on the audience at the Blackfriars. And Alonso, King of Naples, seems to voice not only his own amazement but that of most people in the playhouse: "This must crave --/An if this be at all – a most strange story"; "These are not natural events; they strengthen/From strange to stranger"; "This is as strange a maze as e'er men trod" (5.1.116–17, 229–30, 244). "Strangeness" is a particular characteristic of Shakespeare's late plays (though it is not uncommon in earlier works), possibly in response to qualities of the Blackfriars stage.

Jonson plays the alchemical trick of turning the base metal of everyday life into gold; Shakespeare turns "a most strange story" into a moving enactment of remorse, redemption and reconciliation, where "Prospero [did find] his dukedom/In a poor isle; and all of us ourselves/When no man was his own" (Gonzalo, 5.1.213–15). But at heart what both of them are doing is dramatizing the experience of theatre itself. For Jonson, acting is always a confidence trick, and his three principals are all actors: Subtle pretending to be an alchemist or cunning man, Dol playing the Queen of Faery, and Face, the con-artist par excellence, who shifts from Captain to Lungs to Jeremy butler at a farcical pace. While they collaborate their "venture tripartite" is invincible, each bearing up the others' credibility; they string along a dizzying succession of different dramas to satisfy each of the gulls they lure into Lovewit's house. The return of Lovewit, however, confronts all these fantasies with a blunt common sense, exploding them all *in fumo* – only to leave us with a wry twist in which Lovewit's restored mastery is seen to be a scenario which Jeremy/Face continues to control.

Prospero's "so potent art" (5.1.50) is a very different medium, one confident that the audience will meet him halfway in sustaining a mystery. If they are being conned they know it and willingly share in a suspension of disbelief for the pleasure and emotional release it will bring. It is, perhaps literally, perhaps metaphorically, a collective act of faith, most majestic but also most vulnerable when – in an obseisance of sorts to Jonson – Prospero stages the masque of Juno, Ceres, and Iris to mark the betrothal of Ferdinand and Miranda (4.1.60–142). He calls it "Some vanity of mine art" and confirms to Ferdinand that the actors are indeed "Spirits, which by mine art/I have from their confines called to enact/My present fancies" (41, 120–2). On New Year's Day 1611 the latest of Jonson's masques, *Oberon*, was magnificently staged at court by Inigo Jones; as usual the speaking parts were performed by members of the King's Men. So here Shakespeare likens his fellow actors (who of course also played the roles of Juno, Ceres, and Iris) to "spirits" summoned by "mine art." Theatre is a piece of magic which entraps even the magician himself, which is why in the Epilogue Prospero has to invoke the power of prayer, the ultimate expression of faith:

> Now I want
> Spirits to enforce, art to enchant,
> And my ending is despair,
> Unless I be relieved by prayer.
>   (13–16)

The rivalry between Shakespeare and Jonson brought out the best in both of them, and in these plays both of them produced supremely effective plays at polar opposites of theatrical style and philosophy. Both plays, we must assume, performed equally well at the Blackfriars playhouse for which they were written. But it is likely that they were transferred at times to the Globe and we know that they were both performed at court – *The Tempest* is recorded on November 1, 1611, while both it and *The Alchemist* were among the twenty plays the King's Men put on over the Revels season of 1612–13, which included the wedding of James's daughter, Princess Elizabeth, to the Elector Palatine.[20] Whatever the playhouse, the plays had to be transportable.

One of the advantages that the Blackfriars shared with the Globe was that it was closely adjacent to the Thames, which made the process of transporting the actors, costumes, and properties to court – especially to nearby Whitehall, where James usually stayed over Christmas – much easier than it had been from the Theatre or the Curtain. It was perfectly possible for them to perform as usual in the afternoon, ending around 5 p.m., and be set up to to appear at court after supper, around 9 p.m. The court, as have noted, was always a major factor in the flourishing of Shakespeare's company, and it is in his late plays that we see some tangible effects of this. *The Winter's Tale*, for example, contains "*a dance of twelve Satyrs*" (4.4.342.1), which was clearly borrowed (costumes and all) from the antimasque to *Oberon*, an entertainment in which numerous satyrs appear. The same play, notoriously, contains the stage direction "*Exit, pursued by a bear.*" This has generated much hilarity over the ages but also a serious debate over whether it could have been a real bear, brought in from one of the nearby bear-baiting pits. The discussion has even been refined recently by the discovery that in 1609 King James was presented with two polar bear cubs, from a Muscovy Company expedition. Could it have been one of those – rather safer than a full-grown fighting bear? It would still have been extremely difficult to control it.

We should consider that in *Oberon* Henry, the Prince of Wales, was brought on stage in a chariot pulled by two bears. There was no way that the safety of the heir to the throne was going to be compromised by the use of live bears: these were men in bear suits. And the coincidence of timing makes it extremely likely that the bear in *The Winter's Tale* was also a man in one of those suits. Such a suit was presumably court property, though it is possible that the King's Men might borrow or lease it by arrangement with the Revels Office, which cared for costumes used in court entertainments. But such questions lie behind Tiffany Stern's wider questioning about these court/playhouse interactions: "was the masque [of satyrs] added specifically, and perhaps only, for a *court* performance of the play (like the one that took place on 5 November 1611) as a reprise of a loved event? In other words, is *Masque of Oberons*'s antimasque successfully and permanently melded into Shakespeare's play, or is it only a temporary visitor there?" (2009*a*, 151). The fact is that we do not know.

We only have a single version of all Shakespeare's plays written after *King Lear* (1606) and can never be certain what venue or occasion that version was prepared for.[21]

Prospero's prayer for release at the end of *The Tempest* is popularly and understandably thought to speak for Shakespeare himself. But the biographical evidence does not really bear this out. *The Tempest* was evidently written 1610/11. Shakespeare was still to write *Henry VIII*, *The Two Noble Kinsmen* and (apparently) the lost *Cardenio*, which meant that he was still writing (in regular collaboration now with John Fletcher) until 1613 at least, possibly even 1614; Fletcher was the man who was to succeed Shakespeare as the company's contracted "ordinary poet," though he was never an actor or sharer in the company (but see E. Collins, 2007). Moreover in March 1613 Shakespeare finally bought a property in London, after a career spent in rented accommodation. And it was in the Blackfriars gateway complex, barely 200 yards from the playhouse (Schoenbaum, 272–5).

None of this speaks to a man urgently preparing to retire. But in fact he never seems to have lived in his Blackfriars property and it is difficult to locate him in any theatrical activity after 1614. In the will Shakespeare drew up shortly before his death in April 1616 there is no mention of his share in the King's Men or his shares in either of their playhouses. He had evidently made a clean break by then, selling off all his holdings. We do not know who he sold the shares in the Globe and the Blackfriars to, but since no outsiders can be traced who might have acquired them, it seems likely that he sold them to colleagues, keeping it all in the company.

But what was left of the company that he co-founded? There is some measure of this in John Webster's *The Duchess of Malfi*, which was first performed in 1613/14, "privately, at the Blackfriars; and publicly at the Globe" (1623 title-page). It is the first English play ever printed which included itemized details of its original cast and so gives us a snapshot of the company around the moment Shakespeare withdrew. John Lowin played Bosola; Richard Burbage played Duke Ferdinand; Henry Condell played the Cardinal; William Ostler played Antonio; John Underwood played Delio; Nicholas Tooley played Forobosco (Underwood and Tooley also played some of the madmen).[22] For some of these roles a second name is given, evidently relating to a revival of the play circa 1621/2. So the dead Burbage was replaced by Joseph Taylor, who had transferred to the King's Men from Lady Elizabeth's Men – he was also to pick up other Burbage roles, including Hamlet. Condell was replaced by Richard Robinson; he had not died but this is perhaps a marker that, like Heminge (who does not appear here at all) he had retired from playing, though he remained in some capacity as a sharer. Robert Benfield, an addition to the company by 1616, replaced the dead Ostler.

Lower down the cast the information seems all to relate to the revival. John Rice is allocated the role of the Marquis of Pescara; he had left the King's Men in 1611, still a boy, and may not have returned until 1619 (see pp. 183, 186–7). Richard Sharpe is named as the Duchess, but had surely been too young for the role in 1613/14; we encountered him earlier in Herbert's Protection List of 1624, when he was still on the point of becoming a sharer – he might well have played the Duchess in 1621/22. As noted earlier, it seems most likely to have been Richard Robinson, the company's leading boy actor at that date, who created the role (see p. 187).

So in 1613/14 only Burbage and Condell of the original group that assembled in 1594/5 were still acting; Heminge had moved exclusively into management. These were the three Shakespeare was to remember with gold rings in his will. Richard Cowley was still officially with the company, but Webster does not credit him with a role. Bryan, Pope, Phillips, Kemp, Sly, and Fletcher had all died or left the company; even Armin had retired circa 1611. The Globe itself burned down on June 29, 1613. As Sir Henry Wotton wryly observed: "This was the fatal period of that virtuous fabric, wherein yet nothing did perish but wood and straw, and a few forsaken cloaks; only one man had his breeches set on fire, that would perhaps have broiled him, if he had not by the benefit of a provident wit put it out with bottled ale" (quoted in Schoenbaum, 1987, 276–7). This was in the middle of a performance of *All is True* (*Henry VIII*), with Lowin in the title role, which was fortuitous since it meant that all the company personnel were on hand to help save the essentials, including "allowed books," plots, parts, costumes, and props. (This contrasts with the burning down of the Fortune in 1621, when the Revels Company lost all its plays and properties.) The experience evidently demonstrated the benefit of having two playhouses, and the sharers rebuilt the Globe, on a brick foundation and with a tiled, rather than thatched, roof; it was completed in less than a year, a testament to the value of what it was replacing.

But probably without Shakespeare's involvement. His last work for the company, as far as we can tell, was *The Two Noble Kinsmen*, co-written with John Fletcher, the only one of his plays published (though not until 1634) as only performed at the Blackfriars. And in it the theatre of the era completes a circuit, since the play tells the same tale of Palamon and Arcite, taken from Chaucer's *The Knight's Tale*, as Richard Edwardes' *Palamon and Arcite*, performed before Elizabeth at Oxford in 1566. It seems to have been staged late in 1613 or early 1614, and demonstrates the authors' complete command of Blackfriars staging.

The Two Noble Kinsmen is a play of ceremonial, of ritual, of chivalric display. It has what might be described as a carefully scheduled soundtrack, which must have been particularly effective in the enclosed confines of the Blackfriars, modulating between the music of courtly ceremony, song, country dancing, repeated sennets on the battlefield and the shrill of cornetts, outcries of passion from offstage. It opens with a spectacular procession:

> *Music. Enter Hymen with a torch burning; a boy in a white robe before, singing and strewing flowers. After Hymen a nymph, encompassed in her tresses, bearing a wheaten garland. Then Theseus between two other*

> *nymphs with wheaten chaplets on their heads. Then Hippolyta, the bride, led by Pirithous, and another holding a garland over her head (her tresses likewise hanging). After her Emilia, holding up her train.* (B1)[23]

The situation is that at the beginning of *A Midsummer Night's Dream*, but the tone and mood are very different. It is reminiscent of some of Jonson's court masques, notably his wedding masque, *Hymenaei*, of 1606. The text then prints the boy's song, "Roses their sharp spines being gone." Immediately there is another ceremonial, but contrasting, entry: "*Enter three Queens in black, with veils stained, with imperial crowns. The first Queen falls down at the foot of Theseus; the second falls down at the foot of Hippolytta; the third before Emilia*" (B1v).

Theseus agrees to defer his wedding to help the three queens bury their dead husbands, which can only be achieved by force of arms: "*Cornetts. A Battle struck within. Then a retreat: Flourish. Then enter Theseus (victor); the three queens meet him, and fall on their faces before him*" (C4). The stage of the Blackfriars was too small to handle battle scenes, all the more so when it had members of the audience sitting, standing, or reclining on it. So Shakespeare and Fletcher handle the violence of the play offstage, generating something of the tension of classical drama, which likewise did not portray violent acts. But here the soundtrack makes them almost tangible. The next scene begins: "*Music. Enter the Queens with the hearses of their knights, in a funeral solemnity, &c*" (C4v).

In the middle of the play a different tone is introduced, with various Maying activities. It appears first at the start of Act 3 ("*Cornetts in sundry places. Noise and hallowing as people a-maying*"), when an angry confrontation between Palamon and Arcite is counterpointed by the repeated sounding of horns, from Theseus and Hippolyta engaged in the Maying offstage. We can, incidentally, talk confidently about "acts" in this play; they are the units of dramatic action, not a printer's affectation. The Maying culminates in morris dancing, flagged by the direction: "*Enter a Schoolmaster, four Countrymen: and [one dressed as a baboon]. Two or three wenches, with a Taborer*" (G2). The taborer, who would almost certainly also have been playing a pipe, signals that we are in the festive mode of a Tarlton or Kemp (see p. 44 and Figure 2.1).But this is foolery that has been fully absorbed into the aesthetics of the court. The sequence had in fact been scripted by Fletcher's former partner, Francis Beaumont, as the second antimasque in the *Masque of the Inner Temple and Gray's Inn*, presented on February 20, 1613 at Whitehall as part of the festivities for the marriage of Princess Elizabeth to the Elector Palatine. It is introduced here like the dance of satyrs in *The Winter's Tale*, suggesting the sexual passion that lies behind the wooing of Theseus and Hippolyta, and Palamon, Arcite, Emilia and the Jailor's Daughter (p. 288). But its energy is not allowed to degenerate into a version of Kemp's jigging.

By the fifth act ceremony and ritual reassert themselves, as the contest between Palamon and Arcite for Emilia takes on the form of a stylized Jacobean tourney, though here a tourney in deadly earnest. To a *"flourish"* of cornetts, *"Enter Palamon and Arcite and their knights."* Arcite and his knights pray to Mars, falling on their faces and then kneeling. When he asks Mars for a sign *"Here they fall on their faces as formerly, and there is heard clanging of armour, with a short thunder as the burst of a battle, whereupon they all rise and bow to the altar"* (K4v). As they leave, Palamon and his knights return and they repeat these rituals, but praying to Venus rather than Mars. When he asks for a sign: *"Here music is heard. Doves are seen to flutter. They fall again upon their faces, then on their knees"* (L1v). Doves were sacred to Venus; perhaps they were real doves, released behind the altar, perhaps it was an effect created by casting shadows on a screen.

They return to the conflict. Emilia enters to pray to Diana, goddess of chastity.

> *Still music of recorders. Enter Emilia in white, her hair about her shoulders, a wheaten wreath. One in white holding up her train, her hair stuck with flowers. One before her carrying a silver Hind, in which is conveyed incense and sweet odours, which being set upon the Altar, her maids standing aloof, she sets fire to it, then they curtsey and kneel.* (L1v)

"Still" means that the recorders played throughout. As Emilia's prayer progresses: *"Here the Hind vanishes under the altar: and in the place ascends a rose tree, having one rose upon it"* and shortly thereafter *"Here is heard a sudden twang of instruments, and the rose falls from the tree,"* symbolizing – despite her wish to remain a virgin – her imminent marriage.

The contest between Palamon and Arcite takes place offstage in the penultimate scene, which is repeatedly punctuated with cornetts, cries, shouts, and noises offstage, eventually announcing *"Arcite, victory."* In the final scene Palamon is brought to the scaffold, his penalty for losing. But at the last moment he is saved by news that Arcite has been thrown from his horse, crushed and mortally wounded, thus leaving Palamon the winner of Emilia's hand, by an inscrutable stroke of fate.

I have barely alluded here to the secondary plot of the Jailor's Daughter, which is unremarkable in its staging, but offers as it were occasional respite from the intense stylization of the main story. The latter is perfectly attuned to the confined space of the Blackfriars auditorium, which doubtless reinforced its intensity as what I have described as the soundtrack is played out, with wooden cornetts heavily in evidence, but softer recorders at one poignant moment, repeated cries offstage, and crucially *"a sudden twang of instruments"* as Emilia's rose falls. The demands on the stage are actually minimal: nothing that requires descent machinery, a discovery space or even a trapdoor, unless one was needed to effect the sudden vanishing of Emilia's hind. The most remarkable effects are those involving the altar: the fluttering of the doves, the disappearance of the hind (which is, of course, alight), the growth of the rose tree, and the fall of the rose. All doubtless very effective in a small auditorium, as would be the *"incense and sweet odours"* carried in the hind.

One of the play's most memorable pieces of staging seems to have been the one use of an upper stage: *"Enter Palamon and Arcite above"* (D1v); the next stage direction clarifies that they are in fact in prison, following Theseus's victory. This is where they first catch sight of Emilia, love for whom shatters their long friendship. I call this memorable, because Jonson thought it worthy of parody in *Bartholomew Fair*. As M. C. Bradbrook observed: "The puppeteer shows two faithful friends Damon and Pythias falling out for love of Hero, and abusing each other ... *Bartholomew Fair*, with its puppets leaning out of the booth, must visually have evoked the two prisoners [in *The Two Noble Kinsmen*] leaning out of their prison window: it testifies to the earlier show's success, for Jonson would not waste his satire on a failure" (1976, 241). The joke for Jonson would doubtless have been all the sweeter if *The Two Noble Kinsmen* had been performed at court, so that the satire would be appreciated there when *Bartholomew Fair* led off the 1614/15 Revels season.

Court staging would in many respects have resembled that at the Blackfriars, though the surroundings would have been more lavish and the lighting brighter (see pp. 2, 119). But is this a play that would have transferred comfortably to the Globe? There is nothing in it that precludes its being played there, but it is difficult to believe that the effects of the music, the smells and the miracles at the altar would be as intense on a much larger stage, in sunlight and the open air. Shakespeare and Fletcher had constructed something that would always be most comfortable and effective in small, élite auditoria.

It was now, rather than with *The Tempest*, that Shakespeare finally bowed out. He had mastered every kind of theatrical venue that the King's Men would ever perform in, down to its dissolution in the Civil War. And he left them an unrivalled, time-honored collection of plays, most of which were crafted and recrafted to suit any and all of those venues – a solid core in their repertoire and fortunes going forward. That was what the 1623 First Folio of his *Comedies, Histories and Tragedies* was to acknowledge when Heminge and Condell compiled it, "to keep the memory of so worthy a friend and fellow alive as was our Shakespeare" (Dedication to the Earls of Pembroke and Montgomery, A2v). They were the last survivors of the 1594 company and had prospered more than any from its success. They knew that Shakespeare was a central factor in that success, not only an incomparable poet but a man who understood what worked on their stages.

It tells us everything that in the winter of 1604/5, the second of King James's reign, when his players were called to perform at Whitehall a total of eleven times, eight of those plays were Shakespeare's: *Othello, Merry Wives, Measure for Measure, The Comedy of Errors, Love's Labour's Lost, Henry the Fifth*, and *The Merchant of Venice* twice (apparently because Prince Henry missed the first performance: *ES*, 4: 171–2). One wonders what they had performed the previous year, the first of the reign – *Hamlet*? *Much Ado*? *1 Henry IV*? *As You Like It*? There was a phenomenal back-catalogue already to draw on. But, as is usually the case, that information has not survived. By the same token we do not know why Shakespeare chose to retire after *The Two Noble Kinsmen*. Possibly his looming fiftieth birthday was cause enough. His revels, however, had certainly now ended.

Notes

1 The "Secretary of Florence" was the personal representative of the Grand Duke of Tuscany, though he did not have full ambassadorial status. The habit of ambassadors and foreign royalty visiting playhouses gradually became more common. In 1610 Prince Frederick Lewis of Württemberg brought a large entourage to the Globe to see *Othello*; in 1621 the Spanish Ambassador, Count Gondomar, visited the Fortune in a major act of self-display (Gurr, 2004*b*, 83–4).
2 In 1609/10 the Duke of York's (i.e. Prince Charles') Men performed at court for the first time, and in 1611/12 they were joined by Lady (i.e. Princess) Elizabeth's. But by then the Whitefriars (latterly Queen's Revels) company was ailing. The total number of companies resident in London at any one time never rose above five and was usually less. Only Queen Henrietta's Men from 1625 to 1636 seriously rivalled the King's Men.
3 James Wright in *Historia Histrionica* speaks of the Blackfriars and the Globe in the 1630s as "a winter and a summer house" (B3; 1699). Roslyn Knutson has warned against taking this too literally and against the assumption that the Blackfriars was immediately the King's Men's *primary* playhouse (2002).
4 It may even have *been* Henry Evans; such confusions of names were common enough. Evans was censured by the Court of Star Chamber in 1602 for his part in impressing the children of gentlemen to be trained as actors, an abuse of the powers associated with taking up children for the royal choirs He thereafter distanced himself from the Blackfriars management, though he retained an interest (*ES*, 2: 43–5).
5 *Troilus and Cressida* did also appear with alternative front-matter, apparently denying any public performance at all ("never staled with the stage, never clapper-clawed with the palms of the vulgar").
6 *Richard III*, reprinted in quarto eight times between 1597 and 1634, was never associated with any playhouse. Nor was *Hamlet*, reprinted (the 1604 Q2 version) four times between 1611 and 1637. For such information see *DEEP: Database of Early English Playbooks*, created by Alan Farmer and Zachary Lesser (http://deep.sas.upenn.edu/).

7 Thurles came onstage and stood, blocking the view of Essex and his lady in their box. Essex objected; Thurles ignored him. Essex attempted to push him aside and Thurles attacked him with his sword. The affair ended up in Star Chamber (Gurr, 2004b, 33–4).
8 Dr Cohen is the driving force behind the *third* Blackfriars theatre, in Staunton, Virginia.
9 On the rushes, see pp. 180–1.
10 The frontispiece of Francis Kirkham's *The Wits, Or Sport upon Sport* (1662) shows an unnamed theatre with two candelabra hanging over its stage. They contain a total of sixteen candles. But this has no pretentions to realism. See https://en.wikipedia.org/wiki/Francis_Kirkman.
11 No play by Shakespeare was printed with act divisions prior to the 1623 First Folio, and even there the practice is patchy. *Othello, A Midsummer Night's Dream*, and *King Lear* are fully divided into acts and scenes. *Romeo and Juliet* and *Antony and Cleopatra*, by contrast, start out with a confident *Actus Primus, Scena Prima* – but no further divisions are marked. *Hamlet* marks as far as the second scene of Act 2 but then gives up. It is far from clear in most instances whether those who compiled the First Folio were attempting to mark Blackfriars practice or to emulate Ben Jonson, who consistently printed his plays in the classical manner, with act/scene divisions, most notably in the 1616 folio of his *Works*.
12 The early modern cornet, often spelled "cornett" for distinction, was a woodwind instrument, a long conical pipe with finger holes, unrelated to the modern brass instrument.
13 Pinning the precise number of sharers at any one time is not easy. Fifteen members of the King's Men were granted black livery for the funeral of James I in March 1625; but only twelve are listed that June in the licence granted to the company by the new king, Charles. Moreover, the oldest of them, John Heminge and Henry Condell, were no longer playing by this date, though they appear on both lists. There were perhaps ten performing sharers at this date.
14 In 1628 John Heminge had Byland and Henry Wilson arrested, describing both as "fidlers" (Cutts, 102). Notice that Byland, a member of the Drapers' Company, was able to take on apprentice players, even though he was not a sharer in the acting company.
15 The reference here is to Simon Forman's *Book of Plays*, a manuscript that details four trips he made to the playhouse. The date and venue for *Cymbeline* are not explicit. But the other three plays – in addition to *The Winter's Tale* he saw *Macbeth* and an otherwise unknown play about Richard II – were all at the Globe, and all in 1610/11 (Rowse, 1974, 308–11).
16 Wells and Taylor say of this passage in *Cymbeline* that it "suggest[s] that as Shakespeare wrote he may have had in mind the audience and the stage equipment of the Blackfriars theatre … and stylistic evidence places the play about 1610–11" (1986, 1131).

17 Among the items Henslowe bought for the Admiral's Men was "a robe for to go invisible," evidently a familiar convention, like the impenetrability of disguises in general (*Henslowe*, 325).

18 Cited from Middleton, 2007*f*. The same edition contains a version of *Macbeth* by Gary Taylor, with speculative reconstructions of Middleton's work on/additions to the text (2007*d*).

19 There is in fact one other possibility about the longest texts in the Shakespeare canon, including ones like *Cymbeline* with spectacular effects. That is that they were versions prepared for court, where there were resources to stage virtually anything the players required. I explore this possibility in Dutton, 2016.

20 I have already speculated that *The Alchemist* was first performed at court in the Revels season of 1610/11 and, if suspicions that Shakespeare responded directly to it are correct, *The Tempest* might have been too; see p. 310.

21 Most of these appear only in the 1623 First Folio: *Antony and Cleopatra, Coliolanus, Cymbeline, The Winter's Tale, The Tempest, Henry VIII*. *Pericles* (1609) and *The Two Noble Kinsmen* (1634) each appeared in a single quarto. *Cardenio* has not survived at all.

22 John Russell Brown suspects that Tooley's allocation to Forobosco is a mistake for Malateste; he discusses all the castings and apparent errors in the text in Webster, 2009, 47–51.

23 I am citing from the original 1634 quarto text because modern editors have a habit of tinkering with the stage directions to flesh out what they believe is going on.

Appendix

Chamberlain's/King's Men's Plays 1594–1614,
Other than by Shakespeare

We know precious little about plays written for Shakespeare's company while he was with them other than by Shakespeare himself. We are almost entirely dependent on the luck of plays being published with this information or titles being preserved when they were played at court. In Shakespeare's own time with the company (circa 1594–1614) the only other playwrights we can identify are Ben Jonson, Thomas Dekker, John Marston, Thomas Middleton, George Wilkins, Barnabe Barnes, John Fletcher (alone or with Francis Beaumont, Nathan Field or Philip Massinger), John Webster, Cyril Tourneur, Richard Niccols, and John Ford. It is a small pool, compared with the many names that crop up in Henslowe's *Diary* over a much shorter period. The plays by Tourneur and Niccols have not survived; those by Dekker (*Satiromastix*) and Marston (*The Malcontent*) only came to the company through special circumstances. In all twenty-three such plays up to 1614 are extant; six of those are by Jonson; nine are by Fletcher, with or without collaborators. There are also six anonymous texts associated with the company (seven, if we include *Mucedorus*, an old play they revived). And nine for which we have titles but no texts.

Extant Texts, with Dates of Performance and Publication, and Probable Playhouse of First Performance

These lists are inevitably conjectural in places. None of the plays ascribed to Middleton was associated with him at the time. The dating of most Beaumont and Fletcher plays is guesswork, so some may actually be ineligible for this list, while eligible titles may be missing. We do not know to what extent the Globe and Blackfriars repertories were interchangeable; where I have identified post-1608 texts with one or other it is based on circumstantial evidence (e.g. *The Alchemist*) or title-page assertions, but these are often long after the date of composition. And we cannot assume that texts as printed necessarily reflect their earliest staging.

Anon

Mucedorus (pre-1594; first pub. 1598; revised ed. 1610, after performance at court)
A Warning for Fair Women (early; pub. 1599; Theatre?)
A Larum for London (circa 1601; pub. 1602; Globe)
Thomas, Lord Cromwell (circa 1601; pub. 1602; Globe)
The Fair Maid of Bristow (circa 1603; pub. 1605; Globe)
The London Prodigal (circa 1603; pub. 1605; Globe)
The Merry Devil of Edmonton (circa 1606; pub. 1608; Globe)

Barnabe Barnes, *The Devil's Charter* (1607; pub. 1608; Globe)
Thomas Dekker, *Satiromastix* (1601; pub. 1602; Globe, also staged by Paul's Boys at their own playhouse in the War of the Theatres)
Ben Jonson, *Every Man In His Humour* (1598; pub. 1601, Curtain)
  Every Man Out of His Humour (1599; pub. 1600; Globe)
  Sejanus (1603; pub. 1605; Globe)
  Volpone (1606; pub. 1607; Globe)
  The Alchemist (1610; pub. 1612; Blackfriars)
  Catiline (1611; pub. 1611; Globe)
John Marston, *The Malcontent* (1602–4; transferred from Blackfriars to Globe; Globe version pub. 1604)
Thomas Middleton, *The Revenger's Tragedy* (circa 1606; pub. 1607; Globe)
  A Yorkshire Tragedy (circa 1607; pub. 1608; Globe)
  The Second Maiden's Tragedy (circa 1611; survives in manuscript; Globe or Blackfriars)
John Fletcher (alone or predominant author), *Bonduca* (circa 1609; pub. 1647; Globe or Blackfriars)
  The Woman's Prize (circa 1611; pub. 1647; Globe or Blackfriars)
  Valentinian (circa 1612/13; pub. 1647; Globe or Blackfriars)
  Monsieur Thomas (>1616; pub. 1647; Globe or Blackfriars)
John Fletcher (with Francis Beaumont) *Philaster* (circa 1610; pub. 1620; Globe)
  The Maid's Tragedy (circa 1611; pub. 1619; Blackfriars)
  A King and No King (1611; pub. 1619; Globe)
  The Captain (circa 1612; pub. 1647; Globe or Blackfriars)
  Love's Pilgrimage (circa 1614; pub. 1647; Globe or Blackfriars)
John Webster, *The Duchess of Malfi* (1614; pub. 1623; Globe and Blackfriars)

Non-Extant or Unidentified Plays Associated with the Company

2 The Seven Deadly Sins (Richard Tarlton, pre-1588; at the Curtain circa 1597)
The Tragedy of Gowrie (anon; mentioned in correspondence 1604; Globe)
The Spanish Maze (at court, Shrove Monday 1605; Globe)
Jeronimo (mentioned in Induction to *The Malcontent*, 1604, as a King's Men's play; see pp. 283–4 and Note 4)
Cloth Breeches and Velvet Hose (entered in Stationers' Register, 1600; Globe)
The Freeman's Honour (by Wentworth Smith? circa 1601; Globe)
Knot of Fools (at court 1612–13; Globe or Blackfriars)
A Bad Beginning Makes a Good Ending (by John Ford? at court, 1612–13; Globe or Blackfriars)
The Nobleman (Cyril Tourneur; at court 1612–13; Globe or Blackfriars)
The Twins' Tragedy (Richard Niccols; at court 1612–13; Globe or Blackfriars)

Bibliography

Primary Material from the Sixteenth and Seventeenth Centuries

Where no modern edition is indicated, I have consulted the work on *Early English Books Online* (*EEBO*). All quotations have been silently modernized. Most early books were not paginated. They did, however, carry "signatures" on some (though not all) pages to help the printer assemble them in the right order. Most of the books included here were in quarto format – a large sheet of paper had been folded to give four pages, eight sides. The first such folding might be marked intermittently A1, A2, A3, A4, on the front (recto) side of pages only; it was implicit that the reverse side was A1 verso etc., often expressed A1v. The next folding would be B1, B2, and so on. Hence the perhaps unfamiliar "pagination" given in my text.

Anon. (1609). *Every Woman In Her Humour*. London.
Anon. (1605). *The Fair Maid of Bristow*. London.
Anon. (1968). *Gesta Grayorum*, ed. Desmond Bland. Liverpool: Liverpool University Press.
Anon. (1605). *The London Prodigal*. London.
Anon. (1608). *The Merry Devil of Edmonton*. London.
Anon. (1949). *The Second Part of the Return to Parnassus*. In *The Three Parnassus Plays (1598–1601)*, ed. J. B. Leishman. London: Ivor Nicholson and Watson, Ltd.
Anon. [Anthony Munday?] (1580). *A Third Blast of Retreat From Plays and Theatres*. London.
Anon. (1602). *Thomas, Lord Cromwell*. London.
Anon. (1599). *A Warning for Fair Women*. London.
Barnes, Barnabe (1999). *The Devil's Charter*, ed. Nick de Somogyi. London: Nick Hern Books.

Shakespeare's Theatre: A History, First Edition. Richard Dutton.
© 2018 Richard Dutton. Published 2018 by John Wiley & Sons Ltd.

Birch, Thomas (1754). *Memoirs of the Reign of Queen Elizabeth from the Year 1581 to her Death*. 2 vols. London.
Braithwait, Richard (1631). *English Gentlewoman*. London.
Brome, Richard (2010). *Richard Brome Online*, gen. ed. Richard Cave. (http://www.hrionline.ac.uk/brome, 12 January 2017).
Brome, Richard (2010a). *The Antipodes*, ed. Richard Cave. Modern Text. In Brome, 2010.
Brome, Richard (2010b). *The Court Beggar*, ed. Marion O'Connor. Modern Text. In Brome, 2010.
Buck [Buc], Sir George (1982 [1979]). *A History of King Richard the Third*, ed. A. N. Kincaid. Stroud: Sutton Publishing.
Chamberlain, John (1939). *The Letters of John Chamberlain*, ed. N. E. McClure. 2 vols. Philadelphia: American Philosophical Society.
Chapman, George (1874–5). *The Works of George Chapman*, ed. R. H. Shepherd and A. C. Swinburne, 3 vols. London: Chatto & Windus.
Chettle, Henry (1592). *Kind–Heart's Dream*. London.
Collins, A. (1746). ed. *Letters and Memorials of State. Written and Collected by Sir Henry Sydney, Sir Philip Sydney, Sir Robert Sidney, etc.* 2 vols. London.
Dekker, Thomas (1609). *The Gull's Horn-Book*. London.
Dekker, Thomas (1612). *An Apology for Actors*. London.
Dekker, Thomas (1953–61). *Satiromastix*. In *Thomas Dekker: Dramatic Works*, ed. Fredson Bowers. 4 vols. Cambridge: Cambridge University Press. 1.299–395.
Edwards, Richard (2001). *The Works of Richard Edwards*, ed. Ros King. Manchester: Manchester University Press.
Flecknoe, Richard (1653). *Miscellania*. London.
Fletcher, John and Philip Massinger (1980). *Sir John Van Olden Barnavelt*, ed. T. H. Howard- Hill. Oxford: Malone Society Reprints.
Fletcher, John and William Rowley (1647). *The Maid in the Mill*. Printed in Francis Beaumont and John Fletcher, *Comedies and Tragedies*. London. (Each play separately paginated.)
Gascoigne, George (1576). *The Princely Pleasures at the Court at Kenilworth*. London.
Golding, Arthur (1573). *A Brief Discourse of the Late Murder of Master George Saunders*. London.
Greene, Robert (1964). *Friar Bacon and Friar Bungay*, ed. Daniel Seltzer. London: Edward Arnold.
Greene, Robert (1592). *The Third and Last Part of Conny-Catching*. London.
Henslowe, Philip (2002). *Henslowe's Diary*, ed. R. A. Foakes. 2nd ed. Cambridge: Cambridge University Press.
Jonson, Ben (2012), *The Cambridge Edition of the Works of Ben Jonson*, gen. eds David Bevington, Ian Donaldson, and Martin Butler. 7 vols. Cambridge: Cambridge University Press.
Jonson, Ben (2012a). *The Alchemist*. ed. Peter Holland and William Sherman. In Jonson 2012, 3: 541–710.

Jonson, Ben (2012*b*). *Bartholomew Fair.* ed. John Creaser. In Jonson 2012, 4: 251–428.
Jonson, Ben (2012*c*). *Cynthia's Revels,* quarto version. ed. Eric Rasmussen and Matthew Steggle. In Jonson 2012, 2: 427–547.
Jonson, Ben (2012*d*). *The Devil is an Ass.* ed. Anthony Parr. In Jonson 2012, 4: 465–609.
Jonson, Ben (2012*e*). *Eastward Ho!,* by Jonson, Chapman and Marston. ed. Suzanne Gossett and W. David Kay. In Jonson 2012, 2: 529–640.
Jonson, Ben (2012*f*). *The Entertainment at Althorp.* ed. James Knowles. In Jonson 2012, 2: 393–412.
Jonson, Ben (2012*g*). *Every Man In His Humour,* quarto version. ed. David Bevington. In Jonson 2012, 1: 111–227.
Jonson, Ben (2012*h*). *Every Man In His Humour,* folio version. ed. David Bevington. In Jonson 2012, 4: 617–728.
Jonson, Ben (2012*i*). *Every Man Out of His Humour.* ed. Randall Martin. In Jonson 2012, 1.233–428.
Jonson, Ben (2012*j*). *Hymenaei.* ed. David Lindley. In Jonson 2012, 2: 657–712,
Jonson, Ben (2012*k*). *Informations to William Drummond of Hawthornden.* ed. Ian Donaldson. Jonson 2012, 5: 351–91.
Jonson, Ben (2012*l*). *Love Restored.* ed. David Lindley. In Jonson 2012, 4: 197–212.
Jonson, Ben (2012*m*) *Sejanus.* ed. Tom Cain. In Jonson 2012, 2: 195–391.
Jonson, Ben (2012*n*). *Songs from the Entertainment for the Merchant Taylors' Company.* ed. James Knowles. In Jonson 2012, 3: 217–25.
Jonson, Ben (2012*o*). *The Staple of News.* ed. Joseph Loewenstein. In Jonson 2012, 6: 1–157.
Jonson, Ben (2012*p*). *Volpone.* ed. Richard Dutton. In Jonson 2012, 3: 1–193.
Langham, Robert (1575), *A letter wherein part of the Entertainment unto the Queen's Majesty at Kenilworth Castle in Warwickshire in this summer's Progress 1575 is signified/from a friend officer attendant in court unto his friend, a citizen and merchant of London.* London.
Lodge, Thomas (1596). *Wit's Misery.* London.
Malone, Edmund, ed. (1790). *The Plays and Poems of William Shakespeare.* 10 vols. London: H. Baldwin.
Marlowe, Christopher (1995). *Dr Faustus and Other Plays.* ed. David Bevington and Eric Rasmussen. World's Classics. Oxford: Oxford University Press.
Marston, John (1975*a*). *The Dutch Courtesan.* In *Four Jacobean City Comedies,* ed. Gāmini Salgādo. Harmondsworth: Penguin Books.
Marston, John (1975*b*). *The Malcontent.* ed. G. K. Hunter. Revels Plays. Manchester Manchester University Press.
Marston, John (1978). *Antonio's Revenge.* ed. W. Reavley Gair. Revels Plays. Manchester: Manchester University Press.
Marston, John (1598). *The Scourge of Villainy.* London.
Middleton, Thomas (1993). *A Game at Chess.* ed. T. H. Howard–Hill. The Revels Plays. Manchester: Manchester University Press.

Middleton, Thomas (2007). *Thomas Middleton: The Collected Works*, gen. eds Gary Taylor and John Lavagnino. Oxford: Clarendon Press.

Middleton, Thomas (2007*a*). *The Black Book*. ed. G. B. Shand. In Middleton, 2007, 204–18.

Middleton, Thomas (2007*b*). *A Chaste Maid in Cheapside*. ed. Linda Woodbridge. In Middleton, 2007: 907–58.

Middleton, Thomas (2007*c*). *A Mad World, My Masters*. ed. Peter Saccio. In Middleton, 2007, 414–51.

Middleton, Thomas (2007*d*). *Macbeth*. ed. Gary Taylor. In Middleton, 2007, 1165–1201.

Middleton, Thomas (2007*e*). *The Revenger's Tragedy*. ed. MacDonald P. Jackson. In Middleton, 2007: 543–93.

Middleton, Thomas (2007*f*). *The Witch*. ed. Marion O'Connor. In Middleton, 2007, 1124–64.

Nashe, Thomas (1592). *Pierce Penniless, His Supplication to the Devil*. London.

Nashe, Thomas (1904–10), *Works*. ed. R. B. McKerrow. 5 vols. London: A. H. Bullen.

Prynne, William (1633). *Histriomastix*. London.

Puttenham, George (2007). *The Art of English Poesy*, ed. Frank Wigham and Wayne Rebhorn. Ithaca: Cornell University Press.

Rainolds, Dr John (1599). *Th'Overthrow of Stage-Plays*. Middelburg, Holland.

Rowlands, Samuel (1600). *The Letting of Humour's Blood*. London.

Rowlands, Samuel (1617). *The Bride*. London.

Shakespeare, William (1962). *The Comedy of Errors*, ed. R. A. Foakes. Arden 2. London: Methuen.

Shakespeare, William (1974). *The History of King Henry the Fourth, as revised by Sir Edward Dering, Bart.*, ed. G. W. Williams and G. B. Evans. Charlottesville: University of Virginia for the Folger Library.

Shakespeare, William (1980). *Romeo and Juliet*, ed. Brian Gibbons. Arden 2. London: Methuen, 1980.

Shakespeare, William (1986). *The Complete Works*. Gen. eds Stanley Wells and Gary Taylor. The Oxford Shakespeare. Oxford: Clarendon Press.

Shakespeare, William (2006). *As You Like It*, ed. Juliet Dusinberre. Arden 3. London: Thomson Learning.

Shakespeare, William (2009). *The Complete Works of Shakespeare*. ed. David Bevington. 6th ed. New York and London: Pearson Longman.

Shakespeare, William and John Fletcher (1989). *The Two Noble Kinsmen*. ed. Eugene M. Waith. Oxford: Clarendon Press.

Shakespeare, William and John Fletcher (1634). *The Two Noble Kinsmen*. London.

Stow, John (1605). *Annals, or a General Chronicle of England*. London.

Tayor, John (1638). *Taylor's Feast*. London.

Tilney, Edmund (1992). *The Flower of Friendship: A Renaissance Dialogue Contesting Marriage*, ed. Valerie Wayne. Ithaca: Cornell University Press.

Webster, John (2009; 1974). 2nd ed. *The Duchess of Malfi*, ed. John Russell Brown. The Revels Plays. Manchester: Manchester University Press.
Webster, John and Thomas Dekker (1607). *Northward Ho!* London.
Wilkins, George (1607). *The Miseries of Enforced Marriage*. London.

Secondary Material

Andrews, John F. (1987). "William Shakespeare." In *The Dictionary of Literary Biography, Vol. 62: Elizabethan Dramatists*, ed. Fredson Bowers. Detroit: Gale Research. 267–353.
Astington, John H. (1991). "A Drawing of the Great Chamber at Whitehall in 1601." *REED Newsletter* 16:1, 6–11.
Astington, John H. (1999). *English Court Theatre, 1558–1642*. Cambridge: Cambridge University Press.
Astington, John H. (2009). "Court Theatre." In Dutton, 2009: 307–22.
Astington, John H. (2010). *Actors and Acting in Shakespeare's Time: The Art of Stage Playing*. Cambridge: Cambridge University Press.
Astington, John H. (2014). "An Afterpiece and its Afterlife: a Jacobean Jig [with text]." *English Literary Renaissance* 44: 108–28.
Baker, Oliver (1937). *In Shakespeare's Warwickshire*. London: Simpkin Marshall & Co.
Baldwin, T. W. (1927). *The Organisation and Personnel of the Shakespearean Company*. Princeton: Princeton University Press.
Barker, R. (March 1, 2009). "'Not One Thing Exactly': Gender, Performance and Critical Debates over the Early Modern Boy-Actress." *Literature Compass*, 6, 2: 460–481.
Barroll, J. Leeds. (1988). "A New History for Shakespeare and His Time." *Shakespeare Quarterly* 39: 441–64.
Barroll, J. Leeds (1991). *Politics, Plague, and Shakespeare's Theater: The Stuart Years*. Ithaca and London: Cornell University Press.
Barroll, J. Leeds (2005). "Shakespeare and the Second Blackfriars Theater." *Shakespeare Studies* 33: 156–70.
Barroll, J. Leeds, Alexander Leggatt, Richard Hosley and Alvin Kernan (1975). *Revels History of Drama in English*. 3: 1576–1613. London: Routledge.
Bate, Jonathan and Eric Rasmussen, gen. eds. (2013). *William Shakespeare and Others: Collaborative Plays*. The RSC Shakespeare. Basingstoke: Palgrave Macmillan.
Bawcutt, N. W., ed. (1996). *The Control and Censorship of Caroline Drama*. Oxford: Clarendon Press. Cited parenthetically as *Herbert*.
Bearman, Robert (2002). "'Was William Shakespeare William Shakeshafte?' Revisited." *Shakespeare Quarterly* 53: 83–94.
Beckerman, Bernard (1962). *Shakespeare at the Globe 1599–1609*. New York: Macmillan.

Bednarz, James P. (2001). *Shakespeare and The Poets' War*. New York: Columbia University Press.
Beier, A. L. (1985), *Masterless Men: The Vagrancy Problem in England 1560–1640*. London: Methuen.
Bentley, G. E. (1941–1968). *The Jacobean and Caroline Stage*. 7 vols. Oxford: Clarendon Press.
Bentley, G. E. (1984). *The Profession of Player in Shakespeare's Time, 1590–1642*. Princeton: Princeton University Press.
Bergeron, David (2003; 1971). *English Civic Pageantry 1558–1642*, 2nd ed. Tempe: Arizona State University Press.
Berry, Herbert (1986). *The Boar's Head Playhouse*. Washington: Folger Shakespeare Library.
Berry, Herbert (2002). "Playhouses." In *A Companion to Renaissance Drama*. ed. Arthur Kinney. Oxford and Malden, MA: Blackwell. 147–62.
Bly, Mary (2000). *Queer Virgins and Virgin Queans on the Early Modern Stage*. Oxford: Oxford University Press.
Bly, Mary (2009). "The Boy Companies 1599–1613." In Dutton 2009, 136–50.
Boddy, G. W. (1976). "Players of Interludes in North Yorkshire in the Early Seventeenth Century." In North Yorkshire County Records Office Publications, 10, *Journal* 3: 95–130.
Brown, Pamela A. and Peter Parolin, eds (2005). *Women Players in Early Modern England, 1500–1660*. Aldershot: Ashgate.
Bourus, Terri (2014). *Young Shakespeare's Young Hamlet: Print, Piracy and Performance*. New York: Palgrave Macmillan.
Bowsher, Julian M. C. (2007). "The Rose and Its Stages." *Shakespeare Survey* 60: 36–48.
Bowsher, Julian M. C. (2012). *Shakespeare's London Theatreland*. London: Museum of London Archaeology.
Bowsher, Julian and Pat Miller. (2009). *The Rose and the Globe: Playhouses of Shakespeare's Bankside, Southwark: Excavations, 1988–90*. London: Museum of London Archaeology.
Bradbrook, M. C. (1976). *The Living Monument: Shakespeare and the Theatre of His Time*. Cambridge: Cambridge University Press.
Bullough, Geoffrey (1957–75). *Narrative and Dramatic Sources of Shakespeare*. 8 vols. London: Routledge and Kegan Paul.
Butler, Martin (1992). "Ecclesiastical Censorship of Early Modern Drama: The Case of Jonson's *The Magnetic Lady*." *Modern Philology* 89: 469–81.
Calderwood, David (1842–49). *Historie of the Kirk of Scotland*. 8 vols. Edinburgh: Wodrow Society.
Calendar of State Papers, Domestic: Elizabeth 1598–1601 (1870). ed. Mary Anne Everett Green. London: HMSO.
Callaghan, Dympna (2000). *Shakespeare Without Women: Representing Gender and Race on the Renaissance Stage*. London: Routledge.

Cerasano, Susan P. (2004a). "Alleyn, Edward." (1566–1626). *Oxford Dictionary of National Biography*, Oxford University Press; online edn, Jan 2008 [http://www.oxforddnb.com.proxy.lib.ohio-state.edu/view/article/398, accessed 7 Jan 2014].

Cerasano, Susan P. (2004b). "Henslowe, Philip (c.1555–1616)." In *The Oxford Dictionary of National Biography*, Oxford University Press; online edn, Jan 2008. [http://www.oxforddnb.com.proxy.lib.ohio-state.edu/view/article/12991, accessed 4 Feb 2014].

Cerasano, Susan P. and Marion Wynne-Davies, eds (1996). *Renaissance Drama by Women*. London: Routledge.

Chambers, E. K. (1923). *The Elizabethan Stage*. 4 vols. Oxford: Clarendon Press. Cited parenthetically as *ES*.

Chambers, E. K. (1930). *William Shakespeare: A Study of Facts and Problems*. 2 vols. Oxford: Clarendon Press.

Chernaik, Warren (2014). "Shakespeare as Co-Author: The Case of *1 Henry VI*." *Medieval and Renaissance Drama in England* 27: 192–220.

Clegg, Cyndia Susan (1997). "'By the Choice and Inuitation of Al the Realm': *Richard II* and Elizabethan Press Censorship." *Shakespeare Quarterly* 48: 432–48.

Cohen, Ralph Alan (2009). "'The Most Convenient Place': The Second Blackfriars Theater and Its Appeal." In Dutton, 2009: 209–24.

Collins, Eleanor (2007). "Richard Brome's Contract and the Relationship of Dramatist to Company in the Early Modern Period." *Early Theatre* 10: 116–28.

Collins, Eleanor (2013). "Ghosts in the Archive: Edmond Malone, Craven Ord, and the Missing Texts of Henry Herbert's 'office-book.'" *Critical Quarterly* 55: 30–41.

Cook, Ann Jennalie (1981). *The Privileged Playgoers of Shakespeare's London, 1576–1642*. Princeton: Princeton University Press.

Crockett, Peter (2009). "Performing the Queen's Men." In Ostovich *et al.*, 2009, 229–42.

Cutts, John P. (1966). "New Findings with Regard to the 1624 Protection List." *Shakespeare Survey* 19: 101–7.

Dawson, Anthony and Paul Yachnin (2001). *The Culture of Playgoing in Shakespeare's England: A Collaborative Debate*. Cambridge: Cambridge University Press.

Dibdin, James C. (1888). *Annals of the Edinburgh Stage*. Edinburgh: Cameron.

Donaldson, Ian (2011). *Ben Jonson: A Life*. Oxford: Oxford University Press.

Dusinberre, Juliet (2003). "Pancakes and a Date for *As You Like It*." *Shakespeare Quarterly* 54: 371–405.

Dutton, Richard (1988). "*Hamlet, An Apology for Actors* and the Sign of the Globe." *Shakespeare Survey* 41: 35–43.

Dutton, Richard (1991). *Mastering the Revels: the Regulation and Censorship of English Renaissance Drama*. Basingstoke: Macmillan.

Dutton, Richard (1998). "'Discourse in the Players, But No Disobedience': Sir Henry Herbert's Problems with the Players and Archbishop Laud, 1632–34." *Ben Jonson Journal* 5: 37–62.

Dutton, Richard (2000). *Licensing, Censorship and Authorship in Early Modern England*. London: Palgrave.

Dutton, Richard (2006). "The St Werburgh Street Theater, Dublin." In Adam Zucker and Alan B. Farmer, eds. *Localizing Caroline Drama: Politics and Economics of the Early Modern English Stage, 1625–1642*. New York: Palgrave Macmillan. 129–56

Dutton, Richard ed. (2009). *The Oxford Handbook of Early Modern Theatre*. Oxford: Oxford University Press.

Dutton, Richard (2016). *Shakespeare, Court Dramatist*. Oxford: Oxford University Press.

Dutton, Richard, Alison Findlay and Richard Wilson, eds (2004). *Region, Religion and Patronage: Lancastrian Shakespeare*. Manchester: Manchester University Press.

Eccles, Mark (1961). *Shakespeare in Warwickshire*. Madison: University of Wisconsin.

Eccles, Mark (1993). "Elizabethan Actors IV: S to End." *Notes and Queries* 238: 165–76.

Edmond, Mary (2004). "Burbage, James (c.1531–1597)." *Oxford Dictionary of National Biography*. Oxford University Press, 2004; online edn, Jan 2008 [http://www.oxforddnb.com.proxy.lib.ohio–state.edu/view/article/3950, accessed 4 Feb 2014].

Egan, Gabriel (1997). "The Situation of the 'Lords Room': A Revaluation." *The Review of English Studies* 48: 297–309.

Egan, Gabriel (2009). "The Theatre in Shoreditch, 1576–1599." In Dutton, 2009, 168–85.

Elliott, John R.Jr. and Alan H. Nelson (University); Alexandra F. Johnston and Diana Wyatt (City) (2004). *Records of Early English Drama: Oxford*. 2 vols. Toronto: University of Toronto Press.

Erne, Lukas (2003). *Shakespeare as Literary Dramatist*. Cambridge: Cambridge University Press.

Evans, Robert C. (1989). *Ben Jonson and the Poetics of Patronage*. Lewisburg, PA: Bucknell University Press.

Feuillerat, Albert (1908). *Documents Relating to the Office of the Revels in the Time of Queen Elizabeth*. Leuven: Ustpruyst.

Findlay, Alison and Stephanie Hodgson-Wright, with Gweno Williams (2000). *Women and Dramatic Production, 1550–1700*. Harlow: Pearson.

Fisher, Will (2006). *Materialising Gender in Early Modern English Culture*. Cambridge: Cambridge University Press.

Foakes, R. A. (1993). "The Image of the Swan Theatre." In Andre Lascombes (ed.), *Spectacle and Image in Renaissance Europe: Selected Papers of the XXXIInd*

Conference at the Centre d'Études Supérieures de la Renaissance de Tours, 29 June–8 July 1989. Leiden: E. J. Brill. 337–57.
Foakes, R.A. ed. (2002). *Henslowe's Diary*. 2nd ed. Cambridge: Cambridge University Press. Cited parenthetically as *Henslowe*.
Foakes, R. A. (2004). "Henslowe's Rose/Shakespeare's Globe." In *From Script to Stage in Early Modern England*. Eds Peter Holland and Stephen Orgel. Basingstoke: Palgrave. 11–31.
Freedman, Barbara (1994). "Shakespearean Chronology, Ideological Complicity, and Floating Texts: Something is Rotten in Windsor." *Shakespeare Quarterly* 45: 190–210.
Galloway, David, ed. (1984). *Records of Early English Drama: Norwich 1540–1642*. Toronto: University of Toronto Press.
George, David, ed. (1991). *Records of Early English Drama: Lancashire*. Toronto: University of Toronto Press.
George, David (2004). "The Playhouse at Prescot and the 1592–94 Plague." In Dutton, Findlay and Wilson, 2004: 227–42.
Gibson, James M. ed. (2002). *Records of Early English Drama, Kent: The Diocese of Canterbury, vol. 1*. Toronto: University of Toronto.
Gillies, John ed. (1998). *Playing the Globe: Genre and Geography in English Renaissance Drama*. Madison, NJ: Fairleigh Dickinson University Press.
Graham, Elspeth and Rosemary Tyler (2011). "'So Unbridled & Badde an Handfull of England': The Social and Cultural Ecology of the Elizabethan Playhouse in Prescot." In Mike Benbough-Jackson and Sam Davies, eds, *Merseyside: Culture and Place*. Newcastle: Cambridge Scholars Publishing. 109–39.
Graves, R. B. (2009). "Lighting." In Dutton 2009, 528–42.
Greenfield, Jon (2007). "Reconstructing the Rose: Development of the Playhouse Building between 1587 and 1592." *Shakespeare Survey* 60: 23–35.
Greenfield, Peter H. (1983). "Entertainments of Henry, Lord Berkeley, 1593–4 and 1600–05." *Records of Early English Drama Newsletter* 8: 1, 12–24.
Greenfield, Peter H. (1988). "Professional Players at Gloucester: Conditions of Provincial Performing." In C. E. McGee, ed. *Elizabethan Theatre X*. Port Credit, Ontario: P. D. Meany, 73–92.
Greenfield, Peter H. (2009). "Touring." In Dutton 2009, 292–306.
Greenstreet, James (1889). "The Whitefriars Theatre in the Time of Shakespeare." In *New Shakespeare Society Transactions*. Serial 1, Part 3. London: Kegan Paul, Trench, Trübner: 269.
Greg, W. W. (1907). *Henslowe Papers*. London: A. H. Bullen.
Greg, W. W. (1931). *Dramatic Documents from the Elizabethan Playhouses. Stage Plots: Actors' Parts: Prompt Books*. 2 vols. Oxford: Clarendon Press.
Grose, Francis (1808). *The Antiquarian Repertory*. 2 vols. London.
Gurr, Andrew (1993). "The Chimera of Amalgamation." *Theatre Research International*: 85–93.

Gurr, Andrew (1996). *The Shakespearian Playing Companies*. Oxford: Clarendon Press.
Gurr, Andrew (2002). "Privy Councilors as Theatre Patrons." In White and Westfall, 2002, 221–45.
Gurr, Andrew (2004*a*). *The Shakespeare Company, 1594–1642*. Cambridge: Cambridge University Press.
Gurr, Andrew (2004*b*; 1987). *Playgoing in Shakespeare's London*. 3rd ed. Cambridge: Cambridge University Press.
Gurr, Andrew (2005). "Henry Carey's peculiar letter." *Shakespeare Quarterly*. 56: 51–75.
Gurr, Andrew (2007). "The Work of Elizabethan Plotters, and *2 The Seven Deadly Sins*." *Early Theatre* 10: 67–87.
Gurr, Andrew (2009; 1970, 1992). *The Shakespearean Stage, 1574–1642*, 3rd ed. Cambridge: Cambridge University Press.
Gurr, Andrew and Mariko Ichikawa. (2000). *Staging in Shakespeare's Theatres*. Oxford: Oxford University Press.
Haaker, Ann (1968). "The Plague, the Theatre and the Poet." *Renaissance Drama* n.s. 1: 296–306.
Hackett, Helen (2012). "'As the diall hand tells ore': the Case for Dekker, not Shakespeare, as Author." *Review of English Studies* 63: 34–57.
Harbage, Alfred (1941). *Shakespeare's Audience*. New York: Columbia University Press.
Harington, Sir John (1960). *The Metamorphosis of Ajax*, ed. Elizabeth S. Donno. New York: Columbia University Press.
Hattaway, Michael (2009). "Dating *As You Like It* and the Problems of 'As the *Dial Hand Tells O'er*." *Shakespeare Quarterly* 60: 154–67.
Herbert, Sir Henry: see Bawcutt 1996.
Hildy, Franklin (1993). "If You Build It They Will Come." In *The Design of the Globe*, 2nd ed. Ed. Margaret Shewring, J. R. Mulryne and Andrew Gurr. London: International Shakespeare Globe Centre: 89–106.
Honigmann, E. A. J. (1985). *Shakespeare: The "Lost Years."* Manchester: Manchester University Press.
Honigmann, E. A. J. and Susan Brock, eds (1995). *Playhouse Wills, 1558–1642: An Edition of Wills by Shakespeare and His Contemporaries in the London Theatre*. Manchester: Manchester University Press.
Hosley, Richard (1957). "The Gallery over the Stage in the Public Playhouse of Shakespeare's Time." *Shakespeare Quarterly* 8: 15–31.
Hotson, Leslie (1931). *Shakespeare versus Shallow*. London: Nonesuch Press.
Hotson, Leslie (1954). *The First Night of Twelfth Night*. New York: Macmillan.
Hotson, Leslie (1960). *Shakespeare's Wooden O*. London: Macmillan.
Ingram, William (1992). *The Business of Playing: The Beginnings of the Adult Professional Theatre in Elizabethan London*. Ithaca: Cornell University Press.
Ingram, William (1999). "The Economics of Playing." In *A Companion to Shakespeare*, ed. David S. Kastan. Oxford: Blackwell. 313–27.

Jackson, MacDonald P. (2003). *Defining Shakespeare: Pericles as Test Case.* Oxford: Oxford University Press.

Jensen, Phebe (2004). "Recusancy, Festivity and Community: the Simpsons at Gowlthwaite Hall." In *Region, Religion and Patronage: Lancastrian Shakespeare,* ed. Richard Dutton, Alison Findlay and Richard Wilson. Manchester: Manchester University Press. 101–20.

Joseph, B. L. (1951). *Elizabethan Acting.* New York: Oxford University Press.

Jowett, John (2005). " *Sir Thomas More* and the Play of Body", *Actes des congrès de la Société française Shakespeare [online],* 23 | 2005, mis en ligne le 15 mars 2007, accessed September 8, 2014: http://shakespeare.revues.org/661.

Kathman, David (2004a). "Reconsidering *The Seven Deadly Sins*." *Early Theatre* 7.1: 13–44.

Kathman, David (2004b). "Grocers, Goldsmiths, and Drapers: Freemen and Apprentices in the Elizabethan Theater." *Shakespeare Quarterly* 55: 1–49.

Kathman, David (2004c). "Stanley, Ferdinando, Fifth Earl of Derby (1559?–1594)." *Oxford Dictionary of National Biography.* Oxford University Press, 2004; online edn, Sept 2013 [http://www.oxforddnb.com.proxy.lib.ohio- state.edu/view/article/26269, accessed 11 Feb 2015].

Kathman, David (2005). "How Old Were Shakespeare's Boy Actors?" *Shakespeare Survey* 58: 220–46.

Kathman, David (2006). "Richard Tarlton and the Haberdashers." *Notes and Queries* 252: 440–2.

Kathman, David (2009a). "London Inns as Playing Venues for the Queen's Men." In Ostovich et al 2009: 65–76.

Kathman, David (2009b). "Inn-Yard Playhouses." In Dutton 2009: 153–67.

Kathman, David (2009c). "Alice Layston and the Cross Keys." *Medieval and Renaissance Drama in English* 22: 144–78.

Kathman, David (2009d). "Players, Livery Companies, and Apprentices." In Dutton 2009: 413–28.

Kathman, David (2011). "*The Seven Deadly Sins* and Theatrical Apprenticeship." *Early Theatre* 14: 121–39.

Kernan, Alvin (1995). *Shakespeare, the King's Playwright: Theater in the Stuart Court, 1603– 1613.* New Haven and London: Yale University Press.

Kernodle, George (1944). *From Art to Theatre: Form and Convention in the Renaissance.* Chicago: Chicago University Press.

King, Ros (2004). "Introduction." In *The Comedy of Errors,* ed. T. S. Dorsch, rev. ed. Cambridge: Cambridge University Press.

Knutson, Roslyn L. (1991). *The Repertory of Shakespeare's Company, 1594–1613.* Fayetteville: University of Arkansas Press.

Knutson, Roslyn L. (1995). "Falconer to the Little Eyases: A New Date and Commercial Agenda for the 'Little Eyases' Passage in *Hamlet*." *Shakespeare Quarterly* 46: 1–31.

Knutson, Roslyn L. (2001). *Playing Companies and Commerce in Shakespeare's Time.* Cambridge: Cambridge University Press.

Knutson, Roslyn L. (2002). "Two Playhouses, Both Alike In Dignity." *Shakespeare Studies* 30: 111–17.
Korda, Natasha (2009). "Women in the Theatre." In Dutton 2009, 456–73.
Korda, Natasha (2011). *Labors Lost: Women's Work and the Early Modern English Stage*. Philadelphia: University of Pennsylvania Press.
Krivatsky, Nati H. and Laetitia Yeandle (1992). "Sir Edward Dering." In R. J. Fehrenbach and E. S. Leedham-Green, eds, *Private Libraries in Renaissance England: A Collection and Catalogue of Tudor and Early Stuart Book-Lists*. Binghampton, NY: Medieval and Renaissance Texts and Studies. 1.137–269.
Lancashire, Anne (2009). "London Street Theater." In Dutton, 2009: 323–39
Law, Ernest (1910). *Shakespeare as a Groom of the Chamber*. London: G. Bell and Sons.
Lawrence, W. J. (1912). *The Elizabethan Playhouse*. Stratford-upon-Avon: The Shakespeare Head Press.
Levin, Harry (1971). "Two Magician Comedies: *The Tempest* and *The Alchemist*." *Shakespeare Survey* 22: 47–58.
Long, William B. (1985). "'A Bed/for Woodstock': a Warning for the Unwary." *Medieval and Renaissance Drama in England* 2: 91–118.
Long, William B. (1999). "'Precious Few': English Manuscript Playbooks." In *A Companion to Shakespeare*, ed. David Scott Kastan. Oxford: Blackwell. 414–33.
MacLean, Sally-Beth (2001). "Alternative Theatres: The Use of Urban Space by Touring Entertainers in Early Modern England." Unpublished paper invited for the 2001 North American Conference on British Studies.
MacLean, Sally-Beth (2002). "Tracking Leicester's Men: the patronage of a performance troupe." In White and Westfall, 2002: 246–71.
MacLean, Sally-Beth (2004). "A Family Tradition: Dramatic Patronage by the Earls of Derby." In Dutton, Findlay and Wilson: 205–26.
Manley, Lawrence and Sally-Beth MacLean (2014). *Lord Strange's Men and their Plays*. New Haven: Yale University Press.
Marcus, Leah (1988). *Puzzling Shakespeare: Local Reading and Its Discontents*. Berkeley, CA: University of California Press.
Mateer, David (2006). "New Light on the Early History of the Theatre in Shoreditch [with texts]." *English Literary Renaissance* 36: 335–75.
McLuskie, Kathleen (1985). "The Patriarchal Bard." In Jonathan Dollimore and Alan Sinfield, eds. *Political Shakespeare: New Essays in Cultural Materialism*. Manchester: Manchester University Press: 88–108.
McManus, Clare (2002). *Women on the Renaissance Stage: Anne of Denmark and Female Masquing in the Stuart Court*. Manchester: Manchester University Press.
McMillin, Scott (1987). *The Elizabethan Theatre and the "Book of Sir Thomas More."* Ithaca: Cornell University Press.
McMillin, Scott and Sally-Beth MacLean (1999). *The Queen's Men and their Plays*. Cambridge: Cambridge University Press.

Menzer, Paul, ed. (2006a). *Inside Shakespeare: Essays on the Blackfriars Stage*. Selinsgrove: Susquehanna University Press.

Menzer, Paul (2006b). "The Tragedians of the City? Q1 *Hamlet* and the Settlements of the 1590s." *Shakespeare Quarterly* 57: 162–82.

Montrose, Louis (1983). "'Shaping Fantasies': Figurations of Gender and Power in Elizabethan Culture." *Representations* 2: 61–94.

Mullany, Steven (1988). *The Place of the Stage: Licence, Play, and Power in Renaissance England*. Chicago: Chicago University Press.

Mullholland, P. A. (1977). "The Date of *The Roaring Girl*." *Review of English Studies,n.s.* 29: 19–31.

Mulryne, J. R. (2007). "Professional Players in Stratford-upon-Avon." *Shakespeare Survey* 61: 1–22.

Munro, Lucy (2005). *Children of the Queen's Revels: A Jacobean Theatre Repertory*. Cambridge: Cambridge University Press.

Munro, Lucy (2009). "Music and Sound." In Dutton, 2009, 543–59.

Neill, Michael (1978). "'Wit's Most Accomplished Senate': the Audience of the Caroline Private Theaters." *Studies in English Literature* 18: 341–60.

Nelson, Alan H. ed. (1989). *Records of Early English Drama, Cambridge*. 2 vols. Toronto: University of Toronto Press.

Nelson, Alan H. (1992). "Hall Screens and Elizabethan Playhouses: Counter-Evidence from Cambridge." In J. Astington, ed., *The Development of Shakespeare's Theater*. New York: AMS Press. 57–76.

Nelson, Alan H. (1994). *Early Cambridge Theatres: College, University, and Town Stages, 1464–1720*. Cambridge: Cambridge University Press.

Nelson, Alan H. (1997). "The Universities: Early Staging in Cambridge." In *A New History of Early English Drama*, eds David S. Kastan and John D. Cox. New York: Columbia University Press.

Nelson, Alan H. (1998). "George Buc, William Shakespeare, and the Folger *George a Greene*." *Shakespeare Quarterly* 49: 74–83.

Nelson, Alan H. (2009). "The Universities and the Inns of Court." In Dutton, 2009, 280–91.

Nicholl, Charles (2008). *The Lodger: Shakespeare on Silver Street*. New York: Viking.

Nicoll, Allardyce (1976). *The World of Harlequin: A Critical Study of the Commedia Dell' Arte*. Cambridge: Cambridge University Press.

Orrell, John (1983). *The Quest for Shakespeare's Globe*. Cambridge: Cambridge University Press.

Orrell, John (1988). *The Human Stage: English Theatre Design, 1567–1640*. Cambridge: Cambridge University Press.

Ostovich, Helen, Holger Schott Syme, and Andrew Griffin, eds (2009). *Locating the Queen's Men, 1583–1603*. Aldershot: Ashgate.

Platter, Thomas (1937). *Travels in England*, trans. Clare Williams. London: Jonathan Cape.

Plett, Heinrich F. R. (2004). *Rhetoric and Renaissance Culture*. Berlin: Walter De Gruyter Inc.

Postlewait, Thomas (2009). "Eyewitnesses to History: Visual Evidence for Theater in Early Modern England." In Dutton 2009: 575–606.

Rackin, Phyllis (2005). *Shakespeare and Women*. Oxford: Oxford University Press.

Riddell, James (1969). "Some Actors in Ben Jonson's Plays." *Shakespeare Studies* 9: 285–98.

Roberts-Smith, Jennifer (2006). "The Red Lion and the White Horse: Inns Used by Patronized Performers in Norwich, 1583–1624." *Early Theatre* 9.2: 109–44.

Robbins, Robin (2003). "Poets, Friends and Patrons: Donne and his Circle, Ben and his Tribe." In *A Companion to English Renaissance Literature and Culture*, ed. Michael Hattaway. Oxford: Blackwell. 419–41.

Rosenberg, Marvin (1968). "Elizabethan Actors: Men or Marionettes?" In *The Seventeenth Century Stage: A Collection of Critical Essays*, ed. G. E. Bentley. Chicago: University of Chicago Press: 94–109.

Rowse, A. L. (1974). *The Casebooks of Simon Forman: Sex and Society in Shakespeare's Age*. London: Weidenfeld and Nicholson.

Royce, Jaclyn (2009). "Early Modern Naturalistic Acting: the Role of the Globe in the Development of Personation." In Dutton 2009, 477–495.

Schoenbaum, Samuel (1987). *William Shakespeare: A Documentary Life*. Rev. edn. Oxford: Oxford University Press.

Schoone-Jongen, Terence G. (2008). *Shakespeare's Companies*. Aldershot: Ashgate.

Shapiro, Michael (1977). *Children of the Revels: The Boy Companies of Shakespeare's Time and their Plays*. New York: Columbia University Press.

Shapiro, Michael (1989). "Lady Mary Wroth Describes a 'Boy Actress.'" *Medieval and Renaissance Drama in England* 4: 187–93.

Shapiro, Michael (2009). "Early (Pre-1590) Boy Companies and their Acting Venues." In Dutton 2009: 120–35.

Sharpe, Kevin (1979). *Sir Robert Cotton, 1586–1631: History and Politics in Early Modern England*. Oxford: Oxford University Press.

Simpson, Catherine (2013). http://findingshakespeare.co.uk/shakespeares-world-in-100-objects-number-76-a-money-pot.

Smith, Bruce R. (1999). *The Acoustic World of Early Modern England*. Chicago: Chicago University Press.

Smith, Irwin (1964). *Shakespeare's Blackfriars Playhouse: Its History and Design*. New York: New York University Press.

Somerset, J. A. B. ed. (1994). *Records of Early English Drama: Shropshire*, 2 vols. Toronto: Toronto University Press.

Somerset, J. A. B. (2006). "The Blackfriars on Tour: Provincial Analogies." In Menzer, 2006*a*, 80–5.

Southern, Richard (1973). *The Staging of Plays before Shakespeare*. London: Faber and Faber.

Steggle, Matthew (1998). *Wars of the Theatres: The Poetics of Personation in the Age of Jonson*. Victoria, BC: English Literary Studies.

Stern, Tiffany (2006). "'On each Wall and Corner Poast': Playbills, Title-pages, and Advertising in Early Modern London." *English Literary Renaissance* 36: 57–89.

Stern, Tiffany (2009a). *Documents of Performance in Early Modern England*. Cambridge: Cambridge University Press.

Stern, Tiffany (2009b). "Actors' Parts." In Dutton 2009, 496–512.

Stern, Tiffany (2009c). "'The Curtain is Yours.'" In Ostovich *et al.*, 2009, 77–96.

Streitberger, W. R. (1986a). *Edmond Tyllney, Master of the Revels and Censor of Plays: A Descriptive Index to His Diplomatic Manual on Europe*. New York: AMS Press.

Streitberger, W. R.. ed. (1986b). *Jacobean and Caroline Revels Accounts, 1603–1642*. Oxford: Malone Society Collections, 13.

Streitberger, W. R. (2016). *The Masters of the Revels and Elizabeth I's Court Theatre*. Oxford: Oxford University Press.

Sutton, Dana. F. (2006). *Henry Jackson: A Letter*. The Philological Museum. (http://www.philological.bham.ac.uk/jackson/).

Syme, Holger Schott (2010). "The Meaning of Success: Stories of 1594 and Its Aftermath." *Shakespeare Quarterly* 61: 490–525.

Taylor, Gary (1985). "The Fortunes of Oldcastle." *Shakespeare Survey* 38: 85–100.

Taylor, Gary (1987). "William Shakespeare, Richard James and the House of Cobham." *RES* 38: 334–54.

Taylor, Gary (1995). "Shakespeare and Others: The Authorship of *Henry the Sixth, Part One*." *Medieval and Renaissance Drama in England* 7: 145–205.

Thompson, Peter (1997). "Rogues and Rhetoricians: Acting Styles in Early English Drama." In *A New History of Early English Drama*, ed. John D. Cox and David S. Kastan. New York: Columbia University Press: 321–36.

Tomson, Leslie (2010). "Playgoers on the Outdoor Stages of Early Modern London." *Theatre Notebook* 64: 3–11.

Thomson, W. G. (1930; 1906). *A History of Tapestry*. 2nd ed. London.

Tiner, Elza C. (2006). "Professional Players in Stratford-on-Avon, 1587–1602." In Menzer, 2006a, 86–92.

Tittler, Robert. *Architecture and Power: The Town Hall and the English Urban Community c. 1500–1640*. Oxford: Oxford University Press 1991.

Tillotson, Geoffrey (1933). "*Othello* and *The Alchemist* at Oxford." *TLS*, July 20, 494.

Tribble, Evelyn (2009). "Marlowe's Boy Actors." *Shakespeare Bulletin* 27: 5–17.

Van Es, Bart (2013). *Shakespeare in Company*. Oxford: Oxford University Press.

Vickers, Brian (2007). "Incomplete Shakespeare; or, Denying co-Authorship in *1 Henry VI*." *Shakespeare Quarterly* 58: 311–57.

Wallace, C. W. (1913). *The First London Theatre: Materials for a History*. Lincoln: University of Nebraska.

Warner, George (1881). *The Catalogue of the Manuscripts and Muniments of Alleyn's College of God's Gift at Dulwich*. London: Longmans, Green, and Co.

West, William N. (2009). "When is the Jig Up – and What is it Up To?" In Ostovich *et al.*, 2009, 201–15.

Westfall, Suzanne (1990). *Patrons and Performance: Early Tudor Household Revels*. Oxford: Clarendon Press.

Westfall, Suzanne (2009). "'He who Pays the Piper Calls the Tune': Household Entertainments." In Dutton 2009, 263–79.

White, Paul Whitfield (2009). "The Queen's Men in Elizabethan Cambridge." In Ostovich *et al.*, 2009: 41–50.

White, Paul Whitfield and Suzanne R. Westfall, eds (2002). *Shakespeare and Theatrical Patronage in Early Modern England*. Cambridge: Cambridge University Press.

Wickham, Glynne, Herbert Berry and William Ingram, eds (2000). *English Professional Theatre, 1530–1660*. Cambridge: Cambridge University Press. Cited parenthetically as *EPT*.

Wiggins, M. J. (2005). "Copies for Ruff and Cuff". *Around the Globe* 30: 20–1.

Wiles, David (1987). *Shakespeare's Clown: Actor and Text on the Elizabethan Stage*. Cambridge: Cambridge University Press.

Williamson, Elizabeth (2016). *Religion and Drama in Early Modern England: the Performance of Religion in Renaissance Drama*. London: Routledge.

Wills, Gary (2011). *Verdi's Shakespeare: Men of the Theater*. New York: Penguin.

Wilson, Richard (2004). *Secret Shakespeare*. Manchester: Manchester University Press.

Wilson, Richard and Richard Dutton, eds (1992). *New Historicism and Renaissance Drama*. London: Longman.

Winstanley, Michael, "Shakespeare, Catholicism and Lancashire: A Reappraisal of John Cottom, Stratford Schoolmaster', *Shakespeare Quarterly* 68 (2017), 172-91.

Wynne-Davies, Marion (1992). "The Queen's Masque: Renaissance Women and the Seventeenth-Century Court Masque." In S. P. Cerasano and Marion Wynne-Davies, eds, *Gloriana's Face: Women, Public and Private in the English Renaissance*. New York: Harvester Wheatsheaf. 79–104.

Wynne-Davies, Marion (2009). "Orange-Women, Female Spectators, and Roaring Girls: Women and Theater in Early Modern England." *Medieval and Renaissance Drama in England* 22: 19–26.

Yachnin, Paul (2005). "'The Perfection of Ten': Populuxe Art and Artisanal Value in *Troilus and Cressida*." *Shakespeare Quarterly* 56: 306–27.

Index

Page numbers in *italics* refer to figures.

a

Act for the Punishment of Rogues and Vagabonds (1598)   222
Act for the Punishment of Vagabonds (1572)   29, 59
acting styles   257–260
Act of Abuses (1606)   179
Act of the Common Council (1574)   84, 91–92, 115
actors, hired   157–159
Actors' Remonstrance, The (unk.)   159, 167
Adams, John   41, 45
adaptability   36, 71, 134–135
Admiral's Men; *see also* Prince Henry's Men
  Alleyn *see* Alleyn, Edward
  costumes   170–173
  court performances   82, 278
  court privileges   100
  duopoly with Chamberlain's Men   77–78, 80
  at the Fortune   14, 269, 270
  at Greenwich Palace   118
  hired men, women and boys   158, 168, 173, 184
  leaving Theatre   32, 61
  musical instruments   176
  at Newington Butts   75, *76*, 77
  number of players   44
  patronage   197
  Pembroke's Men, rivalry with   221
  petitions against   221
  props   247, 253, 255
  purchase of plays   147
  repertoire   148
  at the Rose   13, 77–78, 80, 100
  sharers   44
  Sir John Oldcastle   197
  Slater, Martin   144
  special licences   222, 270
  turnover of plays   106–107
advertising   106, 144, 181–182
Alchemist, The (Jonson)   150, 158, 183, 208, 292, 308, 309–311
"Alice Layston and the Cross Keys" (Kathman)   116
Allen, Giles   32, 92, 193, 223
Alleyn, Edward
  acting style   261
  in Admiral's Men   78, 82, 129

Alleyn, Edward (cont'd)
  Admiral's Men property lists 170–173, 176
  apprentices 184
  back-stage plots 113, 178
  Fortune construction contract 230–231
  gatherers 166, 167
  Henslowe, relationship with 11, 13–14, 151, 164
  hired men 157–158
  letters 64–65, 184
  portrait *11*
  retirement 278
  stature 21
  in Strange's Men 62, 63
  as theater owner 13–14, 14–15, 151
  in Worcester's Men 19
Alleyn, Joan Henslowe 13, 62, 64–65, 165, 184
Alleyn, John 61–62
All's Well that Ends Well (Shakespeare) 269
Almond for a Parrot, An (unk.) 103
amphitheater model 8–10, 83, 97–99
animals, live 256
Annals (Stow) 88, 124
Anne of Denmark 34, 127, 135–136, 145, 165, 168, 277, 280, 284, 287-288; *see also* Queen Anne's Men *and* Children of the Queen's Revels
Antipodes (Brome) 180
Antonio and Mellida (Marston) 270
Antonio's Revenge (Marston) 174, 228 Note 11, 270, 309
Antony and Cleopatra (Shakespeare) 235, 248–249, 251–252, 269
Apology for Actors (Heywood) 85, 97–98, 284–285

apprentices 111, 155, 176, 182–188, 207–208
Architettura (Serlio) 93
Armin, Robert
  apprentices 183
  background 264–265
  in Chandos's Men 19
  comedies by 266
  comic style 265–266
  Malcontent, The (Marston) 283
  motley 105
  multiple minor roles 150, 217
  musical abilities 176, 266
  in Phillips' will 155
  portrait *265*
  replacement for Kemp 261
  retirement 315
  royal licence 279
  Shakespeare's writing for 266, 269
  trade guild associations 28
Arthur, Prince of Wales 118–119
Arundel's Men 100
ascent / descent machinery 96, 252–253, 256, 303–307
Assheton, Nicholas 68
Astington, John H. 5, 118–119, 185
Astraea (Mary Herbert) 161
As You Like It (Shakespeare) 105, 176, 183, 189, 209, 247, 252, 269, 306
Aubrey, John 51, 54
audiences; *see also* seating
  accidents 3
  diversity 16, 225, 238
  as participants 4–5
  women 133, 162–163

b

Bacon, Francis 153–154
Barnavelt, Sir John Van Olden 87–88
Barnes, Barnabe 243, 251, 252–253;
Baron, The (Buc) 88–89

Index | 343

Bartholomew Fair (Jonson)   14, 45, 121, 134, 177–178, 180, 297, 318
Baskerville, James   165
Baskerville, Susan   165–166
bear-baiting   9, 13, 14, 180, 247
Beare, James   117
Beaumont, Francis   163, 177, 288, 294, 304, 316
Beckerman, Bernard   240, 241, 278
Beeston, Christopher   140, 141–142, 155, 157, 158, 164, 207–208, 217
Bell inn, Gracechurch Street, London   49, 115, 116, 185
Bell Savage inn, Ludgate Hill, London   95, 115, 116
below-stage space   245; *see also* trapdoors
Belte, Thomas   150, 183, 207, 208
Benfield, Robert   314
Bentley, G. E.   17, 20, 47, 145, 157, 178
Bentley, John   39–40
Bereblock, John   1, 2, 3, 22
Berkeley, Henry, 7th Baron   125
Berkeley, Sir Thomas   125
Berkeley's (Bartlett's) Men   19
Berry, Herbert   190 Note 10, 293
Birch, George   150, 183
Birch, Thomas   121
Bird (Borne), William   107, 155, 164, 166
bird whistles   198–199
Blackfriars Boys
  as competition for Men's companies   225, 238, 270
  disbanded   15, 286
  entry fees   116
  fall from favor   91, 284–286
  Jonson's plays   271, 310
  Malcontent, The (Marston)   241
  Queen Anne's patronage   277
  revenge plays   284
  revival   70, 83, 225, 238
  transition to Men's companies   176
Blackfriars playhouse (Burbage's)
  apprentices   185
  boxes   294
  Boys company *see* Blackfriars Boys
  business plan and failure   194
  Chamberlain's Men   32
  Condell's shares   167
  court records   15
  descents   252, 256, 305–309
  discovery space   307
  entry fee   83, 116
  freehold passed to Richard Burbage   222
  galleries   293, 294
  Globe plays performed at   292–293
  Heminge's shares   151, 164
  housekeepers   160
  housekeeper shares   224
  King's Men *see* Blackfriars residency of King's Men
  liberties   198
  lighting   58, 299, 300
  music and musicians   174, 176–177, 282, 292, 300–301, 303
  night-time scenes   299–300
  political writing and consequences   284–286
  protests against   32, 117, 129–130, 175, 194, 195–197, 197–198
  purchase   193
  Queen Henrietta Maria's attendance   163
  seating   239, 241, 283, 293, 295–298
  size and structure 293–294
  stage   293–294
  time of performances   298-299
  tiring house   293
  trapdoors   307
  upper stage   307

Blackfriars residency of King's Men
   Alchemist, The (Jonson) 310,
      311–312
   Blackfriars Boys joining 292
   delayed by plague 17, 291
   entry fees 116
   Globe/Blackfriars
      adjustments 292–293
   Globe/Blackfriars
      arrangement 291–292
   Henry VIII (Shakespeare) 304
   hired men and women 156–157
   lighting 299–300
   Macbeth (Shakespeare) 307–308
   Malcontent, The (Marston) 306
   music and musicians
      300–303, 304
   night-time scenes 299–300
   performances of Shakespeare's
      plays 35
   reacquisition 290
   repertoire 303–305, 305–306
   revenge plays 284
   romances and tragicomedies
      304–35
   Shakespeare writing for 309–314,
      315–318
   sharers 291–292
   Tempest, The (Shakespeare)
      306–307
   Two Noble Kinsmen, The
      (Shakespeare/Fletcher)
      315–318
Blackfriars theater (1576,
   Farrant's) 32, 193, 196
Boar's Head playhouse,
   Whitechapel 78, 115, 158,
   165, 270–271
book-keepers 108, 110, 112,
   177–180
Book of Martyrs (Fox) 238–239
boy actors 35, 59, 150–151, 182–188,
   209, 295–296

boys companies 49, 70, 83, 116, 177,
   225, 238, 270; *see also specific*
   companies
Bradbrook, M. C. 316
Braithwait, Richard 162
Brayne, John 30–31, 92–93, 99,
   109, 185
Brayne, Margaret 31–32, 61, 92, 164
Brayne, Thomas 30
Bristow, James 184
Brome, Richard 148–149, 185–186
Brown, Edmund 39–40
Brown, Henry 40
Browne, Anne 165
Browne, Robert 165, 167
Browne, William 165
Bryan, George 63, 140, 157, 205, 206,
   207, 208, 217
Buc, Sir George 15, 87–89, 121,
   310–311
Bullard, Alexander 302
Bull inn, Bishopsgate Street,
   London 44, 49, 115–116
Burbage, Cuthbert 30, 32, 102, 159,
   207, 222–223, 224
Burbage, Ellen Brayne 30
Burbage, James
   Admiral's Men, tensions
      with 61–62
   apprentices 185
   background 30
   Blackfriars playhouse *see* Blackfriars
      playhouse (Burbage's)
   Brayne, partnership with 30–31
   Brayne's widow, lawsuit by 31–32,
      61–62
   Chamberlain's Men 31
   death 32, 222–223
   family 30
   Fleetwood, confrontation with
      28–29, 31, 100
   Hind brothers 185
   Lanman, arrangement with 99, 198

Leicester's Men 30
stubbornness 31–32
Theatre *see* Theatre, Shoreditch
Burbage, Richard
  acting style 259, 261, 263
  background 102
  birth 30
  Blackfriars Boys 225, 238
  Blackfriars consortium 291–292
  Chamberlain's Men sharer 81, 140, 152, 207
  Cuthbert, cooperation with 222–223
  death 264
  doubling roles 102–103
  Duchess of Malfi, The (Webster) 314
  and father's creditors 15, 31–32, 61–62
  King's Men sharer 279
  Malcontent, The (Marston) 241, 283
  portrait *262*
  Prince Henry's water pageant 187
  revenge plays 284
  as Richard III 263
  Seven Deadly Sins, 2 The (Tarlton) 205
  Shakespeare, friendship with 263–264, 313
  Shakespeare writing for 102–103
  swordsmanship 46
  Tarlton's influence 46
Burbage, Robert 92
Burghley House, Lincolnshire 124–125
Byland, Ambrose 302

C

Callaghan, Dympna 162
Cambridge University 22–23, 35–36, 271
cannons 249
canopies *see* "heavens"
Captain, The (Beaumont and Fletcher) 177
Cardenio (Shakespeare) 89, 305, 314
Carey, Elizabeth 125
Carey, George *see* Hunsdon, George Carey, 2nd Baron
Carey, Henry *see* Hunsdon, Henry Carey, 1st Baron
Carey, Sir George 125
Cary, Elizabeth 161, 163
Catherine of Aragon 118–119
Catholicism 27, 51, 58, 59–60
Catiline (Jonson) 141, 150, 158, 208, 268
Cecil, Sir Robert 88, 125, 135–136, 196, 278
Cecil, William 3, 5, 125, 129
censorship of plays *see* licensing and censorship of plays
Chamberlain's Men
  from 1603 *see* King's Men
  apprentices 182–188
  boys companies, competition from 270
  comics/clowns/fools 103–106
  costumes and properties 146
  Derby-Oxford wedding 124–125
  dismantling Theatre 223
  duopoly with Admiral's Men 77–78, 80
  formation 129
  founder-members 63
  hired men and women 156–157
    actors 157–159
    book-keepers 177–180
    gatherers 159–160, 166–167
    musicians 174–177
    stage-keepers 180–182
    tiremen 169–174
    tirewomen 167–169
  jigs 218, 220, 225–226
  Kemp's departure 224–227, 261

Chamberlain's Men (cont'd)
  as Lord Hunsdon's Men   130, 198
  loss of 1st Lord Hunsdon   129–130
  number of players   44
  ordinary poets   147–148
  petitions against   32, 129–130
  Phillips, Augustine   152–155
  private commissions   135
  repertoire   94, 101, 112, 122–123, 322–324
  salaries   278–279
  Shakespeare as "ordinary poet" 147–148, 149–150
  sharer/housekeeper issues   224
  sharers   44, 63, 81, 127–128, 140–143, 146, 217
  special licences   222
  turnover of plays   101
  venues   124–125
    Blackfriars   194, 197–198
    court   81–82, 85, 117–123
    Cross Keys Inn   80, 114–117
    Curtain *see* Curtain residency of Chamberlain's Men
    Globe *see* Globe playhouse
    Gray's Inn   82, 130–136
    Greenwich Palace   118–123
    Newington Butts   75, 76, 77
    Theatre *see* Theatre residency of Chamberlain's Men
Chambers, E. K.   6, 44, 97, 234, 240, 272, 309
Chambers, William   302
Chandos's Men   19, 264
Chapman, George   35, 91, 271, 284
Chaste Maid in Cheapside, A (Middleton)   10, 309
Chettle, Henry   44, 107, 284
Children of Bristol   71
Children of Paul's   33, 35, 70, 83, 127, 225, 270, 272, 277, 300
Children of the Blackfriars *see* Blackfriars Boys

Children of the Chapel *see* Blackfriars Boys
Children of the King's Revels   143–146, 156, 188
Children of the Queen's Chapel   35, 225, 270
Children of the Queen's Revels *see* Blackfriars Boys
Children of the Whitefriars   291, 301, 310
Cholmely, Sir Richard   58–59
Chomley, John   12–13, 109
Christ Church Hall, Oxford   1-5, 22
Christmas Revels   54
City of London authorities   28–29, 31, 33, 49, 80, 84, 91–92, 197, 290; *see also* Lord Mayor of London
civic venues   21, 23
Clegg, Cyndia Susan   89–90
clocks   200, 246, 254
clothing   105–106, 123; *see also* costumes
clowns   44–46, 103–106, *104*, 206, 217–220, 227, 261; *see also* fools
Cobham, Henry Brooke, 11th Baron   195, 196, 197
Cobham, William Brooke, 10th Baron   130, 195, 196
cockfighting   68
Cohen, Ralph Alan   294
Collins, Jeffery   302
color   23, 99, 173, 242, 257
Comedy of Errors, The (Shakespeare)   35, 82, 94, 122–123, 130–134, 319
composers   177, 186
concession stands   13, 31, 109–110
Condell, Henry
  bequest to servant   167
  Blackfriars consortium   292
  Chamberlain's Men
    apprentice   207–208
    compilation of First Folio   318

Duchess of Malfi, The (Webster) 314, 315
Every Man In His Humour (Jonson) 140
Globe housekeeper 291-293
King's Men sharer 157, 207, 279, 292
Malcontent, The (Marston) 241, 283
  in Phillips' will 155
  retirement 314
Seven Deadly Sins, 2 The (Tarlton) 207–208
  in Shakespeare's will 264
continental companies 161
contracts
  hired men's/boy's 157–158, 184, 185
  Shakespeare's 147–151
  sharers' 140, 141–143
Cook, Ann Jennalie 238
Cooke, Alexander 150, 155, 159, 176, 183, 207, 208–209
Cope, Sir Walter 135–136
Coriolanus (Shakespeare) 242–243, 269
costs 47–48, 156, 176–177
costumes
  Alleyn's list 170–173
  as characterizations 258
  color 257
  costs 109, 169–170
  leased from theater 143
  owned by company 143, 146
  storage 13, 100, 109
  supplied by Master of Revels 84, 313
  tiremen 169, 170, 173–174
Cottam, John 51
Countess of Montgomery's Urania, The (Wroth) 187–188
Court Beggar, The (Brome) 185–186

court performances; *see also* Masters of the Revels
  Chamberlain's Men 61, 81–82, 117–118, 122–123, 124–125, 193
  court records 15
  Greenwich Palace 117–123
  increase under James I 277
  King's Men 122, 243, 277, 281, 291, 310, 318–319
  lighting 58, 121–122
  masques 34, 161, 168, 177, 287-288, 312
  monarch's centrality 4–7, 121
  payment for 81
  Queen's Men 49–50, 121
  sets, luxurious 22–23
  Shakespeare's plays 35, 318–319
court/playhouse interactions 313–314
Coventry, Warwickshire 20, 27–28
Cowley, Richard 67, 106, 141, 155, 159, 206, 207, 217, 279, 315
cross-dressing 4, 182, 183, 186–188
Cross Keys inn, Gracechurch Street, London 61, 78, 80, 114–117
currency 16–17
Curtain residency of Chamberlain's Men
  beginning 198
  duration 199
  Every Man In His Humour (Jonson) 199–200, 200–201, 202, 217
  Every Man Out of His Humour (Jonson) 225
  Henry V (Shakespeare) 202–203
  Kemp, Will 217–218
  Romeo and Juliet (Shakespeare) 201
  Seven Deadly Sins, 2 The (Tarlton) *see Seven Deadly Sins, 2 The* (Tarlton)
  A Warning for Fair Women (unk.) 203–205

Curtain theater, Shoreditch
  archeological excavations   198
  bird whistle   198–199
  Burbage - Fleetwood
    confrontation   100
  Chamberlain's Men see Curtain
    residency of Chamberlain's Men
  destruction   270
  destruction order   221
  discovery space   200, 200–201,
    213–214
  fencing matches   202
  layout   198
  protests against   31, 100
  Queen's Men   48, 49, 78
  Theatre, arrangement with   99, 198
  touring companies   100, 199
  women in audience   163
Cutts, John P.   302
Cymbeline (Shakespeare)   177, 197,
  254, 299, 304, 305–306
Cynthia's Revels (Jonson)   178, 310

d

Daborne, Robert   181
Daniel, John   71
Daniel, Samuel   123, 281, 283, 284
Daphnis Polystephanos (Buc)   88
Dawes, Robert   142–143
dead bodies, removal of   134–135
Dekker, Thomas
  Gull's Hornbook, The   234, 240,
    295–297, 298
  payment for plays   107–108
  Roaring Girl, The (Middleton and
    Dekker)   161
  Satiromastix   175, 232–233,
    267–268, 272, 273
  *Seven Deadly Sins of London,
    The*   300
  War of the Theaters   271–273
Derby, Elizabeth de Vere, Countess
  of   124–125

Derby, Earls of see Stanley family
Derby's Men   19, 44, 65, 127, 165, 271;
  see also Strange's Men
Dering, Sir Edward   55
descent machinery   96, 252–253, 256,
  305–309
Devil is An Ass, The (Jonson)   38, 43,
  187, 294–295
Devil's Charter, The (Barnes)   257
  author   243
  black magic   244–246
  discovery space   249–250
  entry points   247
  firearms   248–249
  fireworks   244–245
  music   247, 248, 250–251, 251–252
  night-time scenes   246
  performed at court   243
  Prologue   244
  stage devils   245
  story   243–244
  trapdoors   245
  upper stage   247–248
De Witt, Johannes   8–10, 93, 97
discovery spaces   10, 96–97, 110,
  112, 200–201, 249–251,
  253–255, 307
Ditchfield, James   69
Downton, Thomas   67, 107, 109, 144,
  158, 184
Dr Faustus (Marlowe)   200, 253
drums
  announcing performance   106, 114,
    174–175, 181, 280
  in performances   175, 247–248, 303
Duchess of Malfi, The (Webster)   102,
  158, 183, 187, 314–315
duels   39
Duke, John   140, 157, 206, 217
Dulwich College   15
Dunkenhalgh Hall, Lancashire   52
Dutton, John   41, 49–50
Dutton, Laurence   29, 34, 49–50

e

Eastward Ho! (Jonson, Chapman, Marston)   90–91, 284
Ecclestone, William   207, 208
Edinburgh Kirk   279–280
Edwardes, Richard   1–5
Elizabeth I
   Christmas courts   117–118
   cultural presence   5, 6, 121
   Derby-Oxford wedding   124–125
   at Kenilworth Castle   25–27, 28
   monopolies, granting of   279
   at *Palamon and Arcite* performance   1–5
   Queen's Men   41, 121
   Queen's "reward"   81
   on the stage   3, 4–5
English Traveller, The (Heywood)   147
entry fees   16–17, 83, 95, 159–160, 232–233, 239
Epigrams (Davies)   240
Essex, Robert Devereux, 2nd Earl   135, 153–154, 196
Essex's Men   19, 48, 53, 69
Evans, Henry   292
Evans, Thomas   292
evensong   80, 117
Every Man In His Humour (Jonson)   140, 150, 199–201, 207, 217–218, 226, 244–245, 246, 254
Every Man Out of His Humour (Jonson)   150, 224, 225, 234, 240, 241, 243, 256, 267
Every Woman In Her Humour (anon.)   178
Excellent Actor, An (Webster)   259, 261, 263

f

Fair Maid of Bristow, The (anon.)   204
Falstaff, character of   7, 102, 130, 194–197
Famous Victories of Henry the Fifth, The (unk.)   44, 47, 50, 195
Farrant, Richard   32
fencing matches   202
Ferabosco, Alphonso   177
festival holy-days   80
Field, Nathan   147, 176, 261, 262
firearms   248–249
fires   17, 249, 257, 315
fireworks   215–216, 227, 244–245, 307
First Book of Consort Lessons (Morley)   301
Flecknoe, Richard   181–182
Fleetwood, William   28–29, 31, 100
Fletcher, John   55, 87, 147, 303–304, 314
Fletcher, Lawrence   144, 155, 279, 280, 292
Flower of Friendship (Tilney)   85–86
Foakes, R. A.   8–9
Follie's Anatomy (Hutton)   241
fools   105–106, 206–207, 264–266, 269; *see also* clowns
Forman, Simon   163, 304, 306, 307, 320 Note 15
Fortune theater, Shoreditch
   audiences   238
   construction contract   13–14, 230–232
   fire   17, 313
   galleries   233, 237–238
   Globe as model   230–231, 232
   Henslowe *Diary*   13
   jigs   220, 226
   Privy Council licence   270
   repertoire   238–239
   seating   233
   size and structure   230–231, 236
   stage   93
   women   161, 165

Four Plays in One (unk.) 216
Franklin, John 116, 117
Funeral Elegy for Richard Burbage, March 1619, A 264

g

Gascoigne, George 26–27, 34
Gascoyne, William 302
gatekeepers 40
gatherers 159–160, 166–167
Gawthorpe Hall, Lancashire 52
George, David 66–67, 69
Gerschow, Frederic 300–301
Gesta Grayorum 130–136
Gibbons, Brian 101
Gillies, John 113
Gillom, Fulke 51–52
Globe playhouse
  acting style 257–260, 263
  Antony and Cleopatra (Shakespeare) 235
  archeological excavations 231, 237
  Armin 264–271
  audiences 238–242
  Blackfriars, plays performed at 281–284, 292–293, 308–309
  blazing star 255
  cannons and other arms 249
  celebrity culture 283
  color 257
  contentions about 236–242
  costumes 257, 268
  Cymbeline (Shakespeare) 305–306
  descent machinery 252–253
  discovery space 249–250, 251, 254, 255, 257
  entry fees 232, 233
  Every Man Out of His Humour (Jonson) 234
  financial success 290–291

fire 315
galleries 232–234, 237–238, 268
"heavens" and posts 246–247, 252–253
hell mouth 253
Henry VIII (Shakespeare) 304
housekeepers 224
housekeeper shares 224
impression on visitors 97
Julius Caesar (Shakespeare) 267, 268
lease of site 224
live animals 256
London Prodigal, The 255–256
Lords' room 234–236, 238–242
Malcontent, The (Marston) 281–284
Merry Devil of Edmonton, The 253–254
Miseries of Enforced Marriage, The (Wilkins) 256
as model for Fortune 230–231, 232
Mucedorus 256
music and musicians 282, 301, 308–309
night-time scenes 299–300
Privy Council licence 270
rebuilding 315
repertoire 308
Revenger's Tragedy, The (Middleton) 255
romances and tragicomedies 304–305
"roof-house" 268
seating 233, 238–242, 283
severed head 254
Shakespeare's plays 267–271
sharers 153
sightlines 232
size and structure 13, 230–232, 236–237, 242
soundings 267

space below stage   245
spoken word   257–261, 263–264
stage   240, 242
stage directions   242–243, 256–257
  Devil's Charter, The (Barnes)   243–253, 257
  live animals   256
  London Prodigal, The   255–256
  Merry Devil of Edmonton, The   253–254
  Mucedorus   256
  Revenger's Tragedy, The (Middleton)   255
  Thomas, Lord Cromwell   254
timbers from Theatre   15
time of performances   80, 267, 298
tiring house   234
trapdoors   245, 257
upper stage   235–236, 247–249, 257
War of the Theaters   271–273
Winter's Tale, The (Shakespeare)   304, 311, 313
Goodale, Thomas   206
Gough, Robert   155, 164, 207, 208
Gouthwaite Hall, Yorkshire   58
Gowrie (anon.)   90–91
Graham, Elspeth   66, 67, 68
Gray's Inn, London   130–136
Greene, Robert   4, 115
Greene, Thomas   144, 165
Greenwich Palace   22, 35, 82, 118–123, 124–125
Griggs, John   12, 65
Guild Hall, Stratford   20–22, 41
Gull's Hornbook, The (Dekker)   234, 240, 241, 295–297
Gurr, Andrew
  audience, Shakespeare's   239
  Christmas Revels   33
  duopoly, Admiral's Men and Chamberlain's Men   77–78

inns as venues   49
Kemp   206
King Lear (Shakespeare)   85, 126
sitting on the stage   241
Slater, Martin   145–146
social hierarchy   234, 238
Tempest, The (Shakespeare)   306–307, 311
touring   47
women in theaters   163

h

Halsall, Sir Cuthbert   52
Halsall's Men   52, 53
Hamlet (Shakespeare)
  acting style   260
  arras   200
  Burbage in title role   46, 103
  connection to other plays   270
  dumb shows   176, 203
  Henslowe's diary   77
  Kemp, references to   227
  little eyases   35, 225, 285
  music   176, 186, 251
  mystery plays   27
  night-clothes   246
  removal of body   134–135
  revenge play   284
  re-writings   269
  sword-fights   46
  trap door   94, 257
Hampton Court   119
Harbage, Alfred   238
Harington, Sir John   6, 36
Harrington, Percival   67
Harrington, Richard   66, 67–69, 70
Harte, Sir John   61
Harvey, George   213
Hatton, Sir Christopher   100
hautboys   175–176, 251–252, 303
"heavens"   9, 10, 95–96, 99, 247, 252–253
hell mouths   253

Heminge, John
  apprentices   150, 183, 185, 208
  Blackfriars housekeeper   292
  Chamberlain's Men
    business manager   150–151
    payee   81, 107, 140, 150
    sharer   140, 150–151, 153
  co-executor of Phillip's will   155
  compilation of First Folio   318
  Globe housekeeper   224, 290
  Globe tapster   109–110
  King's Men sharer   154, 279
  lawsuit by daughter   15, 151, 164
  marriage   164
  roles in *Seven Deadly Sins*
    206–207
  in Shakespeare's will   263–264, 315
  Strange's Men   63
Heminge, Thomasin   164
Henrietta Maria of France   163
1 Henry IV (Shakespeare)   35, 50, 55,
    94, 103, 130, 194, 260, 284
2 Henry IV (Shakespeare)   7, 50, 55,
    94, 130, 268, 284
Henry V (Shakespeare)   50, 101, 102,
    202–203, 267
1 Henry VI (Shakespeare and
    others)   63–64, 94, 101,
    148, 197
2 Henry VI (Shakespeare)   94, 101,
    125–126, 148, 175, 254
3 Henry VI (Shakespeare)   94, 101,
    125–126, 148, 175
Henry VIII (Shakespeare)   101, 249,
    257, 267, 304, 314, 315
Henry Frederick, Prince of Wales
    187, 197
Henslowe, Agnes   12, 14, 164
Henslowe, Philip; *see also* Henslowe
    Diary
  Alleyn, relationship to   62
  background   10–11, 12
  boy actors   184

civic and church duties   14
Dawes contract   142–143
philanthropy   15
theater owner   10, 12–14; *see also*
    Fortune theater, Shoreditch;
    Hope theater, Southwark; Rose
    theater, Southwark
Henslowe *Diary*
  costumes and properties   109,
    169–170
  dates   16
  dealings with companies   13
  "Harey the vi"   63–64
  loan to nephew   141
  Lord's rooms   234
  new plays   106–108
  overview   10–11, 13
  performances in Lent   112
  plague, impact of   75, 76, 77
  repertoires   148
  Slater   144
  Strange's Men at Rose
    theater   62
  Swan theater rivalry   221
  takings   63, 64, 160
  tiremen   173–174
  tirewomen   168
  turnover of plays   106
Herbert, Mary, Countess of
    Pembroke   161
Herbert, Sir Henry   15, 90, 112,
    179–180, 301
Hertford's Men   69, 144
Hesketh, Sir Thomas   51, 52, 53,
    55–56, 60
Hewes, Joan   167
Heywood, Thomas   72, 85, 97–98,
    127, 147, 284–285
Hind brothers   185
hired men and women   156–157
  actors   157–159
  book-keepers   177–180
  gatherers   159–160, 166–167

musicians   174–177
stage-keepers   180–182
tiremen   169–174
tirewomen   167–169
History of King Richard the Third (Buc)   88
history plays before Shakespeare   47
Hoghton, Alexander   50–60
Hoghton, Thomas   51–52
Holcombe, Thomas   183
Holland, Aaron   166
Holland, John   206
Holland, Peter   310
Holland, Thomas   40
Hollar, Wenceslas   236, *237*
Hope theater, Southwark   13, 14, 178, 180, 232, 247, 270
Hosley, Richard   235–236
Hotson, Leslie   5, 105, 126, 239–240
housekeepers   154, 156, 160, 224, 290, 291–292
Howard, Charles, 1st Earl of Nottingham, 2nd Baron Howard of Effingham   49, 77–78, 88, 100, 129, 185, 197; *see also* Admiral's Men
Howard-Hill, T. H.   87
Hunsdon, George Carey, 2nd Baron   32, 128, 130, 194, 195, 196; *see also* Chamberlain's Men
Hunsdon, Henry Carey, 1st Baron; *see also* Chamberlain's Men
  Burbage - Fleetwood confrontation   28–29, 31
  Cross Keys permission request   78, 80, 114, 116–117, 175
  death   194, 196
  duopoly, Admiral's Men and Chamberlain's Men   77–78
  overview   128–130
  portrait   *128*

Hunsdon's Men   130, 198
Hutchinson, Elizabeth   164
Hymenaei (masque, Jonson)   168, 177, 314

i

Ichikawa, Mariko   307
Ill May Day riots   86
Ingram, William   17, 48
inns as venues
  Act of the Common Council (1574)   92
  indoor and outdoor performances   48, 49
  Lancashire   69
  London   34, 35, 49, 114–117
    the Bell   49, 115, 116, 185
    the Bell Savage   95, 115, 116
    the Bull   44, 49, 115–116
    the Cross Keys   61, 78, 80, 114–117
  payment   40
  profitability   48
  Stratford   25
Inns of Court   130–136
Isle of Dogs, The (Nashe and Jonson)   39, 221, 272–273

j

James I   126–127, 154, 277, 279, 280, 281, 286; *see also* King's Men
Jephtha (unk.)   107–108, 109
Jew of Malta, The (Marlowe)   64, 77
jigs   46, 105, 218–220, 225–226, 227
Johnson, Robert   177
Jonson, Ben; *see also specific plays*
  Alleyn, Edward   261
  background   273
  Blackfriars, writing for   310, 311–313
  court masques   34, 127, 287–288
  legal cases   179, 272–273

Jonson, Ben (*cont'd*)
  London theaters, references to   38
  music   177, 307
  Robinson, Richard   187
  Satiromastix (Dekker)   272, 273
  Shakespeare, relationship
    with   311–313
  Spenser, Gabriel, duel with   39,
    202, 273
  Tarlton, Richard   45
  tirewomen   167
  trade guild associations   28
  turnover of plays   106–107
  War of the Theaters   271–273
  writing for patrons   127, 280
Julius Caesar (Shakespeare)   8, 200,
  202, 226–227, 246–247,
  267–268, 269

k

Kathman, David   49, 116, 183,
  205–209, 213
Kemp, Will
  Armin's difference from   265–266
  Chamberlain's Men   81, 140
  Chamberlain's Men, departure
    from   224–227, 261
  Every Man In His Humour
    (Jonson)   217–218
  experience   103
  jigs   218, 219–220
  Kemp's Nine Days' Wonder
    104, 226
  language inadequacies   104–105
  morris dance from London to
    Norwich   226
  motley   105–106
  in *Romeo and Juliet*   110–111, 112
  in *Seven Deadly Sins*   206
  Shakespeare roles   102–104
  Strange's Men   61, 63
  Tarlton's influence   46
  Worcester's Men   227

Kendall, William   157–158
Kenilworth Castle, Warwickshire
  25–27, 28
Keys, Isabel   164
Kiechel, Samuel   94
King, Ros   132
King and No King, A (Beaumont and
  Fletcher)   304
King Edward VI School, Stratford-
  upon-Avon   4, 21
King John (Shakespeare)   50, 94,
  101, 200
King Lear (Shakespeare)   50, 85, 102,
  126, 243, 250–251, 266, 269
King Leir (unk.)   50
King's Men
  before 1603 *see* Chamberlain's Men
  1624 "Protection List"   301–303
  actors, hired   157, 158, 159
  after Shakespeare   314–315
  apprentices   184–185
  at Blackfriars *see* Blackfriars
    residency of King's Men
  book-keepers   179–180
  court performances   277, 291,
    318–319
  court-playhouse
    interactions   313–314
  Duchess of Malfi, The
    (Webster)   314–315
  Edinburgh performances   279–280
  Fletcher, John   279
  formation   278
  at Globe *see* Globe playhouse
  Globe/Blackfriars
    arrangement   291–292
  housekeepers, quarrels with   156
  in court masques   287-288
  Inns of Court performances   134
  Malcontent, The (Marston)   241,
    281–284
  Masters of the Revels, relationship
    with   90

Index | 355

music and musicians 174, 176–177, 186, 300–301, 302–303
ordinary poets 147
patent from James I 154
Pericles for French Ambassador 122
plague, impact of 280–281, 291
private homes, performances in 52, 135–136
repertoire 148, 301–303, 322–324
revenge plays 284
romances and tragicomedies 9303–305
royal livery 281
salaries 278–279
sharers 207, 279
Knack to Know a Knave, A (unk.) 6, 64, 103
Knell, William 39, 49, 164
Knight, Edward 179–180, 301
Knutson, Roslyn 78, 285
Korda, Natasha 164
Kyd, Thomas 283–284

l

Lady Elizabeth's Men 14, 142, 147, 178, 314
Lake, Sir Thomas 286
Lambarde, William 95, 233
Lane, Sir Ralph 29
Laneham, John 41, 49–50
Langham, Robert 26, 27
Langley, Francis 78, 169, 221–222
Lanman, Henry 99, 198
Larum for London, A (anon.) 249
Lathom House, Lancashire 60–61
lawsuits 15, 165–166
Layston, Alice 116, 117
Layston, William 117
Lea Hall, Lancashire 51, 52
Legh, Sir Peter 52–53
Legh's Men 52–53
Leicester, Robert Dudley, 1st Earl 25–27, 28, 29–30, 124

Leicester's Men
Act for the Punishment of Vagabonds, response to 29–30, 43
Burbage, James 30
dissolution 61
founding 30
number of players 43
payment for performances 48
players lost to Queen's Men 41
royal patent 30, 33–34, 80, 84
the Theatre 77, 100
touring 19, 69, 124
Lessons for Consorts (Rosseter) 301
Letting of Humour's Blood, The (Rowlands) 263
liberties, the 198
licensing and censorship of plays 15, 30, 33–34, 86, 89–90, 91, 108, 281, 283
lighting 58, 119, 121–122, 156, 292, 298, 299–300, 318
Lincoln, Admiral Edward Clinton, 1st Earl 29
Lodge, Thomas 94
Lodger, The (Nicholl) 168
London from the Bankside (Hollar) 237
London playhouses, map of 79
London Prodigal, The (anon.) 255–256
Long, William B. 178
Long View of London (Hollar) 236, *237*
Lord Mayor of London
banning of bills 181
Lord Hunsdon's request 114, 175, 196
persecution of players 61, 117, 129–130, 197
prayers for 6
Privy Council requests 33–34, 80
Show 35
Warwick, letter to 175

Lord Strange's Men and their Plays
(Manley and MacLean) 61
Love Restored (Jonson) 167
Love's Labour's Lost
(Shakespeare) 54–55, 66,
82, 85, 94, 126, 135–136,
292–293, 319
Lowin, John 158, 241, 261, 283, 314
Lyly, John 49, 88, 177
Lyzard, William 22–23

m

Macbeth (Shakespeare) 46, 169,
176, 251, 254, 269, 306,
307–308
MacLean, Sally-Beth 23, 61, 125–126,
133–134
Maggett, Steven 173
Mago, William 302
Maid in the Mill, The (Fletcher and
Rowley) 180
Maid's Tragedy, The (Beaumont and
Fletcher) 294
Malbon, Thomas 70
Malcontent, The (Marston) 102, 158,
174, 241, 270, 281–284, 306
Malloy, Christopher 59
managers 141–142
Manley, Lawrence 60, 61, 125–126
Manningham, John 134, 269
Marston, John
   Antonio's Revenge 174
   Children of Paul's, writing for
      70, 270
   Dutch Courtesan, The 293
   Eastward Ho! (Jonson, Chapman,
      Marston) 284
   Malcontent, The 102, 208, 241,
      281–284
   Scourge of Villainy 201, 218
   Sophonisba 301
   War of the Theaters 271–273
   What You Will 174

Martholme, Lancashire 52
Martin Marprelate scandal 86
Masque of Blackness, The
   (Jonson) 177, 287
*Masque of the Inner Temple and Gray's
   Inn* (Beaumont) 288
Masque of Oberon (Jonson) 252, 286,
   289 Note 5, 312, 313
Masque of Queens (Jonson), 287-288
Massey, Charles 141
Massinger, Philip 87, 147, 302
Masters of the Revels
   benefits, personal 90
   Buc 15, 87–89, 121, 310–311
   censorship of plays 89–90
   court performances, approving/
      censoring 33, 84–85, 126
   editing plays 86–88
   expenses, reducing 84
   failure to censor plays 90–91
   Herbert, Sir Henry 90
   history 84
   public performances, licensing/
      censorship of 6, 15, 33,
      84, 108
   Queen's Men 41
   Revels calendar allocations 62, 84
   Tilney *see* Tilney, Edmund
Maurice of Nassau (later Prince of
   Orange) 87, 88
Mayne, Jasper 309
McLuskie, Kathleen 161–162
McMillin, Scott 50, 133–134
Mead, Thomas 66, 67
Meade, Jacob 13, 14, 142–143
Measure for Measure (Shakespeare)
   254, 269
Menzer, Paul 117
Merchant of Venice, The (Shakespeare)
   94, 102, 103, 105, 183, 205,
   220, 319
Merry Devil of Edmonton, The
   (anon.) 253–254, 256

Merry Wives of Windsor, The
(Shakespeare) 82, 126,
130, 168–169, 177, 196–197,
284, 318
Meyrick, Sir Gelly 135, 153–154
Middleton, Thomas
Black Book, The 240, 245
Chaste Maid in Cheapside, A
10, 307
Mad World, My Masters, A 6
Revenger's Tragedy, The 244,
255, 284
Roaring Girl, The (Middleton and
Dekker) 161
Robinson, Richard 187
Witch, The 177, 186, 308
Midsummer Night's Dream, A
(Shakespeare)
acts 300
Brooke's influence 101
Burbage as Theseus 102
Chamberlain's Men 124–125, 127
cultural presence of the monarch 5
Kenilworth, reference to 26
marriages associated with 130
music 302
plays-within-plays 43
at the Theatre 94
Titania 169
traveling players 38, 54
Miles, Robert 31–32
Miseries of Enforced Marriage, The
(Wilkins) 204, 256
monarch, the; *see also* Elizabeth I;
James I
authority 7
centrality of 4, 5, 119, 121
cultural presence of 5, 6–7
prayers for 6–7
Montrose, Louis 5
More, Sir Thomas 42–43, 86–87, 263
More, Sir William 193, 195, 196
"motley" 105–106

Mountjoy, Marie 168
Mount Tabor (Willis) 20
Mucedorus (anon.) 256, 293, 322
Much Ado About Nothing
(Shakespeare) 94, 103, 141,
168, 183, 205
Mulryne, J. R. 21
Munday, Anthony 86–87, 108,
162, 197
Munro, Lucy 175–176
musical instruments 112, 174–176,
252, 300–301, 302, 303; *see also*
drums; trumpets
musicians 174–177
ambiguity in records 52–53
at Blackfriars 174, 292, 300–303
boys 176, 186, 209
at the Globe 308, 309
household 124
housing for 308–309
Musicorum Chorus 282
women 161
music rooms 309
mystery plays 27–28

n

Nashe, Thomas 45–46, 62, 63,
129–130, 196, 218–219, 221
Nelson, Alan H. 22, 23, 134
Newington Butts theater,
Southwark 10–11, 77
Nicholson, George 279
night-time scenes 111, 246, 299–300
Northbrooke, John 99
Northumberland, Henry Percy, 5th
Earl 54
Norton, Thomas 161

o

occasional drama 34–35
Oldcastle, Sir John 7, 135,
194–197, 284; *see also*
Falstaff, character of

Old Wives Tale, The (Peele)   133–134
ordinary poets   147–151
Orlando Furioso (Greene)   108
Orrell, John   93, 236
Ostler, Thomasine   15, 151, 164
Ostler, William   151, 164, 176, 207, 292, 314
Othello (Shakespeare)   24, 135, 176, 186–187, 245, 269, 292, 299, 318
Overthrow of Stage Plays, Th' (Rainolds)   4, 186
Oxford, Edward de Vere, 17th Earl   271
Oxford's Boys   49
Oxford's Men   19, 34, 41
Oxford University   1–5, 22–23, 35–36, 186–187

P

Palamon and Arcite (Edwardes)   1–5, 186
Palladis Tamia (Meres)   127
Pallant, Robert (the Elder)   206
Pallant, Robert (the Younger)   150, 183, 302
Palsgrave's Men   14
Pant, Thomas   59
parts   108
Patrick, William   302
patronage
　aristocratic, exclusively   6, 29, 43
　of companies   124, 127–130
　defining   123
　economic impact   123
　falsification   145–146
　hereditary duty   32, 196
　of individuals   123–124
　loss of   196, 284
　protection   28–29, 29–30, 129–130, 196
　royal   6, 41, 197, 277; *see also* King's Men; Queen's Men

Shakespeare and the Stanleys   125–126
　writing for patrons   124–130, 197
Paul's Boys *see* Children of Paul's
payment for performances; *see also* entry fees; salaries, sharers'
　at court   49–50, 81, 82, 150, 207, 277, 281
　at inns   40, 117
　at playhouses   13, 107
　on tour   47–48, 53
Pembroke, William Herbert, 3rd Earl   145–146, 264, 278
Pembroke's Men   39, 169, 221
penny-by-penny entrance system   95, 116, 159–160
Perambulation of Kent (Lambarde)   95
performances, typical   110–112
performing rights   101, 283
Pericles (Shakespeare)   58, 122, 169, 243, 252–253, 256, 264, 290, 292, 304
Perkins, Richard   184
Phillips, Augustine
　apprentices   183, 186
　Chamberlain's Men   63, 140
　examination by Chief Justice   153–154, 272
　family and residence   152–153
　Globe sharer   153, 224
　King's Men   154, 207, 279
　Phillips His Slipper jig   105–106, 226
　Seven Deadly Sins, 2 The (Tarlton)   205, 206
　Strange's Men   63, 152
　will and bequests   154–155, 157, 176, 208
Phillips, Mary   164, 167
Philotas (Daniel)   284
Pierce Penniless, His Supplication to the Devil (Nashe)   62, 63
Pig/Pyk, John   184

plague
  concerns about spread of   8, 33, 91
  impact on companies   17, 64, 75, 77, 145, 149, 270, 280–281, 291
  number of deaths   75
Platter, Thomas   8, 78, 80, 95, 110, 159–160, 169, 225, 235, 267–268
Playgoing in Shakespeare's London (Gurr)   163
Play of St Christopher, The (trad.)   58–59
plays-within-plays   42–43
plots/plats, back-stage   113–114
Pope, Thomas
  Chamberlain's Men   63, 106, 206, 207
  Globe sharer   153, 224
  Phillips' stepbrother   154–155
  retirement   157, 279
  Seven Deadly Sins, 2 The (Tarlton)   205, 206, 207
  Strange's Men   63, 140
  will and bequests   208
portability   36, 134, 313
Prescot playhouse, Lancashire   66–71
Prince Henry's Men   141, 166, 197, 277, 284, 291
private commissions   135, 153–154
private homes as venues   48, 52–53, 55, 56–58, *56, 57*, 135–136
Privy Council
  1600 theater restrictions   270–271
  Blackfriars Boys disbanded   286
  Blackfriars petitions   32, 194, 195, 198
  Burbage - Fleetwood confrontation   28–29, 100
  vs. City of London authorities   28–29, 33–34, 49, 80
  duopoly, Admiral's Men and Chamberlain's Men   77–78

festival holy-days   80
Gowrie, displeasure with   90–91
plague, responses to   64, 75
playhouse destruction orders   221
prayers for   6
Queen's Men   41, 48–49
special licences   33–34, 63, 64, 67, 152, 222
propaganda, national/religious   47
properties; *see also* costumes
  acquisition   109
  Alleyn's list   171
  emblematic nature   134
  storage   95, 100
  supplied by Master of Revels   84
  supplied by playhouse owners   13, 143
public vs. private playhouses   83
Puritan attacks   4, 27–28, 99, 174–175, 186, 188
Puttenham, George   97

q

Queen Anne's Men; *see also* Worcester's Men
  formation   207, 277
  Greene, Robert   165
  Heywood, Thomas   147
  jigs   227
  manager   141
  Prescot playhouse, Lancashire   69–70
  Red Bull   146, 166, 167, 189 Note 9, 227, 230, 290
  Slater, Martin   144, 145
  special licence   75
Queen Henrietta's Men   142, 148–149
Queen's Men (i.e. Queen Elizabeth's)
  decline   50
  dominance   49
  formation   41, 129
  holy days petition   80
  "houses"   133–134

360 | Index

Queen's Men (i.e. Queen Elizabeth's) (cont'd)
   at inns   115
   Laneham-Dutton split   49–50
   London venues   48–49
   number of players   41, 43–44
   sale of plays   213
   Shakespeare's association with   39–41, 43–44
   Shakespeare's plots, influence on   50
   Tarlton   44–50, *45*
   at the Theatre   46, 48, 100
   touring   19, 25, 39, 46–48, 69
   violence among players   39–40
Queen's "reward"   81
Quest for Shakespeare's Globe, The (Orrell)   236

r

Rackin, Phyllis   161
Rainolds, John   4, 186
Rape of Lucrece, The (Shakespeare)   123
Records of Early English Drama project   19
Red Bull playhouse, Clerkenwell   115, 165, 166, 167, 215–216, 220, 226, 238–239, 240, 290
Red Lion, Aldgate   30–31, 92, 94, 242
rehearsals   109, 143
Revels season   54
revenge plays   284
Revenger's Tragedy, The (Middleton)   244, 254, 255, 284
Rhodes, John   300
Rice, John   168, 183, 187, 314
Richard II (Shakespeare)   89–90, 94–95, 101, 102, 293, 309
Richard III (Shakespeare)
   Burbage in title role   102, 261, 263
   King's Men repertoire   148

metatheatricality   258, 261, 263
music   175
music rooms   309
popularity   101
Queen's Men repertoire   47, 50
Stanley   60, 125
sword-fights   46
the Theatre, Shoreditch   94
Richmond Palace   118–119
Rickner, George   302
Roaring Girl, The (Middleton and Dekker)   161
Robinson, Bishop Nicholas   1–2, 2–3
Robinson, Richard   164, 187, 314
romances   303–304
Roman theaters, imitation of   97–99
Romeo and Juliet (Shakespeare)
   actors and roles   103–104, 105
   balcony scene   24
   bird whistle   198–199
   book-keeper   178
   Brooke's influence   101
   Curtain discovery space   201
   A Day at the Theatre   106–114
   prompter   180
   stage directions   235
   sword-fights   46
   the Theatre, Shoreditch   94, 96–97, 235
   upper acting space   95
Romeus and Juliet (Brooke)   101
Rosenberg, Marvin   258, 259
Rose theater, Southwark
   1592 refurbishment   233
   Admiral's Men   13, 32, 100, 148
   Admiral's Men departure   269
   concession stands   109
   days open   77
   destruction order   221
   duopoly, Admiral's Men and Chamberlain's Men   77–78

investment and profit   17, 62
location benefits   92, 152
Lords' room   234
management   12–13, 151
purchase   10–11
repertoire   148, 216
size and structure 93–94, 237
Strange's Men   13, 32, 62, 64, 216
Worcester's Men   14, 158, 269
Rosseter, Philip   301
royal patents   30, 33–34, 80, 84, 277
Royce, Jacalyn   261, 263
Rufford Hall, Lancashire   51–52, 54, 55–56, *56*, *57*
Russell, John   166

S

St Saviour's Church, Southwark   14, 152, 208
St Werburgh Street playhouse, Dublin   71
saint's plays   58
salaries, sharers'   17, 47–48, 81, 149, 278–279
Salisbury Court playhouse   148, 297
Satiromastix (Dekker)   175, 232–233, 267, 272, 273
Saunders, William   302
Savage, Jerome   77
Schoenbaum, Samuel   60, 195
Schoone-Jongen, Terence G.   38, 66
Scourge of Villainy (Marston)   201, 217–218
seating
  at court performances 119–120, *120*
  entry fee variations   16–17, 63, 95, 159–160, 270
  Globe and Fortune   233–234
  at inns   133
  social hierarchy   22–24, 119–120, 238–240, 295–296
  on-stage   5, 240–242, 292–296
Sejanus (Jonson)   90, 141, 150, 153, 158, 208, 243, 268, 282
Seven Deadly Sins of London, The (Dekker)   300
Seven Deadly Sins, 1 The (Tarlton)   205, 216
Seven Deadly Sins, 2 The (Tarlton)
  adult actors   205–207
  authorship   213
  boy actors   207–209
  Chamberlain's Men   205, 206, 217
  dating   213, 217
  four plays in one   216–217
  hired actors   208
  "plot"
    purpose   209, 210
    text   213
    transcription   211–212
  scenes   213–216
  stories   209–210
severed head props   254
Shackerly, Edward   302
Shakespeare, Edmund   207, 208
Shakespeare, John   20, 25, 51
Shakespeare, Mary Arden   26
Shakespeare, William; *see also specific play*
  acting   150
  Blackfriars, writing for   309–314, 315–318
  Blackfriars management, condemnation of   285-286
  Blackfriars property   314
  Blackfriars sharer   292
  Burbage, friendship with   263–264
  Catholicism   51
  Chamberlain's Men
    contract as ordinary poet   147–148, 149–150
    sharer   81, 127–128, 140, 290
    turnover of plays   101

Shakespeare, William (cont'd)
  early experiences, possible
    Kenilworth 25, 26, 27
    mystery plays 27
    Stratford Guild Hall 20, 25
    Stratford inns 25
  early life 7
  education 4
  festive comedies 267, 269
  First Folio published 318
  Fletcher, collaboration with
    314, 315ff
  Globe, plays written for the
    267–271
  histories 267
  Jonson, relationship with
    311–313
  Kemp, jibes at 226–227
  Kemp, roles for 219–220
  King's Men sharer 279
  "lost years"
    Hoghton Theory 50–60
    Queen's Men Theory 39–41,
      43–44
    Strange's Men theory 63,
      65–66
  marriage and children 7
  monarch, centrality of 4, 5
  motley 105–106
  patronage 123, 124–128
  private house performances,
    references to 38
  problem comedies 269
  reading 27
  retirement 314, 318
  romances and tragicomedies
    304–305
  selling shares 314
  Seven Deadly Sins, role in
    206–207
  Strange's Men 125–126
  tirewomen 168–169
  War of the Theaters 271–273

will and bequests 313
work as teacher/tutor/school
  master 54–55
in written records 81–82
Shakespeare's Motley (Hotson) 105
Shakespeare's Wooden O (Hotson) 5,
  239–240
Shank, John 141, 184–185
Shapiro, Michael 187
sharers 140–143, 146
Sharers' Papers 160, 224
Sharpe, Richard 183, 302,
  314–315
Sherman, William 310
Shirley, James 71, 147, 308
Shrewsbury, Francis Talbot, 5th
  Earl 124
Simpson, Christopher and
  Robert 58–59
Sincler (Sinklo), John 206, 208, 241
Singer, John 39–40
Singing Simpkin jig (Kemp) 219
Sir John Oldcastle (unk.) 135,
  197, 284
Sir John Van Olden Barnavelt
  (Fletcher and Massinger)
  87–88, 183, 302
Sir Thomas More (Munday) 42–43,
  86–87
Skialetheia (Guilpin) 218
Slater, Martin 143–146, 186
Sly, William
  Blackfriars sharer 292
  Every Man In His Humour
    (Jonson) 140
  executor of Phillips' will 155
  Globe sharer 290
  Malcontent, The (Marston) 158
  Seven Deadly Sins, 2 The
    (Tarlton) 205, 206, 207, 208
  sharer 157, 279
Smith, Irwin 198, 294
Smithills Hall, Lancashire 52–53

Index | 363

social hierarchy   22, 23, 24, 235, 239–240, 297–298
Somerset, Alan   19, 21, 48
Sophonisba (Marston)   301
soundings   9, 110, 249, 267
Southampton, Henry Wriothesley, 3rd Earl   67, 123, 135–136
Spanish Curate, The (Fletcher)   55
Spanish Tragedy, The (Kyd)   162, 273, 283–284
Spenser, Edmund   162
Spenser, Gabriel   39, 202, 273
Stafford's Men   19
stage-keepers   177–178, 180–182
Staging of Plays before Shakespeare, The (Southern)   24
staging practices   22–24, 133–134
Stanley family
   Ferdinando, 5th Earl of Derby, 13th Baron Strange   53–54, 65, 68
   Henry, 4th Earl of Derby, 12th Baron Strange   53–54, 65, 68
   Lathom House hall screen   60–61
   patronizing players   61, 68; *see also* Derby's Men; Strange's Men
   Prescot and Knowsley   67–68
   Shakespeare's treatment of 125–126
   Thomas, 1st Earl of Derby   60
   William, 6th Earl of Derby   67, 68, 70, 124–125, 127, 271
Staple of News, The (Jonson)   174
starting time of plays   78, 80, 81
Stepmothers' Tragedy, The (Chettle)   107
Stern, Tiffany   108, 113, 201, 202, 313
Stockwood, John   99, 174–175
Strange's Men; *see also* Derby's Men
   1593/94 tour   65
   Admiral's Men, association with 61–62, 129
   ascendancy of   50
   become Derby's Men   65
   contempt for Lord Mayor   61
   Four Plays in One   216
   hired men   67
   leaving Theatre   32
   loss of patron   65
   number of performances   61, 62
   number of players   62–63
   plague, impact of   64
   repertoire   63
   Rose theater   13, 62
   Shakespeare's association with   60, 63, 65–66, 67, 125–126
   special licences   63, 67
   touring   66, 67
Stratford-upon-Avon
   Guild Hall   20–22, 23–24, 25, 41
   "Mayor's play"   20–21, 25, 41
   performances in inns   25
   theater companies performing in   19
Street, Peter   13–14, 223, 230–232, 242
Surrenden Dering, Kent   55
Sussex's Men   41
Swan theater, Bankside   8–10, 24, 78, 97, 99, 221–222, 233, 235, 247, 268, 309
Swinnerton, Thomas   145–146, 166
sword-fights   46
Syme, Holger Schott   78

t

Tamer Tamed, The (Fletcher)   90, 112, 179–180
Taming of the Shrew, The (Shakespeare)   38, 54, 55, 94, 292
Tanner of Denmark, The (unk.)   64, 147
tapestries   61, 119, 123
Tarlton, Richard   39–40, 41, 44–50, 45, 105, 182, 213, 218, 261; *see also Seven Deadly Sins, 2 The* (Tarlton)

Tarlton's Jests (Tarlton) 44
Tawyer, William 302
Taylor, John 179
Taylor, Joseph 314
Tempest, The (Shakespeare) 10, 38, 177, 216, 298, 304–307, 311, 313, 314
theater, types of 34–35
Theatre, Shoreditch
  apprentices 185
  Burbage - Fleetwood confrontation 28–29, 100
  canopy, lack of 95–96
  concession stands 109–110
  costumes and properties 109
  Curtain, association with the 99, 198
  decoration 99
  destruction order 221
  discovery space 96–97, 112
  dismantling 15, 223
  early use 100
  entry fees 95
  everyday work 112
  fencing matches 202
  financial difficulties 92
  galleries 93, 94
  house-rent 143
  impression on visitors 97
  lease of land 193
  Leicester's Men 100
  location 83–84, 91–92
  protests/complaints against 31
  Puritan attacks 99
  Queen's Men 46, 48
  rehearsals 109
  Romeo and Juliet performance 110–112
  seating 95
  size and structure 31, 92–94
  stage 93–94
  Strange's Men 61
  tiring house 95
  trapdoor 94
  upper acting space 94–95, 235
Theatre residency of Chamberlain's Men
  advantages of residency 81, 100–101
  duopoly with Admiral's Men 77–78
  jigs 220
  naturalistic acting 263
  repertoire 94–95, 101–102
  Shakespeare's importance 101–102
  typical day 106–112
Thomas, Lord Cromwell (unk.) 254
Thompson, Peter 260, 261
Thomson, John 184–185
Thomson, Leslie 240–241
Tilney, Edmund
  attendance fees 84–85
  Chamberlain's Men 85
  Elizabeth I, relation to 85
  expenses, reducing 84
  Flower of Friendship 85–86
  licensing and censorship of plays 15, 86–87, 89–90, 126–127
  performing rights 283
  Queen's Men 41, 50
  Shakespeare, collaboration with 85–86
  special licences 222
  Strange's Men 62
  Topographical Descriptions, Regiments, and Policies 86
Timon of Athens (Shakespeare) 176, 257, 269, 288
tiremen 169–174
tirewomen 167–169
tiring houses
  canvas booths 24–25, 121, 134
  costumes and properties storage 13, 100, 109
  Swan sketch 9, 10

Tittler, Robert   23
Titus Andronicus (Shakespeare)   36, 65, 75, 77, 94, 101, 148, 210
Titus and Vespacia (unk.)   64
Tooley, Nicholas   155, 159, 207, 208, 292, 314
Topcliffe, Richard   221
Topographical Descriptions, Regiments, and Policies (Tilney)   86
touring   20, 25, 46–48, 69–70
Towne, John   39
trade guilds   27–28, 34–35
Tragedy of Mariam (Carey)   161
tragicomedies   303–305
trapdoors   36, 94, 216, 245
Trigge, William   183
Troilus and Cressida (Shakespeare)   251, 269, 292
Troublesome Reign of King John, The (unk.)   47, 50
True Tragedy of Richard III, The (unk.)   47, 50
trumpets
 announcing performance   106, 114, 174–175, 181, 280
 in performances   175, 247–248, 303
Tuckfield, Thomas   301
turnover of plays   101, 106–107
Twelfth Night (Shakespeare)   27, 133, 134, 176, 183, 247, 252, 266, 269
Two Gentlemen of Verona, The (Shakespeare)   94, 168, 256
Two Noble Kinsmen, The (Shakespeare/Fletcher)   89, 288, 315–318
Two Wise Men And All The Rest Fools (unk.)   6–7
Tyler, Rosemary   66, 67, 68

U

Underhill, Nicholas   302
Underwood, John   176, 292, 314
universities   1–5, 22–23, 35–36

V

Valentinian (Fletcher)   175, 177, 186
Valiant Welshman, The (R.A.)   197
van Buchell, Arendt   8–10
Venus and Adonis (Shakespeare)   67, 123
Vernon, George   302
Verreyken, Louis   135
Vincent, Thomas   179, 207, 209
Volpone (Jonson)   141, 150, 158, 177, 183, 208, 243, 257

W

Walmesley, Thomas   52
Walsingham, Sir Francis   41, 181
Warning for Fair Women, A (anon.)   203–205
War of the Theaters   271–273
Warren's Men   52, 53
Warwick's Men   19, 34, 77, 175
Webster, John   141, 150, 263, 282–283, 314
What You Will (Marston)   174
Whitehall, Palace of   118, 120, *120*, 313, 316, 318–319
widows of actors/owners   164–165
Wiles, David   105, 106, 217–218, 219–220, 265–266
Wilkins, George   256
Willis, R.   20, 25, 47–48
Wilson, Henry   302
Wilson, John   150, 183, 186
Wilson, Thomas (Robert)   41, 44
Windsor, Miles   2, 3
Winter's Tale, The (Shakespeare)   177, 252, 304, 306, 311, 313
Witch, The (Middleton)   177, 186, 308
wives of actors/owners   164
Wolsey's Men   42–43, 112
women in theaters   161–166, 167, 182

Worcester, Edward Somerset, 4th
    Earl   127, 271
Worcester's Men; *see also* Queen
    Anne's Men
  Beeston, Christopher   158, 207
  Boar's Head   165
  Henslowe's loan to   170
  Kemp, Will   227
  Lowin, John   158
  Oxford's Men, merger with   271
Rose theater   14, 173, 269
  touring   19
Wotton, Sir Henry   257, 315
Wroth, Lady Mary   187

y

Yorke, Sir John and Lady
    Juliana   58–59
Yorkshire Tragedy, A (Middleton)
    204, 216

Made in the USA
Monee, IL
03 May 2026

49437979R00213